Goals for Living

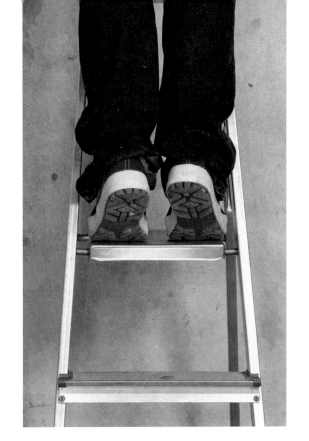

Managing Your Resources

Nancy Wehlage
Portage, Wisconsin

Mary Larson-Kennedy, CFCS
Delavan, Wisconsin

Publisher
The Goodheart-Willcox Company, Inc.
Tinley Park, Illinois
www.g-w.com

Manufactured in the United States of America.

Library of Congress Catalog Card Number 00-057829

ISBN-13: 978-1-59070-412-7
ISBN-10: 1-59070-412-6

2 3 4 5 6 7 8 9 10 – 06 – 11 10 09 08 07 06

The Goodheart-Willcox Company, Inc. Brand Disclaimer: Brand names, company names, and illustrations for products and services included in this text are provided for educational purposes only, and do not represent or imply endorsement or recommendation by the author or the publisher.

Library of Congress Cataloging-in-Publication Data

Wehlage, Nancy.
Goals for Living: managing your resources/Nancy Wehlage,
Mary Larson-Kennedy.

p. cm.
First published in 1989.
Includes index.
ISBN 1-59070-412-6
1. Life skills--United States. 2. Home economics--United States I. Title.

HQ209.U6 W44 2001
640--dc21

00-057829
CIP

Cover Image: Getty Images

Introduction

Goals for Living: Managing Your Resources is a comprehensive text designed to help you manage the challenges of daily life now and in the future.

The text begins with a basic introduction to the management process. The remaining parts of the book represent areas of your life in which you make management decisions daily. Managing personal and family life, relationships with others, child care and guidance, physical and mental health, finances, consumer concerns, meal planning and preparation, clothing, housing, and career choices are covered. *Goals for Living: Managing Your Resources* emphasizes how management skills can help you control your life in these areas.

As you read the text, you will become more aware of the important decisions you will be making throughout your life. As a result, you will be better prepared to face future challenges. You will also find that this knowledge can help you to better understand the decisions made by others. This can lead to a better understanding of society in general.

About the Authors

Nancy Wehlage's experience ranges from teaching at both the junior high and high school levels to working in the financial planning field. She earned both bachelor's and master's degrees at the University of Illinois. This textbook began to evolve as she was completing additional graduate work at the University of Wisconsin-Madison. Her work at the University of Wisconsin-Madison included serving as project director on a statewide curriculum development project with a strong management emphasis. Nancy served as the executive director of the Wisconsin Association of Family and Consumer Sciences.

Mary Larson-Kennedy is a Family and Consumer Sciences teacher. She earned bachelor's and master's degrees from the University of Wisconsin-Stout. Her teaching experience ranges from the middle school to high school and technical college levels. Mary is the recipient of such prestigious awards as the Wisconsin Outstanding Vocational Educator, Wisconsin Family and Consumer Sciences Teacher of the Year, American Association of Family and Consumer Sciences National Teacher of the Year–Top Ten Finalist, The Gateway Technical College Image Award, and the Senator Herb Kohl Teacher Fellowship Award.

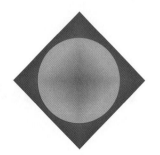

Brief Contents

Contents

Part Two
Development Across the Life Span

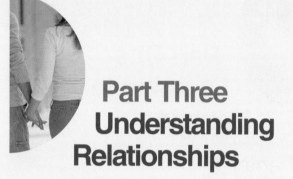

Part Three
Understanding Relationships

Part Four
Family Living

Part Five
Managing Health and Wellness

Part Six
Managing Finances

Part Seven
Managing as a Consumer

Part Eight
Managing Food

Part Nine
Managing
Clothing

Chapter 27
Planning and Shopping for Clothes 479

Chapter 28
Caring for Clothing 503

Part Ten
Managing
Housing

Chapter 29
Planning and Selecting Housing 517

Chapter 30
Furnishing and Caring for the Home 552

Part Eleven
Preparing for
Your Career

Chapter 31
Career Planning 583

Chapter 32
Finding a Job 604

Part One
Learning to Manage

Chapter 1
Decision Making in Your Daily Life
Certain factors influence decisions
you make every day, including
goals, values, and resources.
Recognizing the steps in the
decision-making process can
help you make and evaluate
your decisions more carefully.

Chapter 2
**Your Values, Goals, and
Standards**
Your values and goals form
and change throughout your
life. As you grow older, you
will establish standards to
measure your progress in
attaining goals.

Chapter 3
Managing Your Resources
You have access to many different
resources. The management process
can be used to help you identify
your resources and make them work
for you.

Chapter 4
Technology as a Resource
Technology impacts your life every day. As
technology continues to advance, it will bring
about greater benefits as well as greater
concerns.

1

Decision Making in Your Daily Life

To Know

managers
goals
resources
stages in life
role
values
decision-making process
alternatives
consequences
evaluation

Objectives

After studying this chapter, you will be able to
- recognize how the decisions you make affect your life.
- describe how the changing world affects your decision making.
- explain how values, goals, and resources influence management decisions.
- apply the decision-making process to your daily life.

Have you ever thought of yourself as a manager, managing your daily life? Think of the decisions you make each day. What will you do this weekend? What will you wear to school? When will you study for your math test? The way you answer these and other questions will affect the way you manage your life. Just what is a manager? How do people manage?

Managers are people who make choices or decisions that move them toward specific goals. **Goals** are the ends toward which they work—what they desire to achieve. The coach of a basketball team, who represents the manager, makes decisions to move the team toward their goal of winning. See 1-1. The manager of a clothing store makes certain decisions so business will move toward the goal of profit. The principal represents the manager of a school. He or she makes decisions that will move students toward the goal of a good education.

Managers have resources, which help them reach their goals. **Resources** are the ways and means of reaching specific goals.

Texas Tech Women's Basketball

1-1 **The coach represents the manager of the basketball team. As the manager, she makes decisions aimed at the team's goal of winning.**

The manager of a basketball team has various resources available to help the team win games. The players' skills and the manager's knowledge of the game are examples. Resources available to the manager of the clothing store might include the store's location, advertisements, and salespeople. The principal has the skills of the teachers and textbooks as resources to help reach educational goals.

The challenge to managers is deciding which resources to use to reach certain goals. The basketball coach must decide which players to use throughout the game. Which plays will be used? When should a substitution be made? When is a good time to call a time-out? All these are resources available to the coach. The coach must decide which resources will be most helpful in reaching the goal of winning the game. See 1-2.

As you can see, management occurs when there is a problem to be solved or a decision to be made. A manager's decision is guided by his or her goals.

Managers are not just found in stores or coaching teams. You, too, are a manager. You manage your daily living. Many times throughout the day you make decisions. Those decisions lead you toward something you want to achieve, something that is important to you. They lead you toward your goals in daily living.

Some of the decisions you make are very important and require a lot of thought. Others are so routine you hardly even notice you are making decisions. The important point to remember is you are making the decision. You are in control of the decisions. You are managing your daily life.

Decisions You Make Daily

One of the first steps in becoming an effective manager is to become aware of the many decisions you make daily. Then you will be ready to learn how to manage and how to improve your decision-making ability.

Decisions—Your Stage in Life

Certain decisions you make are related to your **stages in life.** Words such as *infant, preschooler, teenager, young adult, middle-aged adult,* and *older adults* describe these stages. High school juniors and seniors may be making decisions about what they will do after graduation. Will they begin careers right away or continue their education in a college or technical school? See 1-3. Many

Texas Tech Women's Basketball

1-2 The coach uses her knowledge of the game, the skill of certain players, and the strength of certain plays as resources in moving the team toward their goal of victory.

1-3 Decisions about life after high school are some of the most important that teens must make.

*Getting*Involved

Connect with a local service organization, such as Food Pantry, Big Brothers or Sisters, and volunteer to help out as a role model for wise decision making. Then, write a report on how decision making helps both services and people being helped by the services.

decisions are made about relationships with others. Young people in their twenties might be making decisions about whether or not to get married. Many people in the middle years of life are faced with financial decisions concerning their children. People later in life often have to make decisions about changing their living arrangements. This may occur after retirement or following the death of a spouse.

Decisions—Your Roles in Life

Choices and decisions are often related to your roles in life. A specific **role** refers to a certain function you assume in life. Your roles may be those of a family member, an employee, or a member of a peer group. In your role as an individual, you make many decisions involving your personal self, such as the style of clothing you like to wear. In your role as a family member, you make decisions that involve other members of the family. For instance, you may decide to join the basketball team for personal satisfaction. However, your decision may affect other members of the family. It might mean adjusting evening meals around practice time and arranging for transportation to and from practice. It might also mean having less time to continue regular responsibilities at home. See 1-4.

Many of the decisions you make are related to your role as a member of a peer group. For example, you and your friends make decisions about what to do on a

1-4 **Teens must often plan other decisions around one of their most important roles— that of student.**

Saturday evening. You might go to a movie. If so, which movie will you see? What will you do for transportation? What will you do after the movie?

If your role is that of a parent, you make decisions involving your children. Research shows that decisions made even before the birth of a baby can influence that child's life. The pregnant woman who chooses to eat nutritious, well-balanced meals during pregnancy will affect her child's life in a positive way. Parents make many decisions affecting their children, particularly during childhood and teenage years.

If you work, you make decisions related to your work role. These decisions may include how to do your job more efficiently or how to improve relations with other employees. Decisions might also include whether to accept another job.

In your role as a community member, you make decisions that can affect the entire community. By voting, you help decide who will represent you in government. When you decide to do volunteer work in the community, you are making a decision that will benefit that community. By being a law-abiding citizen, you are also taking an action that affects your community in a positive way.

Decisions–Daily Living

The decisions you make throughout life and in your various roles involve all aspects of daily living. These decisions can involve your personal life, your relationships with others, the food you eat, the clothes you wear, and what you buy.

The decisions you make about your personal life may be simple or complex. A simple decision might involve deciding what you are going to do on a particular day. Deciding whether to attend college after high school would be a more complex decision. You make decisions about your relationships with other people. These decisions range from whom to invite to a party to whether you want to marry a certain person. Some decisions involve your health, such as what you are going to eat for lunch or whether to start smoking. You manage your life through your decisions.

Decisions–Relationships

Relationships with friends, family members, teachers, and others have strong influences on your decisions. Their opinions and requests may affect your decisions in many ways. For instance, your friend may want to go to a movie with you. Your father may want you to rake leaves. Your teacher may expect an assignment from you in a week. You must make decisions about how or whether to meet each of these requests.

Decisions–Attitudes

Attitudes and feelings are also involved in your decisions. If you feel good about yourself, you are more likely to make decisions with confidence. The results of your decisions are more likely to be positive. Having a healthy attitude toward yourself tends to result in more positive relationships with others. See 1-5.

Factors Affecting Decisions

Decision making seems to become more challenging year by year. Changing social

1-5 **A positive attitude can help you make decisions for the right reasons.**

Brainstorming

As a class, list as many roles as you can that people assume and suggest decisions typically made in each role. Do any of the roles seem to conflict with any other roles? Why? Give suggestions for handling role conflicts.

customs result in new situations and sometimes new problems for individuals and families. These include changes involving families, lifestyles, and roles of men and women. Changing attitudes related to social behaviors, premarital sex, and divorce have added pressures to decision making.

Advances in technology have resulted in new products that affect family life. When television became a part of family lives, it created new pleasures as well as many challenges for the family. Today, computers and the Internet also have a significant effect on family members.

Consumer decisions are more challenging today. One reason is that there are so many more products from which to choose. Even a simple decision, such as choosing a sweatshirt, may be confusing. The average clothing store has several different styles from which to choose. The brands and prices differ. They come in different colors and are made of different fabrics. All these factors will make your decision making more complex. In addition, the Internet offers many consumer products. Making purchases through the Internet brings forth even more decision-making challenges.

As you can see, the changing world affects many of your decisions in life. Although you have little control over these external forces, it is helpful to be aware of them and how they may influence your life.

Although outside forces strongly influence you, most of what goes into shaping your life comes from within you. The more skilled you become in managing daily living, the greater control you have over your life. As you become more effective at managing your decisions, you will be better able to adjust to those changes that you cannot easily control.

Values, Goals, and Resources Influence Decisions

Management goes on at all times, sometimes effectively and sometimes ineffectively. The ability to manage well can be acquired through observation and practice. You can observe how the results of a decision can affect individual lives. You can see how practice in making decisions can lead to more effective decision making.

As you make decisions about daily living, you improve your managerial skills. You can begin by understanding more about your values, goals, and resources. You can also learn to use what is called the decision-making process.

Values and Goals

Management occurs when there is a problem to solve or a decision to make. Your decisions are guided by your goals. You set goals to achieve something important to you—something you value.

Values are what is important to you. They provide a motivating force. For instance, if you value a certain friendship, you are motivated to treat that friend in a special way. If you value having your own car, you may be motivated to get a job in order to earn money to buy the car. Values

Hercules, Inc.

1-6 **If you value cleanliness, you are motivated to shower or bathe regularly.**

M. Bruce

1-7 **Because this young man values having spending money, his goal is to find a job.**

may also motivate you to dress a certain way or to follow a certain grooming routine. See 1-6.

While values provide the motivation, goals provide direction. Goals are the ends or purposes toward which you strive. In setting goals, you project yourself into the future. See 1-7. To buy a car within the next year might be a goal of yours. However, you may value other things that cost money, such as clothes, DVDs, and going out on weekends. When you are deciding whether to spend money on clothes or to put the money in your savings account, your goal of buying a car may influence or direct your decision. That goal helps guide your decision making. *Standards* help you decide if you have reached your goal. They help measure your performance.

Resources

When you make decisions, you have many resources available to use in reaching your goals. A particular skill, money, and good health are just three examples. You may have used money to help reach a goal such as having some new clothes. You may have used the skill of playing a musical instrument to help you reach the goal of being in the school band. Your good health is a resource that might be helpful in

reaching a goal of finishing a difficult job. If you did not have good health as a resource, you might not have had the stamina to complete the task.

Many resources go unused because people do not recognize their resources or their possible uses. This textbook will help you become aware of the many resources that are available or that can be developed to help you reach your goals in daily living. See 1-8.

1-8 **If a friend tells you of a job opening or helps you prepare for an interview, he or she is acting as a valuable resource.**

Using the Decision-Making Process

To be able to manage decisions effectively is a valuable resource. The skills you use as you make decisions include the ability to clarify your values. This skill helps you be sure the goals toward which you are working represent those things most important to you. Another management skill is being aware of your resources and using them wisely.

Every day of your life you make decisions. Many of these decisions are routine. For instance, you decide what to wear to school or what to eat for lunch with little thought. On the other hand, you make many more complex decisions that help you solve problems or reach goals. Deciding where to go to college or how to solve the problem of poor grades are examples of difficult decisions. These decisions have a significant effect on your life. Learning to think through your decisions and focus on possible future outcomes will help you in solving both life's large and small problems. By doing so, you will be developing a helpful skill in managing daily living.

Each person makes decisions based on his or her knowledge, skills, values, and past experiences. Therefore, each person's decision making is different from any other person's. Although two people may make the same decision, their reasoning behind that decision may differ. For instance, two girls may apply for the same summer job as a lifeguard. One girl wants the job to help with her family's financial problems. The other girl has different reasons for wanting the job. She would like to spend the summer at the beach and save money for new fall school clothes. Both girls have decided to apply for the job, but they have different reasons for wanting the job.

Because you are a unique person, your decisions will be based on your unique values and goals. Decisions you make will be aimed at what is right for you.

The **decision-making process** is a valuable resource to help you solve problems and reach your goals. See 1-9. Whether you are deciding what to eat for dinner or what job to take, you can follow the steps of the decision-making process.

Identify the Problem to Be Solved or Decision to Be Made

Many of the problems and goals in your life are quite obvious. For instance, being hungry is an obvious problem. Wanting to have a party for your best friend's birthday is an obvious goal. Unfortunately, not all problems and goals are so easily identified. Sometimes the real problem remains hidden among the events that are happening in your life. For instance, two months ago Kiesha began working after school and on weekends at a women's clothing store. Since she began working, she hasn't been getting enough rest, and her grades in school are slipping. Her social life has become limited, too. She is considering quitting her job because she feels that her job is the problem. However, one of her close friends points out that maybe Kiesha is just not using her time well. Perhaps that is the real problem. She mentions how Kiesha spends her free hour

Use Your Reasoning Skills

Consider a decision you need to make. Use the five steps of the decision-making process to guide your decision making. Analyze how the process helps your decision making easier.

Decision-Making Process

1. **Identify the problem to be solved or decision to be made.**
State your problems as goals to focus on the positive and on the future.

2. **Consider all possible alternatives to reach that goal.**
List any option you can think of, even ones that may seem farfetched at first.

3. **Recognize the consequences of each alternative.**
Thoroughly examine each alternative and its outcome.

4. **Choose the best alternative.**
Plan and implement that alternative.

5. **Evaluate the decision and the process.**
Was the problem or goal clearly identified? Was the goal reached, and was the problem solved? If not, what other alternative might be used? What have you learned from this process that will be helpful to you in the future?

1-9 Skill in using the decision-making process is an important resource very helpful in daily living.

at school in the cafeteria visiting with friends. She also spends a lot of time watching television. She seems to waste study time calling friends to find out about assignments and then visiting on the phone. Kiesha's problem is not her part-time job, but instead the way she manages her time.

Sometimes people find it difficult to admit that a problem exists. It is their way of defending themselves in that situation. Paulo got a poor grade on his report card in math. He told his parents that it was because his teacher didn't like him. He found it difficult to admit to them and to himself that he really hadn't been working very hard on his math during the past few months. Paulo offered an explanation for his behavior that avoided the real problem.

One helpful step when identifying a problem is to state it in terms of a goal to achieve. Stating your problem as a goal forces you to deal with conflicting values. It forces you to decide which values are most important and to then set your goal according to those values. Kiesha's goal could be to improve her time management skills. Paulo's problem, stated as a goal, is to raise his math grade. It is helpful to focus on the future and the positive by stating the problem as a goal. See 1-10.

There is another advantage in stating the problem in terms of a goal. This technique helps you decide if you have identified the true problem. Ask yourself, "If I achieve this goal, will it solve the problem?" Paulo might have rationalized that his goal was to get his teacher to like him better. He might question, "If the teacher likes me better, will that make my math grade better?" If he is honest with himself, he will answer "No." He will develop another goal that identifies the real problem—lack of studying.

Consider All Possible Alternatives

In this second step of the decision-making process, alternative ways to solve the problems are considered. **Alternatives** are the various options available from which to choose. Ideally, you would be aware of all the possibilities. However, this is not always possible due to a lack of time or a lack of knowledge. Often, people limit themselves to two or three obvious alternatives. It might be more helpful to "brainstorm." This is a technique where you allow ideas to flow freely into your mind no matter how outrageous they may seem to be. This may result in new and creative alternatives to be considered.

Stating a Problem in Terms of a Goal	
Problem	Tim is discouraged because his parents don't seem to trust him. He wanted to take the car out of town to a football game, but they would not let him. He wanted to go to a rock concert in a nearby city with some friends, but they were against it. Tim knows he made some mistakes in the past that led to his parents' lack of trust. However, he thinks they ought to give him another chance.
Goal	Tim realizes the real problem is not being able to take the car out of town or to go to a concert. Instead, Tim's real problem is that his parents do not trust him. His goal is to prove he is trustworthy.
Advantages of Working with a Goal Rather Than a Problem	
A Goal Focuses on the Positive	By emphasizing the goal rather than the problem, Tim thinks of ways to prove he can be trusted. This will lead his parents to react more positively than if he tried to get around his parents' distrust.
A Goal Calls for Action	To prove that he can be trusted, Tim must take action. He must decide how to prove he is trustworthy. If he emphasized the problem rather than the goal, Tim might spend most of his time moping about not being able to do what he wanted to do.
A Goal Focuses on the Future	As Tim makes future decisions, he will keep his goal in mind. He will try to make each decision to help prove that he is trustworthy. Then each action will help Tim reach his goal of proving he can be trusted.

1-10 In solving problems, it is helpful to state the problem in terms of a goal.

Recognize the Consequences of Each Alternative

As you gather information about each alternative, you consider the consequences of each. **Consequences** are the end results of each option. Consider the following example. Robyn and her sister have decided they want to go to a movie tonight. They would like to choose from three good movies. Their goal is to decide which of the three movies to see.

Consider all the facts about each alternative. In this example, one of the movies is downtown and will require taking the bus. The movie starts at 6:30 and ends at 9:00. Because it is 5:00 now, the girls will have to rush, grab a quick bite to eat, and hurry to the bus stop.

One of the other movies is not on the bus route, so they would need to make arrangements for a ride. The third movie also is downtown and starts later. However, that movie will not be over until after the last bus. They would have to find another ride home.

Each of the three choices has advantages and disadvantages. No choice stands out as the best alternative. Robyn and her sister would have to consider each and decide on their priorities related to time, money, and convenience. The main disadvantage of the first choice is having to eat hurriedly and rush to get to the bus stop. The second choice would be inconvenient in terms of arranging transportation since their brother is using the family car for a date. Transportation is also the disadvantage of the third choice since they would have to arrange for a ride home. Calling a taxi would be a problem in terms of money. It would probably cost more for the ride than for the movie. The two resources involved in this choice seem to be time and money. To make a choice, Robyn and her sister have to set priorities.

Considering alternatives as done here takes only a matter of seconds in your head. However, both the problems and the alternatives are often more complicated. You will find in such cases that writing down the facts about each alternative can be very helpful. See 1-11.

Choosing a college is an important decision that can be difficult and involved. You may need to write down the advantages and disadvantages of each alternative in order to consider all aspects of each one. This is how Tony decided what college to

attend. He considered the alternatives of the local community college, a private college, and a state university.

Most of Tony's friends were going to attend the local community college, and it was also the least expensive alternative. Tony figured he could live at home and keep his part-time job. However, this school did not offer a program in engineering, Tony's area of interest. This was a definite disadvantage since one of Tony's goals was to become an engineer.

The prestigious private school Tony was interested in offered one of the best engineering programs in the nation. Two of Tony's friends were planning to attend this school. However, it was 750 miles from home and the most expensive alternative. Tony would need to take out a large loan and get a part-time job to help with expenses.

Using the Decision-Making Process

State the Problem or Decision as a Goal	List Possible Alternatives	List Consequences of Each Alternative	Choose the Best Alternative Based on Your Standards
To select the movie it would be most convenient to see	6:30 movie downtown	• Will have to hurry • Little time to eat • Can take bus down and back	Best alternative for persons whose standards include economy over personal appearance and eating well
	7:00 movie at mall	• Will have to find a ride—not on bus route • Brother using family car	Not a possible alternative as no car is available
	8:30 movie downtown	• Plenty of time to eat and catch bus • Will have to find a ride home • Taxi fare is expensive	Best alternative for persons whose standards include eating well and good grooming over economy

1-11 **The decision-making process will help the girls choose the best alternative.**

The state school Tony considered had a good reputation for its engineering program and was also nationally known. However, it was not as prestigious as the private school. Although it cost more than the community college, it was one-third the cost of the private college. Tony figured a part-time job on campus would help provide him with spending money. Although he would definitely have to live at school, Tony would be close enough to go home on weekends. He was concerned, however, that none of his high school friends would be attending school there.

Writing down the advantages and disadvantages of each school was very helpful to Tony. By reviewing this information, he was able to weigh the alternatives and make what he felt was the best decision.

Choose the Best Alternative

It is not always easy to choose the best alternative. You have to consider the benefits of each as well as the disadvantages or costs. Your values, goals, and standards will guide you in making your choice. See 1-12. In Tony's case, he needed to decide what characteristics he valued most in a school. Was he determined to reach his goal of achieving a degree in engineering? What standards did he use to measure a good college and a good education?

Tony thought through each of the alternatives. He strongly valued a good education, and his goal of becoming an engineer was very important to him. Therefore, he could not attend the community college with his friends. It did not meet his standards because it offered no program in engineering.

The state and the private schools had both advantages and disadvantages. The private school offered prestige and two of Tony's friends were going there. Tony knew the state school had a good reputation, too, and tuition was one-third the cost of the private school. Tony decided that he valued a good education, but prestige was not that important to him. Prestige was not worth

1-12 When making a difficult decision, leave yourself enough time to consider each alternative carefully so you don't feel rushed.

 1-13 **Choosing a college is a difficult decision for many people.**

such a large difference in cost. Tony could reach his goal of becoming an engineer just as well at the state school. Tony also knew that he would meet many new friends at school. At the same time, he would be close enough to go home and visit his old friends on weekends.

Ultimately, Tony decided the state school was his best alternative. It is wise to examine each of your alternatives in a thoughtful, logical manner like Tony did. Then you, too, will be able to select the alternative that will most help you reach your goal.

Evaluate the Decision and the Process

When a problem is stated as a goal, you can use your standards to judge whether you have reached the goal. This is the process of **evaluation**. In other words, you judge your decision based on your standards.

Keep in mind that people's standards will vary. In the example of choosing a movie, one person might consider rushing to get to a movie very inconvenient. That

person might rather pay the extra money for cab fare home following a later movie. Another person might decide the opposite. The two people have different standards for measuring the goal related to choosing the movie.

In choosing a college, prestige might be more important to one person than cost, 1-13. That person might choose the private college. To another person, being with friends and family might be more important than reaching the goal of becoming an engineer. That person might attend the community college.

Evaluating the decision-making process is important, particularly when the decision does not seem to have been the best one. Ask yourself the following questions: Did you clearly identify the problem or the goal? Were the alternatives possible? Did you think through the outcomes of each alternative?

In the example of choosing a movie, the bus may have been late after the girls hurried to get to the bus stop on time. Then they would have missed the beginning of the movie. In evaluating the process used, Robyn and her sister should have planned for the possibility of a late bus.

Careful evaluation of the decision-making process can be a helpful guide in making other decisions. The evaluation is successful if the information gained is used to prevent future mistakes, even if the decision made was a wrong one. Everyone makes occasional mistakes in decision making. However, the wise person learns to profit from those mistakes.

Evaluating your decisions is a major step in learning to use the decision-making process successfully.

Summary

Every day you make decisions aimed at reaching your goals. To become an effective manager, it is helpful to be aware of the kinds of decisions you make each day. The decisions you make will be influenced by your values, goals, and resources. They will also be influenced by your ability to use the decision-making process.

Decision making has become a challenging activity in today's changing world. However, skill in using each step of the decision-making process is important in effectively managing your daily life.

To Review

1. Managers make _____ that move them toward their _____.
2. List two resources available to each of the following individuals to help reach their goals: manager of a team, manager of a clothing store, and a high school principal.
3. List four terms that can be used to describe stages in life.
4. Name four roles you may assume in your lifetime.
5. Explain how decisions you make might affect other members of your family.
6. Give examples of three decisions you might make in managing your daily life.
7. Describe three forces outside the family that have made managing daily living more difficult.
8. Your decisions are guided by your _____, which are based on your _____.
9. List the five steps in the decision-making process.
10. In the decision-making process, it is helpful to state the problem in terms of a _____.

To Do with the Class

1. Choose class members to represent various stages in life. Suggest a variety of decisions that are related to each life stage.
2. Work in small groups to solve a given problem following the steps in the decision-making process.
3. Practice with others to state problems in terms of a goal.
4. Share examples of decisions you make that may seem unimportant, but could have a significant impact on your life if repeated on a regular basis.

To Do with Your Community

1. Interview someone in your community who is in a management position. Discuss with that person the decision-making process. Ask for an example of how that person has used the process.
2. Talk with some older adults in your community about how decision making might have differed for them in different stages of life. How was it the same?
3. Select three or four people who each represent a different stage in life. Interview them about the major decision they have had to make related to their particular stage in life. What values and goals do they hold?
4. Invite someone in your community who is involved in community leadership to speak to the class. Ask the person to discuss the importance of decision making within the community.

To Challenge Your Thinking

1. Describe at least five decisions a young person might make in a typical day. Categorize the decisions as simple decisions or decisions that are more complex.
2. Think of four persons you know who are at different life stages. List two decisions each person might possibly make that are related to his or her particular stage in life.
3. Choose two roles you feel you may assume in life and list five decisions you might have to make in each role.
4. Identify values and goals that might be involved in the decisions you described in #1.

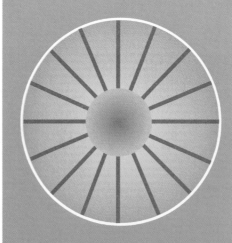

2

Your Values, Goals, and Standards

To Know

value indicators
higher values
instrumental values
moral values
human need values
needs
aesthetic values
culture
peer group
short-term goals
long-term goals
standards
objective standards
subjective standards
conventional standards
flexible standards

Objectives

After studying this chapter, you will be able to

- identify values.
- explain how needs and values influence your behavior.
- distinguish between higher values and instrumental values.
- describe how values form and change.
- analyze the relationship between values, goals, and standards.
- describe the importance of flexible standards.
- use your values, goals, and standards to become a better manager.

As a manager, you make many decisions that are based on your needs and values. These decisions move you toward your goals. Your standards help you judge when you have reached your goals. Understanding your needs, values, goals, and standards will help improve your decision-making ability.

Understanding Your Values

When you value something, you believe it is important—that it is worthwhile. Values are more than just ideas you discuss. You use them to judge the worth of people, objects, ideas, actions, and situations.

You show others what you value by what you say and do. See 2-1. What you say and do are **value indicators.** Other value indicators are your attitudes, beliefs, interests, actions, and activities. They reveal your values. For instance, saving money to buy a car would show that owning a car is one of your values. Doing volunteer work at a local hospital would show that you value helping others.

Do you know what you value? To better understand your values, you might think of them as fitting into two categories. Most values can be described as either higher values or instrumental values.

2-1 **2-1 This action indicates these two people value exercise and good health.**

Love, honesty, beauty, and security are examples of **higher values.** Examples of **instrumental values** might include your friends, home, stereo, dog, or car. As you can see by these examples, a higher value is more abstract than an instrumental value. When something is abstract, it is not a material object. For this reason, it is more difficult to understand. However, an instrumental value is usually a more specific value. Its meaning is usually clearer. It is often a material item.

Higher Values

Most higher values fit into three categories. These are moral values, human need values, and aesthetic values.

Moral Values

Moral values have to do with conduct—right and wrong behavior. They indicate what is right, just, and good. In everyday life we see examples of specific moral values such as honesty, respect, fairness, and responsibility.

Your beliefs and actions will indicate your moral values. Returning a lost wallet to the owner shows the moral value of honesty. Listening to the opinion of someone whose ideas differ from yours is an example of respect. Getting to work on time shows you value responsibility.

In the society of this country, human dignity is a moral value. *Human dignity* is the belief that each individual has worth and is equal to others. Laws were designed to protect democratic rights such as freedom of speech, religious freedom, and equal opportunity. These rights are intended to promote human dignity. These higher values are quite abstract and, therefore, can be difficult to understand.

Human Need Values

Human need values are related to your basic fundamental needs, both physical and psychological. You have these values because you have a need for them. Human beings share the same basic needs. **Needs** are the basic items you must have to live.

Physical needs include the need for food, water, air, and rest. Another physical need is to protect yourself from exposure. Unless these needs are met, you cannot stay alive. You help meet these needs through your choices of food, clothing, and shelter.

Psychological needs involve what you think and how you feel. These include your need to feel safe and secure. You also need acceptance as part of a group. Persons at any age need to love and to feel that they are loved. They need to know the warmth of human affection. Other psychological needs include the need for respect and recognition from others. You need to feel that you are a worthwhile person and that others also feel you are a worthwhile person. Self-fulfillment is another psychological need. This is your need to become all that you are capable of becoming. It involves your desire for growth—physically, socially, emotionally, and intellectually. Self-fulfillment involves your need to be creative and to succeed.

There are several theories regarding human needs. A system devised by psychiatrist, Abraham Maslow, states that humans are motivated by the same basic needs. These basic needs are arranged in an order of urgency. Physical needs are the most urgent of these needs. To reach self-fulfillment, all other needs must be at least partially met. See 2-2.

Aesthetic Values

Aesthetic values are related to the five senses: touch, smell, taste, sight, and

Maslow's Hierarchy of Human Needs

Self-Fulfillment Needs
Meeting these needs involves doing what you must to become fully yourself, developing individuality, and becoming everything you are capable of becoming.

Ego and Esteem Needs
Meeting these needs means developing respect and liking for yourself and others. Having strength, competence, status, achievement, freedom, and/or fame helps meet these needs.

Love Needs–Social Needs
Feelings of acceptance, membership, affection, belonging, and being loved and wanted help meet these needs.

Safety Needs
These needs include protection from physical and psychological threat, fear, and anxiety, and the need for order, structure, and security.

Physical/Survival Needs
These include needs for food, water, shelter, and clothing.

2-2 According to Maslow, as human needs are met, beginning with physical needs, the goal of self-fulfillment can be achieved.

hearing. Your senses combine with your thoughts to develop an appreciation—an aesthetic sense. Enjoying a beautiful sunset, a delicious meal, or the sound of your favorite musical group are examples of aesthetic values.

Aesthetic values pertain to an appreciation of function as well as looks. You might appreciate how well a car runs or the ease of using a particular computer program. You value how it functions. You may also appreciate the skill of a musician, a surgeon, or an athlete. They have skills that you have learned to appreciate and value.

Instrumental Values

These values are more specific. Instrumental values are the means you have of attaining higher level values. For instance, everyone has a need for respect and recognition. These are higher level human need values. However, people have differing instrumental values that lead to respect and recognition.

For instance, a man might value a rebuilt car from the 1950s because other people admire it. Their admiration gives him feelings of respect and recognition. A teenager might value her position on the soccer team. She experiences feelings of respect and recognition from other people because of this status.

Instrumental values, such as the rebuilt car and being a member of the soccer team, are more specific than higher level values. These instrumental values are held primarily because of the higher level values to which they lead.

Influences on Value Formation

The formation of values is a personal process that continues throughout life. As life experiences broaden your awareness, new values develop. Values develop from experiences related to your basic needs, family, culture, peers, and everyday life. See 2-3.

Basic Needs

Values develop as basic needs are met. Early in childhood, you learned to value your parents as they met your need for security. They held you close and cared for you. This became important to you because it made you feel good. You felt secure and valued the security they provided.

2-3 Belonging to a group of friends often gives teenagers feelings of self-worth and recognition.

Experiences throughout life continue to meet basic human needs. A teenage girl values getting her driver's license. It helps satisfy her need for independence and self-worth. A young man values his promotion at work because it helps satisfy his need for respect and recognition. An older woman values the letters she gets from her children and grandchildren. The letters make her feel loved and needed.

Family

Your family influences your values. Through their actions and words, members of your family demonstrate their values. See 2-4. They act as models for you to follow. Your parents may attend religious services because religion is important to them. They demonstrate this value by setting an example.

Families also influence the formation of values by distinguishing right from wrong. They may have made such statements as, "You should always tell the truth," or "It is wrong to steal." Such statements indicate their values.

2-4 **These parents demonstrate their feelings about the value of learning by often reading to their daughter.**

Culture

Values develop from the culture in which you live. These values are often closely related to the values of parents and family. **Culture** refers to the beliefs, social customs, and traits of a particular social group. Cultural values may determine foods eaten, the way holidays are celebrated, and methods of education. Family structures and patterns also vary from culture to culture. You would not expect a child raised in London, England, to have the same values as a child growing up in a jungle village in Brazil. The two children would have been exposed to very different cultural experiences. See 2-5.

Peers

Values are strongly influenced by peer groups. A **peer group** consists of persons similar to you in age or status. The influence of the peer group is thought to be greatest during your adolescence. It is a period when you are meeting new people. You are becoming aware of the values of others even though these values may differ from those of your own family.

Everyday Living

Your daily activities and the people with whom you interact have an influence on your values. Television and advertising have been shown to influence individual values. Your values may also be influenced by world politics, environmental problems, and the nation's economy.

2-5 **Daily experiences of young people who live in the city vary greatly from those who live in the country.**

New experiences in your everyday living give more meaning to past experiences. Your feelings about education may be a good example. When you were young, you may have complained about studying math in school. It is difficult to value something when you don't understand its importance. Later, through new experiences, perhaps a new job as a cashier, you may better understand the importance of what you were studying. Then the value of education may have more meaning for you. See 2-6.

Many times people learn to value something when it is no longer available. You have heard the saying, "You don't know what you have 'til it's gone." Often people are not aware of the value of something until it is gone. For example, this may occur when there is a fuel shortage and the car cannot be driven as much. People then learn to value the freedom they had to use the car before the shortage of fuel. This recognition of value also happens in relationships. The teenage boy may normally think of his younger sister as a nuisance. He learns to value their relationship when she goes to stay with their grandparents for a month and he realizes he does miss her.

Values Change

Throughout life, you will continue to do new things and meet new people. Through these experiences, you may either develop new values or modify old ones. For instance, you may become involved in a sport new to you, such as tennis. As you learn the game and enjoy playing, you develop a new value.

Perhaps while you are ill, a friend takes careful notes for you in class and comes to visit you often. Because your friend is so thoughtful, your value of that friendship becomes stronger.

In situations involving other people, remember that every person has his or her own unique values. Those values are based on that person's particular life experiences. They are neither right nor wrong, but they show what that person feels is strongly influencing his or her life.

As you manage your life, making decisions and solving problems, you will be making certain discoveries. You will be learning what is important and meaningful to you—what you value.

Value Conflicts

You will become quite aware of your values when you experience a conflict in values. Value conflicts occur often in everyday living. Sometimes conflicting

2-6 As you get closer to entering the workforce on a full-time basis, education may become more important to you.

*Getting*Involved

Select a service organization or club. What do they value in members? Find out how they contribute to the community. How could you become involved in this club? What value would the club find in your efforts? How does the community value the club?

values involve fairly simple choices. For instance, should you have a candy bar or an apple for a snack? Your value of good health may conflict with the pleasure of eating the candy bar.

Many situations involving value conflicts are not so simple. They can create stress in a person's life. For example, Jim's best friend confides in him that he has stolen a copy of the final exam for their math course. The teacher asks Jim if he knows who stole the exam. In this situation, Jim experiences a conflict of values. Jim has strong feelings about honesty, but he also values the other boy's friendship.

Whether you are making choices in simple or stressful situations, you may have to decide which value is more important to you. When you experience value conflict, you are forced to make a choice.

Value conflicts occur both between persons and within a person. When parents insist their children be home by a certain time, a value conflict may occur. The parents' decision may reflect their values of health and safety. Their child, who disagrees with the time limit, may value his or her freedom and independence. This is a value conflict between persons.

Value conflicts are often experienced within a person. A teenage girl who has a midnight curfew experiences a value conflict when her friends ask her to stay longer at a party. On one side, she values having fun with her friends at the party. On the other side, she values the feelings of her parents. She must make a choice, deciding which values take priority.

Understanding Your Goals

As you know, a *goal* is something you desire to have or achieve at a given point. How do goals relate to values? Your goals develop from your values. Because you value something, you set certain goals. When a goal is achieved, you have realized something of value in your life.

Types of Goals

To help you understand goals, think of them in terms of time periods: short-term goals and long-term goals. **Short-term goals** indicate what you want to accomplish soon. This may mean within hours or days—in the immediate future. **Long-term goals** are what you want to accomplish later. This may mean next year or even years from now, 2-7.

2-7 **This young woman's short-term goal was to finish the race. Her long-term goal is to be healthy.**

Brainstorming

Describe situations illustrating value conflicts within an individual. Are there any recurring elements in your examples? What does this indicate about the most common value conflicts of your age group?

Short-term goals tend to be clearly defined and identified. They tend to have a single purpose. Finishing your English assignment, opening a savings account, or getting to school on time are examples of short-term goals.

Making specific plans for reaching your short-term goals will help you reach them more easily. For instance, if Judy's goal is to raise her math grade from a B to an A, she can make plans for reaching this goal. The first step of her plan might be to discuss her goal with her teacher. Then she might spend more time each day studying math and also do some extra credit. Finally, Judy might plan to study harder for her math tests. Following this plan will make it easier for Judy to reach her goal.

Many long-term goals are more general and more abstract than short-term goals. To get married and have a happy family life is an example of a general, more abstract long-term goal. A more specific long-term goal might be to become a commercial airline pilot.

Whether the goal is general or specific, many short-term goals will lead to the long-term goal. For instance, to become a commercial airline pilot flying a 757 might involve the following short-term goals: (1) get a private pilot's license, (2) get a commercial instrument rating, (3) get a multi-engine rating, (4) get a type rating for a 757 pilot. It is necessary to accomplish these short-term goals in order to reach that desired long-term goal.

Goals Change

As you have new experiences that result in value changes, goals change accordingly. For instance, a young woman in business school had a goal of buying a car after she got her first job. However, her first job was in the downtown area of a very large city. Parking was a problem, but public transportation was quite good. Because of this new situation, the car did not seem so important to her. She changed goals, planning instead to buy furniture for her new apartment.

Many goals change because they are unreasonable. Maria, a high school sophomore, loves horses and has always had the goal of owning her own horse. As time has passed, Maria has realized that her goal is unreasonable. She lives in a city where horses are not allowed. It would be too expensive to rent space to keep the horse in the country. It also would be too difficult to get to where the horse was stabled. She realized this goal would not be possible at this stage of her life.

Standards as Measures

As you strive to reach your goals, certain measures or clues will show your progress. These measures or clues are your **standards.** They help measure performance and tell you when a goal has been reached to your satisfaction. They help you identify what is acceptable and what is not acceptable to you.

When you describe something you value, you often do so by describing your standards. If you are asked to describe a good friend, you might say, "A good friend is someone I can talk to about private matters. A friend is someone I enjoy being with and someone who shares many of my interests." These are your standards for a good friend.

Objective and Subjective Standards

As with values and goals, there are different ways of classifying standards. Think of standards in terms of objective and subjective standards.

Objective standards are specific and easy to measure. Points in a test, requirements for graduation, and the number of inches in a foot are examples of objective standards. These standards are the same for everyone.

Subjective standards come from your own value system and are based on your own experiences. Subjective standards cannot be specifically measured. Each person's subjective standards vary. See 2-8. For instance, people have differing standards for a good book, good music, and an enjoyable vacation. See 2-9.

Differing standards may cause conflict. For example, a mother asked her teenage son to clean the kitchen. Although he felt he did a good job, his mother was disappointed. Their standards regarding a clean kitchen were different.

2-9 **People have differing standards about what is a good restaurant.**

Standards for a Good Summer Job According to Three Teenagers	
Randy	Don't have to work hard Get plenty of money Don't have to work nights
Joan	Good pay Convenient hours Physical rather than office work
Jermaine	Don't have to work weekends Good pay Outdoor work

2-8 **Although you may have the same goal as someone else, you have your own standards for judging progress toward that goal.**

Use Your Reasoning Skills

Analyze yourself in terms of "changing values." What did you value as a ten-year-old compared with what you value now? What might be some reasons for these value changes? Do you still have some of the same values? Do you see these as consistency in your character or lack of personal growth?

Some subjective standards are referred to as **conventional standards.** These standards are generally accepted in our society. These often are related to traditions, social customs, and social behavior. For instance, conventional standards for behavior in a movie theater would include sitting and being quiet.

Flexible Standards

When you have **flexible standards,** you are willing to adapt those standards when necessary. Research shows that families who have flexible standards are likely to be more relaxed and have closer relationships.

Recall the situation involving the teenage boy who had differing standards for a clean kitchen from those of his mother. The mother might have become angry because she felt the cleaning job was poorly done. However, if her standards were more flexible, she could adapt them to the situation. She might realize her son may not have enough experience to know the best way to clean certain parts of the kitchen. For instance, he might not know how to clean the oven or get the marks out of the sink. The mother might then show her son how these particular tasks can be done.

As pressure builds in your various roles, being able to use flexible standards may help you avoid or relieve stress. For instance, many mothers who are employed outside the home have more flexible standards related to the neatness of the home. Many fathers in these same homes have developed more flexible standards regarding their "homemaker role." They are more willing to help with the cooking and cleaning. When both the father and the mother have flexible standards, stress is less likely to occur.

Summary

By better understanding your own needs and values, it will be easier to make the choices most important to you. Understanding how values develop will help you understand and resolve conflicting values. Value conflicts will occur both within yourself and with other people.

Goals develop from your values. You will be developing both long-term and short-term goals throughout life. Standards are measurements used to evaluate your progress toward your goals. You will find that flexible standards can help you move toward your goals.

To Review

1. List four examples of how people might reveal their values.
2. Which of the following are higher values and which are instrumental values?
   A. Self-respect.
   B. Money.
   C. Painting skill.
   D. Human dignity.
   E. Education.
   F. Truth.
3. _____ needs include the need for food, water, air, and rest. _____ needs involve what you think and how you feel.
4. Describe five psychological needs.
5. Give an example of conflicting values you might experience.
6. Value conflicts occur both _____ individuals and _____ an individual.
7. List five sources of values.
8. List three examples of short-term goals and three examples of long-term goals.
9. What is the purpose of standards?
10. Which of the following would be defined by objective standards and which would be defined by subjective standards?
    A. A good dinner.
    B. A passing test score.
    C. An exciting football game.
    D. A clean room.
    E. College entrance requirements.
    F. A quart of milk.

To Do with the Class

1. Choose a specific higher value and discuss ways people might express this value through their behavior. Suggest behavior that might indicate a lack of that same value.
2. Describe situations illustrating value conflicts between two teenage friends.
3. Discuss how the following might influence a person's values:
   A. Watching television.
   B. An unhappy home life.
   C. Living in a period of economic recession.
   D. Death of a family member in an automobile accident.
   E. Living in a foreign country for six months.
4. Describe situations that illustrate persons using flexible standards.

To Challenge Your Thinking

1. Look through the comic section of newspapers and find cartoons related to values. Analyze how they reflect certain values. Bring them to class to contribute to a bulletin board on values.
2. Make a list of some of the decisions you have made today. Decide what value or values were involved in making each decision. In which situations did you experience conflicting values?
3. Talk with your parents or other parents to find out what values they want their children to learn from them. If you have children in the future, what values will you want your children to learn from you?
4. Make a list of short-term goals you have accomplished recently or hope to accomplish in the near future. Make a list of your long-term goals. How do these two lists compare?

To Do with Your Community

1. Identify values held by the community in which you live. What are examples that show these values? (For instance, aesthetic values are shown through lovely parks.)
2. Collect advertisements from local publications. Analyze them as to what values they seem to illustrate.
3. Invite a panel of individuals representing various ages, lifestyles, and ethnic groups to discuss influences on value formation.
4. Arrange for a group of parents and teens to debate the following: Values cannot be taught, but they can be learned.

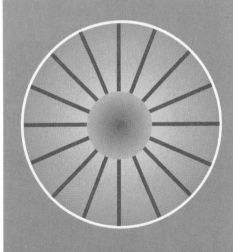

3

Managing Your Resources

To Know

human resources
motivation
nonhuman resources
credit
community resources
natural resources
exchanging resources
developing resources
sharing resources
use-cost
management process
planning
sequence
implementing
controlling
evaluating
work simplification

Objectives

After studying this chapter, you will be able to

◇ identify a variety of human and nonhuman resources.

◇ explain how resources change throughout a person's life.

◇ describe ways to use your resources.

apply responsible use of resources to your daily life.

◇ identify existing resources and resources that can be developed.

◇ describe how the management process will help you achieve your goals.

How do you reach the goals you have developed? You do it by using your resources. Your resources help you reach your goals and maintain control over your life. A person who manages well is aware of the resources available and how they can be developed and used.

Types of Resources

In order to make wise choices about the use of resources, you need to be able to recognize the many resources that are available. You can only use a resource if you can recognize it. Then you can consider using it to help you reach a goal.

Many resources are available. Some are abundant and some are scarce. Some are your own, while others have to be shared. Some are inherited at birth, yet others have to be developed. Resources can be divided into two major groups: human resources and nonhuman resources.

Human Resources

Human resources are the resources that come from within a person. Your own human resources exist because of the person you have become as you have matured. Your experiences in life influence your human resources. These resources include your time, energy, personal qualities, knowledge, talents, and skills. See 3-1.

Time is a human resource because each person must decide how to use the 24 hours in each day. How each person uses that time as a resource differs.

Personal qualities that are human resources include good physical and mental health. Strength, energy, and the absence of sickness indicate good physical health. Good mental health is indicated when a person is happy, self-confident, and emotionally stable. These can be effective resources. **Motivation**, having a strong desire to achieve a goal, may also be included in this list of human resources.

Knowledge, talents, and skills make up a wide range of human resources. Your mental abilities affect your ability to reason and deal with problems. They include how well you communicate with others. These can be helpful human resources.

Hercules, Inc.

3-1 **A pleasant personality is a human resource.**

Your talents are areas in which you perform well. Some talents and skills may be the result of genetics, such as a beautiful singing voice. Many others can be developed throughout life. You can develop such talents and skills as painting, playing a musical instrument, or building furniture.

Other persons are also important human resources. These may be family members, friends, or persons in the community who provide services to you. The members of your family, through their loving, caring, and helping, can be a valuable resource in your life. See 3-2. Skills of other persons can also be important resources in your life. Your teachers, coaches, and employers share their skills to help you reach certain goals.

3-2 **Special relationships are also human resources.**

personal belongings. Your bike, CD player, and clothing are all nonhuman resources.

Your money and purchasing power are resources that include any wages, salary, or allowance you receive. This also includes money you might have in a checking or savings account and money you receive as gifts. **Credit**, a promise to pay later for goods or services used now, can be a part of your purchasing power. Using credit by borrowing money from a bank or savings and loan is a way to use your purchasing power as a resource.

Community resources exist not only within your local community but also throughout your state and nation. Citizens usually share these resources. The government provides some through tax monies. City, county, and state parks; police and fire protection; libraries; and city services such as trash collection are examples. Private firms such as banks and department stores provide other community resources. Citizen groups like the Chamber of Commerce and the Better Business Bureau are other examples. **Natural resources**—water, energy, air, and other resources that occur in nature—are community resources because all people share them. See 3-3.

Many human resources are never used. You may have many personal resources available to use that you have yet to discover.

Nonhuman Resources

Nonhuman resources include material possessions, money or purchasing power, and community resources. Nonhuman resources are somewhat easier to recognize than human resources. They are not physically or mentally a part of an individual.

Your personal and family belongings are material possessions. These include your home, your furniture, and all your

Scarcity of Resources

No one has unlimited resources. Human resources, such as time and energy, as well as nonhuman resources, such as money and possessions, are all limited or scarce.

For many young people, money is a good example of a scarce resource. Most teens do not have enough money to buy everything they want to buy or to do everything they would like to do. For instance, Janet may have to choose between buying a new pair of jeans and attending a rock concert. Juan may have to settle for a used car rather than that new car he would have preferred. Because resources are limited, it helps to understand how to further develop and use your resources. Learning to conserve your resources and use them to effectively satisfy your most important needs and wants is important.

Changing Resources

Often, the amount of resources and the types of resources you have are related to your stage in life. For instance, most teenagers have plenty of energy, which can be a valuable resource. However, money is often a limited resource for teens.

During a family's expanding stage, resources are often limited. As children are added, costs become greater. Additional work is related to the expanding family. In many cases, parents may devote more of their time and energy to activities other than their wage-earning responsibilities.

As children mature and develop skills and abilities through education, these skills and abilities become valuable resources. These resources can enhance their lives and often provide a method to earn an income. As young people leave home and become financially independent from their parents, there is often a change in the resources available to their parents. They may be in a better financial position, but they will no longer have their children's help with responsibilities at home.

As people age, their needs and resources often change. For instance, they may have more time available for activities, but their energy level may diminish with age. Financial resources may also affect the quality of life in these aging years.

Glad Wrap & Bags

3-3 **A variety of human and nonhuman resources helped make this public service project a success.**

Using Your Resources

Because most resources are limited, the wise manager carefully chooses which resources to use and how to use them.

Understanding the different ways resources might be used may help you manage effectively. Resources can be used in the following ways:

◆ They can be exchanged or traded.
◆ They can be developed or expanded.
◆ They can be shared.

Exchanging Resources

Long ago, **exchanging resources** was common. People would trade one resource for another. The early settlers might have traded blankets to the Native Americans for meat. Now you go to the store and exchange your money for food. See 3-4. Many people who go to work each day exchange their knowledge, skills, time, and energy for money. When your family eats out, you are exchanging money for food. You are also paying for the time and energy you would normally use to prepare the food at home. As consumers, you exchange money for goods and services.

Think of the possible exchange of resources that can take place within the family. Some examples are obvious. A mother and father go to work each day so the family will have money for their needs and wants. In exchange, their children may have certain jobs to do at home, such as cooking, cleaning, and lawn mowing. See 3-5.

Less obvious but very important are the exchanges of emotional resources within the family. These involve the loving, caring, comforting, and supporting that take place among family members. You see an example of this in the young child who runs into the house after a fall from a tricycle. The child is eager to have a parent provide comfort and take care of the scraped knee. The child gives the parent a hug after the bandage has been placed over

3-5 **These children help wash the family car on weekends.**

M. Bruce

3-4 **Money is exchanged for food products.**

the cut. This emotional resource, the hug of a child, is a positive factor in parenting. Parent and child have helped each other in an exchange of emotional resources.

In today's busy world, some people choose to help organize their lives by contracting services. In other words, they have other people do some of their work at home for them. Doing so may give them more time for leisure activities, hobbies, or time with the family. Families where both parents work or single-parent families could especially benefit from these services. For example, a family might decide to pay a person to come to their home and do the cleaning or the cooking. Another family might decide to have someone do their laundry or their yard work. By contracting to have these services done, families are increasing their available time. They are trading one resource, money, for another resource, time.

Developing Resources

Knowledge and skills are human resources that are closely related. The possibilities for **developing resources**—increasing or expanding them—are practically unlimited. Being a student is an opportunity for you to expand your human resources.

Radio, television, books, and magazines can be helpful in developing knowledge and skills. The Internet provides an excellent opportunity for research and problem solving. You can also increase these resources through your experiences with other people. See 3-6. Practice will develop your skills as well.

The human resources that are related to your personal qualities can also be developed. Your health can be improved by eating nutritious foods. Daily exercise will help keep you physically fit.

Material resources increase as you buy new items or as they are given to you. Money and purchasing power can be

3-6 **Meeting new people and making new friends are ways of developing resources.**

expanded as you earn and save more money. A savings account or investments can help you expand your money resources. By managing your money wisely, you may find you have more money available to use as you wish.

Community resources are constantly being developed and expanded. New stores, banks, and services appear in many communities, adding to the existing resources. As certain social needs arise, public and private services are added or changed to help meet those needs.

Sharing Resources

Many resources are shared. **Sharing resources** means more than one person is using them. Each day families share such resources as the family car, computer, and television. Facilities in the home such as the bathroom and kitchen are also shared.

Personal resources are often shared. You might lend a friend a DVD that he wants to see. You might borrow your neighbor's lawn mower while yours is being repaired. Perhaps your brother is low on cash and would like to borrow some money from you.

All the family may share income earned by one or two family members. Material possessions in the home are used by different family members. If one person uses these resources carelessly, other family members are forced to limit their use of those resources.

Community resources are also shared. Many people in the community use resources such as libraries, parks, schools, and religious facilities. Many local support groups, such as Parents Without Partners, Battered Women's Support Group, and Alcoholics Anonymous are open to the public. As a nation, we share natural resources such as the air we breathe and the water we drink. See 3-7.

On a national level, conservation of natural resources is a current issue. People are aware there is not an endless supply of natural resources in the world. Wasteful use of resources such as gas and oil causes shortages and results in higher prices. Misuse of some resources causes pollution of air and water. Many public and private groups are striving to better inform people about conserving natural resources.

Almost all resources are limited. If they are used carelessly, there is less available for everyone to use. Sharing resources, whether among family members or on a national level, requires wise use of those resources. If groups are going to use their resources wisely, all members of the group must act responsibly.

Managing Resources Effectively

Managing your resources means more than just using them. When you manage, you control the use of resources so a goal is reached. Identifying your resources and

3-7 **Water and trees are natural resources that we share throughout our nation.**

carefully planning their use are two skills you can develop to help you. Use of various management skills is an additional process that will help in managing your resources.

Identifying Your Resources

The skill of managing resources can be learned. The first step is to become aware of your existing resources and how they might be developed. Without recognizing a resource, you cannot take advantage of its use. Too often money is considered the one major resource to use in achieving goals. However, many other resources are available or could be developed.

First, consider your human resources—your personal qualities. Is your health good? Do you have a normal amount of strength and energy for your age? If so, you have these valuable human resources to help you in many situations. If your health is not good, you could take steps to improve it. You could see a doctor, improve your eating habits, or get more rest. See 3-8.

Your personality can be another valuable human resource. If you get along well with other people and have a positive attitude toward daily challenges, you have two valuable resources. However, if you have trouble getting along with people, or often feel depressed, you can take action. Talking with a parent, counselor, religious leader, or good friend might help you understand how you can improve your personality.

Can you identify your special abilities, talents, and skills? You can learn additional skills through classes, from other people, or by reading about those skills. There are "how to" books written about almost every skill that exists.

Your material resources, particularly your material possessions and money, are somewhat easier to identify. The quality of your material possessions may depend on how you have cared for them.

3-8 **Improving your health and appearance through exercise is a way of developing resources.**

Your purchasing power is a resource that might be developed or expanded. You can become aware of ways to make your money "grow." Various types of savings and investment plans can become valuable resources for you.

Effective managers are aware of various community resources. The resources you need depend on the goal you are working to achieve. Although it is a challenge to identify resources, the local Chamber of Commerce, local government offices, or public library can help.

Sometimes you may feel that your resources are limited compared with those of other people. Some individuals and families do have more resources available to them. However, people with more resources will not necessarily be more successful in reaching their goals. People reach goals not because of the number or amount of resources they have available. Instead, they reach goals because they have made wise use of their limited resources. The case study in 3-9 is an example of this.

In deciding which one of several resources to use, consider the **use-cost** of each resource. In most cases, using a resource reduces the amount that is available for future use. If a resource is important to you but is limited, it has a high use-cost. In this case, you might prefer to use another resource instead. If a resource is readily available to you, it has a low use-cost.

For example, time and money are two resources that are often weighed and compared in daily situations. For a retired person, time might have a low use-cost. See 3-10. On the other hand, money would have a high use-cost for a retiree with a limited income. Time has a very high use-cost for a financially successful business person who is very busy.

Mr. and Mrs. Johnson lived quite comfortably when their children were teenagers.
Mr. Johnson's business was doing very well. They built a new home, bought a big boat, had several cars, and took many vacation trips. After a few years, due to changes in the economy, Mr. Johnson's business declined. They found it necessary to sell their home. Their home had become run-down because they had not taken proper care of it. The selling price was not as high as they had hoped it would be. The cost of living was going up, but their income and the value of their possessions were going down. They were caught in a very difficult situation.

In contrast to the Johnson situation, the Mendozas lived through the same period but used their limited resources wisely. Mr. Mendoza had a modest income. However, early in their married lives, the Mendozas made plans for their future.

They decided on their priorities and long-range goals. They put a small amount of money away each month for their retirement. They also set up a savings plan for their children's education. Mr. Mendoza learned many skills that were useful in caring for a home such as carpentry and plumbing. Mrs. Mendoza sewed curtains and draperies and reupholstered furniture. These combined skills provided them with a modest but comfortable and attractive home. After their children left home, the Mendozas were able to sell the house. That money, along with some of the money that had been put in the retirement plan, made it possible for them to buy a small home near the lake. They were able to achieve one of their long-term goals through effective management.

3-9 **This case study illustrates the difference between having many resources and using limited resources wisely.**

Ask the following questions when figuring use-cost:
- How important is the resource to you?
- How much of the resource will be used?
- Can the resource be replaced?

Figuring this cost helps you set priorities in the use of your resources.

Using the Management Process

The **management process** is a resource managers use each day to make decisions and solve problems. The management process involves three steps: (1) planning, (2) implementing and controlling, and (3) evaluating. See 3-11.

Planning

You need guidance to reach the desired outcome—your goal. **Planning** provides this guidance. It involves first identifying the activities necessary to carry out the plan. It also includes arranging activities in a logical sequence. Finally, planning

Anderson Corp.

3-10 **For this older man, time has a low "use-cost."**

Management Process
What is my goal?

Planning
What steps are necessary to reach my goal? What is the logical sequence of these steps? Can some steps be combined or coordinated?

Implementing and Controlling
Is each step progressing as planned? Does the plan need any adjustment?

Evaluating
Did I reach my goal? How could I have improved my plans? What have I learned from this process?

3-11 Ask yourself these questions as you manage any situation.

involves grouping activities and coordinating different parts of the plan.

With some decisions, very little planning is necessary. For instance, if you are deciding how to get downtown and have made the decision to take a bus, little planning is required. It is all done quickly in your head. It is just a matter of getting to the bus stop on time.

Other decisions require much more planning. For instance, you might decide to have a large going-away party for a friend. You would begin planning for the event by identifying what must be done. This might involve deciding on the date for the party and who will be invited. Deciding what food to have, shopping for the food, cleaning the house, and fixing the snacks are other tasks that might need to be done.

The next step in planning is to establish a **sequence** of activities. This means you will place the activities in a logical order. For instance, it would be logical to develop the list of guests before making the shopping list so you will know how much food to buy.

GettingInvolved

Talk with parents, neighbors, or friends who seem to have busy schedules to find what suggestions they have for better time management. Share some of the ideas you have gained from this chapter with them. Volunteer to work with them to adjust their schedules.

Coordinating planned activities often makes things go more efficiently. For instance, you might plan to coordinate the activities of cleaning the house and baking cookies. While each batch of cookies is baking, you could be doing some cleaning. This would make good use of your time.

Implementing and Controlling

The next step of the management process involves implementing and controlling the plan. **Implementing** simply means moving ahead with the activities planned.

Once the plan is underway, you will need to check the progress regularly and adjust the plan where necessary. This is the **controlling** step of the process.

You will need to see if the activities are done in the correct order. You will also be checking to see if the resources are being used as planned. Finally, you will be checking to see if your plan is going according to the time schedule.

While checking, you will be able to see if any changes in the plan are necessary. For instance, perhaps some of the food selected for the party was not available. It would be necessary to substitute another food. In other words, it would be necessary to adjust the plan.

If changes are necessary, the successful manager must be flexible. You may need to make some adjustments in the plan. The person who is not willing to be flexible often becomes frustrated and is unable to reach desired goals.

Evaluating

The step of the management process that involves judging the entire process and the end result is **evaluating**. You can see that evaluation goes on to some extent during the implementation stage. It is also involved in controlling the plan. You judge the progress by whether or not the plan is moving along as it should be. You are evaluating the progress.

Evaluation of the outcome and the process gives you information that can be helpful to you in the future. It will point out the areas in which you need to improve your skills. It will also show you the areas in which you are quite skillful. Evaluation gives you an opportunity to learn from your mistakes and from your accomplishments.

The Management Process in Action

At this point, you may feel the management process seems quite complicated and not very practical for your use. Actually, it can be very simple and quite effective in helping you reach your everyday goals. For instance, you can use the management process to get your homework done as Britt does in the following example.

Britt has homework to complete but would also like to watch a special television program. She can use the management process to reach both goals—complete her homework and watch the television special.

- *Planning.* Britt must first determine just what she has to do to complete her homework. See 3-12. She has 10 pages of math to do, a chapter to read in science, and a paper to write for history class. The television program she would like to watch is on from 9:00 to 10:00. After some thought, she decides on the following schedule. She will do her science first while her mind is fresh. She will then do her math assignment. After that, she will write her history paper. Hopefully, she will finish before 9:00 when the television program begins.

- *Implementing and Controlling.* Britt proceeds as planned. She finishes her science and math assignments more quickly than she had expected. Her schedule is going very well. She begins writing her history paper, but first she needs to do some research on the Internet. While searching the Internet, she gets an instant message from a friend and chats awhile online. Britt then realizes she will not finish her work before the television program begins. She must either adjust her plan or give up the television program. Britt has about one-third of the paper remaining to write. She decides to watch television and finish writing the paper before she goes to bed.

3-12 **Britt identifies the homework she must do. Then she decides on a schedule for completing it.**

◆ *Evaluating.* The next morning, as Britt walks to school, she wonders whether she made the right decisions in her planning. She is actually in the evaluating step of the management process. Britt feels good about her plan because she did finish her work and she got to watch the television show. However, she recalls that after watching television, it took her as long to write the last one-third of the paper as it had the first part. That was probably because she was tired. She decides that in a similar situation, she will wait and finish writing early in the morning. That way her mind will be fresher, and she will be less likely to make mistakes. By evaluating the management process, Britt will be able to profit from this mistake when she makes similar plans in the future.

Management Skills

Certain skills can be developed in addition to using the management process. These skills can help you be a more effective manager.

Time is a resource that everyone has. It is a unique resource because everyone has the same amount of hours in each day. Some people use their time wisely; others do not. Time management involves organizing your day to accomplish the things that need to be done. It is an important organizational skill. Energy is also a resource to be managed. Work simplification is a process that helps manage both time and energy more efficiently. Technology and the use of computers can also have a major impact on management skills.

Time Management

How can you judge if time is being used effectively? A person might be busy every minute of the day but not be using that time wisely. Effective time use is an individual matter. You as an individual have certain goals you wish to accomplish. Some goals are more important than others, so you set priorities. When a person uses his or her time effectively, it is being used to accomplish the most important goals of that day.

For most people, much of their time use is predetermined. See 3-13. For instance, as a high school student, an average 24-hour-day involves school from perhaps 8:00 to 3:00 and sleep from 10:30 to 6:30. In other words, those two time periods involving fifteen hours of the 24-hour-day are already set. Other things you want or need to do that day must be done in the remaining nine hours.

3-13 As a student, you spend a certain amount of time in school almost every day.

Have you ever considered how you use your time? It is used for a variety of activities, such as working, eating, socializing, reading, surfing the Internet, watching television, and personal grooming. You also spend time thinking, planning, and creating. The way you use time is constantly changing as you develop new interests and assume new responsibilities. Your use of time as a seven-year-old was certainly different from the way you use your time now. See 3-14.

One of the first steps in improving time use is to keep a record of how you presently use your time. Keep a record for about a week. You will then have a basis for evaluating your time use. A time record or log can be helpful in identifying time wasters.

Identifying your goals and setting priorities is another important step in time management. To use time effectively, it should be used for the things that are most important to you. It will be more helpful if goals are specific so you can focus on the

tasks to be done. For example, your parents may have asked you to save your Saturday morning for helping with some jobs around the house. When you ask what needs to be done, you may be told that there is some yard work to do. Also, the garage needs straightening, and there is some work in the basement. You get up Saturday morning with a rather vague idea about what needs to be done. You are not too enthusiastic since you would rather go to the mall and wonder if you will have time.

If goals are more specific, time management is easier. Often, your attitude is more positive. Your parents might have told you specifically that they wanted you to mow the lawn and sweep out the garage. They would also like you to get the camping equipment out from winter storage in the basement. This would mean airing the tent and putting the rest of the equipment on the shelf in the garage. Since these jobs, or goals, are more specific, you know just what needs to be done. You also know just about how long it will take you. You can see that there will be plenty of time for you to go to the mall later in the day. You are likely to be more enthusiastic about planning your morning work.

When a resource is limited, careful planning for the use of that resource becomes very important. For the parent who works outside the home, time becomes a very limited resource that must be managed carefully. There are meals to be prepared for the family and cleaning, shopping, and laundry to be done. In contrast, for a child who has few tasks to assume, time is not such a limited resource. Therefore, the child does not feel the pressure to manage time well.

Time management helps you organize your day and your life. Ideally, it will allow you the extra time you need to do special things you want to do.

Tyke Corporation

3-14 This child's use of time will change as she develops new interests.

Brainstorming

On the chalkboard, list the various categories into which resources can be divided. Have someone write down the various resources mentioned in class discussion in the appropriate category. At the end of the class period, discuss which category has the most resources. Why do you think this is the case?

Energy Management

Unlike time, people have different amounts of energy. The average 17-year-old boy is likely to have more energy than either of his grandparents. However, the boy's energy level will also vary throughout the day.

Your energy level is the amount of energy you have at a given time. Your age, diet, sleep, rest, and physical activities affect your energy level. Age is the least significant of these factors until a person becomes elderly. Following a nutritious diet plan will help you be more energetic. Getting adequate sleep and rest will also give you the energy you need to go about your daily activities.

How active a person is will affect the amount of energy that person has. A busy Saturday of mowing the lawn, trimming some shrubs, and running errands on your bike will use a lot of energy. A normal day in the classroom at school will require much less.

When you feel weary and your energy level is very low, you experience fatigue. Fatigue can be caused by both physical activity and environmental factors. After a long day of physical labor, you will naturally experience fatigue. Temperature, humidity, and noise are environmental factors that can also cause fatigue.

Many people have definite energy patterns. Some like to get up early and are at their best early in the day. They can accomplish many tasks during that time. Others move slowly in the morning. It takes them awhile to wake up and get going. They can accomplish more later in the day or even in the evening. Each individual tends to have a peak time period when his or her energy level is at its greatest.

The two resources of time and energy are very closely related. In fact, it is almost impossible to consider one of the two resources apart from the other. If you are trying to complete certain tasks in a given period of time, your energy level will greatly influence whether or not you are successful. See 3-15.

Can you identify problems related to time and energy management? Some might be wasting time or not getting enough done. Hurrying so fast that tasks are not done well might be a problem. In addition, many projects take longer than expected. What can be done about these problems?

Work Simplification

One way to manage your time more wisely is through **work simplification**. Begin by breaking down an activity into a detailed listing of what needs to be done. Then ask yourself these questions:

- Are there any unnecessary steps? If so, eliminate them. They are wasting your time. Are the steps arranged in a logical order? You may be able to reorganize the steps to work more efficiently.

- Can some steps be combined? For instance, you can press your clothes as you launder them. That will save you time when getting dressed in the morning. Sometimes you can also combine activities. You could balance your checkbook while you wait for your clothes to dry at the laundromat.

3-15 **You may have scheduled time to do homework after playing basketball with your friends. However, your energy level may be reduced.**

Use *Your* Reasoning Skills

Analyze your time use in the last few days. How much of your time was predetermined? Was the remainder of your time used related to those things most important to you? How could you use this analysis to adjust your schedule in the future to make the most of your time?

the tent out to air. Cleaning off the shelf and sweeping the garage would also come before storing the camping equipment there. Do the most important activities first and set deadlines for yourself on each activity. By taking these precautions, you will be avoiding unnecessary activities that waste time.

Managing your schedule well takes time, but also saves time. Taking time to plan to do things right saves the time of having to do them over again. Putting your plans in writing is often helpful. Many times it is difficult to remember all the details. At other times, the planning can all be done in your head.

◆ Are supplies and equipment available for use? They should be kept in a place that is easily accessible for that activity. Having to search for supplies contributes to poor time management. See 3-16.

You might find it helpful to divide the activities into two lists—*must do* and *should do*. You can then list the most important activities first in each of these lists. Your next step would be to estimate the time needed for each activity. You can then decide on a logical sequence of activities. In the situation described earlier, mowing the lawn would logically come before putting

Time can be saved...

...if supplies and equipment have a definite storage spot known by all who use them.

...if these items are stored near to where they are used most often.

...if the most frequently used items are stored in easy to reach areas.

...if these items are returned to their storage place after being used.

3-16 **Work simplification techniques such as these can save you valuable time.**

Summary

Many human and nonhuman resources are available to help you reach your goals. Being able to recognize these resources and understand how they can be developed and used is important to effective management.

As you manage, you control a situation so you reach a goal through wise use of your resources. Management skills and the management process are resources that can help you meet the challenge of decision making.

32
31
30
29
28
27
26
25
24
23
22
21
20
19
18
17
16
15
14
13
12
11
10
9
8
7
6
5
4
3
2
1

To Review

To Review
To Review

1. Name 10 human resources.
2. Name 10 nonhuman resources.
3. Often, the amount of resources and the types of resources you have are related to your _____ in life.
4. Indicate whether each of the following is an example of exchanging resources, developing resources, or sharing resources:
   A. Carlos deposits $40 in his savings account.
   B. Mr. Kelly is taking a class in "Repairing Small Appliances."
   C. Doug lifts weights daily to prepare for football season.
   D. John writes a check for his tuition costs as he registers for his first semester in college.
   E. Julie and Emily both attend West High School.
   F. Twanda is going to learn to play the piano.
   G. Amy takes the children to the city park.
   H. Celia, who is baking cookies, borrows a cup of sugar from a neighbor, then later, takes her some cookies.
5. True or false?
   A. People who have many resources can always reach their goals.
   B. Use-cost of a resource depends on how important the resource is to you, how much will be used, and whether or not it can be replaced.
   C. Money as a resource is always more limited than time.
6. When you _____, you control the use of _____ so a goal is reached.
7. Explain the meaning of use-cost.
8. List the steps of the management process.
9. Name five factors that might affect your energy level.
10. Describe what is meant by *work simplification*.

To Do with the Class

1. Describe situations that illustrate the sharing of resources by family members.
2. Share ideas of ways that resources could be expanded or developed.
3. Think of examples of decisions made that may seem unimportant, but could have a significant effect on your life if repeated on a regular basis.
4. Think of the many opportunities you have during the day for thinking and planning. Discuss situations that illustrate how the wise use of this time could improve your time management habits.

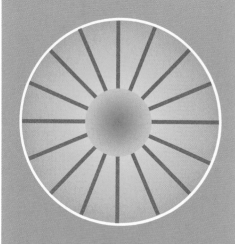

To Challenge Your Thinking

1. Think of many of your activities in the past two days. Make a list of the resources you have used.
2. Develop a list of your own material resources.
3. Describe a recent situation in which you consciously or unconsciously used the management process.
4. In the situation described in #3, explain which activities were a part of:
   ◆ the planning stage
   ◆ the implementing and controlling stage
   ◆ the evaluation stage

To Do with Your Community

1. Investigate organizations in your community that are resources related to the following:
   A. care of small children
   B. care of older people
   C. family recreation
   D. alcohol or drug problems
2. Make a list of school resources that are shared by students who attend your school. Compare lists with others in the class.
3. Investigate any examples that indicate irresponsible use of resources in your community.
4. Invite someone from your community who is involved in physical recreation, such as a physical education teacher or a personal trainer from a gym, to speak on energy management.

4

Technology as a Resource

To Know

technology
network
Internet
multimedia
electronic funds transfer (EFT)
biotechnology
genetics
telecommuters

Objectives

After studying this chapter, you will be able to
◆ identify some of the technological advances used in the world today.
◆ determine forms of technology that will help you manage your resources.
◆ explain how technology can benefit individuals, families, and society.
◆ summarize some of the concerns related to technology.

Technology is a constantly changing body of scientific knowledge that is used to solve practical problems. Family life has been transformed by the application of scientific discoveries to everyday living. New devices and products are constantly being developed that make daily tasks easier to accomplish. Access to the latest information is at your fingertips. A technological revolution is turning science fiction into reality, transforming the world in which you live. See 4-1.

Apple

4-1 **Most of today's students grow up using computer technology.**

Technology has had a profound impact on society. You probably use some forms of technology to manage your life every day. Knowledge of these applications will be helpful to you in understanding the impact of technology, the benefits it provides, and the concerns it raises.

Technology as a Resource in Daily Living

Advances in technology provide families with products and services that can be helpful in managing their day-to-day lives. By becoming more aware of the options available, you will better understand the impact they can have on various aspects of daily living.

Actual results of technology surround you all the time. Consider a typical day. You awake to a digital alarm clock, dress in clothes of synthetic fibers, microwave your breakfast, and ride to school in a car while listening to a CD. The rest of your day is similarly affected by technology you may never consider.

Computers

Personal computers (or PCs) have become the most popular communication tool in the United States. They are used for many different functions. For instance, they can be used to do homework, conduct research, and e-mail friends. Above all, computers serve as a source of information. See 4-2.

The price of basic computers has gone down somewhat, making them available to more families. Shopping for computers is less intimidating. They can now be found in a variety of stores. Major manufacturers back up their products with toll-free help lines and reassuring guarantees.

Personal computers have also become easier to use. They are manufactured for ease of setup with a minimum of connections. In some models, the hard drive and monitor combine to form an all-in-one unit. Computer supplies include both hardware and software.

Courtesy of International Business Machines Corporation. Unauthorized use not permitted.

4-2 **Computer packages such as this one are the industry standard.**

Processor speed is measured in gigahertz (GHz). Computers can be purchased with processor speeds of over 1 GHz. Currently, computers are typically purchased with anywhere from 128 megabytes (MB) to more than 1 gigabyte (GB) of *Random Access Memory*, or *RAM*.

A computer might have 7 to 15 GB of hard drive space. The most common storage method today is writable CDs. See 4-3. You can write any information to a CD-R one time or a CD-RW numerous times. These can hold about 800 MB of data. A special drive is needed to save data to a rewritable CD.

Software is the set of instructions that tells the computer what to do. The *operating system* is the software that gives the computer its basic operation instructions.

Application software is instructions for a specific function, such as word processing.

Software developers have created thousands of programs on health care, finances, and home repair, as well as educational packages and games for the entire family. Software can be purchased on CD-ROMs, and many software programs can be downloaded from the Internet.

The industry continues to move toward more compact computer equipment. In the near future, computers may consist of poster-like screens attached to walls or laid out flat on desks. These computers would use voice recognition for input instead of devices such as the keyboard or mouse.

Internet Access

When a group of computers is linked together to share data, they form a **network**. The **Internet** is a global network of computers also known as the "Information Superhighway." The multimedia section of the Internet is the *World Wide Web*. **Multimedia** refers to the combination of sound, graphics, animation, and information in one presentation. Connecting to the Internet is known as going *online*.

A computer can be connected to the Internet using a modem and telephone lines. Many people are now using *digital subscriber lines (DSL)*, a form of Internet service that transmits data much faster than dial-up service. This type of service also allows you to use your telephone at the same time you are using the Internet.

The Internet allows millions of people to exchange information on a worldwide basis. Using the Internet, you have access to services such as communication, information, business, and leisure. It can bring you a world of new choices in education, medical care, e-commerce, entertainment, and employment. Anyone connected to the Internet can tap into an array of library catalogs, databases, and electronic discussion groups. See 4-4.

The Internet has revolutionized our nation politically, economically, and culturally. Internet services will continue to grow as more people become connected. However, many questions have been raised about this technological advancement. Who will control the Internet? Should its benefits go only to those who can afford to go online?

E-Mail

Electronic mail, or *e-mail*, is another tool that has made communication more convenient. Using e-mail, you can send and receive messages instantly as they are entered on the keyboard. People who are accustomed to using the computer on a daily basis may find e-mail a preferred method of communication. Some find it faster than handwriting letters to distant family members. For business purposes, it can clarify information that could get confused in a spoken conversation. Also, information such as document files or photographs can be attached and sent through e-mail.

Handheld Computers

Handheld computers, also known as *personal digital assistants (PDAs)*, are about the size of a calculator. They are convenient organizers commonly used for both business and personal needs. These minicomputers contain calendars and address books. Many also allow Internet and e-mail access. Some PDAs include digital cameras or MP3 players. See 4-5.

PDAs are useful because they can hold a great deal of data, yet they are small. A slim handheld can hold the same information as a date book, address book, to-do list, and calculator. With the right software, it can take the place of your camera and CD player.

Entertainment and Recreation

One of the most common uses of technology is entertainment. This has been true since moving pictures and phonographs were invented. The technology of the entertainment industry has progressed a great deal since then. The changes reflect the

4-4 **How much time do you spend online? What do you use the Internet for most?**

palmOne

4-5 **Handheld computers are popular because users have access to many tools in a compact format at any time and place.**

ever-growing need for streamlined products with better quality and more capacity.

Digital cameras have become quite popular. These devices capture images to digital files instead of film. You can buy different size memory cards to insert in the camera. With more memory, you can take more pictures at higher resolutions. The image files are saved to the memory card. They can then be downloaded to a computer. When a picture is taken, it can be viewed on a digital screen and deleted if its quality is unacceptable. The pictures are printed out on quality printers. Different types of paper can be purchased to get higher-quality printouts. There is no wait time for film development. Image files can be quickly e-mailed to long-distance family members.

A recent addition to the entertainment field is the *MP3 player*. MP3 files are digital music files. They can be purchased and downloaded from the Internet. The files can then be stored in the MP3 player. This eliminates the need for packaging and physical media such as CDs. These factors contribute to the lower cost of the music. They also reduce the need for storage space and simplify organization.

4-6 **Playing challenging videogames can be fun for people of all ages.**

Computerized games have been a popular form of family recreation for many years. These range from simple games for young children to quite complex and challenging games for adults, 4-6. Games are constantly being upgraded to have more options, better controls, and lifelike graphics. Most games now have memory or memory cards so longer, more complex games can be saved.

Cellular Phones

Everywhere you look, you can see people using cellular phones, or cell phones. Many people have become dependent on these technological tools. They are popular with people of all ages. Many use them to stay in touch with business associates while they are away from the workplace. Others use cell phones for emergency purposes. Some simply enjoy the convenience of being able to be reached at any time.

Like PDAs, cell phones can include address books, Internet access, and text messaging. Newer models come with digital cameras and MP3 players. Some even have video capability.

Schools may allow cell phones so parents can have immediate communication with their children in case of a crisis. However, many schools ban the use of cell phones during school hours. Some also ban them from school buses, and still others prohibit them on school campus altogether. The main reason is because cell phone use can distract students from the learning process.

The use of cell phones while driving has become a major problem. Many accidents have occurred as a result of cell phone use. Some cities and states have laws against cell phone usage by drivers of vehicles.

The growth in the use of cell phones has created a need for rules of courtesy to be followed by wireless phone users. By being aware of these rules of courtesy, cell phone users are less likely to offend others around them. See 4-7.

Electronic Shopping

Online shopping is one of the most popular ways to buy items. Books, music, clothing, magazine subscriptions, theater and travel tickets, and even groceries can all be purchased over the Internet.

Convenience is the main reason people give for online shopping. With the click of a mouse, you can find exactly what you want. Hard-to-find or out-of-stock items can be purchased immediately. This saves the time and effort of driving from store to store. Although shipping costs must be taken into

account, many online stores offer discount prices. The discount will often offset shipping costs. Some stores offer rush shipping for an additional fee. See 4-8.

Caution must be used when shopping online. Before entering a credit card number, make sure you are using a secure site. This prevents others from stealing your credit card information. A secure site may be identified by an icon such as a closed padlock at the bottom of your screen. In addition, many people apply for low-limit credit cards for the sole purpose of online shopping. This way, if the number should be stolen, no major purchases could be charged to the account.

Electronic Banking

In banking and bill paying, technology is moving toward a cashless society. An

---

Cell Phone Courtesy

- Let your voicemail take your calls when you are in public areas such as restaurants. If you must speak to the caller, excuse yourself and find a secluded area.

- Speak in your regular conversational tone. There is no need to speak louder on your cell phone than you would on any other phone.

- Turn off your phone in public places such as movie theaters, libraries, churches, and museums.

- If you are expecting a call that can't be postponed, tell your companions ahead of time and excuse yourself when the call comes in. The people you are with should take precedence over calls you want to make or receive.

- Change the ringing tones on your phone to match your environment. Use a loud ring for outdoors, but inside, use the silent or vibrating options.

4-7 Following these guidelines can help you be considerate of others when you are using a cell phone.

4-8 Online shopping can be done any time of day from the convenience of your own home.

electronic funds transfer (EFT) is a system of carrying out financial transactions by computer rather than using checks and cash. Automatic paycheck deposits, automatic bill paying, automatic savings, and automated teller machines are examples of this technology. You will learn more about these options in Chapter 20, "Financial Management."

Computer-based bank-at-home systems can also be used for financial transactions. In addition to the computer, Internet access and special software are necessary. A home banking setup lets you instruct your bank to pay your bills. This is done by electronically transferring money from your account to various merchants.

These options affect the convenience of handling money. However, they may make record keeping and managing of saving and spending more difficult for some people. Using these conveniences requires care in recording credits and payments in your accounts.

Home Appliances

Many of the technological advances in the home have taken place in the kitchen. Most new products and appliances are designed to save time and energy. Many also aid in preserving the environment and conserving natural resources. The newest refrigerators, for example, use 50 percent less energy than their counterparts did only two decades ago.

The latest appliances generally feature added convenience, performance, and durability. Ovens have more accurate temperature controls. Products such as bread machines and dishwashers have become standards in many households.

New cleaning products and appliances have been introduced. The latest laundry appliances feature thermostatically controlled water temperatures, self-cleaning lint filters, one-button programming, electronic dryness monitors, and increased energy efficiency.

New and developing technologies can enhance home security. New surveillance cameras are available that are smaller, more reliable, and less expensive than their tube-based predecessors. They could be used in a baby's room or a front entrance. An outdoor camera might serve as a deterrent to would-be burglars. Motion or heat detectors can turn on an outside light when someone approaches after dark. Smoke alarms seem to have artificial senses by "smelling" fumes in different ways to set off alarms. See 4-9.

The trend in home appliances seems to be combining items into one device. In the future, homes may contain a single computer-like device that will provide everything from telephone service to music to DVDs. The computer of the future may integrate appliances like televisions and telephones and even home security systems into one unit.

S. Hamilton

4-9 A home security system can be easy to use and provides a high degree of security.

Brainstorming

Brainstorm a list of ways a home computer can benefit a family. How many of these ideas are you already practicing at home? Which ideas would you like to put into

Manufacturers are developing appliances that "talk to one another" through microprocessors and a home's electrical wiring. You could have a vacuum cleaner that shuts off when the phone rings or the doorbell chimes. You could have lights that turn on and off in semi-random fashion when you are away from home.

A home management system is being developed that will monitor home energy use so homeowners can act immediately to conserve energy. This would help people take steps to conserve energy before the monthly utility bill arrives. Through this system, a person can learn how much it costs to run a certain appliance. The percentage of the electric bill generated by the appliance would be indicated, too. Computers will also be able to control some appliances. For example, a computer could be programmed to raise or lower the thermostat. Special sensors may indicate appliance problems or failures.

Medical Technology

Medical issues are also a part of the technological revolution. Many of these issues relate to prevention of illnesses and diseases. Others involve diagnosis, treatments, and cures. Every day new developments in medical technology significantly impact health and well-being.

Ultrasound imaging devices now help not only pregnant women, but also persons with heart disease and other health problems. New medical technology can help control costs; shorten procedures; and provide safer, more accurate health assessment. Surgical procedures are more often done by laser, which results in less pain and recovery time. Miniature cameras can transmit color video images to a recorder worn externally. The data provided serves as a diagnostic tool for determining various conditions. Other technology helps determine bone density, monitor patients, and provide mobility to people with disabilities. Power scooters, motorized wheelchairs, and lift chairs have improved the capabilities of those who need them on a daily basis.

Biotechnology

New research results may influence people's lives as much as the Internet. Prominent in this revolution is a field called **biotechnology**, or applied biological science. Biotechnologists apply technological advances to everything from growing better crops to curing human diseases. See 4-10. New drugs are constantly being manufactured, tested and marketed. These medications can relieve symptoms of everyday annoyances such as allergies and indigestion. Other drugs perform lifesaving or life-prolonging tasks, such as blocking the replication of HIV-infected cells.

A cornerstone of the biotech industry is **genetics**, the study of inherited traits in living things. Scientists are learning to manipulate genes and alter the makeup of living things. In the hands of biotech engineers, these techniques may alter the very concept of life.

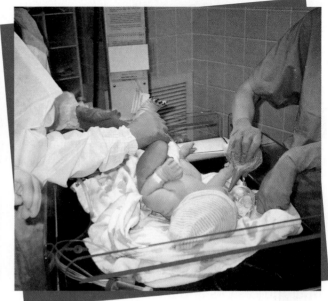

Schrader

4-11 **It is possible that in the future parents may select traits they want in their child. What questions does this raise?**

4-10 **Today's research in the field of biotechnology may lead to more healthful living tomorrow.**

The science of genetics has the potential for incredible developments. Genes in millions of different combinations make each person unique. In recent years, scientists have learned that defective genes are the source of thousands of inherited diseases, including diabetes, some cancers, and cystic fibrosis. Some researchers believe identifying every gene is a boon to human health, enabling doctors to isolate defective genes while replacing them with healthy ones. It may even be possible for parents in the future to select their baby's characteristics. See 4-11.

The Workplace at Home

With computers and other electronic gear dropping in price even as they become more powerful and versatile, more people are working out of home offices. Although many of these people are self-employed, the great majority are **telecommuters**—employees working at home. Telecommuters represent one of the fastest-growing segments of the workforce. Although the computer is the main tool of the telecommuter, other multifunction devices combine printing, faxing, scanning, and copying into one machine.

Studies have shown that the increased flexibility of working at home often boosts worker productivity. Telecommuters may also use the time they save by not commuting to work on family responsibilities. Another advantage to business is individuals, not the companies, usually pay for the office equipment.

Working at home does have its disadvantages. People who like being around other people may have trouble adjusting to the isolation. Some home workers join a networking group or communicate online. Full-time telecommuters may also have concerns about their careers. They worry they might be passed over for a promotion or bonus if they are not actually in the company office.

A key benefit to working at home is the chance to be close to family members. See 4-12. Some working parents may even be able to avoid the cost of child care. Those who do work at home find they must set ground rules both for themselves and their families. They may set definite work hours and have a separate room for their workspace. Having some way of letting family members know they are not to be disturbed is important. At-home workers have to be able to say "No, I am working now."

Benefits of Technology

Learning about the changes brought about by technology and the possible changes that lie ahead often raises questions. Have people really benefited from technology? Are people better off today than they were in the past? Will they be better off tomorrow? In answering these questions, several main benefits of technology are identified.

4-12 Telecommuters have more personal time to spend with their families and on household tasks.

Technology has led to tremendous increases in the production of goods and services. For example, in the past a farmer worked from dawn to dusk, yet produced enough food for only about four people. Today, machines do most of the work on U.S. farms. As a result of machinery and fertilizers, as well as advances in agricultural technology, one farmer can now produce enough food for about 100 people each day.

The amount of labor needed to produce goods and services has been reduced by technology. Powerful machines have made it possible to produce the same amount of goods and services with less labor. Most factories use mass-production techniques and have largely replaced hand labor with powered machinery. Labor-saving devices in the home are also the result of technology.

The workplace is also safer and the work less physically demanding. For example, in the early 1900s, miners toiled all day with picks and shovels to produce a few tons of coal. Many mines were dark, poorly ventilated, and dangerous. Today, better lighting and ventilation and improved safety devices have reduced these hazards. Machines perform most of the hard labor.

Use Your Reasoning Skills

Select a technological development to research. Report to the class, giving a full description of the technology, its benefits, and its concerns. Are you or anyone in the class currently affected by this technology? Is the personal effect positive or negative? How does this influence your report?

Because of technology, many new jobs have been created. Computers are an invaluable aid in almost every job you can think of, from astronaut to zookeeper. In fact, almost every job is involved in some way with computers.

Technology has given people higher living standards. The United States and the other industrial nations have the world's highest standards of living. Most people in these nations enjoy a healthier, more comfortable life now than at any other time in history. Most people also live longer due to advances in technology.

Since more families now have computers at home, research has been done to determine how they affect children. The results show that children benefit in many ways. According to studies, children who use computers tend to watch less television. The computer helps them develop fundamental skills like reading, writing, and math. Educational software has been developed that targets particular skill development. For instance, children can be challenged to identify similarities and differences of orders and patterns. They can also learn basic music skills. The skill levels adjust automatically based on the child's responses or can be set by the parent. See 4-13.

Pointing and clicking with the computer mouse is much easier for young hands to master than pencil, crayons, and paintbrushes. This allows very young children to focus more on imagination and creativity and less on how to manipulate tools. As children grow older, eye-hand coordination and general reaction time can improve with use of the computers.

The Internet gives families access to a wealth of information and a new form of communication. They can quickly research information that ordinarily required a trip to the library. They can also post messages on electronic bulletin boards and communicate with other people who have similar interests.

Apple

4-13 **Parents can help their children learn basic skills on the computer.**

Concerns in the Use of Technology

Though people have benefited greatly from technology, there are still some important concerns. The undesirable effects include environmental pollution and the depletion of natural resources. Technological unemployment, which occurs when human workers are replaced by machines, creates job concerns for many Americans.

There is concern about both the direct and indirect effects of many technological advances. Almost every technology introduced for its intended benefits produces some negative and unplanned side effects, 4-14. For instance, pesticides to improve agricultural productivity are sometimes poisonous. Nuclear plants generate both power and dangerous waste. Jet aircraft create objectionable noise. These are direct effects. The indirect effects may be more subtle but even more potent.

Advocates for the poor feel a strong effort must be made to see that poor people have access to technology. Such access will be crucial to obtaining high-quality education and getting good jobs. See 4-15.

People are also concerned about advertisers moving in on the Internet and exploiting it for profit. Meanwhile, racists and child pornographers have also used the Internet as a tool to circulate their materials. Cases such as these might influence the government to step in and regulate the Internet.

Parents have been strongly cautioned to protect their children from Internet predators. These people use a different identity online to lure children or teens to a public place. For your own safety, *never* agree to meet in person anyone you have met online.

In many instances, people have become "addicted" to the Internet. Because

D. Riehle

4-14 **One of the negative side effects of technology is the challenge of disposing of radioactive substances.**

Technology involving computers, the Internet, and multimedia is very exciting, but brings certain negative issues. The availability of information has made life easier in many ways. However, as computers compile more information, a person's constitutional right to privacy is threatened. Unfortunately, laws that protect personal privacy have not kept up with technology. Hundreds of lawsuits over the last decade involve the invasion of privacy. The more people connect electronically, the more chance there is that someone will be eavesdropping on others, examining their buying habits, checking their tax records, or stealing credit card numbers. Activities such as these have even led to cases of identity theft.

Apple

4-15 **It is important to society that all students have access to emerging technologies.**

the Internet offers such an incredible wealth of information, a person can spend hours online yet never even scratch the surface of what is available. Both children and parents are drawn away from spending time with their families. Also, not all computer time is spent in worthwhile learning. Hours spent playing games or chatting could be better used reading or participating in physical activities.

Another technology concern that has surfaced is that of cyberbullying. *Cyberbullying* involves the use of communication technology such as e-mail, cell phone and pager text messages, instant messaging, offensive Web sites, and offensive online personal polling. These forms of communication are being used to harm others through deliberate, repeated, and hostile messages. This not only shows poor behavior on the part of those posting or sending the messages. It also displays a lack of respect for those who can be harmed personally and professionally on a large scale. Cyberbullies can be either individuals or groups.

There is also the problem of hackers. *Hacking* originally meant tinkering with computer systems and figuring out what they could do. Now, there are those who use their skills to break into other people's computer systems. These computer intruders hack into business or government computers mainly to prove they can. Unfortunately, the more malicious hackers think nothing of tampering with data, crashing entire systems, and disrupting businesses. Many hackers have created viruses that are transmitted through e-mail. Some of these viruses have caused worldwide problems.

Cost is another concern about technology. Most new technology is expensive. The expense may be felt by families as they

GettingInvolved

Develop a brochure or flyer with information on using technology wisely. Address topics such as cell phone safety, chat room safety, and Internet shopping. Make the flyers available to the public at the local library or a grocery store.

budget for the latest labor-saving appliances or newest forms of at-home entertainment. They may also be hit by high costs if they are hospitalized for any reason. Hospitals often have the latest lifesaving equipment, but the cost of this equipment is enormous. These costs are passed on to consumers either directly or through their health insurance providers.

Genetic manipulation is also controversial. Many feel that scientists, by trying to alter the genetic makeup of the human body, might end up creating even more horrible diseases than the ones they are trying to cure.

Use of high-tech life support systems has created controversy. Technology has made it possible to prolong the lives of brain-dead patients for years. Many families now have to make an agonizing decision: Should they let their loved ones linger, or choose to have the machines that keep them breathing unplugged?

Many scientists believe the harmful effects of technology can be prevented. They believe that any proposed large-scale technology should be thoroughly tested before it is put into use. Other experts believe it is not possible to discover all the undesirable effects of a technology before it is put into use.

Forecasts for technology in the future are abundant and amazing, 4-16. No doubt some will come true and others will not. No one knows exactly where these changes are leading. Experts agree, however, that technological breakthroughs will continue to reshape the ways you manage your life.

Forecasts
• Within 15 years, standard desktop computers will be 1,000% more powerful than they are today and capable of being hundreds of times smaller. They'll be carried around in our pockets, on our wrists, or even in our wrists.
• Within a couple of decades, all money could be digital. People could make purchases by using their thumbprints as identification. This would eliminate the need to carry cash or cards.
• Smart houses will have systems that allow you to program the entertainment center, set the alarm clock, start cooking dinner, or turn on lights from any location by voice command.
• Homes will be built with materials that have chemical and electronic sensors that can transmit an alert to a central home-monitoring station when there is a leak or other hidden problem.
• Photoelectric windows will react to light conditions outside, letting in more light in the winter and less in the summer.
• Furniture and carpets will be made of dust-rejecting materials. A constant air-cleaning system would simply suck the dust and dirt out of the air and dirt-scavenging robots will clean continuously.
• Closets will have automatic cleaning centers. Close the closet door and flip a switch to activate automatic dry-cleaning, done with an electrostatic charge or a chemical gas.
• There will be smart pantries. They will track your inventory of food, order more as needed, and suggest meals that can be prepared from what is on hand. A smart refrigerator will tell you when the milk is spoiled.
• Many homes will be equipped with health-monitoring equipment, such as a toilet that analyzes urine for sugar, protein, and red and white blood cells, or equipment that measures cholesterol and blood temperature and can relay the information to a doctor.
• Looking for a new home will be made easier when virtual reality will allow out-of-town house hunters to walk through dozens of homes in a couple of hours.
• Shopping for clothing via virtual reality will eliminate a trip to the mall. If you need a new pair of pants, your computer will show you some choices. You can try them on your virtual reality self-image without leaving home. Once you make a choice, your order will be transmitted to a factory, where they will be custom cut to fit and shipped to you the next day.
• When traveling, you'll be able to merge into a special automated highway lane, where a computer will note your destination. A collision-avoidance system will automatically decelerate when it senses you are too close to the car ahead. Instrument panels will be voice activated. You'll be free to turn on your laptop computer or watch a movie. A "driver-performance monitor" will make sure you are not sleeping when it's time to exit the highway and resume driving.

4-16 **Technology will continue to play a vital role in the future. Which of these forecasts would you find most useful?**

Summary

Technological change has greatly affected our world. Changes in the area of communications are constantly taking place. Sound, graphics, animation, and information are combined into multimedia offerings. Unlimited choices are already available in relation to information, communication, business and leisure. Medical and biological research has produced technological advances that could strongly affect society.

The present and proposed changes have definite benefits. However, there are also many concerns to be considered. Understanding both these benefits and concerns will be helpful to you in understanding the impact of technology on the family. This knowledge will then guide you in the decisions you make and the resources you use to reach your goals.

New advances will continue to change your management options and methods. You will need to determine the effect of these changes in terms of your needs, values, and management goals.

To Review

1. _____ is a constantly changing body of scientific knowledge that is used to solve practical problems.
2. The _____ is a global network of computers.
3. List three examples of technology used as entertainment.
4. List two reasons people choose to shop online.
5. A system of carrying out financial transactions by computer is called _____ _____ _____.
6. _____ is the study of inherited traits in living things.
7. List two advantages and two disadvantages of working from your home.
8. Describe three benefits of technology.
9. As computers compile more information, a person's constitutional right to _____ is threatened.
10. Describe three concerns related to technology.

To Do
with the Class

1. Brainstorm specific examples of technological advances you make use of each day.
2. Develop a display of a variety of technological toys, games, and entertainment devices. Discuss benefits and concerns related to their use.
3. Develop a bulletin board display of various Internet services. Highlight the differences in cost, speed, and available package options.
4. Tour a new supermarket or other retail store to view the electronic devices used to make shopping easier. Ask the store manager to explain the electronic devices used behind the scenes.

To Challenge
Your Thinking

1. Find a newspaper or magazine article related to the Internet and report its contents to the class.
2. Choose an appliance that has electronic controls. Research information related to that appliance and report to the class, identifying and describing the electronic control parts.
3. Research how e-commerce is affecting the retail industry.
4. Interview someone at a bank to discover the processes and costs involved in using computerized banking services.

To Do
with Your Community

1. Visit a local business and identify the many examples of technology used by its employees and customers.
2. Invite a panel of medical professionals to discuss the benefits and concerns of new technology in the areas of health and wellness.
3. Analyze how technology has either improved or become a detriment to the daily life in your community.
4. Invite persons involved in telecommuting to discuss their work.

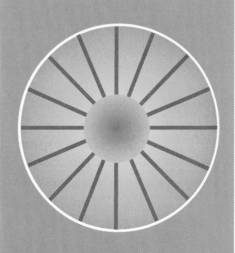

Part Two
Development Across the Life Span

Chapter 5
Understanding Development
Heredity and environment affect the way you grow physically, socially, emotionally, and intellectually. Part of this growth is the development of your character and your self-concept.

Chapter 6
Development During the Early Years
Children follow similar patterns of development by achieving skills as infants, toddlers, preschoolers, and school-age children.

Chapter 7
Developmental Tasks of Childhood
Developmental tasks are behaviors and skills learned at each stage of development. Children need to accomplish developmental tasks on one level before they can successfully move to the next level.

Chapter 8
Developmental Tasks from Adolescence Throughout Life
Adolescents, young adults, middle-age people, and older adults also strive to achieve developmental tasks. These tasks center on becoming independent and reaching life goals.

5

Understanding Development

To Know

self-concept
heredity
genes
chromosomes
genetic disease
genetic counseling
environmental influences
neurons
secure attachments
maturation
physical growth and development
social growth and development
emotional growth and development
intellectual growth and development
character
personal self
social self
ideal self
extended self
identification
peers
self-concept core
healthy self-concept
self-esteem
realistic self-concept
complete self-concept
peer pressure

Objectives

After studying this chapter, you will be able to

◆ explain how heredity and the environment influence human development.

◆ describe the patterns of human development.

◆ explain the significance of character formation in human development.

◆ identify the forces that shape your self-concept.

◆ describe the components of a healthy self-concept.

The growth and development of an individual is an extremely complex process. However, learning more about human development will help you better understand yourself. It will also help you understand other people around you.

There are different ways to examine human development. One way is to study how heredity and the environment influence development. A second approach is to study the patterns of development that lead to maturity. Research has shown that people follow a similar sequence as they develop physically, socially, emotionally, and intellectually. On the other hand, each person has a unique growth pattern and rate of development. No two people pass through developmental patterns in exactly the same way. See 5-1.

Character formation is a part of human development. Certain traits, such as respect and responsibility, help build strong character in a person. These positive traits or values can lead children to become socially and morally responsible adults.

Another factor in human development is self-concept. As you develop physically, socially, emotionally, and intellectually, you acquire certain ideas or impressions about yourself. These ideas or impressions are your **self-concept**. Understanding your self-concept will help you identify your strengths and weaknesses. You can use your strengths to help reach goals. You also can make plans for doing something about your weaknesses.

5-1 **A mother can expect her children to go through the same sequences of development, but at different rates.**

The Role of Heredity and Environment

All persons differ from one another in how they look, how they feel, and what they think. These differences are due to hereditary or environmental influences.

Hereditary Influences

You were born with certain characteristics and possibilities for your development. You inherited these. The process of passing on biological characteristics from one generation to the next is called **heredity**. You have inherited all the traits passed from your parents and ancestors to you. These traits affect not only the way you look, but also your behavior.

Inherited traits are passed from generation to generation by means of **genes**, the basic unit of heredity. Human beings have tens of thousands of genes. Each gene carries potential for specific traits. The genes are contained in threadlike structures called **chromosomes**. Each cell in the human body contains 23 pairs of chromosomes.

At conception, a unique individual is created when the egg from the mother unites with the sperm from the father. The egg and the sperm each contain 23 chromosomes. The sex of the individual is determined at conception. The chromosomes from the egg and the sperm pass on certain hereditary traits. For instance, you might have inherited your mother's brown eyes or your father's red hair.

At the moment of conception, the presence or absence of certain disease conditions or abnormalities is also established. Scientists have learned a great deal about inherited abnormalities and health problems through research. See 5-2. The science that studies the transmission of genes is known as *human genetics*. Scientists have

Genetic Diseases	
Disease	**Description**
Cystic Fibrosis	This glandular dysfunction damages the process of breathing and digestion. It is often fatal.
Down Syndrome	This chromosome abnormality causes varying degrees of retardation. Physical defects may include a thick tongue, slanty eyes, and a flat face.
Hemophilia	This blood disease is characterized by poor clotting ability. Bleeding varies from mild to severe.
Phenylketonuria (PKU)	This disease is caused by the body's inability to break down a protein called phenylalanine. Severe brain damage may occur. It may cause retardation, hyperactivity, and destructiveness.
Sickle-Cell Anemia	This blood abnormality occurs mostly in African Americans and causes excruciating pain.
Tay-Sachs Disease	This enzyme deficiency causes deterioration of the brain and central nervous system.

5-2 Some of the more common inherited abnormalities are described in this chart.

made many recent discoveries about human genetics and genetic disease. **Genetic diseases** or disabilities are inherited. They are passed from one generation to another.

Genetic counseling is a service provided for people who have a special concern about the role of genetics in their lives. This service may be used by a couple who are going to be parents or just thinking about starting a family. It may be used by anyone who is affected with a disease or at risk for a disease. People who have a child with a disability may want to see if the disability is genetic. This could tell them the chances of a second child being born with the same condition. People who have a family history of hereditary illness may also wish to use such a service.

Genetic counseling involves more than just communicating complex medical information to families. It also involves helping families cope with the consequences of genetic disease. Genetic counseling can raise complex ethical questions that do not have clear and simple answers. However, this knowledge can be helpful to couples who are making decisions about having children.

Environmental Influences

Environmental influences consist of everything around you that affects you. This includes your family, home, friends, community, and all your life experiences.

The environment can affect your looks, growth, and health. It can influence how you get along with other people and how well you understand yourself. It can also affect your creativity, communication, thinking, and problem-solving skills.

Heredity and environment work together to influence your development.

Heredity determines the potential for your development; the environment determines if or how that potential will be developed. Poor eating habits or certain forms of disease may prevent a person from reaching his or her genetically determined height. However, environmental factors cannot make that person grow above his or her inherited height. Experts are not certain whether some human traits result more from heredity factors or environmental factors. Human traits such as mental health are examples.

Early Brain Development

Recent scientific research shows how heredity and environment interact in the development of the brain. Scientists have learned much about brain development, particularly in the early years of life. You already know that a baby's body needs food to grow. In the same way, positive experiences in the earliest years are necessary for healthy brain growth. A mixture of social, emotional, physical, and intellectual experiences is important. These experiences will help shape the way people learn, think, and behave for the rest of their lives.

At birth, the infant's brain has 100 billion nerve cells called **neurons**. Heredity affects how many neurons a baby will have throughout his or her life. This network of fibers is called the brain's *wiring*. Messages travel between neurons along pathways of fibers that carry messages from cell to cell. This network, which grows daily in the young brain, forms the foundation upon which a child builds a lifetime of skills. Various body functions, such as thinking, seeing, hearing, moving, and expressing emotion, are controlled by the network.

The brain needs experiences to create new networks for learning. Every new experience establishes a new network link. Therefore, the environment is crucial. A child's early experiences can increase or decrease the brain's potential by as much as 25 percent. The brain physically changes due to these experiences. It is from early infancy to early childhood that many of the vital connections in the brain's wiring are made permanent. See 5-3.

Rich sensory experiences such as being talked to, exploring a toy, and hearing music strengthen and refine the brain's wiring. Repeating a positive experience strengthens the connection. Over time and with additional experiences, the brain strengthens some pathways but begins to weed out the unused ones. This process of weeding out weak connections between neurons is called *pruning*. Only those connections that are frequently used are retained. Lack of use results in the disappearance of these connections and, therefore, a lack of development. The effects this has on future learning potential can be lifelong.

However, during early childhood the brain retains its ability to remember information it has discarded. This ability is referred to as the brain's *plasticity*. You might think of this as putting something into the temporary deletion storage bin on your computer. You can still retrieve that information as long as the storage bin has

5-3 **This child's network links are being simulated by her mother, the environment, and the activity.**

not been emptied. After a child reaches age 10, this plasticity is lost.

When children are loved and receive warm, responsive care, they are more likely to feel safe and secure with the adults who take care of them. These strong relationships, sometimes referred to as **secure attachments**, are the basis of a child's future relationships. Early secure attachments actually affect the way the brain works and grows.

Touch is how an infant first knows he is loved. Holding and stroking the infant stimulates the brain to release important hormones necessary for growth. Research has shown that gently massaging premature infants three times per day for 15 minutes helped them gain weight, be more alert, and cry less. These infants were released from the hospital sooner than infants who were not massaged.

Interaction with others is important. Infants see expressions on a person's face. They hear cooing, singing, and talking. Infants don't grasp the meaning of words, but these early "conversations" help develop the parts of the brain that affect speech and language. The more language infants hear, the more those parts of the brain will grow and develop. See 5-4.

5-4 **By interacting with his child, this father is already helping develop language skills.**

Talking to babies encourages them to begin babbling, which is the first step in learning to speak. As they get older, young children need to hear people talk to them about what they are seeing and experiencing. This helps their brains to fully develop language skills.

Picture books and stories can be read to very young children—even infants. By about six months of age, infants show excitement when looking at a book with pictures of familiar objects. They do this by widening their eyes and moving their arms and legs.

How children are read to also makes a difference. Stories can be read in a way that encourages older babies and toddlers to answer questions, point out pictures, and repeat rhymes. It may seem boring to tell the same stories or sing the same songs over and over, but it is not boring to children. They learn through repetition.

If a child is in an environment with little stimulus or an abusive environment, he or she can suffer effects that can be very difficult to reverse. For instance, children who have little experience of being talked to or read to may fail to develop critical language skills.

It is also important to realize that parts of the brain are not fully developed until well past puberty, and the brain changes throughout life. The human brain is capable of learning and developing new brain wiring until old age. However, this fact does not reduce the importance of the first three years of development.

Patterns in Growth and Development

As people mature, they move toward full development. During the process of **maturation**, growth occurs and certain personal and behavioral characteristics begin to appear. This growth cannot be measured by specific standards. It is judged instead by progression through an orderly sequence of development.

There are four types of growth and development patterns: physical, social, emotional, and intellectual. Each person follows a similar sequence of growth and development in these four areas. However, each person has his or her own unique growth pattern and rate of development. See 5-5.

Physical Growth and Development

Physical growth and development are body changes affecting the outside appearance of the body and the internal structure. The internal changes affect the functions of the muscles, organs, and nervous system. As the body matures, new and more complex physical abilities develop.

Physical growth is most rapid during the early years of life. Although actual growth stops in the late teens or early

5-5 **Although both girls are the same age, one is much taller than the other.**

twenties, physical changes continue throughout life until death. Biological aging occurs at greatly varying rates among older people. Some factors that influence aging are genetic inheritance, physical activity, and physical environment. Other factors include nutrition, medical care, and stress.

Social Growth and Development

Social growth and development refers to the way people behave and react to others. Because most people do not live in isolation, learning to get along with others is important.

Moving toward social maturity involves learning acceptable behavior patterns. As you live in an environment with others, you become aware of the rules or appropriate behaviors for living within that environment. When a toddler hits a playmate who will not share a toy, the child is guided toward a more appropriate response. This is a small step toward social maturity. For an adult to hit someone who would not share would be considered inappropriate behavior. It would indicate social immaturity.

As you develop socially, you move from being totally dependent to being more independent. Infants depend on their parents for everything. On the other hand, a young adult who requires a parent's help in making many daily decisions is considered socially immature.

As you develop socially, you move away from being totally self-centered. You develop an increased awareness and acceptance of others. The socially mature person is sensitive to the feelings of others and values feelings of self-respect and self-worth.

Social development is largely influenced by the environment. This includes a person's culture, family, peers, social institutions, and the mass media. However, researchers have shown that temperament and certain other behavior patterns appear to be inherited. Heredity's role in social growth and development tends to be less clear than with physical characteristics.

Emotional Growth and Development

Emotional growth and development involves feelings or emotions and their control. Emotional reactions are feelings you have when your desires or interests are either satisfied or frustrated. Examples of human emotions are love, anger, sadness, worry, jealousy, fear, happiness, and loneliness.

As you mature emotionally, you are better able to recognize and control your emotions. The ability to control your emotions depends greatly on your understanding of yourself and your relationships with other people.

When you learn to control your emotions, you do not allow them to have a negative effect on your behavior. For example, fear of taking a test can be so strong it almost paralyzes the mind. Feelings of anger can be so strong they may cause injury to another person. Learning to control such emotions will have a positive effect on development.

Strong emotions can also be accompanied by physical changes. Some of these are harmless, such as a more rapid heartbeat or heavy perspiration. However, emotionally stressful situations can also have negative physical effects. For instance, high blood pressure and heart problems may result.

Emotional growth is influenced mainly by the environment. A child's emotional development is determined greatly by experiences with adults in that child's environment. Parents and other family members provide guidance and set an example for the younger children, 5-6. As children

Lynn Hellmuth

5-6 **The way teenagers express emotions is greatly influenced by their parents and other family members.**

mature emotionally, they learn acceptable ways to express negative or unpleasant feelings as well as pleasant ones.

Intellectual Growth and Development

Intellectual growth and development refers to intelligence. Intelligence indicates a person's ability to learn, adapt to new situations, and solve problems.

Like other areas of development, people vary greatly in their levels of intellectual ability. These differences are related to heredity and all aspects of a person's environment. Hereditary factors have a

Use Your Reasoning Skills

Explain the following statement: "Nature provides capacities; culture converts them into abilities." Think of two famous people and apply this statement to them. How does this statement apply to yourself?

strong influence on a person's intelligence. However, whether this inherited potential will be reached depends on the person's environmental experiences. Environmental influences include life experiences, opportunities for education, home environment, and relationship experiences.

Various systems within the body affect intelligence. The brain controls thinking, concept formation, reasoning, and problem solving. It coordinates intelligent behavior. The development of intelligence is also highly dependent on the sense organs. Perceptions result from looking, listening, tasting, smelling, and touching.

Language is extremely important to mental growth. A child learns language by first understanding the speech of others, then pronouncing words, building a vocabulary, and combining words into sentences. Learning to read and express thoughts clearly and accurately through writing are important steps in intellectual development.

Your Character

Certain personal qualities make up your **character**. These are the traits that make each individual unique. They include qualities such as trustworthiness, respect, responsibility, fairness, caring, and citizenship. These traits have to do with how people think and behave related to issues such as right and wrong, justice and equality, and other areas of human conduct. See 5-7.

Character development begins as early as the preschool years. Children begin to learn which behaviors are acceptable and which are not. This helps them develop standards that guide their behavior. As children have new experiences, they become more aware of right and wrong. Their characters continue to grow. A person whose actions show traits such as honesty, fairness, and responsibility is said to have strong character. However, a person who seldom shows these traits has a weak character.

Qualities of Character	
Qualities	**Actions That Show These Qualities**
Trustworthiness	Act with integrity, honesty, reliability, and loyalty; stand up for beliefs; tell the truth; keep promises; honor commitments
Respect	Be accepting of others, resolve disagreements peacefully, treat others with courtesy
Responsibility	Meet obligations, accept consequences of actions, work hard, set realistic goals, be self-disciplined
Fairness	Treat people equally, act without being influenced by favoritism or prejudice, consider others' points of view, be open-minded
Caring	Act with concern for others, be considerate and grateful, forgive others, work to make others' lives better
Citizenship	Do your share, respect authority and the law, volunteer, follow rules, participate in committees and voice your opinion

5-7 The way a person behaves indicates the traits that make up his or her character. Character Counts!

*Getting*Involved

Parents, caregivers, teachers, and community members help children build positive character qualities. They help develop the knowledge, skills, and abilities that encourage children to make informed and responsible choices. Religion can also be a strong influence on character development.

Your Self-Concept

Your self-concept, the impressions you have of yourself, affects decisions you make throughout life. It greatly influences how satisfying your life will be. Self-concept changes as you develop and have new life experiences.

Your self-concept is based on how you see yourself and feel about yourself. It includes how you see

◆ your personal self

◆ your social self

◆ your ideal self

◆ your extended self

Your self-concept in terms of your **personal self** includes how you see yourself physically. This might include being male or female and tall or short. It might also include whether you see yourself as physically fit or not in very good physical shape. Other ways you view your personal self may involve aspects of your personality. Do you see yourself as happy, shy, responsible, immature, well-liked, moody, or disorganized? Your personal self includes your feelings about your skills and talents, too.

How you see your **social self** depends on how you view yourself in relation to other people. Would you describe yourself as sociable, at ease in talking with others, and easily able to make friends? Are you a good sport, and do you try to understand why others behave as they do? Do you like group activities or would you rather be alone? These images indicate your social self-concept.

Your **ideal self** is the image you have of the person you would like to be. These images often begin in your youth. You admire someone, perhaps from television or sports, and want to be just like that person. Your actions tend to imitate that person. Later, as you become more mature, you recognize admirable traits in many people. You then form ideas about an ideal self made up of traits from many people rather than just one person.

Self-concept may also include ideas or images outside the individual self. This is known as the **extended self**. Sometimes possessions or people extremely important to you become a part of extended self. This extension of self is referred to as **identification**. It indicates a feeling of oneness as you identify with a person, group of people, or object. You may identify with a social group—your team, friends, or club, 5-8. If a person from one of these special groups is insulted, your "self" reacts as though you were offended.

All these images of your personal self, social self, ideal self, and extended self make up your self-concept. Self-concept includes all that you know and believe about yourself.

Self-Concept and Behavior

Your self-concept influences your behavior. It is considered by many to be the

5-8 **As an active member of the band, an individual identifies with the group and takes pride in the band's accomplishments.**

key to human behavior and personality. How you act in a situation depends on how you see yourself in relation to that situation.

Your self-concept is the center of your universe. It serves as a yardstick for making judgments. Things are near or far, right or wrong, better or worse when judged in relation to yourself. How you find yourself compared to these other factors creates either a positive or negative feeling about yourself.

A positive self-concept will usually influence behavior in positive ways. You will feel confident in your relationships with others. You will be more willing to accept challenges. See 5-9.

A negative self-concept will have a negative influence. People who have developed negative self-concepts may have difficulty accepting themselves. They may make poor personal and social adjustments. Teens who have negative feelings about their social selves may avoid group activities. People with negative self-concepts tend to react to challenges negatively. They will think they can't handle a situation or feel they don't even want to try.

Experiences Shape Your Self-Concept

You are continually developing your self-concept throughout life. It is based on your values, your life experiences, and the people around you. Most of your self-concept is determined by your response to experiences with other people, especially your parents, family, and peers.

Experiences with Parents and Family

Infancy is a most important time in the development of self-concept. The infant is constantly exploring and discovering. Parents' reactions to these experiences have a great influence on the child's self-concept. When a child is given care, encouragement, security, love, and guidance by parents, a positive self-concept will likely develop. However, those children who are rejected, discouraged, and often punished are likely to develop negative images of themselves.

5-9 **Having achieved their goal of high school graduation, these young people have confidence in furthering their education.**

The nature of your family can strongly affect how you perceive yourself. The number of children and order of birth may affect self-concept. The oldest child often has many expectations to meet. He or she is to set a good example for the younger children. This oldest child often takes on a more adult or serious self-concept than younger children do. Parents usually relax and are more casual with their second and third children. These children, being under less pressure, are often more carefree and independent.

Brainstorming

Describe experiences that illustrate how sense of self changes as a person grows from childhood to adulthood. Do people realize their sense of self is changing as they are growing? Why or why not?

Expectations or goals that parents have for their children also affect self-concept. For instance, a father who was an outstanding athlete as a young man might expect his son to have similar interests. His son, however, may not have the same interest or ability in athletics. He may have negative feelings about himself because he can't live up to his father's expectations.

The quality of family relationships influences the self-concept, 5-10. The influence of a home where there is a lot of fighting and strained family relations is often negative. A more positive self-concept is likely to result from a home where each person's opinion is respected. In such a family, decisions are likely to be made in a democratic manner.

Parents who are overprotective may cause their children to lack self-confidence. This can cause a negative self-concept. Overprotection limits the child's experiences in meeting challenges. Proper guidance can help the child learn from new experiences and yet avoid situations that are too challenging.

Dennis Corcoran

5-10 **Children get good feelings about themselves when they are given love and security by a parent.**

Experiences Outside the Family

As children grow up, they learn much about themselves from the way they are treated by people outside the family. This results in a continual altering of the self-concept.

Your **peers** are friends and classmates in your age group. Peers can have a strong influence on your self-concept. They can play an important role in your life by providing you with friendships and a sense of belonging.

Peer group influence can become very strong early in childhood and continue throughout the early teens. Young people often identify strongly with their peer groups. The peer group becomes a part of the extended self.

Neighbors, teachers, and other individuals may also have a strong influence on a person's self-concept. See 5-11. These people are important for various reasons. An eight-year-old boy who idolizes the teenage boy next door may be very concerned about what that teen thinks about him. The teen might have a positive or a negative influence on this young boy's self-concept.

Kent Hayward

5-11 **Experiences within the school setting can greatly affect self-concept.**

The Self-Concept Changes

Your self-concept is always changing as you grow, develop, and respond to the changing world. However, you have a **self-concept core** that is not easily changed. The self-concept core is developed in the early years and is usually related to basic beliefs. The core changes only over a long period of time through repeated daily experiences. This fact is unfortunate for persons who were victims of their environments as children. As a result, they may have developed negative self-concept cores when they were young. Changing their self-concepts takes a long time and a lot of work. This cannot be done in a few hours or a few days.

As your world expands and you have new experiences, your sense of self changes. As you face each new challenge, a new sense of self develops as a result. For example, you may take on the new challenge of playing on the soccer team. Your experiences as a team member will affect your self-concept.

Although people important to you influence your self-concept, you do have some control over shaping your self-image. By increasing your understanding of human behavior, you can improve your relationships with family and peers. You develop skills and talents. You can improve your performance in school. If you feel you need help, you can seek it.

Parts of a Healthy Self-Concept

If you have a **healthy self-concept**, you have an honest, accurate, and positive view of yourself. You are able to realistically judge the facts about yourself. You know what your strengths and weaknesses are. You feel positive about your good points. You may not like your bad points, but with a healthy self-concept, you accept them. The result is a feeling of being a worthwhile person.

A healthy self-concept evolves when a person has

- high self-esteem
- a realistic self-concept
- a complete self-concept

High Self-Esteem

How you feel about yourself indicates your **self-esteem**. If you feel good about yourself, high self-esteem exists. If you have a negative feeling about yourself, you have low self-esteem. Everyone has a need for high self-esteem. This means having feelings of worth, success, self-respect, and confidence in facing the world.

High self-esteem is a part of a healthy self-concept. People with high esteem feel they are worthwhile. They behave like worthwhile persons. This feeling of self-esteem gives them confidence. They feel personally secure. It is easier for them to face challenges. They are more independent and trust themselves rather than "following the crowd."

People with low self-esteem lack self-confidence. You may be able to think of someone you know who does not feel good about himself or herself. You might hear that person say "There's no point in my trying— I'd never be able to do it" or "I can't do anything right." These comments indicate low self-esteem. Such negative feelings cause fear, insecurity, and inferiority. People with low self-esteem often feel threatened by new experiences and other people.

Feelings of high esteem give you confidence to deal with new experiences. People with high self-esteem still make mistakes, but they are able to deal with these events. They do not lose their sense of self-worth. For example, Brian was an outstanding wrestler at his high school. He lost a wrestling match in the semi-finals of the state tournament. Brian was disappointed, of course, since he was hoping to win the state title. However, he knew he had worked hard and tried his best. His opponent had just done better in that match. Brian had not lost self-esteem.

Realistic Self-Concept

High self-esteem is good as long as it is built on a realistic self-concept. For instance, sometimes people have high self-esteem that is faulty because they can't admit they have any weaknesses, 5-12. You may know someone who has false high self-esteem. You might describe that person as "cocky" or "over-confident." That person does not seem to have a realistic self-concept.

Dennis Corcoran

5-12 Some people who receive a lot of praise and recognition have a hard time maintaining a realistic self-concept.

You have a **realistic self-concept** if what you know about yourself is accurate. You see yourself as you really are, not as what you would like to be. This is not easy because your feelings and abilities change with each new experience. You may have to work hard to see the facts as they are.

People often see themselves differently from the way others see them. A young girl who feels she is ugly because she has a large nose might be considered attractive by other people. They notice her well-groomed hair, pretty eyes, and happy smile instead.

The ideal self is good in that it moves you to develop traits and abilities you admire in others. It helps you set goals for improvement. However, if this ideal self is too unrealistic and those goals are too difficult to reach, you are likely to become discouraged. In people with low self-esteem, the gap between what they would like to be and how they actually perform is often wide. They are not being realistic.

By carefully judging the facts about yourself, you will be more realistic. You will be more likely to set realistic goals and not aim for the impossible. See 5-13.

Complete Self-Concept

A healthy self-concept results from not only a realistic self-concept, but also a **complete self-concept**. The more you know about yourself, the more complete your self-concept will be.

Have you ever watched someone do a task that looked very easy? When you tried to do the task yourself, it may have been very hard. Because you had not experienced that particular task before, your self-concept in relation to the activity was not complete.

Self-concepts tend to set limits determining what a person can and cannot do. Involving yourself in new experiences expands your self-concept. This also expands what you can do. You develop a more complete self-concept when you take advantage of opportunities to try new

5-13 People with realistic self-concepts are more likely to meet goals they set for themselves.

things. The self-concept becomes more complete as you mature.

Being with a variety of people is important to a complete self-concept. If children are around only a few people in their daily lives, their self-concepts will be incomplete. As they move beyond the family and are with other children and teachers at school, they develop a more complete self-concept. This is especially so in terms of their ability to relate to others.

As you mature and your self-concept becomes more complete, concepts about yourself also become more precise. For instance, your self-concept regarding your size may be very clear. You are a certain height and a certain weight. This self-concept is precise.

In contrast, your self-concept regarding your personality may be less precise. For example, sometimes you may feel quite confident about decisions you make. At other times you may lack self-confidence. Your concept regarding this part of your personality, self-confidence, is not very clear. As you mature and are involved in a variety of life experiences, your self-concept will become more precise and complete.

As you have new experiences, your self-concept also becomes stable. This is important to a healthy self-concept. Each new experience tests your self-concept core, making it stronger over time. This gives you the added confidence of knowing who you are, what you think, and how you feel.

Psychological problems are often related to a less-than-stable self-concept. Some people go through life without attaining a stable self-concept. It is difficult for such people to make choices. They are confused about who they are, what they believe, and what they want in life.

A healthy self-concept involves accepting and liking yourself. It is not the same as being conceited or selfish. It means you judge your traits and feel good about your good points, but accept your weaknesses, 5-14. This self-awareness also helps you decide which aspects you would like to improve. You can then set goals based on those traits most important to you.

Teenagers can be influenced both positively and negatively by their peers. This is known as **peer pressure**. Although peers can provide friendship, they can also try to influence you to do things that might not reflect your beliefs.

A healthy self-concept is a valuable resource in responding to negative peer pressure. People with healthy self-concepts are able to stand up for what they feel is right. With a healthy self-concept, you are more likely to be firm about your beliefs. This helps you avoid being influenced by the group in ways that might be harmful to you and others.

Do You Have a Healthy Self-Concept?

A Healthy Self-Concept
- In general, do you feel good about yourself?
- Do you recognize your strengths and weaknesses? Do you accept those weaknesses you cannot change?

High Self-Esteem
- What do you like and dislike about yourself?
- What can you change about yourself to raise your self-esteem?

Realistic Self-Concept
- Do you see yourself as you really are in terms of your personal self, abilities, and relationships with others?
- Do other people see you differently from the way you see yourself? If so, why?

Complete Self-Concept
- Have you had experiences similar to those of other people your age?
- What new experiences could make your self-concept more complete?
- What aspects of yourself would you like to develop or improve?

5-14 Do you have a healthy self-concept? Thinking about these questions may help you understand your feelings about "self."

32
31
30
29
28
27
26
25
24
23
22
21
20
19
18
17
16
15
14
13
12
11
10
9
8
7
6
5
4
3
2
1

Summary

You can better understand yourself and others by knowing how heredity and environment influence human development throughout life. Recent scientific research has shown the importance of both heredity and environmental experiences on brain development in the early years of life. This knowledge will help you recognize what factors in your own development and in the development of others that you can influence.

People develop physically, socially, emotionally, and intellectually. By understanding each pattern of development, you will be better prepared to make choices that influence your life in a positive way. You will also have a better understanding of others and their development.

The formation of positive character traits helps guide your behavior. These traits are values that will influence your decisions throughout life.

Your self-concept is what you know and believe about yourself. Understanding the importance of the self-concept and how it is formed will help you understand yourself and others.

Because your self-concept is constantly forming and changing throughout life, you can influence that development. You can make decisions to move toward the goal of developing a healthy self-concept. Self-concept influences decisions you make throughout life. It has a large influence on how satisfying your life will be.

To Review

To Review
To Review

1. _____ determines the potential for your development while _____ determines how or even if that potential will be developed.
2. What physical changes can occur when strong emotions are experienced?
3. As you develop socially, you move from being totally _____ to being more _____.
4. True or false? All people have the same inherited ability for intelligence.
5. _____ changes as you develop and have new life experiences.
6. Indicate whether each of the following describes your personal self, social self, ideal self, or extended self.
   A. your team
   B. enjoying group activities
   C. being female
   D. desire to be rich
   E. moodiness
   F. desire to get married
   G. having a lot of friends
   H. being shy and self-conscious
7. Which of the following would be related to the formation of a positive self-concept, and which would be related to the formation of a negative self-concept?
   A. praise
   B. encouragement
   C. overprotection
   D. concern
   E. rejection
   F. love
   G. hostility
   H. respect
8. True or false?
   A. The self-concept core is easily changed.
   B. Your self-concept becomes stable as you have new experiences.
   C. As you face new challenges, you develop a sense of self in relation to that experience.
9. Describe the difference between a realistic self-concept and a complete self-concept.
10. Define *peer pressure*.

To Do
with the Class

1. Write and perform role-plays in which couples consult a genetic counselor. Include situations in which couples face the possibility of having children with certain diseases or genetic abnormalities.
2. Develop case situations that show how an adolescent might mature socially through a specific social experience. Share case situations with the entire class.
3. Relate an incident you have experienced or seen that would enhance a person's self-concept. Give a similar example of an experience that may cause a person to feel inferior.
4. Practice making positive comments about people by saying something nice to other students in your class. Ask them how they feel when they are complimented. How do you feel when you are complimented by others?

To Challenge
Your Thinking

1. Think of a person whom you consider mature. What physical, social, emotional, and intellectual characteristics indicate this maturity?
2. List qualities or characteristics you would like people to know you have.
3. Think of how your self-concept has changed over the past five years. List reasons for that change.
4. Write a brief description of someone with an unrealistic self-concept. What are some qualities this person has that are related to the unrealistic self-concept?

To Do
with Your Community

1. Find resources available in the community to encourage physical development and share them with the class.
2. Watch and listen to a group of people. Then list behaviors or comments that illustrate their self-concepts.
3. Observe persons in your community. Describe actions of people that might indicate low self-esteem. Include examples for people of all ages.
4. Consider ways in which being involved in your community can help make your self-concept more complete. Share you ideas with others in the class.

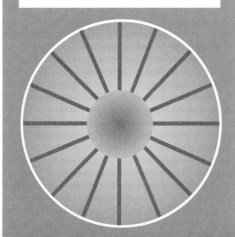

6 Development During the Early Years

To Know

patterns of development
reflexes
motor skills
eye-hand coordination
stranger anxiety
parallel play
cooperative play
sibling rivalry
symbolic play
perception
moral development

Objectives

After studying this chapter, you will be able to

◆ describe the patterns of physical, social, emotional, and intellectual development during the early years.

◆ predict what development to expect at various ages.

◆ describe influences on the development of a child's self-concept.

◆ explain the importance of the skill of self-observation.

Most people have some contact with small children. You may have a younger brother or sister. You may babysit with young children, or perhaps there are young children in your neighborhood. What you do, what you say, and how you act can influence a child's development.

Children are strongly influenced by other people because they are not yet sure how they feel about themselves. Opinions and reactions from others can have a significant effect on them. The people most important to children, such as parents and other family members, have the most influence.

You may influence a child more than you realize. For instance, the young boy who lives next door may idolize you. You may represent what the boy hopes to be. You are a role model. He may try to copy you, hoping to be just like you. You can imagine the influence your actions might have on the young boy.

Each child is unique, with his or her own growth pattern and rate of development. However, all children follow similar patterns of development. Understanding these patterns will help you understand

children and how you might influence their development.

Patterns of Development During the Early Years

As children develop, they display certain characteristics in an orderly and predictable sequence. These are referred to as **patterns of development**. Many researchers agree on four patterns of development: physical, social, emotional, and intellectual. See 6-1.

Development of Children				
	Physical Development	**Social Development**	**Emotional Development**	**Intellectual Development**
Infants and Toddlers	Show reflex actions Turn head and kick Begin developing hand-eye coordination Roll over Reach for objects Hold head steady Sit Crawl Experience eruption of teeth Handle a cup awkwardly Pass toys from hand to hand Use spoon in feeding Show hand preference Climb stairs Learning bowel control Jump Constructive play with toys Learning bladder control Run Climb	Smile Show awareness Listen to voices Develop special attachment to mother Show fear of strangers Seek attention of others Like playing with others—throwing objects and retrieving them Exhibit parallel play but not cooperative play Like to imitate parents' work	Cry as response to anything unpleasant Have normal fears, such as loud noises and falling Strong emotional attachment to mother Express feelings openly and strongly (toddlers)	Make simple perceptions Show interest in the world around them Recognize sounds and familiar voices Show interest in putting things together Understand simple commands May repeat familiar words Are very curious

(Continued)

6-1 As a child develops physically, socially, emotionally, and intellectually, certain characteristics can be observed.

Development of Children				
	Physical Development	**Social Development**	**Emotional Development**	**Intellectual Development**
Preschool Children	Walk and run with good balance Need some help dressing Alternate feet climbing stairs Ride a tricycle Establish a toileting routine Skip Can enjoy most athletic activities such as jumping and acrobatics Show advanced small muscle development and improved finger dexterity	Realize importance of friends Learn many social skills through trial and error with friends Play in a more cooperative manner Commonly have imaginary playmates Like to talk a lot	Demand a lot of parental attention. Experience compulsive patterns such as stuttering and thumb-sucking Express jealousy Have frequent frightening dreams	Understand new concepts based on many new experiences Progress rapidly in language development Gradually develop skill in reasoning Learn to count Can print
School-Age Children	Are very active physically Can dress themselves Experience emergence of first permanent molars Like physical games and sports Show more individual variations in growth Show much more advanced finger dexterity Show traces of approaching adolescence (especially girls)	Show strong interest in having and being with friends Get along better with older than younger siblings Become more accepting and more sensitive of the needs of others Are less likely to exhibit anti-social behavior Often fight with siblings Often have a special friend their own age Become involved in clubs or organized groups	Exhibit more stable emotions Begin to accept responsibility for their behavior Are more controlled and cautious about expressing themselves Act happy, less tearful during this stage	Develop ethical sense Show increased enjoyment of reading Develop mathematical skills Use language fluently Can form abstract ideas

6-1 *(Continued)*

Understanding these patterns helps you predict what development to expect. Then you can plan activities to encourage each step in development and help the child practice new skills. Being aware of these patterns can also help parents notice any signs that indicate their child is not progressing normally. They then might consult a physician. Children do follow a similar sequence of growth and development. It is important to remember, though, that each child's growth pattern and rate of development will be somewhat different.

Physical Development

Physical development refers to the growth of the body's muscle, bone, and tissue. This includes changes in the internal organs such as the brain and growth of the circulatory, digestive, and nervous systems.

Physical Development of the Infant and Toddler

Infants are born with certain physical reflexes that are related to survival and protection. **Reflexes** are automatic, unlearned behaviors. One of these is the rooting reflex. Infants search for something to suck on when their faces are touched. This reflex helps infants get nourishment necessary for life. Another reflex, the blinking of the eye, is a way of providing protection. The infant's kicking legs and moving arms are also reflexes.

As physical development occurs, children gain control over their bodies and develop what are referred to as **motor skills**—voluntary, directed movements. To develop motor skills, coordination of the muscular system, nervous system, and senses must steadily improve. The muscles strengthen, the nervous system matures, and the senses develop. These three systems work together to help the child control movements. During the first few years of life, there are great changes in the child's

Getting Involved

Visit a child care center and observe the physical development of the children in a particular age group. Are the children similar in development? How are they different? Do you think developmental differences are alarming to parents?

motor skill development. As the body continues to mature physically, the child is able to perform more complex movements.

Infants show evidence of motor coordination by first turning the head from side to side and then lifting it. At around three to four months, the infant sits with some support. The child sits alone at five to seven months. Following these advancements, the infant rolls over, crawls or scoots, and stands. Between the ages of 10 and 16 months the child begins to walk.

Infants must reach a certain point in physical maturity before they can develop these skills. Until certain muscles develop, an infant cannot stand, no matter how much practice and encouragement family members offer. Children give certain cues when they are ready for each new step. Encouragement and practice might help then, but not before that time.

Although it isn't possible to hurry a child's development, it is possible to cause a delay in development. For instance, infants learn to handle objects in a clear sequence of stages. If an infant is not allowed to play with objects or toys, this development may be delayed. Children should be encouraged to explore their world within safe bounds.

Development of **eye-hand coordination** begins in the early months when infants begin to notice their hands and some objects, like a bottle or a toy. They begin to coordinate what they see with the way they move their hands. As infants mature, they work to move their hands toward objects. Eventually children are able to grasp objects. This physical development involves the senses as well as the nervous and muscular systems. Children develop skill in manipulating objects rapidly between one and two years of age.

Children grow rapidly during the first two years, and their proportions change. During the first year, children's height usually increases about one and one-half times their length at birth. Most children triple their birthweights during the first year, and they gain only about one-fourth of that during the second year. As babies grow taller and heavier, their bones and teeth are also developing.

The baby's teeth are actually formed before the baby is born. At about six months of age, the teeth begin to erupt through the gums. The front teeth are usually the first teeth to appear. Several teeth usually appear before the baby's first birthday.

Development of the senses is also a part of physical development. The newborn is able to use all the senses, but a baby's senses are not as highly developed as an adult's. However, some babies seem particularly sensitive to touch and loud noises.

Physical Development of the Preschool Child

During the preschool years, motor skills and physical coordination develop rapidly. Both small and large muscle development become advanced as the preschooler is involved in a variety of physical activities. See 6-2 and 6-3. Preschoolers are able to perform many everyday tasks on their own.

During this period, growth slows down compared with the earlier years. Changing body proportions become quite noticeable. Preschoolers lose their baby fat. Their muscles and bones become more developed.

Physical Development of the School-Age Child

Children grow regularly but more slowly during the school-age years from 6 to 10.

Nancy Henke-Konopasek

6-2 **Painting this small object with a brush indicates improvement of dexterity of the hands and fingers.**

Proportions change somewhat as the children grow taller and thinner. Boys tend to be slightly taller and heavier than girls early in this period. However, girls often experience preadolescent growth spurts and find themselves taller than many of the boys.

During this period, growth takes place in spurts. The growth spurts vary in each individual. There is a wide range in height and weight among normal children.

Motor abilities and coordination continue to develop during the school-age years. Because large muscles develop before small muscles, many of the children's activities involve running, climbing, and ball games. Later in this period of life, the activities indicate small muscle development. Crafts, model building, and other activities that help improve finger dexterity are common.

Along with each child's level of maturity, environment plays an important role in what children can do physically. Being

6-3 **Being able to run and kick the ball indicates large muscle development and coordination.**

aware of the steps in physical development can help parents choose activities that will enhance their child's physical development.

Social Development

Social development involves getting along with others and accepting new responsibilities. As children mature socially, they move from a self-centered attitude to behavior that recognizes other people's feelings.

All people have basic needs related to love, affection, belonging, and self-worth. These basic needs motivate children to develop socially. Children quickly learn that certain things they do help satisfy these needs.

Children vary in their rates of social development. These variations have to do with differences in personalities and abilities. Also, the home environment greatly affects social development. Children need contact with people and acceptance from others. No child can develop normally if isolated in an environment with limited contacts. Children develop socially as they have the opportunity to be with others, cooperate with others, and assume responsibilities.

Social Development of the Infant and Toddler

Babies quickly learn to respond in a way that will satisfy their needs. Early in life, infants make sucking noises and other mouth movements when their mothers come in view. Later, infants show increased awareness by smiling. By the time babies are about three months of age, they respond to voices and follow the movements of nearby people. At around four and five months of age, babies begin to desire companionship, especially from family members. Babies need people for social as well as physical reasons. See 6-4.

Once children develop a feeling of security with their caregivers, mainly family members, they may experience **stranger anxiety**. Between the ages of five and seven months, children often feel anxious or afraid around unfamiliar people. At this stage, children recognize the difference between their secure attachments and the world that is strange and different.

6-4 **By smiling and laughing, babies show they recognize family members and feel comfortable with them.**

As children continue through the first year of life, they become more socially oriented and want to be with others. They begin playing, throwing and retrieving objects, and imitating others. Near the end of the first year, children can follow simple instructions. During this period they learn parents approve and disapprove of certain behaviors. Approval means a lot to toddlers. They learn quickly which actions please their parents.

Because toddlers are very self-centered, they need to mix with other children. They will involve themselves in **parallel play**. This means they will play next to another child but not with the child in a cooperative way. Although they are too young to understand sharing with each other, toddlers do enjoy each other's company.

Social Development of the Preschool Child

Rapidly developing speech is an important factor in a preschool child's social development. This new skill allows children to interact with all age groups. The more children interact, the more their language skills improve.

Three-year-olds become involved in **cooperative play**. This means children interact with others. They like to pretend with other children and play simple games. These play situations help children learn about other people's needs and how to adjust to different personalities.

Many children attend nursery schools or child care centers where they can make more social contacts and learn new social skills. Children learn to fit into the group, cooperate, and contribute. See 6-5.

During this period, friendships become more important, and children become less self-centered. Through these friendships, children learn how people differ in their physical looks, personalities, habits, and lifestyles.

Social Development of the School-Age Child

School greatly influences the socialization of the child. School provides increased contact with other children of the same age. When children begin school, most of the other children are strangers. School is a new social world requiring many adjustments. The child who has had a variety of social experiences will adjust more easily. The child who is shy, has had limited social contact, and is self-centered is likely to have more trouble adjusting.

6-5 At this age, children need the companionship of others—not just to have fun, but also to learn how to get along with others.

Increased contact with peers affects a child's social development. The peer group gives children a chance to meet others and learn to cooperate in the group. The peer group also helps children develop a feeling of identity. See 6-6. Children tend to copy the clothes, interests, and mannerisms of others in the group.

During these years, children become more understanding and accepting of other people. They become more sensitive to the needs and rights of others. Friendships differ now—they are more the result of careful selection than a matter of convenience.

School-age children are developing a conscience. They learn to control their impulses and are less likely to exhibit anti-social behavior.

As school-age children grow older, they become interested in clubs and organized groups. These groups give them greater responsibilities and continue to provide the opportunity for identity. Scouts, 4-H groups, and sports teams are examples of these groups.

Emotional Development

Emotional growth and development involves recognizing emotions, expressing them in a healthy manner, and controlling them. Emotions have a strong influence on a person's life. A child's behavior is an indication of that child's emotional development. Children whose emotional needs are met are interested in life, happy and relaxed, and free from unusual strain or tension. They react to everyday situations in a manner appropriate to their age. Each person, whether a child or an adult, needs to be loved, be wanted, and belong. Everyone also has the need for self-confidence. If these needs are not met, it is more difficult for children to grow and mature emotionally.

6-6 **Playing together helps children develop a spirit of cooperation and a feeling of belongingness.**

Children are more self-confident when their emotional needs are met. Self-confidence gives the child the initiative to move ahead, be curious, and learn more.

Emotional Development of the Infant and Toddler

Babies experience feelings or emotions that lay the foundation for their ability to love, trust, and feel secure with other people. The first emotional relationship a child has with another person is usually with the mother. The mother-child relationship forms the basis for emotional relationships with all other human beings.

Infants experience positive feelings when their needs are met. This happens when they are held closely and when they are fed. They learn to expect more of the same. Early emotional experiences resulting from contact with family members greatly influence emotional development throughout life. These secure attachments are the basis of a child's future relationships.

Babies are capable of expressing delight, distress, fear, anger, and affection. They communicate early in life mostly by crying. This crying is usually related to some discomfort, such as hunger, a dirty diaper, or a loud noise. See 6-7.

Babies may express anger by crying while waiting for food or when feeding is interrupted. Anger may also be related to discomfort, such as when clothing or a blanket is too tight.

A happy, cheerful baby often smiles and gurgles. Babies laugh out loud at about four months of age. The infant displays affection by snuggling close and the older child by hugging. Each of these emotional responses is related to satisfying basic needs.

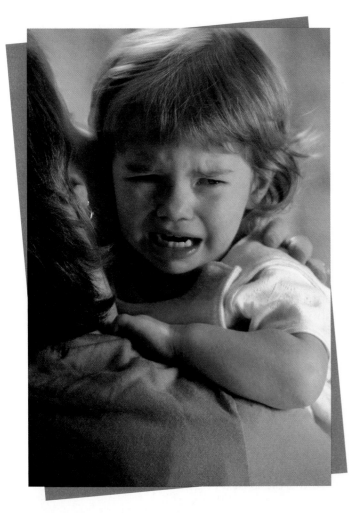

6-7 **Crying is a baby's way of expressing emotions such as discomfort and anger.**

Infants have certain normal fears. Some of these fears, such as the fear of falling and the fear of loud noises, are inborn. They result from the babies' need to protect themselves. Reassurance and comfort will help calm frightened babies.

Emotions are intense for toddlers, who can be very moody. They express their feelings openly and strongly. Toddlers express a range of feelings from love to aggression. They sometimes strike others or throw objects. Tantrums are not unusual for toddlers. Tantrums occur when children need to assert themselves but cannot express their emotions in a healthy, socially accepted way.

Emotional Development of the Preschool Child

Like the toddler, the preschooler displays a variety of emotions, usually at an intense level. The preschooler may quickly switch from laughter to tears or from joy to anger. Preschoolers are quite open about letting others know how they feel.

Fears seem to develop more during the preschool years. This may be caused by having frightening experiences or hearing about scary things. Preschoolers have imaginations that can "run wild." Fear of the dark, panic at being left alone, and concern about death are not uncommon at this stage.

Jealousy is common among preschoolers. **Sibling rivalry**—competition between two or more children in a family—often creates jealousy. As children become more competitive, there is also jealousy among peers. Normally this jealousy fades with maturity. See 6-8.

Emotional Development of the School-Age Child

As children grow older, they are exposed to more people and more ideas. They become more independent and self-sufficient, and begin to accept responsibility

Sandra Balfour

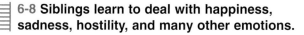
6-8 Siblings learn to deal with happiness, sadness, hostility, and many other emotions.

for their behavior. Their emotions are more stable. Older children begin to hide their feelings. They are more controlled and cautious about expressing themselves. Although they still get angry, they are not likely to express this anger in a physical manner.

During the school-age years, children learn many new skills. They want to do well and gain a sense of achievement. If they do not do well at something, they may feel they are not good enough. If this occurs often, it may have a negative effect on the child's development toward emotional maturity.

The emotions of affection, love, joy, and happiness are positive forces in a child's life. Other emotions, such as anger, fear, worry, anxiety, and jealousy, can be a problem. They are not bad emotions. However, they can be destructive unless the child accepts them and learns to deal with them in a constructive manner.

Intellectual Development

Intellectual development involves many different abilities. The abilities to use the senses and verbal and written symbols are a part of this development. The abilities to perceive, think, reason, form concepts,

Brainstorming

Brainstorm ideas of play equipment and materials that promote sensory-motor development during infancy and the toddler period. What cautions should be taken with this equipment? How do adults need to be involved in this kind of play?

and solve problems are also included. Children learn in many ways. They learn through their senses, reinforcement, insight, and models. Other opportunities for learning are daily experiences, contact with others, and play.

Play and Intellectual Development

Young children acquire much of their knowledge through play. You can help make learning an easier, more enjoyable task. Encouraging certain activities, providing certain toys, and making arrangements for play with others can help children learn. Children who are deprived of play experiences do not learn as effectively as children who have participated in a variety of play situations.

Play is a wonderful way for children to learn about themselves and the world. As they play with their toys and other children, they see how things work in new and different ways. They form new concepts or ideas from these experiences. Children also help develop communication skills by talking with others and listening to them.

Watching others is an important way in which children learn. During their playtime, children imitate adults in various activities. These experiences help children learn more about people and things. They also help children learn how to get along with others.

Children often use symbols in their play, such as when a cardboard box is used as a car. **Symbolic play** indicates that children have the ability to hold mental images from past experience—in this case, the car. Symbolic play can be helpful to a child when he or she starts learning to read. Reading is easier when past experiences create many mental images relating to printed words.

Many simple play experiences help children develop concepts related to mathematical ideas, such as number and measurement. Playing in the sandbox with containers that are graduated in size helps children learn about small, bigger, and biggest. When playing with clay, children learn about "how many" by counting out their products.

Pretend play is valuable in many ways. It develops symbolic thought in young children and flexibility in their thinking. Young children, particularly toddlers and young preschoolers, live in their own world. They have not learned to adjust to different ideas and different ways of doing things. Pretend play helps children learn other responses and other ways of life. As a result, the children may become more flexible and adaptable. Pretend play gives children many opportunities for decision making and problem solving. See 6-9.

One of the major benefits of play is its impact on the development of thinking skills. Most children are basically curious. As they play they ask many questions about what they are doing or what they are using. With each new activity, children ask questions and find answers.

The ability to classify objects into certain categories is another thinking skill. Children develop this ability gradually as they begin to put things together according to likenesses or differences. This ability becomes noticeable as children arrange groups of objects according to color, size, or shape. This skill indicates reasoning ability and is an important basis for most thought processes.

6-9 Children learn new ideas and have new experiences through pretend play.

Young children learn much about the world through their senses—by touching, seeing, hearing, tasting, and smelling. The brain uses the information gained by the senses, and the child reacts. A skill such as eye-hand coordination is important for young children. Babies see a toy, but are not physically mature enough to reach for it. As babies develop, they are eventually able to see a toy and take hold of it. Many play activities can help children develop motor skills like eye-hand coordination. See 6-10.

Unfortunately, many people do not recognize the value of play. They tend to look at play as the opposite of work; they see work as positive and play as negative. These people do not realize what a powerful learning tool play is for children.

6-10 **The ability to reach for a toy shows the development of hand-eye coordination in infants.**

Intellectual Development of Infants and Toddlers

Recent discoveries regarding early brain development were presented earlier in this textbook. This scientific research emphasizes the importance of brain development during the first three years of a child's life. Stimulation of the brain comes from the child's experiences and surroundings. In a favorable environment, this stimulation has positive effects on brain development. However, in an environment where stimulation is limited and stress exists, these conditions have negative effects.

Research has shown that knowledge and understanding first come through the senses. However, infants must go through a process known as **perception** in order to understand what their senses are telling them. Perception involves a relationship between an impression from the senses and

some past experience. For instance, a baby sees a bottle and associates it with the good feeling of drinking milk. Perception might be described as the process that reads the messages sent by the senses.

Perceptual ability grows gradually. At only a few days old, an infant is not physically mature enough to recognize the bottle. Perceptual ability of the eyes, ears, nose, mouth, and skin gradually increases. The older infant is able to interpret information from previous experiences. For example, an infant begins to look at faces at about six or seven weeks old. However, by four months of age, the infant has enough perceptual ability to recognize faces.

The infant's first step in communicating with others is through crying. At first the crying is a reflex action. Later the baby learns to associate crying with the response of a parent. For example, crying is a way of signaling hunger. This shows the baby experienced a step in learning. Parents usually learn to distinguish between cries of hunger, pain, and general unhappiness.

The next stage in language development is babbling. These sounds represent the infant's attempts to copy the language of his or her parents. Just as parents teach infants to smile by smiling at them, parents can improve infants' language development by talking to them. At around six or eight months of age, the infant begins to make repetitive sounds such as *da-da*. Soon afterward the infant starts to form single words.

Using a single word is an important step in language development. Simple words often stand for complex ideas. When the child says "Daddy," the child may mean "Look at Daddy," "Pick me up, Daddy," or "Daddy is home." Parents can usually understand what the child means by considering the situation.

From this point, language development progresses rather rapidly. The toddler learns to make different sounds, connect meaningful words, and associate new words with particular objects. Toddlers often become frustrated during their second year as they try to make themselves understood through words. Tantrums may result from this frustration.

Children's language development progresses quickly at this time when they can walk and are discovering much more about themselves and the world. Toddlers are learning many new concepts through their experiences. Much of children's learning comes from body movements and through their senses. Their understanding of these new concepts also grows stronger. The many new experiences children have are important to their learning. Children cannot learn how to use words as symbols until they have had some experience with the objects those words represent.

Toddlers develop many intellectual skills as they learn they are a part of a much larger world. Children develop skill in reasoning gradually during the first few years. During this time, simple concepts of objects, space, time, and cause and effect also develop. Toddlers can achieve simple problem-solving tasks. During this stage of experimenting and curiosity, children learn much through trial and error.

Curiosity is a positive trait wisely fostered by parents. Before children can develop concepts or ideas, they need to actually touch, see, and hear the things around them. Being patient with children and giving them time to look at what interests them is important. Children's curiosity is a valuable tool for learning. See 6-11.

Intellectual Development of the Preschool Child

The growth of mental abilities during the preschool years is as remarkable as the physical development during infancy. The growth of language in particular is dramatic. From simple sentences during the second year, children progress to rather complex sentence construction by age four or five.

6-11 **Play provides a wonderful way for children to learn.**

By three years of age, children are very talkative and constantly ask questions. Their vocabulary doubles between the ages of three and five. By the time they are six, most children have generally mastered speech.

Language is a basic part of children's mental development. During the time when language development progresses so quickly, children are also strengthening their basic learning skills.

Perceptual development continues to progress during the preschool years. Countless opportunities to use the senses help children develop intellectually.

Preschoolers learn to identify and distinguish among various objects in their everyday world. For example, they learn the difference between apples and oranges. Their ability to identify, classify, and compare objects improves swiftly.

Children rapidly develop the ability to reason in this age period. They learn how objects are related to each other. They can create wholes out of parts and group objects together. As children near school age, they are able to more fully understand the meaning of cause and effect. They develop more advanced concepts regarding time, numbers, space, and form. See 6-12. Children have their own conceptual world just like adults do. Growing up involves learning about the world of adults and gradually giving up the world of early childhood.

A sense of right or wrong, sometimes referred to as **moral development**, begins during the preschool years. When adults guide, restrain, or reprimand a child, the child begins to internalize these ideas of right and wrong. Children near school age begin to show concern about what others might think of their actions. They also begin to consider how their actions might affect others. This is the beginning stages of the development of a child's character. *Character* refers to a sense of right and wrong that guides a child's behavior.

6-12 **Preschoolers enjoy play that involves the development of their reasoning skills.**

Intellectual Development of the School-Age Child

During elementary school years, language develops considerably as the children learn to use many new terms. They begin to use language fluently by carrying on conversations and expressing their ideas. Children learn how to listen, speak, read, and write more effectively through their schoolwork. Improving their language abilities enhances other abilities related to memory, problem solving, and reasoning.

School-age children are more capable of forming abstract ideas. They have little problem grouping objects together or arranging them in order.

Children are active explorers and investigators at this time. Questions are frequent and more complex than the simple "why" questions of preschoolers. More thought is given to moral issues such as truth and honesty. School-age children show increasing growth in understanding by making decisions based on prior knowledge. The school-age child learns to judge what to do in situations based on past experience.

The Self-Concept During the Early Years

A child's self-concept indicates how the child thinks about himself or herself. Self-concept might include thoughts of being good or bad, helpful or troublesome, happy or sad. These feelings may influence the behavior of children.

Most decisions children make are based on the feelings they have about themselves. For instance, a boy may go to the park and see a group of children having fun in a sandbox. If the boy is confident that he gets along well with others, he may hurry over and join the group. If the boy lacks confidence and feels threatened by the other children, he may decide to play alone. The decision is related to his self-concept either way.

Although self-concept strongly influences behavior, a child's self-concept is not fully formed. Children are easily influenced because they are not sure of what they believe about themselves. Children who are treated as if they are special are more likely to believe they are special. See 6-13. Children who are treated as if they are inadequate are more likely to believe they can't do many things well. Children learn to defend themselves from criticism as they grow older. While they are very young, they feel parents, family members, and other adults know more than they do about themselves.

As children mature and have more experiences, their self-concept becomes stronger and is less easily changed. Ideally, the self-concept becomes more complete through experience. Experience helps children see themselves in relation to the rest of the world and make judgments accordingly. This helps them develop a more complete self-concept.

The more experiences children have, the more opportunity they have to develop a realistic self-concept. This means what they know about themselves is accurate. Experiences with other people in daily life and play help young children develop a realistic self-concept. A little girl may think she can throw a ball as far as her older brother. She may learn this is an unrealistic self-concept when her ball goes only half as far. A preschooler in a child care center doesn't think he paints very well. However, when the teacher shows the class his nice painting, his self-concept about his painting skills begins to change. The boy begins to develop a more realistic attitude about his skill.

One of the finest characteristics a child can develop is high self-esteem, 6-14. Children who have high self-esteem have greater self-confidence and can confront challenges more easily than children with low self-esteem.

6-14 **New experiences can have a positive effect on self-esteem.**

6-13 **It is important to get older children involved in welcoming a new baby in the family. This will help them feel special also.**

Self-Concept and Basic Needs

The development of self-concept is closely related to the way the child's basic needs are satisfied. A child's needs reach beyond the obvious physical needs for food, clothing, and shelter. He or she needs to be loved and accepted, be secure, belong, and be recognized as a person of worth.

Most human behavior is an attempt to satisfy one of these needs. For example, a three-year-old hits her baby brother because she feels a lack of attention, and her mother is very busy with the infant. The mother could reinforce a positive self-concept by anticipating this jealousy and need for attention. She could make special efforts to provide the three-year-old with love and caring. On the other hand, the mother could also reinforce a negative self-concept. Scolding the child without satisfying her need for attention would do this. If negative reinforcement occurs regularly, the little girl will begin to think of herself as bad. She may misbehave on purpose just to get attention. Children who do not receive attention often misbehave just to be recognized.

When children's basic needs are met, they develop an inner stability. They feel positive about themselves and the world. This stability is important to children as they confront the many challenges in their daily lives.

Self-Concept and Experiences with Others

Self-concept develops mainly as a result of experiences with others, 6-15. Children form or change their self-concepts because of what they feel others think of them and how others treat them. It is as if they were looking

6-15 **Positive experiences at school can help a child develop self-esteem.**

at themselves through the eyes of others.

Early in life, most of these experiences are with parents and family members. Children who are given care, encouragement, security, love, and guidance are likely to develop a positive self-image. Children who are rejected, discouraged, and punished are more likely to develop a negative self-image.

Older children have more experiences outside the family with playmates, relatives, neighbors, and friends of the family. These experiences may cause children to change their feelings about themselves.

Many experiences that affect self-concept are closely related to the child's development. Experiences related to physical, social, emotional, and intellectual development affect the child's self-concept. It is helpful if the people who have an influence on younger children are familiar with these growth patterns. These people can then attempt to influence the child's changing self-concept in a positive manner.

In the early years, much of the development of self-concept is related to physical development. Children feel positive about themselves when they succeed. When a toddler throws the ball directly to her father, this indicates a degree of physical development. She feels good about herself when her daddy shouts, "Good throw!" At every age, children want to be noticed and recognized as they practice their skills. For example, babies clap their hands and one-year-olds begin to feed themselves. Two-year-olds become toilet trained and preschoolers learn to ride their tricycles. Children develop self-confidence as other people recognize these accomplishments. See 6-16.

Self-concept plays an important role in social development. Children who develop healthy self-concepts relate to other children and adults in positive ways. Having experiences with others helps them develop communication skills. As they learn to communicate with others more effectively, they feel good about themselves and act with more self-confidence. Experiences with others are important to emotional development as well. As children grow older and learn to control their emotions better, encouragement and praise from others helps strengthen their positive self-concept.

Daily experiences teach children what they can or cannot do and strongly influence intellectual development. Providing opportunities for children to develop skills also helps children enhance their self-concepts. As the toddler learns to stack blocks so they will not fall over, she feels good about herself. As the preschooler recognizes that the robin in the tree is just like the bird in his book, he feels proud.

Hercules, Inc.

6-16 **Learning to blow bubbles and being able to ride a bike are exciting accomplishments for young children. When adults recognize their achievements, children gain self-confidence.**

Skill in Self-Observation

The way children feel about themselves depends on how they look at what they have done. Young children do not have stable self-concepts since everything in life is so new. However, children learn to identify feelings about themselves as they grow older. Eventually children learn to make decisions based on these feelings.

You can help children develop skills in self-observation. For instance, you can comment on a job done well or poorly. This will help the child think about that activity in relation to the self-concept. Self-observation skills help children make decisions. The little boy who did not think he could paint well learned differently when his teacher showed his fine painting to the class. If this had not happened, the boy would have remained unsure of his painting skill. He might even have had negative feelings.

People such as parents and teachers have a great influence on children. They can help encourage positive self-concepts by helping children recognize their good characteristics. See 6-17. It is also important, though, to encourage a realistic self-concept.

Undeserved compliments or praise can actually harm children by causing them to develop unrealistic self-concepts. Sometimes this occurs in a family when a child is constantly praised, given in to, and seldom challenged. These practices may result in a spoiled child with an unrealistic self-concept. Children like this can have problems getting along with their peers.

Young children may have difficulty observing themselves accurately. However, encouraging self-observation skills at a young age will help. As children grow older, they will learn that understanding themselves better is a key to effectively managing daily living.

6-17 **Parents and teachers can help children form positive self-concepts in the early years by offering encouragement.**

32
31
30
29
28
27
26
25
24
23
22
21
20
19
18
17
16
15
14
13
12
11
10
9
8
7
6
5
4
3
2
1

Summary

As children develop, they display certain characteristics in an orderly and predictable sequence. By understanding the four patterns of development, you can predict what development to expect. You can then plan activities to encourage that step in development.

Children who have high self-esteem have greater confidence in confronting challenges and facing difficulties than children with low self-esteem. When you understand influences on the development of self-concept, you can guide children toward developing a healthy self-concept.

To Review

To Review
To Review

1. Name the four patterns of development.
2. To develop motor skills, coordination of the _____ system, _____ system, and _____ must steadily improve.
3. Development of _____ coordination begins in the early months when infants begin to notice their hands and some objects.
4. True or false?
   A. Many boys experience preadolescent growth spurts.
   B. As children mature socially, they become more self-centered.
5. Describe three ways a peer group contributes to the social development of a school-age child.
6. Toddlers engage in _____ play, which means they will play next to but not with another child.
7. Decide whether each of the following statements about emotional development describes the infant and toddler, the preschooler, or the school-age child.
   A. Fears seem to develop more during these years.
   B. Emotions are more stable.
   C. The main method of communication is crying.
   D. Their imaginations can "run wild."
   E. Children begin to hide feelings.
   F. Jealousy is common at this stage.
8. Briefly describe three ways play can benefit a child.
9. Describe steps in language development.
10. List two advantages of high self-esteem.

To Do with the Class

1. Discuss ways parents and others can influence motor development.
2. Interview several people to learn the advantages and disadvantages of having children attend a child care center or preschool.
3. Give examples of how choice of clothing, food, and activities might be influenced by peers.
4. Discuss the meaning of the following: Children can learn to control their actions, but they cannot learn to control their feelings.

To Challenge Your Thinking

1. Research information on stranger anxiety. Discuss your findings with others in the class.
2. Read several articles about the fears of preschool children. Discuss what influences these fears.
3. Use references to help you understand the thought processes usually developed in the school-age child.
4. Think about how you might help children like themselves. Observe a young child in several situations. Recall incidents and the child's responses to them. Then evaluate whether these incidents might help a child like himself or herself.

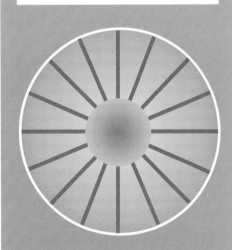

To Do with Your Community

1. Survey your community to find out if there is an adequate number of child care centers to meet the needs of your community.
2. Invite a panel of teachers to discuss intellectual development.
3. Investigate what resources your community has to promote intellectual development in children.
4. Visit a playground in your community. Describe situations that illustrate different types of development taking place.

7 Developmental Tasks of Childhood

To Know

developmental tasks
demand feeding
weaning
security object
toilet training
family rituals

Objectives

After studying this chapter, you will be able to

◆ describe the developmental tasks of infants, toddlers, preschoolers, and school-age children.

◆ suggest ways children can be encouraged to achieve these developmental tasks.

Specialists in human development often refer to growth in terms of life stages. These include infancy, early childhood, middle childhood, adolescence, young adulthood, middle adult years, and late adulthood.

Children's growth toward maturity is often described in stages, from the infant and toddler to the preschooler to the school-age child. Researchers have found that certain behaviors and skills, known as **developmental tasks**, are expected to be learned at each stage of development.

Developmental tasks might be considered goals of growth toward maturity. When a child reaches one goal, the child can move on to the next related goal. If the child does not reach that goal, moving on to another goal will be difficult. For example, a child's development depends greatly on what foods are eaten. Establishing poor eating habits as a preschooler can later affect a child's ability to lead a physically active life.

Developmental tasks result from physical, psychological, and cultural needs. Eating the right foods so the body can develop normally is a physical need. Eating in a manner that is acceptable to other people is a cultural need. In this culture, school-age children are expected to use a knife, fork, and spoon when eating a meal. It would be unusual to see a school-age child eating mashed potatoes with his or her fingers.

Children achieve their developmental tasks easier when they have encouragement and support from people who are important to them. When you know the developmental tasks common to children at each stage, you can help guide them toward maturity. Parents, other family members, close friends, teachers, and neighbors can all encourage a child's growth in a positive way.

Developmental Tasks of Infants and Toddlers

All infants and toddlers follow similar patterns of development, but each child is unique. See 7-1. Though heredity is important, the environment also affects a child's development and uniqueness. Factors such as the emotional climate in a home and interaction with parents and family have a strong influence on a child's development. Understanding ways you might affect the infant and toddler's development can help you influence their positive growth.

Developmental Tasks of Infants and Toddlers	
Task One:	Develop good eating and sleeping habits
Task Two:	Become aware of what the body can do
Task Three:	Learn about elimination
Task Four:	Learn to relate to others
Task Five:	Learn to experience and express feelings
Task Six:	Develop self-awareness

7-1 It is important for all infants and toddlers to achieve these developmental tasks. How and when children achieve the tasks will vary.

Developing Good Eating and Sleeping Habits

Foundations for the development of good eating habits begin when infants have their hunger satisfied. When infants are fed, they become conditioned to the natural sequence of hunger—being fed, satisfaction, physical well-being, and contentment. Infants soon learn that eating means contentment.

The technique used to feed babies is as essential to social development as it is to physical development. In other words, the way babies are fed is just as important as the food they eat. All their senses are stimulated as they are fed. When babies are held close and fed in a parent's arms, they are touched, looked at, talked to, and cuddled. Each of these benefits adds to the infant's feelings of security.

Before a baby is born, the parents will make the decision to formula-feed or breast-feed the baby. There are pros and cons to each alternative. Breast milk provides all the nutrients a baby needs as well as some antibodies. It is a natural food for babies and is easy for them to digest. However, some mothers find breast-feeding inconvenient. The mother is the only one who can feed the baby unless she also uses the bottle-feeding method. The mother may need an alternative if she will be returning to work.

Formula-feeding can be more convenient and allows others to feed the baby. Some women also prefer the modesty of bottle-feeding over breast-feeding. On the other hand, formula can be expensive. The bottles must be washed and prepared before use. The formula must also be warmed to just the right temperature.

Those in favor of breast-feeding consider closeness to be one of its major advantages. Other people believe the same closeness can exist with bottle-feeding as long as the child is held. Parents should choose the feeding method they find most comfortable. If the infant is held closely and talked to, the feeding will have a positive effect. This will make feeding time most enjoyable for the infant and parent.

Eating patterns are quite irregular for young infants. Doctors formerly suggested that babies stick to a strict eating schedule, eating every so many hours. Today, doctors recognize individual differences in food needs. They now suggest more flexibility in feeding schedules. Because infants indicate hunger by waking, crying, or being restless, doctors suggest demand feeding. With **demand feeding**, a child's "inner clock" determines feeding, and it may differ slightly from day to day. The child is fed when he or she is hungry. However, the parent can still exercise some control over the feeding times. This feeding method seems to benefit both the infant and the parent.

Although babies may start on solid foods during the first few months, many doctors prefer waiting about six months.

Introducing new foods one at a time is a good idea. That way digestive problems or allergies to a particular food can be identified more easily.

At about six months of age, the infant may be given finger foods such as fruit, cooked vegetables, or crackers. This important step represents the child's first opportunity to show independence in eating. Eating experiences may create a mess. However, the child's pleasure may far outweigh the disadvantage of some extra cleanup. Some doctors suggest having one food the baby can eat by hand at each family meal. The child benefits by gaining independence and trying a variety of new foods. See 7-2.

7-2 Young children take great enjoyment in learning to eat on their own.

Giving the infant a variety of foods has advantages. It can help children accept new foods easier later in childhood. The infant becomes familiar with different flavors and textures. This also helps the infant learn to chew properly and benefits the teeth and gums.

During the second half of the first year, babies may give clues that they are ready to be weaned. **Weaning** is when babies learn to drink from a container instead of from the bottle or breast. Weaning is a gradual process; it does not happen overnight. When babies are ready to be weaned, they may show interest in drinking from a cup. They may also become more interested in playing with the bottle than drinking from it.

Patience is important during this gradual process. There are many types of nonspill cups available to help through this period. There may be spills and messes, but a positive attitude and encouragement will help the child meet the challenge.

During the second year, children begin to feed themselves. Independence in eating, like most growth steps, comes gradually. Children need some help to learn to eat with utensils. Using a special rounded spoon with a large handle is helpful. The age when children are able to use the cup, spoon, and fork varies widely.

Growth begins to slow down later in the second year, and the appetite usually diminishes some. Fluctuation of appetite is normal. On some days children eat well and on other days they do not. This eating pattern is typical. It should not concern parents as long as the good days balance the bad days.

Eating rituals can be very important and helpful during the second year. By their second birthdays children may become very impatient and stubborn about mealtime. Having mealtime rituals or routines that give children a good idea of what to expect can be helpful. A warning

Brainstorming

Brainstorm characteristics of a child that may indicate the child's sleeping patterns suit him or her. Also brainstorm characteristics of a child that may indicate the child is not getting enough rest.

that mealtime is coming helps children prepare for the fact that playtime will end soon. The routine continues with washing hands and coming to the table.

Establishing good eating habits during this period is extremely important. The family's food practices strongly affect the young child's developing food attitudes. At this stage, children develop food likes and dislikes. Children are more likely to have open attitudes toward food choices if their families eat a variety of foods. Serving children only certain foods may cause them to be less open to trying new foods. The attractive appearance of food can affect a child's appetite just as much as it affects an adult's.

Present nutritional concerns stress avoiding junk foods and limiting the intake of sweets and fats. A chubby child may have developed fat cells that can present a lifelong problem. Along with causing health problems, obesity can limit a child's normal physical play activities.

To satisfy their basic needs, babies develop cycles of rest and activity. They need rest to conserve energy so their bodies can grow. Babies awaken when their bodies need nourishment. Newborns sleep most of the time, usually 14 to 20 hours a day.

Sleep habits of babies vary as do the sleep habits of adults. The way babies look and act usually indicates whether they are getting enough sleep, 7-3. Unusual sleep-lessness may be a sign of illness. Therefore, a physician should be consulted to determine the cause.

The sleep pattern changes as the infant matures. By five months of age the infant sleeps less and takes two or three naps a day. By two years of age most children sleep about 13 hours and take an afternoon nap one to two hours long. However, the range of sleep needs is wide for children of this age.

Just as with eating, a routine at bedtime is important at this age. Children do not like to stop playing even though they are tired. A bath and a story to warn that bedtime is coming are typical steps in the bedtime routine. Many toddlers want some security object at bedtime—perhaps a toy, blanket, or pacifier. **Security objects** are items children carry that make them feel safe and protected. Security objects are important to children at the time, but they will give up these attachments as they grow older.

Becoming Aware of What the Body Can Do

You can encourage an infant's physical development in various ways. As large muscles develop from head to foot and from trunk to extremities, infants need opportunities to exercise, move, and kick without being confined by clothing.

Parents can help stimulate the senses by choosing toys wisely. At birth, infants can distinguish some patterns and shapes. Infants' sense organs are stimulated by colorful objects with interesting shapes. Infants enjoy playing with and watching rattles, beads, and brightly colored mobiles. See 7-4. Infants also respond positively to the pleasant sounds of a music box or musical toy.

One of the earliest signs of coordination is when infants put their hands in their mouths. Gradually infants learn to use the thumb and fingers to grasp a toy. Young children who lack small muscle control tend to play with easy-to-grasp objects like stuffed toys or large balls. To be safe, toys should have no sharp edges or parts that can come loose.

As the child matures, toys can be selected to encourage small muscle control and eye-hand coordination. Children develop skill in manipulating objects rapidly from one to two years of age.

The child's sitting, crawling, standing, and walking are steps in physical development. Walking is an exciting achievement for the child and is soon followed by

7-3 **Young infants are asleep more often than not. The way they look and act will help indicate when they need to be sleeping.**

fingers. They may turn the pages of books, use small scissors, hold crayons properly, button clothes, hold drinking glasses, and eat with forks and spoons.

Physical development varies depending on the maturity of the child and the learning opportunities each child has had. Achieving physical skills is important to children. As they experience success, they feel more positive about themselves. Parents and other family members can reinforce this success by praising their children. Sometimes children may not be mature enough to play with a certain toy in the intended way. When this happens, the toy can be put away for a while and brought out again at the proper time. This avoids frustration for the child.

7-4 **Brightly colored toys stimulate a child's senses and make the child more aware of his or her surroundings.**

running, jumping, and climbing stairs. To mature physically and stay fit, children need activities that promote vigorous action. Play is one of the best ways to provide these activities. Playing with push toys, wagons, wheelbarrows, and small bikes without pedals can promote large muscle development.

As children mature, they are able to make more complex movements with the fine muscles of their hands and fingers. It is helpful for children to have toys that encourage small muscle control. Children can practice these skills by stacking blocks, playing with toy rhythm instruments and simple puzzles, and stringing beads. See 7-5. Near the third birthday, children become skillful with their hands and

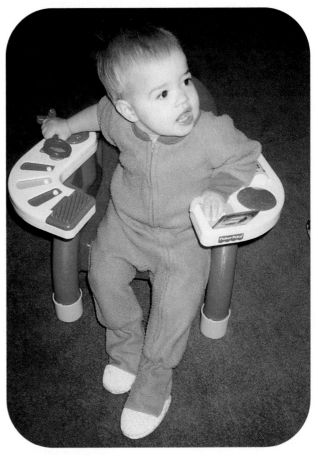

7-5 **A play seat like this encourages development of muscle coordination in the hands and fingers.**

Parents and family members can help promote a child's development by being aware of patterns of physical development. Being aware of these patterns also helps them recognize when expected development does not occur. Early diagnosis of a problem may mean it can be corrected and prevent future complications.

Learning About Elimination

The process of urination and bowel movement is an involuntary reflex for the newborn and young infant. Infants do not understand these functions. However, during the first year, they begin to show signs of discomfort when they have a wet or dirty diaper. The diaper should be changed as soon as possible after becoming wet or after a bowel movement. Doing this helps avoid diaper rash or infection.

Toilet training is the time when children learn bladder and bowel control. Toilet training usually begins in the child's second year, but it depends more on physical and emotional readiness than age. Toilet training is a waste of time until children are physically developed enough to control the muscles that restrain elimination. Parents often make toilet training more difficult by trying to force the child before the child is physically able. Most children are easily toilet trained if they are allowed to proceed at their own rate with guidance.

Before children can learn physical control, they also must learn the proper place to eliminate. There is some controversy over whether the potty chair or a training seat on the regular toilet is best to use. The major advantage of the separate potty chair is that children can get on and off as they please. The chair can be placed in the bathroom sometime before it is expected to be used so the child can become familiar with it.

In time, children will become familiar with the feeling that indicates the need for elimination. Learning this new behavior takes time and patience. Eventually children learn to tighten their muscles to avoid elimination until they are in the proper place. Young children are proud of their accomplishments and are quite willing to learn if properly guided.

Children will show signs of having a bowel movement. They may stop what they are doing or get a distracted look. Showing children the soiled diaper in a matter-of-fact way helps them understand toilet training. Often bowel training comes first and then bladder control. Children should be encouraged to urinate before and after taking a nap. If a two-year-old stays dry for two hours, the child can be encouraged to go to the bathroom. Once children have learned daytime bladder control, nighttime control will eventually follow.

Adults help this learning process by watching for clues of readiness and patiently providing guidance. By praising successes and calmly accepting failures, adults can help children accomplish this step in maturity more easily.

*Getting*Involved

Have a panel made up of a pediatrician, parents, and educators. Discuss answering preschool children's questions about mature subjects such as sex, death, and religion. Be sure the discussion includes ways people your age, who may care for children, should respond to these questions. Then write a pamphlet of information from the panel and give it to parents you know.

Learning to Relate to Others

Although the newborn makes no social response, the infant becomes quite sociable during the next six months. Infants mature socially as their basic needs for food, comfort, and security are satisfied. The infant develops a positive feeling—trust—toward the person satisfying the needs.

Early in the infant's life, many of the warm, close relationships are between the parents and their child. Babies may be cuddled and loved by people other than their parents, though. Children are likely to feel more secure socially if they develop positive relationships with a variety of individuals. This might include their brothers, sisters, grandparents, and friends. See 7-6.

The baby's smile is one of the first indications of a conscious effort to communicate. Crying is another way of communicating. Parents and family members learn that different cries have different meanings. Perhaps the baby is tired, angry, hungry, or in pain.

Communication can be encouraged in many ways during infancy. During the first months, smiling, talking, and singing to the infant helps encourage a social response. Repeating rhymes during routine, daily events like bathing and diaper changes encourages imitation. Playing simple games such as pat-a-cake encourages communication. Soon infants smile, coo, and babble.

Children begin saying words and talking at different rates. The home environment has a strong influence on this step in maturity. Babies who have been talked to frequently seem to learn to speak earlier than those who have not. During the first two years, children learn to associate many objects with their names, speak many words, and form short sentences.

Although toddlers do not understand how to play cooperatively with others, they do enjoy companionship. By allowing toddlers to be with other small children, parents are helping prepare them to learn to play cooperatively.

Learning to Experience and Express Feelings

During the first two years of life, children express their feelings strongly and with very little control. Crying is the first emotion an infant expresses. It is a challenge to know just how to react to a baby's cries. How parents respond to those cries affects the developing relationship between the baby and parents.

Babies cry for many reasons. It may be because of a dirty diaper, hunger, or discomfort. Babies may also cry when they are left alone or when they awaken suddenly from sleep. Parents learn to

7-6 **This little boy learns about positive relationships when he is with his older sister.**

interpret the sound of each cry and associate it with a particular problem. The parent may ignore the cry that indicates the child has awakened suddenly from sleep. Soon the baby will be sleeping soundly. Another crying sound may cause the parent to check the baby. This time the child might be cold because the blanket has been kicked off.

Movement and soothing sounds can calm the crying baby. Babies get a positive and secure feeling when they are held. The benefits of this feeling far outweigh the concerns for spoiling infants by picking them up when they cry.

During their first year, children form the basis for their ability to love and be loved. The infant first experiences love through being cuddled and fed through contact comfort. Today, many hospitals allow babies to room with their mothers. Research shows that important bonds are formed within those few days following birth. See 7-7.

Just holding an infant does not automatically cause love to form. Babies seem to sense when someone who is not at ease holds them. This makes the baby feel tense. For this reason, it is important for fathers and other family members to feel comfortable holding the infant. However, only sisters and brothers who are old enough to be responsible for the baby's safety should hold him or her. As these family members learn to care for the baby confidently, they will experience a loving relationship with the baby.

The cuddling, talking, and smiling the infant receives from family members all help create pleasant feelings. The infant then feels more secure and develops trust toward those who helped create this good feeling.

Infants can be expected to express anger and dissatisfaction with certain actions or routines. At first they express this anger by crying. During the second year, the toddler may throw temper tantrums. Children of this age are too young to

understand reasoning. Therefore, ignoring the tantrum is usually best. When the child sees that the outburst is not getting any results, the tantrum usually ends. Changing activities can often distract children. This makes them forget what upset them.

Comforting the young child is the best way to deal with fears. The children are too young to understand explanations about fears. Comforting by rocking them or just holding them helps renew infants' trust in the world that suddenly seemed threatening.

Young toddlers often rely on a security object when they experience something threatening. Thumbsucking, use of a pacifier, or fondness for a blanket or a stuffed

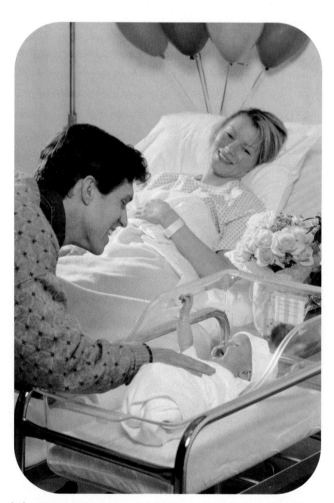

7-7 Most hospitals allow "rooming in" so the parents have more time to bond with their baby immediately.

animal can substitute for that warm, trusting feeling of being held closely. Thumbsucking and use of a pacifier are controversial, although most children outgrow their use. Unless the child experiences other problems in development, ignoring these habits is probably best.

Developing Self-Awareness

Until infants learn to see a relationship between people, objects, and themselves, self-awareness does not exist. Being sure of when this sense of self develops is difficult. Certain clues seem to indicate that it is happening. Reaching for a rattle, thumbsucking, and crying when their mother leaves the room may indicate self-control. These are small steps in the change from total dependency to a more independent relationship.

Toddlers are very self-oriented-interested in taking care of themselves. They show independence by wanting to feed and undress themselves, 7-8. The toddler stage is often a difficult time for parents. One reason is the self-oriented attitude. Another reason is toddlers are very curious and yet too young to understand risks to their safety. When toddlers are restricted from certain activities, such as playing with something sharp, they often express themselves through temper tantrums.

As toddlers are given opportunities to succeed, they gain feelings of confidence. These feelings are important to the development of their self-concepts. They need to feel good about their abilities.

Family members may have to develop flexible standards for judging the toddler's success at certain tasks. For instance, learning to feed themselves can be a messy experience. Toddlers often get more food in

7-8 **Toddlers show their independence by wanting to feed themselves.**

their hair and on the floor than in their mouths. As toddlers learn, encouragement is very helpful, even though their efforts are not really successful by adult standards.

Developmental Tasks of the Preschool Child

No specific age in terms of years and months defines when the preschool stage begins. Instead, the preschool stage begins when the child begins to show a great deal of independence, initiative, and imagination. These years are a time of much intellectual development. For most children, the preschool years include the period from three through five or six years of age. See 7-9.

Developing Healthy Daily Routines

The preschool years are important in laying the foundation for physical growth. How well children develop depends not only on maturation, but also on their diet and the physical care they receive.

A child's development depends greatly on what foods are eaten. Malnourishment can slow bone and tooth development and result in illness. It is helpful if parents and other caretakers are aware of guidelines for helping preschoolers learn about food and good eating habits.

Having a realistic view of what children can eat is important. Offering preschoolers

Developmental Tasks of the Preschool Child	
Task One:	Develop healthy daily routines
Task Two:	Develop physical skills
Task Three:	Learn through new experiences and more effective communication
Task Four:	Learn to express feelings and control actions
Task Five:	Be an active member of the family
Task Six:	Strengthen self-concept while becoming more independent

7-9 These developmental tasks are the goals of the preschool child.

food in small portions is better because then they can have more if they want. Preschoolers like to have some say about what they eat and how much they eat.

If mealtime is pleasant and relaxing, there seems to be fewer problems. Many food problems occur when parents are impatient and concerned. Most appetite problems of young children can be handled with ease if parents do not make them a major issue. Healthy children eat what their bodies need if meals are appealing and nutritionally balanced.

Sometimes children have good reasons for not eating well, such as when they are overtired or excited. Children's appetites may also lessen before, during, and after an illness, but their appetites return when they are well. Poor snack habits can create eating problems. If children are going to have a midmorning or afternoon snack, fruit, raw vegetables, or crackers are best. It is best to avoid junk foods and sweets. Sugar in the diet is linked with problems of obesity, tooth decay, and hyperactivity in children.

During this busy, active period, children find it hard to accept bedtime. Established routines at bedtime will be helpful. Setting a definite bedtime hour helps avoid arguments. A child needs some "winding down" activities to smooth the transition from active play to bedtime. Taking a bath, looking at picture books, reading stories, or listening to music can be part of the bedtime ritual.

Imaginations are active at this point in life. Fears and nightmares are on the rise, so wakefulness and crying are not unusual. Hugs and reassurances can be helpful. Some children may want to have a night-light, while others may find a favorite stuffed animal or a soft doll consoling. See 7-10.

Preschool children seem to have boundless energy. Most preschoolers require a

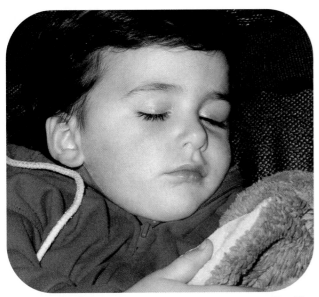

Starr King

7-10 **A favorite toy often helps a child feel more secure while napping or sleeping at night.**

nap or rest time until they are four or five years of age. Rest time may involve looking at picture books, listening to music, or playing quietly with small toys on the bed.

The child's growing feeling of independence can be used to help develop routines related to dressing and cleanliness. By age four most preschoolers are able to dress and undress themselves with little help. They are able to bathe, wash their hands and faces, and brush their teeth. Routines for these activities are important for the busy preschooler. Without routines, stopping their many activities for these chores can be difficult. Children feel a sense of accomplishment when they assume daily responsibilities with their parents' help and encouragement.

Developing Physical Skills

Large muscle coordination greatly improves during the preschool years. Preschoolers need ample opportunity to use and develop their large muscles to discover their physical abilities. They can gain much

self-confidence through physical play. Ideally, play activities should be challenging enough to be interesting and promote learning. However, they should not be so challenging they cause frustration.

Many of the physical activities preschoolers enjoy immensely require no equipment—just playmates. Tag and hide-and-seek are examples of these activities. Playground equipment, tricycles, and other transportation toys provide opportunities for large muscle activity.

Art materials and toys that encourage sorting, matching, and fitting help develop small muscle control and eye-hand coordination. Many wonderful toys are available to encourage this type of development.

Preschool children may need some protection as they learn because they are too young to understand certain possible dangers. See 7-11. They need to be protected from being hurt by a breakable object or falling down the stairs. On the other hand, being overprotective by having too many

7-11 **This boy needs close supervision while playing near the water. He can be taught to be cautious.**

rules can discourage children from learning motor skills through physical play.

Learning Through New Experiences and More Effective Communication

Language development is important not only in communication, but also in developing other mental abilities. Parents and other family members can influence language development in many ways. Children enjoy having rhymes and simple stories read or told to them. They like books with a lot of pictures. Preschoolers tend to like stories about real-life situations more than fantasy. They like stories about what people do and stories about other children and their families. The preschool age is an excellent time for children to visit the local library and learn about the services it offers.

Many opportunities for new experiences provide new words and ideas. Going to a zoo, walking in the woods, visiting the fire station, and watching a parade are activities preschool children enjoy. Local groups often offer inexpensive courses in rhythm, music, sculpture, and crafts for preschoolers. These experiences, along with playing new games and playing with new toys, all result in new learnings and ideas to share.

Effective communication involves listening as well as speaking. Listening is more than just hearing. It also involves trying to understand the message, perhaps an underlying message, in what the person is saying. People who communicate well are often those who accept and understand other people's feelings. One of the best ways to teach a child to listen is to set an example and be a good listener. If children are surrounded by people who listen carefully, they are likely to learn this skill.

Preschoolers are fascinated with words, and they may learn some words their parents do not like. Usually it is best not to make an issue over such a matter. Parents might make a comment about the use of the word and then quickly turn their attention to another matter. If parents make too much fuss, these words might be repeated just to gain attention.

Language development in preschoolers is closely related to their social development. As they improve communication skills, they are also involved with more children and learn to play cooperatively. Through cooperative play and much pretend play, preschoolers practice and improve communication skills. See 7-12.

Parents can help their preschoolers by providing opportunities to play with other

Sandra Balfour

7-12 This boy pretends to be like the "grownups." At the same time, he works on his communication skills.

children. They may play in groups of neighborhood children or with children of their parents' friends. Child care groups and preschool groups also provide opportunities for children to play with others. A preschooler who is isolated and does not play with others may have some difficulty adjusting to school. The child is likely to be shy and lack self-confidence in a group.

Learning to Express Feelings and Control Actions

Preschoolers are quite open about letting others know how they feel. However, they sometimes express emotions through actions that hide their true feelings. For example, Jim's family is excitedly straightening the house before his sixth birthday party. In the midst of the preparations, four-year-old Tom dumps out his toy box in the middle of the living room. In situations like this, it is important for parents to understand the difference between feelings and actions. Actions are children's outward behavior. In this case, the action is dumping the toy box in the living room. The internal emotions are the feelings. In this situation, Tom feels jealous because all the attention is being aimed at Jim and his birthday.

Although children cannot control their feelings, they can learn to control their actions. In this case, the wise parent would recognize Tom's problem and insist he help

pick up the toys. Then they could do something special together to get ready for the party. In fact, Tom's family might have avoided this situation altogether. Family members could have anticipated the common problem of jealousy and somehow involved Tom in the excitement of the plans.

Before children can learn to control their actions, they must become aware of their feelings. Again, parents and other family members can guide children by expressing their own feelings. Comments from parents such as "I feel happy when you eat so well at lunchtime" or "I feel very disappointed when you make such a mess and do not help clean it up" make the child aware of other people's feelings. Parents can also make comments to help children become aware of their own feelings. They may say "Doesn't helping someone make you feel happy?" or "Are you disappointed and angry because the boys would not play with you?" Children need help in understanding their feelings. They need to realize feelings are not wrong, but learning to express them in a healthy manner is important.

As children mature emotionally, they learn to recognize their feelings and attempt to control them. They learn to express their feelings in a way that does not hurt themselves or others.

Although anger, fear, and jealousy are not bad emotions, they do need to be controlled. Anger is a normal part of human experiences that often indicates the child's identity is threatened. It is important for parents to teach their children to understand angry feelings and express them in a positive way.

By age five, children show progress in emotional maturity by using fewer aggressive actions such as hitting or pushing. Parents and family can assist in this maturing by encouraging *openness*—discussion of feelings. Suppressing these strong, negative feelings may create internal stress in a child.

Being an Active Member of the Family

The family is important to children in providing for the basic needs of security, worth, and love. Children need to feel they are an important part of their family unit. See 7-13.

Certain values help promote family spirit. When family members respect one another, the child develops a warm feeling toward family. That child's feelings are respected. In some homes, children's feelings are dismissed as unimportant. When they attempt to contribute, they are often laughed at and not taken seriously. Those homes are likely to lack family unity.

One way to develop family spirit is through family rituals. **Family rituals** are events or activities observed at certain times by the family. These rituals may range from activities on certain holidays like Thanksgiving to weekly rituals like special family breakfasts on Sunday mornings. Family rituals are a special and private happening. They generate a feeling of togetherness and a sense of belonging. Preschoolers love rituals for the fun of something special and the security of knowing what is going to happen.

Certain responsibilities come with any special relationship, especially within a family. As part of the family group, children feel the need to assume responsibility as family members. When children feel this responsibility, they think of the family in terms of *we*, *us*, and *ours* rather than *I*, *me*, and *mine*. This bonding, a feeling of oneness and support, can be a valuable resource in many aspects of children's daily lives.

Helping their parents with simple tasks makes preschoolers feel good about their contribution to the family, 7-14. In assigning tasks or responsibilities, it is important for parents to consider each child's age and abilities as well as safety.

7-13 **These parents promote their child's feelings of self-worth by stressing her role in the family unit.**

7-14 **Preschoolers like to feel they are helping.**

Parents and family will also want to allow time for training children to assume responsibilities. If parents do not help children learn to do a task the right way, they might have to correct them. This could discourage rather than encourage children to assume that responsibility. Preschoolers can help set the table, dust, empty wastebaskets, and do some yard work. As children mature, they may be trusted with certain errands like taking something to a neighbor or going to a nearby store.

It is important for parents and family not to judge a child's early attempts at these responsibilities by adult standards. Too much criticism may destroy a child's desire to help. Parents can help build a child's self-confidence by planning experiences that are likely to be successful. As children learn to accept responsibilities, they begin to enjoy being responsible.

Strengthening Self-Concept While Becoming More Independent

Preschoolers' self-concepts are partially based on how others respond to them. Young children see themselves as they feel others see them. Preschoolers unconsciously see themselves in terms of their personal self, social self, and ideal self.

Family members can bring about positive feelings by praising children for their physical accomplishments. Praise for everything from being able to ride a scooter to cutting their meat with a knife can benefit a child. That praise makes children feel good about their personal selves.

Their social selves are strengthened when preschoolers are praised for their good behavior in a group, such as when sharing toys. This positive influence gives preschoolers confidence in being with and relating to others.

Preschoolers also tend to evaluate themselves as good or bad in terms of their social responsibility. Parents need to be careful about their use of praise. It is important to praise the action rather than the child. "I am happy you ate a good dinner" is better than "You are a good girl." The first response emphasizes the action. The child will develop positive self feelings and want to repeat the action. A preschooler might not even recognize the reason for the comment "You are a good girl."

The ideal self relates to who the child would like to be. At first preschoolers tend to identify with the parent of the same sex. Little girls want to be like their mothers, and little boys like their fathers. Much of the child's *identity*—sense of self—results from the way parents and others close to them cope and behave.

During this age period, children consciously or unconsciously develop perceptions related to being male or being female. In American culture, sex role expectations are becoming less rigid. However, sex typing develops rapidly during the preschool period and can strongly affect the self-concept.

Curiosity is an outstanding trait of preschoolers. Having the chance to see, touch, and hear helps preschoolers develop new concepts and ideas. Each new experience expands the self-concept. Family members can encourage this interest in learning by giving preschoolers the opportunity to explore and answering their questions. Although a questioning child can challenge an adult's patience, these questions and answers are very important to the child's learning.

Parents can encourage learning by placing the emphasis on "Can you do it yourself?" rather than "Let me show you how to do it." Children who believe they can learn have the self-confidence to try new things. Along with this encouragement should come guidance and caution. Preschoolers need help in recognizing situations that might be dangerous.

Developmental Tasks of the School-Age Child

As children begin school, peer groups and other adults outside the family begin to have a greater influence on them. Although the family is still very important, the peer group becomes more significant. Other adults, particularly teachers, can also have much influence on a child. See 7-15.

Developing and Improving Physical Skills

Individual differences become increasingly obvious among school-age children. Wide ranges in height and weight exist.

Developmental Tasks of the School-Age Child	
Task One:	Develop and improve physical skills
Task Two:	Maintain healthful habits
Task Three:	Continue to develop basic learning skills
Task Four:	Increase ability to relate to others
Task Five:	Participate in family life as a responsible member
Task Six:	Continue to move toward a more complete self

7-15 **Other people have a great influence on the way school-age children achieve these developmental tasks.**

Physical skills also vary greatly. Although maturation plays a large part in the development of physical skills, environmental and cultural influences are also important. Children tend to be influenced by what other people expect of them. Many seven- and eight-year-old children are encouraged by their parents to join a sports team. However, a child who is smaller and quieter might be considered more intellectual. This child might be given a beginner's chemistry set rather than a baseball and glove. The tendency to stereotype children in relation to physical stature has a strong influence on the interests a child develops. Encouraging a variety of activities would show more respect to the child as a person. This freedom would give the child a chance to find where his or her skills and interests seem to be.

School-age children are constantly involved in activities that involve the large muscles—running, jumping, throwing, and balancing. See 7-16. In order to strengthen large muscles and develop body control, children need to be active. They also need encouragement from their parents. Children want to develop skills other people will admire. There is a close relationship between physical development and self-esteem.

7-16 **Many activities, such as riding a bike, help make the large muscles strong.**

During this active period, children go through a transition. They move from playing running games, jumping, and throwing to more organized play that is usually more competitive. Older school-age children and teenagers seem to get an overdose of competition. Therefore, parents may want to encourage these children to play games for fun, healthful development. This could help keep the competition within reasonable limits.

School activities such as cutting, drawing, coloring, and painting tend to encourage the child's small muscle development. By 9 or 10 years of age, children often become interested in other activities that involve small muscles. These might include model building and craft activities. Many of these activities can be very helpful in developing the child's intellectual skills as well.

7-17 Parents who emphasize healthful snacks have an important influence on their children's good health.

Maintaining Healthful Daily Habits

At this very busy physical stage of life, children do a lot of snacking. Parents can encourage healthful snacking by keeping certain types of foods at home. See 7-17. A hungry child will eat a healthful snack if fresh fruit, carrot sticks, cheese and crackers, and fruit juice are available rather than soft drinks, cookies, and candy. Many healthful snack foods are available, and recipes for healthful snack foods are published in popular magazines.

Snacks and other foods children eat can certainly have an effect on their teeth. During this stage of life, the permanent teeth are all coming in. Regular tooth care habits are important in addition to good eating habits. Soft foods that cling to the teeth seem to cause decay. Crisper foods, such as apples or carrot sticks, are much healthier for the child. These types of foods have a cleansing effect on the teeth. In

addition, crisp foods stimulate the gums and make them healthier.

These years are an excellent time for parents to encourage children to appreciate their healthy bodies. It is important for children to realize that many of the decisions they make will affect their health and can have long-term consequences. This is also a good time for children to become conscious of sitting and standing correctly. The best approach for parents is to teach children why good posture is desirable and set a good example. This is much more effective than nagging and scolding them about their posture.

Continuing to Develop Basic Learning Skills

Skills in reading, writing, problem solving, and working with numbers are extremely important to the child's success in school. See 7-18. Parents and other family members can do a lot to encourage these skills and influence a child's attitude toward learning. Parents can stimulate skills like these through encouraging conversation, listening carefully, answering questions, and above all, stimulating curiosity.

Children who have regular opportunities for stimulating conversation usually feel good about themselves. They confidently enter into conversation and participate willingly at school. To learn effectively, the child needs self-confidence. Research suggests that self-esteem may affect a child's chances for success in school even more than intelligence. Children of high intelligence and low self-esteem often do poorly in school. On the other hand, children of average intelligence and high self-esteem are often successful. Children with low self-esteem tend to get little satisfaction from school and lose interest easily. Lack of interest usually results in poor performance. The poor performance reinforces low self-esteem. The child who experiences more success than failure usually maintains a confident attitude. Family members can greatly influence the child's successes.

The effects of watching television and using the computer are very controversial. Both expose children to many new concepts. However, there are concerns about exposure to elements parents would rather have their children avoid. Also, children who spend a lot of time watching television and being on the computer read less, do not engage in as much conversation, and are usually not as physically active as they could be.

Many adults give children the impression that beginning school involves leaving the world of play and entering into the world of work. Children who enjoy their play do not happily accept this idea. Fortunately, play and academic learning at school do not have to be separated. Many toys, games, and other activities parents encourage are stimulating and help children learn basic skills.

At this age, a child needs some type of a table or desk where he or she can read, write, or do other creative work or play. Stimulating play materials, such as books, puzzles, hobby crafts, models, educational computer games, and science projects make excellent gifts for children.

7-18 **With family help and encouragement, this boy learns to enjoy schoolwork and gains greater self-esteem.**

Increasing Ability to Relate to Others

During these years, children experience much more social interaction with other children and adults. Social experiences help children understand and accept other people's rights and needs. Therefore, they learn to understand themselves better. See 7-19.

A child's ability to adjust to new experiences such as going to school is strongly influenced by his or her experiences at home. A sense of respect, caring, and security in the home help make new experiences less threatening.

Happy children who have high self-esteem generally have good relationships with others. Children with low self-esteem are often either overly aggressive or very shy. Relationships are important to everyone, especially to the child with low self-esteem. Through relationships, they seek the support and approval they cannot give to themselves.

School-age children tend to imitate adult behavior. For this reason, warm and caring relationships with special adults are extremely important to children. Parents, teachers, neighbors, and family friends can be a positive influence. Children will also identify with heroes or heroines, such as sports stars, movie stars, and television

performers. Children develop their ideal selves based on the adults they admire. Children want to be like these adults and try to copy their characteristics.

The peer group becomes a powerful influence on a child's life during this stage. It serves a positive purpose by starting to pull the child away from the dependency on the family toward the independence necessary for maturity.

Parents sometimes have difficulty accepting some of their child's friends. However, children need the chance to choose their own friends without parents' interference. They are learning to be with a variety of people. They are learning to sort out those who are honest, respectful, and enjoyable from those who are disloyal, disrespectful, and have undesirable habits.

If a child has difficulty making friends, it will become obvious during this stage in development. Parents and others close to the child can help encourage the development of friendships. Some ways to do this might include encouraging the child to invite friends home to play. Other ideas would be to help the child become involved in small group situations such as a scout troop or a team sport such as soccer.

Helping children develop social skills is important at this stage. If social skills are neglected, children are apt to become more and more socially isolated as they grow older. This would affect many aspects of their lives.

Participating in Family Life as a Responsible Member

The parent-child relationship continues to be a strong influence in the child's development. Although the school-age child is more involved in life outside the home, the family is no less important. The child's feelings of security and self-confidence result from good relationships with parents.

7-19 At school, children learn to make friends and develop social skills.

School-age children are anxious to behave like grown-ups. They tend to imitate the actions and mannerisms of adults, particularly their parents. This is an opportune time for parents and older brothers and sisters to encourage responsible behavior. During these early school-age years, children are capable of taking part in family decision making and sharing family responsibilities.

One of the best ways to prepare children for effective decision making is to let them observe and then participate in family decision making. This gives the child the opportunity to see the decision-making process in action and perhaps participate in the discussion. Children are more likely to learn cooperation when they are allowed to participate in decision making that affects them directly. This sharing helps children learn how to work together to solve problems for the good of the family. Through family decision making, children learn how people make decisions and how to plan for and implement those decisions. Being able to voice their opinions and have them respectfully considered makes children feel they are important to the group. This helps children become more self-confident.

To become responsible, children need to assume responsibilities. In every family, a variety of tasks must be done regularly. Assuming some of these tasks gives children the opportunity to learn skills, contribute to the family, and become more independent. Children gain self-confidence as they accomplish tasks. However, it is important for parents to be sure the resources needed to do the tasks are available and children have the necessary skills. Doing this will help children succeed and develop self-confidence. See 7-20.

The more children assume responsibilities in the home, the more likely they are to develop a respect for order and organization. The 10-year-old who fixes a casserole for dinner learns why promptness at mealtime is important. Imagine an eight-year-old leaves the towels he folded on the dryer instead of

7-20 Children can start learning responsibility through tasks they find fun, such as washing the family dog.

taking them to the bathroom closet. He understands more about order as he hears his parent shout, "Where's my towel?"

Because children will not succeed at all responsibilities they assume, parents need to help them cope with failure. Parents can do so by helping the child analyze a failure. Children need to understand what happened in order to prevent it from happening again. It is important for the child to understand that failure is an event, not a personal characteristic. It is in the past and can be avoided in the future.

These early school years are a perfect time for children to learn responsibilities with money. For some children, having a set allowance each week helps them develop confidence in handling money. They can make their own small purchases and save some of each week's allowance for a specific goal such as a toy, book, or gift.

Continuing to Move Toward a More Complete Self

During this stage, children gain a great deal of independence. Many experiences lead them to question certain values and develop some that are new. Parents and others close to children can encourage them to mature by helping them recognize and understand their values. They can be helped to understand that they will have conflicting values at times, which will result in the need to set value priorities.

Although parents have certain values they hope their children will share, values cannot be forced on children. The most effective way for parents and other family members to influence children's values is through modeling. See 7-21. If parents value honesty, they will be honest people. If they value openness, they will be open. If parents value maturity and independence, they will encourage their children to grow while still being willing to "let go." This gives their children the opportunity for new experiences on their own.

The new experiences children have during the school-age years lead toward a more complete self-concept. The more they know about themselves, the more complete their self-concepts become.

Parents can teach their children skills in self-observation. These skills help children feel good about their positive characteristics and accept their weaknesses. Parents can also help children decide which aspects

of themselves they would like to develop or improve. With this understanding, children can take steps toward self-improvement. Parents can be role models for their children by working on improving their own weaknesses. When family members help children learn more about themselves and their strengths, their self-confidence grows. As a result, the children develop a feeling of control over their lives and their futures.

7-21 **Parents can show they value family togetherness by spending special time with their children.**

32
31
30
29
28
27
26
25
24
23
22
21
20
19
18
17
16
15
14
13
12
11
10
9
8
7
6
5
4
3
2
1

Summary

Developmental tasks are important steps in a child's growth toward maturity. Infants, toddlers, preschoolers, and school-age children each have certain developmental tasks as goals. Adults can help guide children in these steps toward maturity.

Children achieve their developmental tasks easier when they have encouragement and support from people who are important to them. Parents, other family members, close friends, teachers, and neighbors can all encourage the child's growth in a positive way.

To Review

1. Explain why it is important for people who have a strong influence on children to be familiar with the developmental tasks of children.
2. List three ways to help infants and toddlers develop good eating habits.
3. Large muscles develop from _____ to _____ and from _____ to _____.
4. True or false?
   A. The time children learn bladder and bowel control depends more on their age than their physical or emotional readiness.
   B. Babies who have been talked to often learn to speak before those who have not.
5. Describe ways that babies communicate.
6. Name three security objects commonly used by toddlers.
7. Suggest four methods of helping a child accept bedtime.
8. List five ways parents and other family members can influence language development of children.
9. How is the peer group a positive influence on the school-age child?
10. The most effective way for parents to influence their children's values is through _____.

To Do with the Class

1. Security is a basic psychological need of an infant. Brainstorm ways adults and others can give security to an infant or young child.
2. Discuss ways family members might slow down a child's speech development.
3. Brainstorm listing ways families influence language development. What guidelines or suggestions would you have for parents?
4. Divide into groups for an activity on understanding the thought process of school-age children. One group can deal with developing concepts, another with developing logical thought in problem solving, and another with developing cause-and-effect relationships. List ways the family might influence the type of development you have been assigned. Share the lists with other groups and discuss.

To Challenge Your Thinking

1. Invite local pediatricians to debate issues related to developing good eating habits in children. Prepare questions for the pediatricians in advance.
2. Use library resources to learn about conflicting beliefs on the possible impact of toilet training on personality. Report your findings.
3. Organize a panel made up of parents of preschool and school-age children. Develop a list of questions for them to answer related to guiding their children's development.
4. Make a list of tasks that a preschool child could do in the home. Make a list of tasks school-age children could do.

To Do with Your Community

1. Interview the parent or parents of three unrelated children. Ask what they do to help their child develop good sleeping behaviors.
2. Talk with several elementary school teachers to get suggestions on how to influence a child's attitude toward learning.
3. Invite a pediatrician to speak to the class on toilet training. Ask the person to cover the physiological changes involved as well as the psychological involvement.
4. Invite a qualified individual from the community to speak on skills children can develop by participating in family discussions and decision making.

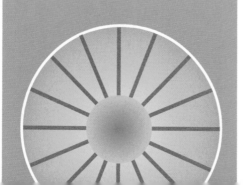

8

Developmental Tasks from Adolescence Throughout Life

To Know

personal resources
avocational interests
menopause

Objective

After studying this chapter, you will be able to

◇ relate the developmental tasks of adolescence, young adulthood, middle age, and late adulthood to your life goals.

In this chapter, you will become familiar with developmental tasks of adolescence and the adult years. Becoming aware of developmental tasks will help you better understand yourself and others. It will also help you set goals for the future and develop plans to meet these goals. See 8-1.

Developmental Tasks	
Developmental Tasks of Adolescence	• Accept and manage your changing body • Participate in a variety of social experiences • Assume more responsibility while moving toward greater independence • Develop personal resources helpful in reaching future goals • Continue to develop a healthy self-concept
Developmental Tasks of Young Adulthood	• Prepare for and become successfully involved in a vocation • Expand social relationships and assume social responsibilities • Exercise management skills related to daily living • Continue self-enriching pursuits • Assess readiness for marriage • Adjust to marriage • Assess readiness for parenthood • Assume responsibilities of parenthood • Develop a husband-wife relationship beyond the children
Developmental Tasks of Middle Age	• Continue self-enriching vocational and avocational pursuits • Adjust to physiological changes • Continue family responsibilities • Further the growth of the husband-wife relationship
Developmental Tasks of Late Adulthood	• Care for the physical self • Continue self-enriching pursuits • Maintain family contacts and responsibilities • Adjust retirement and changes in income and living arrangements • Adapt positively to the certainty of death

8-1 Human growth and development does not stop when a person reaches physical maturity. Certain behaviors and skills are expected to be learned at each stage in life.

Developmental Tasks of Adolescence

Adolescence is an exciting period of your life when many changes occur. However, it is also a time of many challenges. Both the excitement and challenges of this period involve making many decisions. These decisions are ideally based on your values and lead to reaching your goals. By achieving these goals, the developmental tasks of adolescence, you are better prepared for young adulthood.

Accept and Manage Your Changing Body

Because of biological changes that occur during adolescence, sharp physical differences occur both within each sex and between sexes. Young adolescents are usually quite concerned about their physical appearance. Growth spurts during this age period vary widely, and individual differences are quite normal.

Adolescents experience many changes in their bodies. Many of the changes are related to the ability to reproduce. These changes cause adolescents to experience a normal heightened sexual drive. Some adolescents lack the maturity and control to deal with their capacity for reproduction even when they understand it. This is one reason teenage pregnancy has become a major social problem in the United States.

In today's society, there tends to be more openness and honesty about sexual matters. Adolescents make more healthy adjustments when they feel they can talk to their parents and other adults about their concerns. No matter how open and helpful the communication is, however, you have the final responsibility for managing and controlling your own actions. The social and moral changes that have occurred today make this responsibility a challenging and important one.

Participate in a Variety of Social Experiences

You will be involved with other people throughout life. You deal with people whether you participate in work, leisure, or school activities. Adolescence is an ideal time to have a variety of social experiences both at school and through other daily experiences. These may include part-time jobs and organizations outside school. See 8-2.

These experiences give you the opportunity to learn and practice social skills. You will move from a feeling of social awkwardness to a more confident feeling of social poise. A variety of experiences points out the great differences between people—the uniqueness of each person. As you meet more people, you will begin to understand

8-2 **Being on a team helps these girls develop friendships and improve their social skills.**

how and why they have different thoughts and feelings. You will become more tolerant of others.

A sense of belonging or feeling like a part of a group is a basic human need throughout life. Adolescents are no longer children and yet not considered adults. Therefore, they create a group or culture of their own. Peer groups play an important role in an adolescent's development. Many adolescents conform to the values, customs, and fads of the group. The power of the peer group may be either positive or negative. Either way, it has a strong influence on the adolescent.

People develop deeper relationships with their peers during adolescence. Having a special friend you trust and are open and honest with is a special experience. See 8-3. Friendships like this prepare adolescents for later adult relationships. Close friendships give you the opportunity to learn about the values, personalities, and family backgrounds of others. Friendships also give you the opportunity to interact with a variety of individuals and further develop your communication skills.

Not all teenagers show an interest in dating at the same time. Some young people are deeply involved in hobbies or activities that leave few hours or little desire for

8-3 **Close friendships play an important role in a person's development.**

dating relationships. It is important to recognize that not everyone is interested in dating relationships during adolescence.

Most people have ample opportunity to move toward social maturity during adolescence. If a person does not achieve this developmental task during adolescence, it will be more difficult to achieve later in young adult life. Young adults with feelings of personal inadequacy and social isolation often have difficulty with new social experiences as they get older.

Assume More Responsibility While Moving Toward Greater Independence

Adolescents want the freedom to test their own ideas and become independent. This is perfectly normal. You may experience frustration as you desire independence, yet realize how you depend on your parents financially and emotionally.

Becoming more independent means gradually assuming responsibility for yourself. Infants are almost totally dependent on their parents for both physical and emotional needs. Children become less dependent as they grow older. By adolescence, a person is able to assume many responsibilities of daily living.

An adolescent's ability to move toward independence depends to a large degree on the attitude of the parents. Parents who provide guidance and control rather than domination make the task of becoming independent easier for their children. They encourage adolescents to solve problems and make decisions. When parents give adolescents real responsibilities and encourage them to participate in family affairs, those adolescents are practicing skills they will use in the future. They are preparing for adult living.

As adolescents accept more responsibilities, parents develop more trust. Therefore, additional privileges are extended. See 8-4. As more trust develops, the relationship between parents and adolescents often undergoes a special change. Parents become friends who provide guidance. This is an important step toward greater independence.

Develop Personal Resources Helpful in Reaching Future Goals

Personal resources include your personal qualities, capabilities, talents, and skills. Although some personal resources are inherited, many can be developed and expanded. Adolescence is a period in life when you have many opportunities to expand and develop your resources. Physical stamina, opportunities for education, and spirit to improve yourself are all strong during adolescence.

8-4 Borrowing the car is a privilege that parents may allow as a teen proves he or she is trustworthy.

As you have read, certain personal qualities make up *character*. These qualities include personality traits such as tolerance, generosity, honesty, trustworthiness, and fairness. Character traits develop over time, and the growth of character continues throughout life. An individual with a strong character shows these positive personality traits through his or her actions.

Physical health, mental health, and personality are valuable personal resources you can assess and strengthen. Improved diet, exercise, and proper health care can build your physical health. In terms of mental health, most adolescents are aware of shortcomings in their personalities. Perhaps they know they can be stubborn, unfriendly, moody, or aggressive. Other adolescents may feel they have personality problems because they have trouble communicating with their peers. Maybe their peers seem to avoid them. These adolescents may have trouble identifying their actual problem. School and community resources are available to help.

Most adolescents do realize a good education is one of the greatest resources available. Attending school gives you the opportunity to expand your knowledge and develop countless talents and skills. Skills in reading, writing, speaking, and listening help you communicate with others. Course work helps you develop abilities to reason. Learning to solve problems helps adolescents deal with increasing challenges. A student's performance in school will affect his or her future as far as job possibilities, additional schooling, and a career.

With additional knowledge, adolescents have a more complete sense of the world and a more complete feeling of self. It helps you set more realistic personal goals based on what is most important to you.

Continue to Develop a Healthy Self-Concept

Daily new experiences, educational opportunities, and social experiences all affect your self-concept. When you understand the meaning and importance of a healthy self-concept, you can assume responsibility for shaping your own self-image. See 8-5.

Ideally, adolescents move from a vague self-concept to a more complete one. They become more aware of their abilities and interests and more accurately perceive their values. They also become aware of their uniqueness as individuals.

If your ideal self is realistic, it can help motivate you toward certain goals. It can help you prepare for your career goals and goals involving marriage and family life.

When you begin to consider career goals, assess your abilities, aptitudes, interests, personality characteristics, and general physical condition. This will help you choose realistic career goals. Having positive feelings about your choice of a career helps improve your self-concept.

Many adolescents begin to form goals related to marriage and family life. Adolescents who have assumed responsibilities in the family are better prepared for the challenges of marriage and family.

Mike Deatherage

8-5 **Developing a new skill has a positive influence on a person's self-concept.**

Developmental Tasks of Young Adulthood

It is difficult to specify when young adulthood begins. The transition into young adulthood varies greatly depending on social and economic factors. People who choose careers that require many years of education may not achieve financial independence until their late twenties. Others may get a job right out of high school. Some people marry and start a family in their early adult years while others postpone marriage or decide against it. Some people are independent during their early adult years. They focus on their careers, leisure-time activities, and social lives.

Life as a young adult is a highly individual matter. However, for any young adult there are certain developmental tasks. If the tasks are achieved during these years, adjustments during the middle and later years will be less challenging. People who choose not to marry or have children are not involved in the tasks related to marriage and parenthood.

Prepare for and Become Successfully Involved in a Career

In today's society, young adults are expected to become financially independent. The choice of a career or occupation is important in the way it affects your life. Where you live, the clothes you wear, the food you eat, your daily schedule, and your social life all depend on your job. Even your health and self-concept are related to the job you choose.

Although most people work to earn a living, their jobs may also be important for other reasons. Some people may gain respect and a feeling of self-worth through their work. For others, work may be an opportunity to be involved socially. A job may also be an opportunity to express creativity.

Social and technological changes have a constant effect on opportunities in the world of work. The amount of education or training required depends on the occupation. See 8-6. Most jobs have possibilities for advancement through increased skill or seniority. Some do not have this potential.

8-6 **The amount of knowledge involved in a job determines its education requirements.**

Although being employed can have many immediate rewards, it is wise to consider the long-term effects of employment. A person's occupation involves a great investment of time, emotional energy, and commitment. Because of this, a person's life at work and home are interrelated. Positive or negative factors at work or at home can affect the success or failure of each.

Expand Social Relationships and Assume Social Responsibilities

The self-concept has become more stable for young adults, and they have a clearer sense of values. This growing understanding of self and others makes young adults become more selective in their relationships. They learn to appreciate others for their unique qualities. Young adults develop a deeper caring and concern for others.

Many young adults date as they are exploring deeper relationships. Dating provides experience with members of the opposite sex that can improve communication and increase social maturity. Young adults have social experiences with a variety of people. This gives them the opportunity to consider what personal qualities are important in selecting a marriage partner.

Because of their age, young adults automatically assume certain social obligations. Just one example is the responsibility to voice opinions by voting on issues involving the community or the country. Interest in community and political activities varies greatly among individuals. Involvement in organizations satisfies personal needs for recognition and self-worth for many people, 8-7.

8-7 **Young adults often assume social obligations by doing volunteer work.**

Schools are just one example of volunteer opportunities for young adults. Through personal involvement in schools, they learn to recognize problems that teachers and administrators face. They can then explain these challenges to friends and family members who have less knowledge of local educational issues.

Use Management Skills Related to Daily Living

Keeping yourself healthy, eating well, maintaining a place to live, and managing your finances are some of the challenges involved with everyday living. Using management skills will help keep your life running smoothly.

The management and decision-making processes are valuable resources to use in dealing with daily challenges. Organizational skills such as time and energy management also are important resources in daily living.

Young adults need to be aware of how their daily decisions affect their health. Many *lifestyle diseases*—diseases that are closely related to behavior—can begin in the young adult years. Eating right, exercising, and making intelligent decisions involving your health are valuable management skills.

Management skills contribute to the organization and maintenance of the home. A person's home might be a room, apartment, or house. Consumer skills are helpful in selecting food, clothing, household equipment, and other financial and personal needs.

Skill in financial management is important in guiding the use of the money earned and also in planning for future financial security. Understanding the use of credit and the importance of insurance to financial security will also help the young adult.

Continue Self-Enriching Pursuits

Many young adults are "on top of the world." They have become independent of their parents, mainly because of a job and their own income. They have moved toward a more clearly defined self. Many young adults choose a period of personal freedom before settling down to the responsibilities of marriage and family life.

This time presents an opportunity for young adults to pursue **avocational interests**—interests outside their occupation—in depth. Time may be used to establish leisure interests that promote physical, social, emotional, and intellectual health and growth. These interests developed in young adulthood are often the basis for activities that will be enjoyed throughout life.

Assess Readiness for Marriage

This developmental task involves examining qualities that would contribute to stability in marriage. It also includes examining the compatibility of a possible spouse and becoming aware of marital responsibilities and adjustments, 8-8. Personal qualities that contribute to stability in marriage are the same qualities that contribute to other good interpersonal relationships. Trust, concern, respect, openness, and a sense of responsibility help any relationship succeed. A mature love between two people implies they are able to care about the well-being of each other. They will realistically accept the other person. With this mature attitude, deciding on issues they can live with and how to negotiate priorities will be less challenging.

One of the most valuable resources of a couple is communication. This involves both speaking and listening. The ability to communicate well increases the chances of a lasting marriage. Exchanging ideas related to desired lifestyle will help a couple decide if they are truly compatible. Couples who understand each other's needs can develop satisfying plans for careers and financial management as well as home and family living. Discussing attitudes toward sex helps prepare the couple for their expectations in marriage.

Agreement on family planning is also important to the success of a marriage. Through most of the past century, society assumed that when a couple married, they would have children. More recently, however, many couples are making a conscious choice not to have any children.

Before marriage, the two people involved will benefit from discussing important issues related to the success of their marriage. They may both revise some of their ideas and even change their behavior. Working to establish a united identity as a married couple does not mean each person gives up his or her identity. With mutual respect and trust, each person is free to establish and maintain individual role expectations.

An understanding of marital adjustments and the responsibilities of parenthood is important to the success of a marriage. This awareness helps create a realistic view of marriage and family life.

Professional resources are available to help a couple assess readiness for marriage. Using these resources can help create a stable marriage.

8-8 This young man and woman considering marriage have developed mature love and an open, stable relationship.

Adjust to Marriage

An understanding that a successful marriage requires adjustments is important. Adjustments take time, effort, and cooperation.

Conflicts occur in all human relationships, including marriage. Knowing the techniques that can be used to resolve conflicts helps a marriage succeed. A happy marriage relationship depends on the conscious effort of both marriage partners. The relationship is more likely to be stable if both people cooperate in assuming responsibilities of the marriage.

Assess Readiness for Parenthood

It is important for a couple to appraise their readiness for parenthood. Physical and emotional maturity of the couple are extremely important to the welfare of the child and parents. Adding a child to the family will not be quite as challenging if the couple has had time to make their own early marital adjustments.

Choosing to have children is a serious decision. See 8-9. A couple should consider their reasons for starting a family to be sure they are wise, mature decisions. Having a baby because of pressure from family and friends or to strengthen a shaky marriage are not good reasons for such an important decision. It is important that both husband and wife want a child. For them, having a child is an expression of the love they have for one another. They want to share in the joys and responsibilities of guiding their child's development. For many young adults considering parenthood, family is important. They have had positive family experiences and wish to continue this tradition.

Parenthood brings many adjustments. When a child is born, husband-wife relationships require adjustments in role

8-9 **Becoming a parent is assuming a responsibility that lasts a lifetime.**

patterns and daily living patterns. Pregnancy and parenthood may require adjustments in relationships with relatives and friends. With the birth of a child, parents also take on a huge financial responsibility.

Being aware of parental responsibilities is important to the couple thinking about parenthood. Seriously considering these responsibilities gives them a more realistic view of marriage and family life.

Assume Responsibilities of Parenthood

Parenthood is a lifelong responsibility that involves giving and guiding. By recognizing the responsibilities of raising a family, parents can help their children be healthier both physically and mentally.

Every child has the right to receive love, care, understanding, and opportunities for development. The responsibility to provide these is the challenge of parenthood. Children have physical, social, emotional, and intellectual needs that parents can help meet. Parents provide more effective guidance when they understand needs and the factors that influence human development.

Develop a Husband-Wife Relationship Beyond the Children

Making a special effort to strengthen the relationship between husband and wife is important to happiness in marriage. Participating in social and recreational interests together and spending time alone together helps a couple strengthen their marriage. A good marriage relationship is a valuable resource a couple will use to face challenges in their future.

Developmental Tasks of Middle Age

Keep in mind that people within any age group vary greatly from one another. This is particularly true with middle-age adults. This period spans many years and involves major changes in life situations. In spite of individual differences, certain common challenges are shared by most middle-age adults.

Continue Self-Enriching Vocational and Avocational Pursuits

Middle age is often a time when men and women take inventory. They assess what they have accomplished and decide what resources they have or need to face the future.

It is not uncommon for middle-age people to experience a conflict between earlier dreams for the future and actual achievement in their careers. At this stage in life, they may consider still trying to achieve those dreams, or they may develop other interests. Other people realize the limitation of their abilities and make adjustments by setting more realistic goals.

Middle-age adults may have mastered their occupations and find little challenge and excitement in work. This can create a feeling of stagnation. They might be able to seek challenge through avocational interests, 8-10. They might even want to consider a career change.

Parents who have invested much of their time in child rearing may wish to return to a part-time or full-time job during middle age. The change will force the family to make adjustments in responsibilities assumed in the household. Making these changes will be easier if they are worked out to satisfy all family members.

Expanding interests beyond the occupation can provide great satisfaction. This is especially true at a time when people have more leisure time than in the past.

8-10 **Middle-aged people who spend many hours at work take special enjoyment in relaxation and recreation.**

Imagine you are a middle-age person. What changes might you be experiencing? How might you handle the achievement of developmental tasks? Do you think middle-age people think of themselves as achieving developmental tasks? Why or why not?

Art, music, literature, sports, and volunteer work can give a person a feeling of accomplishment. Many community organizations rely on middle-age adults for leadership. Their time and life experiences are valuable resources to the community. Opportunities for volunteer work are available through schools, hospitals, retirement centers, nursing homes, homeless shelters, and neighborhood centers. Many of these volunteer opportunities can be a source of interest and pleasure during later adult years when leisure hours are even greater.

Adjust to Physiological Changes

Physical changes that occur during middle-age years may cause emotional anxiety to people who do not accept them. Mature adults accept the reality of these changes and do not become obsessed with restoring youthful vigor. Instead, they aim at making the most of their potential.

Menopause occurs when a woman's menstrual periods cease and she is no longer able to have children. This physical change may also have psychological implications for certain women. How well a woman adjusts to these changes depends on the physical problems that occur and her ability to adapt to change. Both medical

and psychological support systems are available for help.

Men also experience hormonal changes during middle age. However, little is known about the effects of these changes on physical or psychological well-being.

Anxiety about sex can be a problem during middle age. These anxieties may not concern actual problems. Instead, they can occur because of myths about how age affects sexual capacity. If marriage partners are open and respect each other, each will better understand anxieties the other is experiencing. Then they will be more likely to support one another in their marriage.

Continue Family Responsibilities

During this period, married couples may be under both financial and psychological strain. The costs of rearing children can be financially draining, 8-11. Guiding adolescent development often causes psychological

Lynn Hellmuth

8-11 **Middle-aged adults often face the challenge of financing their children's education.**

Brainstorming

Brainstorm a list of problems many people have in their later years. Discuss whether some of these problems could be lessened or avoided if certain steps are taken early in life. Do you ever think about taking these types of steps now?

strain. Mutual respect between parents and children makes the transition from adolescence to adulthood less difficult for everyone. As young adults assume more responsibility for themselves, parents can help by letting go while standing by with encouragement and reassurance.

During middle age, some people must provide some form of care for their aging parents. Many American families now look after aging relatives and manage these responsibilities well. Understanding the changes that are likely to occur during later adulthood helps the adult children. They can better prepare themselves and their aging parents for those changes and problems that might be likely to occur. This period may bring difficult choices related to housing for a parent who needs help in everyday living; managing financial drain from parent's medical bills and other care costs; and dealing with medications, doctors, and legal documents such as wills. In addition, most of these middle-age adults are juggling jobs along with the care of both their own children and their aging parents.

Middle-age adults must strike a balance between meeting the needs of aging parents and meeting their own needs. Ideally, aging parents maintain their independence as long as they can do so comfortably and safely. Their independence is an advantage to both the aging parents and the adult children.

Further the Growth of the Husband-Wife Relationship

A growing relationship between husband and wife can continue during the middle-age years. Even when a strong relationship exists, certain adjustments are required at this time. People who have planned for these adjustments will usually find them less challenging.

With children leaving home, a couple has an opportunity to redefine their relationship in terms of their own needs. This new start can be a special challenge to the couple. Both marriage partners may feel the need to renew their own self-esteem and respect for each other. To continue a satisfying life together, a spirit of mutual cooperation is helpful.

Maintaining personal identity is very important to the middle-age person. For the marriage relationship to keep growing, each person must respect the other person's right to have a life of his or her own. Freedom from family responsibilities and increased leisure time may give people an opportunity to strengthen their self-concepts. Two people who are certain of their own identities are more likely to have a healthy, loving relationship.

Manage Daily Living and Prepare for Later Years

Being flexible is important in every stage of life. If middle-age adults continue to assess their goals, they may find certain changes would help them better meet those goals. Change is often difficult, but being open to new ideas and different ways of doing things will help adults avoid problems caused by being too rigid.

Managing resources related to health needs is especially important during this period. To manage their health, middle-age people need to assess their lifestyles and how it affects their health. Diet, stress, and exercise affect that person's health and future well-being. See 8-12.

Managing financial resources is also important during middle age. Financial planning for retirement can begin during young adulthood. However, it is highly motivated during middle-age years. Full knowledge of financial affairs is important to an individual or a husband and wife in preparing for the future. The financial world continues to become more and more complex. Some people may wish to take classes to help them develop the skills and knowledge they need to manage their finances.

Preretirement programs and classes are presented in many communities. The classes help prepare middle-age people for the challenges they will face as they retire. This is also a good time to be thinking about plans regarding arrangements in later life and discussing them with other family members. Families need to talk about finances, housing, and legal concerns.

Developmental Tasks of Late Adulthood

The age at which a person enters late adulthood has more to do with physical characteristics than a specific chronological age. Unfortunately, myths and negative stereotypes about aging are common among many Americans. These myths do have an impact on the well-being of older adults. The stereotypes deny older people their individuality by considering them all alike.

Kent Hayward

8-12 **The pressures of life make it difficult for middle-aged adults to schedule time for exercise. However, exercise is very important during these years.**

*Getting*Involved

Invite community leaders, including educators, clergy, and extension personnel to join a panel. Ask the panel to familiarize the class with programs offered that help equip young men and women to become competent husbands, wives, fathers, and mothers. Compile brochures on the information and pass them out at community centers.

This is not true. Older people are individuals with different levels of functioning, both physically and mentally. See 8-13.

Aging is a natural process that cannot be avoided. Many puzzling questions about the process of aging have not yet been answered. Older people do undergo significant physical and psychological changes. However, many changes are more of an inconvenience than a true handicap. Late adulthood can be a special time for people who plan ahead and are aware of the changes that will take place.

Care for the Physical Self

No one can avoid certain physical changes related to aging. Over the years, the

8-13 This woman is 83 years old. She is still physically able to care for her home, garden, and great-grandchildren.

skin becomes more wrinkled and joints stiffen. The spinal discs compress to produce shorter, bent posture. Muscular strength lessens, reaction time decreases, and hearing and eyesight decline. The age at which people experience these changes varies.

The problems that occur as a result of physical changes often involve the person's self-concept. Being aware that most of these changes will occur helps people accept and cope with the changes effectively. Knowing the changes occur gradually helps people adjust. It also helps to know that other older adults are going through the same changes.

Disease is a very important influence during late adulthood. Disease is not the same as aging. In the absence of disease, the effects of aging are less harmful.

Although physical changes and problems cannot be avoided, resourceful people can remain physically active. They are able to manage the strength and energy they have. Maintaining good practices related to diet, exercise, accident prevention, and physical exams benefits an aging person.

Continue Self-Enriching Pursuits

Many myths about old age often cause older people to lose self-esteem. However, older people who are informed can plan and take steps to continue to satisfy their basic human needs. These needs include the need to be respected, loved, needed, and esteemed. These basic needs do not decrease with age.

Throughout life, personal appearance affects a person's self-concept. Keeping fit through exercise and having a well-groomed appearance can have a positive effect on older people.

All people feel better about themselves when they feel their behavior is meaningful and worthwhile, 8-14. A common misconception is that older people will enjoy

8-14 **Creating a beautiful painting is self-enriching for this woman.**

usefulness. Working with children in schools gives a renewed enthusiasm for life and a chance to pass on lessons learned and skills mastered during a lifetime of experience. In today's mobile society, grandparents and children are often separated by many miles. Children grow up with little or no contact with older people, and older persons who live alone or in communities with others their age seldom talk to children. Through the adult's volunteer work in schools, child care, or children's organizations, the two generations are able to learn more about one another.

Many types of avocational interests are either continued or discovered in late adulthood. Being involved in activities, especially with other people, stimulates and exercises a person's mind. This is important in maintaining mental skills. During late adulthood, people have the time to become involved in new activities and additional new knowledge.

Like people of all ages, older people desire companionship. Being an active member of a group gives them a meaningful role in life at a time when their responsibilities have lessened. Group activities satisfy a person's need to belong. In addition, these activities fill free hours constructively and provide opportunities for happiness and companionship. Many senior citizen centers and groups throughout the country provide a place to find companionship along with cultural, recreational, and educational activities. In social situations like this, older people share the events of their daily lives. They find many people whose situations are much like their own.

another's taking care of them. Instead, most prefer to be given as much choice and control as possible. Older people want to be useful. With no pressures of an occupation, they are able to explore interests and become involved in new activities. Helping others through volunteer work in hospitals or schools gives older people a feeling of

Maintain Family Contacts and Responsibilities

In their older years, people are usually more sentimental and nostalgic. Family is

8-15 **Family relationships are very meaningful in the later years of life.**

an important part of their lives, 8-15. Older parents who live near their children tend to see their family often. Those relationships are very important to them.

Being a grandparent is a special human experience. Grandparents have additional time available to be involved with their grandchildren. Grandparents have a wisdom that comes from age and experience. They may not have had the same understanding with their own children. Grandchildren are a part of the grandparents that will continue to live after they have gone.

Relationships with brothers and sisters tend to be more important during later life than in middle age. One reason for this is that immediate family activities and pressures are greater during middle age. People have more time to be with their brothers and sisters during late adulthood. These relationships become very important. Brothers and sisters may serve as a substitute after the death of a spouse or close friends.

As in any other stage in life, certain family responsibilities are to be assumed by the aging adult. Family members at all age

levels can be helpful to one another. Years of experience provide aging parents with helpful advice to pass on to younger family members. On the other hand, wise parents carefully assess each situation before they give advice. They make sure they are being respectful to their adult children or grandchildren in the way they give advice.

The desire for independence at this age is just as strong as it was in adolescence and other stages in life. However, the aging adult must gradually begin to depend on others. When this happens, the pride of being self-sufficient becomes very strong. However, an older person who is wise faces and accepts dependency when necessary. An important ingredient in good relationships is openness. Those in late adulthood today grew up in a period when they were taught to keep a stiff upper lip and suffer in silence. It is difficult for many to know how to ask for help or say how they feel. This confuses their children, who grew up at a time when persons were more open about their feelings.

Adjust to Retirement and Changes in Income and Living Arrangements

The way a person adjusts to retirement depends on whether that person has achieved the developmental tasks in the preceding stages of life. People who have planned financially, maintained their physical and mental health, and developed avocational interests are prepared for retirement. Retirement should not cause many problems for people who are well prepared.

The retired person has a new status, social position, and role. The challenges and expectations of the new role may be very exciting. People who think about the new challenges and expectations rather than worry about their previous positions in life are more likely to successfully adjust to retirement. See 8-16.

Reduced income is one of the greatest problems of retirement. Due to constant changes in the economy, financial plans developed earlier may no longer meet financial needs. This may cause people to change their standards of living and alter their plans.

Changes in health and finances cause many older adults to become dependent on others. This causes many retired people to make changes in their living arrangements. The death of a spouse may also cause a change in living arrangements. An older adult whose spouse has died may consider moving in with an adult child or moving to a retirement or nursing home.

Although people need suitable living arrangements at any age, they are especially important to older people. Older people spend more time at home than those who are younger. For older people, housing is more than just a shelter. It may mean memories, a social center, or an anchor for children and other family members. The place they live may represent status, independence, or an investment to others. To some older people, their home becomes a financial and housekeeping burden.

Adapt Positively to the Certainty of Death

Death is a reality. It is the final stage of human development. Aging adults who accept the certainty of death are usually the people who focus most on life. See 8-17. These people know each day could be their last day of life. They set their priorities and live to make the most of each day.

8-16 **Some retired people spend more of their free time with family members. Others plan to travel and devote time to hobbies.**

Courtesy of Avon Products

8-17 **This woman has accepted the certainty of death, but she continues to enjoy each day of her life.**

Most people who have a positive attitude toward death are open with others about the subject. They rely on their knowledge, values, and beliefs to give them strength.

Death frequently breaks close personal ties for the older adult. Being prepared for the possible death of a spouse or close friend is important. Married people who have shared daily living responsibilities adapt better to the death of a spouse. For the spouse who has never done any cooking or shared in keeping financial records, adjustments may be very difficult.

People vary in the way they react to death and grief. There is no way to deal painlessly with the death of someone close to you or to face your own death with no pain. However, people can prepare for death and adjust to it over time.

Most people who are facing death go through stages in letting go of life. These stages begin with denial that death will occur. Then there are feelings of anger, resentment, and possible rage. The person is angry that he or she must die while others will continue to live. Depression is the next stage. The person begins to withdraw from the world and may also reject family and friends. Acceptance is the final stage. The person is able to accept death and calmly prepare for it.

People who are grieving the loss of a loved one go through similar stages. These stages also begin with denial that death has occurred. People who are grieving may then go through a period of anger. They may be angry at God or the person who died. Depression is another stage. It often occurs as the grieving person is trying to get life back in order. Feelings of guilt are often present at this time. Acceptance of the loved one's death is the final stage of grief. Some people reach this stage more quickly than others. The length of the grieving process varies from person to person. The order of these stages may also vary.

Summary

There are certain developmental tasks in the adolescent and adult stages and life just as there are in childhood. Achieving these tasks or goals of growth leads toward a more satisfying life. Knowledge of developmental tasks will help you set goals for your own future and understand people at each stage in life.

To Review

1. List and describe the developmental tasks of adolescents.
2. Which of the following statements about developmental tasks of adolescents are true?
   A. Peer groups are very important to the adolescent.
   B. An adolescent's ability to move toward independence depends to a large degree on the attitude of his or her parents.
   C. Ideally, adolescents move from a vague self-concept to a more complete one.
3. List four personal resources available to most adolescents.
4. True or false. All people enter into young adulthood at the same age.
5. Describe five personal qualities that contribute toward stability in marriage.
6. True or false. Parenthood brings many responsibilities, but requires little adjustment in the parents' lives.
7. Financial planning for retirement becomes highly motivated during the _____ years.
   A. adolescent
   B. young adult
   C. middle age
   D. late adult
8. _____ occurs when a woman's menstrual period's cease and she is no longer able to have children.
9. Why are avocational interests so important to people in the late adulthood stage?
10. Describe the stages older adults go through when they are faced with death.

To Do with the Class

1. Write a case study that shows how an adolescent might mature socially through a specific social experience. Share your case study with others in the class.
2. Discuss how having a variety of interests helps an individual become more interesting to others.
3. Brainstorm identifying citizenship responsibilities any adult citizen is expected to assume.
4. List responsibilities of parenthood throughout the life cycle. Discuss how being aware of these responsibilities gives the young adult a more realistic view of marriage and family life.

To Do with Your Community

1. Interview adult workers of various ages about whether they would choose their present vocation if they were young adults again. Keep a list of their responses and discuss them with the class.
2. Research to find agencies and individuals in your community who assist couples experiencing difficulties in marriage adjustment. Discuss their programs in class.
3. Interview happy, active older adults to discover what self-enriching activities they enjoy. Did they begin these activities during the young adult, middle age, or late adult years?
4. Invite a banker, an investment broker, and someone to represent retirement and social security concerns to speak on money and retirement. Prepare questions for the speakers that will help you understand the importance of planning for financial security in the later years.

To Challenge Your Thinking

1. Make a list of responsibilities an adolescent could assume in a family to prepare for marriage and family life in the future.
2. Make a list of advantages to the adolescent of mixing with people of all ages.
3. A person's self-esteem is strengthened by achieving certain developmental tasks. Choose a developmental task and describe a situation that illustrates how achieving this task affects self-esteem.
4. Investigate to find ways aging individuals might benefit a community through their activities.

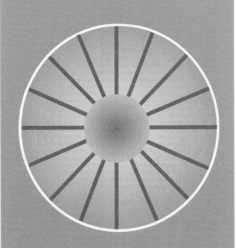

The achievement of developmental tasks begins when a child is born and continues throughout life.

Part Three
Understanding Relationships

Chapter 9
Successful Relationships
Positive relationships are those in which respect, trust, responsibility, and openness are valued. As you mature, you develop personal relationships with people other than family members.

Chapter 10
Effective Communication
Understanding different types of communication can help you communicate with others more effectively. Communication is especially important in conflict resolution.

9

Successful Relationships

To Know

personal relationships
functional relationships
respect
stereotype
mutual respect
trust
openness
empathy
dating
infatuation

Objectives

After studying this chapter, you will be able to

◇ analyze the importance of respect, trust, responsibility, and openness to successful relationships.

◇ examine the importance of relationships throughout life.

◇ identify the benefits of relationships within the family and relationships outside the family.

Throughout life you will be in contact with many people. Some of these contacts will develop into close personal relationships. See 9-1. **Personal relationships** are those you may have with your parents, close friends, and eventually with a marriage partner and your own children.

Other contacts with people are on a more functional level. **Functional relationships** are relationships such as those with your teachers, employer, or fellow employees. These contacts may not develop into close personal relationships. However, functional relationships can be important to you. For instance, if you do not get along well with your employer, your job might be threatened.

The relationships you share with other people have a great effect on the quality of your life. These relationships are important to you for many reasons, and you want them to be successful. Understanding the basis of good relationships and the importance of relationships throughout life will help you reach the goal of developing successful relationships with others.

Characteristics of Positive Relationships

Think of two people you know who have developed a good relationship with each other. You may think of two good friends, a father and son, a husband and wife, or a sister and brother. Why do you think these positive relationships have developed? Most positive relationships have several characteristics in common: respect, trust, responsibility, and openness.

Respect

Respect is an important ingredient in a good relationship. Everyone has the need for a feeling of worth as a person. Respecting a person is different from liking that person. **Respect** means seeing someone as a worthwhile individual. Examples of respect or lack of respect are all around us. A teenage boy shows respect when he gives his bus seat to an elderly man. A student shows respect when she waits for the

9-1 **Having close relationships with others is important for people of any age.**

teacher to finish speaking before asking a question. A father respects his daughter's individuality by not criticizing her latest hairstyle.

A girl shows lack of respect when she will not listen to her friend's side of a disagreement. Parents may also show lack of respect to their children. Consider the boy who wants to join the debate team instead of the football team, which his father has suggested. If the boy's father becomes angry, he is showing lack of respect for his son's interests.

Sometimes people stereotype others. A **stereotype** is a belief that all members of a group share characteristics that may only belong to some members of the group. Some comments that stereotype are "Old people are slow," "Women are too emotional," and "He's a dumb athlete." Stereotyping usually indicates a lack of respect. When you lack knowledge about the unique characteristics of people within a group, you are likely to stereotype.

As you spend time with certain people day after day and continue to show them respect, a positive relationship develops. Mutual respect is necessary for a special relationship to exist between you and another person. **Mutual respect** shows that each of you accepts the other as a worthwhile person.

Trust

Trust means believing a person is honest and reliable. You trust people when you believe their word represents what they will actually do. Honesty is an important part of trust. It is difficult to trust people when they say one thing and do another.

Both words and actions communicate trust. A baby girl develops trust as her basic needs are satisfied. When she feels hungry and cries, her parents or caregiver feed her. She learns to trust them to satisfy her needs. See 9-2. Other feelings of love and security come from this feeling of trust.

The key to building trust in a relationship is being trustworthy. Developing trust takes time; trust does not appear overnight. Parents develop trust in their teenage son if he drives responsibly and cares for the family car. A husband and wife develop a trusting relationship over the years as they meet each other's needs.

Although trust takes time to develop, it can be easily destroyed. If you violate your word, the other person may question whether you can be trusted. For instance, you may have shared many secrets with a long-time friend. Consider what might happen if you share one of these secrets with another friend. If the first friend discovers what you have done, he or she may not be able to trust you in the future.

9-2 As this baby's basic needs are satisfied, she learns to trust those who care for her.

You have shown a lack of responsibility toward this special relationship. Trust and responsibility are very closely related.

Responsibility

Responsible people are dependable and reliable. They are accountable for their actions. Responsible people live within the written and unwritten rules. They obey our laws, which are the written rules. They also abide by the unwritten rules, which are standards of behavior acceptable to people around them. A person's sense of responsibility usually increases with maturity.

All relationships carry certain assumed responsibilities with them. An employer-employee relationship requires responsibilities of both parties. The employee exchanges skill and hours of work for pay and fringe benefits from the employer. Parent-child and husband-wife relationships also require certain responsible behaviors. These behaviors depend somewhat on the values and standards of the people involved. See 9-3.

Irresponsible actions have a negative effect on relationships. If you are often irresponsible, other people will begin to lose trust in you. In addition, people may develop a lack of respect for you.

Openness

Openness—letting another person know your thoughts, opinions, and feelings—is important to a successful relationship. In a good relationship, two people trust each other to be open.

Being open involves a degree of risk. When you are open with someone, you risk causing hurt feelings, embarrassment, or insult. However, the risk may be even greater if you are not open with that person.

When being open, it is important to be tactful rather than blunt or rude. For instance, you may have a rather chubby friend who asks how you like her new red sweatpants. You could tactfully answer, "You do look nice in red, but the outfit you wore yesterday was more flattering to your figure."

When you are open you are also accepting. You are accepting the openness someone is sharing with you. You respect the other person's opinions and feelings even though you may not agree. It is easier to be open with someone who is accepting. Accepting people have **empathy** for your feelings. When they empathize, they see things from another person's point of view. They try to understand your feelings without judging whether you are right or wrong.

People who share information about themselves promote openness in others. By being open, people learn more about others. As a result, they often learn more about themselves. Being open with people of different backgrounds and different ideas will give you the opportunity to

9-3 **Work relationships involve the responsibilities of fulfilling duties and acting appropriately in the workplace.**

consider new information, ideas, and values. These experiences lead to a more complete self.

The Importance of Relationships

Relationships involve sharing feelings, experiences, problems, interests, and activities. Through close relationships, people share and work toward common goals. Successful relationships can be an enriching factor throughout life, meeting basic needs and contributing to personal development.

Relationships as Resources

Every person needs to be accepted, respected, cared for, and needed. These are lifelong needs. These needs are met through relationships that are formed both inside and outside the family. Relationships with others are as important when you are 70 years old as when you are seven years old.

Your happiness and success in life are closely related to your ability to form meaningful relationships with others. See 9-4. Whether you have successful relationships with others can have a strong influence on your self-concept. Good relationships with others result in a more positive self-concept and higher self-esteem.

Social experiences with others also influence your emotional development. You learn to deal with both positive and negative emotions through your relationships. You learn to express your emotions in socially acceptable ways.

When you have the chance to develop relationships with a variety of people, you learn to accept differences among people. You become aware of new and different values. You weigh these values and decide how important they are to you. These

Nancy Henke-Konopasek

9-4 The special friendship these girls have developed results in higher self-esteem for both of them.

experiences help you to know and understand yourself better. They help you mature and become a more open and accepting individual.

The depth of relationships you develop throughout your life will vary. Some relationships are very personal. Others are more functional.

Personal relationships are those that fulfill basic human needs such as the needs to belong, be cared for, and be loved. Relationships with family members and friends are very important in meeting these needs and to happiness throughout life.

Many relationships are more functional than personal. Functional relationships involve everyday needs and interests. For instance, Julie is a checkout clerk at a grocery store. Julie relates to many people throughout the day. These are functional relationships. This does not indicate that they are unimportant. Julie's success at her job depends on how she relates to customers. How they perceive her and communicate with her may affect their attitudes toward the store.

Relationships Within the Family

Your first personal relationships occur within the family as family members meet your basic needs. Young infants develop positive feelings when they are held closely. Their need for security is being satisfied. Young children develop positive feelings as their brothers or sisters smile, talk, and play with them. They feel happy, secure, and loved. These family relationships satisfy the basic human needs.

Family members are teachers and role models. They teach children about relationships by guiding the young child's social behaviors and attitudes. Young children learn by observing the way family members relate to each other and people outside the family. See 9-5. Modeling strongly influences a child's skill at interpersonal relationships. When family members show respect for one another and accept and share responsibilities, they are an effective model of relationship skills.

Relationships Outside the Family

Family relationships are very important in satisfying human needs and developing relationship skills. The relationships you develop outside the family also strongly

⊟ 9-5 **These parents act as role models for their child.**

influence your happiness and quality of life. Your friends, teachers, fellow workers, and other people with whom you come in contact all influence your life. You benefit personally by establishing positive relationships with all these people.

You will meet many people outside your family. Each new acquaintance will be different because every person is unique. As you meet a variety of people, you will learn more about the differences that exist among people. There will be differences in the way people look, talk, act, think, and feel. The experiences you have with these people will influence many choices you make in your life.

Relationships of the Young Child

Young children learn about relationships by interacting with other children in the same way they learn within their families. Young children in a neighborhood group, child care center, or a nursery school learn what behaviors strengthen relationships with friends and what behaviors cause problems. Children learn a great deal through trial and error. The young child learns that pushing to the front of the line makes other children unhappy. Children learn that they feel good when they help others. See 9-6. They learn that giving compliments gives them a good feeling.

Children in group situations are not only learning how to manage relationships. They are also learning how to satisfy their own needs. A little boy feels happy and cared for when his friends run to greet him as he enters the classroom. A little girl gains a more positive self-concept when a boy tells her he likes the picture she is drawing.

These social experiences are very important to young children. Being with other children provides a wonderful opportunity to learn and practice relationship skills. Children become less self-centered as they become aware of the needs of other children around them.

Relationships of School-Age Children

The peer group has a strong influence on school-age children, especially teens. The peer group is made up of people of the same age or status. Close association with

9-6 Sharing his toy with the younger child makes this little boy feel happy.

the peer group is normal during the process of growing up and establishing independence from the family.

The peer group satisfies basic needs by providing for the need to belong and to be recognized. The peer group gives the young person opportunities to develop a social identity—to be recognized as a part of a group. See 9-7. A peer group may be a mixed group of friends or a special interest group like the band, the wrestling team, or a computer club. Being accepted into a group of peers influences a person's self-concept and his or her relationships with others.

School-age children often develop special relationships with adults. They might admire a neighbor, a teacher, an entertainer, or an athlete. These adults serve as role models to school-age children. This relationship gives the children an opportunity to consider qualities that they might like to develop in themselves.

As young people mature socially, they become more independent of their families. During this time, they may develop friendships with people of different backgrounds, cultures, and values. They will develop close friendships from this variety of casual friendships. Learning to be a good friend and maintaining that friendship is a step toward social maturity and adulthood.

Boy-Girl Relationships

Developing and maintaining relationships with people of the opposite sex is part of growing up and learning to live in our society. See 9-8. You relate to people of both sexes in all aspects of life—at school, at work, and in the community.

During the teen years, friendships become very important. Friends provide a sense of identity and importance. In the early teens, boys and girls tend to be more involved in group activities. At first, time is spent more with groups of the same sex. Next, there is a trend toward mixed group activities, and then pairing off for boy-girl friendships. Teens may feel nervous about their first dates, but in time, they develop more self-confidence.

Dating gives teens the opportunity to become close to someone of the opposite sex outside their own family. This new experience helps them improve their communication skills as they share opinions, attitudes, values, and goals with

Nancy Henke-Konopasek

9-7 The peer group satisfies the need to belong.

9-8 As young people mature, they have the opportunity to develop close friendships with people of both sexes.

Getting Involved

Visit an assisted living facility to develop a relationship with an older resident. Share life stories, read, or play games with the person. How do you think an older person is affected by a "fun" relationship? How do you think this relationship influences your relationship skills?

others. Through dating, they gain an understanding of various personalities and an appreciation of respect, love, and caring from others. They learn to appreciate unique qualities of different individuals. This helps them realize the fallacy of certain stereotypes such as "girls always do this" or "guys are all like that." Dating experiences also provide occasions for the teens to learn to deal with misunderstandings and hurt feelings. Dating is an important experience in the lives of teens as they approach adulthood.

With dating often comes romance and love. Teenagers and young adults may fall in love many times. Feelings of romantic excitement can sometimes gradually lead to genuine love. However, in most cases, teens can be fooled into thinking they are in love when instead they are infatuated. **Infatuation** is a powerful but short-lived attraction to another person. This experience is sometimes referred to as "puppy love." Infatuation or puppy love is highly self-centered and temporary.

Love is difficult to define, partly because the word is used in so many different ways. You may love chocolate chip cookies or you may love football. These examples clearly aren't the same as loving another person. To make it even more complicated, there are different types of person-to-person love. How you love your parents or grandparents, for example, is very different from how you feel about a boyfriend or girlfriend with whom you may be in love.

Social maturity comes to different people at different times. Therefore, not all young people show an interest in dating at the same time. People who have had negative experiences with members of the opposite sex may see dating as a threatening experience. People who have had limited experience with members of the opposite sex may also be reluctant to date. It is important to recognize that everyone is not ready to date at the same time of life.

Adult Relationships Outside the Family

Relationships outside the family are important throughout life. Friends are as important to adults as they are to children. Adult friendships develop with fellow employees, neighbors, parents of children's friends, and other adults who share the same interests. Having such a variety of relationships often makes a person become more interesting.

Work relationships, both with the employer and fellow employees, are important to job success. A work atmosphere in which employees work well together is usually more productive than when there are conflicts.

Brainstorming

Think of examples that illustrate how adults and young people show respect for one another. Then consider ways adults and young people sometimes fail to show respect for one another. Do people always realize whether they are showing respect or disrespect? Why do you think this is the case?

During young adulthood, deeper, more caring personal relationships are often formed. See 9-9. These relationships tend to be less selfishly based than relationships formed during the early teen years. Adults enjoy friends for their unique qualities.

Young adults become more selective about relationships with people of the opposite sex. As their feelings grow about the person they are dating, marriage in the future may become a consideration. Mature, young adults carefully assess the personal qualities in a partner that would help create a stable, happy marriage. They carefully consider whether they are experiencing genuine love. Genuine love requires a certain measure of maturity. This type of dedicated love is only possible for those who have the ability to give of themselves.

Real love is being able to contribute to the happiness of another person without expecting anything in return. That type of unselfishness demands considerable maturity. Love is more than just a feeling. It also involves a commitment, a determination to make the relationship succeed.

People in love experience conflict. That is normal. The conflict is a warning signal, and mature adults will make the conflict constructive. They will examine the cause and set goals to avoid that conflict in their future together. Love takes hard work and much creative energy.

Relationships during the middle and late adult years can also be very meaningful. See 9-10. As children mature and move away from home, adult friendships may become even more important to the parents.

Just as in the early years of life, friendships help meet basic human needs for older adults. Older adults can participate in activities with friends, such as joining a bowling league, volunteering at a hospital, or taking a class to develop a new skill. These are all ways to satisfy the need to belong, be accepted, and feel of worth. Upon the death of a spouse, friends can be very helpful and caring.

Kent Hayward

9-9 College students often develop close relationships that will last a lifetime.

9-10 Relationships outside the family are important at any age.

32
31
30
29
28
27
26
25
24
23
22
21
20
19
18
17
16
15
14
13
12
11
10
9
8
7
6
5
4
3
2
1

Summary

Respect, trust, responsibility, and openness are the basic factors that influence relationships. When you understand these factors, you can analyze your own relationships. This understanding will guide you as you develop new relationships and improve current ones.

Your ability to form meaningful relationships with others can greatly affect your happiness and success in life. Relationships within your family are very important. However, your relationships outside the family as a young child, a school-age child, a teenager, and an adult also strongly influence your satisfaction in life.

To Review

1. True or false?
   A. Respecting a person is the same as liking that person.
   B. A person's sense of responsibility usually increases with maturity.
   C. Being open with someone carries a certain degree of risk.
2. Give three examples of stereotypes and explain why they are stereo types.
3. Explain what is meant by empathy.
4. Describe three ways relationships can be a resource.
5. What is the difference between a personal relationship and a functional relationship? Give examples to contrast the two types of relationships.
6. Name three ways relationships can benefit a young child.
7. School-age children, especially young teens, are strongly influenced by their _____ group.
8. Learning to be a good friend and maintaining that friendship indicates a step toward _____ maturity and adulthood.
9. _____ provides an opportunity to get to know someone of the opposite sex outside your own family.
10. Name several ways adult relationships outside the family can benefit a person.

To Do
with the Class

1. Discuss how a young child might be affected by associating with only one friend.
2. Brainstorm as a class to list the benefits of peer influence.
3. Discuss 10 important ways you can develop trust.
4. Discuss the meaning of the following statement: Developing trust takes time.

To Do
with Your Community

1. Volunteer at a community group, such as a religious organization, homeless shelter, or Big Brothers/Big Sisters organization. Develop friendly, fun relationships through planned and spontaneous activities.
2. Interview two couples, one who has been married 10 years or less and one 10 years or more. What factors have contributed to the success of their relationships
3. Talk with a local business person. What does he or she feel contributes to a positive employer/employee relationship? Ask someone who works for that person the same question. Compare responses.
4. In school, what activities help students form lasting friendships? What are the traits common to you and your best friends?

To Challenge
Your Thinking

1. Talk with a nursery school or child care worker. Ask that person how a child benefits from relationships with other children.
2. Describe two situations that show lack of responsibility in a relationship.
3. List examples of trust and lack of trust in the family setting.
4. Teenagers sometimes break ties with their parents through disrespectful criticism. Give several examples that illustrate this.

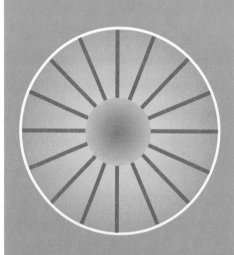

10 Effective Communication

To Know

communication
verbal communication
nonverbal communication
inner communication
open communication
informational level
hidden messages
emotional level
body language
behavioral level
listening
feedback
conflict
negotiation
compromise
"I" messages
"you" messages
problem ownership

Objectives

After studying this chapter, you will be able to

◆ describe various communication skills.
◆ examine listening as an important step in communication.
◆ explain guidelines in conflict resolution.
◆ apply positive conflict resolution to your own life.

Communication is more than just talking. It involves the sharing of ideas and feelings with others. It also involves getting to know your own feelings.

Consider whether you communicate effectively. Effective communication occurs when you express yourself so the other person understands what you are saying and feeling. You communicate your values, ideas, feelings, and interests. Ideally, the message the other person receives should be the same as the message you send.

Effective communication is challenging in many situations. For instance, when you are not sure of your own feelings, you may not be able to effectively communicate them to another person. If your feelings are hurt, you may be afraid to say how you feel. Sometimes you may be afraid of hurting someone else's feelings. At other times, the way you say something gives the other person the wrong impression. Sometimes communication breaks down simply because people are not listening carefully. You can overcome many of these problems by learning and practicing effective communication skills. See 10-1.

10-1 **In a special friendship, communication channels are always open.**

Types of Communication

There are various types of communication used in sending and receiving messages. Being aware of these will help you to be understood more accurately. It will also help you better understand others.

Verbal and Nonverbal Communication

People communicate both verbally and nonverbally. **Verbal communication** involves speaking and/or writing. **Nonverbal communication** includes the inflection of the voice, movements of the body, and emotions shown. Eye contact with others, facial expressions, and gestures are examples of nonverbal communication. See 10-2.

Inner Communication

Inner communication involves getting in touch with yourself—with your own feelings. Understanding yourself is very important. If you cannot communicate with yourself, it will be difficult to communicate effectively with others.

Feelings are your reactions to everything that goes on about you. They strongly influence your perception of the world. Your feelings may vary from day to day. The way you feel on one day may cause you to react differently to a situation from the way you would react on another day. You may notice this in other people, too. For instance, one day four-year-old Jimmy walked into the house with chocolate smeared all over his face. His mother laughed and kidded about his funny face. Then she took him to the bathroom to wash off the chocolate. Another day, his mother was tired and things had not gone well. If all sending you different messages. Often these voices send conflicting messages based on different values and goals.

In effective inner communication, you train yourself to identify all the voices and feelings inside yourself. See 10-3. This helps you see which voices or feelings are influencing what you say and do. You consider the values they represent and decide if you are reacting as you want to. In other words, you set value priorities. Learning and practicing this skill in inner communication will give you more control over what you communicate.

Open Communication

Open communication means being honest and letting the other person know your true thoughts and feelings. Open communication also means you accept the other person's ideas and feelings.

10-2 The look on a person's face can communicate a broad range of emotions. What feelings are suggested by the facial expressions in these pictures?

Jimmy had come in with a dirty face on that day, his mother might have become angry with him. Her feelings strongly influence her perception of a situation and the way she reacts to it.

Because so much of what you do depends on your feelings, being in touch with those feelings is extremely important. This inner communication can be like communicating with several people. You feel as if there are several voices inside you,

10-3 Learning to communicate with yourself puts you in touch with your feelings and gives you more control over what you communicate to others.

Mutual respect goes hand-in-hand with open communication. Respect and openness allows you to be honest without worrying that the other person will be angry or think you are silly.

Open communication also involves responsibility. When you communicate openly, there is no place for rudeness. Instead, you try to be honest about your feelings without being disrespectful.

Levels of Communication

Communication is complete when the other person understands your exact message. Unfortunately, communication between people is not always complete. Incomplete communication may give the wrong impression or cause a misunderstanding. If communication occurs on several levels, however, the message is more likely to be understood. The three levels that lead toward full communication are the informational level, emotional level, and behavioral level.

The Informational Level

At the **informational level**, you communicate thoughts, ideas, plans, beliefs, or stories. See 10-4. Although communicating on the informational level seems simple, words are often misused or misunderstood. Hidden messages are another problem at this level of communication. **Hidden messages** occur when someone says one thing, but is really implying another. For instance, a brother may say to his sister, "Your hair looked really nice before you got it cut." The brother is really saying, "I don't like the way you are wearing your hair now." Hidden messages are often misunderstood and insulting. Hidden messages do not belong in open,

M.T. Crave

10-4 **Plans for an upcoming event are shared at the informational level.**

honest communication. However, hidden messages are sometimes unconsciously sent.

The Emotional Level

The second level toward full communication is the **emotional level**. This level involves communicating feelings. You show your feelings through nonverbal communication. Sometimes nonverbal communication tells you more about a person's thoughts, needs, and feelings than verbal communication. Giving a hug, crying, and slamming a door are emotional actions that communicate a certain message. See 10-5. Nonverbal communication usually reinforces verbal communication, thus moving toward full communication.

Many forms of nonverbal communication have a major impact. For instance, a friend may be talking to you about an important problem. If you do not give your friend your undivided attention, you may communicate that you are not interested in what he or she is saying.

Becoming aware of what your body language means will help you communicate more effectively. **Body language** consists of emotions in many different ways. A strong hug and a kiss may indicate a caring relationship for one person. However, a warm grasp of the hand might be just as meaningful to another person.

Another reason emotions are difficult to interpret is that stronger, more violent emotions may overshadow the gentler ones. Angry emotions tend to be more obvious than caring, feeling emotions.

10-5 **Giving a hug can communicate love to a child.**

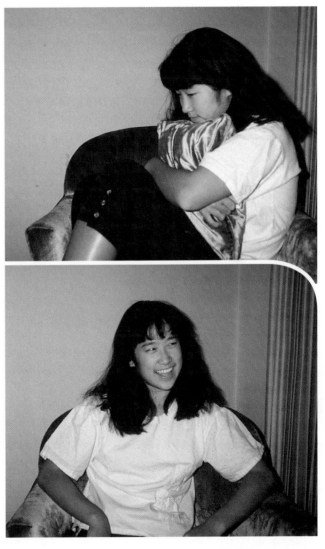

10-6 **This girl's body language tells a lot about her feelings. In which picture would you be more likely to approach her?**

your body movements, facial expressions, and posture. For instance, if you maintain good eye contact as you speak to someone, you show that you want him or her to understand what you are saying. If you avoid looking a person in the eye as you speak, you are signaling uneasiness. The other person may think you have something to hide. A forced smile looks quite different from a genuine smile and indicates insincerity. Becoming aware of what body language means can help you understand yourself and other people. See 10-6.

Emotional expression is difficult to interpret because people display their

The Behavioral Level

The third level of communication is the **behavioral level**. This level involves "doing." If you tell someone you like him or her, you are communicating at the informational level. If you hug that person, you are communicating your fondness at the emotional level. If you do nice things for that person, you are communicating on a behavioral level. See 10-7.

The three levels of communication are not always reached in the same order. Some people can communicate their feelings better through actions than through words. A friend may communicate caring by doing something special for you when you are feeling low. Sometimes you may communicate accurately emotionally without communicating accurately verbally. For instance, your words may say you are not angry, but your eyes say you are. If you are only able to communicate on one level, others are more likely to misinterpret the meaning of your message.

When you communicate at all three levels, you are less likely to be misunderstood. In full communication, your mind is working, you feel emotions, and your body shows action.

The Importance of Active Listening

Communication is a two-way process. One person signals while the other person interprets the signals. When you have full communication, you have skill in both signaling and in interpreting signals. You speak and listen well.

Hearing and listening are sometimes different. You can hear words without really listening for meaning. **Listening** requires a conscious, active effort to understand the message. When you really listen to people, you are letting them know you value them and their thoughts and ideas. It indicates a caring attitude about what the other person is saying. Good listening skills are important because they motivate people to share ideas, opinions, and knowledge, and they enhance relationships. See 10-8.

Good listeners give **feedback** to what the speaker is saying by repeating what they thought was said. A good listener might say, "What I hear you saying is…" or "Do you mean…?" Feedback gives the sender an opportunity to clarify the message. This provides a "mirror" that helps the sender decide if the message has been received. Good listeners ask questions if they are not sure of what is being said.

When you listen well, you show interest and stay focused. You think about the feelings that lie behind the words. Then you respond to those emotions. A good

10-7 A father communicates caring to his child by spending quiet time reading to her.

10-8 **These good friends have open communication and a caring relationship. Whether listening or speaking, each keeps in mind the feelings of the others.**

listener searches for feelings and learns how to read between the lines by picking up nonverbal clues. The speaker's body language can reveal things about what they are saying.

A good listener listens for hidden messages. A child may ask his mother to hold his hand when he goes into nursery school. He might really mean that he is feeling insecure about a new experience. Having his mother close would make him feel better. An insensitive parent who did not really listen might say that big boys don't hold hands. She might make the boy walk in by himself.

People take the time to listen in respectful, caring relationships. Listening is an important responsibility to be assumed in your special relationships.

Skill in Conflict Resolution

Some conflict is normal in any close relationship. See 10-9. **Conflict** occurs in a relationship when there is disagreement. The presence of conflict is normal, natural, and inevitable. You should not fear conflict or be ashamed of it.

Conflicts occur for many reasons. Perhaps the most obvious reason for conflict is differing values. Friends may argue because they cannot agree on where to go for a special weekend outing. Parents and children may have conflicts over the use of time. A father may feel that his teenage daughter spends too much time talking on the phone. A married couple may argue over whose parents to visit during the holidays. All these conflicts involve values.

10-9 **Even friends experience conflict at times. Learning to handle these conflicts in a positive way is important.**

Sometimes conflicts occur because of poor communication. In some cases, a message is not sent clearly. At other times, the message may not be received accurately, or it may be misinterpreted.

Although you cannot eliminate conflicts, you can control them. You can avoid anger, shouting, and rudeness by handling conflicts in acceptable, positive ways. If conflicts are handled in a positive way, relationships are often actually strengthened.

Relationships are seldom threatened because of a single event. Instead, small, everyday conflicts, if unresolved, may eventually destroy a relationship. By practicing positive conflict resolution in day-to-day conflicts, a build-up of tension and problems can be avoided.

Steps in Conflict Resolution

You can use the problem-solving process to successfully solve personal conflicts. The first step is to define the problem—to pinpoint the issue. It is important for the two people involved in the conflict to work together to define the problem. Working together openly and respectfully gives you a better understanding of the other person's point of view. See 10-10.

After defining the problem, the next step is to find out what caused the conflict between you and the other person. When you can identify and understand the cause of a conflict, you can avoid that conflict in the future.

Next, change the problem into a mutually acceptable goal. A goal is positive and focuses on the future. Goals present the problem in a constructive manner that calls for action.

Seeking alternatives for reaching the goal is the next step. This involves **negotiation**. This means working together to find a solution to a problem. As you work together, you evaluate each alternative to select the most constructive one. Evaluate each alternative and choose the most constructive one. This step will often involve **compromise**, in which each person is willing to give something up in order to resolve the conflict. Then, it is time to implement the plan.

After a period of time, evaluate the situation. Did that alternative meet your goal and solve the problem? If not, why didn't it work? You may need to implement a different alternative.

Guidelines in Conflict Resolution

Keep respect, trust, responsibility, and openness in mind while working together to resolve interpersonal conflicts. If any of

10-10 **Relationships may even be strengthened when you learn to work through conflicts in a positive way.**

these factors are violated, additional problems may occur.

Attack the problem, not the person. When you have a personal relationship with a friend or a family member, you care for that person. Constructive conflict resolution attacks the problem itself. Destructive conflict resolution attacks the other person. Don't be afraid to admit your negative feelings, but control your aggressive feelings. You can express your anger without insult.

Using "I" messages can help you resolve conflict. **"I" messages** help the other person understand how you perceive the situation.

An "I" message usually has two parts: your feelings about the situation and a statement of the behavior or situation that bothers you. For instance, a mother might say to her daughter, "I feel so frustrated when I look in your room and see clothing all over the floor."

"I" messages can also include how a behavior or situation inconveniences you. For instance, a father might say to his son, "I feel angry when I come home and have to get out of the car to move your bike from the driveway."

Often, in times of conflict, people tend to use "you" messages. **"You" messages** attack the person rather than the problem. Some examples are "You had better get that done, or else!" or "You never can do anything right!" "You" messages are a dead-end approach. They create more hostility without resolving the problem.

If an "I" message is used instead, the emphasis is on resolving the conflict. "I" messages create a challenge for the other person in the conflict. That person has to decide what to do about your feelings. See 10-11.

Use of "I" Messages in Confict Resolution

Situation	"You" Message	"I" Message
A mother comes into the kitchen and finds her son has made a mess baking cookies.	You are so sloppy. Just look at the mess you have made of this kitchen.	I am glad you enjoy baking, but I feel very frustrated when I leave the kitchen clean and come back to find it such a mess.
Parents are upset because their son had the family car and did not get home until an hour after he said he would.	You are so irresponsible and inconsiderate when you don't come home when you said you would. You don't even call and let us know you are going to be late.	We're glad you are home now, but we felt concerned when you didn't come home when you said you would. We are also disappointed that you did not at least call to let us know you were safe and when you would be home.
A young man wonders why his wife hasn't spoken to him all evening.	You are so moody. Why don't you lighten up or else go somewhere else and sulk?	I can tell something is bothering you. Would you like to talk with me about it?
A teenager is upset because her friend made the basketball team and she was cut.	You think you are so smart because you made the basketball team.	I feel very envious of you since you made the team and I didn't.
A father is concerned because his overweight teenage daughter is eating junk food.	You are so dumb to eat that stuff. You are getting fatter every day.	Your health is important to me, so I am concerned when I see you eating that kind of food instead of a snack food that would have fewer calories.

10-11 **When you use "I" messages rather than "you" messages to resolve conflict, the other person tends to react more positively. "I" messages attack the problem rather than the person.**

Brainstorming

Make a list of topics young people find difficult to discuss with their parents. Why are these topics difficult to discuss? How might good communication skills make them easier to discuss with parents?

Problem Ownership

Considering the idea of problem ownership can often help in conflict situations. In **problem ownership**, you try to determine whose problem it is. The person concerned or upset about the situation is said to own the problem. For instance, you may not like having your younger sister play in your room when you are not home. You own this problem. Solving the problem is your responsibility.

Unfortunately, many parents assume ownership of their children's problems. Assuming ownership of someone else's problem is a mistake and can cause more difficulties in the long run. It deprives the other person of a chance to learn to handle problems more effectively and to mature through experience.

For instance, Sheri's father told her she could not use the car because she did not wash it as she had promised. She stomped furiously into the house to see her mother. Sheri complained that she had been running errands for her mother and had been too busy to wash the car. Sheri's mother went to her father and explained why Sheri had not done the work. Reluctantly, Sheri's father let her use the car. Although Sheri owned the problem, her mother assumed ownership.

Sheri needs to practice resolving conflicts with her father and stop relying on her mother. In this situation, Sheri could have used her own "I" message to help resolve the conflict. She could have said, "I am terribly disappointed that you will not let me use the car. I meant to wash it, but I have been busy all day running errands for Mom." Sheri's father would probably have reacted more positively if Sheri had come to him with that message. Sheri and her father are likely to develop a better relationship if Sheri learns to resolve her own problems.

If another person's behavior bothers you, it is your problem. However, you should think about the situation before you demand a change. You may be able to accept that person's behavior, respecting his or her feelings and actions. If you cannot accept the behavior because it violates important values, then be open with the person about your concern. If you indicate genuine concern about this behavior, the other person is likely to be more receptive than if you demand a behavior change.

Summary

Relationships are more likely to continue in a positive way when respect, trust, responsibility, and openness exist. You can communicate these qualities by using communication skills effectively.

In order to communicate effectively with others, it is helpful to develop skill in communicating with yourself. When you become skillful in open, full communication, others will better understand you. Skill in listening is an important part of effective two-way communication. Being a good listener shows that you care about what the other person is saying.

Because conflicts will occur in any close relationship, conflict resolution skills are necessary for effective communication. You cannot eliminate conflicts, but you can control them. You can learn to successfully resolve personal conflicts.

To Review

1. In_____ communication, you train yourself to identify what is influencing what you say and do.
2. _____ communication means letting the other person know your true thoughts and feelings.
3. Describe the three levels that lead to full communication.
4. Give an example of a statement that indicates a hidden message. Explain what the statement might really mean.
5. What is body language? Explain how body language helps a person to communicate effectively.
6. Give three examples of feedback in communication.
7. Give an example of a parent-child conflict that might occur because of differing values.
8. List the steps in positive conflict resolution.
9. Which of the following statements are true?
    A. Caring emotions tend to be more obvious than angry emotions.
    B. Conflict occurs in most relationships.
    C. You can express anger without insulting the other person.
    D. Destructive conflict resolution attacks the problem itself.
    E. Using "you" messages tends to attack the person rather than the problem.
10. When using problem ownership during conflict resolution, who is said to own the problem?

To Do with the Class

1. Act out nonverbal expressions to see if your classmates recognize them.
2. Discuss implications of the following statement: "I don't talk to you because you don't listen."
3. Role-play situations in which communication is healthy and open. Then role-play situations in which communication is unhealthy and closed. Discuss.
4. Write anonymous descriptions of parent-child conflicts. Trade descriptions with others in the class. Use positive conflict resolution to role-play how you might handle that situation.

To Challenge Your Thinking

1. Write examples of six "I" messages.
2. Watch a television drama and give examples of the different ways people communicated.
3. Choose a partner and take turns discussing a problem. Practice listening, not just hearing the other person's problem. Offer feedback and watch for emotions and nonverbal communications. Then discuss how it felt to have someone really listen to your problem.
4. Practice positive conflict resolution with one of your own interpersonal conflict situations. How well did it work? How could you have improved the way you resolved the conflict?

To Do with Your Community

1. Read the front page of a local newspaper. How do the headlines persuade you? Do the articles have a slightly different view once you read them? How are stories or ideas communicated through written or verbal communication?
2. Observe signs, billboards and advertising in your community. What visual messages are being communicated?
3. Invite a school counselor or psychologist to share strategies and insights about conflict resolution. Role-play scenarios using "I" messages.
4. Observe people in school, at a community event, or in a shopping mall. What are the nonverbal messages you can identify through others' body language?

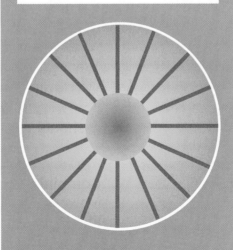

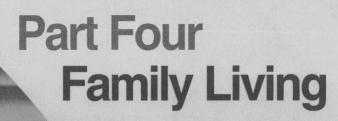

Part Four
Family Living

11

The Family Today

To Know

interdependent
caring family
responsible
respect
concern
open expression
sharing
leveling
accepting
crises
domestic violence
physical abuse
emotional abuse
sexual abuse
child abuse
incest
child neglect
physical neglect
emotional neglect
substance abuse
divorce
custody
joint custody
suicide
support group

Objectives

After studying this chapter, you will be able to

⬦ explain why the family survives as an institution.

⬦ describe ways families meet basic human needs.

⬦ analyze challenges the family faces due to social and technological changes.

⬦ cite the characteristics of a functional family.

⬦ describe crises that can have major effects on a family.

⬦ describe resources available to families.

Few people live in isolation. Instead, most people interact with others to meet their goals. Most people are involved in some type of family living.

No one definition describes the variety of families that exists in our society today. See 11-1. Nuclear families, single-parent families, stepfamilies, and extended families are just a few examples of the many family forms. Chart 11-2 describes these family forms.

The Importance of Families

Although family forms differ, each family shares a common characteristic. Each type of family meets the basic human needs of family members. Because of this common characteristic, families have been able to survive many challenges over centuries of time.

Families—Meeting Human Needs

Every human being has certain basic needs. These include the need for love, acceptance, and feelings of self-worth. People also need respect, recognition from others, and room to grow and develop their own capabilities.

11-1 Traditionally, the term "family" indicated father, mother, and children.

The family can provide a quality environment that encourages human growth and development. The family can offer shelter and security during challenging times. It can provide an opportunity to care, love, be accepted, and share.

Families can pass on values from generation to generation. These values may form the basis for family goals. The family also gives family members the opportunity to work together for the good of the group. Family members assume responsibility for the well-being of one another. See 11-3.

Families can give you the opportunity to learn and practice skills that are important to your development in today's world. Communication skills, relationship skills, and management skills are all practiced within the family structure.

Families and Change

Families have gone through many changes in the past century. At the turn of the century, the father was the power figure in the typical family. He provided income for the family and made important family decisions. The mother's major responsibilities were to take care of the household and to raise the children. The father made decisions he thought would be "best for the family."

In the past, many of the family's material needs were taken care of at home. Food needs were satisfied through gardening, raising animals, and hunting. Children learned trades and skills in daily living from their parents. Although these families lived in a world much different from our world today, they did function to meet basic human needs. Families provided physical care for their members and helped children gain skills that would prepare them to live in that society.

Today's world is very different. Change is constant. Technological and social

Family Forms		
Family Form	**Definition**	**Description**
Nuclear or traditional family	A married couple lives in their own home with their children if they have any.	The family is independent from their other relatives. Children leave home when they become adults. One or both parents may work outside the home. Nuclear families are less common today than they were in past years.
Single-parent family	One adult lives with one or more children.	The number of single-parent families in the United States is rising quickly. Most single-parent families are not planned. They usually result from divorce or separation, death of a spouse, or having children outside of marriage. Single parents are under a great deal of stress because they are fully responsible for the family. Cooperation is very important in single-parent families.
Stepfamily	A single parent becomes married. Stepparents and stepchildren are included as well as parents and children.	Either the husband, the wife, or both may have been previously married. There may be children from a past marriage. In a stepfamily, family members are adjusting to a new life together and relationships with each other. The increased family size may create additional financial concerns.
Extended family	Several generations of a family live together under one roof. This may include grandparents, parents, children, aunts, uncles, and cousins.	This type of family is less common in the United States. However, it is more common in some foreign countries. Extended families provide care for the young and the old. They allow for the daily sharing of resources among several generations.

11-2 **Each of the family forms described can successfully meet the basic human needs of family members.**

changes strongly influence everyone's lives. Although children are still influenced by their parents, they are also influenced by many factors outside the home. The Internet, television, radio, movies, magazines, and books have a major influence on children's lives. Advertising, travel, education, and association with people from other cultures expose children to other values, beliefs, and teachings. Parents can help children accept these differences.

During this period of rapid social change, many beliefs associated with the traditional family have been questioned. Family roles have changed, divorce has increased, and economic conditions have put an increasing strain on families. However, the family continues to survive as an institution because it still meets basic human needs better than any other single institution. Change will continue, and in order to survive, families need to understand and adjust to those changes. The family who cares and understands how to meet basic human needs in spite of constant change will be the family who survives.

11-3 **Families face many challenges as they grow together throughout life. However, the benefits are great for people who have this experience.**

The Functional Family

The functional family is a valuable resource to members of the group because it supports their basic needs. This functional family also helps its members deal with stress and crises. What are the characteristics of this resource, this special family, that make it unique?

Family Members Are Interdependent

Family members do not live in complete isolation; they are **interdependent**. This means events that affect one member of the family often affect others either consciously or unconsciously. For example, when Tara decided she wanted to go to college, her decision affected other members of her family. She took a part-time job to help with college expenses. Although her job helped with the finances, she did not have as much time to help out at home. Money that would otherwise be going to other family goals had to be put aside to help meet her college expenses. Because her family values education, this was a priority in relation to family finances.

The interdependence of the family requires a cooperative use of resources. Many services are performed by one family member for another. Family members also share many human and nonhuman resources. The human resources that families share include time and energy, as well as love and affection. Husbands, wives, parents, and children all need to be cared for and to give care to others. Nonhuman resources shared may include equipment, such as the television or the washer and dryer, or facilities, such as the bathroom.

The family is a resource that belongs to all members, and each member is able to contribute to the group. Each person depends on the others. The basis of the family unit depends on the actions of each member of the group. In a **caring family**, each person sees the relationship between his or her behavior and the success of the family as a unit. See 11-4. Therefore, each family member understands the importance of assuming his or her responsibilities.

Kent Hayward

11-4 **Assuming a sense of responsibility toward schoolwork is one way of contributing to the family.**

Family Members Are Responsible and Trustworthy

The responsible actions of family members are closely related to the interdependence of the family. Being **responsible** means being dependable and reliable. Each family member's responsible actions are important in a caring family.

Trust develops as basic needs are met within the family. Responsibility and trust are closely related. It is said that responsibility breeds trust. In other words, if you prove you are a responsible person, then you are trusted. When you trust someone, you believe in his or her honesty, reliability, and sense of responsibility. However, unless a person is given a certain degree of trust, that person cannot practice responsibility. If parents do not trust their teenager to drive the family car, can that teenager become a responsible driver? The two characteristics are very closely related.

Family Members Show Respect and Concern

In a caring family, every member, regardless of age, is treated as a person in his or her own right. Every family member is entitled to respect and consideration. Respect does not mean always agreeing with others and approving of their opinions and feelings. Instead, **respect** means showing consideration by accepting each person's rights to have opinions and feelings. Families who have this basic respect are characterized by feelings such as acceptance, warmth, understanding, and love.

Children need to feel they have the respect and concern of their parents under all circumstances. Knowing their parents will always show care and concern gives children the confidence they need.

Respect and concern, like trust and responsibility, are very closely related. If family members respect one another as people with special feelings and special needs, then family members are concerned about those feelings and needs. **Concern** means having a special interest in what happens in the lives of other family members. See 11-5. If a member of a caring family has suffered a great disappointment and is feeling low, other family members do not ignore the situation. Instead, they show concern for the person's feelings and do what they can to help.

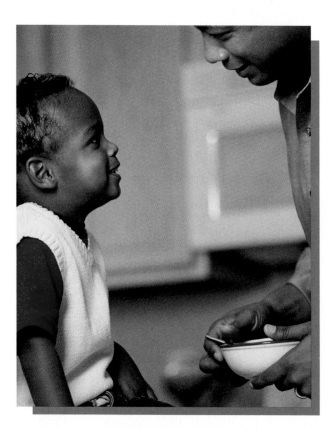

11-5 In a functional, caring family, a young child learns the importance of special caring and concern for others.

Family Members Openly Express and Accept Feelings

Expressing yourself openly involves several aspects. **Open expression** means sharing, leveling, and accepting. First, **sharing** is letting others in the family know your personal thoughts, feelings, and opinions. In a caring family, people are not afraid to express themselves honestly. They do not fear losing the love of other family members. They know that other members of the family respect their right to their own feelings and opinions.

The second aspect of open expression is **leveling** or letting others know how you feel about them and their behavior. This can be challenging when sharing critical feelings. However, caring family members can do this in a way that does not offend the other person.

Accepting is the third aspect of openness. This means respecting the other person's right to his or her own opinions and feelings, even if you don't agree. Everyone's feelings are recognized—even angry feelings. In a caring family, voicing angry feelings is permissible and should be encouraged. When negative feelings are acknowledged and accepted, they are not likely to pile up to a crisis point.

If each member of the family is open and can expect the same openness from other family members, then trust will exist within that caring family. Family members can be trusted to let others know their feelings, to share them, and to accept the feelings of others. Open expression is necessary for trust to develop and continue in a family.

Family Members Are Open to Change

Change is inevitable both today and in the future. In the past, families prepared children for very definite life roles. Life was full of "shoulds" and "should nots." These ideas were not open to discussion or change.

Today, functional, caring families prepare family members to deal with change. They look at change as an opportunity for personal growth. Family members are encouraged to wonder, question, speak their own thoughts, and broaden their interests. Caring families encourage exploring new ways of living that will offer the promise of enriching individual and family life. See 11-6.

Families in Crisis

All families have day-to-day problems, many with which they are able to cope or to solve. However, many families experience major problems that have a great effect on the people involved. These situations are **crises**. Family violence, child abuse and neglect, substance abuse, divorce, and suicide are realities faced by some families. These crises often affect the people involved in physical, social, and emotional ways. These crises are quite often

11-6 Even a happy change, such as a new baby, can be stressful to young children. They may handle the change better if their involvement is encouraged.

interrelated. For instance, substance abuse might be the cause of divorce. In other situations perhaps the opposite is true, with substance abuse being the outcome of divorce. Either way, the people involved are greatly affected. Crisis situations may also result in spin-off problems such as juvenile delinquency, runaway adolescents, teenage pregnancy, and criminal behavior.

An awareness of what family members often go through in a crisis can be a resource to you. This understanding can help prepare you to cope with a family crisis or to lend support to persons who may be experiencing a crisis. In addition, this understanding may influence you to set goals for yourself that can help you avoid or deal with these crises in your future.

Family Violence and Abuse

Statistics reveal that family violence, spouse abuse, and child abuse and neglect are major concerns in society. Some family members, mostly women and children, struggle to survive the harmful effects of the violence they encounter in their own homes. Although women and children are most often the victims of abuse, some men are abused as well. In recent years, elder abuse has been recognized as significant in family violence. Abuse can occur between parents and children, mothers and fathers, and among brothers and sisters.

Abuse can occur in many forms. Family violence, also referred to as **domestic violence**, indicates **physical abuse** of a family member. It may involve hitting, kicking, tripping, choking, biting, or threatening with a weapon. In some cases, physical abuse can result in serious injury or death. Many women endure spousal abuse because they think it is normal, having seen it in their childhood. Some are embarrassed, afraid, or too poor to leave home.

Emotional abuse is purposely harming the self-concept of a family member by insulting and undermining a person's

Use Your Reasoning Skills

List three crises with which you, your family, or your friends have had to deal. What resources were used at the time of the crises? What are several other possible resources that could have been used? Which resources would help most in dealing with the crises?

confidence. The abused individual may suffer personality changes. Most suffer low self-esteem.

Another form of family violence involves sexual abuse. **Sexual abuse** involves unwanted sexual contact.

Abuse has powerful effects on children and teenagers. **Child abuse** has been defined as the physical or mental injury, sexual abuse, negligent treatment, or maltreatment of a child under the age of 18. Apart from the physical pain that is obviously endured as a result of physical abuse, the psychological effects can be devastating. Abused children often feel worthless and unloved.

Sexual abuse can harm children physically and can cause emotional problems throughout life. Sexual abusers of children usually do not use force but instead gain the cooperation of children through bribes, threats, or use of their position of authority. In many cases, incest is involved. **Incest** is sexual activity between persons who are closely related.

In addition to physical, sexual, and emotional abuse, children can also be victims of neglect. **Child neglect** is failure to meet a child's physical or emotional needs.

Children suffer **physical neglect** if parents or persons legally responsible for them don't supply food, clothing, shelter, education, and medical care. Physical neglect can also occur without proper guidance and supervision. Children who are abandoned or left alone for long periods of time are also considered to be neglected.

Emotional neglect is the failure to provide children with love and affection. Like emotional abuse, it is difficult to identify but is acutely felt by the children and teenagers who are its targets. Some lifelong effects of emotional abuse and neglect may include depression, eating disorders, substance abuse, and difficulties with relationships and careers.

Family violence often occurs as families change and pressures and demands increase. Unemployment, alcoholism, or marriage pressures are examples of stress that can lead to abuse and neglect. Child abusers are often emotionally immature. They are often so concerned about their own needs that they neglect the needs of their children. Many child abusers were abused when they were children. They are not aware of any other way of acting. They tend to feel it is normal to vent their anger on children. Neglect of children may result when parents do not understand how to care for their children.

Substance Abuse

Substance abuse involves misusing drugs, including alcohol, to a potentially harmful level. Substance or drug abuse occurs when a person's mood is altered or his or her perceptions change. Substance abusers may lose control, lose their inhibitions, and not be able to distinguish between what is right and what is wrong. Sometimes they may become involved in physical and sexual abuse.

Substance abuse subjects all members of a family to constant stress and fear. To one degree or another, all members of a family are affected. Among families in which substance abuse exists, high rates of domestic violence, separation, divorce, and child neglect and abuse occur. The abuser may have trouble holding a steady job. Lack of work usually causes financial strain on the family. Sometimes loss of a job or family stress results in substance abuse.

Substance abusers not only harm their own lives, but also the lives of people around them. Family members, friends, neighbors, and coworkers are all affected. Substance abuse is also strongly associated with legal problems.

Divorce

In the United States, the incidence of divorce has grown to one divorce for every two marriages. **Divorce** occurs as a result of stress in various areas, such as tension in marriage, financial problems, family violence, and substance abuse.

Divorce often requires many adjustments for the family members involved. See 11-7. Because divorce usually involves strong emotions, adjustments are not easy. Some of the initial reactions to divorce are similar to the reaction to the death of a family member.

When divorce occurs, it is not unusual for children to feel embarrassment, disappointment, and anger because of the loss of their sense of security and well-being. Overeating or loss of appetite and poor school performance are common. Unfortunately, guilt is seen in children of all ages when their families separate.

11-7 **Parents may strive to spend more time with their children during a divorce, but adjustments are not always easy.**

Disagreements over the division of property and over child custody can add stress and affect each person involved. **Custody** is the assumption by a parent of the responsibility for the day-to-day decisions affecting the health, education, and welfare of the children. **Joint custody** means the parents share equally in the responsibility for the children, with each parent having equal rights in decision making and spending time with the children.

Divorce often results in economic pressures and strained relationships. When parents divorce, separate households are established. This can result in additional costs. Divorce can also affect relationships with extended family and friends.

Suicide

Suicide, the taking of one's own life, is one of the leading causes of death among young people. The impact on family, friends, and the community is one of great sadness, confusion, guilt, anger, and loss.

Although there is no single symptom or cause of suicide, some situations are likely to cause people to think about suicide. These include

- loss of a loved one
- a major disappointment or humiliation
- loss of job
- inability to compete
- lack of a stable family life

People thinking about suicide often send out many warning signals and clues that might allow others to save them. These include

- a change in personality such as sadness
- withdrawal from usual activities or a feeling of worthlessness
- changes in eating or sleeping habits
- decline in grades or job performance
- expressing thoughts of despair, death, or suicide
- putting affairs in order such as suddenly giving away possessions or discarding things
- suicide attempts

Communication is an important first step toward suicide prevention. Don't be afraid to talk to someone who is thinking about suicide. Remind him or her that even seemingly unsolvable problems can almost always be worked out. If someone you know exhibits any of the warning signals of suicide, especially over a period of days or weeks, seek professional help. Doctors, social workers, teachers, and clergy can be valuable sources of help. Local suicide crisis numbers can also be helpful in preventing suicide.

Brainstorming

Brainstorm a list of ways families help meet individual human needs. How does having these needs met help an individual develop? What can happen if these needs are *not* met through the family?

Resources for Families

When serious family troubles arise, help is often needed. Parents who are experiencing major problems need help, and children need protection and guidance. It is important to be able to reach out for help when it is needed. In crisis situations, both adults and children often feel alone. However, this is not the case. There are many people who not only understand their situations, but also can help and want to help. Talking with someone outside the family is often necessary. Someone who is not affected by the problem can often give a neutral viewpoint.

Children in families in crisis need to know they have a right to get help. They need to understand that help is available. Family doctors, religious leaders, teachers, school nurses, or guidance counselors may be able to provide assistance. Social workers, physicians, and the police often work together to help families in crisis.

The chart in 11-8 lists several community resources for families. Some of the resources listed are national organizations that may have local chapters. These resources are often called support groups. A **support group** is a group of people who share a similar problem or concern. In a support group, members can talk to other people who have similar problems. They can listen to and encourage one another as they learn how to cope with their problems. It is a good idea to become familiar with the support groups available in your community. You can do this by checking the phone book or contacting your local public library.

_Getting_Involved

Collect food, clothing, toiletries, toys, etc. to donate to a local community group such as a food pantry or homeless shelter that helps families in need or crisis. By doing this, how _are you_ acting as part of the family that benefits from your support?

Specific Organizations Aimed at Family Problems	
Organization	**Purpose**
Al-Anon	To help people whose lives have been affected by the alcoholism of a family member.
Alateen	To help teens deal with their parent's alcoholism.
Alcoholics Anonymous	To help people solve their problems with alcohol.
Alzheimer's Disease Support Group	To help family members of Alzheimer's Disease victims.
American Association of Suicidology	Supplies information about local specialists as well as educational materials.
Battered Women's Support Group	To help women who are victims of domestic violence.
Narcotics Anonymous	To help people seek ways to break their addictions.
Parents Anonymous	To help parents overcome abusive tendencies. (It offers a 24-hour telephone service, Heart Line, that provides information and counseling.)
Parents Helping Partners	To help families who have children with special needs (covers all handicapping conditions).
Parents Without Partners	To help meet individual needs of members of single-parent families.
Resolve	To help couples who are trying to become parents.
Tough Love	To help parents who are going through adjustment/addiction problems with their teenage children.

11-8 **These organizations can be valuable resources to families.**

32
31
30
29
28
27
26
25
24
23
22
21
20
19
18
17
16
15
14
13
12
11
10
9
8
7
6
5
4
3
2
1

Summary

Although the family has gone through many changes in the past century, the need for family survives. Most families meet basic human needs better than any other social institution.

The family can provide an environment that encourages human growth and development. The family can also meet basic human needs for love, acceptance, and self-worth. It can offer each member of the family respect and recognition from others. The family encourages growth and development of capabilities.

Caring families have certain characteristics. They are interdependent, responsible, and trustful. They show respect and concern for each other and openly express and accept feelings.

Within a family, members interact with each other to meet their goals. In a caring family, this interaction provides the support—the caring—that is important to each family member. Two valuable resources can help you promote a functional, caring family. They are an understanding of the importance of the family and knowledge of the characteristics of a supportive family.

Many families are struggling to survive the harmful effects of such crises as family violence, substance abuse, suicide, and divorce. Support groups have been developed to help people facing these crises. Understanding how these crises occur may influence you to set goals for yourself that can help you avoid or deal effectively with these crises in your future.

To Review

1. A _____ family consists of a married couple and their children if they have any.
2. A _____ family results when one adult lives with one or more children.
3. A _____ is formed when a single parent marries.
4. An _____ family is where several generations of a family live together under one roof.
5. Name four basic human needs that can be met by families.
6. True or false? Technological and social changes have affected the family very little.
7. List five characteristics of a functional family.
8. List a variety of resources, both human and nonhuman, that are shared by the family.
9. The part of open expression that involves letting others know how you feel about them and their behavior is called _____.
10. Describe three crises that can have major effects on a family.

To Do
with the Class

1. Debate the following statement: Some human needs are met even in families where a lot of conflict exists.
2. Investigate support systems for families that exist in your community. Report on the functions of these support groups.
3. Suggest ways to help a friend who is feeling stressed or experiencing a family crisis. What might you as supportive friends do or say to help?
4. Role-play real life scenarios where crises have occurred. Include strategies for successful use of resources.

To Do
with Your Community

1. Identify at least six resources within your community that can help families experiencing difficulties, stress, and/or crises.
2. Invite a person from the community to speak about how their group or organization helps families.
3. Invite a marriage counselor to talk about marital, family, and relationship stressors. Include strategies to deal with these and how to promote supportive, caring relationships.
4. Invite an intergenerational panel to compare and contrast causes of stress and coping strategies at various stages of the life cycle.

To Challenge
Your Thinking

1. List and describe some of the family forms that exist among people you know.
2. Ask five people of different ages to tell you how their family helps them meet goals.
3. Make a list of resources your family shares in your home.
4. Describe five specific incidents that show lack of respect among family members.

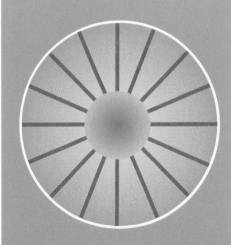

12

The Marriage Relationship

To Know

maturity
social maturity
emotional maturity
intellectual maturity
mature love
companionship
commitment
lifestyle

Objectives

After studying this chapter, you will be able to

◆ explain the factors that influence marital success.

◆ analyze the importance of mutual expectations in a marriage.

◆ recognize marriage adjustments commonly made throughout married life.

◆ explain the advantage of anticipating adjustments and of mutual efforts in solving problems.

Many books and articles suggest how to successfully choose a marriage partner. However, the divorce rate remains very high. No book can explain the "right" way to choose the person with whom you would like to spend the rest of your life. However, there are factors that seem to affect marital success. Being aware of these factors is helpful to a person considering marriage.

The husband-wife relationship does not continue throughout life the same as it was at the time of marriage. Times, circumstances, and people change. Both marriage partners must make continual adjustments to maintain this special relationship.

Factors Influencing Marital Success

In today's world, making a marriage succeed is challenging. See 12-1. A marriage has a better chance of being successful if both marriage partners are committed to that goal. Even then, marriage is a definite challenge to couples who share this commitment. Many now question whether young people today are as committed to the goal of a successful marriage as their grandparents were. People who are not committed are not likely to accept the challenges of marriage. Therefore, their marriage is less likely to succeed.

Certain personal characteristics of each person in a marriage may have a strong influence on that couple's ability to have a successful marriage. Being aware of these factors can help a couple assess their chances for reaching the goal of having a successful marriage.

12-1 **A successful marriage does not just happen. It requires hard work and patience.**

Maturity

Age and maturity are two different concepts. Some people are extremely mature when they are 20 years old. Other 20-year-olds are mature intellectually, but immature socially. Still other 20-year-olds are mature physically, but immature emotionally. By their late teens, most people are physically mature. Social and emotional maturity takes more time to develop as people have various life experiences.

Maturity indicates moving toward full development. Mature people have learned to be comfortable with themselves. They recognize their abilities and accept their shortcomings.

When you can accept yourself as you really are, you are more likely to be able to develop and maintain a relationship with another person. This is particularly so in a commitment such as marriage. You will find it difficult to respect, trust, and care for another person if you are not comfortable with yourself.

Social maturity indicates you have moved from a dependent self to a more independent self. You have become less self-centered and more concerned about others.

You are socially mature when you are sensitive to situations and feelings of others. Social maturity makes you aware of basic individual values such as self-respect and self-worth. A successful marriage requires sensitivity to another person's feelings.

Emotional maturity involves your ability to understand and control your emotions. It also involves being able to express your emotions, such as anger, in appropriate ways. Your feelings—your emotions—influence much of what you say and do. Therefore, your emotions are critical to the success of any interpersonal relationship.

Intellectual maturity refers to your ability to communicate, solve problems, and reason. It also includes your ability to learn from daily experiences and to adapt to new situations. These aspects of intellectual maturity are essential to a marriage.

The overall maturity of a husband and wife strongly influences their chances for a successful marriage. The more mature the couple are, the greater the chance their marriage will succeed. See 12-2. Marriages are most likely to succeed when both people have had ample time and experiences to mature. People who marry very young are less likely to have successful marriages.

Developing mature love is important when choosing a marriage partner. Often people confuse infatuation with mature love. When mature love exists, each person cares about the well-being of the other person. They realistically accept each other for their positive characteristics along with those that are not as desirable. **Mature love** is characterized by mutual trust—feelings of confidence and security in one another.

As the expression "opposites attract" indicates, people who have successful marriages often complement each other. When you experience mature love, you accept and recognize these differences as a resource for strengthening the marriage.

With immature love, you tend to try to change the other person to be more like yourself.

When you experience mature love, the other person becomes an extension of yourself. Marriage partners identify with each other as an extension of self. This identification and feeling of oneness occurs at times of achievement, sorrow, and happiness.

Cultural and Family Influences

Families and culture have a strong influence on values. Values related to race, religion, and education may influence marital success. Research also shows that values related to day-to-day rituals and experiences are extremely important. Values related to foods, holiday traditions, care of the home, and leisure activities can be significant in marital adjustment. To live together successfully, both husband and wife must accept some values that differ

Jeffrey Jordan Photography

12-2 Men and women who are mature when they marry are more likely to have successful marriages.

from their own. They must learn to communicate effectively to deal with the values they cannot accept.

Parental approval or disapproval is often a strong factor regarding marriage success. Two mature young people who are economically and emotionally independent from their parents will have a greater chance of success in marriage. Unhealthy dependency often strains the relationship between the couple and their parents. This also causes the marriage relationship to be strained.

Shared Interests

Companionship and friendship are vital ingredients in a successful marriage. Common social and recreational interests may develop before or after marriage. However, a marriage is likely to succeed when a couple has **companionship**—they share similar interests and enjoy doing activities together. See 12-3. In many successful marriages, husbands and wives say they are

12-3 **Having common interests and spending time together help "bind" a marriage throughout life.**

best friends. They have fun together and enjoy their special time together.

Having fun together is beneficial for married couples, but each couple's idea of fun is different. One couple may enjoy taking walks together while another couple may like golfing or bowling. Common interests are a strong bond that holds husband and wife together.

Mutual Expectations About Marriage

When two people are entering a marriage, sharing their expectations regarding their marriage is necessary. This point cannot be overemphasized. During this time of great social change and varying attitudes toward the marriage commitment, sharing expectations is even more important.

Expectations Related to Marriage as a Commitment

In the past, marriage was a permanent arrangement. Two people publicly agreed to live with each other for the rest of their lives. In today's changing world, the decision to marry is only one of several options. Whether or not a person stays married is also a matter of choice.

A **commitment** is similar to a pledge or a promise. Being committed to a marriage means promising to work to bind that marriage together. See 12-4. For people considering marriage, this is a key issue to discuss. When both partners agree that marriage is a lifelong commitment, the marriage is more likely to succeed. Marital adjustments would be very challenging if one partner believed in traditional commitment and the other partner saw marriage as only a temporary arrangement.

12-4 **Couples who have experienced a successful marriage over many years find the commitment is very worthwhile.**

Expectations Related to Roles

Male and female roles in marriage have greatly changed in recent years. Many of these changes have been influenced by the women's movement and the fact that more and more women are working. Today, both career and family role expectations vary.

Family roles have certainly changed. The stereotype of the father as patriarch and decision maker is no longer true in most families. Today, in most marriages, the husband and wife share more equally in decision making. The man of the house is not always the "breadwinner" today. Many women help support their families financially.

Families usually have certain expectations regarding roles related to daily living responsibilities. In the past, keeping house and raising the children were mainly the mother's responsibilities. Today, men assume many of these responsibilities.

Being open with each other about role expectations is important for two people considering marriage. When two people have different role expectations, problems arise. Both people need to make adjustments. Discussing role expectations prior to marriage will allow the couple to work out those adjustments then. Marriage results in many other normal adjustments that will be easier if role expectations are already established. In some cases, adjustments or compromises are not possible. Discovering this before marriage rather than after marriage creates fewer problems. See 12-5.

Expectations Related to Future Goals

Couples develop many common goals after their marriage. However, young people develop goals related to lifestyle, careers, and raising a family even before they meet a potential marriage partner. Attitudes toward these goals can affect the success of a marriage.

12-5 **Establishing roles early in a relationship helps a couple run a household in harmony.**

Lifestyle refers to the way you live your life. A couple's possessions and what they do create their pattern of living. Different types of people bring different lifestyles to mind. A business executive who commutes from a beautiful home in the suburbs to a large city has a certain lifestyle. A rural person who farms for a living has a different lifestyle. In some lifestyles, material possessions are very important. New experiences seem more important in other lifestyles. In still others, the opportunity to be creative and enjoy creativity are most important. No one lifestyle is right or wrong. However, two people who have very different lifestyle goals must be willing to adjust or marriage will be very difficult.

Lifestyle and career choices are closely related. Choosing to become a commercial airline pilot greatly affects your lifestyle. You will be away from your home and family for several days at a time. Many career choices have advantages and disadvantages that may affect a couple's happiness in marriage. A couple should openly discuss their own preferences for career choices.

In the past, lifestyle choices and career decisions centered around the husband. Today, both men and women may have careers. The compatibility of a couple's careers and future goals may certainly affect the success of the marriage. Each person should be well aware of their own and their potential partner's career expectations.

Past generations assumed that a couple would have children when they married. That is no longer the case. More couples are giving a great deal of consideration to the choice of whether to have a family. See 12-6. Through contraception and family planning, couples are able to make that choice and space their children as they choose. It is essential that couples discuss their views regarding children *before* marriage. Discussion of family size and ideas about discipline and child rearing will help a couple decide how compatible their viewpoints are.

12-6 **Compatible views on the training and guidance of children are important to a good marriage relationship.**

Mutual Adjustments in Marriage

All married couples make marriage adjustments throughout life. These adjustments may be caused by changes in circumstances or differences of opinion. Not all adjustments are caused by a conflict. Making marriage adjustments takes time and patience. When each marriage partner makes a conscious effort, problems can be solved to satisfy each of them.

Adjustments Early in Marriage

Certain adjustments are common to almost all couples early in their married years. These adjustments involve day-to-day situations caused by two people living together.

Brainstorming

Make a list of topics to discuss or decide on before marriage. Why do you think these should be discussed *before* a marriage takes place? What can happen if these discussions are delayed? Should some topics be discussed even before a relationship starts to become serious? Why?

Mutual openness is crucial in marriage. Openness helps newly married couples make the needed adjustments more easily. When marriage partners are open and honest from the very beginning, problems are less likely to build. Along with openness, mutual efforts based on respect, trust, and responsibility influence successful adjustment.

Consider what might happen if two newlyweds are not open with each other. Charlene, a newly married woman, is annoyed that her husband, Jim, leaves his dirty clothes all over the bedroom floor. Because they are newlyweds, Charlene decides not to say anything that might make Jim angry. She picks up his clothes and puts them where they belong.

Charlene is not being open with her husband. If she does this task over a long period of time, her anger will build and there will be a conflict situation. Charlene could have been honest and open if she had respectfully said, "I feel good when our bedroom is tidy, but all these clothes on the floor makes it look very messy." The responsibility would have been "thrown" to her husband, Jim. He would have responded with his feelings about the situation. Most people would assume that Jim would consider picking up his clothes his own responsibility. However, Jim's mother may have picked up his clothes for him throughout his growing-up years.

During that period of adjustments related to day-to-day living, acceptance and respect are also important. Two people who have done things their own way for years are now living together. Accepting new ways and respecting the other person's rights makes many adjustments easier. "That's not the way my mother did it" is an often quoted phrase early in marriage. However, the wise person remembers that there are many ways to reach a certain goal. That person is open and willing to consider alternatives. That person is even willing to accept a new way of doing something.

Successful division of responsibilities in a marriage is challenging. There is no easy formula to show who should do what. Ideally, decisions are made on the basis of openness, respect, and concern for each other. In some marriages, the husband works full-time and the wife works part-time. In this case, the wife is likely to assume more responsibilities in the home than her husband. However, if both husband and wife are working full-time, they probably share responsibilities at home more equally. An agreeable arrangement is based on each marriage partner's willingness to be open and to respect the other person's rights.

Problems develop when marriage partners do not settle on a division of responsibilities in the home that satisfies them both. Juanita works full-time and does the cooking, laundry, and most of the house cleaning. She does not want to complain to her husband, Jose, because he is paid much more than she. However, Juanita does admit to feeling bitter that Jose has so much time for relaxation and recreation. Juanita says she is too tired to enjoy what little free time she has. You may think that Jose should see that his wife assumes more than her share of their household responsibilities. However, Juanita is also at fault. In the beginning, Juanita could have openly

*Getting*Involved

suggested that Jose help with the household duties. Then Jose might have accepted his fair share of household responsibilities. Jose does not realize the amount of work Juanita does because he has not shared any of these responsibilities. Jose, as well as other family members, could help with some of the household tasks.

Couples make many adjustments during the early years of marriage. These adjustments involve the couple's social life, financial matters, and sexual life. Adjustments are more likely to be successful if each person is willing to openly and respectfully express concerns with each other. After identifying each problem, the couple can develop a goal toward which they can both work. Making successful adjustments gives couples a sense of satisfaction that can help strengthen their marriage relationship.

Adjustments Throughout Married Life

Although couples experience unanticipated adjustments throughout married life, specific stages in married life almost always require adjustments. Anticipating changes and adjustments makes problem solving easier. Identifying and planning for adjustment requires time and effort. However,

planning for adjustment is always better than looking back to see what you should have done.

The birth of the first child usually causes adjustments for both husband and wife. These adjustments are less traumatic if the couple has had enough time to make early marital adjustments. See 12-7. The birth of the first child, a joyous event in most families, brings many changes. The couple, who had only each other, now has another person with whom to share their lives. The birth of a child creates new responsibilities. Either the husband, the wife, or both of them must assume responsibility for the baby. Similar views on guidance and discipline of children are important to a good marriage relationship.

When a couple have children, they will experience many changes in their lives. During this time, they should make a special effort to strengthen their own relationship. Attending social and recreational activities together is a good way to do this. Couples face many challenges and adjustments as their children grow older. A strong marriage relationship is a resource that can make adjustments easier throughout the years.

12-7 The birth of a child is the beginning of many adjustments for a husband and wife.

When children leave home, further adjustments are usually required in husband-wife relationships. This adjustment is easier if husband and wife have developed and maintained a strong relationship beyond their children. However, when the children leave home, many couples must relearn being husband and wife. Because their lives have revolved around their children, they may have grown away from each other.

When either the husband or the wife retires, more adjustments must be made. If these adjustments are anticipated, they will not cause problems. However, retirement can be a difficult adjustment for a couple who has not planned for it. A man unprepared for retirement faces a great adjustment in his relationship with his wife. The wife may have plenty of activities to keep her busy and happy. Then her husband suddenly has nothing to do and demands most of her time. People who are involved in interests and activities beyond their occupation make these adjustments better. See 12-8. Planning ahead helps avoid these conflict situations.

12-8 Couples who have shared interests and activities for many years often adjust to retirement better than couples who have not.

32
31
30
29
28
27
26
25
24
23
22
21
20
19
18
17
16
15
14
13
12
11
10
9
8
7
6
5
4
3
2
1

Summary

Being aware of factors influencing husband-wife relationships is helpful to couples considering marriage. By understanding characteristics that influence success, couples can more accurately assess their chances for that success.

Being aware of common adjustments in marriage helps a couple prepare to solve those problems. By anticipating adjustments and making mutual efforts to resolve situations, the couple has a better opportunity for a successful marriage.

To Review

1. True or false? The husband-wife relationship continues throughout life the same as it was at the time of marriage.
2. _____ maturity indicates you have moved from a dependent self to a more independent self.
3. _____ maturity involves your ability to understand your feelings.
4. _____ maturity refers to your ability to communicate, solve problems, and reason.
5. List five characteristics of a mature person.
6. Describe what being committed to a marriage means.
7. Discuss what is meant by *lifestyle*.
8. Describe how a man and woman considering marriage might have different expectations regarding commitment, roles, and future goals.
9. What can newly married people do to make their marriage adjustments easier?
10. List two reasons why marriage adjustments may be necessary at each of the following stages of life:
    A. at the birth of the first child
    B. when children leave home
    C. at retirement

To Do
with the Class

1. Discuss the meaning of the following statement: A happy marriage is an accomplishment.
2. Listen to a panel of married people discuss adjustments in marriage.
3. Discuss the importance of long-range goals when considering marriage.
4. Discuss what is meant by a husband-wife relationship beyond the children.

To Challenge
Your Thinking

1. Write a report on two current articles relating to teenage marriage.
2. Think of some positive and some negative aspects of becoming a parent. How might these affect husband-wife relationships?
3. Research the causes of divorce by reading books and magazine articles on that topic. Describe how the causes of divorce relate to the factors that influence marital success.
4. Make a list of traits or qualities you would like in a potential marriage partner. Of those listed, which ones are compatible with your personal traits?

To Do
with Your Community

1. Ask married people to share what factors have helped or hindered their relationship as a couple.
2. Interview couples who have been married a number of years. Find out what they think are the factors that influence marital success. Prepare a summary of your findings.
3. Invite married couples to speak to the class about what makes marriage successful.
4. Invite family or marriage counselors to share their views, strategies, and advice on partner relationships.

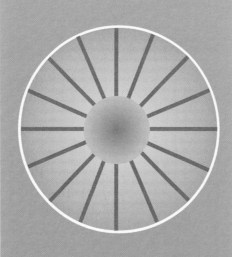

13 Parenting

To Know

parental responsibilities
physical needs
psychological needs
discipline
guidance
role model
independence
dependence
interdependence

Objectives

After studying this chapter, you will be able to

◆ describe responsibilities of parents to their children.

◆ explain how parental responsibilities influence the parent-child relationship.

◆ describe the stages of dependency children pass through as they mature.

Respect, trust, responsibility, and openness are just as important to parent-child relationships as they are to any other relationship. In addition to these factors, communication and conflict resolution skills are also needed to maintain a satisfying parent-child relationship.

The relationship between parents and their children is a unique one. Parents take on a huge responsibility when a child is born. They have such a strong influence on their children's development. In the parent-child relationship, there is also a constant struggle between independence and dependence.

Rewards of Parenting

Children bring a sense of fulfillment to a marriage. Most men and women want children. Parents want them to grow up strong and capable of dealing with the everyday world. Parents experience endless rewards as they watch and guide their children from birth through adulthood.

Responsibilities of Parenting

The quality of the parent-child relationship is extremely important. The quality of this relationship is largely determined by how well parents assume their parental responsibilities. When parents bring a child into the world, they automatically assume certain responsibilities. **Parental responsibilities** involve meeting basic physical and psychological human needs. Raising a child involves providing care, support, guidance, and education to lead that child toward maturity. Parents are the most important influence on a child's life. How well they assume these responsibilities has an enormous effect on the growth of a child's body and mind. See 13-1.

Recent findings on early brain development have great significance to parents and their responsibilities. This research shows that the way that parents relate and respond to their children directly affects brain development. Many basic activities, such as talking to infants, reading to them, and helping them play simple games, have lasting effects. Parents play the most important role in the nurturing and stimulation required for early brain development.

13-1 Parents who recognize the responsibilities of raising a child can better provide for the child's physical and mental health.

Meeting Physical Needs

Children depend on their parents to meet their **physical needs**—the needs for warmth, shelter, food, clothing, and safety. Infants develop a sense of trust as parents respond to these basic physical needs. Parents meet these needs by feeding the hungry baby, dressing the baby in warm clothes on a cold day, and giving the baby a place to sleep and play.

As children grow and mature, they learn how to meet some of their own physical needs by observing their parents. Housing, clothing, and furnishings selected by parents influence a child's future perceptions and expectations. The home acts as a small world to which the child relates.

Meeting Psychological Needs

Psychological needs relate to mental well-being and a sense of worth. Parents can meet the psychological needs of their children in a number of ways.

By Accepting and Respecting Each Child As a Worthwhile Individual

Children need to feel that they are accepted and valued as worthwhile individuals. One of the best ways parents can influence their children is to show the children they respect them and care about their feelings and opinions.

Parents may feel they accept their children. However, children may not feel accepted if their parents do not express this acceptance. Phrases such as "I see, " "I understand," or "I know what you mean" help the child feel this acceptance. Sometimes parents communicate acceptance through nonverbal clues such as a smile or a pat on the back.

Accepting the child does not mean accepting all the child's behavior. Parents can reject certain behaviors without rejecting the child as a person. They can communicate negative feelings about certain behaviors and still communicate that the child is valued. Young people need to know that their parents accept them and care about them, even when their actions are not acceptable. This reassurance helps young people grow toward maturity.

By Caring for the Child and Loving the Child

Children need to be cared for and wanted. Parents provide warmth, human closeness, pleasure, and tenderness. Infants feel this caring early in life as they react to the emotional atmosphere of the home.

Parents communicate caring to their children in many ways. First, they can give their children genuine attention. Caring parents provide for physical and psychological needs. They are available to their children and are willing to spend time listening and responding to them. See 13-2. All children, from infants to teens, need to know their parents care about them.

Kent Hayward

13-2 **As this mother and daughter spend time together playing tennis and sharing ideas and feelings, their mother-daughter relationship strengthens.**

From this caring evolves love. Children are born with the capacity to love. However, the ability to love is learned through experience. Parents greatly influence their child's ability to love.

By Helping Children Feel Good About Themselves

Children need to feel good about themselves. They need to have a sense of worth or self-esteem. This sense of self begins developing in infancy and is strongly influenced during the early developing years.

Parents strongly influence the development of a child's self-image. They can help a child develop self-esteem in many ways. By expressing encouragement and showing appreciation to a child, parents are contributing to the child's self-esteem. The child can assume responsibilities in the home. A child can also be included in family discussions and can help make family decisions. When children are raised in this type of atmosphere, they learn to think of themselves as separate and valuable family members.

By Providing Opportunities for the Child to Assume Responsibilities

Children have a healthier self-image and greater feelings of worth when their parents allow them to assume responsibilities. See 13-3. Parents should give their children responsibilities appropriate to each child's age and maturity. This helps children grow without becoming frustrated. Even the young toddler can be responsible for putting away toys and getting dressed. When parents do not allow their children to do things for themselves, those children are missing an important learning opportunity.

As children become teenagers, they can assume greater responsibilities. Teenagers are helped to mature by becoming responsible for their routine decisions and by realizing their own limitations. Wise parents allow their children to assume as much freedom and responsibility as they can handle.

By Providing Opportunity for Growth

Children have the right to grow physically, socially, emotionally, and intellectually. Effective parenting involves learning about children's needs, wants, and growth patterns in each of these areas.

Exposing children to many experiences helps them to grow and to develop a more complete self. They will understand more about people and the environment in relation to themselves. See 13-4. As children have new experiences, they discover special talents and abilities that parents can encourage them to develop.

By Transmitting Values and Character

Parents strongly influence their children's values through the atmosphere in their home. Consider the fact that all choices a person makes are based on his or her values. Therefore, having a large

13-3 **By helping his parents clean the garage, this young boy feels good about himself and assuming this responsibility.**

13-4 **By planning experiences for this young child to learn new things, this parent is providing opportunities for growth.**

influence on a child's values is an awesome responsibility. See 13-5.

Parents act as role models for all types of values. Values related to how people treat one another; values related to respect for individuals and life; and values related to caring, love, and affection are learned from parents.

Many of these values are related to the development of character. When parents help children recognize the importance of their decisions, they encourage the development of skills that will serve children all through their lives. Major decisions are those that involve trust, respect, responsibility, fairness, caring, and good citizenship.

By caring for one another and spending time together, families reinforce the value of the family. When parents consciously plan for leisure time together with their family and include their children in the planning, family relationships are strengthened and enriched. When the family attends sporting events or concerts in which one of the children is participating, it shows they value that child. Sharing their pride as a family strengthens their family relationship.

13-5 **These parents have transmitted their value of education by encouraging and supporting their daughter.**

Brainstorming

Brainstorm a list of problems that occur as adolescents become independent. These problems may relate to the teenager's room, the way he or she looks or dresses, the use of the telephone, household chores, television privileges, or other problem situations. What do these situations have to do with independence? How can teenagers use these problems to promote their independence instead of limit it?

By Guiding and Disciplining

Children need understanding and guidance to help them grow. When children are born, they cannot take care of themselves. They are completely dependent on their parents. **Discipline** is a process aimed at self-control and self-direction. Discipline guides children in the direction of independence and self-discipline. **Guidance** is all the words and actions used to influence a child's behavior. Every child is unique and needs a special kind of guidance. A wise parent considers a child's age, personality, and temperament differences in guiding that child.

Effective guidance and discipline helps children develop a sense of right and wrong. Parents define the boundaries and establish limits to help children learn appropriate behaviors. Limits that are clearly defined and consistently maintained give children a sense of security and direction. Limits provide structure; they are not a penalty. Limits must be clearly stated so the child understands what conduct is unacceptable. If limits are unclear, children have more difficulty making decisions related to those limits.

Children learn acceptable social behaviors, referred to as *etiquette*, through parental guidance. By learning and practicing social skills, children become more self-confident. An example of such social skills are table manners. A child's knowledge of good table manners will allow him or her to relax and enjoy eating with others rather than feeling anxious about doing something wrong. This becomes important in adolescence in relation to boy-girl relationships and continues throughout life as people are judged by their actions.

Parental guidance in developing skill in coping with stress is also important to the child's growth. Understanding how to confront and cope with stress is a valuable resource for everyone. These skills will be learned largely through the parents' actions as they serve as role models. A **role model** is a person who, through his or her actions, affects the attitude and actions of another person.

The parental role changes as a child matures and becomes more independent. Parents provide teenagers with less structure and limits and become more of a consultant. They help their children reason and volunteer opinions about possible consequences. See 13-6. Teenagers go to their parents to discuss problems rather than to be told how to solve them. The support and guidance a parent can offer in these situations is helpful in further strengthening the parent-child relationship.

By Encouraging Independence

Parents can encourage independence by helping their children experiment and develop their unique capabilities. Children have many opportunities to function independently as they grow. They have these opportunities in schoolwork, in relationships with peers, and in money matters.

Independence means not requiring or relying on the help of others. Poor choices may be made, but children learn a lot through their own mistakes. Sometimes overprotective parents interfere with their

13-6 As children grow, a parent's role regarding guidance also changes.

children's decision making, making the decisions themselves. These parents do not realize the importance of letting their children fail. When children always succeed as a result of parental interference, they have trouble accepting failure when it does occur. When children are not allowed to be independent, they are robbed of their security and self-confidence.

Consider a boy who is always reluctant to do his homework. His parents help him with it and must coax him to do it daily. They repeatedly remind the boy to take the homework back to school the next day. Although the boy is completing his

Use *Your* Reasoning Skills

Think of common examples of unrequested advice and attention parents give teenagers. How does this advice and attention affect the way teenagers assume responsibilities? Why might parents give unrequested advice? What might this indicate about the way parents learned to assume responsibility?

*Getting*Involved

homework, he is not learning independence. One day, the boy's parents do not remind him to do his homework, so he forgets about it. The next day his teacher may discipline him in some way for failing to complete the assignment. Only after this kind of experience does the boy learn to do his homework without his parents' coaxing and assistance. After doing his schoolwork independently, the boy will gain new confidence in his own ability.

Changes in Dependency

Everyone is aware of the struggle that goes on between parents and their children. Parents want to guide and control, while children want to be independent and make their own choices. Understanding this struggle and knowing it is normal can make it less threatening to relationships.

Dependence

When you cannot take care of your own needs, you depend on others to help you. **Dependence** means relying on others to satisfy your needs.

Children move away from total dependence. They do this by gradually assuming responsibility for themselves.

During the teen years, the desire for independence is very strong. Even so, teenagers are still quite dependent on their

parents for basic needs such as food, clothing, and shelter. There is also a dependency for psychological needs. Love, encouragement, and guidance from parents help children grow toward independence and maturity.

Dependence is not a negative characteristic. It becomes negative only when it prevents children from maturing and learning to function effectively on their own.

Independence

The desire for independence begins in early childhood. Early in life, children want to take care of themselves and make their own decisions. They want to stop relying on others to satisfy all their needs. A wise parent will encourage this independence.

There is often a period of strain during the teen years when the desire for independence is quite strong. Teenagers are struggling to establish their own identities and become independent of their parents. See 13-7. At times, teens may resent their parents' advice because of their strong desire to be self-sufficient.

Independence is a necessary step in development. When young adults become independent, they are able to make choices based on what they feel is right and wrong. As they establish this independence, there may be a period of withdrawal and

Mark Felstehausen

13-7 **Being able to drive gives teenagers a feeling of great independence.**

separation from their parents. This allows the young adult to assess his or her ability to be independent. To become fully mature, young people must separate from their parents both physically and emotionally.

Interdependence

A caring family recognizes the importance of mutual trust, responsibility, and openness. A healthy atmosphere exists in this type of family. In this atmosphere, there is a balance between dependence and independence. This desirable relationship is called **interdependence**. Interdependence indicates working together and sharing each other's resources. A sense of give-and-take exists, yet family members maintain their own identities. Interdependence is a balance between freedom and responsibility.

Mutual Respect

The foundation for interdependence is mutual respect. When parents respect their children and children respect their parents, wholesome growth takes place. In addition, children's self-respect grows when they are shown respect by people who are important to them. See 13-8. Children learn to respect others when their parents respect their ideas and opinions. Children observe how their parents respond to each other and learn from their behavior. Parents teach their children respect through the way they lead their own lives and by the way they deal with their children.

Mutual Trust and Responsibility

Maturity and wise judgment come to children as they learn to make decisions and profit from those experiences. Unfortunately, parents often have difficulty trusting a child to make wise decisions in new situations. Parents who attempt to protect their children from mistakes by making decisions for them are only keeping their children from learning.

When children make their own decisions, they learn to accept the consequences of those decisions. Eventually, children develop skill in making choices and learn to trust their own judgment. If a child's parents permit this learning to take place, they learn to trust the young person. Parents and children develop a mutual trust for one another. This trust can guide that child through difficult times in growing up.

When mutual trust and respect exist in a parent-child relationship, openness is not a problem. Anything can be freely discussed. Openness gives children the confidence to seek their parents' opinion and guidance. The children know their parents will respect them and will not laugh at them. This allows children to learn from their parent's experiences and knowledge. An atmosphere of openness encourages mutual support and helps avoid anger, rebellion, and depression.

13-8 **This father and son have a close relationship based on mutual respect. Each person cares for the other and his interests.**

32
31
30
29
28
27
26
25
24
23
22
21
20
19
18
17
16
15
14
13
12
11
10
9
8
7
6
5
4
3
2
1

Summary

The type of environment parents create in their home has an enormous effect on their children and on parent-child relationships. Parents have the responsibility to meet their children's basic physical and psychological needs.

Basic relationship skills are as important to parent-child relationships as they are to other relationships. The changes in dependency in the parent-child relationship create a challenge that does not exist in other relationships. Understanding this challenge may help you understand yourself and your relationship with your parents.

To Review

1. In the parent-child relationship, there is a constant struggle between _____ and _____.
2. Name four ways parents might meet an infant's physical needs.
3. List six psychological needs of a child and describe a situation for each that illustrates a parent meeting these needs.
4. As children mature, they gradually assume responsibility for some of their own needs and become less _____ on their parents.
5. Parent-child relationships may be strained during the teen years when teenagers try to establish their identity and become _____ of their parents.
6. True or false? Dependency is always a negative characteristic.
7. True or false? When you are independent, you have the ability to make your own choices based on what you feel is right or wrong.
8. Give an example of respect being shown a child by a parent.
9. Give an example of respect being shown a parent by a child.
10. _____ is a balance between freedom and responsibility.

To Do
with the Class

1. Discuss the meaning of the following: People may be directly affected by decisions made by others.
2. Discuss instances when dependence is appropriate and instances when it becomes harmful to a person.
3. Discuss ways that children, even as married adults, may be dependent on their parents.
4. Form two groups. Let one group represent parents and the other group represent children. Work in pairs—one "parent" with one "child." Have each person indicate how he or she can show respect, trust, responsibility, and openness to the other.

To Challenge
Your Thinking

1. Make a list of ways a parent might help a child become more self-sufficient.
2. List aspects of daily living in which most teenagers are independent. Then list other aspects in which teenagers are dependent.
3. Make a list of ways parents can help children feel good about themselves.
4. Talk with people outside the class about responsibilities they were expected to assume during their childhood and teenage years. Share your findings with others in the class.

To Do
with Your Community

1. Ask a panel of parents to share with your class the responsibilities of parenting.
2. Invite persons in careers dealing with children, such as a pediatrician, counselor, police officer, or social worker, to share their views about the challenges of raising responsible children and how their job is important to families in today's society.
3. Find a single parent or new parents and offer to help babysit to encourage time out for the parents.
4. Investigate to find what support groups for parenting there are in your community.

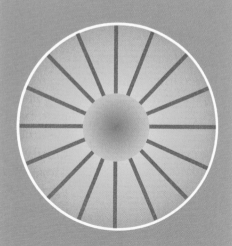

14 Family Management

To Know

family management
family composition
family life cycle
role expectations
concession
family management tasks

Objectives

After studying this chapter, you will be able to

◇ explain the factors that affect family management.

◇ list the steps in family decision making.

◇ describe challenges to making family decisions.

◇ recognize the importance of sharing family responsibilities.

◇ discuss guidelines for sharing family responsibilities.

Family management occurs when members of a family help make choices and assume responsibilities for the group. Each family member can help a family function more successfully. The family is an interdependent group. You will understand how each family member can affect family management after studying three areas:

- factors that affect family management
- the importance of skill in family decision making
- ways of sharing family management responsibilities

Factors Affecting Family Management

Families are made up of individuals who have unique values. These individuals form family values, goals, and resources. Because each family's values and goals differ, each family approaches management tasks differently. However, many factors other than values, goals, and resources also affect the way a family manages.

Family Composition

Family composition, the number of people in the family and the spacing in age of the children, influences family management. See 14-1. A larger family requires more resources for daily living than a smaller family. However, the human resources available increase because there are more people to help with tasks.

The spacing in age of the children influences management of the family. Even a young child can assume simple management responsibilities. An older child can help the family by assuming increasing responsibilities.

The Family Life Cycle

Families go through basic stages as they grow and develop. These stages are often referred to as the **family life cycle** and are the result of changes occurring in family structure and composition. Each stage produces varying demands on family resources.

14-1 **Effective family management is always a challenge. This is especially true in a family with four active children.**

Beginning Stage

A couple is in the beginning stage when they make a commitment to marriage and establish a home. During this time, household routines and habits are developing as the couple adjusts to their life together. They develop habits in communication that will greatly affect how they manage their lives.

Expanding Stage

The family moves into the expanding stage after their first child is born. The addition of the first child and others in the future requires many adjustments. Goals involving the responsibilities of parenthood now become an important focus, resulting in changing demands on time, energy, finances, and freedom. These changes will affect the couple's relationship, social life, and work. Material goods begin to accumulate during this period, resulting in additional household management demands.

Developing Stage

The management emphasis during this stage is on meeting needs related to personal growth, interpersonal relationships, and education as related to the expanding world of school-age children. Child care and shared responsibility in the home are often the major challenges of this stage. School, social activities, and clothing needs increase the challenge of managing time, energy, and finances. Often, both parents find it necessary to be employed during this period.

Contracting Stage (Launching Stage)

The family moves into the contracting stage when the first child leaves home for college, the military, a job, or marriage. Family expenses usually become less challenging as children begin to support themselves, although providing care of aging parents may occur during this stage.

When the children are gone, the couple again are independent. Now that their time is no longer focused on rearing children, they often turn to other activities. Their management emphasis changes as they plan more for retirement and later years.

Later Years (Aging Stage)

This stage is greatly influenced by income and health. The death of one spouse leaves the surviving spouse to make major adjustments. Often, changes in living arrangements are necessary. Much of what occurs at this stage is largely dependent on earlier stages.

Family Stability

Family stability affects managerial actions and behavior. If family members cooperate with one another, they are more likely to reach their goals. The type of relationship the husband and wife have developed in their marriage greatly influences family management. Couples who have a positive relationship and communicate openly help the family succeed in reaching their goals. In contrast, reaching family goals will be more difficult for couples who have a strained, angry relationship.

Each family member can influence management outcomes by thinking of the family as a team. Ideally, each person assumes the responsibility of working for the well-being of the others. Therefore, family members work together to achieve family goals.

Role Expectations

Role expectations are behaviors expected in certain positions of responsibility. Roles differ from person to person and from family to family. Each person has different role expectations for a parent, wage earner, and homemaker. See 14-2. Families manage better when roles are clear and family members have similar role expectations.

Change in Family Circumstances

Many events and conditions occur that are beyond the control of the family. Uncontrollable events may change management patterns by making demands on

Management Skills

Families who develop management skills have more influence and control over the events in their lives. See 14-3. Family management is challenging. In addition to managing their own lives, family members also help manage the family as a group. Managerial action takes place at the same time on two different levels.

Understanding values is an important management skill. When families understand their values, they can make choices directed toward their goals—goals based on their values. When resources are limited, families, as well as individuals, must set priorities. Setting priorities is challenging in family management because several people are involved. However, setting family management priorities is less difficult when family members have respect and consideration for one another.

Families develop standards through effective communication and mutual understanding. These standards serve as

14-2 **Role expectations are changing in today's world. More men are involved in nurturing their children, and more women are involved in careers that have been traditionally male.**

family resources. For instance, a recession may force a family who has been living well, buying both needs and wants, to decrease their spending. Family crises, such as the death of a family member or divorce, are two events that cause many changes for the family.

Effective family management requires:
• understanding values
• setting priorities
• communicating effectively
• having flexible standards
• using resources wisely
• having organizational skills
• managing time and energy
• having decision-making and problem-solving skills

14-3 **Effective family management requires a cooperative effort from all family members.**

accepted levels of performance, which guide the behavior of family members. A wise family develops flexible standards. No single standard is suitable for all situations, people, or families.

The family uses its resources to help reach goals. Families can more easily reach these goals by becoming aware of their existing resources and resources they might develop. Each person in the family has personal resources that can contribute to family management. Because most resources are limited, careful use of family resources is important.

Organizational skills are management skills that involve the conservation of time and energy. You can conserve time and energy by planning carefully and simplifying work procedures. By planning ahead and anticipating problems, families will be more organized.

Effective family management requires a positive attitude, an openness to change, and a desire for improvement. Learning to change problems into goals, accepting the certainty of change, and being motivated toward accomplishing goals are examples of these skills.

Decision-making and problem-solving skills are essential for effective management. They are two of the major resources in family management.

Family Decision Making

Decision making is a basic activity of the family group. It is often used to solve problems. Problem solving involves discovering the problem and clearly identifying it. After the problem is identified, it can be changed to a goal. The decision-making process is used to decide how to reach that goal.

There are five steps in the decision-making process:

- identifying the problem or the need for a decision

- considering all possible alternatives
- recognizing the consequences of each alternative
- choosing the best alternative
- evaluating the decision and the process

Not every decision made within the family needs to be a group decision. Many decisions are simple and do not require group discussion. Other decisions are more complex and may involve a high degree of risk. These decisions may have serious consequences. Because of this, family members who have the experience and knowledge to make the best decision usually make complex decisions. In a caring family, decisions and the reasons for the decisions are often shared with younger, less experienced members of the family.

Caring families approach decision making by discussing issues with all members of the family. The preferences of each family member are heard and acknowledged. The advantages and disadvantages of each alternative are considered. Then the group tries to find the most acceptable solution.

Caring families make a definite effort to involve all family members in the decision-making process. Family members differ widely in knowledge and life experiences. However, each family member can be involved in the decision-making process in some way.

Family members can express their preferences freely in an open, caring family. The family respects each person's opinion. The caring family focuses on what is appropriate and best for all.

Taking part in effective family decision making is a valuable experience. Being able to speak your own opinion and know you will be listened to with respect helps build self-confidence. See 14-4. Family decision making also helps develop your own decision-making ability.

Challenges of Family Decision Making

Family decision making is challenging because the family is made up of many personalities. Each person has unique values and goals that influence each step of the decision-making process.

Making decisions may be difficult when family members are not considering the same values. Consider the following situation. Mrs. Esparsa announces that her Uncle Carlos will be in town on Saturday

M. Bruce

14-4 One way young children can learn decision-making skills is to be involved in making shopping decisions.

night. She would like each family member to spend some time with him. Mr. Esparsa cringes because his favorite football team is on television that night and he wants to watch the game. Their daughter, Maria, has already accepted a date with a boy she has wanted to go out with for months.

Juan, their son, planned to meet some friends and practice basketball since tryouts are next week. Each person sees the problem in a different way and would probably state the problem in terms of their own values.

The Esparsa's challenge is to identify the real problem and turn it into a goal. After discussion, the Esparsa family might decide the problem is rather simple. Uncle Carlos is going to be there, and everyone except mother has other plans. Their goal might be to work out a plan that would allow each person to spend some time with Uncle Carlos and also continue with their own plans.

The family may choose to decide on possible alternatives together. In other instances one or two family members might identify alternatives and let others respond to them. There is no reason to limit the number of alternatives. Creative thinking may bring up new ideas that are much better than the first two.

There is often no "right" choice in family decision making. Family members negotiate as they consider the various alternatives. They work together to find the best solution to the problem. Often they have to compromise. A compromise occurs when family members give up some things in order to reach the best decision. The final solution contains some of each of their views.

For instance, in the example of the Esparsa family, Uncle Carlos is coming to visit and they must choose the best alternative. The Esparsas may plan to have dinner together at home. They could work out their schedules so each family member would have time for a visit with Uncle Carlos.

Father might compromise by not watching the entire football game. Juan might compromise by cutting down on his basketball practice time. Maria might compromise by postponing her date until later in the evening. Although Mother would like to have the family home all evening, she decides this plan will work the best for the family. In her way, she compromises.

Unfortunately, not all family decisions work out so smoothly. A compromise is not always possible. Sometimes a **concession** must be made—one family member must give in completely. For instance, that is true in this situation involving financial resources.

Cheri Little's family planned to get her a new coat in November. Cheri had grown several inches in the last year and her present coat was short on her. However, there was trouble with the family car early in November. The mechanic said the car had to be fixed or it would be damaged more. After thinking about alternatives for solving this problem, the family came to a decision. Compromise was not possible. The car would have to be fixed, and Cheri would have to wait for a new coat. Cheri would have to make a concession.

Each family member agreed that they needed to use the family car more than Cheri needed a new coat. Cheri's father suggested they look over the family budget. Maybe Cheri could buy her coat on sale after Christmas. All family members must make sacrifices at one time or another. A caring family considers these sacrifices when making future family decisions.

Family decision making requires give-and-take because the decisions may not please everyone in the group. However, decisions are more likely to be supported if family members are able to voice their feelings and choices. In group decision making, as in family decision making, it is important that each person understand the basic problem. Each person should then have the opportunity to voice his or her opinions regarding possible solutions. Family

members are more committed to the family's goals if they are involved in the decision-making process.

Sharing Family Management Responsibilities

One of the basic human needs is for a feeling of self-worth. Each person needs to feel valued as an individual. One of the most natural ways this need can be met is by accepting responsibilities within the family. See 14-5. Each family member can contribute to the good of the family. Family members

14-5 Oftentimes family responsibilities are more enjoyable when they are shared.

of all ages, except very young children, can make some type of contribution.

Parents can begin encouraging a sense of individual responsibility in their children as soon as possible. Children often do not assume responsibilities because they are not given the chance. In a caring family, human growth and development is valued. Each family member assumes responsibilities that will help develop the skills needed for daily life. A child gains a feeling of self-confidence by assuming responsibility and accomplishing a task. When a child repeats a task, that child develops greater skill and becomes a more self-confident person.

Young adults often move into their first apartment and realize they know very little about preparing their own food. Young people might easily acquire food preparation skills during their childhood and teenage years. In this way, they would be gaining skills as well as assuming family responsibility. Assisting in food preparation is a good way to contribute to the good of the family. See 14-6.

Sharing family management responsibilities is equally as important for parents and older adults. These people might one day become widows, widowers, or single parents. If they have shared in family management responsibilities, making adjustments to living alone again will be less difficult.

Family Management Tasks

Family management tasks include all activities that contribute to the well-being of the family. These activities range from simple to complex. Family management tasks include activities related to preparation, serving, and storage of food; care of clothing; care of the home; and selection of consumer goods and services. Each of these areas involves tasks that can be performed by family members of varying ages and abilities. See 14-7.

Denise Riehle

14-6 Food preparation skills can be learned during the teenage years.

14-7 Young children can learn to do many management tasks.

Family management tasks offer opportunities for brothers, sisters, and parents to share work in a cooperative way. This kind of sharing can increase the bonds between family members and can help the group feel more unified. Sharing promotes give-and-take in planning and trying out new ideas and methods. It provides experience in negotiation—working with one another to resolve a matter. Sharing family management tasks can be a valuable growth experience.

Guidelines for Sharing Family Responsibilities

The emotional tone associated with the delegation and division of family responsibilities is very important. See 14-8. Ideally, family members see assuming these responsibilities as a team effort. When this happens, each family member feels responsible for the other members of the group. When the emotional tone is "right," there are fewer feelings of frustration and anger associated with certain tasks. Each family member's attitude is key to the successful sharing of family responsibilities.

It is important that children be given realistic responsibilities. People feel a sense of well-being and accomplishment after successfully completing a task. However, giving a family member a task that is too difficult may cause frustration and failure. Family members need guidance in how to do specific tasks. See 14-9. Even though a task may have been performed in the home for years, some family members do not know how to perform that task. Flexibility is an important aspect of guidance because there are many ways to perform a particular task. Because people are different, their methods may also differ, but the completed task will have similar results.

Guidelines for Sharing Family Responsibilities

- Develop a team effort attitude in assuming responsibilities.

- Give family members realistic responsibilities.

- Guide family members in doing tasks.

- Be flexible.

- Develop mutual standards.

- Avoid sexist division of responsibilities.

14-8 Following these guidelines will help family members have a positive attitude toward sharing family responsibilities.

Courtesy of Hercules, Inc.

14-9 This girl is expected to feed the family dog regularly. She needs to know when the dog should eat and how much food the dog should be given.

Use Your Reasoning Skills

Consider how lack of organization or poor management can cause friction in family life. In contrast, how can organization help promote family relationships? Why is this the case?

Sharing family responsibilities is easier if family members agree on the standards of a completed task. Negative feelings may result unless there is some agreement on standards. For instance, Mrs. Wilson may suggest to her son, Daniel, that he clean his room. Daniel's idea of a clean room may differ greatly from Mrs. Wilson's standards. She may mean picking up, making the bed, dusting, and vacuuming. Daniel may feel his room is clean when the clothes are picked up and the bed is made. If Daniel cleaned according to his standards, he would be satisfied with the result, but his mother would be disappointed. If Daniel and his mother had agreed on standards for a clean room, each would have been more satisfied with the end result.

Standards for young children often have to be relaxed to gain overall cooperation. Performing tasks for the first time or performing more complex tasks may be very challenging to children. When children perform a task, the results do not always meet the agreed-on standards. However, the child still knows the satisfaction of accomplishing the task if that child tried to do it well. See 14-10. This gives the child the security of having performed the task once and being able to do it again. A child has more positive feelings about the experience if the child is not reprimanded for being less than perfect. A caring parent praises the child for the effort. In a respectful way, the parent can also suggest ways for the child to do it even better the next time.

Kent Hayward

14-10 **Flexible standards are important when children are learning to do a task for the first time.**

Caring parents will avoid sexist division of responsibilities with adult members of the family as well as with children. It is as important for males to be able to prepare food as it is for females to be able to handle the financial records and pay bills. Because of past habits, many parents find this difficult. It seems natural to ask the daughter to dry the dishes and the son to shovel the snow. However, there is no reason why these tasks should not be reversed.

Assuming Management Tasks

Each family has its own way of deciding which family members will assume various tasks. What works for one family may not be successful for another. The entire procedure, including deciding on the responsibilities to be assumed, agreeing on standards, and dividing the various tasks, has a great impact on the attitudes of each of the family members. See 14-11.

Caring families decide on the division of responsibilities through discussion. They consider the feelings and needs of each person and of the family as a unit. When people agree to obligations in advance, they react more favorably than when they are suddenly told to do something.

Some families like to have a specific meeting time, such as Sunday evening, when tasks can be discussed and divided. See 14-12. Other families may set aside a particular time, such as Saturday morning, as "work time." During this time, everyone pitches in to get their jobs done. Some families may discuss these concerns at mealtime.

Families may make a list on the bulletin board and have family members sign up for various tasks.

Because personalities, needs, and resources differ, each family has to create a system of managing family responsibilities that is best for them. In a caring family, management is everyone's responsibility. Children benefit when their parents allow them to assume more responsibilities as they mature. By giving children responsibilities, parents are helping their children grow toward independence, teaching them to be assertive, but cooperative. Some children are not given the opportunity to assume responsibilities. These children often grow into immature young adults who cannot cope with the responsibilities of adulthood.

14-11 **When family members share tasks, they learn to appreciate the skill involved in doing that task well.**

14-12 **Having a schedule of responsibilities often works very well with younger children.**

Summary

Many factors affect family management. These factors include the size of the family, their stage in life, their stability, their role expectations, and other special family circumstances. The more management skills a family develops, the more family members can control their lives.

Families depend on each family member to function successfully. By assuming management responsibilities in the family, family members gain a feeling of self-worth and a sense of responsibility. It provides the opportunity to work cooperatively with others. These experiences allow family members to learn and practice skills they will use throughout life.

To Review

1. Name four factors that affect family management.
2. Identify the stages of the family life cycle.
3. How can the type of relationship the husband and wife have developed in their marriage influence family management?
4. List six ways families can manage more effectively.
5. A challenge of solving family problems is to identify the _____ and turn it into a _____.
6. True or false? Every family decision should be a group decision.
7. True or false? With many family decisions, there is often a "best" decision rather than a "right" decision.
8. Describe a basic need you can satisfy by assuming responsibilities in the home.
9. Sharing family responsibilities is easier if family members agree on the _____ of a completed task.
10. Describe four guidelines for sharing family responsibilities.

To Do with the Class

1. Develop a questionnaire to interview men and women in different stages of the family life cycle. Identify demands on time during the different stages of the family life cycle. Ask questions such as:
A. What are your most time-consuming family responsibilities?
B. How are homemaking responsibilities divided among family members? Conduct several interviews and discuss your results with the class.
2. Select a partner and pretend you are a couple deciding whether the wife should accept employment outside the home. Bring out management adjustments you must make and satisfactions you anticipate.
3. How might a family member create conflict by performing a task that is intended to help the family? Consider what might happen if that person did not act according to the standards of other family members. Discuss how these situations might be avoided.
4. Read the following sentence and discuss its meaning: Happy people are people whose circumstances are good in relation to the standards they set for themselves.

To Challenge Your Thinking

1. Identify resources that are available at each stage of the family life cycle. When is each resource likely to be most plentiful and least plentiful? How does resource availability affect family goals?
2. How do young children benefit by sharing responsibilities in the home?
3. Make a list of home management tasks. Do certain family members usually perform certain tasks? Why? Discuss with others in the class.
4. What strategies does your family use to manage daily living?

To Do with Your Community

1. Identify resources and organizations in your community that help manage or influence family decisions.
2. Interview several families and find out their "secrets" to successful family management. Report your findings to the class.
3. Select a local business. Compare the similarities and differences of that business to one's family management and success. Invite an employee from your selected business to share his or her management strategies.
4. When families encounter management problems or are faced with decisions that require outside help, what are the most likely resources accessed within the community?

15

Combining Family and Workplace Roles

To Know

dual-career families
children in self-care
flextime
flexplace
job sharing
maternity leave
paternity leave
Family Medical Leave Act
Pregnancy Discrimination Act
Child and Dependent Care Tax Credit
family child care
hotlines
bartering

Objectives

After studying this chapter, you will be able to

- describe trends related to family and work.

- identify ways family and work influence each other.

- explain ways that employers, governments, and communities are responding to family needs.

- describe skills helpful in successfully combining family and workplace roles.

The last 20 years have brought dramatic shifts in both the American family and the American workplace. Traditionally, the "man of the house" provided the financial support for the family. The woman's role was to maintain the home and nurture the children. She was to be available to meet the family's needs. In the workplace, employees were expected to make work their first priority even if at the expense of personal and family concerns.

We are now in a time of transition. Women make up an increasingly larger portion of the workforce, and this trend is expected to continue. See 15-1. As a result, more children now live in families where both parents work. More children are also being raised by single parents who must work to provide for the family. The impact of these changes on the family and the workplace is enormous. The challenge of successfully combining work and family roles is complex. However, individuals, employers, and governments all will profit from having productive workers and healthy families.

Trends–Family and Work

An understanding of the trends related to family and work will help you better understand those who are faced with the dual challenges of family and work roles.

Why People Work

Most mothers and fathers work because of economic necessity. They wish to assure financial stability for their children and themselves. Maintaining a family is expensive, and in today's world, it often takes two incomes to do so.

Many divorced, single, and widowed parents must work to avoid poverty. With the divorce rate so high, a person who cannot earn his or her own living is at risk. It is not only divorce that puts an income at risk, but also illness, financial setbacks, accidents, and death.

Although most people in the labor force work primarily because their families need the money, there are other reasons as well. Many people work for their own personal self-actualization, 15-2. Careers can satisfy emotional and psychological needs for people. These persons find that productive work through employment is fulfilling and makes them happier. Many people work because they enjoy the challenge and stimulation. Their work fascinates them. For some people, work is important to their sense of identity. It gives them feelings of status and prestige.

15-1 The large proportion of women in the workforce has had a great effect on society.

15-2 Having a job is satisfying to many women for a variety of reasons.

Work gives many women a greater sense of independence than they experience as wives and mothers. They want to establish a part of themselves as separate from their husbands and children. There are more jobs open to women now than there were 30 years ago. Education offers greater possibilities for women in choosing careers.

Who Is Working?

Today's workforce is comprised of both men and women, with women making up almost half of the labor force. More than half of all married women with children under age six are employed. Fewer than 10 percent of families consist of the traditional unit of a married couple with children in which the husband is the sole provider.

The proportion of households headed by a single adult, usually the mother, has also increased sharply. An increasing number of single mothers are working full-time.

There is also an increasing number of *stay at home dads*. In this type of family, the roles are reversed. The wife is the career person, providing financial support to the family. The husband maintains the home and cares for the children. Some dads stay at home by choice. Others stay at home due to workforce reductions. About one in 20 couples include a dad who stays at home.

Dads who choose to stay at home experience similar struggles with time and completion of household tasks as mothers who stay at home. Although still a minority, more dads are choosing this option. They can get help from support groups that have been organized throughout the country such as Stay At Home Dads (SAHD).

Work Patterns

Men and women follow a variety of work patterns today. Their choices are often based on family goals and values, family member roles, the birth of children, and financial needs.

Most men follow a conventional work pattern. They start working following their schooling. Some may change jobs or have periods of unemployment, but most continue working until retirement. Occasionally, there is the exception to this in the stay at home dad, 15-3.

There is a much greater variety of work patterns for women. Some women choose a full-time career, deciding not to have children. Others start work when they leave school and work until they marry or have children, at which time they quit their jobs.

Later, they return to the work world. They may return after a maternity leave, or they may wait to return to work until their children are older. Some work full-time, while others may work on a part-time basis. When both husband and wife pursue careers, they are referred to as **dual-career families**.

15-3 **This man enjoys caring for his children while his wife provides the family's financial support.**

The Impact of Family and Work

When adult family members are employed, what happens at work often impacts the family. Likewise, what happens at home can impact the workplace. A better understanding of how family and work influence each other may help family members manage both roles more effectively.

Impact of Work on Family Life

There is no question of the great impact parental employment has on family life, both positive and negative. Parents are challenged to meet both their work demands and their families' needs. Children are affected by their parents' employment as well. How the family manages the home is more of a challenge when the adult family members are employed.

Impact Related to the Parents

When both parents are working, time is a major concern. Parents find it difficult to find time for themselves, each other, and their children. There is never enough time to take care of everything that needs to be done.

In addition to time concerns, parents have financial concerns. They may incur additional costs due to their employment. For instance, they may have to purchase clothes that are more appropriate for the workplace. There may be a need for an additional car for transportation to and from work. Quality child care is costly. Couples will want to consider if the two incomes will be greater than the costs involved. If the total income is only slightly higher with two people working, the decision for both to work may not be wise.

Parents may be anxious about their children when they cannot be with them. They wonder how their employment is going to affect them. They may worry that their children will feel neglected or insecure. They may also have concerns about the quality of care their children are receiving in their absence. See 15-4.

Often a parent will attempt to be both the perfect parent and the perfect employee. Achieving both goals is difficult, if not impossible, and stress and guilt often result.

Impact Related to Children

The most significant issue related to children of working parents is the quality

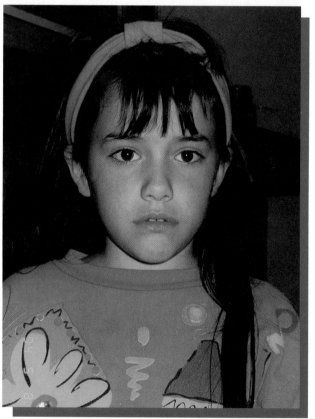

Starr-King

15-4 **Parents do not like to have to leave a child at home alone.**

of child care they receive. Trying to find good child care presents a stressful challenge to many families. Situations exist in which parents are forced to put their children in less than ideal, unlicensed, and even dangerous child care settings because they simply cannot afford anything better.

One of the most disturbing effects of parental employment has been the increase in the number of school-age children who are regularly left alone during some period of the day. **Children in self-care** are also often referred to as latchkey children. Most of these children are school age, although there are children under the age of six who are routinely left alone.

The self-care phenomenon remains low-profile for various reasons. Parents who choose this type of arrangement feel guilty, even though they may also feel they have no other alternative. Parents who choose this type of arrangement also know their children might be in greater physical danger if it were common knowledge that their children were unattended.

Studies of older children with no parent at home are also disturbing. They are beginning to show that preteens and teenagers left alone after school may be far more prone than other kids to be involved with alcohol and illegal drugs.

After-school activities and parental supervision help prevent problems for preteens and teenagers. Extra-curricular activities such as clubs and sports provide skill development under adult supervision during normally unstructured time. Studies have also linked extra-curricular involvement with better grades, lower alcohol and drug use, as well as less sexual activity among teenagers. Positive activities lead to positive behaviors. Parents can encourage participation through support and attendance at such school- or community-related activities.

Impact Related to Home Management

As the nation's labor force approaches being staffed equally by men and women, attitudes about parenting are also changing. Parenting responsibilities are now more often shared by both the mother and the father. Dad may handle the children's nightly baths and drive children to lessons while mom works.

Dual-career families also have to find new ways to manage household chores. Successful arrangements may depend greatly on the attitude of husband and wife regarding role sharing. Even with all the social changes, many couples still follow a more traditional pattern when it comes to household chores. The husbands in these families participate minimally in household work. This is the reason many working women experience more conflict in combining work and family roles than men do. There are more demands on their time and energy.

Men are gradually becoming less bound to the stereotypical "head of the household" role. Women in dual-career families want equity in the home as well as in the workplace. Many desire role sharing in all aspects of the marriage including home maintenance and child care. See 15-5. Some men who still think of themselves in the traditional role of breadwinner of the family have feelings of inadequacy when their wives enter the workforce. For some, it is difficult to adjust to what they see as a threat to their power and privilege. They feel diminished because they no longer enjoy the status and service their fathers took for granted.

Positive Impact of Work on Family Life

Though families are faced with certain challenges when both parents are employed, there are positive aspects to the arrangement. Some people believe dual-career couples attach more importance to their family life. When both spouses work, home life takes on more importance. It becomes a place for reconnecting and revitalizing. Men are more likely to be involved in child care, which contributes to a closer relationship with their children.

Men and women often experience feelings of individual accomplishment and self-fulfillment as a result of their work. Partners who feel better about themselves can offer more to each other and their children.

Many children report less friction in their homes when both parents are working. Their parents have fewer money worries and seem happier because the household income is increased. Increased income can lessen anxiety about money. Even young children have a sense of the role of money in maintaining a certain way of life and meeting the family's needs.

Children are more likely to have more contact with other children and adults through their child care arrangements. These experiences can benefit their social, emotional, and intellectual development.

Children also learn from their parents' work roles. As parents talk about their work and the work environment, children learn about the world of work. See 15-6. They want to understand what their parents do at work and what the world of work is like. It is helpful if explanations about work involve discussing problems as well as satisfactions and accomplishments.

Starr-King

15-5 Both father and children enjoy a special outing together.

M.T. Crave

15-6 Children like to know where their parents work and what they do.

Children learn work can be a positive, integral part of a full life and it can bring happiness as well as frustration. Children also see their parents as competent individuals who have knowledge and abilities to contribute to a job.

Family members can benefit from sharing home management tasks. In dual-career families in which there is a more flexible division of labor, children are less likely to grow up with sexist attitudes. Household management is also likely to be more structured and tightly organized, resulting in greater efficiency in the home.

Involving children in daily household tasks instills a valuable sense of independence and responsibility. It also helps them become more self-confident and resourceful. At any age, children gain a sense of accomplishment and satisfaction from being part of the "family team." See 15-7. The parents, who may not have the time or energy to do everything themselves, will gain from the additional help.

Impact of Family on the Workplace

In the not too distant past, the "perfect employees" put their work above everything else. Their time and commitment belonged to the company. Businesses placed

15-7 The parents and children benefit when the children help take care of the home.

family-related fringe benefits, if they existed at all, far down on their list of priorities.

It is very easy for worries about children to get in the way of an employee giving his or her best to the job. Managers have coined the term "three o'clock syndrome" to describe the concerned glances at the clock around 3:00 p.m. when some employees know their children are now home alone. The stress these working parents experience at home often spills over into the workplace resulting in lower productivity, poorer concentration, and higher absenteeism.

Now, with more dual-career and single-parent families, there is little question that the family exerts a powerful influence on American business. Many families today are looking to their place of employment

*Getting*Involved

for help with child care arrangements. Employers have begun to change their policies. Some companies are providing a variety of family-related services for their employees. Others are making work hours, the workplace, or job demands more compatible with family needs.

Business and industry need families because these are the people who make up the workforce. Employers have much to gain from implementing family-responsive policies and programs, even if some programs appear costly at first glance. Offering employees some options tends to reduce the negative consequences of combining work and family roles and improves worker morale. Absenteeism is reduced and productivity is improved. Family-friendly policies also help in recruiting and retaining good employees. An improved public image is important and indirectly affects the company's success. The results of these changes could provide a balance of social and economic returns for the business.

Employers, Government, and Communities– Responding to Family Needs

Many employers, governments, and communities have undertaken some new options to help dual-career parents and single parents meet the challenges of family and work. The following sections will describe some of the recent changes.

Employer's Response

Although big companies have taken the lead in moving toward more family-friendly policies, changes have occurred in smaller companies, too. Many businesses are making changes that indicate their awareness of and concern for the working parent.

Flexible Personnel Policies

Many working parents benefit from less rigid working arrangements. Some employers have implemented policies that give employees more control over their working conditions. This often allows employees to more easily attend to family needs. These policies include flextime, flexplace, part-time work, job sharing, and family and medical leaves.

Flextime permits employees to determine their own working hours within certain guidelines and limits. There may also be options in the number of days the employee works each week. A compressed workweek is a flextime term referring to a 40-hour workweek in four days. Flextime does not usually reduce the total number of hours in the employee's workweek.

Flextime can allow working couples to arrange their work hours so one parent is with their children at all times. For single-parent families, flextime may allow the parent to work when children are at school or when child care is available.

Flexplace, or work-at-home via computers, is the fastest growing type of alternative work arrangement. See 15-8. The linkup of telephone and computer technology provides extensive possibilities for home employment. Editing and publishing, marketing and sales, research, journalism, technical design, and real estate and

📋 **15-8 With the aid of a computer, this woman is able to work out of her own home.**

financial transactions can be done at home with the aid of a modem and computer.

Permanent part-time work and job sharing are other work options that allow working parents to spend more time with their families. **Job sharing** occurs when two people share the responsibilities of one full-time job. For example, one employee might work mornings and another work afternoons. Their total work hours would equal 40 hours. Often the salary and fringe benefits are also shared by the two employees. These benefits might include health insurance, paid vacations, and sick leave.

Permanent part-time work is another option, but part-time workers often do not receive company benefits. Part-time workers often have less job security.

Many companies have established policies that allow for special leave (absence from work) for parenting activities. Many companies have specified family leave policies. The employer is obligated to allow leaves of absence according to state family leave statutes. Only a little more than half the states have family leave laws in place, and most are very vague.

Policies regarding **maternity leave**, a leave of absence for a mother to care for her newborn child, vary from company to company. There are paid leaves versus unpaid leaves. Unpaid leave results in a financial hardship for many families. In many cases, women do not take off as much time as they are allowed because their family depends on their income for survival. Some companies allow six-week leaves, while others allow up to six months.

Another option available through some companies is **paternity** leave. Paternity leave is time allowed for a father to be absent from his job immediately following the birth of his child. Paternity leave benefits both spouses. It gives the father time to adjust to being a parent and allows both parents to begin parenting together, sharing responsibilities. See 15-9. The leave time can be taken by the father and mother at the same time, which allows sharing the time as a new family. Another option is for the husband to take his leave after the mother's leave ends, which allows them more time to make child care arrangements. It also lets him experience parenting on his own. As more men take advantage of paternity leave, society will move closer to accepting child rearing as a "parental" issue, rather than a "women's" issue.

Another personnel policy that seems to be changing has to do with company transfers and moves. As more couples have dual careers, it is more difficult for them to move when one person is asked to accept a job transfer. One person may have to give up his or her job in order for the other one to advance. Since more couples are resisting such moves, many companies now require fewer moves for advancement. If a move is necessary, many companies will offer some relocation aid for the other spouse, such as providing job leads and paying employment agency fees.

Educational and Support Programs

Some employers are offering a variety of educational programs at the worksite. Many of these programs are aimed at helping parent-employees deal with the frustrations caused by their dual roles. Seminars often help employees become aware of resources both inside and outside the company that can assist them in parenting. Programs also

15-9 Having time off from work to share in the care of his son is a special experience for this father.

help establish networks of people who have similar interests and concerns. Aside from generating goodwill, these programs make good business sense. They minimize the expense of firing, recruiting, and training new staff, which is much more costly than helping current employees through stressful situations.

Employee assistance programs, known as EAPs, were originally set up to help employees overcome alcohol and substance abuse problems. Today they address a wide range of psychological, social, and emotional problems that can interfere with employee performance. EAP staff can help employees with a variety of personal problems such as a serious illness in the family, finding child or elder care, substance abuse, or financial debt. Generally, EAP counselors assess the problem and then refer workers to outside help.

Benefit Packages

Some companies have created flexible or "cafeteria style" benefit packages from which employees may choose. Such plans tend to cover options in five benefit areas: retirement and savings; health insurance; disability insurance; life insurance; and vacation or leave days. Some newer plans are including dependent care options. Employees are given choices as to how they want their benefit dollars allocated. For instance, in dual-career families, both employees may be offered insurance coverage for themselves and their families. Most families do not need dual coverage. With a flexible benefit plan, the employee can choose the type of coverage desired so there is not a duplication of benefits.

Child Care Services

It is estimated that 3,000 companies with more than 100 employees now offer child care assistance in some form. Company-owned child care centers are currently provided by many companies. These range from on-site, company-operated centers to those operated by contracted providers. Many companies offer child care support by providing referral services. Agencies may contract with employers to provide referrals to child care providers who meet certain quality standards.

Some companies help their employees defray the cost of child care by way of subsidies, vouchers, or reimbursement programs. One such corporation in Massachusetts felt that employer-subsidized child care could make it possible for their employee-parents to purchase services of higher quality and greater reliability. They pay a varying percentage of child care expenses for employees earning less than

$25,000 per year. They will pay for care only in licensed child care homes or centers or for care provided by relatives.

Of all the options available to employers for helping working parents with child care, the most visible is the establishment of a child care center on or near the business location. Not only the families benefit from this service, but the business does as well. The presence of on-site child care centers aids in recruitment. Their existence also reduces absenteeism and tardiness. Employees are charged for the child care services provided. Most corporate child care centers only provide care for toddlers or preschoolers. Infant care is very expensive because of the very high child-to-staff ratio required. See 15-10.

Some employers have become involved in family child care networks. The employer recruits providers and may arrange for training and help in licensing. Family child care sites can service employees living in a wide area. Families often prefer these more homelike environments that can keep all siblings together.

D. Kay

15-10 **It is more difficult to find infant care in child care centers because of the expense in staffing.**

Other options are being implemented. One corporation equipped with a sophisticated computer system provides location, fees, limitations, and hours of operation of existing community child care facilities. Another company's program functions as an information and referral service. It includes ongoing screening, monitoring, supervision, and evaluation of all child care providers that are registered with them. A summary of various child care options employers may provide is shown in 15-11.

Government Response

Efforts by the federal and state governments to establish programs to help working family members have been increasing over the years. Government policies are important not only for what they accomplish directly, but also for their symbolic effect in support of families.

The U.S. Congress has supported after-school programs with millions of dollars. These programs are designed to keep children safe as well as provide academic enrichment. Opportunities to participate in recreational activities, such as chorus, band, and technology education, are offered. The programs also provide a safe place for parenting and child development classes, literacy programs, homework centers, and drug and violence prevention counseling.

The United States has moved more slowly than other industrialized nations in support of families in which the adults are in the labor force. Many European nations have established policies making it much easier for men and women to combine work with parenting. Most of these policies involve child care.

Legislation

The **Family and Medical Leave Act**, signed into law in 1993, represents a significant step in promoting workplace rights. This law entitles workers in businesses of 50 or more employees up to 12 weeks a year of unpaid leave for any of the following:

- birth or adoption of a child, or placement in foster care

- care of a child, spouse, or parent with a serious health condition

- the employee's own health condition

In addition, employees are entitled to the same or an equivalent position when returning to work. Health benefits, if offered, must continue during the leave.

Many who are eligible may not be able to afford this benefit since the leaves are unpaid. About one-third of all businesses have less than 50 employees and are therefore not covered under this law.

The **Pregnancy Discrimination Act** of 1978 prohibits discrimination against pregnant women in all areas of employment from hiring to firing. Employers of 15 employees or more are covered by this act. The act states that a physically fit pregnant employee must be allowed to continue to work just as any other physically fit employee would be permitted to work. Secondly, employers must give the same sick leave, disability leave, health insurance, or other benefits to women unable to work due to pregnancy, childbirth, and recovery after childbirth as they would to other employees unable to work for physical reasons.

Other government legislation over time has benefited families, although less directly. Since the 1930's, federal and state governments have been playing a major role in regulating wage and benefit packages. Minimum wage and earned income tax credits for low-wage workers are two other examples of government responses that benefit the family.

Child Care Options for Employers

Option	Description
Sponsor nearby or on-site child care center	A center can be owned or operated by the company, owned by the company and managed by a third party, or owned and operated by a sub-contractor or grantee. The center is primarily for the employees of the sponsoring company.
Support a local child care center	Through a grant or contract, a local child care center can accept funds from a company or a group of companies in exchange for priority enrollment/reduced fees for their employees.
Create or support a family child care network	Provide funds to a body representing a group of family child care homes that will provide slots to employees' children. This is particularly helpful to firms whose employees work evenings or weekends, or have infants.
Create or support after-school care	An employer can help start a program in the community or schools to serve the needs of 6 to 13 year-olds before and after school.
Create or support a vacation/holiday program	Make a program available that serves children when school is out, including summer vacations.
Create or support backup or emergency care	Make a program available that serves children when their regular care arrangements have fallen through or when there is an emergency.
Create or support a sick child care program	Make a program available for mildly-ill children, either as part of an existing child care center, a hospital, a freestanding program near work or in the community, or as an in-home program where qualified people are sent into the child's home.
Offer resource and referral services	Educate employees about their child care choices in the community and provide referrals to programs with openings.
Parenting seminars	Organize informational meetings on parenting issues and child care concerns.
Vouchers	The employer pays for a portion of child care expenses.
Discounts	The employer arranges for employees to be charged a reduced rate at programs of the employer's choosing.
Dependent Care Assistance Plans (DCAPs)	A mechanism that allows for employees to pay for their child care with pre-tax dollars. There is a savings to the employer, although the subsidy is actually paid for by the government.
Corporate contributions	Grants to local organizations to generally improve the supply or quality of child care at the local, state, or national level. Companies might also donate equipment, supplies, or expertise.
Public education	The use of corporate clout can help bring attention to important child care issues. Employer representatives can serve on community-wide task forces, testify at hearings, and publicize child care issues at professional meetings.

Developed by the Families and Work Institute

15-11 **There are many options for employers to consider in helping working parents and their children.**

Tax Benefits

Tax incentives are available for companies offering child care. If a corporation establishes a child care center to increase productivity, then company-supplied startup and operating costs are fully deductible business expenses.

Since 1981, the Internal Revenue Service (IRS) has made a tax-free account for child care available to employers. Employees may deposit up to $5,000 in such accounts to pay child care expenses. This money is not considered salary so it is exempt from taxes (an employee benefit), social security, and state unemployment deductions (an employer benefit).

The **Child and Dependent Care Tax Credit** is a significant type of federal support for child care. By means of this tax credit, families who pay taxes can offset a portion of their tax bill with the expenses they have incurred from paying others to look after their children. However, since this benefit is only for those families who pay taxes, low-income families who pay little or no taxes do not benefit.

Government policies can greatly affect many working parents, particularly single parents. Legislation related to the areas of economic security, equal opportunity, dependent care, and health care could be very helpful to parents trying to balance conflicting responsibilities of work and child rearing.

Community Efforts in Support of Working Parents

A growing number of programs designed in part to assist working parents are being initiated in communities across the nation. Sometimes these programs function with corporate support, sometimes with government support, and sometimes through volunteer efforts of people in the community. Many are businesses that operate for profit.

Child Care Centers

Most communities have child care centers that offer full-day children's programs. Quality centers focus on meeting children's health and safety needs. In addition, many offer educational programs designed for children in each age group in attendance. Some facilities will care for infants and toddlers as well as preschoolers. The curriculum offered will depend on the goals and philosophy of the center. Children benefit from being with other children their own age. Toys and equipment are designed for use by children. See 15-12.

Child care centers may be owned and operated by individuals, corporations, churches, or nongovernment groups. Some are funded by federal or state funds. Child care centers are licensed by state agencies and must meet minimum standards for space, group size, and staff. When selecting a child care center, it is helpful if parents visit programs. They can observe the staff and children and evaluate the facilities. Centers with warm, nurturing environments will benefit the children.

D. Kay

15-12 A good child care center can provide a stimulating environment and good social interaction for children.

Home-Based Child Care

Home-based child care is divided into two broad categories. The care may be provided in the child's own home or in another family's home. Parents selecting care in their own home need to be very cautious in choosing caregivers. Background checks and checking reliable references must be done. Monitoring activities with frequent calls and listening carefully to any complaints their children make regarding their caregivers are wise steps to take in evaluating the care.

Family child care is child care provided in a private home other than the child's own. Family child care constitutes the largest system of child care in this country. At least 90 percent of all family child care consists of unregulated providers who operate informally and independently of any regulatory system. Many states require that family child care providers are licensed or are operated as part of child care systems or networks under the administration of a sponsoring agency.

Family child care was provided historically without charge by relatives. Often child care was bartered between friends and neighbors in an informal exchange of services. Today the nature of informal family child care is changing with the disappearance of the extended family. Fewer parents are at home and are willing to care for their neighbor's children.

If parents need to make child care arrangements for their children, they need to look at the advantages and disadvantages of center-based versus home-based child care. These are summarized in 15-13.

Choosing Child Care		
	Advantages	**Disadvantages**
Child Care Centers	• Licensed child care centers must meet certain safety and health standards, and in some states educational standards as well. • The child care center may be located near or inside the place of employment so the parent can visit the child more easily. • The staff is usually well trained in early childhood development. • There is more opportunity to meet other working parents with children the same age. • The centers are usually well equipped for infant and child care. • The parent does not have to worry about the caregiver becoming ill or quitting. Child care centers are open whether or not a staff member becomes ill or leaves.	• There may be lack of consistency in caregivers: the child can be cared for by several caregivers during the course of the day. There is a very high turnover rate of staff due to the low salaries and demands of the job. • The parents are restricted by the center's hours of operation. • The child is exposed to and thus susceptible to contagious illnesses such as colds, viral infections, chicken pox, etc. A child who is ill cannot be sent to child care. • Many child care centers do not accept newborns or infants. • The costs are usually fairly high.

(Continued)

15-13 **Parents can select the kind of child care that suits their family best by studying the advantages and disadvantages of the two main types.**

Choosing Child Care		
	Advantages	**Disadvantages**
Home-Based Child Care	• The child becomes part of the caregiver's family, providing him or her with more interaction and stimulation in a homey setting. • The child has the security of a consistent caregiver. • This type of child care is usually least expensive. • You have the opportunity to meet other working parents. • There is less exposure to germs and infection than in group child care centers. • There is more potential for individual attention and stimulation because there are fewer children. • There may be more opportunity for flexible scheduling and hours that are available.	• The facility may be unlicensed; most states only require licensing for facilities that accommodate six or more children. If a facility is unlicensed, parents have no guarantee that it follows prescribed health and safety regulations. • Care providers are often untrained and may not have practice dealing with a number of children. • Care provider's child care philosophy may differ from the parents'. • The child may be isolated from other children. • There is no backup when the child is sick. • There is no backup when the care provider or one of her children is sick.

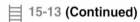 **15-13 (Continued)**

School-Age Child Care

When children are of school age, working parents have to make different arrangements for their children's care. Until recently, there were few options available for after-school child care. Unfortunately, many young children were left alone at an early age. The needs of these children and their parents are being addressed by various community organizations. A variety of programs are now offered.

School-based child care programs supplement the care children receive during the normal school day. These programs take advantage of space that is already available and equipped. Therefore, the programs can operate very economically. In addition, children are already at school so transportation is less of a problem.

Many social agencies are beginning to provide school-age child care. One of the groups most involved in offering a variety of service models is the YMCA.

Schools and community groups are offering training sessions for children in self-care. These sessions train children to cope with situations that may come up when they are alone. Handbooks for young children are really only useful if children get accompanying instructions with them. Parents or other adults need to show children how to handle emergencies and allow them to practice proper procedures.

Safety in three areas is emphasized for children in self-care. First, provide a safe home environment. Doors and windows should be locked, and fire and accident hazards removed. If the child is allowed to use the computer while the parents are away, strict guidelines regarding the use of the computer and/or parental controls should be enforced. A list of emergency telephone numbers should be prepared. Second, rehearse special situations, such as what to do if the doorbell rings and how to answer telephone calls. Actions to take if a fire starts, a stranger approaches, a window is broken, or a door is opened should also be rehearsed. Children should know how to handle simple emergencies. Third, parents should be comfortable with the child's ability to read phone numbers and instructions, comprehend a dangerous situation (such as the sound of the smoke alarm), dial for help in an emergency, provide an address to a neighbor or the police, and leave the house safely in case of a fire, gas leak, or similar situation.

Experts advise that children should not be left at home alone until their parents have confidence in their judgment. A key consideration is the child's own fear about staying alone. Some children, terrified of being by themselves, may panic and do something that exposes them to real danger.

Some community agencies have established telephone **hotlines** that children can call when they need help of any kind. Many of these programs are started as community service projects and are staffed by adult volunteers. Calls come from children who are lonely, scared, or bored. Children might also call for help with homework, help in getting along with siblings, medical problems, or reports of a prowler.

Some nursing homes are combining care for the elderly with care for children in an arrangement that seems to benefit everyone. Many basic principles that apply to care for the elderly also apply to care for the young. The relationships that develop between children and older people can benefit both parties. See 15-14.

15-14 **A positive relationship between an older person and a child benefits both.**

Successfully Combining Family and Work

The challenges related to family and workplace roles and the responses to these challenges have been reviewed. What additional changes might be effective within the family? What new ideas and strategies might allow people to combine family and work more easily?

Satisfaction in combining family and work roles implies success and happiness. However, this does not necessarily mean a life free from problems or stress. Individuals strive for satisfaction in their lives, but those who attain it are generally the ones who have developed personal management skills. These skills help them set priorities, manage their circumstances effectively, and cope with change.

Specific management skills are reviewed at length in other chapters in this book. You may find it helpful to review those chapters as they relate to combining family and work roles.

Some management skills have a direct relationship with successfully combining family and work roles, 15-15. An awareness of these skills will be helpful in meeting that challenge.

Relationship Skills

Effective communication between partners has always been the cornerstone of successful relationships. It is important that couples be sensitive to each other's feelings. Sharing concerns, frustrations, and pleasures is especially important for dual-career couples. Problems can be solved by negotiating and compromising to come up with solutions that will work for both partners.

Management Skills

- Being aware of your values and goals
- Learning to recognize your resources
- Using the management process to reach your goals
- Using decision-making skills in solving problems and reaching goals
- Using time and energy management and work simplification

15-15 These management skills are valuable tools in fulfilling both family and workplace roles.

Older children should be involved in problem solving as well, especially in matters that involve them. A family meeting can be arranged where all parties can express their concerns. Everyone should be allowed to voice possible solutions. A compromise can be reached that will hopefully satisfy everyone's needs. Good communication between family members is the foundation for positive relationships.

Finding time to spend with their children is a primary concern of working parents. Every child wants to feel loved and accepted. There are ways for parents to accomplish this even when they are working full-time.

In many families, dinnertime is the one occasion when all family members are present. Coming together reinforces children's sense of closeness and belonging. Some parents feel very strongly about "connecting with their children" during each day at breakfast, from the office by telephone, at dinner, a special evening hour, and at bedtime. They feel that because they nurture togetherness during each weekday, the weekend connection with their family is even more productive.

For many children, bedtime represents time alone with a parent—having mom or dad all to themselves. It may be the one moment during the entire day when they do not have to share a parent with anyone else. This part of the day can be very important to a child, 15-16.

Although time is a limited resource for the dual-career couple, making a special effort to strengthen their own relationship is important to their marriage. They need to find time to spend alone together. For example, one busy couple decided to do this by hiring a sitter every weekday night for an hour. They paid a high school student to stay with their children after the children had gone to bed so the couple could go for a walk and talk. Another

15-16 Bedtime can be a very special time of the day for both parent and child.

couple made a date at least once a week for some time together outside the home. Couples may have to think of new and creative ways to find time for one another, but their relationship is a valuable resource when dealing with day-to-day challenges.

Skill in Recognizing Resources Available

Managing resources means more than just using them. The first step is being aware of the variety of resources available. Parents concerned about combining family and workplace roles have many resources they can use. There is a variety of support groups available in most communities. Help hotlines can be contacted in emergency situations. Many public and private social service agencies provide beneficial services.

Until the workplace becomes more family-friendly, persons can prepare for the unpredictable by creating their own support networks. Many people can turn to family members, close friends, or neighbors when the going gets tough. Dual-career couples or single parents might form their own support groups. They could ask their employers to consider the possibility of sponsoring working-parent seminars during the lunch hour. They could also contact a senior citizens' center or churches and see whether there is any interest in establishing a foster grandparents program.

Another resource available to any working parent is bartering. **Bartering** is a way of getting what you want by exchanging goods or services instead of spending money. The range of exchangeable goods and services is extensive. One couple who could never find time for themselves bartered with a neighbor who needed after-school care for his nine-year-old. They worked out a plan where one of them would watch his son two afternoons a week. In exchange, he babysits for their two children Friday or Saturday evening so they can go out together.

In a way, bartering is actually role sharing. Working parents can often find financial as well as emotional relief by considering other people who can role-share with them in child care and home management.

Attitude Skills

For working parents, attitude is the key. The happiest and the healthiest working parents are not those who try to do everything perfectly. Instead, they are the ones who decide what is most important to them and then do the best they can. They learn to let go of some higher standards in favor of slightly lower standards. Maybe the house will not be as clean as they would like it to be. Maybe the children will go to school with dirty socks one day if the laundry didn't get done the night before. They also learn to set priorities. They can't do everything, so they decide what must be done.

They set priorities, choosing the important tasks that have to be done each day. Other tasks will have to wait.

A willingness to experiment and be creative is a helpful attitude skill. Maybe a parent is employed in a workplace that has not explored the new family-friendly policies. He or she might consider approaching management with a concrete plan. The plan could show how the company could benefit by supporting its employees through more family-responsive policies.

A person who is deeply torn between parenthood and career may find that a part-time job can be a good balance. See 15-17. This person can spend some time at home with the children, and still continue to advance in a career by staying current and visible. In some families, it might be the father or the mother who chooses the part-time career. If a person is a valued employee, a company might be more willing to allow the parent to work part-time rather than lose his or her talents altogether. It is important to consider the possible loss of company benefits if a person works part-time.

Decision-Making Skills

Working parents have to make many difficult choices. Becoming more skillful in the decision-making process is a valuable resource. For instance, choosing child care is an extremely important decision. The child care provider is one of the most important people in the child's life. Child care providers and teachers have a great influence on children. What they teach, how they teach, and how they interact with children can affect them in many ways.

For parents, following the steps of the decision-making process can be very helpful in reaching decisions and solving problems. The use of this one management tool can help them successfully combine family and workplace roles.

15-17 **In order to have more time with her children, this woman chose to work part-time.**

32
31
30
29
28
27
26
25
24
23
22
21
20
19
18
17
16
15
14
13
12
11
10
9
8
7
6
5
4
3
2
1

Summary

The challenge of successfully combining family and workplace roles is experienced in most families. By being aware of the trends related to family and work, you can better understand those who are faced with these challenges. Parental employment impacts the family in many ways, both positively and negatively. At the same time, families influence the workplace. Business and industry need families because these are the people who make up the workforce. Employers have much to gain from implementing family-responsive policies and programs.

Employers, governments, and communities are responding to family needs. Employers are offering more family-friendly policies. New legislation has been enacted at the federal level that is helpful to working parents. Many communities provide a variety of programs, particularly in the area of child care.

Families can develop personal skills to help meet this challenge. Management skills, relationship skills, attitude skills, and decision-making skills can be very helpful to families in successfully combining multiple roles.

To Review

1. List four reasons people work.
2. Describe two different work patterns women might choose to follow.
3. List two problems that may occur if both parents work outside the home.
4. Describe two ways children benefit when both parents are employed.
5. What is the difference between flex-time and job sharing?
6. What is meant by paternity leave?
7. Describe two of the services employers might provide to help their employees with child care.
8. The _____ entitles workers in businesses of 50 or more employees up to 12 weeks a year of unpaid leave.
9. True or false?
   A. Some child care centers are funded by federal or state funds.
   B. If care is provided in the child's own home, there is no need for parents to monitor the caregiver's activities.
   C. School-based child care programs are often more expensive due to space and equipment costs.
10. Give an example of how working parents might use bartering as a resource.

To Do with the Class

1. Discuss the following statement: "It has always interested me that no one questions whether a man is working as a matter of choice or of economic necessity."
2. Interview a number of adults in your community to determine their work patterns. Compile the results of the interviews and discuss.
3. Invite working parents for a panel discussion of the challenges brought on by their work and how they are attempting to meet these challenges.
4. Discuss the following statement: "The double duty of employed mothers is creating stress, undermining their health, and offering an unfair and impractical model to their children–tomorrow's working parents."

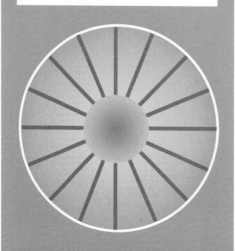

To Challenge Your Thinking

1. Research current statistics of the various categories of individuals making up the workforce in our nation.
2. Discuss factors or criteria used to determine the quality of child care programs.
3. Interview a single parent. Find out the biggest challenges this parent faces in balancing family and work. Discuss with the class.
4. If you have working parents, work with your family in developing a plan to share household tasks.

To Do with Your Community

1. Investigate the child care options in your community. Share your findings with others in the class.
2. Contact a local business to find out what policies and programs they offer that help employees who are parents.
3. Invite several employers from community businesses to participate in a panel. Ask how many of them offer family-friendly policies in the workplace. Hold a debate on the pros and cons of practicing family-friendly policies in the workplace.
4. Survey major businesses in your community to determine how the local companies are helping families in the workplace. What steps could these sites take to become more family-friendly?

Choosing quality childcare may be the most important decision a working parent must make.

Part Five
Managing Health and Wellness

Chapter 16
Physical and Mental Wellness
Influences on your physical and mental health include diet, physical activity, and sleep. The lifestyle decisions you make will also affect your wellness.

Chapter 17
Healthful Eating
The human body needs nutrients such as protein, carbohydrates, and vitamins in order to function. Food guides and meal patterns can help you choose a nutritious diet.

Chapter 18
Coping with Stress
Stress is caused by many events and situations. You can begin to manage stress by understanding its causes.

Chapter 19
Environmental Responsibility
Hazardous situations such as pollution, food contamination, and accidents can threaten your safety. Knowledge of prevention techniques and emergency procedures can help preserve your good health.

16 Physical and Mental Wellness

To Know

wellness
nutrients
MyPyramid
defense mechanisms
rationalization
identification
compensation
displacement
regression
projection
lifestyle diseases
obesity
preventive
  health care
Dietary Guidelines
  for Americans
eating disorders
anorexia nervosa
bulimia
cardiovascular disease
osteoporosis
antioxidants
fiber

hypertension
drugs
drug abuse
alcoholism
sexually transmit-
  ted diseases
  (STDs)
Acquired
  Immune
  Deficiency
  Syndrome
  (AIDS)
Human
  Immuno-
  deficiency
  Virus (HIV)
gonorrhea
syphilis
type II herpes
chlamydia
genital warts

Objectives

After studying this chapter, you will be able to

⬦ explain how good eating habits, physical activity, and rest can affect a person's health.

⬦ analyze good mental health and the healthful use of defense mechanisms.

⬦ identify lifestyle decisions that affect a person's health.

Have you ever known anyone who did not value good health? Good health is a universal value. However, it is an instrumental value. You do not seek health for health's sake. Instead, good health helps you reach other valuable goals. Having good health could help you become a good athlete, do well at your job, and enjoy a satisfying life.

Today, good health means more than just the absence of disease. There is an emphasis on the relationship between health and quality of life. People have become aware of the many factors that lead to **wellness**, or a state of good health. There is more emphasis on preventing illness and taking steps to promote wellness.

You might think of health as a continuum with optimal health—the healthiest you could be—at one end, and poor health at the other. See 16-1. Heredity, the environment, and personal factors determine where you fall on the continuum. Some of these forces are beyond your control, but your health is most influenced by the many decisions you make daily. These decisions will influence your lifestyle and living pattern for most of your life. Now is the time to learn about the factors that contribute to good physical and mental health. It will also be helpful to become aware of decisions that affect good health. These resources can be helpful to you for years to come.

Your good health is largely your responsibility. If you value your health, you will manage it wisely and make your decisions carefully.

Factors That Contribute to Good Health

Think of someone who you would consider very healthy, both physically and mentally. What characteristics come to mind? Healthy people have plenty of energy. They complete their daily activities without becoming overly tired. Their weight is normal for their ages and heights. They have healthy-looking skin. They are good-natured and cooperate with others. They seem to relate well to most people. Do these characteristics describe you? If so, you are a healthy person. See 16-2.

Health on a Continuous Scale		
Poor Health	**Average Health**	**Optimal Health**
Susceptible to life-threatening diseases	Freedom from disease	Freedom from disease
Low energy level		High energy level
May be over-weight or underweight		Ideal body weight
May have difficulty handling the stresses of everyday life		Well-rounded personality

16-1 Good health is more than just freedom from disease. Where do you fall on the health continuum?

16-2 This young woman displays many characteristics of good health.

When describing a healthy person, you discuss both physical and mental health. They go hand-in-hand. If you are physically ill with a bad cold and sore throat, your mental health is also affected. You may be irritable, listless, and moody. If you are emotionally upset because of a quarrel with a good friend, you may develop a bad headache.

If your goal is to be physically and mentally healthy, it is helpful to understand the factors that contribute to good health. Looking at each of these factors will help you make wise decisions about your own health.

Good Eating Habits

A good diet is important to your physical health both now and in the future. The body needs certain substances supplied by the diet in order to function. These necessary food materials are called **nutrients**. You need over 50 nutrients to stay healthy. These nutrients are divided into six groups: carbohydrates, fats, proteins, vitamins, minerals, and water. Although most foods contain more than one nutrient, no one food supplies all the nutrients you need. Therefore, you must eat a variety of foods to assure an adequate diet.

A healthful diet includes the amount and variety of foods your body needs each day. When you have good eating habits, your body tends to be well nourished and free from disease. A healthful diet includes a wide variety of foods with a high proportion of fresh or unprocessed foods. Minimally processed foods, such as canned or frozen foods, are best when you cannot eat fresh food. Foods that are processed have had some substances taken out and other substances added. Processed foods often contain large amounts of sugar and salt. These substances can be harmful in large quantities.

To help you choose foods that contain required nutrients, various guidelines have been developed by the United States Departments of Agriculture and Health and Human Services. **MyPyramid** is a food guidance system designed to help you choose a healthful diet and be active every day. It suggests you eat foods from the grains, fruits, vegetables, milk, meat and beans, and oils groups. The foods within each of the groups supply similar nutrients.

The new MyPyramid replaces the old Food Guide Pyramid. Some experts say that the old Pyramid was made too simple and wrongly promoted all carbohydrates as "good" for you and all the fats as the "enemy." They feel the quality of the carbo-hydrate is important. Carbohydrates that come from whole grains, such as brown rice and oats, provide steady energy over a longer period and keep you full longer than refined carbohydrates, such as white rice and white bread. In terms of fat, those who question the Food Guide Pyramid are concerned that it does not recognize that some fats are good for you and should be eaten in moderation. Monosaturated fats and polyunsaturated fats found in olive oil and other vegetable oils, nuts, whole grains, and fish play active roles in improving cholesterol levels and decreasing the risk of heart disease. The new MyPyramid will be discussed further in Chapter 17.

Brainstorming

Brainstorm examples of recreational or leisure activities that can be used as part of a physical activity plan.

If foods from one or more of the MyPyramid groups are eliminated from the diet, there is a greater possibility of missing necessary nutrients. Nevertheless, vegetarian diets have become an increasingly popular option throughout our society. Nutrition professionals suggest that people following a vegetarian diet eat a wide variety of foods each day. People who are considering eliminating some foods from their diets should consult a nutrition professional about food choices.

If your diet is adequate, you probably do not need to take supplemental vitamins. However, many people have inadequate diets. If nutrition is lost due to the way you store and prepare food, you may also need supplements. Some people need a vitamin-mineral supplement to meet specific nutrient needs related to their stage in life. For example, older adults and people with little exposure to sunlight may need a vitamin D supplement. To reduce the risk of a birth defect, women who could become pregnant are advised to eat foods high in folic acid or to take a folic acid supplement. Pregnant women are advised to take an iron supplement. People who seldom eat dairy products or other rich sources of calcium need a calcium supplement.

When taking vitamin-mineral supplements, be sure not to exceed the recommended dosage. Excessive doses may cause dangerous toxic effects. Dietary supplements include vitamins, minerals, fiber, herbal products, and many other substances offered in over-the-counter form. Although herbal products have become widely used in the past few years, research has not established the value of many of these products. There are few standards for their purity or potency at this time.

Regular and Adequate Physical Activity

Physical activity has positive effects on your physical health. Most everyone recognizes how physical activity benefits the muscular and circulatory systems. However, many people are not aware that it also benefits the digestive, respiratory, and excretory systems. The heart, liver, brain, and lungs all function better after regular physical activity. See 16-3.

People who engage in regular physical activity seem to be able to resist infectious diseases better than those who do not. They also seem to be more emotionally stable. Physical activity helps them release tension and relax. (Developing a physical activity plan is discussed later in this chapter.)

16-3 **Regular physical activity improves your physical fitness and even your attitude toward life.**

Good Mental Health

Good mental health is not a characteristic you have or do not have. Instead, it is a value. Good mental health is an ideal toward which people constantly strive. People who have *good mental health* have the ability to cope effectively with themselves, others, and the world around them.

You can gain a better understanding of good mental health by studying the qualities of mentally healthy people. Then consider how you might develop or improve these qualities in yourself:

- *Mentally healthy people feel comfortable about themselves.* They trust their own sense and feelings and are aware of their capabilities. They know and accept their shortcomings or strive to change them if possible. They seek to satisfy needs that promote personal growth. These people have healthy self-concepts.
- *Mentally healthy people are able to balance independence and dependence on others.* Well-adjusted people are able to think for themselves and take responsibility for their own feelings and actions. However, they also listen to advice or criticism from people they respect.
- *Mentally healthy people can control their emotions.* They are able to deal with frustration without experiencing great stress. They accept disappointment without becoming depressed. Mentally healthy people may get angry but not violent. They are aware of their feelings and are therefore better able to express and control them.
- *Mentally healthy people are able to love.* They are able to experience special interpersonal relationships. These relationships result from the open and caring feelings and sincere respect they communicate to others.

Use Your Reasoning Skills

Keep a list of the food you eat for several days and compare it with the food suggested in MyPyramid. Review your analysis. Were you lacking foods from any of the food groups? How might you adjust your eating habits to compensate for this lack?

Sufficient Sleep

Sleep refreshes your body for activity. During sleep and rest periods, your body "recharges its battery." While you sleep, many of your body's physical functions slow down. Your body temperature falls, muscles relax, heartbeat slows, breathing slows, and blood pressure and pulse rate fall. During sleep, the body recuperates and repairs itself. Living cells of the body are replaced. Cells of the skin divide and make new cells about twice as fast during sleep as in waking hours.

The amount of sleep people need is influenced mainly by rate of growth. Rapidly growing infants need more sleep than children, and children need more than adults. Babies usually sleep 18 to 20 hours a day. During childhood, this period is reduced to 12 to 14 hours. Most adolescents and adults sleep 6 to 8 hours a day, although some need more and some need less. Sleep needs may also change with pregnancy, illness, or unusual stress.

You can best determine your sleep needs by using your own judgment. You have had enough sleep when you awake feeling refreshed and alert. Some people find taking a short nap during the day very beneficial. This first period of sleep is the deepest and most refreshing. Therefore, a short nap can be helpful, especially if you do not get enough sleep at night.

◆ *Mentally healthy people are realistic.* Life is not easy and may sometimes seem unfair. However, mentally healthy people accept life as it is, 16-4. They do not fantasize about how life should be. People who have good mental health recognize what they cannot change. They work to overcome the problems they can change.

◆ *Mentally healthy people are able to accept and adapt to change.* Today's world involves constant change. Mentally healthy people accept these changes and adapt to new roles and challenges. They use change and new experiences to help them learn and grow.

Healthful Use of Defense Mechanisms

Even a self-confident person can feel threatened by the daily world. Fortunately, people have resources that provide temporary relief from stress. These resources are known as **defense mechanisms**.

Defense mechanisms are methods people use to deal with real-life situations and adjust to frustrations. Defense mechanisms help by reducing tensions, protecting self-esteem, and maintaining emotional stability. Using defense mechanisms does not indicate poor mental health. All people use them to some extent. However, defense mechanisms may indicate a definite problem if they are overused. Repeated use often puts off the more constructive approach to solving problems. Excessive use of defense mechanisms may indicate mental illness.

Some commonly used adjustment mechanisms include rationalization, identification, compensation, displacement, regression, and projection. People often use these mechanisms unconsciously.

Rationalization

Offering socially acceptable reasons for a failure or negative situation is called **rationalization**. "The reason I'm overweight must have something to do with hormones," is an example of the use of this mechanism. Rationalization indicates a lack of personal honesty that could interfere with healthy development and maturity.

Identification

Gaining a sense of self-worth by identifying with a person, group, or institution considered special is **identification**. Identification is one of the least harmful defense mechanisms. However, over-identifying with a person or group can cause an individual's personal growth and development to be sharply limited. This may result in a shallow, narrow-minded person with inhibited feelings toward others.

University of Wisconsin Media Center

16-4 Mentally healthy people accept the realities of life and make the best of each situation.

Compensation

People are using **compensation** when they counteract a weakness by emphasizing a desirable characteristic. A person might also make up for frustration by overemphasizing some other need or desire. For instance, a person who boasts and brags might actually be compensating for feelings of inferiority. Compensation usually causes little or no harm. However, you should remember that mentally healthy people are able to face and accept their weaknesses.

Displacement

In the **displacement** process, a person transfers negative feelings toward a threatening person or situation to someone else. For example, your boss may come to work one day right after having an argument with her husband. If she is highly critical of your work that day, she is displacing her anger to you. Displacement does not solve the original problem. In addition, it creates a new problem with the person to whom the displaced negative feelings are directed.

Regression

A person who uses **regression** is reverting to immature, childish behavior when difficulties or frustrations occur. Regression occurs when an older child reverts to thumbsucking or when a teenager throws a temper tantrum. A person who behaves this way often loses the respect of others and even his or her own self-respect.

Projection

Shifting the blame for an undesirable act or thought to someone else is **projection**. It is projecting the blame for something you do not want to acknowledge onto another person. A boy might blame his teacher for his failing a test although he did not study. He might say the teacher made the test too hard. The boy is projecting the responsibility for his failure onto his teacher.

Factors Affecting Good Health

The United States has made great progress in disease control throughout the past century. Diseases such as diphtheria have been controlled and are no longer threats to human lives. However, people in the United States today must be concerned about other disease problems. Heart attacks, strokes, and cancer are leading diseases in this decade. These diseases are called **lifestyle diseases**. They are more closely related to a person's behavior than to infectious agents.

Many in our society are not physically active. This is partly because of the many forms of transportation and modern conveniences available today. Inactive bodies are not as strong and healthy as active bodies. Therefore, they suffer from more diseases. Along with being inactive, many people's diets are high in calories and fat. See 16-5. The combination of these

American Can Company

16-5 Many Americans have poor eating habits. Unfortunately, changing these habits can be very difficult.

Getting Involved

Visit a sports therapy clinic, recreational program, weight clinic, or family health agency to gather information on healthy lifestyles. Share with the class the similarities and information on healthy living. Set up a display at school to share with other students.

factors may lead to **obesity** (being 20 percent or more above desirable weight) and an increased risk of heart and circulatory disorders.

Disease prevention has now become a matter of changing lifestyles—changing habits and customs. Many modern health problems might be considered educational failures rather than medical failures. Being educated about lifestyle and its relation to good health can help you understand the possible hazards of certain lifestyle decisions. Being educated also involves becoming aware of the values that influence your choices. In making lifestyle choices, you decide what you value most and make your choices in line with those priorities.

People in the United States have not traditionally been oriented to the concept of **preventive health care**—maintaining wellness in order to prevent diseases from developing. However, that attitude is changing, and people are beginning to value the importance of improving and maintaining their health. More people are including physical activity in their daily lives and emphasizing healthful foods as preventive health care.

Lifestyle Decisions–A Healthy Diet and Physical Activity

Many health problems are related to diet and lack of physical activity. These problems range from the body's lack of resistance to disease to cardiovascular disease and cancer. Experts say Americans would probably be healthier if they ate more healthfully and were more physically active.

The **Dietary Guidelines for Americans** are recommendations to help people choose healthful eating and fitness patterns, 16-6. They are updated regularly to reflect the most current health and nutrition information. Making the Guidelines part of your lifestyle can help you select nutritionally adequate meals. Following the Guidelines also promotes good health and reduces your risks for heart disease, certain cancers, diabetes, stroke, and osteoporosis.

For some people, choosing to eat more healthfully and improve fitness may involve major lifestyle changes. Understanding some hazards of poor dietary habits may help you clarify your values and set priorities regarding your lifestyle. The following suggestions for a more healthful lifestyle are addressed in the Dietary Guidelines for Americans.

Consume Adequate Nutrients Within Caloric Needs

The latest dietary guidelines emphasize the positive by steering people toward more fruits and vegetables, polyunsaturated and monounsaturated fats, more complex carbohydrates, and lean proteins. For the first time, the guidelines set daily calorie goals. In telling consumers to "make each calorie count," the guidelines make it clear that if people eat the right foods to get the nutrients they need, there won't be many calories left for junk food. They encourage people to consume foods and drinks with "little added sugar" and to keep trans fat consumption as low as possible.

Practice Weight Management

Dietary habits begin early in life. Parents encourage their children to eat a variety of foods for proper growth and

Dietary Guidelines for Americans

Adequate Nutrients Within Calorie Needs	• Consume a variety of nutrient-dense foods and beverages within and among the basic food groups. Choose foods that limit the intake of saturated and trans fats, cholesterol, added sugars, salt, and alcohol. • Meet recommended intakes within energy needs by adopting a balanced eating pattern, such as the USDA Food Guide.
Weight Management	• To maintain body weight in a healthy range, balance calories from foods and beverages with calories expended. • To prevent gradual weight gain over time, make small decreases in food and beverage calories and increase physical activity.
Physical Activity	• Engage in regular physical activity and reduce sedentary activities to promote health, psychological well-being, and a healthy body weight. • Achieve physical fitness by including cardiovascular conditioning, stretching exercises for flexibility, and resistance exercises or calisthenics for muscle strength and endurance.
Food Groups to Encourage	• Consume a sufficient amount of fruits and vegetables while staying within energy needs. Two cups of fruit and 2$\frac{1}{2}$ cups of vegetables per day are recommended for a reference 2,000-calorie intake, with higher or lower amounts depending on the calorie level. • Choose a variety of fruits and vegetables each day. In particular, select from all five vegetable subgroups (dark green, orange, legumes, starchy vegetables, and other vegetables) several times a week • Consume 3 or more ounce-equivalents of whole-grain products per day, with the rest of the recommended grains coming from enriched or whole-grain products. In general, at least half the grains should come from whole grains. • Consume 3 cups per day of fat-free or low-fat milk or equivalent milk products.
Fats	• Consume less than 10 percent of calories from saturated fatty acids and less than 300 mg/day of cholesterol. Keep trans fatty acid consumption as low as possible. • Keep total fat intake between 20 to 35 percent of calories, with most fats coming from sources of polyunsaturated and monounsaturated fatty acids, such as fish, nuts, and vegetable oils. • When selecting and preparing meat, poultry, dry beans, and milk or milk products, make choices that are lean, low-fat, or fat-free. • Limit intake of fats and oils high in saturated and/or trans fatty acids, and choose products low in such fats and oils.

16-6 **Following the Dietary Guidelines for Americans can help you achieve a more healthful lifestyle.**

Dietary Guidelines for Americans	
Carbohydrates	• Choose fiber-rich fruits, vegetables, and whole grains often. • Choose and prepare foods and beverages with little added sugars or caloric sweeteners. • Reduce the incidence of dental caries by practicing good oral hygiene and consuming sugar- and starch-containing foods and beverages less frequently.
Sodium and Potassium	• Consume less than 2,300 mg (approximately 1 teaspoon of salt) of sodium per day. • Choose and prepare foods with little salt. At the same time, consume potassium-rich foods, such as fruits and vegetables.
Alcoholic Beverages	• Alcoholic beverages should not be consumed by some individuals, including those who cannot restrict their alcohol intake, women of childbearing age who may become pregnant, pregnant and lactating women, children and adolescents, individuals taking medications that can interact with alcohol, and those with specific medical conditions. • Alcoholic beverages should be avoided by individuals engaging in activities that require attention, skill, or coordination, such as driving or operating machinery.
Food Safety	• To avoid microbial foodborne illness: • Clean hands, food contact surfaces, and fruits and vegetables. Meat and poultry should be washed or rinsed. • Separate raw, cooked, and ready-to-eat foods while shopping, preparing, or storing foods. • Cook foods to a safe temperature to kill microorganisms. • Chill (refrigerate) perishable food promptly and defrost foods properly. • Avoid raw (unpasteurized) milk or any products made from unpasteurized milk, raw or partially cooked eggs or foods containing raw eggs, raw or undercooked meat and poultry, unpasteurized juices, and raw sprouts.

16-6 Continued.

nutrition. When weight problems begin early and continue into adulthood, many health problems may develop.

Genes are partly responsible for weight, shape, and body composition. If members of your family are large despite relatively healthy habits, pushing yourself to be thin may be unrealistic and even unsafe. On the other hand, overweight that seems to run in a family is sometimes not inherited, but

due to similar sedentary lifestyles and overeating patterns.

Obesity is considered by many health professionals as the number one health problem in the United States. More than 60 percent of Americans are now considered overweight or obese. Twenty-five percent of children are classified as either overweight or at risk for overweight. The health implications of excess weight are becoming clearer. Obesity is linked to an increased risk for cancer and other chronic diseases. The risks of diabetes, high blood pressure, and increased levels of blood fats and cholesterol are greater. Some of these disorders increase the risks of heart attacks and strokes.

People who are overweight or underweight may expect a shorter life and an increased risk of illness. Your doctor can tell you if your weight is appropriate or if you should make changes in your diet.

If you are overweight, you probably eat more food than you need for your lifestyle. You may need to increase your physical activity and eat less fatty foods and sweets, 16-7. One or two pounds of weight loss per week is a safe amount. Diets that cause a faster weight loss may be unsafe.

If you are underweight, eat foods that are high in calories. Instead of eating three times daily, eat five times whether you are hungry or not. You can snack between meals, but avoid ruining your appetite.

USDA

16-7 Cutting down on fats and sweets and increasing your physical activity will help you lose weight.

Eating disorders, or abnormal eating behaviors, interfere with maintaining a desirable weight. Anorexia nervosa and bulimia are eating disorders that can result in serious health problems. Medical care and psychological counseling are needed to help victims overcome these disorders.

A person with **anorexia nervosa** avoids eating. Some victims avoid food to the point of starvation. A person with anorexia nervosa has a distorted self-concept, feeling fat no matter how thin he or she is.

Victims of **bulimia** go on food binges. They eat huge amounts of food. Then they get rid of the food by using inappropriate methods of weight control (purging). These methods include vomiting, fasting, enemas, excessive use of laxatives and diuretics, or compulsive exercising. As with anorexia nervosa, victims of bulimia always feel the need to be thinner.

Family members and friends can often help in recognizing the symptoms and getting treatment for victims of eating disorders. The earlier eating disorders are detected, the better the chances of recovery with no serious medical problems. The symptoms often include:

- depression
- abnormal weight loss or a cycle of weight gains and losses
- vomiting with no other signs of illness
- excessive physical activity
- refusal to eat or binge eating

Plan for Regular and Adequate Physical Activity

Medical experts feel being inactive can be hazardous to your health. Lack of physical activity is often mentioned as a cause of cardiovascular disease. (**Cardiovascular disease**, disease of the heart and blood vessels, is the number one killer in the United States.) Evidence seems to show that long-term physical activity benefits the cardiovascular system. No evidence suggests the healthy heart can be damaged by reasonable amounts of physical activity.

Many people are stuck in a pattern of inactive living though they do not have negative feelings toward physical activity. They go to school or work, watch TV, talk on the phone, and go to movies. Muscles lose strength when they are not used. Therefore, lack of activity could lead to heart problems, contribute to obesity, and increase the risk of high blood pressure.

When developing a plan of physical activity for yourself, keep in mind that regular physical activity benefits your body the most. Daily physical activity is best, but doing some type of physical activity three to six times a week will be helpful. Also, in order to increase your physical development, your muscular and cardiovascular systems should be pushed beyond normal expectations. You develop endurance through physical activity that makes strong demands on the body. This kind of activity increases pulse rate, body temperature, and the rate and depth of breathing. You benefit from physical activity by extending your body beyond its normal activity range.

While a sedentary lifestyle promotes bone loss, weight-bearing physical activity such as walking, jogging, and tennis, can help prevent **osteoporosis**. With this disease, bones deteriorate and become porous as the body takes the calcium it needs from the bones. Physical activity is important for keeping joints and muscles strong, along with promoting flexibility and balance.

The following guidelines may help you develop a physical activity plan:

- Choose a physical activity plan that fits your needs and desires. If you are not happy with the plan, you will probably not stick to it.
- Start your plan gradually. Give your body time to adjust to increased physical demands.
- Choose physical activities that involve both large and small muscles of the body. Jogging may be an excellent physical activity for endurance. However, it should be supplemented with activities that use other muscles, such as the arm, back, and shoulder muscles.
- An effective physical activity session should continue 30 to 60 minutes. A minimum useful period is about 15 minutes.
- People who lack the self-discipline to participate in physical activity on their own may have more success in group programs.

Many forms of physical activity are effective if you follow the above guidelines. Some include swimming, bicycling, tennis, handball, racquetball, jogging, cross-country skiing, and walking. You can supplement these vigorous types of activity with a variety of other recreational activities to improve your physical fitness. See 16-8.

Cautions related to physical activity programs are important. Physical activity plans will vary according to your physical status. Before beginning a physical activity program, be sure there are no medical problems that would prevent involvement in strenuous activity. Having a medical exam will give you this assurance.

Choose Nutritious Foods from the Food Groups

Foods are placed in categories to help guide your food choices. Since no single food provides all of the nutrients that your body needs, eating a variety of foods within each group ensures that you get the necessary nutrients and other substances that promote good health.

Fruits are great sources of vitamins, minerals, and soluble fiber. Except for a few varieties, such as coconuts and avocados, they are low in fat and calories. Fruits offer many sweet choices for eating such as cherries, plums, and tangerines. In fact, practically all fruits fit into a colorful and healthy diet. Whether you eat them as a snack or part of a meal, they offer a variety of nutrients, little fat, and relatively few calories.

Variety is important because different fruits provide different nutrients. Fresh fruit is generally best because it contains the most nutrients. However frozen fruit, fruits canned in their own juice or water, and dried fruit are good alternatives.

Like fruits, vegetables are great sources of vitamins, minerals, and fiber. Because different vegetables provide different nutrients, eating a variety is important. Some

Kent Hayward

16-8 Lifting weights is a good supplementary type of physical activity.

vegetables, such as broccoli, green peppers, and spinach, are also good sources of antioxidants.

Antioxidants are substances that protect the body's cells from damage that can be caused by pollution, exposure to chemicals, tobacco smoke, alcohol, and the by-products of normal metabolism. Oxygen, taken in when you breathe, causes a chemical reaction called *oxidation* in your cells. This process results in the formation of molecules known as *free radicals*, which can damage cells and tissue. If left unchecked, free radical damage may result in cardiovascular disease, certain cancers, and other illnesses.

Eating a variety of fruits and vegetables helps provide antioxidants. One of the easiest ways to recognize foods that are rich in antioxidants is by color, such as in red, yellow, orange, and green fruits and vegetables. *Beta-carotene* is a rich source of antioxidants. Beta-carotene is the fat-soluble pigment that gives fruits and vegetables their bright colors. The body converts beta-carotene into vitamin A. Seeds, legumes, nuts, grains, soy products, teas, and chocolate are also good sources of antioxidants. The best protection comes from eating a variety of antioxidant foods each day.

Grains, also called cereals, are the widely varied seeds of grasses, which are cultivated for food. They are a good source of complex carbohydrates, fiber, and various vitamins and minerals that are naturally low in fat. Choose whole grains as much as possible for more fiber and a wider variety of nutrients.

Grains, including breads, pasta, rice, and noodles, are the main sources of carbohydrate. There are hundreds of ways to prepare them and your whole-grain options are almost limitless.

Milk, cheese, eggs, yogurt, and other dairy products are good sources of calcium, protein, and other vitamins and minerals. However, these foods can be high in cholesterol, fat and calories, so it is important to choose low-fat versions.

Dairy products supply the richest source of calcium. Your body uses calcium to build strong teeth and bones. Also your heart, muscles and nervous system need calcium to function properly. A calcium rich diet may help lower the risk of a variety of diseases, including the bone-thinning disease osteoporosis.

Whole milk dairy products are high in fat, especially saturated fat, and calories. Fat free and low-fat milk products provide the same nutritional benefits without the excess fat and calories.

Avoid Too Much Fat, Saturated Fat, and Trans Fatty Acids

You can avoid too much fat, saturated fats, trans fatty acids, and cholesterol by choosing lean meat, fish, poultry, dry beans, or dry peas as your protein source. See 16-9. Limit your intake of eggs, shellfish,

---

Fat and Cholesterol Terms

Saturated Fats
Foods high in saturated fats tend to raise blood cholesterol. These foods include high-fat dairy products such as cheese, whole milk, cream, butter and full-fat ice cream; fatty fresh and processed meats; the skin and fat of poultry; lard; palm oil; and coconut oil. Keep your intake of these foods low.

Dietary Cholesterol
Cholesterol is a waxy substance required for many important body functions, including forming cell membranes, hormones, and other tissues. The American Heart Association (AHA) recommends your average daily intake of dietary cholesterol should not exceed 300 milligrams.

Foods that are high in cholesterol also tend to raise blood cholesterol. These foods include liver and other organ meats, egg yolks, and dairy fats.

Triglycerides
Triglycerides are fatty substances found in some foods and manufactured by the body from excess alcohol, sugar, and fat in the diet. The AHA recommends a triglyceride level of 150 or less. The primary treatment for elevated triglyceride levels is losing weight. Limiting intake of saturated fats, sugars, sweets, and alcohol may also help.

Trans Fatty Acids
Foods high in trans fatty acids tend to raise blood cholesterol. These foods include those high in partially hydrogenated vegetable oils, such as many hard margarines and shortenings. Foods with high amounts of these ingredients include some commercially fried foods and some bakery goods.

Unsaturated Fats
All kinds of unsaturated fats (oils) help keep blood cholesterol low. Unsaturated fats occur in vegetable oils, most nuts, olives, avocados, and fatty fish like salmon. Unsaturated oils include both *monounsaturated fats* and *polyunsaturated fats.* Olive, canola, and peanut oils are some of the oils high in monounsaturated fats. Vegetable oils such as soybean, corn, and cottonseed oil, as well as many kinds of nuts, are good sources of polyunsaturated fats. Fatty ocean fish have a special type of polyunsaturated fat (omega-3 fatty acids) that may protect you against heart disease. Use moderate amounts of foods high in unsaturated fats, taking care to avoid excess calories.

16-9 Knowledge of these terms can help you choose foods sensibly.

and organ meats such as liver. Also limit your use of butter, cream, shortenings, and foods made from these products. Use reduced fat dairy products instead. Broil, bake, or boil foods rather than fry them. Read labels carefully to learn the amount and types of fat contained in foods.

While your body needs cholesterol to build cell membranes and produce hormones, too much of this type of blood fat is harmful. Foods high in saturated fats, cholesterol, and trans fatty acids all tend to raise blood cholesterol. On the other hand, all kinds of unsaturated fats (oils) tend to keep blood cholesterol low. Unsaturated fats occur in vegetable oils, most nuts, olives, avocados, and fatty fish like salmon.

There has been some controversy related to cholesterol levels and heart disease. Research indicates that people with high blood cholesterol levels have a greater chance of having a heart attack. The population of the United States tends to have high blood cholesterol levels resulting from diets high in saturated fats and cholesterol. However, there are wide cholesterol variations among people due to heredity and the way each person's body uses cholesterol. For this reason, it is important for individuals to discover their own cholesterol levels through their doctors and be aware of the significance of these numbers. Most authorities believe it is wise to adopt a diet low in these substances.

There is increased concern regarding trans fatty acids and hydrogenated fat. *Hydrogenation* is a process that makes fat stable and solid at room temperature. Both hydrogenated fat and partially hydrogenated oils contain significant amounts of trans fatty acids, which have been linked with the development of heart disease. Some of the foods that contain unhealthy hydrogenated fats include butter, margarine, shortenings, crackers, cookies, and French fries.

In the past few years, there has been a great rise in the number of fat replacers used in reduced-fat foods. *Fat replacers* are ingredients that mimic the functions of fat in foods to supply texture, bulk, and flavor and to help consumers meet dietary recommendations for reduced fat intake. They are considered, by many, to be the most promising new method for developing good-tasting, consumer-acceptable foods. Most fat replacers in use today are derived from existing food ingredients whose safety has been established with long-term use in the food supply. However, for others, some side effects, although not life-threatening, may create additional problems. Their use is relatively new, so time and research will provide more definite answers to these issues.

Choose More Complex Carbohydrates and Limit Sugars

Complex carbohydrates include whole grain breads and cereals, fruits and vegetables, beans, peas, nuts, and seeds. These foods contain many essential nutrients, but they are emphasized here because of their contribution to increased fiber in the diet. **Fiber** is a type of complex carbohydrate that humans cannot digest.

The average American diet is relatively low in fiber. This leads to symptoms of chronic constipation, diverticulosis, and some types of irritable bowel. Low-fiber diets also increase the risk of developing cancer of the intestine.

Complex carbohydrate foods have a laxative effect. They provide bulk needed to move other foods through the digestive track and contribute to regular bowel movements.

The use of sugar is associated with an increase in dental decay, heart disease, hardening of the arteries, increases of certain fats in the blood, and diabetes. Americans consume enormous amounts of sugar—approximately 100 pounds per person per year. The link between refined sugar and heart disease has not been proven. Sugar does play a definite role in tooth decay and in obesity. Although obesity may have several different causes, by reducing the amount of sugar, and thus calories, it is possible to lose weight. See 16-10.

You can avoid excessive sugars by using less of all sugars, including white and brown sugar, honey, and syrups. Eat less foods containing sugars, such as candy, soft drinks, ice cream, cakes, and cookies. Select fresh fruits, fruits canned without sugar, or fruits canned with light syrup rather than heavy syrup. Much of the sugar you consume is hidden in pre-prepared and processed foods. Read food labels carefully to find the sugar content. See 16-11.

Limit Intake of Salt, But Increase foods with Potassium

Control of salt intake is a key factor in controlling **hypertension**, or high blood pressure. High blood pressure is often considered a cause of heart disease.

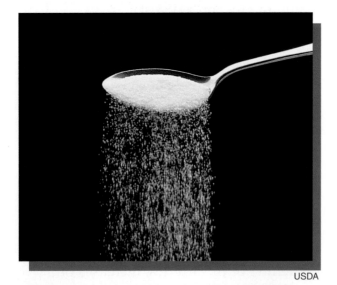

USDA

16-10 Sugar is associated with a variety of health problems. Reducing sugar intake may contribute to better health in general.

Names for Added Sugars That Appear on Food Labels		
Brown sugar	Glucose	Malt syrup
Corn sweetener	High-fructose corn syrup	Molasses
Corn syrup		Raw sugar
Dextrose	Honey	Sucrose
Fructose	Invert sugar	Syrup
Fruit juice concentrate	Lactose	Table sugar
	Maltose	

16-11 A food is likely to be high in sugars if one of these names appears first or second in the ingredient list, or if several names are listed.

The more salt you consume, the more water must flow into your body cells to dilute the salt. Then the cells become swollen and exert pressure on your blood vessels. High salt intake also increases the amount of calcium excreted in urine. Eating less salt may decrease the loss of calcium from bones.

Your body needs very little salt, but salt does bring out the flavor of many foods. When you have eaten foods with salt, you may have difficulty eating them without it. Even if you never touch a saltshaker, you may take in more salt than you need from processed and presalted foods. Read food labels carefully to determine the amounts of salt or sodium in the foods you are selecting. Limit your use of salt, seasoning salts, soy sauce, steak sauce, cheese, pickled foods, and cured meats. See 16-12.

As a public health measure, some table salt is fortified with iodine. If you use table salt to meet your need for iodine, a small amount—about $1/2$ teaspoon of iodized salt—provides more than the daily iodine requirement.

Most Americans get only about half the recommended daily amount of potassium. A potassium-rich diet can help lower blood

USDA

16-12 Think twice before you pick up a salt-shaker. Reducing your salt intake helps decrease your chances of getting high blood pressure later in life.

pressure and reduce the risk of stroke. It may also decrease the risk of some types of kidney stones and help prevent bone loss. Too much potassium can be harmful for people with certain medical conditions so it is wise to consult. with your doctor before increasing your potassium intake.

Potassium is found in many fruits and vegetables. Sweet potatoes, acorn squash, papaya, bananas, dried apricots, pinto beans, and spinach are excellent sources.

Understand the Effects of Alcohol

Heavy drinking reduces life expectancy by 10 to 12 years. Drinking may cause serious conditions, such as scarring or hardening of the liver, that interfere with the body's functions. Evidence also shows heavy alcohol use damages the heart. Many people are unaware that excessive use of alcohol is linked with cancers of the mouth and throat as well as cancers of the liver. Alcohol use by pregnant women is related to birth defects in infants.

Use of alcohol can impair attention, skill, and coordination in activities such as

driving or operating machinery. Further effects of alcohol are discussed later in this chapter.

Practice Food Safety

Foodborne illness is a digestive infection caused by eating contaminated food. Most foods naturally contain small amounts of bacteria. However, when food is poorly handled, improperly cooked, or inadequately stored, bacteria can multiply quickly and cause foodborne illness, also known as food poisoning.

Food supplies in the United States are subject to inspection and are generally safe. However, it is impossible to keep the entire food supply completely free of potentially dangerous bacteria. For this reason, it is important to know how to help prevent foodborne illness in the home. More information related to foodborne illness and safe cooking, handling, and storage of foods will be found in Chapter 19.

Lifestyle Decisions–Drugs and Disease

Drugs are substances other than food that chemically alter the body's structure or functioning. They have been used for many purposes throughout history. Used for proper medical purposes, drugs can help heal illness. However, other uses can cause lasting negative effects. Using alcohol, tobacco, and other drugs can result in damage to such body organs as the heart, kidneys, lungs, and brain. Using these substances may also result in drug dependency, personal and social disorganization, and other serious or fatal diseases.

Drug Abuse

Drug abuse involves using illegal drugs or prescription or over-the-counter drugs in ways other than their intended medical use. Over-the-counter drugs should only be used as directed on the label. Prescription drugs should be taken according to the doctor's instructions or label directions. No one should take a prescription drug that has been prescribed for someone else, 16-13.

Drug is a very general word. A simple classification might help you understand drugs better. They can be divided into three groups:

◆ *Central nervous system depressants.* These substances reduce activity in the brain and spinal cord. They include narcotics, barbiturates, and alcohol.

◆ *Central nervous system stimulants.* These substances stimulate increased activity in the brain or spinal cord. They include cocaine, amphetamines, and caffeine.

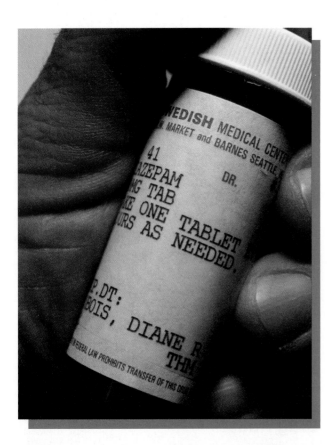

16-13 **Prescription drugs should never be taken by anyone other than the person to whom the drug was prescribed.**

◆ *Hallucinogens.* These substances are capable of producing illusions or hallucinations. They include marijuana, hashish, and LSD.

Inhalants are substances inhaled for their drug effects. These substances are found in such products as spray paint, cigarette lighters, and glues. Inhalant use in this way is deadly serious. Sniffing these volatile substances can cause severe damage to the brain and nervous system. By starving the body of oxygen or forcing the heart to beat more rapidly and erratically, inhalants can kill sniffers, most of whom are adolescents.

Until recently, drinking alcohol and smoking were not perceived as drug-taking behaviors. These activities have been both legal for adults and widely advertised. Many people find drinking alcohol and smoking socially acceptable. Even so, the ethyl alcohol in beer, wine, and distilled alcohol; the caffeine in coffee and tea; and the nicotine in tobacco are all drugs.

Alcohol

Some people consume alcohol because it produces pleasurable sensations of relaxation and provides a relief from tensions. Many people accept the use of alcohol, but alcohol abuse is associated with a number of serious societal ills. These include automobile accidents, on-the-job accidents, domestic abuse, date rape, assault, divorce, and many other social problems. Alcoholism is one of the major medical, social, and economic problems of the United States.

Alcoholism is a progressive disease that involves loss of control over drinking alcoholic beverages. It is both a social and personal problem. See 16-14. Problem drinking affects millions of alcoholics and their families as well as society in general. Alcoholics have higher crime, accident, and divorce rates. The cost of alcoholism in the United States is over a billion dollars a year. This includes care and treatment of alcoholics in hospitals and jails, accidents, lost wages, and support of dependents.

Your choices related to alcohol use depend on your system of values and your maturity. Knowing the effects of excessive use of alcohol may help guide you in setting priorities related to its use. A mature person is able to face the normal stresses of everyday living without using alcohol as an escape.

Smoking

Cigarette smoking is one of the most serious yet preventable health problems. Many people avoid smoking because they understand the serious outcomes of heavy and prolonged smoking. Even so, millions of Americans smoke hundreds of billions of cigarettes each year.

Each year, over 300,000 deaths are related to tobacco use. Long-term effects of smoking include emphysema, chronic bronchitis, heart disease, and cancer of the lungs, mouth, larynx, and esophagus. Women who smoke during pregnancy face other risks. Their babies may be underweight, be stillborn, or die shortly after birth. Therefore, the health risks associated with tobacco are very high.

Cigarette smoking also affects nonsmokers. Carbon monoxide levels in smoke-filled rooms can become high enough to harm the health of nonsmokers. In addition, about 10 to 15 percent of Americans are allergic to tobacco smoke. Studies have shown that children from homes where people smoke are more likely to suffer from respiratory problems than those from smoke-free homes.

Societal Concerns

Drugs are often labeled too simply as either good or bad. Even aspirin can be fatal if a small child takes too much. At the same time, LSD has been used to treat certain mental disorders. No drugs are absolutely safe. All drugs are potentially poisonous and may have side effects. Any drug may be harmful in large enough doses, impure forms, and in combination with other drugs.

Drugs have become a major concern in our society. Although their use is helpful for some physical problems, the major concern about drugs is related to their use socially. Drug use in this way is especially a major concern among teens and young adults.

Each person who uses drugs socially has some kind of excuse. Some people use drugs because of peer pressure. They feel using drugs will help them gain new friends. Others are curious about drugs. Experimenting with the unknown gives them a thrill. Other people use drugs as an escape from reality. They believe drugs may get rid of physical or emotional pain.

Early Warning Signs of Alcoholism

- Difficult to get along with when drinking
- Drinks to relieve depression or calm nerves
- Can't stop drinking until drunk
- Can't remember what happened when drinking
- Hides liquor
- Neglects to eat when drinking
- Neglects family when drinking
- Misses work and performs poorly on the job Remember, alcoholics come from all walks of life and all social classes. Alcoholism is no respecter of age, sex, creed, color, education, or intelligence.

16-14 **Be alert for the warning signs of alcoholism. Someone you know may have an alcohol problem.**

Drug use and abuse creates many risks. When a drug is illegal, there are possibilities of imprisonment and a criminal record or a fine. Drug use can damage physical health or even cause death. These damages may result from the drug itself or from malnutrition and other diseases that are common among users. Drug use and abuse may also cause emotional problems. These might include breakdowns or separation from family, job, school, and friends.

Substance abuse and dependency are not limited to one economic group or a subculture within society. There are many complex causes of substance abuse. A lot of people who abuse substances have poor self-concepts or lack meaningful relationships. People who abuse drugs may feel no one needs them. They do not see themselves as needed, contributing members of a family group, peer group, or society as a whole.

Presenting people with factual evidence on the effects of drug abuse is the best way to help them make rational decisions about substance use. Whether you manage your life with or without the use of drugs is your own decision. However, if you choose to use a drug, it is important to know why you are using it and what effects that drug might have on your body.

Other Lifestyle Diseases

Changing lifestyles since the 1950s have resulted in an increase in **sexually transmitted diseases (STDs)**. STDs are some of the most widespread communicable diseases in the United States. STDs include a group of infections that are almost always transmitted by intimate sexual contact with an infected person. They have reached epidemic proportions among young adults in the United States.

AIDS and HIV

Acquired Immune Deficiency Syndrome (AIDS) is a fatal disease caused by the **Human Immunodeficiency Virus (HIV)**. HIV breaks down the immune system, leaving the body vulnerable to diseases a healthy body could resist. Being infected with the AIDS virus is not the same thing as having AIDS. HIV may live in a person's body for many years without showing symptoms. AIDS is actually the final stage of an HIV infection. For every person with AIDS, there are many more who have been infected with HIV but have not yet developed symptoms of AIDS.

The impact of the AIDS epidemic on society is and will continue to be devastating. When AIDS first appeared in our country, it seemed to be confined mainly to homosexual or bisexual men. However, it is no longer the concern of any one segment of society; it is the concern of all, including heterosexual men and women. AIDS and HIV infection are rising fastest today among teens and young adults.

You cannot get AIDS from casual contact with an infected person. Shaking hands, hugging, or breathing the same air as an infected person will not cause you to contract AIDS. Scientists now believe the only way you can get AIDS is to have a body fluid of an infected person enter your body. HIV is found primarily in body fluids such as semen, blood, and vaginal fluids. AIDS and HIV infection are mainly transmitted through sexual intercourse.

The second-most frequent way of contracting the disease is when intravenous drug users share contaminated needles. Babies in the womb may contract AIDS from mothers who are infected with the AIDS virus. In the past, cases of AIDS have also been linked to the transfusion of blood containing the virus. Today, donated blood is screened for the HIV virus. The chance of getting AIDS from a blood transfusion is very small. Also, any needles used for medical purposes must be disposed of properly to prevent accidental contamination. See 16-15.

When HIV enters the blood, a person may not have the disease. He or she may feel physically fine or may develop only a few symptoms. That person can become a carrier of the disease, though. He or she can pass the virus to others. Blood tests can determine if a person has been exposed to HIV. However, these tests do not distinguish between a carrier and a person with the disease.

Persistent swelling of the lymph glands in the neck, underarm, and groin areas may be an early sign of AIDS. Fevers, unexplained weight loss, night sweats,

unusual blemishes in the mouth, constant tiredness, and frequent diarrhea are other early warnings that the HIV infection may be present. Typically, though, it is the symptoms of other illnesses that develop because of the body's lowered resistance to disease that sends the AIDS patient to the doctor or hospital. The person with AIDS eventually dies from one of these infectious diseases.

Several drugs have been approved by the Food and Drug Administration to fight the virus. A number of vaccines are in various stages of being tested, as are many drugs. However, there is presently no cure for AIDS, nor is there a vaccine to prevent healthy people from becoming infected with HIV.

It is important to realize that AIDS can be prevented. Your best protection is learning what is now known about how the virus is transmitted and keeping informed as new findings are revealed. HIV or AIDS is one of the biggest health concerns of our time. It is difficult to know who has HIV or AIDS. People who have the virus in their blood may not seem sick at all. In fact, many people with the virus don't know they have it. The risk is of coming in contact with HIV or AIDS is the greatest for those who have multiple sexual partners and those who inject illegal drugs.

Other STDs

Gonorrhea is a commonly occurring STD. Symptoms of this disease show up quickly in a person who has been infected. A person with gonorrhea may notice discharge or dripping from the sexual organ or pain when urinating. However, many people have no symptoms of early infection. Left untreated, gonorrhea can cause sterility, heart disease, crippling arthritis, or blindness. Gonorrhea can be diagnosed with a simple test and cured with antibiotics at any stage. However, any damage that the disease has already done cannot be undone.

16-15 **Medical personnel take great care to place used needles in the proper receptacles.**

Syphilis is a destructive STD that can be fatal. After it is transmitted by sexual intercourse, the disease spreads through the bloodstream to various parts of the body in several stages. In the early stages, syphilis may be detected by a blood test and treated with antibiotics.

The first stage consists of a painless sore called a chancre. This chancre occurs at the site of infection and goes away without treatment. Nevertheless, the disease continues to spread. In the second stage a rash appears on the hands, feet, and face. Hair may fall out, the person may feel tired, or there may be sores in the mouth. At this stage, syphilis may be misdiagnosed or overlooked. During these first two stages, the disease is very contagious.

The disease may cure itself at this point, or there may never be further evidence of it. However, most people with syphilis go through the remaining stages. All symptoms may disappear for as long as 30 years. During this stage, the person is not infectious, but pregnant women can still infect their babies. Then the final stage of the disease begins. Bacteria begin to damage body organs. Mental illness, blindness, heart attack, and death may occur.

Type II herpes is another STD. This type of herpes is different from the type that forms fever blisters and cold sores on the lips and mouth. Type II or genital herpes is spread by sexual contact. Symptoms include blisters around the sex organs. These blisters break and form raw sores. Fever, painful urination, and a feeling of sickness may occur.

The herpes virus stays in the body and causes periodic outbreaks. They may be triggered by illness, stress, or physical irritation such as tight clothing. Genital herpes is contagious even days before an outbreak appears. An infected person should avoid sexual contact when blisters are present to prevent spreading the disease.

Women can infect their babies with genital herpes at birth. Women who have herpes are five times more likely to develop cancer of the uterus than women who do not have the disease. There is no cure for herpes, and it can reoccur. Some medicines are helpful; others are not. Warm water and heat lamp treatments relieve some pain.

Chlamydia is the most widespread STD. It attacks the urinary and reproductive systems. Chlamydia can cause permanent damage leading to sterility. Symptoms of the disease are burning and itching around the external reproductive organs, discharge, and burning when urinating. Females may experience pain in the abdomen. Many people have no noticeable symptoms of the disease. A simple test can detect chlamydia. It can then be cured with an antibiotic.

Also becoming more widespread are **genital warts**. Scientists estimate that as many as one million new cases of genital warts are diagnosed in the United States each year. Genital warts are spread by sexual contact with an infected partner and are very contagious. In women, the warts occur on the outside and inside of the vagina, on the cervix, or around the anus. Genital warts are less common in men. If present, they are seen on the penis.

Genital warts may disappear if left untreated. However, in other cases they may eventually develop a fleshy, small raised growth with a cauliflower-like appearance. Because there is no way to predict whether they will grow or disappear, people who suspect they have genital warts should be examined and treated if necessary.

Genital warts may cause a number of problems during pregnancy. Sometimes they enlarge, making urination difficult. If the warts are on the vaginal wall, they can make the vagina less elastic and cause obstruction during delivery.

Prostitution and greater sexual freedom are associated with the spread of STDs. At the same time, many people are afraid to seek treatment for fear of what others will think. They may also be too ashamed to tell their sexual partners they are infected. This only leads to further spreading of the diseases.

Attitudes toward STDs are changing, and treatments are more effective. Becoming educated about STDs should help people avoid them or get prompt and effective treatment. However, the only sure way to prevent STDs is to abstain from sex. Your risk of contracting an STD becomes higher as you have more sexual partners. For people who are at risk of contracting STDs, knowing the early symptoms of the diseases may help them get treatment before they spread a disease to another person.

Summary

By being aware of factors that contribute to good health, you can make wise choices leading to that goal. People who are physically and mentally healthy have certain qualities. If you understand these qualities, you can develop or improve them in yourself.

Good health is largely related to lifestyle. When you understand how lifestyle choices might affect your health, you can make choices to avoid those hazards.

To Review

1. Give an example of how good physical health and mental health are related.
2. Name the six nutrients the body needs to sustain life.
3. List three guidelines for developing a physical activity program and explain why each is important.
4. List four characteristics of mentally healthy people.
5. True or false? Use of defense mechanisms indicates a mental illness.
6. Maintaining wellness in order to prevent diseases from developing is known as _____.
7. Describe four health concerns related to diet and disease.
8. Describe six problems linked with heavy alcohol use.
9. True or false? AIDS and HIV are occurring more frequently among heterosexual men and women.
10. Describe two of the problems in controlling STDs.

To Do
with the Class

1. Work in small groups to develop examples of defense mechanisms typically used by teenagers. Share your ideas with other groups.
2. Research current magazine articles on one of the specific areas of concern related to diet and disease. Report your findings to the class.
3. Take a poll in your class or among friends to find out current attitudes toward the use of drugs. Use the findings of your poll as a basis for class discussion.
4. Talk with people to determine if any of their negative associations toward certain foods influence the eating habits of other people. If so, why?

To Challenge
Your Thinking

1. Develop your own definition of good health and share it with the class.
2. Talk with people you know to learn how they find time for physical activity. Analyze your own schedule and determine where you can fit physical activity into it.
3. Write a paragraph describing what is meant by this statement: Prevention of disease is now becoming a matter of changing lifestyles.
4. Chart your sleep times for one week. Analyze whether you are getting enough, too little, or too much sleep.

To Do
with Your Community

1. Interview or invite a panel of health professionals to share their expertise on achieving a healthy lifestyle for good physical and mental wellness.
2. Think of a person in your community who exhibits good health habits in his or her lifestyle. Ask about the person's values and what he or she does to stay physically and mentally healthy.
3. Find out what community support agencies exist in your area for treatment of people who are chemically dependent.
4. Critique some of the advertisements on television and in print that help teach preventive health care. Do the ads accomplish their aims? How do they do this?

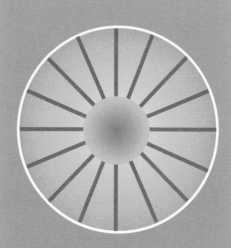

17 **Healthful Eating**

To Know

protein
essential amino acid
complete protein
incomplete protein
complementary
    protein food
carbohydrate
dietary fiber
fat
saturated fat
unsaturated fat
polyunsaturated fats
omega-3 fatty acids
monosaturated fats
trans fatty acids
cholesterol
vitamin
fat-soluble vitamin
water-soluble vitamin
mineral
trace mineral
digestion
enzyme
absorption

metabolism
calorie
Dietary
    Reference
    Intakes (DRIs)

Objectives

After studying this chapter, you will be able to
◆ identify the nutrients the body needs and explain the importance of each.
◆ describe the functions of food in the body.
◆ describe the importance of the food guidance system, MyPyramid.
◆ identify special nutritional needs of people at various stages in the life cycle.
◆ plan diets that meet food guide requirements.
◆ develop menu plans based on various meal patterns.
◆ list resources that can help you make wise choices in selecting nutritious foods.
◆ follow guidelines in selecting nutritious foods when eating out.
◆ identify and explain factors that influence food choices.

Good health is a valuable resource that can help you reach many goals. When you feel well, you are a happier person. You are motivated to perform well and are more likely to get along well with people around you. When you value your good health, you are willing to take preventive steps to stay healthy.

As a young person, you are developing eating habits that can affect you throughout life. The quality of the food you choose affects your growth, development, learning, and behavior. Learning to manage and control the food you eat increases your chances for a healthful life.

Understanding the basic concepts of nutrition will help you make intelligent decisions about your diet. This knowledge helps you make choices at a time when nutritional information and misinformation is abundant. Good diet choices are easier to make when you use a basic food guide and understand the benefits of certain eating patterns.

Basic Concepts of Nutrition

The science of nutrition allows you to understand your body's needs and choose foods important to your health. By using this knowledge to plan meals, you can include the variety and quantity of foods you need.

Nutrients Found in Food

A *nutrient* is a substance supplied by the diet that your body needs to function. Because no single food contains all nutrients, you need to eat a wide variety of foods to be well nourished.

Protein

Protein is an important nutrient for growth and maintenance of body tissues. Your skin, hair, nails, eyes, and muscles are mostly protein. Second only to water, it makes up the greatest percentage of your body weight. It provides the building blocks needed for growing, maintaining, and repairing worn-out cells. Protein helps form enzymes that digest food, hormones that regulate body functions, and antibodies that resist infections and disease.

Protein is made up of amino acids. There are certain essential amino acids that your body cannot produce. **Essential amino acids** must be supplied to the body through certain foods. Protein foods that contain an adequate amount of all the essential amino acids provide **complete protein**. Foods from animals, such as eggs, milk, cheese, meat, fish, and poultry, are examples of complete proteins. See 17-1. (Nutrition experts advise choosing lean varieties of meats to avoid the saturated fat and cholesterol found in many red meats.)

17-1 **The beef in this meal is a good source of protein.**

A protein food that lacks one or more of the essential amino acids is called an **incomplete protein**. Most plant foods, like dried beans, peas, nuts, and enriched or whole grain breads and pastas, are incomplete proteins. Although incomplete proteins do not meet the body's growth needs, one food may provide the amino acids that are missing in another. These foods are referred to as **complementary protein foods**; they supplement one another. Some complementary protein foods include baked beans and brown bread, macaroni and cheese, or peanut butter on whole wheat bread.

Legumes are high-protein seeds such as beans and peas. The soybean is a legume that comes close to being a complete protein by itself. It is consumed in a variety of forms including soy oil, tofu, and soy milk. Eating soy products has been shown to protect against heart disease and cancer and may reduce cholesterol levels.

Carbohydrates

The major function of **carbohydrates** is to provide energy and heat to maintain the body's temperature. Carbohydrates in foods are sugars, starches, or fiber. Sugars are referred to as *simple carbohydrates*. They occur naturally in honey, fruits, and dairy products. They also occur as refined sugar, which comes from either sugarcane or the sugar beet. Since vitamins and minerals of the sugarcane or sugar beet are removed in the refining process, refined sugar contains only "empty" calories. Sugar and honey contain no other nutrients. For this reason, it is wise to choose other carbohydrates and limit your intake of sweets.

When you eat starch, a more complex carbohydrate, the digestive process changes it into simple sugars. See 17-2. Foods high in starch include cereals, rice, flour, and vegetables such as potatoes and corn. Starchy foods are a valuable part of a

17-2   **Breads contain starch, a complex carbohydrate, which is broken down into glucose so the body can use it as energy.**

healthy diet, supplying many key nutrients. However, some starchy foods such as flour, rice, and breakfast cereals may be highly refined. This means a portion of the cereal grain has been removed. The refining process removes fiber as well as many important vitamins and minerals.

Federal law requires that many cereals and cereal products be enriched. The enrichment process adds thiamin, niacin, riboflavin, and iron back into the foods.

Many nutritionists recommend a diet in which most of the carbohydrates come from whole grains which provide the best nutritional value. A healthy diet limits the amount of refined carbohydrates. Eating refined grains can increase blood sugar levels quickly, while the fiber in whole grains slows down the rise in blood sugar.

Dietary fiber, also referred to as cellulose, is a carbohydrate that is not digested. Dietary fiber consists of two types—soluble and insoluble. Soluble fiber is found in all fruits and a few cereals, and as gums added to cereals and other foods. It is the softer, stickier, and thicker fiber. Soluble fiber functions to entrap fatty substances in the intestines, preventing their absorption into the body. This explains how soluble dietary fiber may effectively lower blood cholesterol levels when consumed in adequate amounts.

The largest amount of dietary fiber in our diets is insoluble. It is primarily found in chewy foods like whole wheat products, wheat and corn bran, the skin of fruits, and certain vegetables. Insoluble fiber helps bind water in the intestine and expands the volume of the intestinal contents, resulting in more frequent and softer stools.

Fats

Fats are the most concentrated source of calories. Because they are more slowly digested, they tend to have "staying power." They make you feel full and satisfied.

Fats are broken down and eventually absorbed into the bloodstream. Fat that is not needed immediately is stored as body fat. Since carbohydrates and protein can be converted into fat in the body, they are also potential sources of body fat. Therefore, the amount of stored fat reflects the total amount of food eaten in excess of energy needs.

In addition to providing energy, fats help maintain a constant body temperature by providing effective insulation under the skin. Fat is also used in the production of several hormone-like compounds that help regulate blood pressure, heart rate, blood vessel constriction, blood clotting, and the nervous system. Also, dietary fat carries fat-soluble vitamins from your food throughout your body. In addition, it helps maintain healthy hair and skin.

Fats can be divided into two groups based on their chemical structure. Usually solid or waxy at room temperature, **saturated fat** is most often found in animal products such as red meat, poultry, butter, and whole milk. Most saturated fats can increase blood cholesterol levels and the risk of heart disease.

Unsaturated fats include polyunsaturated fat and monounsaturated fat. Foods high in polyunsaturated fats include vegetable oils such as safflower, corn, sunflower, soy, and cottonseed oils, 17-3. **Polyunsaturated fats** help lower blood cholesterol levels. In addition, they may help reduce the amount of cholesterol deposits in the arteries.

One type of polyunsaturated fat, **omega-3 fatty acids**, may be especially beneficial to your health. These are found mainly in fish, particularly in fatty, cold-water fish, such as salmon, mackerel, and herring. Lesser amounts are in flaxseeds, soybeans, and canola oil. Omega-3 fat appears to decrease the risk of heart attack, protect against irregular heartbeats, and lower blood pressure levels.

Monounsaturated fats are usually liquid at room temperature, but may start to solidify in the refrigerator. Foods high in monounsaturated fats include olive,

USDA

▤ **17-3 Unsaturated fats like corn oil are liquid at room temperature.**

peanut, and canola oils. Avocados and most nuts also have high amounts of monunsaturated fat. If used in place of other fats, monounsaturated fat can lower your risk of heart disease by reducing your blood cholesterol level.

Trans fat, also known as **trans fatty acids**, is a specific type of fat formed when liquid oils are made solid at room temperature through a process called *hydrogenation*. However, a small amount of trans fat is found naturally, primarily in some animal-based foods. Along with saturated fat, trans fatty acids may raise blood cholesterol levels and increase the risk of heart disease. Hydrogenated fat is a common ingredient in commercially baked goods, such as crackers, cookies, and cakes, and in fried foods such as doughnuts and French fries. Shortenings and some margarines are high in trans fat.

Nutrition experts suggest that a good diet will limit fat intake, particularly saturated and trans fats. This diet will also use monounsaturated fats, such as olive and canola oils, when possible.

A diet high in saturated fats may cause you to have a high level of cholesterol. **Cholesterol** is a fatlike substance found in every cell of your body. It is consumed in foods from animal sources and is also manufactured in the body. Although your body needs cholesterol, too much may increase the likelihood of heart disease. Therefore, reducing your intake of saturated fats may be a healthy decision.

Vitamins

Vitamins are compounds required in the diet in extremely small amounts. They are much more important to good nutrition than you might think.

Vitamins regulate body processes, often acting with other substances. Vitamins do not supply energy, but they are vital in the process that releases energy from protein, carbohydrates, and fats. See 17-4.

Vitamins		
Vitamin	**Function**	**Source**
Vitamin A	Helps keep skin clear and smooth and mucus membranes healthy Helps prevent night blindness Helps promote growth	Liver, egg yolk, dark green and yellow fruits and vegetables, butter, whole milk, cream, fortified margarine, ice cream, and cheddar-type cheese
Vitamin D	Helps build strong bones and teeth in children Helps maintain bones in adults	Fortified milk, butter and margarine, fish liver oils, liver, sardines, tuna, egg yolk, and the sun
Vitamin E	Acts as an antioxidant although exact function is not known	Liver and other variety meats, eggs, leafy green vegetables, whole grain cereals, salad oils, shortenings, and other fats and oils
Vitamin K	Helps blood clot	Organ meats, leafy green vegetables, cauliflower, other vegetables, and egg yolk

(Continued)

17-4 **This chart shows the functions and food sources of important vitamins.**

Vitamins

Vitamin C	Promotes healthy gums and tissues Helps wounds heal and broken bones mend Helps body fight infection Helps make cementing materials that hold body cells together	Citrus fruits, strawberries, cantaloupe, broccoli, green peppers, raw cabbage, tomatoes, green leafy vegetables, and potatoes and sweet potatoes cooked in the skin
Thiamin (Vitamin B$_1$)	Helps promote normal appetite and digestion Forms parts of the coenzymes needed for the breakdown of carbohydrates Helps keep nervous system healthy and prevent irritability Helps body release energy from food	Pork, other meats, poultry, fish, eggs, enriched or whole-grain breads and cereals, and dried beans
Riboflavin	Helps cells use oxygen Helps keep skin, tongue, and lips normal Helps prevent scaly, greasy areas around the mouth and nose Forms part of the coenzymes needed for the breakdown of carbohydrates	Milk, all kinds of cheese, ice cream, liver, other meats, fish, poultry, eggs, and dark leafy green vegetables
Niacin	Helps keep nervous system healthy Helps keep skin, mouth, tongue, and digestive tract healthy Helps cells use other nutrients Forms part of two coenzymes involved in complex chemical reactions in the body	Meat, fish, poultry, milk, enriched or whole-grain breads and cereals, peanuts, peanut butter, and dried beans and peas
Vitamin B$_6$	Helps nervous tissue function normally Plays a role in the breakdown of proteins, fats, and carbohydrates Plays a role in the regeneration of red blood cells	Liver, muscle meats, vegetables, and whole-grain cereals
Vitamin B$_{12}$	Protects against anemia Plays a role in the normal functioning of cells	Eggs, fish, liver and other meats, milk, and cheese

17-4 (Continued)

Vitamins are either fat-soluble or water-soluble. The **fat-soluble vitamins** are A, D, E, and K. They tend to accompany fats as they are absorbed in the digestive process. Because fat-soluble vitamins are stored in the body to some extent, supplying them daily may not be necessary.

All the **water-soluble vitamins** except vitamin C are B vitamins. Most water-soluble vitamins are not stored in the body. Excess amounts of these vitamins are excreted into the urine.

Minerals

Minerals function to help regulate body processes. Like vitamins, minerals are needed only in small amounts. However, many of them are essential to healthful living. See 17-5.

Minerals are commonly divided into two groups: minerals present in the body in relatively large amounts and those present in relatively small amounts. Those present in small amounts are referred to as **trace minerals**. Iron, iodine, and zinc are the most common trace minerals. Calcium, phosphorus, magnesium, sodium, potassium, and chlorine are present in larger amounts.

Researchers have found that minerals interact with other nutrients. For instance, vitamin C helps in the absorption of iron.

Minerals		
Mineral	**Function**	**Sources**
Calcium	Helps build bones and teeth Helps blood clot Helps muscles and nerves work Helps regulate the use of other minerals in the body	Milk, cheese, other dairy products, leafy green vegetables, and fish eaten with the bones
Phosphorus	Helps build strong bones and teeth Helps regulate many internal bodily activities	Protein and calcium food sources
Magnesium	Helps cells use protein, fats, and carbohydrates to produce energy Regulates body temperature Helps muscles contract Keeps nervous system working properly Helps balance alkalis and acids	Whole grains and grain products, nuts, beans, meats, and dark green, leafy vegetables
Sodium, Potassium, and Chlorine	Work together to control the flow of fluids in and out of cells through cell walls Help balance alkalis and acids Help the nervous system and muscles function Help cells absorb nutrients	Many animal and plant foods Other source of sodium and chlorine—table salt Other sources of potassium—meat, milk, bananas, citrus fruits, and dark green, leafy vegetables
Iodine	Promotes normal functioning of the thyroid gland	Iodized table salt, saltwater fish, and shellfish
Iron	Combines with protein to make hemoglobin Helps cells use oxygen	Liver, lean meats, egg yolk, dried beans and peas, leafy green vegetables, dried fruits, and enriched and whole-grain breads and cereals

17-5 **This chart explains the functions and sources of important minerals.**

Research to discover other food guides that are used or have been used in the past. Discuss how these guides differ from MyPyramid. List the advantages and disadvantages of each food guide. Why do you think food guides have changed and continue to change?

Minerals also interact with each other. For example, calcium and phosphorus work together to form bones and teeth.

Water

Next to oxygen, water is the most important element for sustaining life. Humans can go for a few weeks without food but only about 48 hours without water. About one-half to three-fourths of your body's weight is made up of water. It is present in your body cells, as part of the blood, and in special tissues.

All the body's chemical processes take place in water. It brings food through the digestive tract and through the intestinal wall into the blood, which is largely composed of water. It helps transport nutrients throughout the body and carries away waste products. It regulates body temperature by taking the heat produced and distributing it throughout the body. Water is involved in every body process: digestion, absorption, circulation, and elimination.

Functions of Food

In order to function properly, your body needs certain nutrients. These nutrients are found in the food you eat. Your body digests them, or breaks them down into simple forms and absorbs them into your bloodstream. Your body uses these nutrients for building and maintaining physical structure, controlling and coordinating body processes, and providing energy for activity and warmth.

Building and Maintaining Physical Structure

Body tissues such as muscle and bone consist mainly of body protein. The body demands the most protein during periods of rapid growth, such as infancy, adolescence, and pregnancy. After adult stature is reached, protein is no longer used to increase body size. However, protein is still needed for body maintenance. Cells are continuously broken down and rebuilt throughout life.

Minerals, mainly calcium and phosphorus, work with protein and vitamins to build bones and teeth. Besides providing a framework for the body, bones serve as a storehouse for the minerals they contain. These minerals can be taken from the bone by the blood whenever they are needed.

Blood and digestive secretions are made up largely of water. However, protein, minerals, and other nutrients are also required to build the blood.

Controlling and Coordinating Body Processes

Nutrients are important to the body processes of digestion, absorption, and metabolism. **Digestion** is the process that modifies and reduces foods mechanically or chemically so they can pass through the intestinal wall into the bloodstream. **Enzymes**, proteins that are found in digestive juices, help break down foods so the body can use them.

Absorption is the process in which nutrients are taken into the bloodstream throughout the walls of the intestine. Fingerlike projections called *villi* are found all along the lining of the small intestine. These villi increase the surface area to help the blood pick up nutrients and transport them to the cells of the body.

_Getting_Involved

Metabolism refers to the processes that take place after food compounds have been absorbed into the bloodstream. This includes the processes that help build, maintain, and repair body cells. Metabolic processes also break down waste products into simple substances that are eliminated by the body. Another metabolic process involves transforming modified foods into energy and heat. A surplus of these foods is stored as fat.

Vitamins and minerals work together to coordinate the body processes. Water helps regulate body temperature. _Hemoglobin_, a protein in the blood, carries oxygen to the tissues and carries some of the carbon dioxide from the tissues back to the lungs.

Fiber is important to the digestive process as well. It provides bulk that helps substances move through the intestine and from the body.

Providing Energy for Activity and Warmth

Your body needs nutrients to provide energy for activities such as the beating of your heart, breathing, and maintenance of muscle tone. Physical activities like standing and walking also require energy.

Carbohydrates, fats, and protein are the three nutrients that supply energy, and each is a potential source of body fat. Energy is released when your body burns or uses food. **Calories** are units that indicate the amount of energy burned. The more calories a food contains, the more energy it can supply. The greater the physical exertion, the greater the number of calories needed to supply energy for that activity.

Food Guides and Eating Patterns

As a result of scientific research, Recommended Dietary Allowances (RDAs) were established for each nutrient. These RDAs, the oldest nutritional guidelines, were designed to prevent nutritional deficiencies in the general population, not to prevent chronic diseases. However, in recent years, as scientists have learned more about the role of specific nutrients in disease prevention, more up-to-date guidelines have been developed. The new tool for nutrition planning is **Dietary Reference Intakes (DRIs)**. The primary goal of having new dietary reference values was not only to prevent nutrient deficiencies. Reducing the risk of chronic diseases such as osteoporosis, cancer, and cardiovascular disease was also a consideration. The Dietary Guidelines for Americans, which were presented in Chapter 16, represent federal nutrition policy. They provide the basis for federal nutrition policy related to nutrition assistance programs, such as the school lunch program, and federal nutrition education messages.

Figuring the exact amount of nutrients you get from the foods you eat daily, however, is difficult. Therefore, the food guidance system, MyPyramid, has been developed to help consumers make healthy food choices. It translates nutritional recommendations from the Dietary Guidelines for Americans and the Dietary Reference Intakes into the kinds and amounts of food to eat each day. It is an educational tool, not intended to be a strict prescription, but a general guide that lets Americans choose a healthful diet that is right for them.

MyPyramid

MyPyramid is part of a food guidance system that emphasizes a more individualized approach to improving diet and lifestyle. The MyPyramid symbol shown in

17-6 MyPryamid is a food guidance system. It is a personalized approach to balancing nutrition and physical activity.

17-6 represents the recommended proportion of foods from each food group. MyPyramid features foods from the following food groups:

◆ Grains

◆ Vegetables

◆ Fruits

◆ Milk

◆ Meat and Beans

◆ Oils

By eating the recommended amounts from each group daily, you should get all the nutrients you need. A description of what counts as a serving is given in 17-7.

It is important for good nutrition to choose a variety of foods from within each food group. Since foods within the same food group differ in their content of nutrients and other beneficial substances, choosing a variety helps you get all the nutrients and fiber you need. You may also find that your meals are more appealing when you choose different foods every day.

Physical activity, represented by the steps and the person climbing them, is a reminder of the importance of daily physical activity. Physical activity can range from sedentary to active. *Sedentary* means a lifestyle that includes only light physical activity associated with typical day-to-day life. *Active* means a lifestyle that includes physical activity equivalent to walking more than 3 miles per day at 3 to 4 miles per hour, in addition to the light physical activity associated with typical day-to-day life. Estimated calorie needs for various age/gender groups are given in 17-8.

By visiting www.MyPyramid.gov, you can find an estimate of what and how much food you should eat from the different food groups by entering your age, gender, and physical activity level.

Grains

This group contains all whole grain and enriched breads and cereals, flour, macaroni, spaghetti, noodles, rice, tortillas,

What Counts as a Serving?
Food Groups

Grains

| 1 slice of bread | 1 ounce of ready-to-eat cereal | 1/2 cup of cooked cereal, rice, or pasta |

Vegetables

| 2 cups of raw leafy vegetables | 1 cup of other vegetables, cooked or chopped raw | 1 cup of vegetable juice |

Fruits

| 1 medium apple, banana, orange | 1 cup of chopped, cooked, or canned fruit | 1 cup of 100% fruit juice; 1/2 cup dried fruit |

Milk

| 1 cup of milk or yogurt | 1 1/2 ounces of natural cheese | 2 ounces of process cheese |

Meat and Beans

| 1 ounce of cooked lean meat, poultry, or fish | 1/4 cup of cooked dry beans, 1 egg, or 1 tablespoon of peanut butter |

17-7 These are typical amounts recommended in the food guidance system, MyPyramid.

and grits. Foods in this group are important sources of B-complex vitamins, iron, protein, and fiber. *Folate*, also called folic acid, is a B-complex vitamin that reduces the risk of serious birth defects. It may also help protect against coronary heart disease and certain cancers. Folic acid is now added to all enriched grain products.

To get the nutrients and fiber you need, choose foods made from whole grains. Foods from this group are often served at breakfast as toast, cereals, muffins, or pancakes. They are also served at lunch and dinner as sandwiches, rolls, pasta dishes, or rice.

Vegetables

This group provides vitamins, such as vitamins A and C, and minerals, such as iron, calcium, and magnesium. Vegetables tend to be low in fat and high in fiber.

Different types of vegetables provide different nutrients. It is a good idea to eat a variety of vegetables every day. Dark green, leafy vegetables, such as spinach and broccoli, are high in vitamins A and C, the B-complex vitamins, calcium, and iron. Deep yellow vegetables, such as carrots and sweet potatoes, are high in vitamin A. Starchy vegetables, such as potatoes,

Estimated Calorie Needs

Age/Gender Group	Calorie Range	
Children	*Sedentary*	*Active*
2-3 years	1,000	1,400
Females		
4-8 years	1,200	1,800
9-13	1,600	2,200
14-18	1,800	2,400
19-30	2,000	2,400
31-50	1,800	2,200
51+	1,600	2,200
Males		
4-8 years	1,400	2,000
9-13	1,800	2,600
14-18	2,200	3,200
19-30	2,400	3,000
31-50	2,200	3,000
51+	2,000	2,800

17-8 The calorie range for each age/gender group is based on physical activity level, from sedentary to active.

supply complex carbohydrates. Vegetables are used both raw and cooked. They are used in salads, casseroles, stews, and soups.

Fruits

This group includes both fruits and fruit juices, 17-9. Fruits supply vitamins A and C and potassium. Fruits are low in fat and provide fiber to the diet. When possible, eat whole fruits since they are higher in fiber than fruit juices. At least one serving per day should be citrus fruit or another fruit that is high in vitamin C. Fruits are often eaten by the piece. They may also be used in salads and desserts.

Milk

This group provides protein, vitamins, and minerals. In fact, milk, yogurt, and cheese are the best sources of calcium. To avoid fat, choose fat free and reduced fat milk and cheese products. Milk is often served as a beverage with a meal or snack. It may also be included in the preparation of main dishes, soups, custards, and puddings.

▤ **17-9 Eating fruit is a delicious, lowfat way to add necessary vitamins to your diet.**

Meat and Beans

This group supplies protein, B-complex vitamins, iron, and zinc. These foods usually appear as the main dish at a meal. They may also be an ingredient in a soup, stew, salad, casserole, or sandwich.

Oils

Oils are fats that are liquid at room temperature, like the vegetable oils used in cooking. Oils come from many different plants and from fish. Some common oils are canola oil, corn oil, and olive oil. Foods that are mainly oil include mayonnaise, certain salad dressings, and soft (tub or squeeze) margarine. Most of the fats you eat should be polyunsaturated or monounsaturated fats. Oils are the major source of these fats in the diet. Polyunsaturated fats contain some fatty acids that are necessary for health—called *essential fatty acids*. The oils found in fish and vegetable oils do not raise LDL("bad") cholesterol levels in the blood. In addition to the essential fatty acids they contain, oils are the major source of vitamin E in typical American diets. While consuming some oil is needed for health, oils still contain calories. In fact, oils and solid fats both contain about 120 calories per tablespoon. Therefore, the amount of oil consumed needs to be limited to balance total calorie intake.

Special Nutritional Needs

Throughout life, everyone needs the same nutrients in varying amounts. Diets lacking in nutrients during any period of life can have serious consequences. There are certain crucial periods in life when nutrient needs are higher than normal. People with special nutritional needs include pregnant and breastfeeding women, infants, children, adolescents, older adults, and athletes.

Pregnant and Breastfeeding Women

A mother's nutritional state at the time she becomes pregnant as well as the quality of her diet during pregnancy are important factors in her health and her baby's health. The many physical changes taking place in the mother and the unborn child during pregnancy increase demands for an intake of nutrients. Some doctors prescribe vitamin and mineral supplements. The additional demands of breastfeeding depend to a great extent on the amount of milk produced and the length of time the baby nurses. Both pregnant and breast-feeding women should eat a variety of nutritious foods and consult their doctors regarding the number of calories their diets should supply each day.

Infants

The requirements for energy and nutrients per unit of body weight are higher in infancy than at any other time of life. Milk is given to infants in the form of breast milk or infant formula. A pediatrician can tell parents when infants should begin the transition from milk to pureed solid foods.

Children

Children have unique food patterns and needs, and many young children do not eat healthful diets. Eating a variety of foods is healthful. Eating foods from each of the major food groups every day is the best way for children to grow well and be healthy.

Adolescents

During the teenage period, nutritional requirements for the body are high. Since teens are undergoing a growth spurt, wise food choices are important to meet increased energy needs.

Two nutrients that typically fall short in a teen's diet are calcium and iron. Calcium builds strong bones, and iron helps carry oxygen through the blood to all parts of the body. Teenage boys need iron to meet the needs of an increase in muscle mass and a greater blood supply. Girls require iron to replace menstrual losses.

Older Adults

Elderly people often expend less energy than other people, 17-10. This reduces their calorie requirements accordingly. Because they often eat less, the selection of foods for elderly people becomes more critical in order to provide needed nutrients. Normal physical changes associated with aging may cause digestive problems. Often, dental problems can make chewing difficult. Modifications in the diets of the elderly may include a shift toward eating smaller meals more frequently and a softer diet.

Often, as people age, the tongue's taste buds become less sensitive and the ability

17-10 Some older people lead less-active lifestyles, especially after retirement.

to smell also changes. The diminishing ability to taste and smell can be a factor in poor nutrition among the elderly. A key to getting older people to eat more is to make their food more appetizing. Also, as the sense of thirst declines with age, it is important for older adults to drink eight or more glasses of water a day.

Special Needs of Athletes

Athletes need more calories and nutrients in general than average people. A healthy diet for an athlete is one that is high in carbohydrates, low in fat, and sufficient but not excessive in protein. Complex carbohydrates, such as whole grain pasta, rice, and bread are absorbed slowly into the body and give a steady energy supply. As a dietary bonus, these foods are also generally high in fiber. Simple carbohydrates like sugars are good for a quick energy boost since they are quickly absorbed into the bloodstream, but the benefits wear off quickly. In selecting sugars, natural sources such as fruit or juice should be selected rather than junk foods like candy, soda, and doughnuts. These foods have plenty of calories and fat, but no essential vitamins or minerals.

Fluids are important. If they are not replaced, the body becomes dehydrated. Chronic dehydration increases risk for kidney stones and bladder cancer. Water is usually the best choice. However, athletes such as long distance runners may need a carbohydrate sports drink for fluid and fuel.

Eating Habits and Patterns

Eating habits and patterns refer to what, when, and where people eat throughout the day. Because factors such as ages, activities, occupations, budgets, and traditions vary, eating habits of individuals and families vary tremendously.

People have traditionally eaten three meals a day, 17-11. However, there has been

17-11 **These pictures show the traditional breakfast, lunch, and dinner.**

much variation within that pattern. For instance, farm families often had their largest meal of the day around noon. Because they had been up early and were doing a lot of physical work, they were very hungry. On the other hand, people from urban areas had their largest meal of the day in the evening. The husband, wife, and children were away from home during the day. The evening meal was the only one they could eat together.

Because lifestyles are changing, a variety of approaches to eating have replaced the traditional three meals a day. More women are working outside the home. Because people are busier, they are using more convenience foods and going to fast-food restaurants. These lifestyle changes have caused changes in eating patterns.

Snacking has become as much a part of the typical eating pattern as a regular meal. When considering the nutritional value of the day's food, be sure to include the snacks you have eaten.

If you have poor snack habits, you probably eat too much junk food. Snacking too much before meals may keep people from eating nutritious foods at mealtimes. Providing children with nutritious snacks can have a tremendous effect on their snack habits and their health throughout life.

Basing meals on patterns makes meal planning easier. Meal patterns list the basic types of foods to include at each meal. They provide a framework for planning nutritious meals. If you do not use a meal pattern, you might easily omit some essential foods.

Meal patterns have been suggested for light, moderate, and heavy meals. See 17-12. This allows people to adapt meal patterns to the way they eat. For instance, if you eat only a light lunch, then you can use a heavier meal pattern for dinner.

The MyPyramid is the nutritional basis for making wise food choices. Meal patterns are an additional resource to help you select foods to provide an adequate diet. No matter what eating pattern you

assume, what you eat is more important than when you eat it.

Selecting Nutritious Foods

Your understanding of basic nutrition concepts will help you make sensible food choices. In addition, nutritional labeling and product dating are other resources to help you make wise choices when selecting foods.

Guidelines for Selecting Nutritious Foods

Many factors can affect the nutritional content of a food, whether it is fresh, frozen, or canned. These guidelines should help you choose more nutritious foods.

- Choose crisp vegetables that are firm in texture and free from blemishes. Vegetables that become too mature have a stringy, woody texture. Wilted vegetables often lose nutritional value.
- The nutritional value of frozen products is often equal to that of fresh foods. Frozen products packed immediately after harvesting may even be superior to fresh foods that have moved from farm to market to consumer, especially if they were improperly handled.
- A fresh fruit or vegetable is usually the most nutritious choice. However, each varies in color, shape, and size. There are no general rules to guide your selection. Knowing what characteristics to look for in each type of fruit and vegetable is important. For instance, avoid potatoes that are shriveled and sprouted as they are too old.
- In selecting fish, odor is one of the most important signs of freshness. Each fish has a natural odor. Once the fish gets older, the odor becomes strong and offensive.

Basic Meal Patterns

Breakfast	Lunch* or Supper	Dinner*
Fruit or fruit juice Main dish or protein food Bread Beverage	Main dish Vegetable and/or fruit Bread Beverage	Main dish Potato, rice, or pasta Vegetable Beverage Salad Bread Dessert Beverage

The basic meal pattern can be modified to provide different levels of food intake.

	Light	Moderate	Heavy
Breakfast	Fruit Cereal and/or bread Beverage	Fruit Cereal and/or bread Protein food Beverage	Fruit Cereal Main dish or bread product Protein food Beverage
Lunch	Soup or salad Bread or sandwich Fruit Beverage	Main dish Vegetable or salad Fruit Beverage	Main dish Vegetable and/or salad Bread Fruit Dessert Beverage
Dinner	Meat, poultry, or fish Vegetable Salad Bread Beverage	Meat, poultry, or fish Potato, rice, or pasta Vegetable Salad Bread Beverage	Soup Meat, poultry, or fish Vegetable Salad Bread Dessert Beverage

*Dinner is considered the largest meal of the day. If this meal is eaten near the middle of the day in your family, you would follow the lunch or supper plan for your evening meal.

17-12 **Meal patterns can be a valuable resource in meal planning.**

- Poultry should have firm, thick flesh with a yellowish tinge. It should never look bluish.
- Check eggs and avoid any with cracked shells. They may contain bacteria that can cause foodborne illness. Eggs should be kept under refrigeration.

Nutrition Labeling

Laws have been established to provide the consumer with safer foods and exact information about the content of processed foods. The name of a food product must not be misleading. For instance, a product cannot be called a beef frankfurter unless the meat it contains is all beef. All the ingredients must be listed on the label in the order of the quantity present.

Food labels are required on almost all packaged foods. These labels, known as Nutrition Facts, carry a nutrition information guide or nutrition panel. See 17-13. This guide can help you in planning a healthy diet. Nutrition Facts will include both mandatory and voluntary dietary components, which must appear in a certain order. See 17-14. The nutrients required on the label reflect current public health concerns. The serving size is given in both conventional and metric measures. The number of servings per container is also given. The number of calories per serving is listed, as well as the amount of calories per serving from fat. This is done to help consumers meet dietary guidelines that recommend people get no more than 30 percent of their calories from fat.

Next on the Nutrition Facts panel is the list of nutrients given in amounts per serving. The nutrients listed include: total fat, saturated fat, trans fat, cholesterol, sodium, total carbohydrate, dietary fiber, sugars, protein, vitamin A, vitamin C, calcium, and iron.

Sample Label for
Macaroni and Cheese

17-13 **Nutrition Facts panels, such as this sample, are required on almost all packaged food labels. This guide serves as a key to help in planning a healthy diet.**

For each nutrient listed, a percent Daily Value shows how a food fits into the overall daily diet. The percent Daily Values are based on a 2,000-calorie diet. Your daily values may be higher or lower depending on your calorie needs. Some of the daily values are maximums, such as that for fat (65 grams or less). Others are minimums, such as that for carbohydrates (300 grams or more).

If a claim is made about any of the voluntary components, or if a food is fortified or enriched with any of them, nutrition information for these components becomes

Voluntary and Mandatory Components

Following are the mandatory (in boldface) and voluntary dietary components and the order in which they must appear on the nutrition label.

Total calories	**Cholesterol**	Other carbohydrate
Calories from fat	**Sodium**	**Protein**
Calories from saturated fat	Potassium	**Vitamin A**
Total fat	**Total carbohydrate**	Percent of vitamin A present as beta-carotene
Saturated fat	**Dietary fiber**	
Trans fat	Soluble fiber	**Vitamin C**
Stearic acid (on meat and poultry products only)	Insoluble fiber	**Calcium**
	Sugars	**Iron**
Polyunsaturated fat	Sugar alcohol	Other essential vitamins and minerals
Monounsaturated fat		

17-14 Dietary components, both mandatory and voluntary, are to appear on the Nutrition Facts panel in this order.

mandatory. The nutrition panel on a food product lists information that can be very helpful to you. For people concerned about their families' diets, time spent reading carefully is extremely worthwhile.

Nutrient Content and Health Claims

Current regulations specify terms that may be used to describe the level of nutrients in a food and how the terms are used. See 17-15. There are also regulations related to nutrient-disease relationship claims. The claim must meet the requirements for authorized health claims. For example, the degree of risk reduction cannot be stated; only *may* or *might* can be used in discussing the nutrient- or food-disease relationship. It must also be stated that other factors play a role in causing the disease. An example of an appropriate claim is "While many

factors affect heart disease, diets low in saturated fat and cholesterol may reduce the risk of this disease."

Ingredient Labeling

Ingredient declaration is required on all foods that have more than one ingredient. Because people may be allergic to certain additives and to help them better avoid them, the ingredient list must include

- FDA-certified color additives

- sources of protein hydrolysates, which are used in many foods as flavors and flavor enhancers

- caseinate as a milk derivative in the ingredient list of foods that claim to be nondairy

- total percentage of juice in beverages that claim to contain juice

FDA Regulations Related to Terms That May Be Used

Free	This term means a product contains either no amount or physiologically inconsequential amounts of one or more of these components: fat, saturated fat, cholesterol, sodium, sugars, and calories.
Low	This term can be used on foods that can be eaten frequently without exceeding dietary guidelines for one or more of these components: fat, saturated fat, cholesterol, sodium, and calories. These descriptors are defined as follows: • *lowfat*: 3 g or less per serving • *low saturated fat*: 1 g or less per serving • *low sodium*: 140 mg or less per serving • *very low sodium*: 35 mg or less per serving • *low cholesterol*: 20 mg or less and 2 g or less of saturated fat per serving • *low calorie*: 40 calories or less per serving
Lean and Extra Lean	These terms can be used to describe the fat content of meat, poultry, seafood, and game meats. • *lean*: less than 10 g fat, 4.5 g or less saturated fat, and less than 95 mg cholesterol per serving • *extra lean*: less than 5 g fat, less than 2 g saturated fat, and less than 95 mg cholesterol per serving
High	This term can be used if the food contains 20 percent or more of the Daily Value for a particular nutrient in a serving.
Good Source	This term means one serving of a food contains 10 to 19 percent of the Daily Value for a particular nutrient.
Reduced	This term means a nutritionally altered product contains at least 25 percent less of a nutrient or of calories than the regular product.
Less	This term means a food, whether altered or not, contains 25 percent less of a nutrient or of calories than the reference food. For example, pretzels that have 25 percent less fat than potato chips could carry a *less* claim. *Fewer* is an acceptable synonym.
Light	This descriptor can mean a nutritionally altered product contains one-third fewer calories or half the fat of the reference food. If the food derives 50 percent or more of its calories from fat, the reduction must be 50 percent of the fat. It can also mean the sodium content of a low-calorie, lowfat food has been reduced by 50 percent. In addition, *light in sodium* may be used on foods in which the sodium content has been reduced by at least 50 percent.
More	This term means that a serving of food, whether altered or not, contains a nutrient that is at least 10 percent of the Daily Value more than the reference food. The 10 percent of Daily Value also applies to *fortified*, *enriched*, *added*, *extra*, and *extra plus* claims, but in those cases, the food must be altered.

17-15 Government regulations spell out what terms may be used to describe the level of a nutrient and how they can be used.

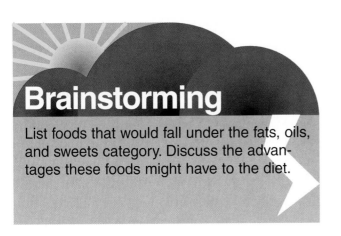

Brainstorming

List foods that would fall under the fats, oils, and sweets category. Discuss the advantages these foods might have to the diet.

Product Dating

Product dating is another valuable aid for consumers who are trying to select nutritious foods. The length of time since the food has been packaged or processed will affect the nutritional quality of the product.

Dating of products is not required by federal law. However, it is required by some local ordinances. The dates listed may be one of the following:

- *pack date*–the date the food was packaged

- *pull date*–the date by which the product should be sold, which is likely to appear on perishable items such as milk, eggs, or poultry

- *quality assurance date*–the date after which the nutrient content may be seriously depleted

- *expiration date*–the last date you should use the product

These dates may be embossed, printed, or stamped on the food products. Store managers can answer your questions about product dating.

Selecting Nutritious Foods When Eating Out

Eating away from home is a growing trend. A large portion of money spent on food away from home is spent in restaurants, many of them fast-food restaurants. A demand for convenience and a change in eating habits have contributed to the popularity of fast food. For most people, an occasional fast-food meal will not upset an otherwise balanced diet. However, for people who eat out regularly, especially families with children, care in selection of foods is necessary.

Fast foods do supply some nutrients. The best nutritional feature of many fast foods is the protein content. Some vitamins and minerals are also provided in moderate to large quantities. However, fast foods tend to provide large amounts of saturated fat, cholesterol, and sodium in addition to many calories. Although salads, fruit juices, and reduced fat milk have been added at most fast-food chains, the selections remain relatively limited. You need some knowledge of food composition and preparation techniques to make wise food choices.

The greatest nutrition problem with typical fast foods is usually the high number of calories. A meal consisting of a quarter-pound cheeseburger, fries, and a shake contains about 1217 calories. This meal probably contains a lot more calories than most dinners prepared at home. Most of the calories in fast foods come from fat. Cheese, mayonnaise, and the popular method of deep frying are rich sources of fat.

Chicken and fish items are usually thought of as the best choices because they are often lower in calories and fat than beef or other red meats. However, these choices are not always good ones if the chicken or fish are deep fried.

Certain menu items, particularly fast-food sandwiches, contain large amounts of sodium, which can contribute to high blood pressure. It is difficult to know by taste how much sodium is in food. Fast foods except for salads and coleslaw are frequently low in fiber. Sources of fiber such as fruits, vegetables, and whole grains have not been traditional fast-food offerings. Some restaurants are trying to meet consumer interest in health, fitness, and nutrition by offering more nutritious foods. When eating at restaurants, it's a good idea to keep these guidelines in mind.

◆ Best breakfast choices would include biscuits or toast with fruit juice and fat free milk. Most other fast-food options tend to be high in fat and calories.

◆ It is a good idea to select basic meat items, such as a regular hamburger instead of a burger with cheese or special sauces.

◆ Choose chicken or fish only if it is roasted, unbreaded, grilled, baked, or broiled. If fried is your only choice, choose regular coating over extra crispy varieties that soak up more oil during cooking.

◆ Consider sandwiches made with whole grain breads and lean meats. A whole grain or white bun has about 135 calories compared to a croissant that averages 400-500 calories.

◆ Instead of fries, take advantage of salad bars, coleslaw, or plain baked potatoes.

◆ When choosing soups, remember that clear soups usually contain less fat than cream soups. Chili with beans is a good choice. Beans are a good source of fiber.

◆ Cheese pizza topped with mushrooms, green peppers, and onions is a good source of protein, calcium, and B-complex vitamins. Avoid the pepperoni, sausage, anchovies, or extra cheese that add unnecessary fat, sodium, and calories.

◆ When choosing a salad, load up on lettuce and fresh vegetables such as carrots, tomatoes, and dark-green vegetables. Avoid high-fat toppings, such as regular dressings, bacon, cheeses, and seeds. See 17-16.

◆ To cut back on sugar, choose fresh fruits instead of canned fruits in heavy syrup.

◆ Soft tacos, tostados, and bean burritos are good calorie and nutrient picks.

◆ Diet beverages, reduced fat milk, fruit juice, yogurt smoothies, or water will help save calories. Shakes and soft drinks are sources of hidden fats and sugars.

◆ Frozen yogurt and reduced fat ice creams are good choices. Ices, sobets, and sherbets generally have less fat and fewer calories.

17-16 **A salad can be a good food choice. Order a side salad instead of fries and request dressing on the side.**

Factors That Influence Food Choices

Eating is one of life's greatest pleasures. Since there are many foods and many ways to build a healthy diet and lifestyle, there is a lot of room for choice. Being aware of the importance of nutritional food choices, factors that contribute to good health, and the influence on lifestyle decisions on your health and well-being will help you make wise choices. Understanding what influences your food choices can also help you make wise decisions.

Food likes and dislikes vary greatly among people. This fact makes planning healthful and satisfying meals a challenge. Understanding why people choose foods and how they develop these attitudes and practices can help you in meal planning.

Societal and Cultural Influences

The availability of foods plays a major role in determining food choices. Obviously, your food choices are limited by the foods available to you. You become familiar with those foods and acquire a taste for them.

Availability of foods is determined by various factors including the climate, production and marketing systems, and economic situation. Some foods grow well only under certain climate conditions. Fish and seafood found in saltwater differ from the freshwater fish found in lakes and streams. Weather extremes, such as drought or excessive rain, can affect the availability of certain foods.

Due to modern marketing and distribution of foods, most foods are available throughout the country. In the past, many fresh fruits and vegetables were available only seasonally. Today these items can be found throughout the year in many supermarkets. However, fruits and vegetables are still most reasonably priced during their peak growing seasons.

Your economic situation also affects your food choices. When your food budget is limited, you avoid certain expensive foods such as steak and lobster. Having a low income automatically limits food choices.

In specific cultures, certain foods are traditionally eaten as a part of special events and celebrations. In the United States, eating turkey for Thanksgiving dinner and cake as a part of a birthday celebration are common traditions. See 17-17.

A person's religion may also influence food choices. Some religions forbid eating certain foods. Specific foods are often associated with religious holidays.

Many ethnic groups continue food traditions to maintain their identity with their heritage. Because the United States has been influenced by so many cultures, eating customs have expanded and changed. Changes in eating habits and food patterns reflect the changes in society as well.

17-17 **A birthday cake is an example of a cultural food custom in the United States.**

Lifestyle Influences

Family lifestyle greatly affects meal management practices and food choices. Meal management responsibilities and mealtime have become difficult to schedule for several reasons. More women are working outside the home. There are more one-parent families. Also, individual family members lead very active lives. Planning menus becomes more and more challenging under these circumstances. Meals are often prepared on the spur of the moment. Because of these lifestyle changes, people are using the wide range of convenience foods for quick meals.

Eating out has become an American habit. There are vending machines, snack bars, lunch counters, drive-in restaurants, cafeterias, and a variety of restaurants. They supply everything from snacks to full meals. Fast-food restaurants provide quick service in an informal atmosphere. You can take the food out and eat it at home or in the car.

Personal Experiences and Associations

Although you eat because you are hungry, you choose certain foods because eating them gives you pleasure. Sense of taste differs greatly among people. Therefore, two people might perceive the taste of the same food in different ways. Your food likes and dislikes result from the way you perceive a food to taste.

Psychological satisfactions or barriers also affect your food choices. These are your attitudes, beliefs, and emotions. Your feelings toward food often result from food experiences in your early childhood. The attitudes a child develops toward food play an important role in determining taste preferences even during later years.

Eating patterns and rituals in the home have a strong influence on children's attitudes toward certain foods. In fact, the home is said to have the greatest influence on food habits. In many families, mealtime is closely related to social values. Eating, sharing food and conversation, and relaxing together represent a pleasant social experience with family or friends for many people.

Because of personal associations, people may have prejudices against certain foods. You may know someone who refuses to eat broccoli because he or she once saw an insect on some broccoli at a supermarket. Another person may refuse to eat chicken because he or she had a pet chicken as a child. Food prejudices are a concern because they may be obstacles to good eating habits. If several family members have food prejudices, meal planning can become much more difficult.

Positive Influences on Eating Habits

The person who plans the family's meals strongly influences the attitudes developed toward food. If that person carefully selects and prepares foods to meet the family's nutritional needs, the family is likely to develop good eating habits.

Positive Attitude

When you have a positive attitude toward meal planning and preparation, these tasks become more enjoyable. Being creative, looking for new ideas and ways to serve foods, and trying new foods can be rewarding. When the person planning and preparing the meals has a positive attitude, other family members are more likely to view this as an enjoyable task.

Variety

Variety is the secret to good food habits. Variety can make nutritious meals both interesting and enjoyable to eat. People too often select certain foods only because they are familiar with them instead of trying something new. Serving a variety of foods in many ways broadens the family's experience with food. Instead of being bored with the same foods time and time again, the family develops new food likes. Most people would resist trying new foods each day. However, an occasional new food or method of preparation gives the family a chance to develop new tastes.

People enjoy eating foods that not only taste good, but are also attractive and have a pleasing texture. By carefully combining foods, you can provide a variety in color, flavor, texture, and type of preparation. See 17-18.

Color

Variety in color is pleasing to the eye and the appetite. The meal is more pleasing when you avoid colors that clash and also avoid too many foods of the same color.

Flavor

After selecting the main dish, decide on a variety of other foods that will create a pleasing combination of flavors. Words such as sweet, sour, salty, strong, tart, and bland describe food flavors. Avoid repeating the same flavors.

Texture

Variety of textures makes a meal more enjoyable. Soft, crisp, creamy, dry, moist, and chewy are words describing different textures. Repetition of texture can make a meal seem boring.

Type of Preparation

Variety in preparation methods creates a more pleasing meal. A meal of all fried foods or all creamy foods would not be appealing. You can find an unlimited number of ways to prepare almost any food by using one of the many available cookbooks.

White Consolidated Industries

17-18 Using a wok in cooking is a simple way to prepare attractive, tasty meals.

Summary

Good health is important. Understanding the basic concepts of nutrition will help you choose foods and plan meals that increase your chances of a healthful life. These choices are easier when you use food guides and meal patterns to help you.

Many factors influence personal food choices. By better understanding how these behaviors develop, you can consider your own attitudes and how you might change them to lead toward a more healthful diet.

To Review

1. Match the following groups of nutrients to the appropriate description.
   _____Fats
   _____Carbohydrates
   _____Minerals
   _____Water
   _____Proteins
   _____Vitamins
   A. important to growth and maintenance of body tissues
   B. makes up about one-half to three-fourths of your body's weight
   C. organic compounds required in the diet in extremely small amounts
   D. main function is to provide energy and heat to maintain the body's temperature
   E. the most concentrated source of calories
   F. inorganic compounds that regulate body functions
2. Describe the difference between an incomplete and a complete protein.
3. Describe four ways water helps the body.
4. Name five fruits and five vegetables that are excellent sources of either vitamin C or vitamin A. Indicate which vitamin each provides.
5. List and describe three functions of food.
6. List the food groups featured in MyPyramid and give an example of a food from each group.
7. True or false? Everyone throughout life needs the same nutrients in varying amounts.
8. What two nutrients are missing in the diets of many adolescents?
9. List four items found on a Nutrition Facts label.
10. Describe five factors that influence food choice.

To Do with the Class

1. Make a list of foods from the meat, poultry, fish, dry beans, eggs, and nuts group using two categories: foods of animal origin and foods of vegetable origin. Research to learn how the two types may differ in protein quality.
2. Identifying appropriate serving sizes in the various food groups is often difficult. Measure and display foods that represent one serving from the various groups. Make a card for each item listing its nutrient content.
3. Plan and develop a bulletin board or poster that will help fellow students consider the healthfulness of their diets. Display it in the cafeteria.
4. Conduct an experiment to determine the presence of fat in food. Rub various food substances onto brown paper. Allow the paper to dry. A translucent spot indicates the presence of fat. Analyze which foods contained the most fat.

To Challenge Your Thinking

1. Watch what people around you are eating for several days. Make a list of the foods that would be considered fats and sweets. Share this list with the class.
2. Plan three days of nutritious meals according to MyPyramid guidelines. Analyze how easy or difficult it would be to eat healthy.
3. Visit the local supermarkets and check Nutrition Facts panels on similar types of foods. For example, compare crackers to whole wheat bread or canned green beans to frozen green beans.
4. Make a list of healthful eating guidelines and share these with school athletes and coaches.

To Do with Your Community

1. Collect nutritious foods and donate these to a local homeless shelter or food pantry.
2. Collect and compare nutrition information from local fast-food restaurants. Identify which food choices are most healthful.
3. Invite a dietitian to speak on the importance of healthful eating in early childhood.
4. Plan a group project that will help familiarize you with the variety of ethnic interests represented in your geographic area.

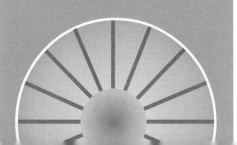

18 Coping with Stress

To Know

stress
coping
self-imposed stress
situational stress

Objectives

After studying this chapter, you will be able to

◆ explain what stress is and describe common reactions to stress.

◆ describe the causes of stress.

◆ apply the problem-solving process to stressful situations in your life.

◆ analyze personal skills for effective stress management.

Stress–emotional, mental, or physical tension–is around you every day; you cannot avoid it. Some stressful situations are caused by major events, such as divorce, the death of a family member, or the loss of a job. See 18-1. However, stressful situations may also result from minor, everyday events. Missing a bus, forgetting an appointment, or arguing with a friend may cause stress. These situations, although seemingly less important, can have harmful effects.

The way you cope with stress has a great impact on your health and happiness. Too much stress on your mind and body is unhealthy. Feeling tense or anxious, being irritable, having headaches, and suffering from nervous indigestion are common symptoms of stress. Stress may have many harmful effects, such as heart problems, ulcers, breathing problems, and depression. Research shows that 50 to 80 percent of all diseases are related to stress. An accumulation of stress may eventually lead to other problems such as alcoholism, drug abuse, and suicide.

Staying healthy by learning to cope with or manage stressful events is a worthwhile goal. **Coping** is any response to a stressful situation that helps prevent, avoid, or control physical and emotional stress. What resources are available to help you cope by managing stress? In this chapter, you will learn more about the understanding of stress, processes for managing stress, and personal skills for coping with stress. These are resources you can develop and use to reach the goal of coping with stress.

Madison, WI Fire Department

18-1 A major crisis, such as a fire, could cause a number of stressful situations. Loss of life, harmful injuries, inability to work, or financial problems may occur.

Understanding Stress

The best way to gain skill in stress management is to learn about stress. You will cope better when you understand the meaning of, reactions to, and possible causes of stress.

Meaning of Stress

The term *stress* can be defined in many different ways, some of which are confusing and contradictory. Stress is sometimes described as a helpful part of living. It can act as a force that helps people achieve. For instance, stress may motivate you to run faster in a race as you near the finish line. The good kind of stress can

encourage you to study harder for a science test. You may know that if you do well on the test, you will pass the course. You may do a better job preparing for the test because of the stress you feel. This kind of stress is a positive force in your life.

Unfortunately, people are more aware of the negative kind of stress and its effects on daily life. This stress makes you feel tense inside. Stress is your body's response to physical and psychological demands made on it. Stress is a mental process that shows itself through physical symptoms. It occurs as you feel threatened or expect future discomfort. Stress indicates a need for you to change your behavior. Your reaction to stress determines how harmful a stressful situation is.

Stressful Reactions

The way your body physically reacts to stress tells you a lot about your stress level. As you experience stress, glandular responses are triggered. Noticeable symptoms follow. These symptoms may include increased heartbeat, faster pulse rate, muscle tenseness, or increased perspiration. As stress builds up, you may experience headaches, irritability, frequent emotional outbursts, and indigestion. Your skill in stress management will affect how you react to stressful situations.

Each person handles stress in a unique way. The way you react to a stressful situation depends on factors such as the intensity of the stress, the duration of the stress, your personality, and your skill in managing stress. For instance, the stress of being involved in a serious automobile accident would be more intense than the stress of forgetting an appointment. The more intense the stress, the stronger the stressful reaction will be.

The period of time a stressful situation continues also affects the strength of your reaction. Losing one tennis match might cause somewhat of a stressful reaction. However, losing many games over a period of time would probably result in a much stronger reaction.

How you react to a stressful situation depends somewhat on your personality. Stress is caused by your perception of the situation, not the situation itself. For instance, a rock flying through the air does not cause a stressful reaction. However, you might feel stressed if you perceive the rock might harm you. Two girls performing a piano duet is not necessarily a stressful situation. It could be stressful if you are one of those girls and you are unsure of yourself.

Different persons may react to the same situation in extremely different ways. A stressful situation may affect one person only slightly, but another person with much greater intensity. For one high school student, performing in a class play might be a very positive experience. However, another student might find performing very stressful. See 18-2.

The same situation may also affect one person differently at different times. One day your mother might react angrily if your younger brother spills a glass of milk on the floor. Another time, she might patiently clean it up, commenting that it was "just an accident." Your mother's actions depend upon how she feels physically and how many other stresses she has experienced that day. In addition to personality, the physical and mental well-being of a person influences that person's reaction to stress.

Mark Felstehausen

18-2 **Speaking in front of a group is a pleasant challenge for this young man, but it might be quite stressful for another person.**

Your skill in managing stress certainly affects the way you react to stressful situations. You can develop personal skills in stress management to improve the way you react to stress.

Everyone uses defense mechanisms to deal with stress. Although some defense mechanisms may relieve stress, they will not usually remove the causes of stress. Instead, defense mechanisms change a person's perception of the real situation to decrease the stress. This may cause the person to become unrealistic and avoid the real problem. For instance, Melanie and her best friend, Trudy, have had a fight at school. When Melanie comes home, she is rude to her family instead of confronting Trudy with their problem. Melanie is using the defense mechanism of displacement. She is relieving her own stress at the moment. However, being rude to her family may only add to her problems.

Mark Hayward

 **18-3 Self-imposed stress can make taking a test even more difficult.**

Causes of Stress

Before you can relieve or control stress, you must recognize the forces that cause stress. In general, there are two types of stress: self-imposed and situational.

Self-Imposed Stress

When you impose unrealistic expectations on yourself, **self-imposed stress** occurs. This stress is caused entirely by your own thought processes. No stress from the outside comes in contact with you. There are many examples of self-imposed stress. Consider the student who is only satisfied with a straight A average or the athlete who must be best on the team. See 18-3. There is also the working woman who wants her home to be spotless. These goals are not wrong, but if goals are unreasonable, the person may experience frustration and stress.

Self-imposed obligations often cause stress. This may happen when you take on projects, accept deadlines, and agree to do tasks that are difficult to complete. In these situations, remember you are the person who obligates yourself. Although others may pressure you, be persuasive, or even be threatening, only you can make something a "must."

Many fears and worries cause self-imposed stress. Mental health authorities believe the fear of losing love is one of the greatest causes of stress. Many people are also afraid of failure. They feel they must succeed according to standards set by themselves or by people important to them.

Situational Stress

Stress caused by events that happen to you or around you is called **situational stress**. This type of stress involves external conditions. Situational stress often involves other people. You may become upset when your little brother and sister come into the room and play noisily while you are trying to study. A teenage boy might react anxiously when he hears his parents quarreling in the next room. These are examples of situational stress.

Sudden or unpleasant changes often cause stressful situations. For instance, a sales executive is ready for a busy workday with tightly scheduled appointments. When her car will not start, she experiences a stressful reaction. A dating situation could also cause stress. When the girl a young man has been dating repeatedly says she wants to go out with other guys, he becomes upset.

Any situation that threatens a person's basic needs is stressful. Although people differ, most will react when their needs for love, security, sense of worth, status, or approval are threatened. A basketball player is devastated when she misses a shot in the last second that would have won the game. Although she is the team's high scorer, she feels she let them down this time. Her sense of worth is suffering.

Certain life conditions tend to contribute to stressful situations. These include

◆ family conflicts and violence, broken homes, crowded living conditions, poverty

◆ hostile and delinquent neighborhoods, high-class and competitive neighborhoods

◆ lack of love in the family and among peers, lack of friends, peer rejection

◆ failure in studies, athletics, friendships, dating

◆ intense motivation or pressure to succeed, unfair competition, no chance to succeed

◆ poor basic skills in reading, math, spelling

◆ physical disabilities and developmental abnormalities

◆ excessive outside activities

◆ inconsistent discipline

◆ physical development and new requirements of maturation

◆ unstable environment

Managing Stress

By managing stress, you can become more productive, improve your relationships, and become more satisfied with your life. Learning how to minimize stress will involve changes that require time and effort. This cannot be done overnight. However, you can learn how to identify stress problems and control or manage them.

Some causes of stress are small and easily managed. Others may overwhelm you by forcing you to adjust to new circumstances. Managing your stress with courage rather than running away in fear is important when coping with stress. One of the essential skills for stress management is the problem-solving process. See 18-4. The steps in the process include defining the problem, developing alternative solutions, taking positive action, and evaluating the process.

Defining the Stress Situation

First, you must learn to recognize your feelings and actions that indicate stress. People under stress often know something is wrong in their lives, but they are not really sure what the problem is. In order to manage stress, first analyze your physical and mental reactions to a stressful situation. Is your heart beating very fast? Does your stomach feel tight or upset? Are you having

Using the Problem-Solving Process to Manage Stress

Sheila is upset with her two closest friends. Lately they have been smoking cigarettes. They give her a hard time because she refuses to join them in this new adventure. Sheila has been a close friend to both girls since they were in junior high school. She is finding this situation quite disturbing.

Define the stress situation: As Sheila thinks through the situation, she realizes her attitude toward smoking is not causing the stress. She knows she does not want to smoke cigarettes. Only two years ago, her Uncle Ted, a chain-smoker, died of lung cancer. At that time she decided there was no reason to take a chance and smoke.

Sheila further analyzes the problem and decides her relationship with her two friends is causing the stress. They are pressuring her to conform to their wishes.

Turn the problem into a goal: Sheila decides her goal is to continue her relationship with her friends and to eliminate the stress she is feeling.

Develop alternative solutions: Sheila thinks of three possible alternatives in dealing with this pressure to conform.

1. She could reconsider her feelings about smoking and go along with her two close friends.
    Advantage: It is wise to constantly evaluate feelings about certain matters.
    Disadvantage: The decision to not smoke hadn't been hers alone. It had also been the decision of both of her parents. It would be disappointing for them to see her change her mind about smoking.

2. She could confront her friends, explaining her disappointment in them for pressuring her to do something she felt strongly against. She could also express to them the importance of their friendship to her.
    Advantage: This would be an honest, direct approach.
    Disadvantage: Her friends might become angry, feeling they were being unfairly criticized.

3. She could just forget about those two friends and let them go their own way.
    Advantage: The stressful feelings would then be gone.
    Disadvantage: She would miss the special friendship she had with the two girls.

Take positive action: After considering all three alternatives carefully, Sheila decides the second alternative offers the best chance for success. To put that alternative into action, Sheila carefully plans her discussion with her two friends. A neighbor in whom she confides encourages her to think about factors that are important in relationships such as trust, respect, and openness.

Sheila makes a list of the points she wants her friends to understand. (1) They are special friends, and they mean a lot to Sheila. (2) Sheila is feeling stress because they are asking her to do something they know she does not want to do. (3) Sheila feels she has very good reasons for making the choice to not smoke. (4) Sheila respects their right to decide whether they want to smoke. (5) Sheila is asking them to respect her right to make her own choice about smoking.

Sheila calls her two friends. She invites them over and explains she has something important to discuss. She feels talking with her friends in this way is much better than just bringing up the subject casually on the way to a movie.

Evaluate the process: As in most cases, it will be necessary for time to pass before Sheila can evaluate the effectiveness of the problem-solving process. After some time has passed, Sheila will notice if the stressful feeling has disappeared. If her action was the right one, she should no longer feel the pressure from her friends to smoke. Their friendship might be stronger now than it ever was. If the pressure continues, Sheila may want to consider acting on one of the other alternatives.

18-4 This example shows how you can use the problem-solving process to help manage stress.

trouble concentrating on what you are doing? Does your head ache? Do you find yourself lashing out at someone for no apparent reason? These all may be signs of stress. They indicate that you need to solve a problem.

After recognizing your stressful reaction, analyze the situation to find what caused the stress. Ask yourself these questions: What is causing this stressful reaction? Is the problem a real problem? Does the problem need a solution?

Try to step back from the situation and consider what is happening. See 18-5. Remember that your perception of threat or discomfort in a situation, not the situation itself, is often the source of the stress.

One major difficulty in dealing with a crisis is in narrowing it down to a specific stress situation. In many crisis situations, stress is caused by several factors. In a divorce situation, there may be several specific causes of stress for the child. These might include living with only one parent, moving to a new location, or adjusting to a new stepparent. You can make the problem-solving process less difficult by breaking large crisis situations down into more manageable units.

Developing Alternative Solutions

After defining the stressful situation and identifying the cause of your stress, you can consider alternative solutions to the problem. These solutions may eliminate the cause of the stress, reduce the stress, or help you accept the cause of the stress.

It is important to use a practical approach in developing alternatives. Ask yourself these questions about each alternative: Is it a workable solution? Are the resources available for putting that solution into action? As you carefully analyze each alternative, decide which one offers the greatest chance for success.

Lynn Hellmuth

18-5 In a stressful situation, it often helps to step back and think about what is really causing the stress.

Sharing your feelings of stress with someone you trust and respect may help you develop alternative solutions. Although you must learn to recognize and solve your own problems, another person's view can be helpful.

Taking Positive Action

Putting the chosen alternative into action requires you to develop a plan and carry it out. Decide what actions are involved, who is involved in the plan, and how you expect the situation to change.

You then control the action you take. Sometimes each step of the plan may not go exactly as you hope. Your plan may require some modification.

Evaluating the Process

By evaluating the problem-solving process, you learn how well your plan worked. Decide what improvement has been made in the situation. You may need to make corrections if the stressful situation has not improved.

Skill in using the problem-solving process to manage stress will improve with practice. Evaluating the process each time you use it will help you solve other problems in the future. By first working through small problems, you will gain the confidence needed to accept and cope with more difficult situations.

Personal Skills for Effective Coping

In many families, children receive guidance in developing skills for coping throughout their childhood. Many of these skills are learned by children as they see them practiced by their parents.

The problem-solving process is one resource for dealing with stressful situations. Other resources for coping with stress involve personal skills. These include skills in self-observation, attitude skills, skills in anticipating stress, personal management skills, relationship skills, and skills in personal health and relaxation.

Having a variety of personal coping skills will help you deal with stress. Certain skills may be very useful in certain situations and less useful in others. You may also find that certain skills work best for you.

Skill in Self-Observation

Learning the skill of self-observation means learning how your body and mind react to stressful situations. When you feel stressed, take the time to read your body. See 18-6. With a little practice, you can learn how your body signals and reacts to stress.

Developing skill in self-observation can help you sense stressful reactions coming on and learn how to solve problems before they become more stressful. This skill also helps you recognize patterns to the stress you are experiencing. For instance, many of your stressful reactions may occur when

Mark Felstehausen

18-6 Taking the time to walk and think may help you solve a problem before it becomes even more stressful.

you are with a certain person. This would indicate a relationship problem. Perhaps you feel stress because you lack the time you need to get certain things done. This pattern would suggest a need for better time management skills. After identifying a pattern in your stressful reactions, you can use the problem-solving process to decide on a course of action. The action you take should improve the situation.

Self-observation skills will guide you in considering your attitude and how it influences your behavior. Learning to view stressful situations in a more positive way requires a change of attitude. This change will be helpful in managing stress. Most pressures can be converted into positive challenges. Be positive and think positively. "I'll just take it one step at a time and do my best," is a more helpful attitude than "I'll never get it finished."

Use Your Reasoning Skills

Make a list of stressful situations you experience during the next month. Note your physical reaction to the stress and the cause of the stress. Analyze the list to find any patterns to your reactions or the causes of stress.

Examine your thoughts from time to time and eliminate those that are negative. Substitute a few positive topics for the negative thoughts that are bothering you. Before long those negative thoughts will come to mind less frequently.

Having a healthy attitude toward yourself helps make you stronger in stressful situations. Healthy feelings about yourself also tend to produce more healthy emotional responses and relationships with others. Healthy feelings give you the confidence to be assertive and let others know your wants, feelings, needs, and ideas. Assertive behavior is different from aggressive behavior. Aggressive behavior often involves accusations while assertive behavior means being honest and expressing your feelings. Being assertive makes you feel better and makes others respect you.

Self-observation will also help you consider your emotions and their effect on your behavior. Try to develop healthy emotions such as cheerfulness, courage, optimism, and a sense of humor. They can be valuable resources in coping with stress. Police officers who have developed a sense of humor about their jobs are most able to adjust to the daily stresses of police work. People who are least troubled by stress are able to laugh at themselves. They generally try to "find a silver lining in every cloud."

Skill in self-observation gives you an opportunity to evaluate your attitude regarding change. Try to develop an open attitude toward change. When a change

occurs that might be considered negative, look at it as a new opportunity to test your resourcefulness. Another positive approach is learning to accept what you cannot change. If you cannot control a problem, try your best to accept it. In the future, the situation may be different and then change may be possible.

Skill in Anticipating Stress

Fear of the unknown, a common cause of stress, often makes situations seem more stressful. The best way to deal with fear of the unknown is to develop skill in anticipating stress and prepare for it emotionally. See 18-7. Before entering any stressful situation, try to acquire as much information or experience as you can.

Mentally rehearsing a stressful situation is a good way to help yourself handle that situation better. This mental rehearsal might help you prepare for the stress of a job interview. You could get ready by finding information on successful interviewing and rehearsing what you and your interviewer might say. This emotional preparation helps reduce your feelings of fear because you focus on success rather

University of Wisconsin Sports Information

18-7 **A goalie must learn to anticipate the stress of missing a puck, accept it if it happens, and think positively about stopping the next shot.**

than on what may go wrong. You experience less stress when you prepare for the situations you think might cause stress.

Personal Management Skills

Your values influence the choices you make. Understanding your values will help you make satisfying choices that are directed toward your goals. Your health, diet, exercise, personal relationships, and other factors affect the quality of your life. You may wish to reexamine your values as you begin to understand more about stress patterns and your reactions to stress. You may want to set new priorities. Being able to clarify your values and prioritize your goals are two management skills that help reduce stress.

You experience less stress when you have flexible standards. When people consciously adapt their standards to a situation, they experience less strain. For instance, a boy's parents may want his friends to be neat, polite, friendly, and thoughtful. However, these standards are likely to be flexible. Many parents would overlook a friend's messy appearance as long as their son felt the child had the qualities of a good friend. They would be adapting their standards to the situation and respecting their son's ability to choose friends.

Organizational and time management skills are other personal skills that can help you deal with stress. When you think of a well-organized person, words like *neat, systematic, methodical,* and *disciplined* come to mind. Those are the characteristics of an orderly person.

Organizational skills involve the ability to plan ahead. Planning is preparing for the future–deciding what you want to do and how you will do it. Record keeping and storage of food, clothing, and other household items can all be planned. You can also make plans about your relationships with others. Planning helps you anticipate and prepare for possible stressful situations in the future.

Time management skills are closely related to organizational skills. Planning helps control the use of your time rather than letting time control you. Time management involves the use of certain resources. In order to manage your time, it is helpful to make written lists such as a list of things that need to be done or a list of things to buy. See 18-8.

18-8 **Using time management skills is an excellent way to reduce stress while accomplishing even more.**

Brainstorming

Share ways that relationship skills help the learning process in the classroom. In what relationship skills does your class excel? Which ones need improvement? How would this improvement help the learning process?

A frequent cause of stress is overextension–trying to do too much in too little time. Successful time management starts with analyzing how you spend your time. By keeping a log of your time use, you can see how much time you spend on various activities. Then you can evaluate your time use by asking these questions:

◆ What activities take up too much of my time and what activities do not take up enough of my time?

◆ What activities do not need to be done?

◆ What activities could I do better?

This type of evaluation helps you set goals and priorities related to your time use. Therefore, by evaluating your time use, you may reduce or eliminate frustrations caused by poor time management.

Relationship Skills

Communication skills are important to interpersonal relationships. Listening attentively, interpreting, and responding to what others say are resources you can use. To deal with stress, you need someone with whom you can talk at a trusting, sharing level. This gives you the opportunity to get feedback from someone whose opinion you

trust. People who have these relationship skills are more likely to understand and care about others. They are also willing to share their own feelings, ideas, and values in conversations.

Relationship skills help you give comfort, support, and direction to people who are experiencing stress. Assisting others gives you respect, esteem, and support that will help you in times of stress.

Effective relationship skills help you avoid and minimize stressful situations with other people. Analyze your own communication behaviors. Do this by studying how others react to the way you treat them. If people who communicate with you feel positive about the experience, they will come back for more. If they don't like the results, they will communicate with you as little as possible. Thinking about how others act toward you will help you identify your behaviors that cause conflict and result in stress. Then you can improve yourself by planning new strategies in interpersonal relationships. Attempt to make all communications with another person rewarding and positive. Then the stress between the two of you will decrease. The following are examples of rewarding and positive behaviors in communication:

◆ giving others a chance to express their own views

◆ listening carefully and hearing the other person out

◆ praising and complimenting others sincerely

Getting Involved

Contact a local hospital or counseling center. What resources are available for people to help them cope with stress? How can you as an individual participate in helping to provide these resources to others?

◆ expressing respect for values and opinions of others

◆ delaying automatic reactions; not "flying off the handle" easily

◆ confronting others constructively on difficult issues

Practicing these behaviors will help you deal with stressful situations in a relationship.

Skill in Personal Health and Relaxation

Taking good care of your health and having a healthy lifestyle clearly reduces stress. However, everyone is likely to experience some stress. Developing skills in relaxation is an important part of stress management. Muscular tension in the form of tightened shoulder or neck muscles or back pain results from stress. Learning to relax is important because when your muscles relax, you relax mentally as well.

People may relax in many different ways. For some people, watching television or going to a movie is a way to relax. For others, time spent gardening or jogging is relaxing. It is important to find the type of activity that relaxes you and reduces your tension. See 18-9.

Spending leisure time together as a family can help family members reduce stress they may be experiencing. However, this time spent together may be even more helpful in preventing crisis situations. A family who shares in activities, such as camping, sports, music, or any other special shared interest, profits from this time together. Relationships can be enhanced through shared activities.

Relaxation skills can help you both prevent and reduce stress. You can prepare for stressful situations by learning to allow your body to relax as much as you can. Yoga is an example of a deep relaxation technique. Skills in deep relaxation may not

prevent a stressful situation from occurring. However, they will probably help keep the stress level down and allow you to function more effectively.

Many people reduce or work off stress through physical activities such as running, gardening, or playing tennis. These exercises reduce stress in various ways. They

Sta-Ride Industries

Kent Hayward

18-9 **Some people might find it relaxing to swim while others might release tension by working on their cars.**

relieve hostile feelings in a positive way. They often provide fresh air, improve physical conditioning, and burn calories.

Creative activities such as art, music, writing, drawing, and painting also help reduce tension. Expressing your creativity in these ways provides an outlet for excess tension.

Momentary relaxation skills can help you deal with everyday stressful situations. Learn to sense when you are beginning to tense up physically or mentally. Taking a relaxation break during those times is an important part of stress management. A relaxing deep breath can help relieve stress. When you find you are about to face a challenging, stressful situation, simply pause a few seconds. Turn your attention to your body and allow your whole body to relax. This will take practice, but you can learn to use this quick relaxation technique. It will help prevent stress buildup that can easily occur in stressful situations.

The ability to handle stress can come from within you rather than through medication. Although many chemicals, including alcohol, may hide stress symptoms, they do not help you adjust to the stress itself. Many of them are habit-forming.

Take time to evaluate the skills you use to manage or cope with stress. Instead of being overcome by stress, you can organize and develop personal resources. By using these resources, you can learn to manage stress rather than let stress control you.

Summary

Your skill in coping with stress will have a great impact on your health and happiness. Recognizing stress and its causes will help you better manage stress in your life.

Certain personal skills can be helpful in stress management. Developing these skills will help you learn to cope with stress.

To Review

1. List three major life events that may result in stressful situations.
2. List three everyday situations that may result in stressful situations.
3. List four physical reactions to stress.
4. Name three resources that can be developed and used to reach the goal of coping with stress.
5. Which of the following examples illustrate self-imposed stress, and which illustrate situational stress?
   A. Marla is nervous about her plans to go swimming with some friends as she has always been afraid of water.
   B. Floyd panics as he sees another car sliding toward him on the icy street.
   C. David is quite irritable with his wife the morning after he had to work the late shift at his job.
   D. Mrs. Sula is upset because the house does not look neat and tidy when some unexpected company drops by.
6. True or false?
   A. If you plan carefully, you can avoid stress.
   B. A great number of diseases are related to stress.
   C. Stress does not affect your health.
7. Stress is the body's response to _____ and _____ demands. Your _____ to stress determines how harmful the stressful situation will be.
8. List three ways that self-observation skills can be beneficial.
9. _____ skills and _____ skills can help you anticipate and prepare for the future.
10. List three examples of positive behaviors in communication.

To Challenge Your Thinking

1. Use the problem-solving process to help cope with a stressful situation in your life. Record the steps of the process as you complete them.
2. Rate your own personal skills for managing stress according to the following scale:
   1. You have those skills.
   2. You need to improve those skills.
   3. You need to develop those skills.
      _____Self-observation skills
      _____Communication skills
      _____Organizational skills
      _____Skill in maintaining good physical and mental health
      _____Time management skills
      _____Skill in anticipating stress
      _____Skill in value clarification
      _____Relaxation skills
3. Create a plan to develop or improve personal skills for managing stress.
4. Describe how you might use personal skills in anticipating stress in the following situations:
   A. going out on a first date
   B. taking a mathematics exam
   C. going to a new school
   D. starting a new job

To Do with the Class

1. Brainstorm examples of stress that result from major events and examples of stress that result from everyday events.
2. Read a recent article about stress or coping with stress. Write a summary of the article and discuss it with the class.
3. Discuss how each of the following factors would affect a person's reaction to a stressful situation: the intensity of the stress, the duration of the stress, and personality.
4. Share healthy ways that classmates try to be organized.

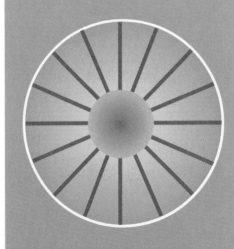

To Do with Your Community

1. Invite a counselor from school or from the community into the classroom to speak on stress management techniques for adolescents.
2. Contact a recreational program director to share program philosophies and ideas that help community members participate in planned activities. How do these programs help members relieve stress?
3. Ask parents, neighbors, and friends to share their ideas on reducing or coping with stressful situations in healthy ways.
4. Visit a shopping mall or public event such as a parade, picnic, or sporting event. What signs of stress and signs of relaxation do you observe? How do these differ by age group?

19

Environmental Responsibility

To Know

biodegradable waste
pollution
noise pollution
recycling
genetic mutation
foodborne illness
additives
carcinogenic
accident
vaccine
first aid

Objectives

After studying this chapter, you will be able to

◈ recognize environmental conditions that are hazardous to your health and safety.

◈ identify actions you can take to protect the environment.

◈ identify preventive techniques that will help you stay safe and healthy.

In the past 100 years, the health and life expectancy of people living in the United States has lengthened by 30 years. See 19-1. Although government agencies have taken steps to help make the environment safer, individual citizens have a great influence on environmental safety. The decisions you and millions of others make determine

- Control of infectious diseases

- Highway safety

- Safer workplaces

- Vaccine development and use

- Decline in vascular disease (heart attack and stroke)

- Better nutrition

- Improvement in perinatal health (pre and postdelivery of babies)

- Family planning

- Water fluoridation

- Identification of tobacco as a major health hazard

19-1 **The top 10 health accomplishments of the past 100 years, as compiled by the Centers for Disease Control and Prevention, are responsible for adding 30 years to Americans' life expectancies.**

your chances of living in a safe environment. For instance, you may slightly reduce air pollution by taking public transportation rather than driving your own car. When thousands of other people make the same decision, problems related to pollution will be greatly reduced.

You can assume environmental responsibility by becoming aware of existing hazardous conditions and what can be done to protect the environment from those conditions. Knowing about hazardous conditions in the environment will help you avoid being harmed by those conditions and change them if possible. Knowledge of prevention techniques gives you guidelines for action that can result in a healthier, safer life.

Hazardous Environmental Conditions

Some hazardous, or dangerous, conditions are brought on by the increase in the human population or by human actions and technology. Other hazardous conditions are related to food and drug concerns or to accidents that occur regularly.

Increase in Population

The population of the world has been increasing at an astonishing rate. According to experts, currently planned programs for food production cannot keep up with the world population growth. Some countries are presently experiencing famine. This will continue to occur if food production is not greatly expanded.

Greater numbers of people creates a need for more consumer goods. Producing these goods uses more energy, requires more factories, and creates more pollution. More people also make greater demands on the world's limited natural resources.

Because so many problems are related to population growth, reducing the birth rate is a desirable goal. Governments of developing countries have started vigorous birth control campaigns. The goal of this approach is to motivate people to want fewer children. For this motivation to take place, people need an understanding of fertility as well as the social issues. Safe and effective methods of birth control are available to couples who have decided to limit reproduction.

Altering the Environment

All forms of life discharge wastes into the environment. Most of these wastes are reusable in one form or another. These are known as **biodegradable wastes.** Natural processes are capable of changing them into useful substances.

Unfortunately, humans have developed non-biodegradable waste products that pollute the air, water, and earth. These wastes create dangers that nature cannot cope with adequately. Non-biodegradable waste products are responsible for pollution. **Pollution** is anything that makes the environment dirty or contaminated.

Air Pollution

Many people have died as a result of air pollution. It has been linked to lung cancer, emphysema, bronchitis, allergies, and other respiratory ailments. Exposure to acute air pollution can be fatal to the elderly, the very young, and people who are ill. Low levels of air pollutants may have similar effects on health and length of life over very long periods of time.

There are many sources of air pollution. One of the major sources is motor vehicles, 19-2. The principal industrial sources are factories, refineries, chemical plants, and power generating plants. The burning of wastes by cities and individual home-owners also creates pollution. Aerosol sprays, pesticide sprays, cigarettes, and cigars are other sources of air pollution. Some chemicals produced by humans are thought to be responsible for affecting the ozone layer so it doesn't block the sun's harmful rays. Without enough ozone to protect us, all living things would suffer.

Water Pollution

All living things need water. Therefore, water pollution by industrial wastes, agricultural drainage, and sewage is a great concern.

Nature has provided streams and rivers that can purify themselves.

19-2 **Most air pollution is created by motor vehicles.**

However, they lose this ability when wastes are dumped into them. They become overloaded with pollutants and are unable to become pure, 19-3. Industrial wastes such as lead, detergents, and chemicals discharged directly into waterways are major sources of water pollution.

Runoff from agricultural lands, animal wastes, and chemicals used on crops also pollute the water supply. Most cities have sewage treatment and water purification systems to ensure clean water. In many rural areas, septic tanks are used to treat sewage. However, water pollution by sewage can still be a problem in areas where the sanitation systems are inadequate.

Lead in drinking water can pose a significant risk to health if too much enters the body. Lead is unusual among drinking water contaminants in that it seldom occurs naturally in water supplies, such as in rivers and lakes. Lead enters drinking water primarily as a result of the corrosion, or wearing away, of materials containing lead in the water distribution system and household plumbing. Despite efforts of public health's actions toward making drinking water safe, lead levels in some homes or buildings can be high. Water tests are essential because it is not possible to see, taste or smell lead in the water.

Noise Pollution

Noise pollution involves sound of any intensity or quality that harms or distresses a person. Millions of people suffer from hearing loss caused directly by excessive sound. Tolerance to increased sound differs from person to person. Research suggests that noise may play a role in the development of heart disease, headaches, and other stress-related ailments.

Noise pollution experts are concerned about people's music listening habits, particularly teenagers. Recent studies indicate that many young people are risking significant hearing loss by listening to loud music.

Excessive noise in the workplace, near airports, and in industrial areas has been recognized as both physically and psychologically harmful. See 19-4. Recent studies have suggested that loud and irritating noises in residential neighborhoods can also cause lasting harm. They suggest sounds made by dishwashers, garbage disposals, electric blenders, or knife sharpeners may injure your hearing over an extended period of time.

The damage done by noise depends on not only how loud it is but also the length of time you are exposed to it. It is wise to wear protective devices, such as earplugs or specially designed earmuffs, when working in noisy settings or with loud equipment.

Pollution by Solid Waste Materials

Unfortunately, many people have a "throw away" attitude; whatever is not needed is thrown away. Solid waste disposal

Mike Deatherage

19-3 **Water pollution can kill plants and animal life.**

19-4 **People who live near airports have to cope with the noise pollution caused by planes taking off and landing.**

has become a major environmental concern. The problem has grown due to the development of disposable, nonreturnable containers and the rapidly increasing population.

Manufacturers and advertisers have learned that many consumers place a high value on convenience and disposability. Many products, such as cans, bottles, and paper products, are designed to be used once and then thrown away. Other consumer goods, ranging from wristwatches all the way to major appliances such as air conditioners, are manufactured in such a way that it is often cheaper to discard and replace them than to have them repaired.

Traditionally, waste materials have been buried in landfills. However, landfills are filling up and closing down in many communities. Even if landfills are available, they are now recognized as health and safety hazards. If waste materials are not well buried, they become a breeding place for rats, cockroaches, and flies. If water percolates through them, they pollute groundwater supplies. Radioactive materials present the ultimate problem of solid waste disposal.

Many measures have been proposed to deal with the problem of solid waste disposal. Heavy taxes might be imposed on any product or wrapping designed to be thrown away rather than returned or recycled. Laws could prohibit the manufacture of products that are neither biodegradable nor recyclable. Large deposits could be required for beverage cans to encourage the return of these containers.

Many communities now provide centers for waste collection of household hazardous materials. Some of these materials are toxic and poisonous, corrosive, flammable, and even explosive. Batteries, acids, paints, aerosol cans, cleaners, disinfectants, and chemicals are examples of some hazardous materials.

Waste Reduction and Product Reuse

Recycling seems to be the most promising alternative. **Recycling,** as its name suggests, is taking a used product and turning it back into something that can be used again. See 19-5. Nature recycles dead plants and animals and the waste products of living ones by turning them into food, energy, and new life.

Out of concern for limited resources–the space required for landfills and the costs associated with incinerators–it makes sense to be more careful in your selection of products. Consider the possibility of products being reused or recycled. Notice how they are packaged. A certain amount of packaging is necessary to keep food fresh, to permit merchandise to be

Recycled

Recyclable

The recycled symbol is used to identify products made entirely or predominately from recycled materials.

The recyclable symbol is used to identify products made from materials that, after use, are suitable for recycling.

19-5 **Recycling materials and using recycled materials is good for the environment. These symbols are used to identify recycled and recyclable products. Look for these symbols when buying products.**

handled and shipped, and to allow shoppers to carry their purchases. However, some packaging is excessive and could be limited in production. Also, consider whether or not you really need the item. Then if you do buy something, use it and, if possible, pass it on to someone else to use. Finally, see that products that can be, are recycled. See 19-6.

Recycling plans in our country are based on trying to keep all types of waste within a cycle of use and reuse as done by nature. This can be accomplished by first turning waste back into the cycle of nature, as when food waste and lawn clippings are composted to make garden soil. Secondly, the plan includes use of materials more than once for the same or similar purposes. This would include using refillable glass bottles instead of disposable plastic ones, printing newspapers on paper made from old newspapers, and making new aluminum beverage cans out of used ones.

Finding new ways to use materials that would otherwise be discarded is also planned. For instance, corporations are developing ways to break down plastic bottles and remake them into different products, such as toys, lawn furniture, and scouring pads. See 19-7.

3M Company, Scotch Brite™

19-7 This scouring pad is made from recycled plastic beverage bottles and uses phosphorus-free soap.

Many communities encourage recycling by having citizens separate aluminum, glass, plastics, cardboard, and newspapers from the rest of the waste products. The degree of recycling and methods of recycling vary from community to community and from state to state. The government has an important role to play in developing recycling policies, passing laws, and supporting the recycling industry. However, the success of recycling rests with individual consumers.

The Mechanics of Recycling

Metal, wood, plastics, paper, glass, motor oil, batteries, tires, and textiles are commonly recycled waste materials. Ideally, people who are concerned about the environment will become familiar with the options for reducing or reusing these waste items.

Recycling Guidelines
RETHINK: Make conscientious product choices.
REDUCE: Buy only what you need and use what you buy.
REUSE: Reuse products whenever possible; pass along to others.
RECYCLE: Decrease the amount of solid waste entering our landfills.

19-6 Protect the environment by following these guidelines.

Plastic recycling is on the increase. Some soft drink bottles can be remanufactured into items such as cassette cases, fiberfill, and textiles. A voluntary coding system for plastics has been developed by the plastics industry. The various types of plastics can be identified by a coded imprint, which is a triangle with a number in the center, on the bottom or the side of the container. Check with your community recycling centers to find out which plastics codes are accepted for recycling.

Opportunities for recycling vary throughout the United States. In many areas, recyclables are picked up by the trash collector or curbside recycling companies. Various methods are used to separate the items.

Some communities conduct recycling drives. Recycling drives are often short-term recycling projects generally run by nonprofit groups such as scout troops or civic organizations. By giving them your recyclables, you can help the environment as well as help the sponsoring organizations support their cause.

Household hazardous waste facilities are special sites that accept toxic materials, such as old paint, motor oil, and antifreeze. Although some communities don't have permanent facilities for this purpose, they arrange for a special day that these items will be collected.

Drop-off centers are places where recyclables can be dropped off. They can be as simple as a few bins at an interstate rest area or as complex as a staffed recycling facility. Drop-off centers are usually located in convenient areas like grocery store parking lots, fire stations, and vacant lots. Many of these are available 24 hours every day.

Buyback centers provide an opportunity to obtain payment for your recyclables. Most are run by private companies. Many of these specialize in aluminum cans, which is the most profitable item. These centers usually have limited hours.

Pollution by Radiation

Throughout the world, people are continuously exposed to background radiation from natural resources–mainly the sun. Other background radiation includes cosmic rays given off by stars and radioactive gases released by soil and rock formations.

Manufactured radiation poses the greatest threat to the environment. Most radiation exposure comes from medical and dental uses of X rays for diagnosis and therapy, 19-8. Exposure also comes from radioactive fallout from testing nuclear weapons. Nuclear reactors that generate electric power are another potential source of radiation exposure. Small amounts of radiation might be released from the reactor. However, the greater concern is the potential for an accident when large amounts of radiation might be released. As the use of the nuclear reactor increases, the need for disposal of radioactive wastes increases. Proper disposal of these wastes is a public concern.

In recent years, a great deal has been learned about the health risks related to the radioactive gas radon. Radon is a natural gas found in the earth. It can become a dangerous

19-8 The amount of radiation a person is exposed to during an X ray is not harmful.

indoor pollutant that can cause lung disease. If a house is located on a site where radon gas is present, the gas may enter the house and be trapped inside. A house can be tested for evidence of radon gas.

Although a single source of exposure to radiation may be small, the cumulative health effects may be significant. The harm caused by radiation depends upon these factors: part of the body exposed, potency of the radiation, and rate at which the radiation is received.

The chief danger of exposure to radiation is that it increases a person's chances of cancer. A second danger is the damage it may do to reproductive cells. Exposure to radiation may damage human genes. As you have read, genes are the basic units of heredity. They carry all the characteristics that are transferred from a parent to a child. When a person's genes are damaged or altered, a **genetic mutation** occurs. Often the damage is not revealed until future generations are born. A third danger of radiation is radiation sickness. This develops when there is considerable exposure to radiation. The symptoms often include nausea, loss of hair, weakness, vomiting, and diarrhea.

Food Contamination

The foods you eat may be contaminated in various ways. Harmful bacteria may develop because of poor processing or handling of the food. The contamination may be due to chemicals added either intentionally or accidentally to the foods. Another threat to food is the possibility of radioactivity resulting from weapons testing or industrial and accidental sources.

Foodborne Illness Caused by Harmful Bacteria

A **foodborne illness** is a disease transmitted through a food product. Foodborne illness is caused by disease-producing bacteria and other bacteria that form

dangerous toxins in the food. Salmonellae are the most common disease-producing bacteria. *Salmonellosis* is the infection caused by this bacteria. It may result from eating foods in which large numbers of the bacteria are growing. Raw or contaminated meat, poultry, milk, or egg yolks may be the source of salmonella. See 19-9. The bacteria survive inadequate cooking and can also be spread by knives, cutting surfaces, or an infected person or a carrier of the infection. The salmonellae bacteria can also be transmitted by insects, rodents, or pets. Symptoms of the illness often include a severe headache followed by vomiting, diarrhea, abdominal cramps, and fever. To prevent salmonella poisoning:

- Cook meat and poultry thoroughly, and don't eat raw or undercooked eggs.
- Avoid unpasteurized milk.
- Keep cutting surfaces clean.
- Wash hands before handling food.

19-9 Careful preparation when cooking poultry, such as turkey, is important in preventing salmonellosis.

Staphylococcal poisoning, or *staph poisoning*, occurs when bacteria in food produce a toxin that is extremely resistant to heat. The bacteria tends to spread through meats, mayonnaise-based salads, cream sauces, and cream-filled pastries that are held at an improper temperature for too long. Staph infection can also be spread by hand contact, coughing, and sneezing. Food handlers may carry the bacteria and transmit it to the food. People contract the infection by eating food that contains the toxin. Symptoms include diarrhea, vomiting, abdominal cramps, lightheadedness, and fever. These symptoms are usually milder than those of other types of foodborne illness. Because of the mild symptoms, staph poisoning may be mistaken for the flu.

The rarest and the deadliest kind of foodborne illness is botulism. *Botulism* results from eating foods containing a toxin formed by certain spores in food. Double vision, inability to swallow, difficulty speaking, and progressive respiratory paralysis are the symptoms of botulism. The fatality rate for botulism is high.

Home canned food that has not been adequately sterilized is the most common source of the organism causing botulism. Fish, fruits, and vegetables may contain the organism. Home canned food must be heated to a high enough temperature to kill the bacterial spores.

Being aware of preventive measures related to these illnesses is important. The Food and Drug Administration (FDA) has been responsible for improvements in the safety of commercially prepared foods. State and local regulations help make the food service industry safe.

Despite government regulations, millions of cases of foodborne illness could be avoided each year. One in every three cases of foodborne illness originates in the home. This means each person must assume a share of the responsibility for safe food. Practicing the following safety tips in the home can decrease your chances of contracting a foodborne illness.

- Avoid buying frozen or fully cooked foods if the package is punctured, torn, partially opened, or damaged in any way.

- Do not purchase frozen products that appear to have been thawed and refrozen.

- Reject all swollen containers or spoiled foods.

- Do not use products that are discolored, moldy, or have an off-odor.

- Do not use products that spurt liquid or foam when the container is open.

- Do not taste the product to determine if it is safe.

- Wash your hands before and after handling food. Clean utensils and surface areas with hot soapy water after use.

- Keep raw and cooked foods separated to prevent cross-contamination.

- Cook foods to a safe temperature.

- Refrigerate perishable foods as soon as possible after purchase. Also refrigerate leftovers within two hours. Thaw foods in the refrigerator, not room temperature.

- Serve foods safely. Keep hot foods hot and cold foods cold. If you question whether a food is still good, throw it away.

Contamination by Chemicals

Additives are chemical substances added to food for a specific purpose. Some are used as preservatives to prevent food-borne illnesses from developing. Others, such as food coloring, are added to give food a more attractive appearance. Food additives prevent foods such as coconut, candy, and marshmallows from drying out and keep salt and baking powder free flowing. Sweeteners are additives used as a substitute for sugar in order to reduce the number of calories.

Additives have been used for many years, and the reasons for their use seem legitimate. However, there has been a growing concern that some additives are harmful to human health. In 1958, the FDA got the power to approve food additives before they were put on the market. See 19-10. Many of the additives used before 1958 were put on what is known as the GRAS list. *GRAS* means *generally recognized as safe*. As time passed, though, some additives that had been used for some time came under attack. As a result of lab testing these additives were banned or restricted in use. For instance, red dye #2, a food coloring, was banned in 1970 by the FDA. Although lab tests never clearly linked the dye to human cancer, there was enough evidence to cause concern.

Sodium nitrite, an additive used as a preservative, is suspected of being **carcinogenic** (cancer-producing). However, sodium nitrite helps prevent growth of deadly botulism-producing bacteria in bacon and some other meats. For this reason, the government established permissible levels of sodium nitrite rather than banning its use.

The FDA regulates the licensing of new food additives. Those who seek to introduce a new additive must show convincing evidence that it will not be harmful. Animal laboratory studies are often conducted to determine any toxicity. On the basis of the

19-10 **All the additives in foods like these must be approved by the Food and Drug Administration.**

best available scientific information, the FDA determines if an additive is safe to use. When the safety of an additive is in question, it is wise to limit your use of that additive.

Chemical contamination of foods from contaminated soil and water is also a concern. Mercury, which can damage the human brain and nervous system, enters water from industrial processes and travels for miles. It can be found in the bodies of many fish.

Soil and vegetation beside major highways can be contaminated by lead compounds from automobile gasoline. Root crops, such as potatoes, and vegetables, such as corn or peas, can accumulate an excessive lead content from the soil. Cows that graze along major highways have an elevated lead concentration in their milk.

Contamination by Radiation

Radiation contamination is not common. However, situations have occurred that make it a concern. In the 1950s, a nuclear reactor accident resulted in large quantities of an isotope being released into the atmosphere. The isotope was rapidly brought to earth and absorbed by plants and grass. Significant quantities of the isotope were found in the milk of cows that had eaten the grass. As the isotopes decompose, radiation is released. Much is yet to be learned about the link between radiation and contamination of food.

Concerns Related to Prescription and Over-the-Counter Drug Use

Because one drug may cause different reactions in two people, the use of prescription drugs should be limited to the individual for whom it was prescribed. Although a doctor may prescribe a drug for you, using the drug is your responsibility. Some drugs must be taken on an empty stomach. Others must be taken after eating. Some drugs react badly with certain foods. Therefore, a person should always ask whether to avoid any specific food or drink when taking a prescribed drug.

Any person can suffer adverse reactions to prescription or over-the-counter drugs. These may be toxic reactions or side effects such as drowsiness. A person might suffer an allergic reaction or a psychological reaction such as depression or hyperactivity.

Experts agree that health professionals could do more to help consumers use their medicines wisely. However, they also agree that consumers should take more responsibility. Part of this responsibility involves knowing the names, purposes, and effects of any drugs they are taking. Keeping track of adverse reactions and informing the doctor about them is important.

Not following directions for taking prescription drugs can have serious consequences. For instance, a person with high blood pressure who doesn't take medicine as prescribed could have a stroke. Misuse can take many forms: skipping doses, failure to finish the course of medications as prescribed, cutting pills in half to make a drug last longer, sharing medications, and failure to heed warnings about drug interactions.

Drug interactions often are the cause of adverse side effects. This is not surprising considering over 25 percent of people over 65 take on average four to five different prescribed drugs a day. Some side effects aren't serious, but others cause illness and even death. Patients can avoid interactions by keeping their doctors up to date on all medicines they take, including over-the-counter drugs, vitamins, and herbal products.

Decisions about prescription and over-the-counter drugs are sometimes very difficult. A person has to weigh the risks against the benefits.

Accidents

Accidents are unplanned events that cause injury or death. Accidents are the leading cause of death for people under 40 years of age. For all age groups, accidents are among the four leading causes of death along with heart disease, cancer, and strokes.

Brainstorming

Drivers between the ages of 18 and 24 are more than twice as likely to have accidents as older drivers. Discuss what might be done to lower the accident rate of young drivers.

Many accidents can be foreseen and avoided. The number of accidents could be lowered if members of society worked together to prevent them. You can lower your personal risk of being in an accident. Being aware of the types of accidents can help you anticipate accidents, identify their causes, and hopefully prevent them. See 19-11.

Accidents rarely have a single cause. A car accident is not usually caused simply by bad driving or a blowout. For instance, Tim had a bad day at school. He did poorly on an exam. Then he fell on the gravel during track practice and scraped his arm. While he was driving home from school, it started to rain. As Tim rounded a corner, a dog ran out in front of the car. What caused the crash that followed? Was it his bad day, his sore arm, the rain, or the dog? No single factor was responsible. Instead, a mixture of risk factors probably caused the accident. Reducing any or all of the risk factors can reduce the risk of an accident.

Motor Vehicle Accidents

More Americans have been killed in traffic accidents than in all the nation's wars. For every person killed in an automobile accident, nearly 35 are injured or partially disabled.

The 18- to 24-year-old is the common victim. More than 10,000 people in this age group die in auto accidents each year. The elderly are also common victims of auto accidents. Admitting that you are too old to drive a car is difficult. However, some older people cannot focus on the road, other vehicles, pedestrians, and traffic signals at the same time. These problems are likely to cause accidents.

Motor vehicle accidents are linked with a variety of factors. These include speed, alcohol, distractions, fatigue, emotions, lack of preparedness, or a combination of these factors. In the 1970s, speed limits were lowered in an effort to conserve fuel.

Kent Hayward

19-11 **Children playing on sidewalks may be out of the motorist's line of vision. Checking behind you before backing out of a driveway can prevent an accident.**

Reducing the speed limit to 55 miles per hour dramatically reduced the number of deaths that occurred.

Alcohol is an important factor in about half of all motor vehicle fatalities. People who have been drinking often mistakenly believe they are fit to drive. However, accidents are likely to occur because alcohol inhibits concentration and slows reaction time.

Accident-prone drivers tend to have problems in emotional adjustment. In a study of high school students, many members of the accident-prone group believed driving relieves tension and associated driving with being an adult. They also had positive attitudes about driving fast and wanted a powerful car. Many accident-prone drivers thought driving was a way of showing confidence in their abilities.

Fatigue definitely affects a person's emotions and ability to drive safely. However, different people may react in various ways when they are driving while very tired. Being tired can make you hostile, nervous, and/or unaware of what is going on around you. All these emotions may have a negative effect on your ability to drive.

Accidents often occur because of the condition of the vehicle. Following the prescribed maintenance on your car is important, 19-12. Mechanical faults, poor brakes, defective turn signals, or worn tires may all result in accidents. Statistics show that seat belts have helped save many lives. However, the seat belts must be in correct working condition and they must be used. Most cars now also have airbags. They inflate rapidly when there is an accident. They are designed to limit head and chest injuries and to keep people from being thrown from the car. However, it is important to remember that air bags are designed to supplement seat belts, not to replace them. Always wear a seat belt.

There are definite precautions related to seat belts and air bags when children are riding in a motor vehicle. Children 12 years of age and younger should always be properly restrained in a child safety seat and/or seat belt and ride in the back seat. Infants and young children should never ride in the front seat of a vehicle with air bags unless there is a switch to disconnect the airbag. This caution also pertains to elderly people and others who are quite small.

Many accidents occur because the driver is not prepared. Many young people are not prepared to handle emergency situations. A brake failure, tire blowout, threatened head-on collision, or stuck accelerator are frightening to anyone. Young drivers may not have the experience that tells them how to react to these problems. Driver's education classes help teach young drivers how to react. These classes have helped prevent many accidents.

Use of cell phones while driving has become a safety issue. Statistics show that many accidents are related to the use of phones while operating a motor vehicle. Some cities have banned cell phone use while driving.

Unfortunately, being a good driver and having your car in good condition is not enough. You must also drive defensively to prevent accidents. You must be constantly aware of other drivers and anticipate what they might do to cause an accident.

A great many deaths and injuries to children have been prevented or reduced through the use of special restraining devices in cars. Different types of devices are available depending upon the age of the child.

Fire Deaths and Injuries

The most frequent victims of fires today are children and the elderly. Ideally, families should conduct fire drills just as schools do. Knowing how to get out safely and planning possible alternative escape routes could save the lives of family members. Surveys show the threat of fire deaths and injuries has been reduced in recent years. Stricter regulations by federal, state, and local governments have made this reduction possible. Safety in the design and construction of new public buildings and multifamily dwellings has improved. Safety officials are concerned about the thousands of older buildings and houses.

Many injuries result from materials used around the home that are extremely hazardous. Gasoline, kerosene, lighter fluid, some paints and thinners, plus alcohol-based

19-12 Making sure your car is in good working condition can help prevent accidents.

products can produce vapors that can ignite. Special care should be taken in storing hazardous cleaning products. Some are highly flammable and can be explosive. Others may be toxic or highly poisonous.

Smoke detectors that reliably warn people of fire are a positive step toward preventing fire deaths and injuries. See 19-13. Fortunately, they can be made and sold at a cost low enough to make them affordable.

Poisonings

Statistics often divide poisoning into two categories. The first is poisoning by solids and liquids. Accidental swallowing of drugs, medicines, poisonous foods, and other commonly recognized poisons are included in this first category. See 19-14. The second category is poisoning by gases and vapors.

Contrary to the stereotype, the vast majority of poisoning deaths are not among young children. The Poison Prevention Packaging Act of 1970 has reduced poisoning accidents involving young children. This act required that various toxic substances be packaged in containers difficult for children to open. The most common type of poisoning death instead

Schrader

19-14 Many products used in the home can cause illness, injury, or fatality if misused. For safety reasons, these items should be kept out of reach of young children.

occurs among adults who mistakenly take a drug overdose.

Accidents and Children

Many children suffer injuries, both minor and serious, as a result of playing with hazardous toys or the use of hazardous equipment. Government safety regulations have helped eliminate many of the causes of injuries. These regulations cover such areas as small parts, sharp points and edges, lead in paint, and safety regulations for electrically operated toys. However, these protective regulations do not cover all safety risks. Unsafe toys and equipment with hazards not covered by these regulations still appear on store shelves. This is why it is important to be aware of dangers in order to protect children from risks.

Consumer Reports has current information available regarding safety in choosing equipment and toys for children. It is published by the Consumers Union, whose mission is to test products, inform the public, and protect consumers.

19-13 Smoke detectors often allow people to escape a burning home and avoid serious injury.

Toys

Toy-related injuries cannot be entirely prevented by government regulations. It is therefore important that toys be checked for possible hazards and that children be guided in safe use of their toys. See 19-15.

Equipment

Following good safety practices in the selection of equipment for infants and young children is the best way to avoid accidents. Fortunately, federal regulations and a voluntary industry standard applies to the design of equipment such as baby cribs and playpens. Older equipment, however, may have slats that are too far apart allowing a baby's head to be caught between the slats. Cribs usually have a single side that lowers. Federal regulations require that lowering mechanisms be built to prevent accidental release by a baby or other young child.

Large puffy quilts and stuffed bedding products are available to the consumer even though the Consumer Product Safety Commission has deemed them unsafe for use in cribs. Use of these products with babies has resulted in suffocation. Sheets will often have a warning that says, "Prevent possible strangulation or entanglement. Never use crib sheet unless it fits securely on the crib mattress."

High chairs usually have a certification sticker on the tray or frame. This indicates that the model meets the minimum requirements of the American Society for Testing and Materials' voluntary standard. It also indicates that its manufacturer participates in the pass/fail certification program administered by the Juvenile Products Manufacturers Association. Certified seats are required to have a passive restraint such as crotch post; a locking device that prevents accidental folding; secure caps and plugs; sturdy, break-resistant trays; wide legs to increase stability; and no springs or dangerous scissoring actions that could entrap little fingers. Safety belts are required to pass force tests.

Other Accidents

Falls, suffocations, electrocutions, and drownings are other types of accidents that can be prevented. Prevention of industrial accidents, farm accidents, and accidents in the home has received more attention in recent years. Publicity on reducing these accidents is distributed through federal, state, and county agencies.

Toy Safety

- Explain to children how to use toys properly and safely.

- Teach children to put their toys safely away on shelves or in a toy chest after playing so no one trips or falls on them.

- Check toy boxes for safety. Both fatalities and permanent brain damage have resulted from toy chest lids falling on children's heads or necks.

- Before buying toys, examine labels for age recommendations. Toys should suit the skills and abilities of children.

- Avoid obvious hazards of poor or fragile construction, sharp edges, and points. For infants and very young children, avoid toys with long strings or cords that may cause strangulation.

- Repair broken toys or discard those that cannot be repaired.

19-15 Protect children from possible dangers by following these toy safety guidelines.

Prevention Techniques

By being aware of the many accidents that often occur and their causes, you can take steps to help prevent these accidents. Many of these accidents commonly occur in the home. Fortunately, you can prevent many home accidents by taking some simple safety measures. See 19-16.

You can take other preventive steps to help assure your good health and safety. These include having medical examinations, keeping adequate medical records, taking precautions to avoid disease, knowing common signs of illness, and learning simple first aid procedures.

Routine Medical Examination

Medical examinations are an important step in preventive safety. They have several advantages. Medical exams might detect life-threatening conditions that can be controlled or cured in the early stages. During an examination, your doctor will add useful information to your health history. This history contains information about the health of close relatives, previous illness, and any other related health problems. Some of the information, such as your blood pressure, forms a basis for comparison during future medical exams.

Safety in the Home

In emergencies...

Keep emergency telephone numbers by the telephone.

Plan fire escape routes and practice using them.

Learn safety procedures for emergencies such as storms, tornadoes, hurricanes, and earthquakes. Find out where the safest places in the home are during emergencies.

With electricity...

Follow instructions when using electrical appliances. Read the information and keep it in a file for later reference.

Make sure electrical cords are not frayed or cracked.

Do not put electrical cords where people may walk or trip over them.

Disconnect electrical cords from the outlet first, then from the appliance. Grasp the plug to disconnect.

Leave space around electrical appliances to prevent heat buildup.

Be cautious in the use of electricity near water. Electric shock can be fatal.

In product use and storage...

Read product labels carefully. Use products as directed. Do not combine cleaning products.

Store medicines and household cleaning products out of the reach of children.

Put all objects in their proper storage places when they are not being used.

To prevent falls...

Do not leave objects on stairs.

Use rugs with nonskid backing.

Place night-lights in hallways and bathrooms.

Place nonskid strips in bathtubs, showers, and sinks.

Use a sturdy step stool for reaching high places.

To ensure security...

Keep windows and doors locked.

Never open the door to a stranger. Look through the peephole or window or ask who it is.

Never let anyone know you are home alone.

Participate in a Neighborhood Watch group.

19-16 **These are some general home safety guidelines. Can you think of others?**

During the physical examination, the doctor can give you useful health guidance. You can ask questions about anything related to your health. This helps reduce any worry and anxiety. During the physical exam, the doctor also updates your immunization records.

Many people consider the annual physical exam necessary. However, in recent years, the annual exam has become controversial for cost reasons. At issue is whether the cost of the exam exceeds the benefits considering the doctor's time and the patient's money.

Certain tests should be performed at least once a year even if they are not part of a complete physical exam. These include a blood pressure test, standard blood and urine tests, and other tests specified by your doctor. People with special concerns might need other diagnostic tests. For instance, a regular smoker might have a chest X ray.

Periodic dental, eye, and ear examinations are important steps in preventive health. Seeing a dentist twice a year is recommended, 19-17. If you have a small cavity properly filled, the decay is stopped and your tooth can be saved. However, if you avoid having dental work done, your tooth may become badly decayed. Then expensive reconstructive work may be necessary.

Medical and Health Records

Accurate medical and health records are a valuable resource and a helpful diagnostic tool. Good records show a relationship between a patient's description of symptoms, results of a physical exam and tests, and past records.

Your medical records should include information about your family as well as your own health records. Blood type, allergies, drug sensitivities, any serious illness, and surgeries should also be included. A checklist of diseases and immunizations indicating dates is also helpful. This infor-

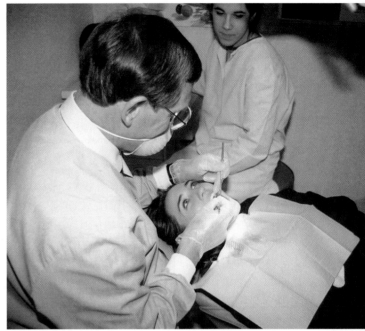

Denise Riehle

19-17 Dental care should begin during childhood and continue throughout life.

mation may help your doctor accurately interpret a symptom that would otherwise mean nothing. The medical history can also help your doctor decide what test to use in diagnosis.

Vaccinations

The average life expectancy for an American born in 1900 was 47 years. Today, Americans can expect to live over 70 years. Vaccines against infectious diseases have played a major role in preventing illness and death at a young age. A **vaccine** is a small amount of dead or weakened bacteria or virus that may be given by mouth or by injection. This stimulates the person's body to build up resistance to a disease. Having proper vaccinations can prevent many diseases or make them less serious. Vaccines are available to prevent polio, diphtheria, whooping cough, tetanus, measles, mumps, and German measles.

*Getting*Involved

For the most part, vaccines are safe and effective, but they do have limitations. Vaccines are not 100 percent effective, and some are occasionally accompanied by adverse reactions. However, the risk of serious complications from not giving a child a vaccine is considered 1,000 or more times greater than the side effects of the vaccine itself. Both old and newly developed vaccines not only go through a massive screening process but also continue to be subject to reviews after they have been used by the public.

Vaccines are not just for children. Many people now get the flu vaccine, particularly those with chronic health conditions, such as lung disease, heart disease, diabetes, or asthma. There is also the concern that when people gather in large groups, such as in a college setting, there is a greater potential for diseases to be transmitted. For a teen heading to college, it is a good idea to make sure he or she is up-to-date on the shots currently recommended by leading medical associations. These may include:

- *Chicken pox*—for teens who never received the vaccine as a child and those who have never had chicken pox. Two shots are administered one month apart.

- *Bacterial Meningitis*—for students living in dorms or other facilities that house numerous people. One shot given.

- *Hepatitis B*—for sexually active teens. Three shots are given over a six-month period.

Awareness of Warning Signals of Illness and Disease

Certain symptoms may indicate a need for medical attention. These symptoms include pain, fever, abnormal bleeding, unusual fatigue, sudden weight change, digestive changes, and respiratory changes. Being aware of these symptoms can help assure you of healthier living.

You don't need to go to the doctor for every little pain. When pain is sudden, sharp, unexplainable, or long lasting, you should see a doctor. Fever indicates illness or infection. Any wart or mole that bleeds may be a sign of cancer.

Many forms of cancer are curable if diagnosed and treated early in the progress of the disease. Therefore, you should be alert to these seven warning signals of cancer. If you experience one of these signs, see your doctor immediately.

- change in bowel or bladder habits

- a sore that does not heal

- unusual bleeding or discharge

- thickening or lump in breast or elsewhere

- indigestion or difficulty in swallowing

- obvious change in wart or mole

- nagging cough or hoarseness

Your mental health is as important as your physical health. It is important for you to be able to recognize the signs of poor mental health. Depression, sudden changes in behavior, inability to feel pleasure, lack of enjoyment in life, and overuse of defense mechanisms indicate poor mental health. These symptoms might eventually lead some people to suicide. Experts agree that most suicides could be prevented if symptoms of poor mental health were recognized.

Emergency Care of the Sick and Injured

First aid, or immediate and temporary care, is required when someone is injured or suddenly becomes ill. First aid helps the victim until he or she can get to a doctor. Since first aid may mean the difference between life and death, only competent people should perform it. Actions involved in first aid, such as promoting breathing, controlling bleeding, and cardiopulmonary resuscitation (CPR) require special training. This training may be available in your high school or through the Red Cross. Many communities also offer first aid courses. You do not become skilled in first aid procedures by simply reading instructions. You instead develop this skill by studying and practicing detailed procedures under an instructor's supervision. People who do not have first aid skills can cause serious injury when they try to help someone in distress.

Every home should be equipped with basic first aid supplies to be used in minor medical situations such as treating small cuts or scrapes and for minor aches and pains. See 19-18 for a list of basic first aid supplies.

The most important rule in first aid is to seek expert medical attention when faced with a serious injury or illness. It is important for people to know how to reach their physicians in case of emergency.

Fortunately, in the United States, legislation has resulted in the 911 emergency number. 911 lines are reserved for emergency calls to report a crime in progress, a fire, or to request an ambulance. Using 911 for non-emergency calls may delay the arrival of help for people in real emergency situations. In some communities, 311 may be used for non-emergency calls to police or other government services.

Other legislation proposes public access to *defibrillation* programs in federal buildings, schools and in other public buildings across the country. This provides ready

Basic First Aid Supplies	
Items	**Use**
Bandages: Adhesive strips Butterfly strips Elastic bandage Sterile bandages, gauze bandages	Cover small cuts Hold cut together Wrap sprains Wrap cuts and burns
Medications: Antibiotic cream Antidiarrheal Antihistamine Antiseptic Aspirin (Do not give to children.) Baking soda Calamine lotion Hydrocortisone cream Hydrogen peroxide	Prevents infection Prevents diarrhea Treats allergic reactions, colds Helps keep small cuts clean Relieves fever and pain Used in soothing baths and for stings Soothes rashes Soothes minor skin irritations Disinfects
Miscellaneous: Adhesive tape Cotton-tip applicators Eye cup Heating pad, hot-water bottle Humidifier, vaporizer Ice bag Scissors Thermometers (rectal and oral)	Use with bandages Use to apply medications Use for irrigating eye Relieve aches and pains Provide aid in breathing Reduces swelling Cuts tape and bandages Take temperatures

19-18 **These supplies should be included in home first aid kit.**

access to the tools needed to improve cardiac arrest (heart attack) survival rates. Early defibrillation is the most critical step in restoring normal cardiac rhythm and resuscitating a victim of sudden cardiac arrest.

Summary

Like all other people in our society, you make choices that affect environmental safety. By first understanding existing hazardous conditions, you can then make decisions that will help you live in a safer environment.

You can take preventive measures to help assure your good health and safety. These include routine medical examinations, accurate medical and health records, and an awareness of warning signs of illness and disease. Knowledge of emergency procedures and how to care for the sick and injured are other preventive resources available to you.

To Review

1. Discuss the problems of over population.
2. Give reasons air pollution, water pollution, and noise pollution are legitimate concerns.
3. Define recycling.
4. List three ways solid waste materials might be limited.
5. Name two health dangers of exposure to radiation.
6. The two most common causes of food contamination are _____ and _____.
7. True or false?
   A. Most accidents are caused by a single factor.
   B. Motor vehicle accidents usually result from speed, alcohol, fatigue, emotions, lack of preparedness, or a combination of these factors.
8. List six facts related to your health that should be included in your health records.
9. Discuss why it is important to be vaccinated against infectious diseases.
10. List five warning signals of cancer.

To Do
with the Class

1. Brainstorm ways you and your family can help reduce solid waste disposal in your community.
2. Invite a physician or other knowledgeable person to speak on the ways various drugs interact.
3. Discuss what might be done regarding the problem of elderly drivers who may not be physically or mentally fit to drive.
4. Invite a trained person to demonstrate simple first aid procedures to your class.

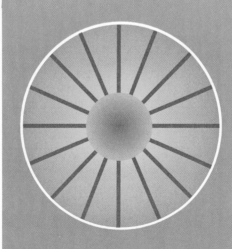

To Challenge
Your Thinking

1. Research the Clean Air Act. Report your findings to the class.
2. Look up information on efforts being made in your area to control water pollution. Discuss your findings with other class members.
3. Make a list of ways you can reduce your chances of being in an accident.
4. Find out if your own medical records are complete. If not, try to get the information necessary to make them complete.

To Do
with Your Community

1. Contact local fire or police departments. Find out how they are prepared to handle community emergencies. Which emergencies are more frequent within your community? How were past emergencies handled? Could there have been improvements?
2. Find out what precautions your community takes to ensure a safe environment. Contact members of the city council, police department, and fire department.
3. Invite an emergency medical technician or a member of the rescue squad to share their views and experiences on accident causes and prevention.
4. What resources and organizations are available in your community to help when emergencies, accidents, or environmental safety issues occur?

Part Six
Managing Finances

Chapter 20
Financial Management
Developing a financial plan can help you achieve goals and avoid financial problems. Making use of banking services and following a budget are important parts of financial management.

Chapter 21
Using Credit Wisely
There are both advantages and disadvantages to using credit. Understanding your credit options can help you make wise decisions.

Chapter 22
Planning for Financial Security
Saving, investing, and buying insurance are all ways to plan for financial security. Learning about retirement plans and estate planning now can help you make decisions and reach goals later in life.

20

Financial Management

To Know

wants
deductions
paycheck stub
gross pay
net pay
exemption
basic checking account
minimum-balance checking account
interest-bearing checking account
blank endorsement
restrictive endorsement
bank statement
automated teller machine (ATM)
debit cards
smart card
preauthorized transfers
telephone transfers
Electronic Funds Transfer Act
financial records
property records
household inventory
personal records
safe deposit box
budget
income
fixed expenses
flexible expenses

Objectives

After studying this chapter, you will be able to

◇ describe financial challenges at various stages of life.

◇ explain the reasons for various pay-check deductions.

◇ manage a checking account.

◇ describe records and papers to keep for financial planning.

◇ explain the importance of a budget.

◇ demonstrate the steps in developing a budget.

Most people handle money almost every day. Whether it is simple day-to-day finances, major spending, or investment, managing money can be difficult. Understanding personal finance and how money works is important. This knowledge can help increase financial well-being, increase your sense of control, and contribute to a more positive outlook on life in general. Learning good habits early in life can make managing money less challenging.

Unfortunately, as many as 50 percent of Americans are struggling to control excessive spending and debt. Financial difficulties can have a serious impact on your mental and physical health, family relationships, and effectiveness at work.

Financial management is necessary to help you reach your desired goals. See 20-1. Being aware of the financial challenges ahead will help you think through these challenges and set meaningful goals based on your priorities.

Financial Management Throughout Life

Both the financial problems and opportunities people face and the strategies needed to deal with them tend to be closely related to age. Although people might encounter financial problems and opportunities at various times throughout their lives, breaking down the major financial

issues by stages in life is helpful in understanding the challenges ahead and in developing a financial plan.

An important lesson in financial management is understanding the difference between needs and wants. *Needs* (as was discussed in Chapter 2) are the basic things in life–food, clothing, and shelter. **Wants** are something unnecessary but desired. Wants help make life more comfortable.

Children

Parents can help children make the distinction between needs and wants. For instance, they can teach their children the difference between *wanting* comic books and candy bars as opposed to *needing* a good breakfast and clothes. Without this foundation, children may have trouble controlling their spending as adults, never appreciating the difference between a luxury and a necessity.

Financial responsibility begins at home. Children learn about money constantly, either directly through observing their parents' spending and saving priorities, or indirectly through casual conversation. Every time children go to a store, restaurant, or ball game, they learn about money and about what adults think is important and valuable. If children are included in some of this financial decision making, they will be taking the first steps in their financial education.

How a family earns, spends, and saves money reveals a lot about their lives and what they value. Parents who talk to their young children about what they do for a living and how working provides shelter, food, clothing, and other necessities are showing them the connection between work and money. Before money can be spent, it first must be earned.

20-1 For many families, it takes careful financial planning to save for goals such as special family trips.

Children start to understand more about the value of money around the age of six. It's a good idea to allow them to begin handling money on a limited basis. Allowances may be started around this age. If they are earned by performing household chores, allowances can be powerful tools for teaching children about the connection between work and money. Even if an allowance is not related to chores, it gives children a sense of pride and responsibility in handling their own money.

The school years are an ideal time for children and teens to learn the basics of personal finance. Learning about banking and banking services, managing a household budget, the importance of saving for future goals, and the consequences and dangers of overspending greatly benefit young people. Parents can teach these financial basics. However, many schools are including money management basics in the curriculum at various levels.

Saving is another important lesson in financial management. If families make savings a top priority and put aside some money before spending it, they are teaching children a valuable lesson. Seeing parents paying bills, keeping track of spending, and setting money aside for savings helps children better understand the difference between needs and wants. See 20-2.

Young Adult Years

If young adults want to be able to afford what they need and want in the future, they will want to set money aside during their 20s and 30s. When it comes to retirement, there is more pressure on young adults now than in the past. Changes in company retirement plans and possible cutbacks or changes in social security require young adults to bear more responsibility for financing their own retirement. This requires some type of saving plan. A commonly suggested savings rate at this stage in life is 10 percent of a person's gross pay.

20-2 **Saving money helps a child learn the basics of financial management.**

For a couple anticipating marriage, discussing how the financial part of the marriage will work is extremely important. Experts say that money–how it is spent and who controls it–is one of those issues that can make or break a marriage. It is not the amount of money, but the management of it that can cause friction between two people.

Unfortunately, many young people form the habit of spending more than they earn. They accumulate big debts through credit cards or other loans and then struggle to pay the interest each month. Credit cards are a convenient method of acquiring goods and services, but paying the balance each month is the ideal step to take in financial management.

When considering buying a home, it is wise to keep in mind that transaction costs involved in buying and selling real estate are steep. Also people often underestimate their housing expenses by not considering such costs as home maintenance, repairs, and improvements.

A safety net during the young adult years is important. Although the chance of such crises as serious illness, home fires, and death are slight, the financial and personal hardships can be huge. Consideration of health benefits, home or rental insurance, and life insurance are important.

Middle Adult Years

The middle adult years can be very challenging financially. Although they may be the high-earning years, there are many financial challenges such as education costs for children, serious planning for retirement, and care of aging parents.

This is the time to contribute as much as possible to tax-advantage retirement plans. If by now, money has not been put away for retirement, financial planners suggest that 20 percent of a person's income be set aside in some type of savings plan.

As in the 20s and 30s, a safety net provided through insurance is important. Would there be enough life insurance to replace family earnings and provide for family members in case of an early death?

Late Adult Years

Some of the important challenges for people in the late adult years is being able to retire, managing financial resources to provide for remaining years, and to arrange financially so a surviving spouse will be financially secure. Health costs and living expenses are a major issue for many senior citizens. More people are taking advantage of long-term health insurance. However, the cost of this insurance is quite high for the older adult. If purchased in middle adult years, the cost is lower.

Most people in their early 60s would like to retire as soon as possible. However, with people living longer, many 60-year-olds can expect to live for another 25 years. They may want to put off retirement until

they are able to afford the lifestyle they would like over an extended time. See 20-3. Working a few more years, often at what is probably the highest earning portion of their career, may have a big impact on their financial resources. Many people continue their working years on a part-time basis.

Understanding Your Paycheck

The amount of your paycheck influences your financial plans. When you receive a paycheck, you may be surprised to find it is smaller than you expected. You may wonder why you don't get to take home all the

20-3 **It is never too early to start saving for leisure time in later years.**

money you earned. This is because part of your earnings are deducted (subtracted) by your employer for tax payments and other expenses. These are called **deductions**. Deductions are listed on the paycheck stub attached to your paycheck. The **paycheck stub** lists the total amount of money you earned as well as deductions. A paycheck stub is shown in 20-4.

Your **gross pay** is the total amount you earn for a pay period before any deductions are subtracted from your paycheck. Your **net pay** is the gross pay minus the deductions.

How does your employer determine how much money to deduct from your paycheck? When you begin a job, you are asked to fill out a W-4 Form. This guides your employer as to how much tax to withhold from your paycheck.

On your paycheck, the amount of social security taxes withheld appears under "Social Security" or "F.I.C.A." The amount of social security tax withheld is a set percentage of your income. The amount of federal income tax deducted appears under "Federal Tax." The amount of federal

income tax withheld depends on how much you earn and the number of exemptions you are allowed. An **exemption** reduces the amount of income on which a person must pay taxes.

Other deductions that may be withheld from your check include state income tax, retirement fund contributions, insurance premiums, and union dues.

Basic Banking

Traditional banking is changing greatly. In addition to different kinds of checking and savings accounts, money market accounts, certificates of deposit, loans, and credit cards, many financial institutions are offering such services as automatic check depositing and bill paying. Many are also offering stock brokerage services and some types of insurance.

No matter what financial institution is used, there are certain fundamentals associated with financial management and

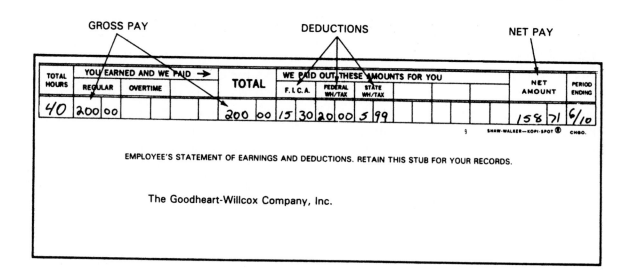

20-4 By studying a paycheck stub you can determine what deductions were made from your total earnings.

banking that are necessary to know. Choosing a checking account, writing and depositing checks, and balancing an account are basic skills in banking.

Checking Accounts

One of the first banking services you are likely to use when you begin earning money is a checking account. Being familiar with banking services and using them wisely is an important step in developing an effective financial plan. (Various savings institutions are described in Chapter 22.) To avoid carrying a lot of cash around and the possibility of it being stolen, many people have checking accounts. A checking account provides a record of spending and receipts of payment. It provides a safe place to keep cash and a convenient way to buy goods and services and pay bills by mail.

Types of Checking Accounts

Types of checking accounts vary from one bank to another. Choose the account that best meets your needs by comparing them carefully. It is important to find out what service charges, check fees, and/or minimum balance requirements are for each type of account.

Three basic types of checking accounts include:

- **Basic checking account**: You are charged a fee for every check you write and/or a monthly service charge. You are not required to keep a minimum balance. This type of an account makes sense for someone who writes few checks or cannot conveniently maintain a minimum balance.

- **Minimum-balance checking account**: You are required to keep a minimum amount of money in the account at all times to avoid paying a service charge. If your account falls below the minimum, there is a charge.

- **Interest-bearing checking account**: You earn interest and are allowed to write checks on the same account. This is a savings and checking account. There is usually a minimum balance requirement.

Opening a Checking Account

Once you have decided on the type of account you want to open, you will be asked to fill out a signature card and make a deposit. You will be asked to sign the signature card the way you plan to sign it on all the checks you write and withdrawal slips. This will be the only signature the bank will honor for your account.

You will receive a checkbook with personalized checks and a register. See 20-5. The checks will have your name, address, and account number on them. Inspect the checks for accuracy. Check the spelling of your name and make sure the correct account number appears on the checks. Report any errors to the bank.

The register will help you to keep track of the checks you write and the deposits you make. If you don't understand a checking procedure, someone at the bank can explain it to you.

You will need to fill out a deposit slip to put money into your checking account. A deposit slip lists what is being deposited—currency, coins, or checks—and the amount of each. Each time you make a deposit, you will be given a receipt. Be sure

*Getting*Involved

Gather information from your community financial institutions. Chart the services and present it to the class or student organizations. Discuss the value of being financially informed.

to enter the amount of the deposit in your checkbook register.

Endorsing Checks

If you want to deposit a check, cash a check, or use a check to pay someone, you must endorse the check. To do this, sign your name on the back of the check at the top left end.

You can endorse a check using a blank endorsement or a restrictive endorsement. A **blank endorsement** requires your signature. Since a check with this type of endorsement can be cashed by anyone who holds it, this type of endorsement should only be used at the time and place the check is being cashed or deposited. A **restrictive endorsement** states what is to be done with the check. Common restrictive endorsements include:

◆ "For deposit only" and your signature

◆ "Pay to the order of," the name of the party to receive the check, and your signature

Writing Checks

Checks must be written correctly in order for them to be processed correctly. A

Banker's System Inc.

20-5 Use the space provided in your checkbook to record all transactions involving your checking account. You will need this information to balance your checkbook when you receive the bank's monthly statement.

properly written check is shown in 20-6. Notice the information on the check that allows the bank to process it.

Every time you write a check, record the check number, date, payee, purpose of the check, and amount of the check in your register. Next, subtract the amount of the check from your balance. This way, you

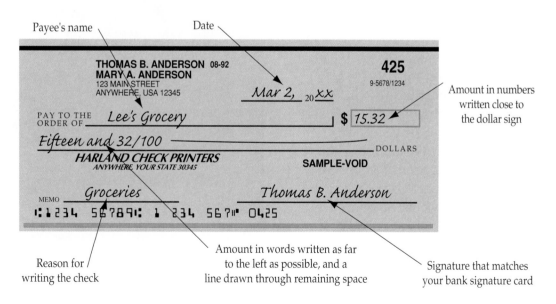

20-6 The information on checks helps banks process them correctly. This check has been written correctly.

will know how much money you have in your account. This can prevent you from writing a check for an amount more than you actually have in your account. If this happens, your account is *overdrawn*. Overdrawn accounts are charged a fee. If you overdraw your account several times, your poor banking record may be reported to a credit-reporting agency. This could cause you to have a low credit rating and make it difficult for you to borrow money or to obtain credit cards.

Balancing a Checkbook

Once you have a checking account, you will receive bank statements. A **bank statement** is a record of the checks, deposits, and charges on your account for a specific length of time, usually monthly. It also may include your canceled checks. These are the checks you have written and your bank has paid. Some banks now use a checkbook that makes a duplicate of each check written. This copy remains in the checkbook. In this case, canceled checks are not included with the bank statement. You already have a copy of each check. Banks may also send you copies of the checks paid instead of the actual checks.

Make sure the balance in your checkbook register matches that on your bank statement. This is called *balancing your checkbook*.

To balance your checkbook, mark off, in your checkbook register, the canceled checks the bank has returned to you. You also need to mark off the deposits that are shown on the statement. Any service charges listed on the bank statement must also be subtracted from your checkbook balance. Any interest that has been earned must be added to the checkbook balance.

Electronic Banking

Many changes have occurred bringing new resources in electronic banking. These new methods allow money to be moved between accounts in a fast, paperless way.

Electronic Fund Transfers

There are several types of electronic fund transfers (EFTs) being used by consumers. By using the **automated teller machine (ATM)**, you can do banking without the assistance of a teller to obtain cash or make deposits, pay bills, or transfer funds from one account to another electronically.

Your employer may offer you the option of automatically depositing your paycheck into your personal account at your financial institution. This is especially convenient for people who travel often or have busy schedules. See 20-7.

Automatic bill paying can be done in a variety of ways. You can request your bank to pay certain bills for you out of your checking account. You enroll with your bank by completing an account-authorization form that lists each company you wish to pay. Funds are either transferred electronically between your account and the

20-7 **If your paycheck is automatically deposited, you can simply make withdrawals through an ATM.**

merchants', or checks are issued and mailed. Some financial institutions offer bank-by-phone accounts. In some systems your spoken instructions are recorded by special equipment. In others, you use a telephone keypad to indicate whom you want to pay, how much, and when.

People are increasingly using another type of EFT–**debit cards**. They transfer money from a checking account to the account of a store or service provider. The bank's computer verifies whether there is enough money to cover the purchase and the sum is deducted from the checking account immediately. Debit cards can be used at locations where credit card logos are displayed.

The advantage of the debit card is it offers the convenience of making purchases with the card without the temptation or the ability to run up credit card debt. It keeps people from spending money they do not have. Also, many people find it is convenient to use debit cards in place of cash or checks. See 20-8.

The debit card does have disadvantages. It's not free. Issuing banks assess a service charge. Also, when using a debit card, maintaining accurate checking account records is very important. Otherwise, you may be facing some insufficient check fund charges.

Credit cards have been available for years, but a new type of card, the **smart card**, is now being used. The cardholder must have money in an account to use the card. As the card is used, money is automatically transferred from the user's account. A computer chip is actually placed in the card itself. This chip stores personal information about cardholder.

A **preauthorized transfer** is a method of automatically depositing to or withdrawing funds from a person's account when the account holder authorizes the bank or a third party to do so. The third party might be an employer. For instance,

20-8 **Debit cards look like credit cards and can be used everywhere credit cards are used, including online stores.**

consumers can authorize direct deposit of wages, social security, or dividend payments to their accounts.

Telephone transfers are used by consumers to transfer funds from one account to another, such as from a savings account to a checking account. Telephone transfer can also be used to order payment of specific bills by phone.

Legislation known as the **Electronic Funds Transfer Act** (EFT Act) functions to protect and inform the consumer. Most consumer concerns center on the fact that EFT systems transmit the information without paper. However, the EFT Act

points out that if you use an ATM or a debit card, you can get a written receipt showing the amount of the transfer, the date it was made, and other information. This receipt is your record of transfers initiated at an electronic terminal.

Also, the EFT points out that your periodic bank statement must also show all electronic transfers. It will also name the party to whom payment has been made and show any fees for EFT services. The way to report errors is somewhat different with EFT services than it is with credit cards. However, as with credit cards, financial institutions must investigate and correct promptly any errors you report.

It is important to be aware of the potential risk in using an EFT card, which differs from the risk of a credit card. With an EFT card, your liability for an unauthorized withdrawal can vary depending upon how quickly you notify the financial institution after learning of loss or theft or your card or code. This liability can range from a limit of $50 if you notify the financial institution within two business days to unlimited loss of the money in your account if you do not report an unauthorized transfer that appears on your statement within 60 days after the statement is mailed to you.

Personal Computer Software

Many software programs are available to personal computer users that make financial management easier. Home banking software allows those with computers to check their balances and receive and pay bills electronically. Some programs can remind you that a bill payment is due. If you are not online, then it can page you on a cellular phone.

Record Keeping

Personal documents, household records, and other important papers may at some time be needed. They may provide evidence of a specific transaction or provide helpful information when developing financial plans. Most important papers fall into the general areas of financial records, property records, and personal records.

Financial Records

A variety of **financial records** can be very helpful to you and would be worth keeping for at least seven to 10 years. See 20-9. These records show how you spend your money. They can help you decide on spending priorities, budgets, figure your income taxes, and prove certain payments have been made. These various financial records include:

- *Cash flow records.* These can also be described as *income and spending records.* They include a variety of income records, such as salary, dividends, interest from money loaned, rent, and money drawn from a savings account. Spending records in this category include cash register receipts, other sales receipts, and other written records of cash spending. Having accurate records of income and spending is extremely valuable in developing a budget.

- *Bank records.* These include canceled checks, statements, deposit receipts, and any other legal documents involving the bank. Cancelled checks that

20-9 **Keeping financial records is essential to financial management.**

substantiate tax deductions, that verify major purchases, or that are particularly significant in other ways are important to keep.

- *Evidence of debts.* These include any type of charge account receipt. These records can be important in settling credit disputes.

- *Savings and investment records.* These include savings account passbooks, records of savings certificates, social security and/or retirement records, information about stock and bond certificates, mutual fund shares, and United States savings bonds.

- *Insurance records.* These include automobile, health, accident, property, life, and any other type of insurance. It is wise to keep a list of the name and address of each of the insurance companies, types of policies, policy numbers, amount of each policy, and place the policies are kept.

- *Tax records.* Tax records for the current year and the six previous years income tax returns should be kept. The IRS generally has three years to examine tax returns, but it has six if there is substantial underreporting of income.

Property Records

Property records may not be as important to developing a budget as financial records. However, they are related and will be important in other areas of financial management. **Property records** include real estate records, household inventory, and records of ownership. Property records can prove ownership, indicate monetary value of possessions, and help determine insurance needs.

Real estate records include deeds, title papers, and mortgage documents. They may include papers showing the price you paid for property or the amount you received when property was sold. Real estate records also include records of capital improvement, such as bills and receipts showing the cost of improvements. These records are very important when preparing income tax forms.

The **household inventory** is a list of personal property including household furniture, furnishings, and equipment. For each item, the date of purchase and the purchase price or appraised value are included. Photos or videos can be a valuable part of the household inventory to help prove ownership and value claims. See 20-10.

Records of ownership include guarantees, warranties, sales slips, and other papers that establish ownership and value of these possessions. Canceled checks also provide a record of proof of ownership.

Personal Records

Like property records, personal records are not used directly in developing a budget, but they are important in financial dealings. **Personal records** include personal documents, health records, education records, and employment records.

Personal documents are important personal papers. They include birth,

Lynn Hellmuth

20-10 A household inventory uses both words and pictures to describe personal property. In case of fire or theft, this information is much more accurate than the information recalled from memory.

marriage, and death certificates; wills, and adoption papers. Other personal documents include divorce and separation decrees; child custody orders; property settlements; citizenship papers; social security cards; and passports.

Health records include dates and details related to immunizations, medical care, allergies, infectious diseases, accidents, and major illness or surgery. These records may also include the blood type of each family member.

Education records include schools attended, graduation date, degree or certificate awarded, record of grades, and important documents, such as diplomas. Both education records and health records may be important when applying for a job.

Employment records may include a list of where and when you were employed and your supervisor's name. Resumes, licenses or permits, certificates of training, union membership information, and job benefits information are also included.

How to Keep the Records

There are many available resources for record keeping. Many workbooks, tax organizers, and record keeping forms are available. Although many important records can be stored in the home, others require a safer place, such as a safe deposit box. A **safe deposit box** is a rented metal box in a fireproof vault, usually at a bank. See 20-11. Records that are irreplaceable or difficult and costly to replace should be kept in a safe deposit box. Photocopies could be made of these records and kept at home with a list of safe deposit box contents.

When you rent a safe deposit box, you receive two identical keys. A master key, kept by the bank, and your key are needed to open the box. You must sign your name each time you open your box.

It may be helpful, also, to develop a *record keeping inventory*. This is a list of all the important papers and where they are stored. It is wise to have two copies of this list, one to keep in the safe deposit box and the other to use at home.

Developing a Budget–A Spending Plan

Most people's needs and wants exceed their incomes. Some have trouble stretching their paychecks from month to month. Some have trouble saving any money. These problems may not be related to the amount of money they have, but instead, how they use that money. Even families with an income that seems comfortable can easily overspend.

M & I Bank Hilldale

20-11 **Safe deposit boxes are available in several different sizes. The rent a person must pay depends upon the size of the box.**

A **budget**, often referred to as a spending plan, is a valuable resource in helping people have the money for the things they need most. See 20-12. The budget controls how they use money. The government, businesses, and many clubs and organizations use budgets to control their finances effectively.

Why Plan?

Budgets should be developed for several very good reasons. First, planning helps you decide your priorities–what is most important to you. It also gives you a better understanding of your financial status. Dealing with specific figures related to income and expenditures, makes it easier to know what changes you must make regarding your finances.

A budget allocates your income so you can purchase as much of what you need as possible. It helps you learn to live within your income. No matter what your level of income, you will make choices about how you spend your money. The budget helps guide your choices so you avoid overspending. It also helps you meet your daily expenses without strain.

A budget helps eliminate wasteful spending. Records help you see the amount of money you spend on nonessential items. Without a plan, many people have no idea how much money they "throw away" on unimportant items.

Budgets can help people achieve long-range goals through monthly saving over a period of time. Many goals that seem impossible can be reached this way. Above all, a budget gives people control over a very important aspect of their lives. This control can be a very positive influence. When you *manage*–plan and control something successfully–you get great psychological satisfaction in return.

A budget can lead toward harmony in the home. Statistics show that financial problems are often major factors that lead toward divorce.

Stig Rahm

20-12 **A spending plan shows just how income and expenses compare. This often gives people incentive to improve their spending habits.**

Developing a Budget

Developing a budget or a spending plan has clear, definite steps. Before you can develop the plan, you must gather information about your expected income and expenditures.

Income

All the money you receive from salaries or wages, money gifts, tips, allowances, and interest earned on a savings account make up your **income**. Income may also include dividends or stocks, income from securities, or income from rental property. Income from a salary should include only take-home pay–the amount you receive after deductions for taxes and other purposes.

Expenditures

Another task prior to developing a spending plan is to estimate expenses. This is usually more difficult. To plan spending, analyze your spending habits. Your ability to do this will depend somewhat on what records of your spending are available. When using these records, try to divide spending into two categories–fixed and flexible expenses.

When expenses occur regularly and stay the same or nearly the same, they are considered **fixed expenses**. Rent or house payments, loan payments, insurance, or property taxes are examples of fixed expenses.

Some fixed expenses are periodic rather than monthly. Bills such as taxes and insurance may be sent once or twice a year. Although these bills are not paid monthly, they are fixed expenses. You plan for these expenses by setting aside a certain amount of the income each month.

Fixed expenses are the easiest part of a spending plan to develop. Calculating the flexible expenses is more complex.

Those expenses that vary both in amount and frequency of occurrence are known as **flexible expenses**. Items such as food, clothing, utilities, transportation, medical care, personal expenses, and recreational expenses are flexible expenses. See 20-13.

Records of past spending form a good basis for estimating future expenses. They help take the guesswork out of planning.

Examining your estimated income compared with your estimated expenses will give you an understanding of your financial position. Planned spending is still very important even if your income appears to be greater than your expenses. The person in this situation must make decisions about what to do with the surplus

20-13 Eating out with friends is an example of a flexible expense.

money that would probably first go into some type of checking or savings account. A young couple may use some of that savings for a down payment on a house. They might also contribute to a specific fund for the education of their children.

If your estimated income is close to or less than estimated expenses, planned spending is extremely important. You must make careful decisions about spending priorities. This is a time to carefully consider the difference between needs and wants. Use your money for what is most important to you.

Determining Goals

The way you use your income depends on your needs and wants. What is a necessity to one person may seem wasteful to another. When your needs and wants exceed your income, you will need to establish priorities.

Spending goals usually focus first on the necessary things. The average American family spends the greatest percentage of income on food and housing. The remainder is divided among taxes, transportation, clothing, medical care, personal care, and entertainment.

Saving part of your income is an important spending goal, even if it is a small monthly amount. It is helpful to have some type of "cushion" amount in case of emergencies. The amount in savings can be earning interest. Putting a set amount in savings each month is a good plan for saving. This might even be done through a payroll deduction plan at work.

Completing a Budget

Once you have collected income and expense figures and considered goals and priorities, you can develop a budget. A variety of budget forms are available at bookstores, stationery stores, and drug stores. Since each family's income and needs differ, many people like to develop their own forms, using the others as guides.

Preparing both an annual budget and a monthly budget can be helpful. An annual budget gives an overall view of your spending and keeps you from forgetting certain expenses that tend to appear throughout the year.

Most people prefer monthly rather than weekly planning. This is convenient because many bills are due monthly and pay periods usually fall into monthly intervals.

By following simple steps, you can develop a budget. See 20-14. This planning, or budgeting, requires practice. It won't work perfectly on your first try. You will

Steps in Developing a Budget

1. Estimate your total income from all sources for a given period of time.

2. Estimate your total fixed and flexible expenses for the same period of time. Use records of your past spending to help you make this estimate.

3. Compare your estimated income with your estimated expenses. It is desirable for income to be greater than expenses.

4. Set spending goals and establish priorities in spending. Decide how much you must spend or want to spend in various categories. Also decide on a savings goal.

5. Complete your budget by putting it in writing on a form you have developed or purchased.

6. Evaluate your budget. Record your actual income and expenditures as they occur and compare them with your estimates. You may need to adjust your plan if the figures differ greatly.

20-14 **By carefully following these steps, you can develop your own budget.**

learn something each month that will make future spending plans more successful.

Being flexible is a positive trait for a successful manager. Sticking to rigid rules and regulations is difficult, if not impossible. Being flexible is just as important in budgeting as in other areas of management. For instance, expenses in a certain area, such as food, may exceed the estimated amount. In this case, you must adjust the budget accordingly. You might use some of the money that had been budgeted for clothing or recreation.

Evaluation

A successful budget requires constant evaluation. At the end of each month, compare actual spending with planned spending. If these figures are not close, you will need to adjust your budget.

If your spending exceeds your income, study the figures to see if they can be changed to become workable. Find a way to either reduce your expenses or to generate additional income. The way a person or a family does this depends on interests, needs, wants, and available resources.

Reducing flexible expenses may be quite difficult for some families. Therefore, they may need to change their fixed expenses. If housing is too great an expense, moving to less costly housing might be necessary.

Families often solve the problem through additional income. This could be accomplished by changing jobs or by having more adults in the family work. In many families today, both husband and wife must work in order to meet expenses.

32
31
30
29
28
27
26
25
24
23
22
21
20
19
18
17
16
15
14
13
12
11
10
9
8
7
6
5
4
3
2
1

Summary

Financial plans help in reaching desired goals. By being aware of financial challenges throughout life, you will be better able to develop both short-term and long-term financial goals.

Certain basic skills are necessary in managing finances. Understanding your paycheck and managing a checking account are two of these skills. A budget is easier to develop if good financial records have been kept. Knowing which records and papers to keep, how they can be organized, and where to store them will aid you in developing an effective budget.

Your income and expense records can help you understand your financial position more clearly. You can then prioritize your spending goals. Before developing a budget, it is also necessary to analyze your needs and wants and consider both short-term and long-term goals. A successful budget requires constant evaluation.

To Review

1. Name at least two deductions that an employer makes from a paycheck.
2. Give three advantages of having a checking account.
3. List the three steps that can be taken to organize record keeping.
4. What are the three categories of important records and papers?
5. Describe a household inventory and explain why it is important.
6. True or false?
   A. Records that cannot be replaced or are difficult and costly to replace should be kept in a safe deposit box.
   B. To get into a safe deposit box, you enter the vault and open the box with your key.
7. List five benefits of using a budget.
8. Describe the difference between fixed and flexible expenses.
9. Why is saving part of your income an important goal?
10. Why is it important to constantly evaluate your spending plan?

To Do with the Class

1. Develop a display of sample budget and record keeping forms.
2. Invite several people to share their record keeping systems with the class. Note the differences and discuss why they might exist.
3. Discuss ways individuals or families could work to change their flexible expenses to fixed expenses. For example, they might develop a spending plan for food that allows a definite amount per month.
4. Look through books and magazines to find examples of completed budget plans. Examine and discuss them in class.

To Challenge Your Thinking

1. List your personal goals. How can a budget help you meet some of those goals?
2. Describe three real-life or fictitious situations that illustrate problems that occur when there is not a system for record keeping. Share these situations with others in the class.
3. Develop a suitable form and record your financial expenditures for a month. Evaluate the form at the end of the month.
4. Research current statistics on the spending habits of American families. Share your findings with others in the class.

To Do with Your Community

1. Visit several banks. Find out about the various types of checking accounts available. Which bank and type of checking account would be best for you? Explain why.
2. Invite a financial planner to share budgeting strategies with the class. What do they consider to be most challenging to a successful budget?
3. Visit a bank in your community and ask about the availability of safe deposit boxes and guidelines for their use. Report your findings to the class.
4. Consider the various businesses in your community. Where do families spend their money? Of those businesses listed, which provide necessities for families? Which supply extras, or wants, rather than needs?

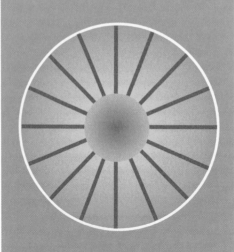

21 Using Credit Wisely

To Know

credit
debtor
creditor
impulse buying
cash credit
sales credit
finance charge
interest
principal
installment loan
single-payment loan
installment credit
regular charge accounts
revolving charge accounts
limited purpose credit cards
multipurpose credit cards
consumer finance companies
consolidation loans
credit unions
capacity
capital
reverse annuity mortgage
credit bureau

Objectives

After studying this chapter, you will be able to

◇ recognize the advantages and disadvantages of credit use.

◇ describe types of credit and types of credit cards.

◇ give examples of various sources of credit and explain how a person obtains credit.

◇ identify and explain various laws governing credit.

Credit has become a way of life for most Americans. Consumers use credit to buy everything from houses to clothing to services and utilities. See 21-1. Most bills you receive in the mail each month are the result of a credit agreement.

Fleetwood Enterprise

21-1 Without credit, purchasing a home would be very difficult for most people.

Credit is the supplying of money, goods, or services in exchange for the promise of future payment by the consumer. When you use credit as a consumer, you are known as a **debtor**. You owe a debt to the **creditor**. Creditors are those who supply you with the money, goods, or services. Credit is based on trust. The creditor trusts the debtor to pay the debt.

Using credit allows the consumer to borrow to enjoy goods and services today and pay for them tomorrow. Americans greatly rely on the use of credit, and many people have financial problems resulting from its overuse. Understanding the advantages and disadvantages of credit and laws and regulations governing its use will help you use credit wisely.

Credit Use

Credit is neither good nor bad. Although it can be used wisely, credit can also be used poorly, creating serious financial problems. Therefore, you must carefully consider the advantages and disadvantages of each credit transaction.

Advantages and Disadvantages of Credit

One of the biggest advantages of credit is that it can be used for so many different purposes. Credit can buy furniture, pay for a meal, or buy an airline ticket. You can use credit to have your car repaired or to pay educational costs. Credit is almost always used to pay utility charges. For instance, you use your gas furnace for a month, the meter is read, and then you are billed for the cost. The utility company lets you use the gas now and then pay for it later.

Credit provides a temporary expansion of your income to meet emergencies or to make major purchases that could not be made without credit. It helps people when their income seems to lag behind their expenses. Credit allows people at least 20 to 30 days before a bill must be paid.

Convenience in shopping is a less important, but significant, advantage of credit. See 21-2. Credit reduces the need to carry a lot of cash. Merchandise is often easier to return if it has been charged. Wise use of credit also helps the consumer build a good credit rating. The consumer receives a receipt when making a credit purchase. He or she also receives a statement that indicates purchases and amount owed. This receipt and statement enable efficient record keeping.

An unfortunate disadvantage of credit is that it encourages many people to over-spend. Many consumers charge beyond their ability to repay. Because charge accounts are so easy to use, they encourage **impulse buying**—buying items that are not really needed.

Using credit creates additional expense in terms of finance charges and the cost of goods. The cost of goods and services must increase to make up for the merchant's costs in time and money to provide the service of credit. Although interest rates on credit card purchases vary, the average

21-2 Using credit to shop online and by phone is another example of convenience.

21-3 Sales credit may be used to purchase expensive toys such as this car.

remains close to 18 percent. This is often twice the going rate of other types of loans and there is no tax deduction.

Credit users must remember that expanding their income through credit now may cause their income to contract in the future. While repaying a debt, your ability to buy is greatly reduced. Events such as illness, job layoffs, or pregnancy leave can also change the amount of available income.

Types of Credit

There are two basic types of credit: cash credit and sales credit. **Cash credit** is used to borrow money. **Sales credit** is used to purchase goods and services. See 21-3. Each of these categories can be further broken down into various types of credit.

With the use of credit, there will often be a finance charge. A **finance charge** is what the consumer pays for the use of credit, including interest charges and any other fees. Understanding interest is another step in financial management. **Interest** is expressed in a percentage of the amount involved. This amount is known as the **principal.** For example, if you borrow $1,000–the principal–at a 10 percent interest rate for one year, you must pay back $1,100–the $1,000 borrowed plus $100 in interest.

If you borrow money for two years, you would probably have to pay a higher rate of interest. This is because more can go wrong over a longer period of time, and that means a greater risk for the lender.

Interest charges often vary for consumer credit, credit cards, store credit, and mortgages. If interest rates go up, borrowers have to pay more. If they go down, they pay less.

Cash Credit

Financial institutions, insurance companies, and credit card agencies extend cash credit. Cash credit is often used to purchase goods and services from sellers who do not give credit. Types of cash credit include installment loans, single-payment loans, and credit card or check credit loans.

When you have an **installment loan**, you borrow a set amount of money and repay it plus finance charges in a series of scheduled payments. When you have a **single-payment loan**, you borrow an amount of money and repay that amount plus finance charges in one payment.

You may also be able to get cash credit through a credit card or check credit loan. You get the cash by using your credit card or writing a check that the bank will cover. There is an agreement between you and the lender regarding how much you can borrow, the way it must be repaid, and the finance charges.

Sales Credit

Businesses who sell goods and services may extend sales credit. Types of sales credit include installment credit, regular charge accounts, and revolving charge accounts.

Installment credit may be used to purchase expensive items like cars or major appliances. With installment credit, the buyer makes payments in regular installments. These installments include the finance charges. See 21-4. A contract is drawn up at the time the purchase is made. The contract includes the amount of the purchase, the amount of the finance charge, and the total amount to be repaid. Cash down payments are often required when a consumer is buying on the installment plan. This down payment acts as a guarantee that the customer will make the installment payments.

Regular charge accounts are a type of sales credit that allow customers to purchase goods and services on credit and pay the bill in full in 30 days. If you do this, you are not charged interest. However, you may be charged interest if you do not pay

21-4 **More costly items such as new appliances might be bought using installment credit.**

the full amount. Regular charge accounts are a convenience for everyday expenses. Utilities, doctor bills, and charge accounts at many stores are examples of regular charge accounts.

Revolving charge accounts differ in that the total amount of the bill does not have to be paid each month. However, a finance charge will be figured on the amount not paid. Additional purchases can be made even though money is owed on previous purchases. The customer's line of credit is usually limited. Credit cards are usually revolving charge accounts.

Credit Cards

Many credit cards used today are limited purpose credit cards. **Limited purpose credit cards** are used only at a specific business or any of its locations. Large department stores have limited purpose cards as do other large businesses such as petroleum companies. Petroleum companies may allow customers to use these cards for auto maintenance, repairs, and emergency services as well as for gas or fuel oil. Some petroleum companies even offer check cashing services and credit at certain hotels and motels throughout the country. Most limited purpose credit cards involve no membership fee or annual charge to the user. The consumer receives a monthly account of spending indicating the total amount owed. If the total amount is not paid by the due date indicated on the statement, there will be a finance charge on the balance of the account.

Many consumers prefer to use one multipurpose credit card such as a bank credit card or a travel and entertainment card. See 21-5. **Multipurpose credit cards**

▤ **21-5 If you have a multipurpose card, many of the limited purpose cards may not be needed.**

Use Your Reasoning Skills

Research your state's consumer credit laws and report your findings to the class. Did any of the information surprise you? How will you benefit from knowing this information now? Why is it important to keep your knowledge of consumer credit laws up-to-date?

will be accepted by a variety of businesses, stores, and restaurants. Some companies charge cardholders an annual fee. There is usually no finance charge if the total bill is paid within 20 to 30 days of the billing date. However, most Americans do not avoid the finance charge and owe billions of dollars in credit card debt. For this reason, it is important to shop for the best deal possible in credit cards. A low interest rate is important, but other factors also affect the cost of a card. For example, some card issuers do not charge interest until 25 days after billing, whereas others start the charges immediately or when the charge is posted.

A wise consumer will consider his or her own bill paying habits when selecting a credit card. It is generally best for people who tend to carry balances to look for the lowest rate. People who regularly pay their balances in full would do better to find a card with no annual fee. If they have two cards, they could have a low-rate card for purchases that they will not be able to pay for right away and a no-fee card for charges that will be paid as soon as they receive the bill. Be alert to special offers. The credit card business is very competitive, with issuers frequently offering inducements to attract new customers.

When you use a credit card, you take the items purchased with you. However, the seller has the legal right to reclaim these items if you fail to pay for them.

If you lose a credit card, the Truth in Lending Law limits your liability to $50 of unauthorized charges per card. To avoid any financial loss, act immediately by contacting your credit card company by phone. As soon as the credit card company is notified, you are no longer responsible for any charges, not even the $50. When you call the company, give them your name, address, and the account number of your card. Make a note of the time you call, and ask the person to whom you speak to do the same. Ask for a written confirmation of your call.

When calling about a missing credit card, have the necessary information close at hand. Keep a list of credit cards that includes the following items:

◇ name of the credit card company or service

◇ names of persons in your household who have copies of each card

◇ account number of each card

◇ address and telephone number to inform the company of a lost or stolen card

◇ expiration date

Credit card companies are legally required to provide you with a self-addressed, stamped form for notifying them of a theft or loss. Be sure to note this address and the number to call.

Sources of Credit

Newspaper, radio, and TV advertisements make it seem like credit is quick and easy to get. You can obtain credit from a variety of sources. Understanding more about each of these sources will help you make decisions about where to seek credit.

Commercial Banks

Commercial banks supply about half of all consumer loans. See 21-6. They are referred to as *full service institutions* because

21-6 **Commercial banks are commonly used as a source of credit.**

they accept deposits, maintain accounts, and perform other functions.

For various reasons, interest rates on loans at commercial banks are often lower than at other institutions. Bank depositors provide most of the funds for bank loans. Their interest rate is low so the bank can afford to make the loans at reasonable rates. Because banks are quite cautious about choosing credit risks, they make few bad loans. Making loans is only one of a variety of services. The bank already has its building, equipment, and employees. The loan department is just one department added to an already functioning business.

Consumer Finance Companies

Institutions that specialize in small consumer loans are called **consumer finance companies**. See 21-7. They range in size from small local companies to nationally known companies. Their rules for qualifying for a loan are less rigid than rules of commercial banks. These companies often make loans to high-risk, low-income consumers who cannot get credit

21-7 **Consumer finance companies often make loans to consumers who are a high credit risk. Therefore, they usually charge a higher interest rate than commercial banks.**

elsewhere. If these companies did not exist, some people would be forced to deal with loan sharks and unlicensed lenders. For many people, finance companies seem much less threatening than the more formal bank situation.

Finance companies, like banks, are important sources of consolidation loans. **Consolidation loans** cover a variety of debts. The borrower arranges for one loan to pay off the total amount of a variety of debts. After paying off these debts, the consumer makes one payment each month to the finance company or other lender.

Finance companies generally have higher finance charges than banks. While banks have depositors to supply their money, finance companies must borrow the money they lend and pay interest on it. Although their loans are small, they require complicated record keeping, which takes time and money. Because finance companies make loans to poor credit risks, they also have greater losses due to nonpayment than banks.

Credit Unions

Financial institutions that are run as a cooperative–owned and operated for the benefit of their members–are known as **credit unions**. See 21-8. They accept deposits and offer loans to only their members. Any group of people who have a common bond may organize a credit union. Groups of teachers, government employees, and union members establish credit unions. Credit unions frequently have the lowest interest charges in the community. The risk of loaning money is less in a credit union since employees have similar jobs and belong to a common organization. Credit unions also have the advantage of being able to deduct loan payments directly from a paycheck. Besides being convenient, this cuts the bookkeeping costs. Since the credit union's sponsor often provides office space and utilities, operating costs are not as great as for independent financial institutions. These reasons contribute to the lower interest rate of credit unions.

21-8 **Credit unions tend to make loans at lower interest rates and pay higher interest on savings than other financial institutions.**

Savings and Loan Associations

Savings and loan associations accept savings deposits from customers and make loans to others. See 21-9.

Originally, savings and loans were established to finance home building. As a result, most of their loans are long-term mortgages for private homes and apartment complexes. To attract depositors, savings and loan associations were given the right to pay more interest on savings accounts. However, they were not able to issue checking accounts to customers. In 1980, these laws were changed so the services of savings and loans and full service banks are now quite similar.

Life Insurance

Another possible source for a loan is a life insurance company. Your life insurance policy may have some cash value in addition to death benefits. If so, you can usually borrow against the cash value and dividends that have accumulated from the time

21-9 **Savings and loan associations have gone through many changes over the years.**

the policy began. Interest rates are usually quite low because many insurance policies were written years ago when other interest rates were low. Once the rates are stated in a policy, they can't be changed.

Loans taken out on insurance policies tend to remain unpaid for long periods of time. There is little pressure on the debtor to repay the loan. In case of death, the insurance company deducts any amount still owed before paying beneficiaries.

Obtaining Credit

Before you can obtain credit, the lender must know whether you are able and willing to repay the debt. See 21-10. The lender will investigate you according to the three Cs of credit: capacity, character, and capital.

Capacity

Your ability to repay debt from your regular income is known as **capacity**. Information on the credit application will help the lender evaluate capacity. The creditor will ask you the following types of questions to learn about your income and expenses:

- How much do you earn?
- How long have you worked?
- What is your occupation?
- Do you have any loan payments?
- How much are your payments and for how long have you made them?
- How many dependents do you have?

BELK CREDIT APPLICATION

| EMPLOYEE NO. | DATE | |

I WANT ☐ REVOLVING ☐ 30-60-90 ☐ BOTH

Type of Account Requested:
☐ INDIVIDUAL ☐ JOINT

PLEASE TELL US ABOUT YOURSELF

| FIRST NAME (TITLES OPTIONAL) | MIDDLE INITIAL | LAST NAME | AGE |

| STREET ADDRESS (IF P.O. BOX — PLEASE GIVE STREET ADDRESS) | CITY | STATE | ZIP |

☐ OWN ☐ LIVE WITH RELATIVE
☐ RENT ☐ OTHER
MONTHLY PAYMENT $
YEARS AT PRESENT ADDRESS
HOME PHONE NO. ( )
NO. OF DEPENDENTS

| PREVIOUS ADDRESS | CITY | STATE | ZIP | HOW LONG |

| NAME OF NEAREST RELATIVE NOT LIVING WITH YOU | RELATIONSHIP | PHONE NO. ( ) |

| ADDRESS | CITY | STATE |

NOW TELL US ABOUT YOUR JOB

| EMPLOYER OR INCOME SOURCE | POSITION/TITLE | HOW LONG EMPLOYED YRS. MOS. | MONTHLY INCOME $ |

| EMPLOYER'S ADDRESS | CITY | STATE | TYPE OF BUSINESS | BUSINESS PHONE ( ) |

| MILITARY RANK (IF NOW IN SERVICE) | SEPARATION DATE | UNIT AND DUTY STATION | SOCIAL SECURITY NO. |

SOURCE OF OTHER INCOME (Alimony, child support, or separate maintenance need not be revealed if you do not wish to have it considered as a basis for repaying this obligation)
SOURCE
INCOME $
☐ MONTHLY ☐ ANNUALLY

AND YOUR CREDIT REFERENCES ARE

NAME AND ADDRESS OF BANK/SAVINGS AND LOAN ☐ CHECKING ☐ SAVINGS ☐ LOAN
PREVIOUS BELK OR LEGGETT ACCOUNT? ☐ YES ☐ NO
ACCOUNT NO.
HOW IS ACCOUNT LISTED?

List Bank cards, Dept. Stores, Finance Co.'s, and other accounts:

NAME	ACCOUNT NO.	BALANCE	PAYMENT
		$	$
		$	$
		$	$
		$	$

INFORMATION REGARDING JOINT APPLICANT

COMPLETE THIS AREA IF ☐ JOINT ACCOUNT IS REQUESTED ☐ YOU ARE RELYING ON SPOUSE'S INCOME OR CREDIT HISTORY TO OBTAIN CREDIT

| FIRST NAME | MIDDLE INITIAL | LAST NAME | AGE | RELATIONSHIP | SOCIAL SECURITY NO. |

JOINT APPLICANT'S ADDRESS IF DIFFERENT FROM APPLICANT
| ADDRESS | CITY | STATE | ZIP |

| JOINT APPLICANT'S PRESENT EMPLOYER | ADDRESS | HOW LONG EMPLOYED YRS. MOS. |

| BUSINESS PHONE ( ) | POSITION/TITLE | MONTHLY INCOME $ |

YOUR SIGNATURE PLEASE

Store Stamp Below

I have read and agree to the Terms and Conditions of the Belk Retail Charge Agreement as set forth on attached. Belk is authorized to investigate my credit record and exchange credit experience with other creditors and Credit Reporting Agencies. This information is given to obtain credit, and is true and complete.

Applicant's Signature _____ Date

Joint Applicant's signature (required if joint applicant section completed) _____ Date

FOR OFFICE USE ONLY
Letter _____
CB. RPT. _____
EMP. VER _____

DATE | EMP. | #CARDS | T/C | CR/LN. | APPROVED

21-10 The lender uses the information on the credit application form to decide if a person is a good credit risk.

Character

By investigating your character, the lender gets an idea of whether or not you are likely to repay the debt. The general behavior, attitude, and personality of the consumer are somewhat difficult to evaluate. However, a person's credit history can demonstrate this. The application may

Brainstorming

Discuss ways lifestyles have changed because of the use of credit. Do you think the overall changes have been more positive or negative? Give reasons to support your opinion.

contain the following questions related to your credit history and stability:

- Where have you obtained credit in the past?
- How much credit have you obtained?
- Have you fully repaid your debts on time?
- How long have you lived at your present address?
- Do you own or rent?
- Do you have life insurance coverage?
- How much life insurance do you have?

Lenders want to issue credit to consumers whose past records show a feeling of moral duty to pay debts when they are due.

Capital

The lender is interested in your financial resources–your **capital**. This includes the property you own and your savings. This gives an indication of whether or not you would be able to repay the debt. The credit application may ask you to list physical assets that could be sold to repay the debt. It may also ask you to list savings account balances, where the savings accounts are located, and any investments, such as stocks, bonds, and real estate.

The creditor can accept or deny you credit. This decision is based on the characteristics just discussed–capacity, character, and capital. However, the importance attached to each of these areas may vary among creditors. To be objective, some creditors have developed a point system for deciding which loan applications to consider and which to deny. This system gives points for various facts that tend to be good credit risk indicators.

Credit is not a right; it is a privilege. However, if you are denied credit, you have a right to know why. In fact, all creditors must follow legal guidelines, and applicants have certain rights. Knowledge of the legalities of credit is an important resource for you as a consumer.

Managing Credit Use Throughout Life

As with other aspects of financial management, managing debt tends to involve different considerations at different stages of life. It is helpful to be aware of the more important debt considerations for people in various age groups.

School Years

Older teens are often directly solicited by credit card companies without the knowledge of their parents. They may sign up without really understanding the commitment they have made. That could lead to big debts at an early age.

Young Adult Years

It is easy for young adults to overuse credit when they are first starting out.

There is the first apartment to rent, clothes for the new job, and a tendency to treat themselves well now that they are finally earning some money. However, this is a time when they are now establishing a credit history, which means it is important to pay bills on time. When they are applying for a mortgage, a car loan, or other credit, lenders will look at the record of credit history in making their decision. Financial advisors suggest that during this period it is best to limit yourself to just one bank credit card and try to charge only what can be paid for every month.

Middle Adult Years

These are usually the peak earning years. Ideally, this is a good time to reduce the debt burden in preparation for retirement. However, this is often the time when people move to a bigger and better house, purchase that bigger and better car, and often times, are sending their children off to college. See 21-11.

For people with sufficient assets, there are many opportunities for financing, such as setting up a home-equity loan, borrowing against a life insurance policy, or borrowing against a retirement plan. However, it is wise to keep in mind that in some ways, having a lot of debt is riskier at this stage of life than in the early adult years. The potential for serious illness is greater, and middle-age people who are laid off as a result of business cutbacks, often have trouble finding another job.

Later Adult Years

It would be ideal if people entering this stage of life could be debt-free. However, it is not unusual for people in their 60s and 70s to have mortgage payments to make and car loans to repay.

21-11 **Having children in college certainly affects a family's use of credit.**

Many older people are uncomfortable with risk. Fixed rate loans are generally better than variable rates, and shorter-term debt is preferable to long-term debt.

Many older people have substantial equity in a home. However, because their home now may be much too big for their needs, they might consider selling and moving to a less expensive, more manageable home. This can lower their costs and give them cash to help meet living expenses.

Another possibility is a **reverse annuity mortgage**. This is a loan based on the equity a homeowner has accumulated. The loan is disbursed as a line of credit in monthly installments over a period of years or as a lump sum. The amount usually depends on the borrower's age and the amount of equity in the home. However, this type of loan is often costly, with added interest charges and other fees. The house typically is sold to repay the loan when the borrower dies or moves out which could leave little or nothing for the homeowner or the homeowner's heirs.

Laws and Regulations Governing Credit

A variety of consumer credit laws have been passed to help both consumers and creditors meet their credit responsibilities. These laws protect and inform consumers.

Truth in Lending Law

The Truth in Lending Law, also referred to as the Consumer Credit Protection Act, helps consumers understand charges for credit. Credit agreements must state charges in a clear, uniform way. See 21-12. The purpose of the law is to let consumers know exactly what the credit charge is. Then they can easily make comparisons of the charges from different credit sources before actually using credit. Creditors must supply the sum of the finance charge. In addition to interest, the finance charge may include several other charges. Among these are a service charge or carrying charge, a fee for checking your credit, or a fee for

---

KEEP THIS NOTICE FOR FUTURE USE
BELK RETAIL CHARGE AGREEMENT

1. Each time I receive the monthly statement (at about the same time each month) I will decide whether to pay the New Balance of the account in full or in part. If full payment of the New Balance shown on the statement is received, by BELK, by the Payment Due Date, No FINANCE CHARGE will be added to the account. Any month I choose not to pay the New Balance in full, I will make at least the minimum partial payment listed on the statement as Minimum Payment Now Due. Each month the Minimum Payment Due will be calculated according to the following schedule:

If New Balance Is	Less Than $10	$10-100	$101-150	$151-200	$201-250	$251-300	Over $300
Minimum Monthly Payment Is	Balance	$10	$15	$20	$25	$30	1/10 of account balance rounded to next highest $5 increment

2. If payment in full is not received by the Payment Due Date, I agree to pay a FINANCE CHARGE at the rate described below for my State of residence.

Annual Percentage Rate for Purchases	10% to 21% (see table below)		
State of Residence	Periodic Rate	Annual Percentage Rate	Portion of Average Daily Balance To Which Applied
DE., KY., VA., MS., GA., OK., MD.	1.75%	21%	ENTIRE
NC., PA., TN., FL., TX and all other states	1.50%	18%	ENTIRE
AL.	1.75%	21%	$750 or less
	1.5%	18%	over $750
WV.	1.5%	18%	$750 or less
	1.0%	12%	over $750
SC.	1.75%	21%	$650 or less
	1.5%	18%	over $650
MO.	1.5%	18%	$1,000 or less
	1.0%	12%	over $1,000
AR.	.083%	10%	ENTIRE
Grace Period:	You have until the next billing date which on average is 23 days if the balance is paid in full, before a finance charge will be imposed.		
Method of Computing the Average Daily Balance.	Average Daily Balance Method: We figure a portion of the finance charge on your account by applying the periodic rate to the "average daily balance" of your account (including current transactions). To get the "average daily balance", we take the beginning balance of your account each day, add any new purchases and subtract any payments or credits, and unpaid finance charges. This gives us the daily balance. Then, we add up all the daily balances for the billing cycle and divide the total by the number of days in the billing cycle. This gives us the "average daily balance".		

3. Credit for returned merchandise will not substitute for a payment.

4. BELK has the right to amend the terms and conditions of this agreement by advising me of its intentions to do so in a manner and to the extent required by law.

5. If any payment is not received by BELK by the Payment Due Date, the full unpaid balance of the account may, at the option of Belk, become due and payable. If the account is referred for collection by Belk to any outside agency and/or attorney, who is not a salaried employee of BELK, I will, to the extent permitted by law, pay all costs including attorney fees.

6. BELK reserves the right to charge a handling fee, not to exceed the amount permitted by law, on any check used for payment on the account that is returned by the bank for insufficient funds or otherwise unpaid.

7. If this is a joint account, both of us agree to be bound by the terms of this agreement and each of us agrees to be jointly and severally liable for payment of all purchases made under this agreement.

8. The credit card issued to me in connection with this account remains the property of BELK and I will surrender it upon request. I understand that BELK is not obligated to extend to me any credit and, without prior notice, may refuse to allow me to make any purchase or incur any other charge on my account. Such refusal will not affect my obligation to pay the balance existing on my account at the time.

9. If any provision of this agreement is found to be invalid or unenforceable, the remainder of this agreement shall not be affected thereby, and the rest of this agreement shall be valid and enforced to the fullest extent permitted by law. No delay, omission, or waiver in the enforcement of any provision of this agreement by BELK will be deemed to be a waiver of any subsequent breach of such provision or of any other provision of this agreement.

10. I hereby authorize BELK, or any credit bureau employed by BELK, to investigate references, statements, and other data contained on my application or obtained from me or any other source pertaining to my credit worthiness. I will furnish further information if requested. I authorize BELK to furnish information concerning its credit experience with me to credit reporting agencies and others who may lawfully receive such information.

11. Except as provided in paragraph 2 above, this agreement will be governed by the laws of the State of North Carolina.

21-12 **Revolving charge accounts have agreements that are similar to this one.**

*Getting*Involved

Prepare a public service brochure, flyer, or pamphlet to make consumers in your community aware of credit pitfalls. Ask permission to leave these in areas where credit card application brochures are also available.

credit insurance. Any of these additional charges must be included in the stated finance charge.

The finance charge must also be stated as an *annual percentage rate*. This figure provides a way for you to compare credit costs regardless of the dollar amount or the length of time payments are made. Even though borrowers must be given this information, it is good to know how to figure the cost of a loan.

When you shop for credit, compare loans by both dollar cost and annual percentage rates. Loans with a lower annual percentage rate will cost you less money than those with higher annual percentage rates.

The Equal Credit Opportunity Act

The Equal Credit Opportunity Act prohibits creditors from discriminating on the basis of sex, marital status, race, national origin, religion, age, or the receipt of public assistance. Credit can be denied only for financial reasons. This law is very important to certain groups of people, such as women and older people, who may have been the victims of credit discrimination.

Before this law was passed, many creditors refused to give a woman credit. They assumed the family's credit was based solely on the husband's ability to pay. Married women often had trouble establishing credit records because most of the financial accounting was listed in their husbands' names. See 21-13. Joint accounts held by

husband and wife are handled differently today. Creditors must now report all credit information in both their names.

In the past, many consumers, particularly retired people, have been denied credit solely on the basis of their age. According to this law, a creditor may ask your age. If you are old enough to sign a binding contract (usually 18 or 21 depending upon state law), a creditor may not deny credit solely because of your age. Instead, credit worthiness must be based on income. Social security, pensions, annuities, and other investments must be considered.

Creditors are allowed to take age into account if it has a bearing on the person's ability to repay the loan. For instance, a creditor may refuse a large loan with a small down payment and a long repayment period to an older person.

21-13 Since the Equal Credit Opportunity Act was passed, women have had less difficulty establishing their own credit.

This law does allow creditors to ask the applicant for age, race, national origin, sex, and marital status. They are also allowed to ask whether or not the person is on welfare and other similar questions. The answers to these kinds of questions can be used only to judge whether or not an applicant can repay a loan. They are not in themselves reasons enough to reject an application.

If an applicant is denied credit, the creditor is required to explain why or tell the applicant in writing how to obtain this information. The creditor must act upon the application within 30 days. If you are denied credit and suspect that denial was based on discrimination, you may take legal action through the state department of justice.

Fair Credit Reporting Act

The Fair Credit Reporting Act ensures that reporting agencies adopt fair and equitable procedures in distributing credit information. It protects the consumer against inaccurate or outdated information in the files of the reporting agency. The **credit bureau**, also referred to as a consumer reporting agency, is a firm that assembles credit information and other information about consumers. They sell this information to creditors, landlords, insurers, employers, and other businesses that are interested in a consumer's ability and willingness to repay loans.

The credit bureau does not make a value judgment about how good or bad a credit risk a particular consumer is. Instead, they simply maintain and report information about the consumer. This information may include a record of who has extended credit to the consumer in the past, repayment patterns on old loans, and how much is still owed. It will also include personal history, employment information, records of any court proceedings against the consumer, and public record information such as divorces. Other information may include neighbors' and friends' views of the person's character, general reputation, and manner of living.

This information is then furnished for a fee to persons or agencies that meet certain requirements. Credit reports are furnished only if they are in consideration for credit, in review of an account, or in consideration for employment or insurance. A credit report may also be issued by a written request from the consumer for a legitimate purpose or when ordered by a court.

If a consumer is denied credit, that person has the right to know why credit was denied. The consumer may request a summary of his or her file from the credit bureau either in writing or in person. See 21-14. If the request is made within 30 days of the credit denial, there is no charge for the information. The summary must tell the sources of the report information and list everyone who has received a copy of the report within the last six months. If the report was used for employment purposes, the summary must list everyone who received a copy within the past two years.

If the consumer finds out-of-date, false, or incomplete data in the report, the credit bureau should be asked to recheck that

21-14 **When consumers need to review their credit reports, they can use the Internet to request copies.**

information. If the bureau finds that information to be incorrect, it must change the report. The bureau must also notify those who had previously received the report of the changes. There is no charge for this to the consumer.

If the disagreement between the consumer and the credit bureau's information cannot be resolved, the consumer has the right to file a brief statement of his or her side of the story, which will be sent in all future reports. The consumer can request that this statement be mailed to anyone who has sought information about his or her credit rating during the last six months.

A recent amendment to the federal Fair Credit Reporting Act requires each of the nationwide consumer reporting companies to provide people with a free copy of their credit report once every 12 months. The Federal Trade Commission, the nation's consumer protection agency, has prepared a brochure explaining your rights and the process for ordering a free annual credit report.

Your credit record will follow you wherever you go. When you move and apply for credit, your files will be transferred to a local agency. If you have a good credit rating, you will have no trouble establishing credit. If your credit rating is unfavorable, you can correct that by paying your bills regularly and avoiding financial overload. After seven years, any unfavorable information on your credit report will be removed.

Fair Credit Billing Act

The Fair Credit Billing Act was passed to help protect consumers against credit card abuses, computerized billing system abuses, and other unfair billing practices. A creditor must mail a bill at least 14 days before the date a finance charge will be added. This gives the consumer time to pay the bill without a finance charge. See 21-15. On the day the creditor receives payment, it must be used to reduce the debt.

Consumers are required to follow a specific procedure to resolve billing errors or other disputes. The consumer must send the creditor written notification of the problem within 60 days. A phone call is not sufficient. The letter should include the consumer's name, address, and account number. It should also describe why the bill is wrong. The consumer must pay the portion of the bill that is not in error by the due date.

The creditor must answer the consumer's letter within 30 days unless the account is corrected. The creditor has no longer than 90 days to either correct the account or tell the consumer why the bill is accurate.

If the creditor made a mistake, the consumer does not pay any finance charges on the disputed amount. The account is credited for either the full amount or a partial amount, and the creditor must explain what the consumer still owes. If the creditor finds no errors in the statement, the consumer must be sent a statement of what is owed. In this case, the creditor may add any finance charges that have accumulated and payments that have been missed while the bill was being questioned.

21-15 **Consumers who pay their credit card bills in full each month are not charged interest, depending on the type of credit card they have.**

32
31
30
29
28
27
26
25
24
23
22
21
20
19
18
17
16
15
14
13
12
11
10
9
8
7
6
5
4
3
2
1

Summary

Credit is a consumer convenience when used wisely. When used poorly, it can create serious financial problems. A thorough understanding of credit use is a valuable resource. Understanding the advantages and disadvantages of credit use, the types of credit available, and the sources of credit will help you use credit wisely. To issue credit to a person, the lender takes into consideration the three Cs of credit–capacity, character, and capital.

Wise use of credit is also based on knowledge of laws and regulations governing credit. Consumer credit laws help the consumer understand charges for credit and protect the consumer from discrimination. They ensure the consumer of fair procedures in distributing credit information. Credit laws also protect the consumer against unfair billing practices.

To Review

1. Describe the difference between an installment loan and a single-payment loan.
2. Describe the difference between a regular charge account and a revolving charge account.
3. List four sources of credit.
4. True or false? The finance charges at consumer finance companies are usually higher than at commercial banks.
5. List the three Cs of credit and describe how they are used to evaluate consumers as credit risks.
6. What can happen to teens who sign up for credit cards without really understanding the commitment they have made?
7. Why is having a lot of debt in the middle adult years often riskier than in the early adult years?
8. A variety of consumer credit laws have been passed to help both consumers and creditors meet their credit ____.
9. Name four important laws governing the use of credit.
10. Describe the procedure to follow if you notice an incorrect charge on a credit account.

To Do
with the Class

1. Obtain and analyze credit applications from local stores. Discuss why various questions are asked.
2. Invite a credit manager from a local business to speak to your class. Ask questions about credit ratings, the work of the credit bureau, and how the credit bureau conforms to the Fair Credit Reporting Act.
3. Interview your parents to find out their ideas on using credit wisely. Share your findings with others in the class and determine the key or most important suggestions.
4. In class groups, develop a service ad or message for wise credit use geared to young adults. Share and discuss.

To Challenge
Your Thinking

1. Ask your parents to share their views and advice on using credit.
2. Collect advertisements for consumer credit to create a classroom display. Discuss the types and sources of credit.
3. Research the kinds and sources of information recorded and utilized by credit bureaus. Share this information with the class.
4. Using the three Cs of credit, where do you stand as a good credit risk? Explain.

To Do
with Your Community

1. Investigate annual fees for multipurpose credit cards available in your community.
2. Interview people in your community from the early, middle, and late adult years. What are their views on credit strategies for using credit wisely? Share your findings with the class.
3. Invite persons from each of the four sources of credit to share credit information with the class.
4. Invite a person from the local credit bureau to share the most current credit information and to discuss the importance of maintaining a good credit rating.

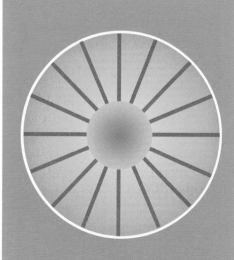

22 Planning for Financial Security

To Know

liquidity
investment
equity investment
fixed income investment
bond
stock
preferred stock
dividend
common stock
market value
mutual fund
stockbroker
insurance
life insurance
premium
death benefit
beneficiary
term insurance
permanent life insurance
annuity
credit life insurance
deductible clause
coinsurance feature
health maintenance organizations (HMOs)
preferred provider organizations (PPOs)
financial responsibility laws
no-fault insurance
vesting
will

Objectives

After studying this chapter, you will be able to

◆ relate savings and investment alternatives to building financial security.

◆ list types of life insurance, health insurance, property insurance, and automobile insurance and describe various features of each.

◆ describe sources of retirement income.

◆ relate estate planning steps toward financial security.

Financial security is a goal for most people. It's never too early to begin financial planning, 22-1. Planning for financial security requires good management of financial resources. When you are financially secure, you have money available for emergencies as well as for long-term and short-term goals you want to achieve.

22-1 **The value of planning for financial security can be learned very early in life.**

There are a variety of ways to build financial security. Many savings and investment options are available at different types of financial institutions. Having life insurance, health insurance, property insurance, and automobile insurance can also contribute to your financial security. Retirement planning and estate planning are other steps in planning for the future. Your goals will help determine your financial plans.

Savings and Investment Alternatives

The type of savings or investment account you choose depends largely on your income and financial responsibilities.

An effective plan for savings requires knowledge of financial institutions and savings programs available. A smart consumer will take advantage of the keen competition between financial institutions and comparison shop for products and services. An array of new services is being offered to the consumer mainly due to computer technology. In addition to the typical services provided by financial institutions, such as credit cards, safe deposit boxes, travelers' checks, and money orders, electronic banking makes it possible to conduct financial transactions during nonbanking hours and in shopping malls or supermarkets. With the use of automatic teller machines (ATMs) and electronic funds transfers (EFTs), certain transactions can be transmitted by computer without a bank teller's assistance.

There are differences between saving and investing. *Saving* is accumulating money for a specific purpose or to use in an emergency. Savings are usually placed in a program that involves no risk of loss. Investing is different. You take a chance when you *invest*. You accept risk with the idea that you may get financial returns higher than your initial investment. With most investments, however, there is the possibility of loss.

Saving is the foundation for investing. Only when you have reached your savings goals should you consider taking the risks involved in investing.

Savings

Choose a form of savings and a savings institution that will provide secure financial returns. When choosing a form of savings, consider earnings, liquidity, and safety.

The major reason for putting money in a savings program is to earn interest. *Interest* is a certain annual percentage of the amount of money in the account. Interest is generally paid daily, monthly, or quarterly. **Liquidity** refers to how easily you can convert an investment into cash when you need it. In some cases, you may have to wait a specified number of days or months before withdrawal is possible. In general, the longer you agree to leave the money in the account without taking any of it out, the higher the rate of interest will be.

Passbook accounts can be obtained through most banks, savings and loan institutions, and credit unions, 22-2. Typically, they pay a relatively low rate of interest. Their chief advantage is that your money is available any time you want it, without paying any penalty for taking it out. Passbook accounts generally do not include check-writing privileges.

M.T. Crave

22-2 Many people find it convenient to have both a checking account and a savings account at the same bank.

Not all passbook accounts are alike, so it is wise to shop around to find the best rate of interest. Also check on any service charges. Some banks impose a monthly service charge on accounts with less than a $300 balance. In addition, ask how interest is credited. Is it compounded annually, semiannually, quarterly, or daily? The more frequently the interest is compounded, the higher the yield. Check also on when interest is credited. In some banks, even though compounding is daily, the money earned may not be credited to your account until the end of a three-month period. If you withdraw money before it is credited, you can lose the interest on it for the entire three-month period.

Time accounts are those in which the money must remain in the account for a fixed period of time. Time accounts may be referred to as certificate accounts, certificate of deposit (CDs), or bonus passbook accounts depending on the institution. Money is deposited for a set period of time, such as 90 days, 6 months, or one year. A fixed rate of interest is paid for that term.

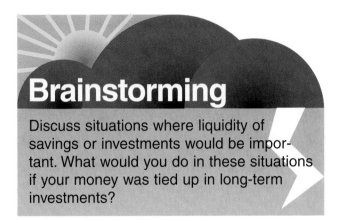

Brainstorming

Discuss situations where liquidity of savings or investments would be important. What would you do in these situations if your money was tied up in long-term investments?

The longer the period of time, the higher the rate of interest will be. There is a penalty for early withdrawal.

Money market accounts generally pay a higher rate of interest than passbook accounts. Rates are based on U.S. Treasury Bill rates and earnings can vary. These accounts often require a minimum deposit, and fees may be charged if your balance falls below a minimum required amount. Checks may be written on these accounts providing cash immediately. However, the number of checks written each month may be limited.

Money market accounts are also available through mutual fund companies. Like bank money market accounts, mutual fund money market accounts offer investors the convenience of writing checks for immediate cash. These check-writing privileges are usually unlimited. *Mutual fund money market accounts* commonly pay interest rates that are comparable to or higher than bank money market accounts. Some require no minimum investment. The mutual fund money market accounts are not federally insured. However, some are privately insured.

The Federal Deposit Insurance Corporation (FDIC), a U.S. government agency, insures deposits up to $100,000 in most banks. If the money in an insured savings account is lost or stolen, it will be replaced by the FDIC. The money will also be replaced if the bank goes bankrupt or

suffers a serious financial loss. When considering any financial institution, be sure it is covered by a guaranteed insurance program.

Financial institutions are constantly developing new services to attract you to their places of business. Take advantage of this competitive situation by regularly evaluating your needs and determining which financial institutions can best meet them.

Investments

When you make an **investment**, you are using money for the purpose of making money. Some people make very successful investments. However, many people lose money by making poor investments. The majority of Americans have modest amounts to invest and want to invest to minimize their chance of loss. Whatever your reason for investing, it is important to understand that a degree of risk comes with each investment. The risk is greater for some investments than for others.

Investments are of two types—equity investments and fixed income investments. An **equity investment** involves owning stock in a company. You own a part of that company no matter how much you invest. You hope to benefit from the company's growth and profits. In a **fixed income investment**, through your investment you are actually lending your money to a corporation or a government agency that issues bonds. A **bond** is a promise to pay the investor a certain amount of money plus interest at a specific time in the future (date of maturity). The interest rate is set, or fixed, when you buy the bond. Common fixed income investments include government securities, government savings bonds, corporate bonds, and tax-exempt bonds.

Putting money in fixed return investments where the income produced is always a fixed percentage is considered a safe investment. However, fixed return investments are less effective ways of producing income, especially in a period of inflation when the purchasing power of the dollar is decreasing.

Careful consideration of your investment objectives combined with knowledge of the types of investments available will help you invest. Knowing where to go for advice, such as to a certified financial planner, will also help you make effective investment decisions.

Government Securities

There are three types of government securities: treasury bills, treasury notes, and treasury bonds. Since the U.S. government borrows billions of dollars a year, government securities are always readily available. These types of securities are issued for definite time periods. The minimum investment is fairly high. Government securities can be purchased directly at any Federal Reserve Bank. They are not taxed at the state or local level.

Government Savings Bonds

If you cannot afford a larger kind of government security, savings bonds might be a good way for you to save. See 22-3. A floating interest rate is paid on savings bonds. The rate will increase if interest rates go up and, if held for five years, the bonds will pay a guaranteed minimum return. The interest is exempt from state and local taxes and no federal tax is due until the bonds mature or are cashed in.

Savings bonds are quite liquid. You can cash them in at any bank after holding them for six months. They are extremely safe, but their yields are lower than other investments that are just as safe.

Corporate Bonds

Corporate bonds are issued by individual firms and banks. The minimum amount is normally $1,000. You buy the bond for a specified length of time. At the date of maturity, the issuer of the bond pays you back the full amount (face value) of the bond. Meanwhile, you receive a fixed rate of interest, paid twice a year in most cases. This rate does not change once the bond is issued even though bond prices fluctuate.

Tax-Exempt Bonds

State and local governments and their agencies issue bonds that are usually called *municipals*. They are used to finance municipal costs and improvements. Their interest yields are not taxed by the federal government. These are usually recommended only for people in high income brackets.

Stocks

A **stock** is a share of ownership in a corporation. When you buy one or more shares of stock, you become a part owner of a corporation. Corporations raise money by selling stock. Stocks are classified as either preferred stock or common stock.

If you own **preferred stock**, the size of the annual dividend is fixed by the corporation and never changes. Dividends for preferred stock are paid before any of the other stockholders receive dividends. A **dividend** is the money paid to stockholders out of the company's earnings.

Common stock entitles the stockholder to share in the profits of the firm if there are any. Common stockholders hope their stock will increase in value and then they can sell their shares for more money than they paid. The price of a stock is called its **market value**. This value changes from day to day as shares are bought and sold. Common stock appeals as an investment because of the potential for increased dividends. Dividends may take the form of a cash payment, additional shares of stock, or a combination of both. Common stockholders also have the right to vote for company directors and on other matters.

Mutual Funds

Investing funds in a wide variety of stocks and bonds is done by mutual fund companies. When you buy shares in a **mutual fund**, you become part owner of investments included in the fund. This way, the rise and fall of any one or two stocks will not have an overall effect. Mutual funds work well for the small investor.

The funds are managed by professionals who devote their full time to studying the market and making investment decisions. There are a wide variety of mutual funds available. They are classified according to their investment objectives, such as growth funds, income funds, and bond funds.

There are a number of advantages to mutual funds. Usually a small minimum investment can get you started. Each share that is purchased provides an interest in a broad range of stocks and bonds. Because of this diversity, it is not so noticeable when one or two of the stocks drop in value. Mutual funds are very liquid. When you want to sell, the company will buy back the shares. Investing in mutual funds is one of the easiest and most convenient ways to begin an investment program.

22-3 **Bonds might be issued to finance a city park.**

Stockbrokers

Buying or selling stocks or bonds is done through a stockbroker. The **stockbroker** is the person who acts as the consumer's agent and handles details of the transaction.

Stockbrokers may provide a variety of services, and they charge for these services. Some provide thorough investment counseling while others simply buy or sell orders. The way to choose a stockbroker is to find one who offers services that best suit your needs.

M.T. Crave

22-4 An independent insurance agent will offer a choice of policies available from many different insurance companies.

Insurance

Insurance protects you against financial risks related to life, health, and property. Before you can decide on the kind and amount of insurance you need, certain information is helpful. Understanding the importance of insurance in people's lives and insurance options available will help. Insurance agents can be a valuable resource for this kind of information. Be sure to choose well-qualified agents who work for financially sound and reputable companies, 22-4. Selecting insurance can be a confusing process and should be given careful, thoughtful consideration. Insurance payments will amount to thousands of dollars over a lifetime.

Life Insurance

People purchase **life insurance** to limit the risk of financial loss. Life insurance is most important to people who are financially responsible for others. If a family's chief wage earner dies, there may be a sudden need for money. There will be debts to pay, dependents to support and educate, and the usual household living expenses. Life insurance protects against these problems.

The insurance policy is the legal contract issued by the insurance company. The **premium** is the amount of money paid by the policy owner, usually the insured. The *face amount* of the policy is the money that will be paid to the beneficiary. The *cash value* is the amount of money the policyholder would receive if the policy is surrendered before the death of the insured or when it matures. If the insured dies while the policy is in force, someone will receive a specified amount of money called the **death benefit**. The person receiving the money is called the **beneficiary** because he or she benefits from receiving it. The death benefit may be received in one lump sum or in monthly installments.

Types of Life Insurance

Life insurance policies fall into two basic categories: term or temporary and permanent. While **term insurance** provides protection for only a specific period of time, **permanent life insurance** remains in force throughout the insured person's life. Consumers will choose the particular type of policy that meets their needs. Although some policies provide protection only in the event of death, others have a savings component in addition to death benefits. Other policies are more closely related to investment strategies. The choice of a particular type of insurance depends on both your immediate and your long-term goals. Knowledge of the various types of policies offered will help you make an appropriate choice.

Term Insurance

The simplest form of insurance is term insurance. The individual's life is insured against death for a certain period of time— a term. The most common terms are 1, 5, 10, or 20 years. The policy terminates at the end of the term period. Benefits are paid only if the policyholder dies within the term.

Term insurance often satisfies short-term needs. For instance, a family who has purchased a new car might purchase term insurance to repay the car loan in the event the wage earner of the family does not live to complete the loan payments.

The main advantage is its low cost in contrast to permanent life insurance. Term insurance has the advantage of offering low premiums to families in the early stages of family life. See 22-5. The cost of term insurance generally goes up as the insured gets older and has a greater chance of dying.

Variations of term insurance have specific provisions that may provide advantages to certain people under certain circumstances.

A *renewable term* policy indicates the company will extend the policy beyond the first term without requiring a medical examination. However, the premium will be higher. *Convertible term* allows you to exchange a term policy for permanent life insurance within a certain amount of time without taking a medical exam.

With *decreasing term* coverage the premiums stay the same, but the amount of coverage becomes smaller. Families might purchase this type of insurance when buying a home to protect against the risk

of the homeowner dying prematurely. In the event of death, the mortgage is paid off by the policy. *Level term* insurance means the amount of protection stays the same throughout the term and the death benefit remains a fixed amount. Level term insurance may be either renewable or nonrenewable.

Permanent Life Insurance

There are variations of permanent life insurance, or cash value life insurance, but some characteristics are common. The annual premium usually remains constant as long as the policy is in force. In addition to the death insurance, a savings account increases in value throughout the life of the policy. If the policyholder dies while the policy is in force, only the death benefit is paid. However, if the policyholder survives, the policy serves as a kind of savings account. The policy increases in value with each premium payment, and the sum of this savings is called the *cash value*. As a policy-holder, you have several choices regarding

22-5 **Term insurance would probably be a good buy for a young family like this one.**

the cash value. You can borrow part of it, use it to pay the premium, convert it into a retirement income, or take it all in a lump sum. Cash value is sometimes referred to as "the living benefit" of life insurance. The longer you have paid premiums, the greater the cash value will be.

The kind of permanent life insurance you buy will depend on your reasons for buying insurance and your ability to pay the premiums. There are various forms of permanent life insurance available: whole life, limited payment, endowment, variable, adjustable, and universal.

Whole life insurance is also referred to as *straight life* or *ordinary life insurance*. See 22-6. The amount of the premium is set at the time the policy is bought. This is the least costly of the permanent life insurance policies.

A *limited payment* insurance policy is like whole life insurance except policyholders pay the principal for only a certain length of time. This may be for 10 years, 20 years, 30 years, or until the policyholder reaches a certain age. Limited payment policies have higher premiums than whole life. Protection is for life, but the premium is paid for only a certain number of years. Because of this, the cash value builds up faster.

Endowment insurance is a form of insured savings. The policyholder makes payments for a certain number of years. After that period of time, the policyholder receives the face value of the policy. If the policyholder dies during that period of time, the beneficiary gets the face value. The premiums are higher for an endowment policy than for whole life or limited life.

With *variable life insurance*, the premiums are fixed but the face amount varies with the performance of a fund in which the premiums are invested. This type of insurance offers the possibility of gaining value if the fund rises. The face amount may not fall below the original amount of the insurance.

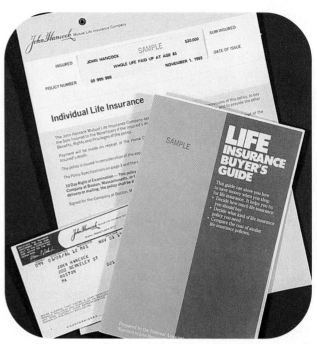

Courtesy of John Hancock Mutual Life Insurance Co

22-6 Whole life insurance is the least costly type of permanent life insurance. The insurance policy explains details about the coverage.

An *adjustable life insurance* policy allows the insured to alter coverage as his or her needs change. The policyholder may raise or lower premiums, the face value, and the premium payment period. The key advantage of this type of policy is its flexibility, but it requires constant monitoring.

Universal life insurance combines the flexibility of an adjustable policy with an investment feature. The cash value is invested to earn interest at current market rates. If interest rates go down, earnings will decrease. Premiums, face value, and level of protection can be altered as needed.

Combination Policies

A variety of insurance policy plans incorporate both cash value and term insurance features. This allows for more flexibility and offers certain advantages.

Annuities

An **annuity** is an investment product sold by life insurance companies that provides payments for a fixed number of years or over a lifetime. The person buying the annuity pays either a lump sum or makes monthly payments over time to pay for the annuity. The money in the annuity accumulates, compounding tax-free until the funds are withdrawn. Taxes are paid when the money is withdrawn. This generally occurs at retirement when the policyholder is in a lower tax bracket. The payout usually begins at retirement and continues for a set number of years or until the death of the policyholder. The insurance company guarantees regular monthly payments. Annuities are widely used to provide supplemental income for people in retirement.

Buying Life Insurance

Life insurance policies are usually purchased by people in one of three ways:

- Individual life insurance policies are purchased through an insurance agent.

- Group life insurance is purchased through a group rather than on an individual basis.

- Credit life insurance policies are written by banks or finance companies.

Individual Life Insurance

Many people choose life insurance policies through an insurance agent who tailors the policy to meet their needs. Once the policy is written, the person is usually required to have a physical examination. On the basis of this physical exam, the company estimates its risk in insuring that person. The poorer the health of the insured person, the higher the insurance premiums and the greater the risk to the insurance company will be.

Group Life Insurance

Those who belong to a particular group of people—perhaps a certain business, government office, or labor union—often purchase life insurance as a group. Group insurance generally does not require a physical exam. The group is large enough to base premiums on the life expectancies of the entire group in that occupation or association.

Group life insurance is less expensive than individual life insurance. In many cases, employers pay part or all of the premium as a fringe benefit for their employees. A master policy for the group states the coverage and what the premium for each member will be. Group insurance is usually, but not always, term insurance. Insurance coverage ends when you leave the group. In some cases, there may be possibilities for converting the policy to another type of insurance.

Credit Life Insurance

Credit life insurance is also referred to as consumer-credit insurance. **Credit life insurance** covers repayment of a loan should the borrower die. Banks and finance companies usually try to persuade their loan customers to insure themselves for the amount of the loan. These policies are usually quite expensive per dollar of insurance for several reasons. They are for small amounts of money, no physical examinations are required, and no adjustment is made for the borrower's life expectancy.

Although credit life insurance policies have been criticized by government regulators, millions of policies are in force each year. Many consumers do not realize these policies are optional. They cannot be a requirement of the loan. Another problem is the policies appear to be relatively inexpensive. They increase the cost of a loan payment by only a few dollars. However, those dollars could be spent more effectively elsewhere. Perhaps they could purchase additional individual life insurance or group life insurance.

Health Insurance

In the past few years, health costs have risen faster than other personal expenses. These costs can account for a large portion of the monthly income of many families. Even a short stay in a hospital can wipe out years of savings. Therefore, most people need health insurance to protect them against the high costs of health care.

Types of Coverage

Health insurance offers two basic kinds of protection: protection against hospital, surgical, and other medical costs, and protection against loss of income during an illness or injury. Health insurance plans may cover the costs of hospitalization, surgery, doctor's fees, nursing care, prescription drugs, X rays, and other major medical expenses. Each kind of coverage may be purchased separately or as part of a package plan. Package plans usually give the most coverage for the least money. Most package plans include basic medical coverage and major medical coverage.

Basic Medical Coverage

Basic medical coverage includes protection against the cost of ordinary hospital care, surgery, and doctors. Hospital coverage usually pays up to a certain amount for each day in the hospital for a limited number of days. See 22-7. It generally pays for the bed or room used and for

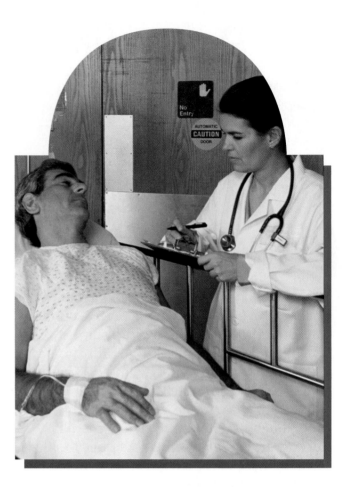

22-7 There are limits on the number of days the insurance covers hospital stay.

services, such as X rays, laboratory tests, use of an operating room, drugs, meals, and nursing care. Because hospital costs have risen so much, some policies now have a **deductible clause**. This means the insured must pay up to a certain point before the insurance company will pay. If the insurance policy has a $250 deductible clause, you will pay $250 before the insurance company begins to pay. A deductible clause lowers the cost of claims for the insurance company and also lowers the cost of premiums for the consumer.

Surgical coverage pays all or part of the doctor's fee for surgical procedures. It usually covers an operation whether it is done in a hospital or a doctor's office. The policy describes the operations covered and the amount or percentage the insurance company will pay per operation. The policyholder must pay the difference if the entire surgeon's bill is not covered by insurance. Protection against doctors' costs provides benefits that pay doctors' fees. This covers nonsurgical care in a hospital, at home, or in a doctor's office.

Major Medical Coverage

Major medical coverage protects people against the risks of prolonged and costly illnesses. Major medical coverage begins where basic hospital and medical coverage stops. You can choose from many major medical plans. Some have a deductible clause that requires the insured to pay a deductible amount of $100 to $500. In other plans, the company pays a certain percentage of the costs of major medical expenses, such as 70 to 80 percent. The policyholder pays the other 20 to 30 percent in addition to the deductible amount. This is often referred to as a **coinsurance feature**.

Dental Coverage

This coverage protects you against the costs of dental services, 22-8. Most dental policies cover part of the costs of all dental care. They include everything from yearly cleaning to surgery and false teeth, but usually exclude work that is primarily cosmetic, such as teeth whitening.

Disability Income Insurance

Anyone who works should have disability income insurance to help replace income lost due to a long-term injury or illness. Disability insurance may also compensate for the loss of an eye, leg, or other body part. There are both long-term and short-term disability plans.

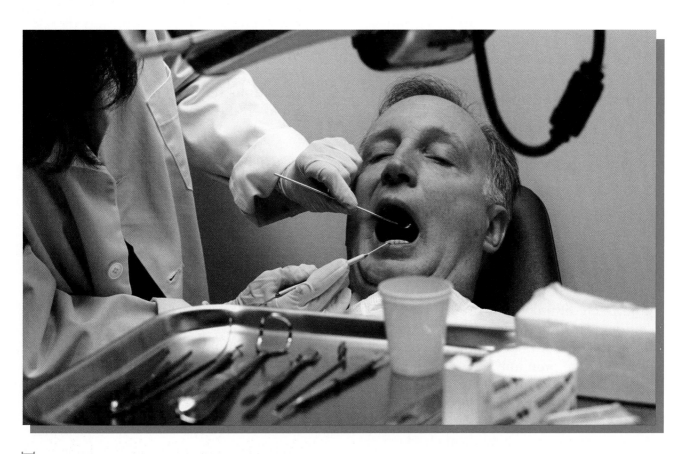

22-8 Dental coverage is often not included in basic health care plans, but must be arranged for separately.

Accident Insurance

Protection against the risk of accidents is provided by accident insurance. These policies are often offered in connection with a school. Such policies cover students if they are injured while attending school or going to and from school. They also cover students while participating in school activities. Accident insurance often does not cover competition in interscholastic sports. However, separate policies can be purchased to cover these activities.

Long-Term Care Insurance

Advances in medical technology, control over infectious diseases, and managed health care are resulting in a large population of older adults. Long-term care costs can quickly use up hard-earned retirement savings. *Long-term care insurance* policies will pay for home health care, adult day care, assisted living, and nursing home care. Each policy provides options for specified daily amounts, inflation protection, length of coverage, and elimination periods.

Kinds of Health Insurance Plans

You can buy or receive health insurance in a variety of ways. Because health care costs are very expensive, you should be aware of the types of plans that are available.

Group Insurance

Insurance companies sell health insurance on a group basis or on an individual basis. Many Americans get group health insurance through their employers, labor unions, credit unions, or professional associations. The employer or organization holds the master policy and often pays all or part of the premium. These premiums are lower than premiums for individual policies because so many people are insured under the same policy. Most group plans do not require a medical checkup. You can join the plan regardless of health. After joining the group, there is a certain

length of time before a person is covered by the insurance. Members of a group plan can often cover their families under the plan, 22-9. Family coverage may mean additional cost depending on the number and ages of the persons covered.

The major disadvantage of group insurance is that it usually ends if the person leaves the company or group through which the insurance exists. Some insurance plans let people change group policies to individual or family policies when they leave the group.

Individual Health Insurance

Special features and provisions are found in individual health insurance policies. The applicant chooses the benefits to be included in the policy. A disadvantage of individual health insurance is the high cost of premiums. In addition, the insured must pay the total cost of the premium.

Health Maintenance and Preferred Provider Organizations

Members of **health maintenance organizations (HMOs)** pay a flat fee each year that entitles them to a specific range of

M.T. Crave

22-9 **When a mother or father is a member of a group insurance plan, coverage is often available for other family members, too.**

health care services. Most HMOs offer emergency care and inpatient and outpatient hospital services. They also offer limited dental care, limited mental care, and certain health care in the home.

HMOs stress preventive medicine, encouraging their members to come in for annual physicals at no additional charge. The philosophy of HMOs is that people use medical services more if they can all be obtained for one fixed fee. Use of these services lowers the risk of becoming seriously ill.

HMOs are the direct result of the rising costs of health care. The competitive nature of HMOs motivates them to provide thorough care as economically as possible. When selecting an HMO, you need to consider several factors. For example, what is the cost for you to be a member of the HMO? What doctors and hospitals are part of the plan? How well is the plan run? State and county health departments should be able to answer your questions concerning various HMOs in the community.

Preferred provider organizations (PPOs) form agreements between insured members and doctors and hospitals to provide reduced fees for services. The agreement is usually with an employer as a health care benefit for employees. The agreement outlines terms and fees for services. The insured members receive reduced fees for services from these preferred providers. The providers gain more patients and receive fee-for-service payments rather than lump sum or per person fees.

HMO and PPO membership is available largely through an employment or union group. As an employee, you may be given a choice between an HMO or PPO plan. Some HMOs and PPOs are open to individuals.

Government Health Insurance

Most people who are employed are covered by worker's compensation and the social security program. Two other government insurance programs are Medicare and Medicaid. Medicare helps pay medical costs for people over age 65 and Medicaid helps pay medical costs for low-income or unemployed people.

Worker's compensation was set up by the states to protect working people who suffer from an illness or injury that happens at work. The benefits of worker's compensation vary somewhat from state to state. If a worker is injured on the job, that person's employer is legally responsible for the injury in most states. It does not matter who caused the injury. Worker's compensation pays two kinds of benefits—for medical costs and loss of income. There is usually a waiting period before employees may get income benefits.

States limit the amount of money paid out each week to a disabled person. A state board or commission looks over each case and considers the seriousness of the illness or injury. Then they decide on the payments that will be made.

If people have health insurance coverage for injuries, they are still eligible for worker's compensation benefits. Health insurance usually pays the medical and hospital bills, but benefits received from worker's compensation will be deducted. This prevents double payments.

Medicare is a two-part program of health insurance for people age 65 and over. It also pays disability benefits to disabled persons under the age of 65. Medicare is a part of the federal social security program and has made hospital care more affordable for the elderly.

Part A, the basic plan, provides for certain in-patient hospital care, follow-up care, nursing home expenses, and some nursing care. It is financed by payroll deductions and employer contributions made during working years. Anyone eligible for social security is automatically covered by Part A.

Medicare hospital insurance requires the consumer to pay a certain percentage of the bill. This is a form of coinsurance. Part A of Medicare pays for only health services that are considered "reasonable and necessary." This is a source of anxiety for people who worry about whether their medical costs will be paid. Unfortunately, a person does not know whether care is considered "reasonable and necessary" until after having that care.

Part B of the Medicare insurance program is voluntary. It pays for both regular medical expense and surgical expense insurance. Starting at age 65, a person can elect to pay a small monthly premium for this insurance. This fee is matched by a contribution from the federal government.

The *Medicaid* program is a joint federal and state program that pays medical expenses to needy people of all ages. Benefits go to families who have enough to cover necessities but cannot pay for adequate health care or large medical bills.

The Medicaid plan is administered by the state and financed with state and federal funds. As a result, state plans may differ as to who is covered and what benefits they will receive.

Property Insurance

Homeowners and renters need protection against the possible loss of a home and its contents due to fire, vandalism, theft, storms, and other hazards. See 22-10. They also need protection against home accidents and lawsuits from people hurt on their property. To guard against these risks, many people buy property insurance. Property and family can be protected by buying several different kinds of coverage. The most common kinds are fire, theft, and liability insurance.

Hart Denoble

22-10 **People who own homes need insurance to protect them from possible losses related to their property.**

Fire Insurance

Standard fire insurance protects the home and personal belongings against damage by fire, lightning, water, and smoke. You can purchase a policy with extended coverage for an extra premium. This may include damage from storms, explosions, wind, hail, or riots. It may also cover crashes by automobiles and aircraft into your property. Additional extended coverage is available to cover items such as vandalism, falling trees, and glass breakage.

If a home is destroyed by fire, the homeowner will not receive the full amount for which the house is insured. Most fire insurance companies have a coinsurance clause in their policies. Many insurance companies pay 80 percent of the loss.

Theft Insurance

Theft insurance protects against theft of personal belongings. It may cover personal belongings in your home or away from home. Most policies do not cover high-cost items such as fine jewelry, furs, or expensive equipment. To cover these items, you can add a mini-policy, referred to as a *rider* or *floater policy*, to your existing policy.

Theft insurance is fairly low in cost. Property away from home can be covered for only a few dollars more. Items stolen from your car are covered by theft insurance as long as the car was locked. In some high crime areas, theft insurance is expensive and difficult to buy.

Personal Liability Insurance

This insurance protects you when accidents happen to someone else in your home. It protects you against lawsuits or claims filed by people who blame you for their injury or damage to their property. This protection covers accidents in the home. Accidents elsewhere are also covered if the injury or damage is caused by you, someone in your family, or your pets.

Homeowner's Policies

Insurance policies can be written for one or more kinds of coverage, but most consumers prefer standard package policies called *homeowner's policies*. The advantage of the homeowner's policy is one policy and one premium protects the policyholder against a number of hazards. The cost is 20 to 30 percent less than separate policies.

Homeowner's policies are available with varying amounts of coverage. In general, the broader the coverage, the higher the premium. Because homeowner's policies do vary, it is important to be aware of any exclusions or limitations in a policy.

Deductible policies reduce the costs because the policyholder pays a deductible amount for every loss. There are different kinds of deductible policies. Some apply a certain deductible amount to all covered losses while others apply the deductible amount only to certain losses.

Another important aspect of homeowner's insurance is the *method of valuation*. This refers to the method used to establish the amount that the policy will pay for the insured property that is damaged or stolen. Payment may be based on the replacement cost or the actual cash value of the property, depending on what the policy states. *Replacement cost* means the company is responsible for the full cost of repair or replacement. *Actual cash value* is based on replacement cost less depreciation. In most homeowner's policies, valuation is at actual cash value unless the policy specifies that replacement cost coverage is provided.

A complete household inventory is extremely important in relation to property insurance. Every property item should be on a list. This list should indicate the original price, current market value, and serial number or identification number if there is one. Some insurance companies provide forms for the household inventory. Some suggest taking pictures of major items. The household inventory should be kept in a safe deposit box or another secure place outside the house. Having a household inventory is important protection against burglary. Without it, many people cannot remember all their personal property. Therefore, they do not get the value they should from their insurance coverage.

Automobile Insurance

No automobile owner or driver can be without automobile insurance. The costs of treating people's injuries and repairing damages to property are often much higher than most people can afford, 22-11. All states now have **financial responsibility laws**. These laws require a driver to have coverage for a minimum amount of damage for which he or she is liable. Financial responsibility laws are intended to keep people who cannot pay for property damages or injuries they cause off the streets. Six kinds of automobile coverage protect most drivers. You can purchase a policy for each type of coverage. However, most people prefer to purchase the six different coverages as a package, as with homeowner's insurance.

Bodily Injury Liability

This coverage applies when your car injures or kills pedestrians, people in other cars, or passengers in your car. Bodily injury liability applies when the policyholder, a member of the immediate family, or another person with permission drives.

Bodily injury claims can be very costly. This liability insurance protects the insured against claims or suits of people injured or killed by the insured's car. It does not cover injuries to the insured or to members of his or her family.

Bodily injury coverage is usually referred to in amounts, such as 10/20, 50/100, or 100/300. The first number is the maximum amount in thousands of dollars the insurance company will pay for the injuries of any one person in any one accident. The second number is the maximum amount in thousands of dollars the insurance company will pay for all injured parties in any one accident.

Unquestionably, this is the most important type of automobile insurance coverage. Injuries or death can bring lawsuits for enormous sums of money. Automobile owners should know the minimum coverage for bodily injury under the financial responsibility laws of their state. However, they should consider buying bodily injury coverage in amounts larger than the minimum.

Property Damage Liability

This coverage applies when the car of the insured damages the property of others. Usually that property is another car. This coverage also applies to damages to other property—lampposts, telephone poles, buildings, traffic equipment, lawns, and store windows. Property damage liability does not cover damage to the insured's automobile.

All members of the family and all those driving the family car with permission are covered by this insurance. If there are claims and suits, this insurance pays for legal defense and pays any damages against the insured up to the policy limits. Property damage liability is usually available in amounts ranging from $5,000 to $100,000. Each state has financial responsibility laws that state a minimum amount for property damage liability.

22-11 Accidents that cause serious injuries can be extremely expensive. For this reason, it is important to have automobile insurance.

Collision

Liability insurance covers injuries and damage to other people. Most people need additional insurance to cover their personal losses and damage to their cars. See 22-12. Collision coverage does not include personal injuries or any damage done to the property of others.

To reduce costs, collision insurance is usually sold with a deductible. The higher the deductible, the lower the premium will be. Costs vary from one geographic area to another and according to driver classification within an area. Unmarried male drivers under 25 years of age pay the highest rate.

Collision coverage is important because a car represents a large investment. If your car is completely destroyed in an accident, the company will pay you the actual cash value of the car. This value depends on the year, make, model, and condition of the car. The value of any car can be found in the "blue book." This book is put out for use by those who buy and sell cars and make car loans. As a car gets older and its value decreases, you should compare the cost of collision coverage with the value of the car. You may eventually wish to drop collision coverage.

Jack Klasey

22-12 In case of an accident, collision insurance covers damage to your car.

Comprehensive Physical Damage

This insurance provides coverage against damage to the insured person's car. It offers protection against fire, theft, glass breakage, falling objects, explosion, windstorm, hail, water, vandalism, civil commotion, and collision with a bird or animal.

Since comprehensive physical damage insurance is relatively inexpensive, most car owners have it. It is often sold with a deductible. This coverage may have certain limitations of which the insured should be aware. Certain extras added to the car, such as a CD player, might need special coverage. Some companies may not insure the car or its contents unless it is kept in a garage. Most insurance companies encourage people to lock their cars at all times. In fact, they may not pay theft claims if the car was left unlocked.

Medical Payments

This insurance pays for medical expenses due to injuries suffered in an automobile accident. It covers the insured, all immediate family members, and any relatives living with them. Family members are covered while riding in the insured's car or someone else's car. They are also covered if they are struck by a car while walking or riding a bicycle. Any passengers riding in the insured's car are covered.

The insurance company will pay reasonable medical expenses incurred as a result of an accident. These expenses must be incurred within one year of the date of the accident. The company will pay only up to the limits of the policy. Coverage includes medical, surgical, X ray, and dental services; ambulance service; hospital care; and professional nursing. The cost of medical payments insurance is fairly low. It is very important coverage for families with children and for families who transport other children as in a car pool situation.

Uninsured Motorists

This insurance is protection for the insured and his or her family. It protects them against risks due to bodily injury by uninsured drivers or hit-and-run drivers. This coverage is usually available only to people who also carry bodily injury liability. It is generally sold in amounts equal to the minimum financial responsibility laws of that state. The cost of this coverage is very low.

Both the policyholder and the company have the right to cancel or stop an insurance policy. A company may cancel a policy in any of the following situations:

- the insured fails to file a written report of an accident
- the insured fails to pay a premium on time
- the insured receives repeated speeding tickets
- the insured is arrested and convicted for driving while taking alcohol or drugs
- the insured lies on an insurance application

If a company does cancel a policy, a written explanation must be provided. People who feel their coverage was canceled unfairly may complain to their state insurance commissioner.

No-fault insurance is an interesting concept that has been implemented in a number of states, but its features vary from state to state. **No-fault insurance** was designed to eliminate lawsuits. Victims are simply reimbursed for their medical expenses by their own insurance companies no matter who caused the accident. No effort is made to collect from the party who caused the accident. If there is serious injury, death, or very high property loss, people still have the right to sue.

Retirement Plans and Estate Planning

For most people, the terms *retirement* and *estate planning* bring to mind the older adult. However, decisions regarding both retirement plans and estate planning are made throughout life. A person should review these plans accordingly as his or her property and needs change, family requirements develop, and economic conditions vary.

Retirement Plans

Several types of retirement plans exist. The most common retirement plans include government plans, private pension plans, and personal pension plans.

Although age 65 is currently considered the age of retirement, some people retire sooner and others choose to work well beyond that age. No matter when a person retires, a successful retirement doesn't just happen. See 22-13. A successful retirement plan requires forethought and constant reevaluation through the years. It is never too soon to start planning for those later years. You can consider various sources of retirement income.

Government Plans

Social security is the most widely used source of retirement income. However, it was not designed to provide all the money people need for retirement. Therefore, social security should not be a person's only source of retirement income. Social security retirement benefits are paid by a tax or contribution taken out of an employee's earnings. These deductions are listed under the Federal Insurance Contributions Act (FICA) on the employee's earning statements. Employees and their employers pay equal amounts of social security tax on those earnings.

Eligibility for social security benefits is based on a person's age and lifetime earnings record. Workers can qualify for

22-13 **By making financial plans for retirement early in life, people are able to get more enjoyment from their retirement years.**

benefits at age 62. However, if they wait until age 67 or older, their benefits will be higher.

You must also be fully insured under social security to be eligible for these benefits. This means you must have worked and made contributions to social security for a certain amount of time. If people are fully insured when they reach retirement age, they will get monthly payments. Certain members of the family may also get payments. If someone is fully insured at death, the family may receive benefits.

The benefits received at retirement depend on a person's average earnings covered by social security. The more a person works, the higher their earnings and the more benefits they will receive. However, there is a limit on the amount per month a person can receive.

Social security benefits are not paid automatically. A person must file an application. This should be done about three months before retirement. The exact amount due a person cannot be accurately figured until that person applies for benefits. This is because benefits are based on a person's total earnings up to the time he or she applies for retirement benefits.

Under the social security program, dependents may also receive benefits if they meet certain requirements. Unmarried children under age 18 or under age 22 for full-time students may receive benefits. Unmarried children 18 or over who are severely disabled before age 22 and are still disabled can receive benefits. A spouse who is at least 62 years of age can also receive benefits. A spouse under age 62 can receive benefits if he or she is caring for the worker's child who is also receiving benefits based on the retired worker's earnings.

Any person contributing to social security should check his or her record occasionally, perhaps every three years, for accuracy. This is especially important for persons who change jobs frequently. A postcard form for requesting a statement of earnings is available at social security offices.

Social security benefits are protected somewhat against inflation. Benefits automatically increase whenever the cost of living climbs three percent or more in a previous year.

In addition to social security, the federal government administers several other retirement plans for federal government and railroad employees. The largest of these is the U.S. Civil Service Retirement System. Employees covered under this plan are not covered by social security. The Veterans Administration provides pensions for survivors of men and women who died while in the Armed Forces. They also provide disability pensions for eligible veterans. The Railroad Retirement System is the only retirement system administered by the Federal Government that covers a single private industry. Many state, county, and city governments operate retirement plans for their employees.

Private Pension Plans

Businesses and industries often offer pension plans, which give monthly income to their employees when they retire. Professional and trade associations and unions also have pension plans. These plans differ from company to company. In order to get a pension, a person must work for a company or belong to an organization for a certain number of years. Some plans are paid entirely by the employer, while others are paid by both the employee and the employer. See 22-14.

Benefits usually depend on how long a person has worked for the company and how much that person was paid. Although the plans vary, benefits provided may include benefits for dependents, disability, death benefits for survivors, and increasing benefits according to the cost of living.

22-14 **Even young people should know about their company's pension plan. This will help them plan for financial security later in life.**

Employees should be aware of exactly how they receive work credit toward the pension. Employees should also be aware of whether a break in service cancels all previously earned credits. Some pension plans allow employees to carry earned pension benefits from one employer's pension plan and invest them in another plan when they change jobs.

Some employees are entitled to a retirement income even though they change jobs and move to a different company. These are employees who have a vested interest in the company's retirement plan. When an employee's contributions are vested, it means they are owned by the employee. **Vesting** is a process by which the employee earns rights over the employer's contributions to the pension plan. Vesting is an important right, and companies that offer pension plans must provide full vesting after a specified number of years of employment with the company.

A serious problem of some employees in the past involved the loss of their pension because their employer managed funds poorly. Congress has passed a law to reduce the problem. Today all pension funds must be managed by a trustee who oversees the financial safety of the fund. However, another problem involves the failure of large businesses and the effect on the employees. If an employee's funds are all in company stock and the company fails, the employee's funds are lost, too.

Personal Pension Plans

Not all companies offer retirement plans, and many people do not work for a company. To help these people, the government has created *Individual Retirement Accounts (IRAs)*. These plans allow many people to make a tax-deductible contribution to a retirement fund. In these plans, the principal continues to grow tax-free until it is withdrawn at retirement. The *principal* is the amount of this investment minus the interest. After age 59 1/2 or at retirement, a person may begin to get this money back with interest. The money is then taxed at a time when the person is in a lower tax bracket.

Under the traditional IRA, a person can place up to $3,000 annually into an IRA account. If his or her age is over 50, the amount is $3,500. The best part about an IRA is that the investments grow tax-free until the money is taken out at retirement.

Another type of IRA, a *Roth IRA*, functions somewhat the opposite of the traditional IRA. Retirement contributions are taxed up front and withdrawals can be made completely tax-free once the person reaches age 59 1/2 and has had a Roth IRA for five years. For some people, paying taxes now to enjoy tax-free income later may actually make more financial sense in the long term. The Roth IRA allows investors to shelter more money for retirement. Although the annual contribution limit is the same for both traditional and Roth IRAs, because the Roth contribution is made with after-tax income, the full $3,000, or $3,500 if over 50, can compound substantially over the years.

The Keogh plan is like an IRA, but it is designed for self-employed people. These people may contribute as much as 25 percent of their income up to a maximum of $40,000 annually. This amount is taken as a deduction from taxable income, deferring tax payments to the time of withdrawal from the account at retirement.

Considerations in Estate Planning

Estate planning allows people to arrange their assets, referred to as "the estate," so the estate can be distributed both before and after death in a manner that best carries out their desires. Careful planning helps minimize income, gift, and death taxes. It also makes the transfer of the estate easier, 22-15.

When property is involved, the manner in which title to the property is held affects how the property can be distributed during a person's life. It also affects who receives the property at the person's death and who is responsible for income taxes, gift taxes, and death taxes.

Central to every estate plan is a will. A **will** is used to designate heirs, identify the property they are to receive, and indicate who will act as administrator of the estate. A person without a will allows the state, according to law, to decide who receives any property. This creates additional

22-15 **Estate planning is important to people who want relatives or friends to inherit their property.**

expenses in settling the estate, and the state may not distribute the property as the person may have wanted.

It is important to understand all aspects of estate planning. It is additionally important to recognize that estate planning will require the help of professionals. Expert advice should be sought in order to ensure your wishes are fulfilled at the minimum tax cost.

Your estate plan should be reviewed occasionally. Tax laws change. Estate sizes change. Minors become adults. Changes in beneficiaries may be desired. People marry, divorce, and remarry. For any of these reasons, an estate plan may need to be revised.

Summary

Planning for financial security means making decisions about financial management so money will be available for emergencies and for short-term and long-term goals. The way you build financial security will depend on your specific goals.

You may use savings, investments, insurance, and/or retirement plans to provide financial security. Thorough knowledge of these alternatives will provide a basis for making your choice.

An effective savings plan requires knowledge of savings institutions and savings plans available. Wise investment choices can be made only when investment objectives are carefully considered and combined with knowledge of types of investments available.

Insurance, another means for building financial security, is protection against financial difficulties resulting from loss, damage, sickness, or death. Understanding the options available will aid in making decisions about the kind and amount of insurance needed.

In each of these areas—savings, investments, and insurance—professionals can provide you with information and guidance to help you in making decisions.

Although retirement may seem unimportant to you now, it is important to realize a successful retirement does not just happen. It requires careful planning and constant reevaluation. Your understanding of sources of retirement income will help guide you.

Working with legal and financial advisers is a necessary step in estate planning. Your understanding of considerations in estate planning along with professional advice will help you minimize taxes and assure ease of transfer of your estate according to your goals and desires.

To Review

1. Match the following terms to their descriptions:
   Time account   Passbook account
   Stock   Bond
   Mutual fund   Money market accounts
   A. a share of ownership in a corporation
   B. may pay a higher interest rate depending on U.S. Treasury Bill rates
   C. a promise to pay the investor a certain amount of money plus interest at a specific time in the future; a loan made to a corporation or to the government
   D. earns the lowest interest and allows money to be withdrawn at any time
   E. an account in which money must be kept for a certain period of time
   F. invests funds in a variety of stocks and bonds
2. Describe the difference between common stock and preferred stock.
3. Which of the following statements describe term insurance, and which describe permanent life insurance?
   A. In general, cost is lower.
   B. Benefits are paid no matter when the insured dies.
   C. After a period of time, the policy ends.
   D. Endowment insurance is included in this category.
   E. Builds a cash value.
4. What two types of coverage do most health insurance package plans provide?
5. True or false?
   A. Group health insurance is more expensive than individual health insurance.
   B. In most group plans, a medical checkup is not necessary.
   C. Group insurance always ends when you leave the group.
6. In which of the following situations would you be covered by personal liability insurance?
   A. An appliance is stolen from your home.
   B. There is fire damage in your kitchen.
   C. A neighbor slips on your sidewalk and breaks his leg.
   D. Your picture window is broken by children playing ball.
7. What is the purpose of financial responsibility laws regarding automobile insurance?
8. When does bodily injury liability insurance apply?
9. Explain why a will is important.
10. True or false? Retirement is the time to begin thinking about financial security for the later adult years.

To Do with the Class

1. Bring newspaper articles to class describing tragedies that illustrate the need to plan for financial security.
2. As a class project, collect various insurance contracts. Identify and discuss the various coverages.
3. Research the HMOs that are available in your area. Compare and discuss the various plans.
4. Invite retired persons to class to discuss the importance of planning for retirement.

To Challenge Your Thinking

1. Interview an older family member or friend. Ask them to share their plans for financial security with you. What do they wish they had done better or differently?
2. Research the most likely reasons for persons to experience financial losses. What steps can be taken to prevent these from wiping out a family's finances?
3. Create an imaginary family situation including the number of drivers and their ages. Shop at several agencies to compare insurance policy coverage and costs.
4. Talk with several people who are considering retirement in the near future. Find out how they feel about the social security system in terms of meeting their retirement needs.

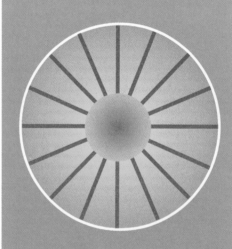

To Do with Your Community

1. Call or visit savings institutions in your community. Find out what types of accounts are available and their interest rates.
2. Invite an insurance agent to speak to your class. Discuss services an agent can provide and criteria for choosing an agent.
3. Invite an insurance adjuster to class to discuss the types of records and evidence necessary to document a loss. Explain how these records should be developed and kept.
4. Invite a lawyer to talk about wills and estate planning in young adulthood.

⊢ Financial advisors can help people make the best plans to meet their needs.

Part Seven
Managing as a Consumer

Chapter 23
Consumer Rights and Responsibilities
Consumers have certain rights that are protected by laws. However, there are also consumer responsibilities that go along with these rights. As a consumer, you should be aware of your rights and responsibilities.

Chapter 24
Consumer Decision Making
The American economy is based on freedom of choice. Using the decision-making process can help you make the best consumer choices.

23

Consumer Rights and Responsibilities

To Know

informative advertising
warranty
full warranty
limited warranty
Consumer Product Safety
　　Commission (CPSC)
Environmental Protection Agency (EPA)
United States Department of
　　Agriculture (USDA)
Food and Drug Administration (FDA)
Federal Trade Commission (FTC)
National Highway Traffic Safety
　　Administration (NHTSA)
monopoly
competition
persuasive advertising
testimonial advertising
institutional advertising
emotional advertising
comparative advertising
deceptive practices
bait and switch
Better Business Bureaus (BBBs)

Objectives

After studying this chapter, you will be able to
◇　describe your rights as a consumer.
◇　describe various ways the consumer can become informed about products and services.
◇　give examples of federal agencies that protect the consumer.
◇　explain the relationship between consumer rights and consumer responsibilities.

In the past 30 years, there has been a growing awareness of consumer problems as well as an effort to achieve better consumer protection. The only voice for consumer interests in the 1940s and 1950s was the magazine *Consumer Reports*. However, there were changes during the 1960s. Consumers became aware of situations that threatened our survival. These were caused by unsafe and unhealthy products, irresponsible use of natural resources, and pollution of water, land, and air. Several books were published on these topics.

During this period, President John F. Kennedy showed enthusiastic support for consumer issues. He gave an important speech in which he stated certain consumer rights. President Lyndon B. Johnson actively worked toward the passage of a set of legislative consumer protection proposals. Throughout the 1960s and 1970s, the consumer protection movement continued growing in impact and importance. Today's consumers are learning to speak out on their own or in groups and are being heard. As a result of the consumer movement, the rights of consumers are being recognized and expanded.

Having a clearer understanding of consumer rights and responsibilities will make you a better consumer. In addition, using your consumer rights and assuming your consumer responsibilities will allow you to promote your own economic welfare.

Consumer Rights

President Kennedy said that consumers have the right to be informed, the right to safety and legal protection, the right to choose among products and services, and the right to express dissatisfaction and be heard. This statement of rights has come to be accepted as a broad outline of what consumers should have in government protection. As a consumer, it is important for you to understand these rights.

Right to Be Informed

The information a consumer receives about products or services may come from several sources–an advertisement, a salesperson, the product, a publication, or a consumer organization. The consumer has the right to be informed through these sources of any claims about the product or service.

Informed Through Advertising

To serve the consumer, advertisers are obligated to inform and not simply persuade people about their products. **Informative advertising** is helpful to consumers in many ways. It lessens the amount of time consumers spend shopping. When more information is provided about the product, consumer decision making becomes easier and quicker.

Advertisements that make both the cost and benefits of the product clear also aid the consumer. Usually, consumers want to become familiar with the uses and benefits of a product before they are willing to buy it. New options in products create more competition, better service, lower prices, and ultimately, greater consumer satisfaction.

Informed by an Honest, Knowledgeable Salesperson

Salespeople can be extremely helpful sources of information about products and

Use Your Reasoning Skills

Watch television commercials and analyze them in terms of what products they promote, the type of person to which they appeal, and the gimmicks they use to persuade. Objectively consider how much you actually learned about the products advertised. Summarize your findings in a written report.

their qualities. See 23-1. Recently, the trend in retail stores has been to have fewer salespeople on the floor to answer customer questions about products or to supply useful information. This is unfortunate for the consumer. However, smaller businesses and specialty shops are still likely to have salespeople who can help the consumer with shopping needs.

Informed Through Product Labeling

Labels, hangtags, and packaging often provide information that is valuable to consumers. This may include information such as features of the products and use and care information.

Some products are required by law to have certain information on their labels. The Permanent Care Labeling Act issued by the Federal Trade Commission is an example. It requires that most clothing and household textiles have a permanent, legible, easily understood care label. The label must list appropriate instructions for washing, bleaching, drying, ironing,

and/or dry cleaning. See 23-2. Another example is the Fair Packaging and Labeling Act, which helps consumers more easily compare food products at the supermarket. Before this act, standard product descriptions and information about container size were not required to be on the package or label. This made comparison shopping extremely difficult.

Another source of consumer information is the presence of a seal that indicates the product has met certain standards of performance. These specified standards cannot be easily verified by the consumer. The appearance of a seal should be one of the criteria consumers use in deciding which product to buy. The best known of these seals is the UL seal, which stands for the Underwriters' Laboratories, a nonprofit testing organization. This seal is found on all equipment, appliances, and materials that could be fire, electric, or accident hazards or used to stop the spread of fire.

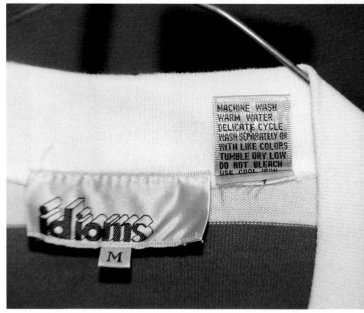

Stig Rahm

23-1 Many consumers rely on knowledgeable salespeople to guide them in making choices.

23-2 The information on this care label is legally required due to the Permanent Care Labeling Act.

Although the seal is not a guarantee, it shows the product has been tested and judged safe for normal use.

Informed Through Warranties

The information on warranties, sometimes called guarantees, tells the consumer in advance what to expect concerning servicing repairs and adjustments. See 23-3. A **warranty** is a guarantee that the product is in good working order and will give good service for a reasonable amount of time. The purpose of the Magnuson-Moss Warranty Act, also known as the Consumer Product Warranties Law, is to simplify the language of a warranty so any consumer can easily understand exactly what is covered for what period of time, and the cost and conditions of service.

Lynn Hellmuth

23-3 A warranty tells what repairs will be paid for by the manufacturer within a certain period of time and what repairs must be paid for by the consumer.

The warranty for products selling for more than $5.00 must include names and addresses of the warrantors, exactly what is covered, a step-by-step description of the consumer's procedures in getting the warranty honored, legal remedies available to the consumer, and the duration of the warranty.

The warranty for products selling for more than $10.00 must state whether it is a full warranty or a limited warranty. A **full warranty** has no specific limitations. In other words, the product is totally guaranteed. Both materials and labor are covered for the length of time specified. If the product does not perform as expected because of poor quality or faulty materials, the manufacturer will replace or repair the product. A **limited warranty** must state what the limitations are. For example, a limited warranty on a radio may indicate that if the radio is not working within six months of purchase, the consumer pays for the labor but the parts would be replaced free of charge.

Informed Through Publications and Consumer Organizations

In 1971, the federal government set up the Office of Consumer Affairs to keep the President and consumers informed about consumer issues. This office publishes the *Consumer's Resource Handbook* to help consumers make informed purchasing decisions and avoid problems in today's complex marketplace.

Another government-supported source of consumer information is the Consumer Information Center. They print guidelines on nearly everything consumers want to buy. These buying tips are available free or for a small cost. You can request a free list of consumer publications from the

Consumer Information Center in Pueblo, Colorado.

Various national nongovernment consumer organizations also work to promote federal legislation and consumer education. Consumers Union is a nonprofit corporation with laboratories and testing facilities for consumer products. Consumers Union publishes the monthly magazine *Consumer Reports*, which presents information related to product testing and educates readers on consumer issues. See 23-4. Consumers Union also publishes a *Buying Guide* with summaries of product test results at the end of each year.

Mark Felstehausen

23-4 *Consumer Reports* is an excellent source of information on consumer products and consumer problems.

The Consumer Federation of America is a prominent national organization that is interested in a wide variety of consumer issues. It supports the consumer through education and legislation. This group publishes a directory of all local and state consumer groups.

Consumer's Research, Inc. is another nonprofit corporation that tests and rates the efficiency of consumer products and provides a consulting service for technical problems. This group publishes the monthly magazine *Consumer's Research*, which contains general consumer information and advice as well as product test results. In October, they publish the *Consumer's Research Annual Guide*, which contains product test results and comparison shopping advice.

Many other national groups are concerned with specific consumer issues. Action for Children's Television is an example of such a group.

Many major businesses have established consumer affairs departments. These departments act as a means of communication between the business and its consumers, including handling consumer complaints. They often produce consumer education newsletters and distribute educational literature related to the product or service they are selling.

Many consumer organizations made up of interested citizens have been formed at the state and local levels. These groups share the belief that only through organized group action will their voices be heard. In addition to promoting consumer legislation, these groups have an interest in consumer information and education.

Other local groups are also involved in consumer education. Newspapers and popular magazines print many articles directed to the consumer. Radio and

Brainstorming

Bring pamphlets on the use and care of appliances to class. Study them carefully and discuss information that relates to active consumer care. Do you think people often read the use-and-care information that comes with products? Why or why not? How does this affect use of the product? How does this affect getting full value of the product?

television stations and newspapers often have some type of "action line" that encourages consumers to share their concerns or problems. High schools and colleges offer courses in various aspects of consumer education. Public libraries contain volumes of books aimed at helping the consumer.

Right to Safety and Legal Protection

Consumers have the right to know the products and services they buy will be safe if used as intended. Government agencies provide consumers with protection and information services. Many of these agencies set and enforce safety standards for products and services.

◇ **Consumer Product Safety Commission (CPSC)**. This agency protects consumers from dangerous products and encourages safe product use in the home, schools, and recreational areas. The CPSC develops safety standards for consumer products and investigates product-related deaths, injuries, and illnesses. This agency has the authority to ban hazardous products and set mandatory safety standards.

◇ **Environmental Protection Agency (EPA)**. Congress formed this agency to protect the nation's land, air, and water systems. The EPA's programs focus on air, noise, radiation, water quality, drinking water, solid waste, hazardous waste, toxic substances, and pesticides.

◇ **United States Department of Agriculture (USDA)**. This department supervises food safety and inspection services. The USDA establishes grades and provides an inspection service for many food products. It also provides nutrition information and has food programs for the needy.

◇ **Food and Drug Administration (FDA)**. This agency assures that all food (other than meat and poultry), food additives, and cosmetics are safe and wholesome. It also assures that drugs and medical devices are properly labeled and safe for intended use. The FDA certifies new drugs and inspects drug and food processing plants.

◇ **Federal Trade Commission (FTC)**. The FTC enforces laws that encourage fair competition among businesses. It also handles consumer problems with credit; price-fixing and fraud; and television, radio, and printed advertising.

◇ **National Highway Traffic Safety Administration (NHTSA)**. This agency works to reduce highway deaths, injuries, and property losses. They do this by enforcing the Federal Motor Vehicle Safety Standards for vehicles and vehicle equipment. This agency can order carmakers to recall cars with unsafe parts.

*Getting*Involved

In addition to the federal government agencies described here, there are also many state and local consumer protection agencies.

Right to Choose Among Products and Services

Consumers have the right to choose from a variety of products and services.

Laws that prohibit most monopolies have been written to preserve this right. When a **monopoly** exists, consumers have no choice of where to buy a good or service. It can be purchased from only one seller. In a monopoly situation, prices tend to be higher than when several sellers are competing for customers.

The Federal Trade Commission (FTC) enforces laws that encourage competition among businesses. When there is **competition**, similar goods and services are offered by more than one seller. See 23-5. This competition creates a larger selection and a lower price of products and services for consumers.

Consumers are also able to choose the businesses at which they shop, 23-6. People quickly learn to avoid businesses that give poor service or set their prices too high. Businesses that continue these practices may eventually fail.

23-5 **Shopping centers create competition and provide a larger selection of products and services.**

23-6 **Consumers reward certain businesses with their dollars and encourage the success of those businesses.**

Consumer Responsibilities

Certain responsibilities go along with consumer rights. These responsibilities cannot be imposed on anyone. Instead, you begin to assume responsibilities because of the values you absorb at home and in the community. Being aware of consumer responsibilities is a valuable resource to every consumer.

Responsibility to Use Consumer Information

The right to be informed carries with it the responsibility to seek out and use information available to help the consumer. See 23-7. Informed consumers make use of consumer agencies and consumer information services. Many good resources are available through the Internet. An informed consumer is in a position to make wise choices. These choices can strongly influence the quality of goods and services available.

Right to Express Dissatisfaction and Be Heard

When a product or service is not satisfactory, the consumer has the right to complain. Consumers have cause to complain when service or repairs are not satisfactory or when they do not receive merchandise or service ordered. Other causes for complaints include defective merchandise, credit billing problems, an unfulfilled guarantee or warranty, or deposits that are not refunded.

You can complain by personal visit, telephone call, or letter. Most complaints can be handled by direct contact with the salespeople. However, you may need to take more difficult problems to department heads or store managers. You might even need to take a complaint to the president of the company or the owner of the store.

M.T. Crave

23-7 **People who are willing to seek out consumer information will find it is available from many sources.**

Use of Information About Misleading Advertising

Business and government have the responsibility to prevent false advertising and encourage informative advertising through product selection. However, consumers also have a responsibility related to advertising. They must analyze advertisements by using the helpful information and ignoring the rest. This leads the consumer to improved buying decisions.

Persuasive Advertising

Persuasive advertising tries to persuade you to buy goods or services using arguments that may or may not be valid. There may be little or no constructive information given about the product or service. A variety of techniques in persuasive advertising are commonly used. Be aware of these techniques so you can avoid being influenced by them. Then you can make choices based on the quality of the product or service.

Testimonial Advertising

Ads that present a recommendation for a product or service from either a celebrity or a typical consumer are **testimonial advertising**, 23-8. Celebrity endorsements are made by movie stars, sports stars, and

23-8 Testimonial advertising tends to be fairly effective whether products are recommended by celebrities or average people.

other national heroes or heroines. For consumers who might doubt the sincerity of famous people, there are testimonial ads from "ordinary people" who give their "honest" feelings about a product.

Institutional Advertising

Companies often use institutional advertising to promote a product or simply promote feelings of goodwill. **Institutional advertising** appeals to values of people, such as patriotism, caring for others, and importance of family. For instance, one Chevrolet ad featured a family at a Fourth of July celebration. The lyrics to the song in the ad were, "Baseball, hot dogs, apple pie, and Chevrolet." The ad's purpose was to get people to associate a type of car with solid American values and feel that car was special.

Emotional Advertising

Ads that aim to satisfy psychological needs are known as **emotional advertising**. They tend to make the consumer feel dissatisfied, insecure, or guilty. For example, these ads may ask, "When was the last time you called home?" or "Doesn't your family deserve the best?" These ads may also use a little "snob appeal" by appealing to the consumer's ego. Ads may tell consumers that using a certain product will put them among the elite.

Comparative Advertising

This type of advertising often includes more information about the product than other persuasive methods. In **comparative advertising**, the company compares its brand with another competing brand. Because price is not included, these ads are often misleading. Also, most products have a variety of characteristics. Comparative advertising emphasizes the more positive ones and avoids the negative ones. Companies must be able to prove what they claim in comparative advertising.

Truth to Convey Falsehood

In this type of advertising, advertisers tell the truth. However, the way they tell the truth deceives the consumer. For instance, an automobile ad may state that a car can go further on a tank of gasoline than its competitor can go. Perhaps this is true, but not because of better gas mileage as most consumers would assume. Instead, it is because the gas tank is larger on that particular car. The ad conveyed a false impression.

Unfortunately, there are times when advertisers attempt to cheat consumers. They use **deceptive practices**. Many of the fraudulent, illegal advertising methods used in the past have been stopped. However, some types of consumer deception are still widely used.

- *Bait and switch.* This deceptive practice involves the consumer's natural urge to get a bargain. With the **bait and switch** technique, the item offered at a low price is the bait. The purpose of the bait is to get consumers in the store. Once consumers are there, advertisers attempt to switch consumers to another, more expensive item. Advertisers do this by saying they are out of the advertised item. Another approach is trying to convince the consumer the advertised item is inadequate for the consumer's needs. Be suspicious if you arrive at a store and the salesperson tells you the advertised product will not work well for you or is not available.

- *Free items.* A commonly used sales strategy is offering some free item or service to consumers who purchase their product. For example, a book company might offer five free books if you join the book club and agree to buy a certain number of monthly selections. The price of those "free" books is actually figured into the cost of the books you buy. They are not really free. This is not illegal because all conditions are advertised.

However, the consumer who takes the time to figure the costs involved can understand the books are not free.

- *Contests—everyone is a winner.* This attempt to deceive consumers is often done either by mail or telephone. The consumer may be informed by mail that he or she has already won a prize. The person may be required to come to the store or business, answer some questions, or fill in a coupon to earn his or her "valuable gift." A catalog or list of merchandise may also be included. This gives the consumer the chance to order more items. The consumer may receive several more prizes and extra incentives for buying from or visiting the business.

- *Limited quantities, irregulars, or seconds.* The problems of limited quantities and irregulars or seconds have been corrected through legal channels. However, the consumer should still be aware of this sales strategy in case it exists. Limited quantities may occur when an item is advertised at a very low price. When the consumer arrives at the place of business, all the items may have been sold. This happens because quantity was very low in the beginning. The true purpose of the ad was to get the consumers to come to the store. Today an advertiser has the duty to inform a consumer if quantities are limited. If irregulars or seconds are offered, the merchant must also say so in the advertising. This information must be on the product as well. Irregulars or seconds can be an excellent buy as long as you don't think you are getting an item in perfect condition. Many flaws have nothing to do with the product's function. For instance, an electric fry pan with a scratch on the outside surface would work just as well as one with no scratch.

Use of Information on Using and Caring for Purchased Products

If consumers expect to receive quality merchandise, they must accept a responsibility. They must read and follow the manufacturer's recommendations included with their product. See 23-9.

Most appliance manufacturers provide booklets that explain how the appliances should be operated and cared for. Failure to follow the instructions can damage the appliance and cause injury.

Consumers are also responsible for reading the warnings printed on package labels. Companies have tested their products and found certain situations to be hazardous. They include this information to ensure that consumers use their products safely. Many accidents occur because consumers do not heed the warnings. Manufacturers also supply information on maintenance that should be done regularly to keep the product in working

order. The wise consumer makes a note of maintenance jobs to be done and keeps this list in a convenient place. Many dissatisfied consumers complain about the poor quality of certain equipment. However, they may be responsible for that poor quality because they have ignored maintenance needs suggested by the manufacturer.

Responsibility to Be an Ethical Consumer

Being an ethical consumer is an important responsibility. Consumer ethics involves each choice you make as a consumer. Each choice is a vote for a product. If you have carefully researched your choice and the product is of quality, that will be a good vote. It will support a quality product in the marketplace. If the choice was made by impulse shopping, it still represents a vote for that product. That choice may be a good one or a bad one. Even if the choice was a poor one, it supports returning the product to the marketplace. All consumers would prefer a market that consists of quality products and services. In order to have this type of market, each consumer must assume the responsibility of making carefully researched choices.

Another responsibility involving consumer ethics involves the choice of reputable merchants. When you purchase an item at a store, you cast a vote of confidence for that merchant. By dealing with reputable merchants only, you are protecting the rights of all consumers.

Consumer ethics also involve careless or dishonest practices of consumers. Honest consumers ultimately pay the price for shoplifting and other dishonest practices. The responsible consumer should be honest, just as merchants and people who do repairs are expected to be honest.

M.T. Crave

23-9 When you read and follow the manufacturer's instructions for the use of a product, you can expect it to perform as advertised.

Responsibility to Protest When You Are Wronged

The right to complain about an unsatisfactory product or service carries with it the responsibility to do so. A consumer who ignores poor quality, defective merchandise, or unsatisfactory repair service is not helping to eliminate deceptive practices. The costs of this complaining process to the consumer may include time, money, and an unpleasant situation. However, the benefits may include a product that now works and personal satisfaction. Hopefully, a corrective measure will be taken so the situation will not happen again.

Whether you complain in person, by telephone, or by letter, it is important to state the problem clearly and concisely. State the complaint with specific facts as briefly as possible without being sarcastic or emotional. Explain what you feel the store or firm should do about the problem. In other words, do you think they should replace the product, repair it, or return your money?

If complaining in person, bring copies of documents, such as sales slips or receipts, canceled checks, warranties, or hangtags to support your request. Keep all original documents on hand for your own reference.

If you complain by telephone, be sure to make a written note of who receives the complaint, the date of the call, and what is said. You may need this information if you get no response to the call.

Sometimes consumers need to write the company about their dissatisfaction. If hangtags or warranties do not list the company's address, this information can be found at a public library.

Your letter to the company should have appropriate paragraph structure and correct spelling. Include very specific information, 23-10. Describe the exact product or service you are complaining about and list model numbers and serial numbers if they apply.

Include what you paid and where and when you made the purchase. State the exact reason you are dissatisfied with the product or service and anything you have already done to try to solve the problem. State what action you wish the company to take to satisfy you. Be reasonable, but firm, about the action you wish to have taken. Include copies of any documents related to your purchase, such as sales slips, canceled checks, or warranties or guarantees. Be sure to include your name, address, and phone number so the company can reach you. Keep copies of all letters you send and receive.

Some industries have organized consumer action panels (CAPS) to help solve consumer disputes. For consumer problems not solved by the local dealer or the manufacturer, a letter to one of the appropriate CAPS may help.

Many states have consumer agencies to help the consumer locate the proper agency to handle a specific consumer problem. Some states have directories that contain names and addresses of agencies that handle specific types of complaints. This information can be found at a public library or on the Internet.

The *Consumer's Resource Handbook* is a valuable source of information on making complaints. It may be obtained by writing to the Consumer Information Center in Pueblo, Colorado. It includes a directory of state and local consumer affairs and protection offices.

Better Business Bureaus (BBBs) are another place you can go to complain. These nonprofit organizations are sponsored by private businesses. They attempt to settle consumer complaints against local businesses.

If the consumer is unable to resolve a complaint through any of the previously suggested channels, legal action may be necessary. In most states, small claims courts quickly solve disputes about small amounts of money up to $3,000. Many consumers fear going to court, but they should not. In small claims court you do not even need a lawyer to file suit. However, you may prefer to hire a lawyer for this effort. Having evidence and witnesses to back up your claims is important. The judgment usually includes court costs.

Many people do not pursue their rights because they fear legal costs. The legal clinic is a resource that has come about in the past few years. In a legal clinic, several lawyers share office space. They select specific types of cases and conduct business only in those categories. These lawyers have fees that are far below what a regular law firm would charge.

519 Liberty
Huntington, MA 03692
February 15, 20XX

Mr. Damon Jackson
Director of Consumer Affairs
Western Hair Dryer Company
1328 North Livingston Road
Alabaster, CA 92365

Dear Mr. Jackson:

On January 25, I purchased hair dryer model number A2X3Z79 at Discount City in Huntington, Massachusetts, for $15.99. A copy of my receipt is enclosed.

After less than two weeks of use, the dryer caught on fire while I was using it. I do understand how quality problems can occur. However, this is a very dangerous problem. Many other consumers could be in danger if other hair dryers are defective.

Although the enclosed copy of my warranty says I am entitled to either a replacement or a refund, Discount City refused to give me either. I would appreciate your refunding my money within the next three weeks.

You may contact me at (436) 555-9589 if you need more information about this problem. I appreciate your help and look forward to your prompt response.

Sincerely,

LaTonya Williams

LaTonya Williams

Enclosures

23-10 If you are dissatisfied with a product or service, you may need to write a complaint letter to the manufacturer before the problem will be solved. Be sure to include information that specifically describes your problem.

Summary

An understanding of your consumer rights and responsibilities will help you become a more effective consumer and promote your own economic welfare. As a consumer, you have certain rights that are protected under the government. Many agencies exist to help you understand and protect your rights.

Along with these consumer rights go certain responsibilities. Putting your rights and responsibilities into practice can send messages to companies about the products and service consumers expect.

To Review

1. What are the four consumer rights as stated by President John F. Kennedy?
2. Describe five sources of consumer information.
3. Describe the difference between a full warranty and a limited warranty.
4. True or false?
   A. The Consumer Product Safety Commission (CPSC) assures that drugs and medical devices are properly labeled and safe for intended use.
   B. The Federal Trade Commission (FTC) enforces laws that encourage fair competition among businesses.
   C. The Food and Drug Administration (FDA) supervises the food safety and inspection services.
5. List four good reasons to complain about a product or service.
6. Explain the deceptive practice called bait and switch.
7. Make a list of the information that should be included in a complaint letter.
8. What are five consumer responsibilities?
9. What is the main role of the Better Business Bureau?
10. Small claims courts settle disputes for small amounts of money up to _____.

To Challenge Your Thinking

1. Use consumer education literature to find examples of situations in which the FTC has requested advertisers to support exaggerated claims about safety, performance, quality, or comparative prices. Discuss these examples with the rest of the class.
2. Look for useful information on labels or tags on foods, clothing, and furniture. Identify information that is required by law. Discuss this with the rest of the class.
3. Check recent items you or your family have purchased for types of warranties and other valuable or useful consumer information. How might this information help you if the product were to break?
4. Analyze consumer-oriented magazines such as *Changing Times*, *Consumer Reports*, and *Consumer's Research*. Determine what help they have available for the consumer and summarize your findings in a written report.

To Do with the Class

1. Discuss your feelings about the following safety laws that inhibit individual freedom.
   A. All children must be restrained while traveling in an automobile.
   B. All motorcyclists must wear helmets.
   C. Skateboarding is not allowed.
2. Look up definitions of *responsibility* in the dictionary. Relate these definitions to consumer responsibility.
3. Discuss the following statement: Knowledge is the consumer's greatest protection.
4. Research the Better Business Bureau for the main reasons for consumer complaints against companies. Share your findings with others in the class.

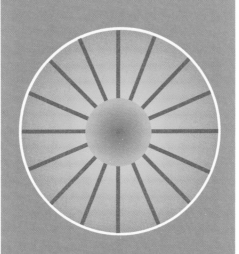

To Do with Your Community

1. Contact your local Better Business Bureau. Invite a representative to share information on the Bureau's role in consumer protection.
2. Analyze the advertising billboards in your community or check your local newspaper for types of advertising gimmicks used.
3. Develop a list of consumer affairs agencies in your area. You may use the *Yellow Pages*, district attorney's office, and other sources of information. Share your list with class members.
4. Invite a lawyer who has dealt with small claims court cases. What are the typical types of cases that might need to go to court?

24 Consumer Decision Making

To Know

economics
socialism
communism
capitalism
mixed economy
economic efficiency
economic stability
inflation
deflation
monetary policies
fiscal policies
private property
profit motivation
market economy
e-commerce

Objectives

After studying this chapter, you will be able to

◇ explain factors affecting consumer decision making.

◇ describe the goals and characteristics of the United States economy.

◇ apply the decision-making process to your own consumer decisions.

You make many decisions as a consumer each day. Whether they are good decisions or bad decisions, they will affect you as a person and society as a whole. Making decisions carefully is in the best interest of both the individual and society. Today's quickly changing society requires consumers to make rational decisions by logically analyzing each situation using the decision-making process. Skill in decision making and knowledge of factors that affect decision making can be valuable resources to you as a consumer.

Factors Affecting Decision Making

The economy of the United States is based on individual participation and decision making. Consumers make choices that have important consequences. The choices of many consumers can combine to strongly influence the entire economic system, 24-1.

Consumers make choices based on their values. The more consumers understand their values, the more consistent and logical their decisions will be. Ability to recognize and use available resources greatly affects the success of your decision making. A vast number of resources are available to consumers. Families also influence many consumer choices. Stages in the family life cycle, family circumstances, family resources, and the values of each family member can greatly affect consumer decision making.

The Economy and Consumer Decision Making

Economics is a study of the process people and societies use to make choices about making and spending their money. A nation's economic system is closely related to its type of government. Three systems frequently compared are socialism, communism, and capitalism.

Socialism is a system in which there is considerable government planning to promote well-being of the citizens. The government owns and operates most industries. The goals of socialism include incentive for each person to earn and government controls for the benefit of society.

In the system of **communism**, the government owns the land and almost all

24-1 **Both large and small consumer decisions influence what products and services are available.**

industries and plans all production. The goals of communism are equal social well-being for all, and for all people to have individuality that is compatible with government doctrine.

Capitalism, the form of government in the United States, allows private ownership of land and producer goods. This system offers people the freedom to use productive resources and purchase consumer goods on their own initiative. The goals of capitalism include individual satisfaction, opportunity, and freedom of choice. The American systems of business and government share the same goals. Under capitalism, consumers basically make the decision as to what shall be produced. However, under socialism and communism, the government almost exclusively makes this decision. See 24-2.

Consumer buying decisions are highly flexible under capitalism, very restricted under communism, and somewhat restricted under socialism. Capitalism supports the consumer's right to be heard and to complain. This right is restricted under both socialism and communism. The consumers in each economic system must adapt and function according to the economic goals of their society.

Economic Goals of the United States

The United States is basically a free-enterprise economy based on economic freedom. Individuals make economic decisions—deciding what jobs they want, what they want to purchase, and what products they want to make. However, the American economy is not completely free; it is called a **mixed economy**. Individuals make most decisions, but the economy is in part regulated by the government. Government regulation is limited.

Any economic system has goals. The following are economic goals of the United States:

Economic Freedom

Economic freedom refers to an individual's freedom to make economic choices. Consumers have the right to choose or reject products or services. They have the right to make their own choices about saving and investing, and they can choose their own careers.

Businesses also have freedoms. People in business have freedom to decide when and where to advertise and how to market

24-2 **American consumers have many choices.**

their products, 24-3. People have the right to start and operate their own business in the private enterprise system.

Economic Efficiency

Making the most efficient use of limited resources is known as **economic efficiency**. Economic efficiency is important from the point of view of the individual consumer, the producer of business, and the nation. For individual consumers, economic efficiency means making the best possible use of their resources such as energy, income, talent, and ability. For businesses, economic efficiency involves keeping their costs down. They move toward economic efficiency by producing a product with the least possible amount of labor, natural resources, and energy. The most efficient businesses stay ahead of their competitors.

The nation as a whole has become more aware of the need for efficiency in the economy. Making wise use of natural resources is a national goal as well as a

24-3 The supermarket is a competitive place. Production and marketing techniques are carefully researched before they are used.

Getting Involved

Visit a local school board or city council meeting. What consumer issues are being discussed? What are the goals, values, and resources being considered in the decision-making process? Interview a member of the board or council to get their views.

personal goal. Conserving fuel in the home through better insulation and lower temperatures is a good example of this. The advantage to families is the decrease in their fuel costs. The advantage to the nation is that energy resources are being conserved.

Economic Growth

Economic growth refers to overall economic progress and an ever-increasing standard of living. An increase in education and a growth in technology cause more goods and services to be produced for each person. Both society and individuals accept economic growth as a basic goal. Through economic growth, the standard of living will continue to improve.

Economic Stability

When there is a high level of employment without inflation or deflation, **economic stability** exists. **Inflation** exists when the prices of goods and services rise without a corresponding increase in the production of goods and services. The demand for goods and services is greater than the supply. Under inflation, money loses much of its purchasing power. **Deflation**, the opposite of inflation, is an undesirable condition that exists when prices are falling. When there is deflation, the supply of goods and services is greater than the demand. The United States experienced severe deflation during the 1930s.

The government uses several methods to influence stability and growth in the economy. Both monetary and fiscal policies are used. **Monetary policies** involve the way the Federal Reserve Board regulates money and credit to achieve a stable and growing economy. **Fiscal policies** involve the way the federal government adjusts taxes and government spending to influence economic conditions.

Economic Security

Economic security refers to people's desire to be able to buy goods and services to at least meet their basic needs. A job is the most basic form of security for a person.

Government programs have been designed to help create economic security for disadvantaged people. Medical insurance programs for the aged and unemployment insurance and government training programs for the unemployed are examples. Aid for depressed areas and farm programs, such as price supports, are other programs.

Most people support some form of economic security. However, there is controversy over what types of government programs should be provided.

Characteristics of the United States Economy

In order to reach the goals of a particular economy, certain customs or characteristics must exist as guidelines. An understanding of the economic characteristics of the United States economy will help you analyze how the economic system is coordinated.

Right to Private Property

The right to private property refers to the right to own, use, and dispose of property in any way. As an income earner, a person must, of course, pay local, state, and federal taxes. After these taxes are paid, people can spend or save as much of their income as they wish. The portion of the income people keep is known as **private property**. They may keep it in the form of material assets,

money, or investments. The right of ownership includes productive resources as well as personal property. The abilities and talents a person has are also a part of that person's private property.

This right of property is an important basic freedom under the Constitution. The right to own property and use it in making a profit provides Americans with an incentive to establish and operate business enterprises. The way people feel about ownership is important. Maintaining and improving something they own often gives people a sense of pride. This ownership also leads people to be more efficient. If their income depends on how they use their private property, people will work harder. By working harder, they will increase their income.

Profit Motivation

Most people work to earn an income, 24-4. This is known as **profit motivation**. A motive is a reason for doing something. People are motivated to work by profits. The income earned is used to meet basic

Safeway

24-4 **A job well done often leads to promotion and higher wages.**

Brainstorming

Discuss current issues in society that indicate conflicting values. (An example would be the conflict between the importance of clean air and the convenience of automobiles.) Do you think that in some cases, a compromise could be reached? Are there issues that seem to have a clear-cut solution, yet the solution is not implemented? What might be some reasons for this?

needs to preserve life. Profits beyond those used for basic needs may be used for pleasure and comfort. These profits may be invested in securities or private property, which may be used to produce additional income. Profits may also be invested in a business. The income from a business would first be applied to the costs of running the business. The portion left over would be profit. Usually, the more efficient a business is, the greater its profits will be. Profits are also used to expand business activities. This, in turn, creates more jobs for more people.

Competition

When two businesses offer the same or similar goods or services, they are in competition. To attract consumers, they offer their products and services at prices that are lower than or comparable to other firms' prices. These businesses are said to be competitors. Competition occurs when two or more businesses act independently to attract customers. There are different degrees of competition in the United States economy. For instance, in the fast-food market, consumers have many choices. When buying a car, choices are more limited. Competition forces business firms to keep searching for more efficient practices so they

can offer better products and services at lower prices.

Competition is not desirable for some products and services. For example, it would be inefficient to have competing water lines, electrical lines, or mass transportation systems. These areas are called *natural monopolies*. A monopoly exists when there is only one seller of a product or service. In the United States, natural monopolies are under tight government regulation.

Freedom of Choice

More than 250 million people in the United States want and need many economic goods and services. Business provides most of these for the consumers. How does business know what consumers want or how much of each good or service to provide? How can business satisfy these demands at prices consumers are willing to pay? The market system of the United States economy answers most of these questions. In a **market economy** such as this, consumers have freedom of choice. Consumer choices influence what will be produced, how much will be produced, and the price that will be paid for goods and services.

The American economy functions in a circular flow of goods, services, and money. This flow is set into motion by the freedom of choice of the consumer. All people are consumers—users of goods and services. Some consumers are also producers—those who create economic goods or services. These people must provide for the needs and wants of those who are not producers.

Businesses use productive services—the labor of consumers—to help produce the goods and services that are used in the economy. Those consumers receive income in the form of salaries or wages in return for their labor. In turn, the consumers spend their income for the goods and services produced. As a result, there is a circular flow of goods and services and a circular flow of money. See 24-5. In order to function, this market economy relies upon the right to private property, profit motivation, competition, and the consumer's freedom of choice. Producers strive to make a profit in goods produced to meet the demands of the consumer. Through their spending habits, consumers are a powerful influence on what goods and services will be produced.

Values and Consumer Decision Making

Making logically consistent decisions without considering your values is difficult. Decisions about what to buy, when to buy, and whether to spend or save are all based on values. Recognizing the importance of values and working to clarify them is an important step toward making more effective consumer decisions.

Many values are transmitted, often unconsciously, by the family. Your religion, customs, traditions, and ethnic or cultural influences will affect your values. Peer groups also have a strong influence on values, particularly during adolescence and young adulthood. See 24-6. Sometimes considering the source of your values can help you analyze them and decide on their importance.

Considering the values of other consumers may be helpful to you as a consumer. This complex society is made up of a variety of people with very different values. Choices in consumer goods that may appear strange to you may actually be quite rational based on another person's values. That consumer with the "strange taste" may have an important influence on choices available to you. Every consumer's choice is like a vote in the marketplace.

Consumer decisions are based on values. When you cast a vote by making a purchase, you need to be sure that purchase is based on your values. The more accurately a person perceives his or her values, the easier it will be to make consumer choices.

Goals and Consumer Decision Making

Values are rather abstract, and for this reason they are difficult to use in planning. However, goals are more specific and are based on values. Goals give you direction—something specific toward which to work.

$ Income Payments (Wages) $

Productive Services (Labor)

Circular Flow of the American Economy

Businesses

Consumers

Goods and Services

$ Consumer Spending $

24-5 Goods, services, and money move in a circular flow in the American economy.

Schrader

24-6 Many teens feel a sports car will give them status with their peers.

As a young person, you may value economic independence. Two goals based on that value are to get a job or work toward a college degree.

Consumer goals are not usually difficult to develop because most consumers have many needs and wants. Prioritizing the goals would be the difficult step. This step would require deciding which goals are most important. Consumer goals usually depend on the resources available.

Resources and Consumer Decision Making

Money is the resource most often used for obtaining consumer goods and services. However, other resources can be used as a substitute for money. Gardening rather than buying vegetables is an example of substituting time and skill for money to get the same type of product.

Skills can be valuable consumer resources. The ability to be a creative cook, repair household equipment, do simple maintenance tasks on your car, and have basic building skills are valuable resources.

In today's rapidly changing world, knowing how to obtain consumer information about a specific product is a valuable resource. Products are constantly being changed and approved. Finding up-to-date information about the latest product is important for the consumer.

The Family's Influence on Consumer Decision Making

Changes in the family as an institution, standards of living, and roles of individual family members have affected consumer decision making and spending patterns. High inflation has made it difficult for some families to reach economic goals. To cope with this problem, more women are working outside the home. In some cases, having two salaries helps raise a family's standard of living.

For a person who lives alone, setting financial goals and making consumer decisions is challenging. This process is even more challenging in families because many of the consumer decisions are made jointly.

Family spending patterns vary according to family composition, the stage in the family life cycle, family income level, the number of family members who work, and values and goals of family members. See 24-7.

The Family Life Cycle

Financial goals, spending patterns, and resources available depend somewhat upon the stage in the family life cycle and the composition of the family. In the beginning stage, as a newly formed family, the young couple develops goals related to career, income, family composition, and standard of living. Many decisions young couples make will affect family income. For

24-7 A couple must work together to determine spending patterns.

example, whether both will work and when and if they will have children will affect their income and standard of living. Their goals related to standard of living will greatly affect the amount of income left once material items have been purchased.

In the past, having children was considered an essential part of marriage. However, today many young couples strongly weigh their options about parenthood. Having children is a long-term commitment that includes a great economic obligation.

During the expanding stage, resources must cover both the parents' needs and the needs of the children. For many families at the low- or moderate-income level, this stage puts heavy demands on the budget. Many of these families have only one income when the children are very young. If the family size grows, need for food, shelter, and medical care increases. For many families, this period involves setting priorities and reducing spending in areas such as clothing and recreation. See 24-8.

The developing stage of the family may vary greatly depending on the size of the family and the spread in ages of the children. Some families reach a certain financial goal, perhaps the final payment on a home or a certain career goal. The costs related to raising children are quite high during this period. Food and clothing costs can be high for adolescents in the family. Paying for children's education or vocational training is a great expense. This may make budgeting a challenge even though the family may be at the peak of their earnings. A way to get some financial relief is to have teenagers work part-time and assume some of their own expenses.

Families gain new financial stability in the contracting or launching stage as children reach adulthood and can support themselves. For many people, financial stability during this period and into retirement depends on whether or not they began planning for later years and retirement earlier in life. People who plan for

24-8 It may be challenging to stretch financial resources so the needs of children and parents are met. Items such as food and clothing are a higher priority than toys.

retirement will have more time together and more money to spend after their children leave home.

Spending patterns often change during the later years or the aging stage, after retirement, particularly for people who have a fixed income. After retirement, spending needs to be planned carefully, especially in times of inflation. People who have planned for retirement earlier in life may have income from pension plans, social security, and investments. For these people, retirement is a time to relax and enjoy hobbies, travel, and other recreational activities.

The later years often pose a special problem for women. Many women spend their last years living alone on a poverty-level income. There are several reasons for this. Men have a shorter life expectancy than women, and husbands are often older than their wives. In addition, widowers who remarry usually marry younger women. Women should anticipate this problem and plan ahead to ease these financial difficulties.

Special Family Situations

The high divorce rate affects income and consumer decisions. Although changes in the law have reduced legal costs and court costs, divorce is still costly both financially and emotionally.

Children of divorce often receive child support from a parent. That parent often also supports a second family who must do without some of their income because of the child support payments. In reality, many people do not receive their child support payments even though they have been required by the courts.

Divorce often means the loss of a wage earner in a family. As a result, the family's standard of living may decrease, and they may have to establish a different household. Single parents often experience increasing expenses, and many of them are living below the poverty level. Most of these households are headed by women.

The career a person chooses is a major factor determining his or her standard of living. Generally, the more education you have, the higher your salary will be and the greater your job security is. Family income has increased because most women are employed outside the home. Along with the additional income from a two-income family come decisions to make. Two-career families often have the challenge of child care decisions, 24-9. Decisions about job advancement can also be challenging. Job promotion may mean a transfer, which could be a poor career move for the other person.

24-9 **Parents who have children as well as a career are faced with many choices.**

In every family, regardless of size, there will be conflicting values and economic goals that differ. It is important for families to set priorities to reach the most important goals. Conflicts will arise between family members when deciding on priorities. However, effective decision making is more likely when family members communicate openly while being sensitive to the needs and desires of others.

The Decision-Making Process in Consumer Choices

Making a choice is a problem in today's society because there are so many alternatives. Consumers are literally overwhelmed by the many goods and services available.

Although some decisions do not require a great deal of thought, consumers are usually more satisfied when they think and plan before they buy. Most consumer problems result from poorly made decisions based on insufficient or inaccurate information. See 24-10.

Rational decisions are choices that result from the process of decision making. You can learn how to make rational consumer decisions by using the decision-making process. You must use this skill regularly to learn it well.

Define the Problem

Even when a problem is obvious, the wise consumer gives careful thought to its definition. Consumers need to think broadly about their problems. Instead, they often think of their needs in terms of a particular product. For instance, when Joe got a job on the other side of town, he immediately decided he needed to buy a car. However, if Joe thought more broadly about the problem, he would realize that he really needed some type of transportation to his workplace. Using mass transportation might be an alternative to the car.

A helpful step in consumer decision making is to state the problem in terms of a goal. Joe's problem was to find a car. His goal could be to find some type of transportation to his workplace. Changing the problem into a goal not only helps clarify the problem, but also gives direction when choosing alternatives. A goal often forces the consumer to deal with values and set priorities. Joe might like to have a car. He values the ease of getting around, comfort, and prestige that might go with owning a car. Joe also values his job because of the money and security it brings him. By stating that his goal is to find some type of transportation to his workplace, Joe is indicating his values. Getting to his job is more important to Joe than having a car.

24-10 **Planning ahead can help you make a decision when you are faced with many alternatives in the store.**

Choose Possible Alternatives

Buying decisions are based on values, goals, and resources. Your consumer choices strongly affect your life. If you carefully consider your real reasons for wanting certain things, you are more likely to make a good choice.

The importance and complexity of a consumer problem will affect the amount of time you use to consider alternatives. The problem of selecting a new washing machine will require more research than selecting new drinking glasses for the kitchen.

In any case, consumers should consider how their values and resources might limit their alternatives. Certain alternatives may not be possible because they are out of range financially. Other alternatives may not be considered because they have features the consumer does not value.

How knowledgeable a consumer is will affect the quality of the alternatives selected and the decision made. The person who understands the many features found on a washing machine and their functions will be more likely to make a wise decision. The person who knows little about what is available and has had limited experience in using such an appliance will probably have difficulty choosing possible alternatives.

Joe, whose goal is to find some type of transportation to his workplace, might decide his alternatives are a car, motorcycle, moped, bicycle, carpool, or mass transportation. However, some of these may not be suitable alternatives. For instance, with his limited income, he could find it difficult to cover all the expenses associated with buying a car. Loan payments, even with a used car, would be challenging for him. Then there would be the additional costs that come with owning a car such as the cost of registration, license fee, insurance, repairs, maintenance, and gas. He would like to be able to save toward buying a car within a year or so, but at this time he feels it is not a suitable alternative for him. The motorcycle also would not be a suitable alternative for the same reasons. In considering mass transportation, Joe could use the city bus lines; however, there are no trains in his town.

Finding suitable alternatives in consumer decision making often takes time and research. Many resources are available to help you get information on specific consumer products. See 24-11. Using these resources will help you develop suitable alternatives for decision making.

Use the computer both to become a more informed consumer and to buy specific items. Millions of people are now shopping regularly from the convenience of their computers. **E-commerce** or shopping online, can save time and money. Many

24-11 **Taking the time to search for product information often helps you make a better choice.**

retailers have Web sites that give you an opportunity to comparison shop to find the best price. If Web site addresses are unknown, a search engine can be used to find possible sites.

Weigh the Costs and Benefits of Each Alternative to Find the Best Choice

Most alternatives have both advantages and disadvantages. Certain product or service features make an alternative desirable, and some product or service consequences may be considered disadvantages. These may be such things as the amount of money involved in the purchase or the amount of time involved in the use of the product.

For many decisions, it might be helpful to make a chart listing costs and benefits of each of the alternatives. Although you can do this mentally, you will probably be surer of your decision if you've written this information. Having the information in black and white makes it easier to weigh the facts and choose the best alternative.

The alternatives Joe is considering for his method of transportation to work are a moped, bicycle, carpool, or bus. A list of costs and benefits of each alternative may be helpful to him in making a final choice. See 24-12.

Evaluate the Choice and Review the Process

Evaluating a consumer decision can be helpful in making other decisions whether the decision was a good one or a poor one. Identifying which step of the process may have led to a poor decision is helpful. Then you can work on improving that particular phase of a decision-making skill. The wise consumer uses evaluation to gain information that will help perfect decision-making skills.

Transportation Choices		
Forms of Transportation	**Advantages**	**Disadvantages**
Moped	• Less expensive than a car or motorcycle • Appropriate for traveling short distances • Better mileage than a car	• Not desirable in climates with frequent rain or snow • Safety is a factor
Bicycle	• Least expensive of two-wheel vehicles • Inexpensive to operate—no fuel costs • Inexpensive to maintain and repair	• Requires human energy • Not desirable in climates with frequent rain and snow • Safety is a factor
Carpool	• Economical • Reduces traffic congestion • Minimizes parking problems • Offers companionship	• Inconvenience—allows little flexibility since needs of all must be considered • Doesn't answer transportation needs outside of carpool
Bus	• Convenient • Less worry than owning other vehicles • Overall cost is less	• Schedule must be adjusted to bus schedule • Getting to and from bus to home during bad weather

24-12 In applying the decision-making process to transportation choices, the advantages and disadvantages among your alternatives must be weighed carefully.

Summary

Consumer decision-making skills and knowledge of the factors that affect consumer decision making are valuable resources. In the United States, the combined choices of many consumers can strongly influence the economy. Knowing the goals and characteristics of the national economic system will help you understand how the economy functions.

Your values, goals, and resources strongly influence your consumer decisions. Your decisions will also be influenced by factors related to your family. These include your family's values, size, and income, and the number of family members working outside the home.

The decision-making process is a valuable resource for making consumer decisions.

To Review

1. Describe economics and explain the type of economic system that exists in the United States.
2. True or false.
   A. The American economic system is completely free.
   B. Freedom, efficiency, growth, stability, and security are goals of the American economy.
   C. A high level of employment is a characteristic of economic stability.
3. What is an advantage of competition to the economy?
4. Why are goals important to consumer decision making?
5. List stages of the family life cycle and give one economic characteristic of each stage.
6. What mistake do many consumers make when defining a consumer problem?
7. How is writing advantages and disadvantages, costs, and benefits helpful in decision making?
8. _____ and _____ limit the consumer's alternatives when making decisions.
9. Finding suitable alternatives for making decisions often takes _____ and _____.
10. Explain how gaining knowledge can aid consumers in decision making, especially if they have limited experience.

To Do with the Class

1. Invite a qualified person to speak to your class on the American economic system, inflation, and deflation. Discuss what consumers can do to help reduce inflationary pressures in the economy.
2. Discuss why competition is not desirable in some areas of business, such as certain utilities.
3. Discuss the family as a resource. What special tasks or services do family members sometimes perform to increase the economic well-being of the entire family?
4. Brainstorm a list of financial needs that often occur at certain stages of the family life cycle.

To Challenge Your Thinking

1. Develop a bulletin board or poster comparing different economic systems. List the advantages and disadvantages of a free enterprise system.
2. Develop a personal economic goal that relates to each national economic goal. Share your ideas with the class.
3. Make a list of your recent purchases and decide if they reflect your personal values.
4. Develop three case studies that illustrate conflict of values of family members in relation to consumer decision making.

To Do with Your Community

1. Invite local business owners to share their views on the role of business in meeting consumer needs.
2. Contact a local co-op, such as food or babysitting co-ops, to speak on barter, trade, and exchange of time for goods and services.
3. Consider what decisions families in your community make on a weekly, monthly, or yearly basis. Where do they go for answers? What community resources are utilized?
4. Select several businesses that offer services. Determine how these are vital to the local economy and in meeting family needs.

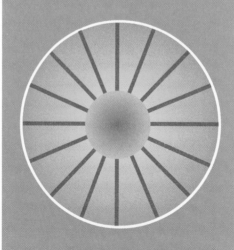

The decision-making process can help you make minor and major consumer decisions.

Part Eight
Managing Food

Chapter 25
Meal Management—Planning and Shopping
By planning in advance, you can save time in food shopping and preparation. Timesaving alternatives such as special equipment and convenience foods can be valuable resources.

Chapter 26
Meal Preparation
You can prepare a meal more efficiently by organizing your workspace and supplies. Selecting the best cooking method for a food can help you retain the food's nutrients.

25

Meal Management— Planning and Shopping

To Know

seasonal foods
promotions
extenders
convenience foods
finished foods
semiprepared foods
comparison shopping
warehouse stores
specialty stores
food cooperatives
national brands
house brands
economy brands
generics
unit pricing

Objectives

After studying this chapter, you will be able to

◇ recognize resources valuable to efficient meal management.

◇ describe guidelines in meal planning.

◇ demonstrate skills in time management leading to efficient planning and shopping.

◇ recognize advantages and disadvantages of shopping at different types of food stores.

◇ relate the choice of brands to intended use.

◇ explain ways to avoid wasting food.

People spend varying amounts on food. This depends on income; family size; lifestyle; available time and energy; and skill in management, shopping, and food preparation.

The amount you spend on food does not necessarily indicate the quality of your meals. With careful planning and preparation, you can create meals superior in quality to those made with more expensive foods. See 25-1.

The key to efficient meal management is in planning ahead and using time management skills. The less time you have for meal preparation, the more important it is to plan ahead.

The United States Department of Agriculture and the Food and Drug Administration have developed many materials to help plan meals to meet budgets. These publications are available through the United States Government Printing Office. The federal government offers programs to increase the purchasing power of people with limited incomes. One of these is the food stamp program. Food stamps can be used to buy most foods and to purchase plants and seeds for gardens.

Guidelines in Meal Planning

Planning meals on a limited budget is a challenge that requires skill in planning and purchasing foods. When you skillfully prepare and store foods, you help assure quality and minimize food waste.

To stay on a budget, careful planning and organization are a must. Planning does not take a lot of time when you have a well-organized, established routine. Thinking ahead and planning meals carefully pays off in the end. In other words, you benefit from managing meal planning effectively.

A variety of ideas can help you plan meals to meet a food budget yet satisfy family members. For example, you might expand your food choices and take advantage of advertisements and special sales. Using the main dish as a basis for your plans is an efficient approach. A shopping list based on planned menus simplifies shopping and helps you stick to the budget. You can always find recipes on the Internet to help you plan.

Expand Food Choices

Your choice of food specials may be limited if you stick to the same pattern of foods week after week. Look for new recipe ideas and try new foods if they are within your budget. See 25-2. The next time you go to the supermarket, look carefully. Note foods you have never tried and check prices to see if they would fit your budget.

Many cookbooks are available in the stores or in the local library. Many of these provide low-cost, nutritionally sound meal ideas. Daily newspapers are another good

25-1 **Many families make a conscious effort to be wise consumers when buying food products.**

25-2 **These shish kebabs are an interesting and appetizing main dish.**

Use Weekly Advertisements

Each week, newspapers advertise food specials in various stores. Using these specials, particularly meat specials, to plan meals can help you limit food costs.

When there are good meat specials, you may want to buy in quantity. Planning ahead and freezing meat for the coming weeks can be economical. Cutting your own meat can help you save money. See 25-3. Instead of buying stew meat, you might buy a large roast on sale. You could cut the roast

source of inexpensive recipes. Collect new ideas from these resources and keep them in a handy spot where you can use them to plan meals.

Look for new ways to use and prepare familiar foods. For instance, you can save money on your milk bill by using nonfat dry milk in a box. Buying this milk in individual packets is more expensive. Some people feel dry milk is more appealing when mixed with equal parts of liquid milk. Some families prefer to use dry milk for cooking and fresh milk for drinking.

Friends can also be an excellent source of new food ideas. Discussing their favorite snacks and meals may give you some new ideas.

Home gardening offers another way to expand your food choices. Many Americans have returned to gardening and home canning, freezing, and preserving foods. Doing this yourself not only helps the budget, but also gives you a sense of satisfaction.

National Cattlemen's Beef Association

25-3 **Keep reasonable serving portions in mind when selecting meat. A few slices of meat rather than an entire steak may be enough to satisfy a person's appetite.**

yourself and use it in various ways, including for stew. Buying poultry whole is also more economical. You can then cut it up according to how you are going to use it. For instance, you might freeze the meaty pieces for later use. The bony pieces might be used for soup or a hot dish like chicken and noodles.

Roasts with the bone removed are usually higher in price than those with the bones. The bone should not be considered waste unless it is unusually large in proportion to the meat. Since bones contain calcium, they add food value to soup stock.

Advertisements often include special prices for meats, canned foods, frozen foods, and produce. To evaluate each advertised special in terms of savings, you would need to know the item's regular price. If you cannot remember prices, you may want to keep a notebook listing the prices of items you often use. It is important to realize that not all foods listed in advertisements have special prices. Some items are listed at their regular prices. Understanding the following terms can help you recognize a good sale.

- **Seasonal foods**. Many items have a peak season during the year. At that time, the price is reduced because the supply is greater than the demand. You can recognize these items by comparing advertisements to see which items are featured at the same time by many stores. See 25-4.

- **Promotions**. Special promotions by major brand companies give that brand a temporary price advantage over the others. For instance, the advertisement might feature a company's full line of products at a special price. It is wise to compare prices carefully because not all items are good buys.

Many stores, newspapers, and magazines offer coupons that can help reduce food costs. Never use coupons to buy items

25-4 **Many fruits and vegetables are less expensive when they are in season.**

you don't want or wouldn't ordinarily buy. If you see a coupon you would like to use, clip it and save it. Coupons are usually valid for several months. As you plan your meals, you can look through the coupons to see which ones might fit into your meal plans.

When the prices of advertised specials are quite low, you may want to buy in quantity. You will first want to consider your budget, needs, storage space, and the storage life of the item on sale. Stocking up on items like this can yield quite a savings.

Plan Around the Main Dish

A large share of the food dollar goes toward the preparation of the main dish. Thrifty planners look for ways to cut the cost of this expensive part of the meal.

One way to cut the cost is to use advertised specials for the main dish. Another way is to make a main dish that combines meat with less costly food mixtures, sometimes called **extenders**. Extenders include macaroni, spaghetti, rice, potatoes, and bread. See 25-5. Soups are another way of extending the meat in a main dish.

You can limit costs for a light meal by eating leftovers from a heavier meal or a nonmeat protein food. For lunch you might reheat some spaghetti, or eat hard cooked eggs or a peanut butter sandwich. Some leftovers can just be reheated, but others require some additional preparation. You might add a sauce to extend some meat or make a dish more appetizing. Leftover chicken might be added to a white sauce to prepare creamed chicken on pasta or biscuits.

Use a Shopping List

Make your shopping list based on the meals you have planned for the week or another convenient period of time. Most people who want to cut food costs find shopping on a weekly basis works very well. Having a complete shopping list makes shopping simpler. A list also helps you avoid impulse buying, which adds to food costs.

Use the Internet

The Internet is a useful source of information and recipes for use in planning family meals. Many Web sites contain recipes, nutritional information, cooking hints, and storage tips. See 25-6. These sites can be found through searches for food-related words or phrases. You can plan an entire meal by accessing recipes for appetizers, main dishes, side dishes, desserts, and snacks.

Using a search engine, try searching for a specific recipe, cooking method, or

25-5 Sausage and rice can be the basis for an economical and tasty dish.

Recipe Web Sites
allrecipes.com
bettycrocker.com
cooksrecipes.com
epicurious.com
foodtv.com
foods.com
ichef.com
meals.com
mealsforyou.com
recipesource.com

25-6 Try visiting these Web sites to find recipes you've never tried before.

ingredient. Many Web sites give information related to holiday or seasonal foods. Some sites may highlight ethnic recipes and regional cooking. Foods for special diets, such as vegetarian, low-calorie, and low fat recipes, can also be found quickly using the Internet. Some sites offer additional entertaining suggestions. Many companies' Web sites promote recipes that use their brand name food products. Most food and gourmet magazines have their own sites. Photos and step-by-step directions can be especially helpful when you are trying a new recipe.

Some sites contain recipes and food information for all ages. Areas of a site intended for children might include easy, nutritional snack recipes. You can spend a great deal of time and learn a lot about cooking and recipes by navigating the Internet.

Time Management in Meal Planning

To plan meals efficiently, decide on meals for a period of time, perhaps one or two weeks. Doing this helps you organize plans for meal preparation. Advance planning saves time in shopping. A variety of resources are available to help you plan meals more efficiently.

A Place to Plan

Ideally, every kitchen would have a desk where planning could be done. This planning area would include drawers and shelves for storing recipe ideas, cookbooks, coupons, and other record-keeping materials related to meal management. However, the kitchen table or any other seating space in the kitchen is a suitable place for planning. You can plan meals more efficiently by using cookbooks, weekly food ads, and coupons as resources.

Storing records so they are easily accessible for meal planning is also important.

A bulletin board is a handy resource that may be used for many purposes. You might post your running list for shopping, coupons, recipe ideas, and grocery ads on the bulletin board. A file folder or box could be used to hold meal or recipe ideas for future use. Watch for ideas for new food dishes that require little preparation time. Casseroles, stews, soups, and other one-dish meals that combine meat with vegetables are often timesaving recipes.

Use Meal Patterns in Planning

Meal planning may go more quickly if you use meal patterns, 25-7. Instead of thinking "What different foods will I plan for dinner on Monday?" use the dinner meal pattern as a resource. Start by deciding on the main dish (the protein food). After making that decision, choose the vegetable, salad, bread, or beverage depending on how heavy the meal is.

25-7 **At lunchtime, sandwiches often serve as the main dish or protein food.**

Making a chart for this is helpful to the inexperienced meal planner. A chart helps avoid repeating the same foods and encourages variety.

Plan to Use Timesaving Equipment

Many homes have a variety of time-saving equipment such as blenders, slow cookers, mixers, and food processors. The microwave oven has become a common appliance. It is an outstanding timesaving appliance in cooking, reheating, and thawing foods. However, the conventional oven can also help you save time. For instance, while the main dish is baking, you can prepare the rest of the meal. With careful planning you can even use the oven for a full meal.

Having an appliance in the kitchen is no guarantee it will save time. Whether you save time depends on how well you use the appliance. When you purchase a major or small appliance, you receive an instruction book that explains how to use the appliance. Recipes and other cooking ideas are often included in this book. These ideas can help you plan meals and use the appliance to its fullest potential. The blender is a good example. Blenders can be used in a variety of ways that save time in meal preparation. However, many people use them only for drinks such as milk shakes.

The blender's instruction booklet includes recipes for sandwich spreads, soups, quick breads, main dishes, and other foods to prepare in the blender. Using these recipes can save time and help you make the most of the blender. See 25-8.

Whether you have a separate freezer or use the freezer compartment in the refrigerator, freezer space is a helpful resource. Having frozen foods on hand is a time-saving convenience.

25-8 **Small appliances can help you prepare nutritious meals and snacks quickly and easily.**

Plan to Use Convenience Foods

Using convenience foods can reduce your food preparation time. **Convenience foods** have had a service added to them. They are either fully or partially prepared at the time you purchase them. Convenience foods that are ready to eat immediately or after heating or thawing them are called **finished foods**. Snack mixes, cold cuts, soups, canned vegetables, and many frozen foods are examples. Convenience foods that require you to perform some additional service are **semiprepared foods**. Cake and cookie mixes that require you to add other ingredients are examples of semiprepared foods.

You can find an abundance of convenience foods in the stores. Most convenience foods are more expensive than the same food prepared from scratch. For many people, though, the time saved is worth the difference in cost.

Plan for Advanced Preparation

As you plan meals, include some foods you can prepare ahead of time. This will help you on a busy day. Advanced preparation might mean fixing food on the weekend to use during the week. This food is usually frozen or refrigerated until needed. You can prepare some food products in large quantity and freeze them. These foods can be used for a meal the next week, or for some other meal in the future. Spaghetti sauce is a good food to prepare in large quantities. By dividing it into portions and freezing it, you can be ready for several future meals. See 25-9.

Advanced preparation may involve only partially preparing a certain dish. For example, you might stew a chicken over the

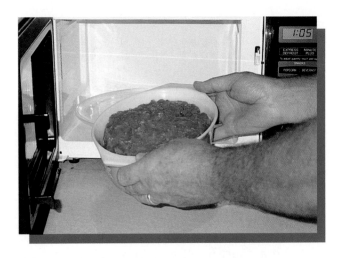

25-9 **Spaghetti and sauce that has been frozen can be quickly reheated when it is needed.**

weekend to use in a main dish during the week. The chicken could be refrigerated or frozen depending on how soon you would use it. You might brown ground beef with some onions or other seasonings. Then you could refrigerate or freeze it to serve in a main dish later in the week. Advanced preparation allows you to quickly fix a meal that would otherwise be much more time-consuming.

Shopping Skills

The next step toward efficient meal planning is the shopping. Good shopping habits are important if you want to limit the money you spend on food. You can develop comparison shopping skills to help you gain the most value from your food dollar. **Comparison shopping** involves looking at different brands or models of the same or similar products in several stores to compare prices, features, and store services.

Shopping can be done most efficiently by using a well-prepared shopping list and timesaving skills while shopping.

*Getting*Involved

A Well-Prepared Shopping List

A complete shopping list is a valuable resource that saves time by helping you avoid extra trips to buy food. A complete list is a combination of the items you need for the meals you are planning and items from a running list. You use a running list to jot down items as you notice the need for them. For instance, you might notice that the salt is almost gone as you are refilling the saltshaker. You would put it on the running list, which usually consists of many staple items such as flour, sugar, paper towels, and napkins. See 25-10.

A variety of resources can help you prepare the shopping list. One of these resources is a chart indicting can sizes and quantity. Such a chart is useful when a recipe indicates only quantity needed. Fortunately, many canned foods now list their quantities in cup amounts.

An equivalent chart is another helpful resource when food quantities are listed differently from the way you will purchase them. For instance, a recipe may call for three cups of cooked rice. An equivalent chart would indicate how much long-cooking or quick-cooking rice you would need. Many basic cookbooks list both the can size chart and the equivalents chart. They may also include other information that will help you develop a shopping list.

Detail may be the difference between a well-prepared shopping list and one that is poorly prepared. As you list food products to be purchased, be sure to include a

Mike Deatherage

25-10 Keeping the grocery list in a special place in the kitchen makes it convenient for family members to add to the list.

complete description. If a salad recipe calls for crushed pineapple, don't just write pineapple. When you are at the store, you may not be able to remember what form of a food you need. Because you can purchase foods in so many different forms today, it is important to clarify exactly which form of the product you need.

Your shopping will be more efficient if your list is made in the order the foods occur in the store. If you are not familiar with the store, you could list foods under their general categories. Some examples are frozen foods, meat, produce, canned goods, paper products, cleaning and laundry products, and bakery items.

Attach any coupons to your shopping list. As you clip the coupons, circle the expiration date. This will serve as a reminder to you and will also save time at the checkout counter.

Saving Time in Shopping

How efficiently you shop depends on the store's location and layout, time of day, and day of the week.

The location of the store is important only if it is a priority. If a budget is your top priority, you may be willing to travel farther for greater dollar savings. However, keep in mind that if you are driving, it also costs money to buy the gasoline to travel. The money you save shopping may be spent on the gas it takes to get there.

Most stores are arranged in a logical order. Once you become familiar with this order, use it to develop your shopping list. This will make shopping more efficient.

If time is a priority, experience will help you decide the best time to shop. Stores are usually crowded later in the week and on weekends. Because many supermarkets have expanded their hours, you can choose to shop when the stores are not crowded.

Where to Shop

A customer's loyalty is valuable in the grocery business. Competition is intense, and different stores use many methods to win the customer.

Food is sold in a variety of stores—supermarkets, neighborhood grocery stores, warehouse stores, specialty stores, and food cooperatives. A supermarket usually offers the greatest overall selection of items. Supermarkets may be large, independent stores or part of a national or regional chain.

Smaller independent neighborhood stores often have trouble competing with large chain stores. They serve loyal local customers who care more about convenience than price. See 25-11.

25-11 **An independent neighborhood store succeeds by building a loyal customer base.**

Small markets feature products that may be locally produced. These items may be fresher and cheaper than those at a supermarket.

Warehouse stores are able to reduce prices by cutting their overhead costs. Warehouse stores include most departments found in supermarkets, but they may offer a reduced selection of brands and sizes. In some warehouse stores, customers are expected to pack their own purchases.

Specialty stores feature specific types of products. Health food stores, cheese shops, butcher shops, and bakeries are examples. The advantage of shopping in a specialty store is you can get more variety in that type of product than at other stores. Specialty stores are generally more expensive than supermarkets, but you may occasionally find a bargain.

Food cooperatives provide a way to save money. They are a group of people who have enough buying power to buy directly from the wholesaler. The members trade work for savings. They profit from buying directly and save the additional money that would have gone to the middleman. Cooperative members are involved in telephoning, taking orders, picking up and delivering groceries, and dividing and repacking bulk orders. Although many cooperatives are developing, they are found mostly in larger cities.

Online shopping for food and other grocery items has become more popular and convenient. People can select grocery items online, pay with debit or credit cards, and then their order is delivered. This way, they shop without even leaving their homes. Working parents, busy professionals, and older people may find this option especially convenient. More stores and food companies will offer this option as time goes on.

Each type of food store has certain advantages and disadvantages. You shop at the store or stores that best meet your needs. Shopping at several places can be expensive in terms of transportation and time costs. Be sure to consider this if you are on a limited budget.

Which Brands?

Deciding which brands are best for you can be challenging. This process becomes easier when you know the categories of brands: national name brands, house brands, economy brands, and generics. Each of the four categories has definite advantages and disadvantages.

National brands are quality products that are widely advertised across the country. They are generally the most expensive products on the market.

House brands or store brands are processed to be distributed by a supermarket chain, an association of independent stores, or other stores with numerous outlets. The top store brand compares in taste and texture to national brands but may be 10 to 20 percent lower in price. Some house brands or store brands are easy to identify because they carry the name of the store. However, large supermarket chains may carry a number of house brands that vary in quality and price.

Economy brands are a form of house brand distributed by many large supermarket chains. Their quality is slightly lower than house and national brands, and they sell for about 25 percent below national brand prices.

Generics are being carried by more food stores. Generic products have plain labels with bold black letters that state the name of the product. Although the price of generics can be much lower, the quality could be well below national brand level. Since no consistent standards are used, the quality of a product may vary from one purchase to the next.

Choosing wisely from the available brands can mean a substantial savings. Remember that the least expensive brand is not necessarily the best product for your needs. First, consider how you intend to use the food and then choose accordingly. If you want to have sliced fruit and a cookie for dessert, you might purchase a house brand. This would give you quality at less expense than a name brand. If you plan to use the fruit in a blender drink instead, you could consider buying a less-expensive and lower-quality choice. An economy or generic brand might be suitable. See 25-12.

Unit Pricing Information

Unit pricing is an important consumer aid. It tells what a product costs per standard unit, such as per pound or per quart. The unit pricing tag is usually located on the edge of the shelf near the product. The left side of the unit price tag lists the unit price: price per pound, quart, dozen, or other measurement. The right side of the tag lists the name, weight, and price of the item.

Unit pricing helps clear up confusion caused by different sizes of packages and cans. This information makes comparison shopping easier since the computing is done for you by the store.

There are certain cautions to remember when taking advantage of unit pricing. Be sure you are looking at comparable items. For instance, a heat-and-serve soup should not be compared with a condensed soup to which you would add water. Products such as paper napkins, paper towels, and toilet tissue may be challenging to compare. Although unit pricing is often stated in terms of a quantity such as price per hundred, some brands may have larger sizes, double thickness, or other variations.

In spite of a few challenges, unit pricing is a valuable aid. If you shop at a store that does not have unit pricing, discuss its value with the manager.

Emergency Situations

No matter where you live, extreme weather conditions can occur. Severe conditions such as snowstorms, hurricanes, or tornadoes can leave people without electricity or a means of preparing or refrigerating food. This is why it's a good idea to stock an emergency food shelf with nonperishable items such as crackers, canned fruits, canned milk, and peanut butter. It would also be wise to have bottled water in case electricity is lost and the water pump does not function.

Another emergency situation might include sickness, such as the flu. When people are recovering from such an illness, doctors recommend a bland diet. Having crackers, clear soups, rice, gelatin, and tea on hand is helpful for such occasions. See 25-13.

Mark Hayward

25-12 **For making a stew or soup, generic or house brand tomatoes would work just as well as a national name brand.**

25-13 **Having soup and crackers on hand will be convenient when family members are ill.**

Avoiding Waste

Avoiding waste is an obvious way to save money. You may have heard the food waste in the United States could feed whole nations. Although eliminating waste is a difficult problem to solve nationwide, it is somewhat easier in the single home. Having less waste gives you more food and a budget savings.

You can begin to eliminate waste by identifying how waste occurs. Once you find the causes of waste you can move toward a solution.

Waste Through Methods of Storage

Waste is sometimes caused by improper storage of food after it is purchased. Meat and poultry should be frozen or stored in the coldest part of the refrigerator. Vegetables that will be eaten raw keep best stored in an airtight container. Most refrigerators have compartments or crisper drawers that can be used to store vegetables and fruits.

Fruits and vegetables stay at their peak longer if you do not wash them until just before they are used. (Moisture left on vegetables and fruits promotes mold and rot.) Eggs keep better when refrigerated in their original carton rather than in the open egg tray in the refrigerator.

Any food that goes into the freezer should be well wrapped and labeled. You may want to indicate the size or weight and date on some foods.

Bread stays fresh stored in its original wrapper at room temperature. However, in hot and humid weather, breads may be stored in the refrigerator to prevent the formation of mold. Cereals and crackers should be stored in tightly closed containers to keep out moisture. Common household insects are attracted to cereal, crackers, flour, herbs, and spices. This is an important reason to keep these items in tightly closed containers.

Waste at the Table

Food left on the plate is a problem in many families for various reasons, 25-14. The first step toward saving money would be to identify the cause and work toward a solution.

Having a permissive or noncaring attitude toward food waste may be the cause. This problem builds over a long period of time with food habits that begin

White Consolidated Industries

25-14 Some food waste at the table may be the result of too much snacking between meals.

early in childhood. If waste is ignored, the child grows up being unconcerned about food waste.

The way the food is served may be another cause of waste. If someone is putting the food on the plates, the portions may be too large. This problem may be eliminated by serving the food family style. The food is set on the table and each person can take as much food as they want. If no one takes more food than he or she can eat, food waste will be minimal.

Leftover Waste

People too often place leftover foods in the refrigerator, forget them, and waste them. Leftovers are easy to overlook if you store them in opaque containers without labels. Losing these foods is also easy if your refrigerator tends to be very full.

You can avoid these problems by storing foods in clear glass or plastic containers so you can see the contents. Organizing your refrigerator storage is a good idea. You might do this by placing leftover containers in a certain section of the refrigerator. You will also have less waste if you make a regular effort to include leftovers in meal plans.

Some environmentally conscious families use leftover food waste to make compost piles. Food waste can be simply dumped in a pile or put into a compost container similar to a large garbage can. As the food decomposes, new nutrient-rich soil is formed. This soil can then be used in gardens or flowerbeds.

Summary

Many resources are available to help cut the cost of food for the family. Understanding the importance of expanding food choices can be very helpful. Using advertisements and special sales will help cut costs.

Time management techniques can be very helpful in meal planning. Having a place to plan; using meal patterns, timesaving equipment, and convenience foods; and preparing foods ahead of time are all time management tips.

Developing shopping skills will help you get the most value from your food dollar and save shopping time. Your selection of food stores and products within those stores will greatly affect the amount you spend. Use of resources within the stores, such as unit pricing, can be helpful to you.

Avoiding waste is a way to save money. If you identify how food waste occurs, you can plan to eliminate those food problems.

To Review

1. List four ways you could expand your food choices.
2. Describe four factors to consider before buying large quantities of an advertised special.
3. List four examples of main dish extenders.
4. Describe how using a shopping list can help you meet your budget.
5. Describe five steps that can be taken to plan meals more efficiently.
6. List three types of equipment that can save time in meal preparation.
7. _____ foods are ready to eat immediately after heating or thawing, while _____ foods require you to perform some additional service.
8. List and describe the four categories of brands.
9. Describe the consumer information found on a unit pricing tag.
10. Describe three common ways food is wasted.

To Do with the Class

1. Brainstorm factors that influence the cost of foods.
2. Discuss how the following factors might influence the amount of money a family spends on food: income, family size, lifestyle, available time and energy, shopping skills, and preparation skills.
3. Gather recipes for economical meal ideas. Either display them on a bulletin board or use them to develop a booklet.
4. Find ideas for meal plans in recent magazines. As a group, analyze them from the standpoint of time management. Which meals would be quick to prepare? What ideas could you suggest to save time?

To Challenge Your Thinking

1. Conduct research on government-funded programs that help low-income families meet their food needs.
2. Compare weekly food advertisements from several stores. What are their similarities and differences? Are seasonal food products advertised?
3. Develop a dinner meal plan starting with a low-cost main dish. Include recipes. Share your meal plan with others in the class.
4. Interview five people to learn where they do their food shopping and why.

To Do with Your Community

1. Go to a supermarket or neighborhood market and make a list of foods you have never eaten. Decide which ones might be possibilities for expanding your food choices.
2. Visit a store where your family often shops for food. Find out what national brands, house brands, and economy brands the store stocks.
3. Invite an experienced cook or a butcher to speak to your class on using meats economically.
4. Invite a local grocer to share information about his or her store's services, foods, and products. The grocer might also discuss career information.

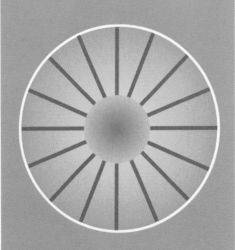

26

Meal Preparation

To Know

work centers
preparation center
cooking and serving center
cleanup center
planning center
family style service
buffet service
multitasking
dovetailing
oxidation
conduction
radiation
convection
microwave
curdle
coagulate
lactose
scorching
emulsion
emulsifying agent
leavening agent
marbling
searing
gelatinization

Objectives

After studying this chapter, you will be able to

- ◇ recognize resources valuable to efficient meal management.

- ◇ relate time management to the organization of the work area.

- ◇ develop time plans for meal preparation and describe work simplification procedures to prepare meals efficiently.

- ◇ describe procedures in food preparation that will help retain nutrients.

- ◇ explain different ways food can be heated.

- ◇ recognize the effect of cooking equipment on food preparation.

- ◇ demonstrate food preparation procedures that can help you avoid common problems.

Developing a standard definition of a good cook is difficult. To some, a good cook is an experienced cook who develops gourmet meals regularly. Others might describe a good cook as someone who develops tasty meals without even using a recipe.

Becoming a good cook takes experience. Young people who share cooking responsibilities in their homes may develop cooking skills as teenagers. Others may not develop cooking skills until they live on their own and are forced to assume this responsibility. Some people never become good cooks.

You learn cooking skills and techniques through experience. Many cookbooks and an abundance of Internet sites are available to help you become a more skillful cook. See 26-1. Cooking shows appear daily on television. These resources often contain a great deal of helpful information in addition to recipes. Using this information can help you develop skills in cooking.

Your attitude toward cooking is a major factor in determining whether or not you become a successful cook. Most people find learning to cook an enjoyable and challenging experience. Unfortunately, some people consider cooking an annoying task. Because everyone must eat to live, making food preparation an enjoyable challenge will make life more pleasant.

Efficient Meal Preparation

Management skills related to meal preparation can make the difference between whether meal preparation is a pleasant or unpleasant experience. People are very busy and are usually interested in efficient meal preparation. Pressures related

26-1 Cookbooks are a fantastic resource whether you are planning a dinner party or a meal for one.

to time management in preparation vary with each individual and family. Time management is usually a priority in single-parent families and families where both parents work outside the home.

Regardless of your family situation, developing certain skills can help you manage meal preparation time well. These skills include organizing the kitchen work area, planning time use, and simplifying procedures. See 26-2. Factors such as family size and the number of people preparing the meal also affect time management. Other important issues are the knowledge and skills of the people preparing the meals. The equipment they use and how well they are organized are also significant.

26-2 Time management skills make a person much more efficient in the kitchen.

Organize the Work Area and Equipment

Efficient organization of space and equipment in your kitchen simplifies meal preparation. This also improves time management. A well-organized kitchen is particularly important when several people share meal management responsibilities. Each person is dependent on the others to take proper care of tools and equipment. It is each person's job to put these tools back where they belong.

Work Centers

Research shows tasks related to meal preparation, serving, and cleanup are done mainly in three areas of the kitchen. These areas are referred to as **work centers**. Storing equipment and supplies you need in the appropriate work center reduces the time it takes to do tasks in that center.

- The **preparation center** includes the refrigerator, freezer, storage cabinets, and counter space for food preparation. Staple items such as flour, sugar, and seasonings are stored here. Equipment used in food preparation, such as the mixer, blender, and baking pans, is also stored in this center.

- The **cooking and serving center** is logically located around the range. The cooking and serving center also includes storage space for pots, pans, other cooking utensils, pot holders, and serving pieces. It is convenient if there is counter space on at least one side of the range if not both sides. This area can be used for ingredients and equipment you need while cooking.

- The **cleanup center** includes the sink area, dishwasher, garbage disposal, storage space for equipment, waste basket, and dishcloths and towels. It is most convenient to have the food preparation center and the cleanup

Brainstorming

Make a list of kitchen utensils and equipment that are essential for someone beginning a household. Explain why each item is important and what might happen if these items aren't available in the kitchen.

center next to each other, 26-3. Many foods such as fruits and vegetables must be washed before they can be used to prepare a food product.

◆ The kitchen might also have a fourth center— the **planning center**. This area might include a desk or some counter space, a recipe file, cookbooks, and record-keeping supplies.

You can efficiently plan a new kitchen based on these work centers. However, adapting an existing kitchen requires flexibility. You may not be able to fit all equipment and supplies into the appropriate work centers.

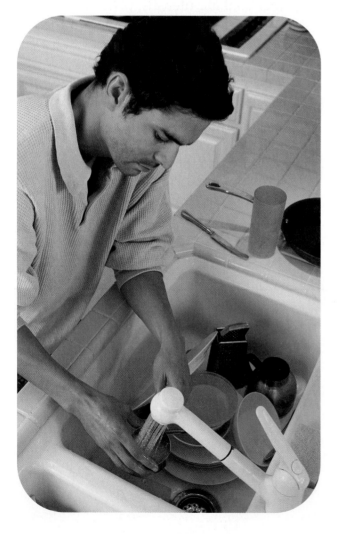

26-3 **In this kitchen, the cleanup center is next to counter space used for food preparation.**

Equipment and Storage

The appliances, cookware, and utensils you have to work with in the kitchen improve time management. For instance, using an electric mixer takes less time than beating by hand. A good sharp knife cuts vegetables more quickly than a dull knife.

When deciding where to store a piece of equipment, first determine in which of the work centers it is most often used. Then consider its frequency of use. The more you use a piece of equipment, the more accessible it should be. For instance, if you place saucepans on a low cupboard shelf, the ones you use most often would go in front. The weight of a piece of equipment also affects its storage place. Heavy items need to be in a place that is easy to reach.

Many devices that help organize storage space are available. You can use racks to store more dishes in the same amount of space. Utensil dividers make utensils more accessible. Some kitchens have pull-out lower shelves that make the items stored toward the back of the shelf much easier to reach.

Use a Time Plan in Meal Preparation

The more knowledge and experience you have in meal preparation, the more skill you will have in time management.

Even experienced cooks use a time plan in meal preparation. However, they may do this in their heads rather than on paper. Writing out a time plan is helpful for a beginning cook.

The time plan helps assure the food will be ready and at the right temperature when it is time to be served, 26-4. Timing is one of the most challenging aspects of meal preparation. This skill develops with repeated experience. A more-detailed time plan is helpful to a beginning cook. As you develop cooking skills, you will need less detail in the time plan.

The first step in developing a time plan for a meal is to determine the time the meal is to be served. To decide when to begin preparing each food, first figure out the amount of time you need to prepare that product. Then, keeping your serving time in mind, decide when to begin preparation. For instance, you may be planning to serve a baked chicken recipe at 6:00. You must decide how much time you need to prepare that dish. You estimate you will need 10 minutes to get the chicken ready to bake. Then it bakes for 45 minutes. Considering this information, you start preparing the chicken at about 5:00. This allows five minutes before serving time for you to take the chicken from the oven and put it on a serving platter.

Next you will need to set up a logical sequence of activities for preparing the different foods. You may be the only person preparing and serving the meal. If this is the case, you may need to include other tasks in your time plan. These include setting the table, getting the serving dishes, and pouring drinks.

The type of service used for the meal also affects time use. In **family style service**, foods are placed on the table in serving dishes and passed. This type of service might not be best on an evening when the family has time pressures. Instead, a modified **buffet service** might be better. With this type of service, family members serve themselves quickly from the serving dishes. Then they carry their plates to the table.

Time plans for the same menu can vary depending upon several factors. The number of people involved in the meal preparation and their cooking skills are important. The amount of food being prepared is also an issue. Each new menu or combination of foods requires a new time plan specifically tailored to that menu.

Use Work Simplification Techniques

Human beings are creatures of habit. They tend to repeat work activities in the same way, with no thought given to a more efficient method. *Work simplification* is a resource you can use to perform a task in the simplest, most efficient way, conserving both time and energy. Work simplification is done by analyzing the activity and breaking it down into detailed steps. Next, decide if you are using any unnecessary steps and if the steps are arranged in a logical order. Also check to see if all the

Time Plan: 1 Hour Preparation

Menu:

Barbecued Chicken
Oven Baked Potatoes
Green Beans
Tossed Salad
Milk
Strawberry Angel Food Dessert

Time	Preparation Task	Time Needed for Tasks	Steps Needed to Accomplish Task
5:00-5:10	Prepare potatoes Prepare chicken	10 minutes	Wash potatoes with a vegetable brush. Pierce each potato a few times with a fork. Place on upper rack in oven. Bake at 350°F for 55 minutes. Wash chicken. Pat dry with paper towels. Place in pan and pour BBQ sauce over chicken. Cover with foil. Put in lower rack in oven for 45-50 minutes.
5:10-5:25	Prepare salad Begin preparing dessert	15 minutes	While potatoes and chicken are baking, wash salad vegetables. Slice tomatoes, carrots, and cucumbers. Arrange salad ingredients into bowls. Cut pre-made angel food cake into slices with a bread knife. Place cut slices into serving dishes. Open frozen strawberries to defrost during meal.
5:25-5:35	Set table	10 minutes	Set table. Get out serving dishes.
5:35-5:40	Prepare vegetable	5 minutes	Pour frozen green beans into glass-covered dish. Add two tablespoons of water. Microwave for 5-8 minutes until fork tender. Let sit until mealtime.
5:40-5:50	Begin kitchen cleanup	10 minutes	Wash dishes and utensils used in meal preparation. Check on potatoes, chicken, and green beans for doneness. Do final salad preparations, such as topping with grated cheese or croutons. Place salad dressing on table.
5:50-5:55	Prepare beverages	5 minutes	Pour milk into glasses just before putting oven and microwave foods on the table.
5:55-6:00	Complete final preparations	5 minutes	Remove potatoes, chicken, and green beans from oven and microwave. Place on serving dishes and place on table.
6:00	Enjoy the meal!		At end of meal, spoon strawberries over angel food cake and add a dollop of whipped cream just before serving.

26-4 Preparing a written time plan can help beginning cooks develop timing skills.

supplies or equipment you need for that activity are available. See 26-5. You may need to reorganize some of the equipment and find a more efficient storage place.

As you develop skill in doing an activity, you do it more efficiently. You learn a lot through trial and error the first time you try something new. As you repeat the activity, you develop skill. The activity becomes less challenging and you accomplish it more efficiently. Do you remember the first time you tried to peel a carrot? It was probably a challenging activity, especially if you were not using the best piece of equipment for the job. By now you may be able to peel a carrot quite efficiently. Through observation, experience, and use of the appropriate tool, you have developed the skill to peel carrots.

An abundance of kitchen tools and equipment is available to simplify meal preparation. The number of tools you own may be limited by their cost and your available storage space. A sharp knife may do the job in one home, while a food processor does the same work more quickly in another. The key to good time management is in learning to use the equipment you have in the most efficient manner.

Multitasking and dovetailing can improve efficiency in the kitchen. These skills help you accomplish more in a shorter period of time. **Multitasking** occurs when you do several tasks at the same time. For example, when you wash the potatoes, you can wash salad vegetables as well. **Dovetailing** involves fitting several tasks together to save time. For example, the salad could be prepared and the table set while the chicken and potatoes are baking in the oven.

As you become more skilled at time management, you will learn to simplify work in the kitchen. With the improvement of time management skills, you will learn

26-5 **Work is simplified when ingredients are gathered before preparation begins.**

to multitask or dovetail meal preparation tasks. All these skills will help you become more efficient.

Nutrition and Meal Preparation

A good cook understands the importance of nutrition to good health. A good cook also knows that cooking procedures may affect nutritional value. This knowledge is important since nutrients cannot be seen. Nutrients are lost in certain preparation procedures. These include soaking certain foods in water, chopping vegetables finely, or storing juice in the refrigerator without a lid. Without a basic understanding of nutrition, you might not realize this.

Learning about how nutrients are lost in food preparation can help you avoid these losses. Simple procedures can reduce losses and result in a more nutritious food product. See 26-6.

Nutrient Loss and Water

The greatest loss of nutrients during food preparation occurs when foods are soaked or cooked in water. Certain nutrients, particularly vitamin C and thiamin, are *soluble*—they dissolve in water.

Of course, washing fresh vegetables before using them is necessary and important. However, washing and soaking are quite different. *Soaking* foods, or letting them stand in water, can greatly affect nutrient content. The nutrients that dissolve into the water are lost because the soaking water is seldom used.

When vegetables are cut into pieces for cooking, more surface area is exposed, increasing the possible loss of nutrients. Washing the fruit or vegetable before cutting will prevent much of the nutrient loss.

By eating raw fruits and vegetables, you avoid the loss of water-soluble nutrients. However, some fruits and vegetables must be cooked to be edible. To lessen nutrient losses, cook them in as little water as possible. Cutting foods into pieces allows them to cook more quickly, but the increased surface area causes more water-soluble nutrients to dissolve. Using medium-size pieces offers a compromise between the two techniques.

Courtesy of Thomas J. Lipton, Inc.

26-6 Foods like these are nutritious as well as appealing to the eye.

The way you use the water after the food is cooked affects the retention of nutrients. By using the liquid for soups, gravies, or sauces, you retain nutrients that would otherwise be lost. See 26-7.

Some vegetables such as potatoes can be boiled in the skin to reduce nutrient loss in the water. Foods can also be steamed to reduce their contact with water. The pressure saucepan is another way to reduce the time the food is in water.

Nutrient Loss and Heat

Heat increases the nutrient losses that occur in water, particularly in the presence of air. Oxygen in the cooking water can cause a loss of vitamin C. This is why boiling water several minutes before

26-7 **Nutrients are retained in the stew because the foods are eaten with the liquid in which they were cooked.**

adding a vegetable is recommended. When the oxygen in the water is expelled, there is less loss of vitamin C.

Enzymes in vegetables can destroy vitamin C if the vegetables are heated slowly during the early stages of cooking. Boiling the water before adding the vegetables makes these enzymes inactive more quickly. The result is less loss of vitamin C.

Thiamin, one of the B vitamins, is especially sensitive to heat in meat cookery. The loss of thiamin increases with the cooking temperature although cooking time is also important. When you stew meat or use other moist heat methods of cooking, the nutrients are lost into the cooking juices. The heat shrinks the protein. However, if you eat the meat with the juices, little nutritional loss occurs.

When foods are reheated, further loss of nutrients occurs. This loss is due to the additional dissolving of nutrients into the liquid as well as the reheating process.

Because heat reduces the nutritional value of many foods containing vitamin C, it is important for these foods to be properly stored. Most foods high in vitamin C should be stored in a cool place.

Nutrient Loss and Oxidation

Nutrient loss due to **oxidation**—exposure to oxygen—occurs in several ways. Foods high in vitamin C require careful storage and preparation to avoid exposure to oxygen. Preparing fruit juices just prior to serving will reduce vitamin loss due to exposure to oxygen. Nutrient loss will also be reduced by storing juices in covered containers to limit exposure to air.

Vitamin C loss due to oxidation also occurs when foods are sliced, cubed, chopped, mashed, ground, or blended. This loss occurs because more surfaces are exposed to oxygen. The nutrient loss is less if these preparations are done as close to cooking or serving time as possible. See 26-8.

Vitamin A is associated with the yellow color of foods such as carrots and some dairy products. This vitamin resists heat, but is sensitive to oxygen. Vitamin A is destroyed by oxygen when foods are cooked at low temperatures for long periods of time. Cooking more quickly or in the absence of oxygen, as in a pressure saucepan, will result in less vitamin A being lost. Fats such as butter and margarine are high in vitamin A and may become rancid through exposure to oxygen. Therefore, they should be stored in a cool place.

Other Causes of Nutrient Loss

Many food preparation techniques affect the nutritional content of food. Nutritional content can be altered by utensils used, substances added to the food, and actual food preparation techniques. Unless you are a nutritional expert, it is difficult to be aware of all the ways nutrient loss can occur. However, an awareness of common nutrient losses can help you take steps to prepare more nutritious food.

Fruits such as apples, pears, and peaches are more nutritious when you eat them without peeling them. Nutrients in many fruits are concentrated just under the skin. Peeling and discarding the skin causes a great loss of nutritional benefits.

26-8 Vitamin C loss is occurring through the cut surfaces of this orange, which are exposed to oxygen. Eating an orange one section at a time will limit oxidation.

Adding some baking soda to green vegetables when cooking makes them retain their bright green color. On the other hand, baking soda destroys vitamin C in green vegetables. If you do use baking soda, use it in very small amounts.

The Significance of Heat in Cooking

Most changes that take place in cooking involve heat. The changes caused by heat may be confusing for beginning cooks. You may wonder why cookies get too brown on the bottom one time and not another. You may not know why milk scorches so quickly in one pan and heats slowly in another.

Cooking involves the transfer of heat from a source to the material being heated. The result of heat transfer depends on three factors. These include the source of the heat, material and finish of the utensil used, and nature of the food being heated.

Source of the Heat

Food may be heated through conduction, radiation, convection, or microwaves. More than one method of heat transfer is involved in most cases.

Conduction

When heat travels by **conduction**, it begins at the heat source, such as the heating element on the range top. The heat travels to the bottom of the pan and through the material of the pan to the substance that is being heated. An object heated by conduction is in direct contact with the source of heat. An example would be a metal pan on the coils of an electric unit. Conduction is a fairly slow method of transferring heat. See 26-9.

26-9 **This soup is being heated through conduction; heat travels from the range top through the pan to the soup.**

26-10 **Radiant heat is being used to cook this barbecued chicken.**

Radiation

Electromagnetic waves or rays are another source of heat. When a food is heated by **radiation**, the energy or heat goes directly from the source to the food being heated. Radiation is unlike conduction because no material is between the heat source and the food being heated. Broilers, toasters, and glowing coals of a barbecue are sources of radiant heat. See 26-10.

Radiation is a rapid method of heating. The farther the food is from the energy source, the less it is heated.

Convection

Heating by **convection** occurs in the oven. Circulating currents of hot air heat the food product. The oven is designed with the heating unit in the bottom because warm air rises and cold air moves downward. As the lower air is heated, it rises. The colder air moves to the bottom where it is heated. This sets up currents of air, which

make the temperature uniform. Heating is likely to be more uniform in the center of the oven while the top and bottom tend to be hotter. If you use more than one baking pan or dish, position them to allow for good air circulation.

Microwave

The energy in the microwave oven is in the form of high-frequency radio waves. **Microwaves** generate heat in the food itself. The water in the food is mainly what absorbs the microwave radiation. Therefore, foods with high water contents cook more rapidly than foods that contain less water. Cooking time in a microwave is much shorter than in a conventional oven. Short cooking time is the greatest advantage of the microwave. Some disadvantages are that foods do not brown or develop crispness. In addition, flavor is sometimes different from foods prepared in a conventional oven.

When you microwave, you must use materials that allow microwaves to pass through. This includes materials such as glass, plastic, or paper. Most metal utensils should not be used. Metal reflects the rays and prevents them from reaching the food. However, some cookware containing metal is designed for microwave use. Check the manufacturer's directions before using any type of metal in the microwave.

The Material and Finish of the Equipment Used

You may have found through experience that different cooking utensils seem to take different lengths of time to heat the same food. How efficiently a piece of equipment conducts heat depends on the material of which it is made, 26-11. Some materials conduct heat better than others. Aluminum, copper, and magnesium are good conductors of heat, while stainless steel and glass are not. Manufacturers of surface cooking utensils have combined the most positive characteristics of different materials to produce cookware that heats efficiently.

In addition to the type of metal, the weight of the metal also affects the efficiency of the cookware. A heavier metal results in more even cooking overall.

A metal's finish is also a factor in cooking. Dark or rough, dull surfaces are good absorbers of radiant energy in the oven. Utensils with light, brightly polished surfaces tend to reflect the rays.

Manufacturers develop improved bakeware by combining qualities. An example of this is a cake pan with a dull, rough bottom and shiny sides. This pan is designed to heat well and produce a cake that cooks more quickly from the bottom. The shiny sides reflect radiant energy and allow the batter to rise and reach a maximum volume before the sides harden.

Mark Hayward

26-11 **There are advantages and disadvantages to each type of cooking equipment.**

The Nature of the Food Being Heated

Foods absorb heat at different rates, largely depending on their moisture content. Water or steam is often used in cooking to soften the cellulose substances. Some foods, such as a baked potato, do not need water added. The water content of the potato is so high it cooks in its own liquid.

Water as a Medium for Heat Transfer

Water is often used in a pan to transmit heat from the heat source to the food. Without using water, food would get hottest in the part of the pan touching the heat source and might scorch or burn. Because water is a good conductor of heat, it quickly gives up its heat to the food. Temperature throughout the water is fairly uniform.

Water is used in larger quantity when boiling foods like potatoes. After the boiling point is reached, the temperature of the water will not go higher no matter how much heat is applied. In other words, the potatoes will not cook more quickly by turning up the heat. After the water boils, reduce the heat to maintain a gentle boiling.

If high heat and vigorous boiling continue, the water changes to steam. It will gradually evaporate and might burn the food. Evaporation occurs more quickly in a wide shallow pan than a deep narrow one because more surface area is exposed. Covering the pan makes a difference. When you cover the pan tightly, the water boils, pressure develops, and a higher temperature results. The pressure saucepan works on this principle. The food cooks more quickly because the pan is sealed. The heat builds up, and little or no evaporation occurs.

Food Preparation Techniques

No one today should have a problem with monotony in cooking. Thousands of recipes are available in cookbooks, magazines, newspapers, and commercial brochures, as well as online. If you follow a recipe carefully, the result will probably be a successful product. However, an inexperienced cook may sometimes have problems that are difficult to understand. You may have followed the recipe exactly, and yet the final product did not turn out right. Why did that happen? What did you do wrong?

Fortunately, you can easily avoid many cooking problems. All you need is a basic knowledge of preparation techniques for cooking or reheating foods. Many experienced cooks have gained this knowledge the hard way—by making mistakes. Over a period of time, they have figured out the correct technique through trial and error. You can avoid many frustrations by learning the facts and using that knowledge in cooking. Doing this will make cooking an enjoyable and creative experience.

Common cooking problems can usually be identified with a specific food group. Becoming aware of these problems and how you can avoid them will improve your cooking skill.

Cooking with Milk

Because milk contains a high percentage of water, it is used as an ingredient in a variety of foods, such as soups, sauces, and puddings. See 26-12. Three common problems can occur when cooking with milk. First, a skin or film can form when the milk is heated. Second, the milk can stick to the bottom and sides of the pan and possibly scorch. Third, the milk may **curdle**, creating small, soft lumps. You can prevent each of these problems by following certain procedures.

26-12 **Milk is an ingredient in this creamy seafood chowder.**

Preventing the Film

As milk is heated, water evaporates from the surface. Milk solids separate and float to the top. This causes a film that can be tough and rubbery. Another disadvantage of the film is that it keeps steam from escaping. This creates a pressure under the film, forcing the milk to break through the film and be more likely to boil over.

You can remove the film if it occurs. However, the nutritive content in the milk solids is lost. Stirring the skin into the milk is undesirable because it results in a lumpy, unappetizing mixture. The best way to solve the problem is to prevent the skin from forming.

You can use several techniques to do this. You might use a covered container or stir the milk while it is heating. Using a rotary beater or a wire whisk to beat the milk creates a layer of foam on the surface and prevents the skin from forming.

Preventing Sticking and Scorching

Milk is extremely sensitive to heat. When heated, some of the milk solids settle out and **coagulate**, or thicken, on the sides and bottom of the pan. Overheating the milk causes the **lactose**—the sugar in the milk solids—to *carmelize* or turn brown. This process, called **scorching**, creates an undesirable flavor.

To prevent sticking and scorching, use low temperatures. Stirring the mixture constantly will also help prevent sticking. Milk is less likely to stick in a pan with a thick bottom that spreads the heat evenly.

Preventing Curdling

Curdling or lumping occurs for various reasons when milk is heated. Curdling occurs when the temperature is too high and when acids are added to the milk. Curdling may also happen when you use milk that is just about to turn sour. Acid develops in milk that has been stored for too long a time.

There are several ways to prevent curdling. Using a low cooking temperature is one suggestion. When you add tomatoes to make cream of tomato soup, you are adding acid to milk. Thicken either the milk or the acid first and then combine it with the remaining mixture. Finally, whenever you cook with milk, be sure it is fresh.

Cooking with Cheese

Cheese is a versatile food that may be used in everything from appetizers to desserts. It can be mixed with meat dishes, vegetable dishes, fruits, and breads. See 26-13.

Cheese contains high amounts of fat and protein. The fat in the cheese is solid in the refrigerator, but it softens at room temperature. Proper cooking procedures soften cheese to an edible consistency. However, overcooking causes the protein in cheese to become tough and rubbery. Overcooking can be caused by either using too high a temperature or cooking too long.

26-13 **There are many kinds of cheese that vary by flavor and texture.**

Cheese is often melted in the oven or under the broiler. Cheese tends to shrink and toughen as it melts. This occurs both because of the evaporation of moisture and the heating of the protein. Because of its low melting point, cheese takes only a few minutes to melt under the broiler and can burn easily. When you use cheese as a topping for a casserole, add it during the last part of the cooking time. This will prevent it from becoming tough and stringy.

Combining cheese with a liquid to make a cheese sauce is a challenge. The liquid must be warm enough to melt the cheese, but not hot enough to toughen the protein. If the liquid is not warm enough, the cheese will not blend with it. If the liquid is too warm, the cheese will toughen and separate. Cheese melts more quickly when sliced, cubed, or grated into smaller pieces.

Cooking with Eggs

Because of their color, flavor, ability to coagulate or thicken, and ability to foam, eggs are used in a variety of recipes. See 26-14. Like other protein foods, eggs toughen when exposed to high temperatures and overcooking.

Eggs are used to thicken liquids. Custards, puddings, sauces, soups, pie fillings, and ice cream are thickened with eggs. Protein in the egg white and yolk coagulates at low temperatures, giving firmness to the food product.

Eggs added to a hot food are likely to curdle. To avoid curdling, add a small amount of the hot mixture to the beaten eggs to condition them. Gradually add them to the remaining hot mixture, stirring constantly. If you use a double boiler, the eggs are less likely to curdle.

Because of the protein, eggs also act as an emulsifying agent. An **emulsion** is a mixture that forms when liquids that do not ordinarily mix, such as oil and vinegar,

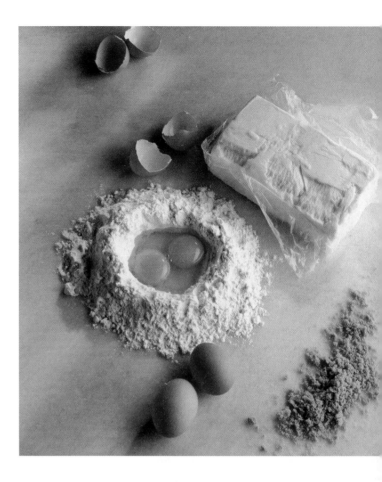

26-14 **The various properties of eggs makes them an important ingredient in many products.**

are combined. An emulsion can be temporary or permanent. The **emulsifying agent** is an ingredient that acts to keep the oil suspended in the water-based liquid.

Homemade French dressing is a temporary emulsion made with oil, vinegar, water, and seasoning. You must shake it vigorously to mix it well before each use. However, using an egg yolk as an emulsifying agent creates a permanent emulsion. The yolk surrounds the oil droplets and keeps them in suspension so they do not separate. Mayonnaise is an example of a permanent emulsion.

Eggs also act as **leavening agents**—they cause a product to increase in volume. As egg whites are beaten, air cells form. Beaten egg whites can hold a large quantity of air and form a foam. The thin film of protein that surrounds each cell gives rigidity to the foam structure. Soufflés, popovers, and angel food cake are foods that depend on eggs for leavening. The amount of air you beat into an egg will determine its effectiveness as a leavening agent. Different products require that eggs be beaten to different stages.

Two factors affect the volume of beaten egg whites: the temperature of the egg whites and the absence of fat. Egg whites whip to their maximum volume at room temperature. Fat interferes with the foaming of the egg whites and reduces the foam volume. Be sure no fat is present. When separating the egg white from the yolk, make sure no yolk, which contains fat, gets in the white. Use a glass, metal, or ceramic bowl. Plastics, especially those that are soft, may retain enough fat to reduce the volume of the beaten egg whites.

Many recipes using egg whites also include an acid, such as cream of tartar. Acid makes the egg white foam more stable. Sugar also increases the stability of the foam. However, sugar is usually not added until most of the volume of the foam has been reached. If you add the sugar too soon, the egg whites will not reach their maximum volume. Once you have beaten the egg whites, use a gentle folding motion to combine them with other ingredients. Stirring the egg whites too vigorously will cause much of the volume to be lost.

Cooking with Meat

Meat consists of muscle tissue, connective tissue, fat, and bone. As meat cooks, the protein in the muscle tissue becomes firmer, the fat melts, and the connective tissue softens. The meat becomes tender and juicy as a result. See 26-15. Too much

National Cattlemen's Beef Association

26-15 **Hamburger contains a certain amount of fat. Otherwise, it would be dry and unappetizing to eat.**

heat causes the muscle tissue to dry out and the fat to drip from the meat. This results in a dry, tough product.

Meat has **marbling** when flecks of fat are evenly distributed throughout the lean meat. Marbling adds moisture to the meat and helps give it aroma and flavor. The best way to cook meat depends on the meat's tenderness and the size of the cut. Meats are usually classified as tender or less tender cuts. Tender cuts come from the section of the animal where the least body movement occurs. The more an animal exercises, the greater the connective tissue development. Muscles in the legs and the neck are less tender because they do more work than muscles along the mid-backbone. Rib and loin muscles are quite tender.

Tender cuts of meat are best cooked using dry heat methods. Less tender cuts are best cooked slowly by moist heat methods. This tenderizes a tougher cut of meat by breaking down most of the connective tissue.

Broiling and Grilling

These dry heat methods are best used for tender meats, 26-16. When meat is broiled or grilled, it is cooked below or above the direct source of heat. When the heat is applied through hot metal in a heavy skillet, it is known as *panbroiling*.

To oven broil meat, preheat the broiler and bring the food to room temperature. Thicker cuts of meat should be placed farther from the heat than thinner cuts. Broiled meat is cooked until brown or seared. **Searing** occurs when the meat is exposed to intense, direct heat long enough to cook the outer layer and form a crust. The sealed surface holds the meat juices inside. When one side of the meat is done, use tongs or two spatulas to turn it over without piercing it. This will minimize the loss of meat juices. Turning the meat only once or as little as possible will also minimize loss of meat juices.

Directions for using the broilers in gas and electric ranges differ slightly. Although the door is closed in gas ranges, the door is left partly open while broiling in electric ranges. Because less air circulates in an electric oven, steam would form if you left the door closed.

When grilling or barbecuing meat, the heat source is under rather than over the meat. When grilling, the same principles of meat cookery apply as when oven broiling.

Broiling and grilling are best for tender cuts of meat such as steaks and chops. Ground meat is also often used in grilling. Some cuts, such as steaks and chops, are usually surrounded by connective tissue. Scoring the tissue every few inches will keep the meat edges from curling while cooking. To score the meat, cut just through the connective tissue but into the muscle tissue as little as possible.

When panbroiling, cook the meat in a heavy skillet without adding fat. If the meat has little marbling, rub the pan with a small amount of fat to keep it from sticking. Place the meat in a hot skillet and sear it on both sides. Then reduce the heat until the meat is done to taste. Pour off any fat that accumulates in the pan.

Panbroiling is suitable for the same tender cuts of meat used in oven broiling. You may prefer to use panbroiling for small, thin cuts of meat.

Roasting

Roasting is done by cooking large cuts of tender meats uncovered in an oven without adding moisture. To prepare meat

National Cattlemen's Beef Association

26-16 Broiling works best for tender cuts of meat that are not too thick.

for roasting, place it uncovered, fat side up, on a rack in a large shallow pan. See 26-17. The melting fat bastes the meat, and the rack keeps the meat out of the drippings.

Roasting is usually done in a slow oven at 325°F or under. Recipes and charts suggest a wide variety of cooking times, but a properly used meat thermometer is the best indication of doneness. Insert the meat thermometer through the thickest muscle in the roast, being sure it does not touch the bone.

Frying

This method of cooking thin pieces of tender meat, ground meat, or small pieces of meat is widely used. Pan frying and sautéing both involve using a small amount of fat or accumulations of fat from the meat itself, 26-18. Cooking a meat by completely immersing it in fat is called *deep-frying*.

National Cattlemen's Beef Association

26-18 **When frying hamburger, it is usually not necessary to use any fat.**

Braising

Less tender cuts of meat can be cooked by braising. When you *braise* meat, you cook it in a tightly covered pan with little or no moisture. See 26-19. The meat is first seared on all sides in fat in a heavy pan. If you did not brown the meat, juices from the raw meat would be released. The meat is more tender and flavorful when it retains these juices.

After searing the meat, add a small amount of liquid and cover the pan tightly. Braising is done at a low temperature either on top of the range or in the oven. The liquid in the pan can be used for a sauce or gravy if desired.

Cooking in Liquid

In this method of moist meat cookery, the meat is covered with liquid. Some meats might be browned before the liquid is added. For instance, this would be done

National Cattlemen's Beef Association

26-17 **Different recipes and charts suggest a variety of times for roasting. A properly used meat thermometer will give you the best indication of doneness.**

National Cattlemen's Beef Association

26-19 **The pan was covered tightly when this meat was cooked. The small amount of moisture helped tenderize the ingredients.**

National Cattlemen's Beef Association

26-20 **Less tender cuts of meat become tender when cooked slowly in liquid.**

in a beef stew, 26-20. To cook other meats, such as corned beef, the meat is placed in the liquid. Seasoning may be added. After covering the meat with liquid, cover the pan and cook the mixture below the boiling point until tender. Add vegetables just long enough before serving to cook them.

In addition to conventional methods of meat cookery, there are other ways to tenderize meat. It can be pounded with a meat tenderizer to break up connective tissue. Meat is more tender when acids such as tomatoes, sour cream, vinegar, or lemon juice make up part of the liquid in which the meat is cooked. Meat can also be marinated in mixtures containing an acid or meat tenderizer. Commercial meat tenderizers that contain protein-digesting enzymes are available. Follow the directions carefully in using these products.

Poultry, fish, and shellfish are generally more tender than beef or pork. They can usually be cooked by either dry or moist heat cooking methods.

Cooking with Grain Products

Products made from grain include breakfast cereals, rice, pasta products, and flours. Two common problems in cooking these products are having a pasty product or a lumpy product. Both problems are linked to the starch content of the products. Because cereals contain a high percentage of starch, cereal cookery is largely starch cookery. When heated, starch granules expand or swell and absorb liquid. As the starch continues to heat, the mixture becomes more clear and thickens. This is known as **gelatinization**.

To prevent lumps from forming, the granules need to swell evenly. You can encourage this by stirring the dry product slowly into rapidly boiling liquid. Stir only enough to prevent the formation of lumps. Excessive stirring can result in a pasty product.

Breakfast Cereals

Although the package directions are probably the most reliable guide, some general guidelines for cooking cereals may also be helpful. You can avoid lumps by slowly adding the cereal such as oatmeal to rapidly boiling water, stirring continually. Because the surface of the granules becomes sticky in boiling water, you will need to continue stirring slowly until the water boils again.

Some fine cereals may be mixed with a small amount of cold water before they are stirred into the boiling water. This method is preferred for fine cereals because lumps easily form when the dry cereals are added to boiling water.

Rice

Rice cooks best in the amount of water it will absorb during the cooking process. During cooking, the rice grains swell and become tender without breaking. The desired product is dry, fluffy grains of rice that stand apart, 26-21. A sticky, gummy product is caused by broken grains. If the rice is stirred only once when the water first comes to a boil, the quality of the products will be better. The rice should be cooked over low heat because rapidly boiling water may break the grains.

Pasta Products

Foods such as macaroni, spaghetti, and noodles are pasta products. Because these are larger than cereal granules, you can more easily separate them when stirring them into boiling water. Add them gradually so the brisk boiling is not disturbed. Adding a little cooking oil to the water will help keep the product from sticking together.

Starch Products as Thickeners

Flour and cornstarch are products derived from grains. They are used to thicken gravies, sauces, puddings, and pie fillings. The starch granules work in the flour or cornstarch just as they do in cooked cereals. The starch swells and absorbs liquid as it is heated. The thickness of the product is determined by the amount of starch you use.

Starch particles in flour and cornstarch tend to lump together easily because they are very fine. To avoid lumps, use one of the techniques to separate the starch granules.

One method for making gravies or white sauces involves first mixing the flour with melted fat. Then the liquid is slowly added. The two are stirred together to distribute the heat and allow the starch granules to swell evenly. This is done over a moderate heat. Using too high a heat may cause the starch to burn and create a bitter flavor. In addition, the starch granules may shrink so they will not be capable of swelling or absorbing the liquid.

Golden Grain Macaroni Co.

26-21 Rice looks like this when properly cooked.

Another method of separating the starch granules is to mix the starch product with a small amount of cold water or liquid before adding it gradually to the hot liquid. This procedure is often used with cornstarch.

You can also mix the starch or flour with other ingredients such as sugar and seasonings to separate the starch. This method is often used for puddings and pie fillings.

Flour as a Structural Ingredient for Leavening Agents

Flour provides the structure or framework for cakes, cookies, yeast breads, and quick breads. When liquid is mixed with flour, a substance called *gluten* is formed from the protein in the flour. Gluten's characteristics of strength and elasticity give structure and volume to the food product.

Gluten formation begins when liquid is combined with the flour. The gluten is further developed by stirring, mixing, or kneading. In some products, such as muffins, you must be careful not to stir too much. See 26-22. This will cause overformation of the gluten and result in a tough product.

Leavening Agents

Various leavening agents are used to make food products increase in volume. Most baked products produce steam. The high temperature to which the products are heated forms the steam, which expands the product's structure. Products such as popovers and cream puffs are leavened almost entirely by steam. Butter cakes use baking powder or baking soda. Carbon dioxide forms when these two products come in contact with liquid, giving volume to the product. The yeast used to leaven yeast breads is actually a microscopic plant. Carbon dioxide forms as the yeast is mixed with a warm liquid and sugar. The gas expands the gluten structure and causes the bread to rise. Egg whites and steam are the leavening agents for angel food cakes. Air

26-22 **Muffins that look like these have been properly mixed and are a quality product.**

is beaten into the egg whites, and steam is produced during the baking.

Cooking with Fats and Oils

You can tell the difference between fats and oils by their physical state. A fat that is liquid at room temperature is called an oil. Those that are solid or semisolid are called fats. Butter, margarine, lard, and vegetable shortenings are examples of fats.

Each type of fat has unique characteristics. Butter is popular because of its good flavor. Since it absorbs odors rapidly, cover the butter during storage. Margarine is usually a blend of animal and vegetable fats. Although it is not quite as flavorful as butter, margarine is less expensive. Lard is a fat that comes from the fatty tissues of hogs. It is a softer, oilier fat than butter or margarine. Lard is often used in biscuits and crusts. Vegetable oils are pressed from common seeds and fruits, such as corn, cottonseed, olive, soybean, sesame, safflower, and sunflower. Vegetable shortenings are made from vegetable oils and are solidified in the hydrogenation process. They may be stored over long periods of time and do not require refrigeration.

Butter and margarine burn or smoke at the lowest temperature of any fat. They are not suitable for frying, but may be used for low heat sautéing. Oils and shortening can be used for frying. They can reach a very high temperature before starting to smoke or burn. See 26-23.

Fats are also used for their shortening effect on flour mixtures. Fat separates the starch and gluten particles to produce a more tender, flaky product. Lard and vegetable shortenings are commonly used in flour mixtures. Vegetable shortenings are preferred for cake products. Because lard is softer and has greater shortening power, it is used in making piecrusts, biscuits, and shortcakes.

26-23 **Olive oil is used to sauté chicken in this dish.**

Salad dressings contain fat in the form of a permanent or semipermanent emulsion. The fat used may be a vegetable oil, such as corn oil or olive oil, or a combination of different types of oils.

Cooking with Fruits

Two common problems seem to occur when cooking with fruits. One is the browning of cut fruits and the other involves the effect of using sugar to cook fruit.

Most raw fruits except those with high acid content tend to turn dark when exposed to air. You can use several methods to reduce or slow down the oxidizing process. One common method is to immerse the cut fruit in an acid, such as lemon or orange juice, to increase its acidity. Another method is to cover the fruit with a sugar solution or glaze to prevent contact with oxygen.

The way you cook the fruit will determine its texture and whether it retains its shape or breaks apart. Fruit cooked in a syrup of sugar and water usually maintains its shape better than fruit cooked in just water. However, if there is too much sugar in the water, the fruit will harden. To make a sauce such as applesauce, cook the fruit in plain water over low heat. The water will soften the cellulose in the fruit and it will break apart. See 26-24.

Dried Fruit

The goal in cooking dried fruits is to get them to absorb most of the moisture lost in the drying process. Ideally, this is done without loss of flavor or texture. Dried fruits are soaked in hot water for a short time and then cooked in the same water. The water passes through the cell membranes into the dried fruit. As it takes up water, the fruit becomes plumper.

Cooking with Vegetables

Cooked vegetables taste best when they retain their color, flavor, and texture. Overcooking affects all these characteristics.

The method to use in cooking a vegetable depends on its color and flavor. See 26-25. Green vegetables such as broccoli and green beans can change from a bright green to a dull greenish brown color when cooked. Green vegetables contain a large amount of *chlorophyll*, a green pigment. Too much heat from overcooking causes the chlorophyll to change color. Leaving the lid partially off during cooking can help. This allows acids that come off the cooked vegetables to escape, thus resulting in a greener color.

Yellow vegetables get their color from a pigment called *carotene*. Although yellow vegetables are not affected much by heat or water, they are best if not overcooked.

White vegetables, such as potatoes and cauliflower, contain a pigment called *flavones*. As these vegetables cook, they may turn from white to yellow to gray. Adding a little acid such as cream of tartar, lemon juice, or vinegar will keep the color white.

Red vegetables such as beets and red cabbage get their color from a substance called *anthocyanins*. This substance bleeds, or gives off its color, in water. To retain their color, cook vegetables such as beets in their skins and peel after cooking. Since red vegetables like acids, you may leave the cover on the pan to keep the red color bright. Overcooking may cause the vegetables to turn purple or blue during cooking.

26-25 If these vegetables had been over-cooked, the dish would lose its touches of bright color.

Serving the Meal

There is no "right" way to set a table. However, the table is set for convenience as well as attractiveness. Table settings vary according to what you are serving, the serving pieces available, and how formal the meal is. For instance, a table set for an elegant, formal dinner, including soup and salad, would be quite different from that set for a quick salad-and-sandwich lunch. A general guideline for setting a table is shown in 26-26.

Just as there is no right way to set a table, there is also no right way to eat a meal. Certain rules of etiquette are suggested. Some of these rules are outlined in 26-27.

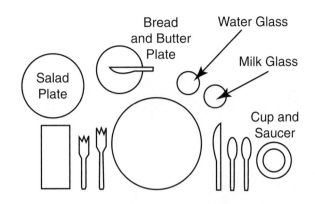

26-26 **This diagram shows the general guidelines for setting a table. Table settings vary according to types of meals. A simpler meal would require fewer pieces of tableware. A more elaborate meal would require more pieces of tableware.**

Dining Do's and Don'ts

DO...place your napkin in your lap as soon as you are seated. It should remain in your lap, except when you are using it, until the meal is over. Following the meal, you should place it neatly on the table.

DO...follow your host's lead if you are not sure which utensil to use.

DO...begin eating only after everyone has been served, unless your host indicates otherwise.

DO...bring your food to your mouth when eating, not your mouth down to your food.

DO...try a little bit of everything, unless you know you are allergic to a certain food.

DO...take small bites, keeping your mouth closed when you chew.

DO...use "Please" and "Thank you."

DO...excuse yourself if you must leave the table before the meal is finished.

DON'T...talk with food in your mouth.

DON'T...put your elbows on the table.

DON'T...engage in distasteful conversation.

DON'T...set a utensil that has been used on the table. Place it back on the plate or saucer.

DON'T...reach across the table or another person if you need something. Ask to have it passed to you.

DON'T...lean back in your chair. Keep all four legs of the chair on the floor.

26-27 **Knowing rules of etiquette for serving and eating food can help you feel confident at mealtime.**

32
31
30
29
28
26
25
24
23
22
21
20
19
18
17
16
15
14
13
12
11
10
9
8
7
6
5
4
3
2
1

Summary

Various resources can help you prepare meals efficiently. Your skill in time management can be greatly affected by the organization of the kitchen work area and the equipment available for use. If the equipment is organized efficiently, meal preparation tasks will be simpler. Skill in managing time and simplifying work procedures will also help you be more efficient.

The way food is prepared affects its nutritional value. By being aware of how food preparation procedures affect nutritional value, you can have a positive influence on your own health and the health of others.

Understanding the changes that take place in foods during heating will help you to avoid the frustrations of mistakes often made. Certain cooking problems are common in specific food groups. By being aware of these problems and how to avoid them, you will improve your cooking skills.

Meal service and table setting will depend on what you are serving, the serving pieces available, and how formal the meal is. Following rules of etiquette can make mealtime an enjoyable experience.

To Review

1. Name the three work centers in the kitchen and list some of the equipment found in each center.
2. List three suggestions regarding the storage of kitchen equipment.
3. Briefly describe how to develop a time plan for the preparation of a meal.
4. Name three ways nutrients are lost in food preparation.
5. Match the methods of heat transfer with their definitions.
   _____ Radiation.
   _____ Convection.
   _____ Microwave.
   _____ Conduction.
   A. Heat begins at the heat source and travels through the bottom of a pan to the substance being heated.
   B. High frequency radio waves generate heat in the food itself.
   C. Circulating currents of hot air heat the food product.
   D. The heat goes directly from the source to the food being heated.
6. List three problems that may occur when cooking with milk.
7. True or false?
   A. Protein is found only in the egg yolk.
   B. Mayonnaise is an example of a permanent emulsion.
   C. Egg whites produce more volume if they are cold when they are whipped.
   D. Fruit will harden when cooked in plain water without sugar.
   E. Overheating has a greater effect on yellow vegetables than on green vegetables.
8. Match the following information about meat.
   _____ Moist meat.
   _____ Tender cuts.
   _____ Dry meat.
   _____ Less tender cuts.
   A. indicates too much heat
   B. indicates greater connective tissue development
   C. indicates the meat comes from parts of the animal in which least body movement occurs
   D. indicates marbling in the meat
9. Name four leavening agents that might give volume to food products and explain how they function.
10. Describe the difference between vegetable oils and vegetable shortenings.

To Do with the Class

1. Divide into three groups. The first group will plan a meal that can be prepared in less than 30 minutes. The second group will plan a meal that can be prepared in 30 to 60 minutes. The third group will plan a meal that takes more than an hour to prepare. Each group should include a brief time plan for the meal preparation.
2. Divide into four groups and develop a demonstration on one of the following: avoiding nutrient loss in water, avoiding nutrient loss to heat, or avoiding nutrient loss to oxidation.
3. Work with a partner to conduct an experiment on beating egg whites under each of the following conditions:
   A. Have one person use cold eggs while the other uses room temperature eggs.
   B. Have one person use pure egg whites while the other uses egg whites with specks of yolk in them.
   C. Have one person use a small deep bowl while the other uses a wide shallow bowl.
   D. Have one person add sugar near the beginning of the beating and the other add sugar near the end.
   Compare and discuss your results.
4. Work with a partner to demonstrate one of the major meat cooking methods. One partner will demonstrate while the other partner explains appropriate cuts of meat for that method.

To Challenge Your Thinking

1. Observe someone doing a meal preparation task in the kitchen. Analyze their steps and suggest ways the task might be done more efficiently.
2. Collect pictures of storage devices for kitchen equipment and utensils. Work with other class members to develop a bulletin board using your pictures.
3. Talk with five people from different families and find out what type of cookware they use (for instance, aluminum or stainless steel). Then find out what they like and do not like about using that material.
4. Heat milk in two pans, one at a high temperature and one at a low temperature. Compare the film or scum formation. Explain the reason for the difference.

To Do with Your Community

1. Interview five people to get suggestions for good management in meal preparation. Develop a list of ideas for meal management and share your results.
2. Visit the store where your family buys most food products. Make a list of all fats and oils that are available. Do not list brand names, but list types such as olive oil or cottonseed oil. Compare your list with others in the class.
3. Invite an experienced cook or a butcher to speak to your class on using meats economically.
4. Invite a dietitian to share current nutrition information and how consumers can best meet their basic nutritional needs.

When parents behave appropriately while eating, they are teaching their children proper table etiquette.

Part Nine
Managing Clothing

Chapter 27
Planning and Shopping for Clothes

Analyzing your clothing needs can help you choose functional and fashionable clothes. Knowledge of construction will help you identify quality garments, while shopping skills will enable you to get the most for your money.

Chapter 28
Caring for Clothing

Clothing care includes repairs, storage, and laundering. When you have learned about care labels and laundry products, you will know the best way to care for each of your garments.

27

Planning and Shopping for Clothes

To Know

conforming
style
fashion
fads
classics
high fashion
clothing inventory
elements of design
structural lines
decorative lines
hue
value
tint
shade
intensity
warm colors
cool colors
texture
natural fibers
synthetic fibers
warp yarns
filling yarns
plain weave
twill weave

satin weave
warp knit
weft knit
fabric finish

Objectives

After studying this chapter, you will be able to

◇ explain how clothing is related to basic human needs.

◇ describe the significance of fashion in clothing selection.

◇ develop a wardrobe plan.

◇ explain how the elements of design relate to clothing.

◇ apply the decision-making process to clothing selection.

◇ describe various shopping guidelines.

◇ explain the factors that influence the performance of a garment.

Clothing is one of your basic needs. Throughout time, people have met the need for clothing in various ways. Fashions have come and gone. In recent years, traditional customs of dress have changed. Clothing means much more than physical protection and comfort. The psychological and social aspects of clothing have become more prominent in our society.

Your choices in clothing depend on both your values and resources. You can gain knowledge and develop skills that will help you reach your personal clothing goals. One of the ways you can do this is by taking inventory of your clothing and then developing a wardrobe plan based on your clothing needs. Learning how the elements of design apply to clothing will help you make the right choices. In addition, you can develop shopping skills to help you make the clothing selections.

The Significance of Clothing

You have probably found yourself sitting in a public place watching the people around you. The variety of dress you see in such situations may be quite interesting. You may see one person and think, "Wow! Is that person ever stylish!" The next person you see may make you wonder, "How could anyone appear in public dressed like that?"

There is little doubt about the significance of clothing. A person's values and lifestyle are strongly reflected in clothing. Many first impressions are based on the clothes people wear. See 27-1. Do you think you are creating the first impression that you want to create? Have you thought about why you choose the clothing you do? What values influence your selection of clothing? Discovering your own values related to clothing will help you understand why other people choose the clothing they do.

Influence of Basic Needs

From a practical point of view, climate strongly influences clothing choices. In

27-1 **Based on the clothing they wear, what do you think these people are like?**

some areas of the country, winter temperatures fall below zero. Clothing choices in these areas will vary greatly from areas where temperatures seldom fall below 40 degrees.

The weather in your area will affect the weight, fiber content, and the number of garments you buy. See 27-2. The wardrobe of a person who lives in Minnesota might include heavy coats for both casual wear and dress, boots, and warm shoes. Someone living in Southern California would probably not need these items.

You select clothing for physical comfort as well as protection. Comfort is influenced by both the fit of the garment and the characteristics of the fabric. For instance, you

27-2 **These jackets are just warm enough for a cool day outdoors.**

may need to choose a shirt to wear when you play tennis. Remember that you will need to move your arms around freely. You will want a loose-fitting garment that does not hamper body movement. You will also want to select a fabric that breathes—a fabric that allows moisture to evaporate from your skin. This makes you feel cooler and more comfortable. In the past 10 to 20 years, the fabric industry has made enormous strides. Today's fabrics are designed to correct problems related to comfort and physical well-being. Some elderly people or people with physical disabilities often base clothing choices on their own physical limitations. The ease of putting on and taking off clothing is of primary importance to them.

Comfort in relation to the feel or texture of certain fibers is a personal choice. Some people cannot tolerate certain wool fabrics because of their roughness and itchiness. Other people may prefer the softness and absorbency of many fabrics made from natural fibers. Comfort is a personal factor based on your physical reactions.

Most clothing choices, however, are based more on psychological than physical

reasons. For instance, you wear certain clothing when you want to impress someone, be fashionable, express yourself, or enhance your self-concept. Most people care about how they look. They understand the clothes they wear send certain messages and strongly influence the impression they make on others. Clothing may convey self-confidence, neatness and organization, conformity, status, independence, or even rebellion.

Desire for social approval can be a strong influence on choices of clothing. You may find yourself **conforming** to a group by wearing only the "right" styles—the styles they accept. Being similar to others provides you with a sense of security and belonging. See 27-3. Although conformity is linked with teenagers, it does occur throughout adult life as well.

The way you dress can also be a way of saying, "I am different." You can use clothing to express your individuality. Groups as well as individuals may use clothing to express nonconformity. Certain

27-3 **Wearing popular clothing styles often gives people a feeling of security and belonging.**

groups develop their own unique styles. These people are nonconformists because they do not meet the standards of society in general. However, they are conformists to their group. While attempting to express independence, they are also showing dependence on acceptance by their group.

Clothing can be a symbol of status. Some people consider designer labels to be prestigious. Having an extensive wardrobe made up of high fashion or expensive clothes may also indicate status.

Your clothing can express your self-image and personality. People have a variety of self-images, and they have clothing that represents each of those images. You may have clothing for school, social events, and work. The way you dress reflects the way you feel about each of your images or roles in life. People present personal identity, attitudes, moods, values, and feelings of self-worth through the way they dress. The way you dress is one of the ways you display and reinforce your self-concept. See 27-4. People who have a positive self-concept are more likely to be independent regarding dress. They are likely to experiment and try new fashions.

During the teen years, when the self-image is developing, clothing choices may seem inconsistent. The self-image becomes more stable as teens progress toward maturity. As this happens, teens begin to develop definite preferences for certain clothing styles.

Values, attitudes, and interests reflect your personality. Values motivate your behavior and decision making. Personal values influence your clothing choices. If social values are a high priority to you, you value what other people think about you. Then you may make clothing choices based on this value. In making clothing choices, values may conflict as they often do in other areas of life. A teenager may experience conflict between wanting to buy a popular style of swimsuit and his or her own feelings of modesty.

27-4 **Dressing neatly and professionally in the workplace can boost your desire for achievement on the job.**

The attitudes you develop as you mature are closely related to your values. They explain how you feel, think, and behave. You personally express your values through your attitude. You express your attitudes toward clothing by the clothing you select and the way you choose to wear it.

When you show an interest in something, you indicate that it appeals to you. The stronger the interest is, the more you emphasize it. People vary greatly in terms of their interest in clothing. Interest in clothing may also vary to a large degree depending on the person's stage in the life cycle.

Style and Fashion

Attitudes toward clothing are greatly influenced by the fashion world. Dressing in fashion—being fashionable—is very important to some people and is not at all important to others. No matter what your attitude is, the fashion of the day is going to affect your clothing choices. For women, current fashion dictates the length of skirts, the shape of shoes, and the height of heels. For men, fashion dictates the fullness of pants, the shape and size of shirt collars, and the width of ties.

Although the words fashion and style are often used interchangeably, they are different. The word **style** refers to specific characteristics or the form or shape of clothing. The A-line skirt or straight-leg jeans are styles of clothing. There are styles of coats, collars, sleeves, and shoes. Being aware of the names of various styles can help you discuss design in clothing.

Fashion refers to the style that is popular at a certain time. If people are wearing the current style, they are said to be "in fashion" or "dressing fashionably." However, phrases such as "being in style" or "looking stylish" have the same meaning as "being in fashion."

Designers and manufacturers regularly create new styles, which offer variations in color, fabric, and design. Certain styles are accepted by a large number of people for only a short period of time. These are referred to as **fads**. Bell-bottom pants are an example of a fad. See 27-5.

Other styles, known as **classics**, are worn year after year by a large segment of the public. The shirtwaist dress, pump shoes, oxford shirt, and trench coat are examples of classics. See 27-6.

High fashion is a term used in the business and fashion world to describe the latest designs. These designs are often extreme and of high quality. These exaggerated versions of new styles are accepted by only a few people who can afford them and like to be different.

Most styles go through a fashion cycle. During their introduction, they are followed by a few daring persons. As a style rises in acceptance, it is copied and adopted by

Pineapple Appeal

27-5 **Wildly colorful pants like these were popular fads of the 1980s.**

27-6 **The suit and blouse worn by this woman are classics.**

those who want to look "smart" and "fashionable." The cycle continues. Through advertising, the fashion gains public attention, often resulting in widespread acceptance and mass conformity. After reaching its peak, the fashion declines and then finally disappears. Unless a style is accepted as a classic, it eventually completes the fashion cycle, and consumers experiment with newer styles.

It is interesting to notice that fashion often repeats itself in somewhat modified versions. The crinoline petticoats of the 1860s returned again in a modified version in the 1950s. The chemise first became popular in the Roaring Twenties, reappeared in the late 1950s, and again in the 1980s.

Many people have a negative view of the fashion world. They see millions of dollars in advertising, extreme styles, and styles that will go "out" in a short time. They may think the fashion world is plotting to keep people spending money and constantly changing their wardrobes. Although this may be true to a certain extent, remember that you make the choices. You decide the way you want to look and the clothing you want to buy. You, along with other consumers, dictate which styles disappear, become fashionable, or become classics.

A change in fashion is often welcome. However, a valuable skill is being able to recognize and use the fashions that meet your needs while ignoring those that don't. The most important skill is controlling your use of fashion rather than letting it control you.

A Wardrobe Plan

You have probably planned clothing for a special occasion or for a vacation. Have you ever thought of making a long-range plan for your entire wardrobe? Have you thought of planning a wardrobe that suits your own personal needs? Without a wardrobe plan, you may find yourself making impulse purchases that can add up to costly mistakes. Many people have

unworn garments in their closets. These are often separates that match nothing in the wardrobe.

Your *wardrobe* consists of all the clothes you have to wear. An adequate wardrobe means you have enough clothing to carry out your daily activities satisfactorily.

To plan an adequate wardrobe, you must consider what clothing and accessories you need for your lifestyle. Be aware of what clothes you have and the activities for which you need clothing. See 27-7. Conducting a personal analysis will help you become aware of personal characteristics that might influence your clothing selections.

A Clothing Inventory

Before you can effectively make decisions about clothing needs, take inventory

27-7 **A person who likes to ski needs the proper clothing and equipment for this activity.**

of your clothing. A **clothing inventory** is simply a list of your clothing and accessories. You can use suggested forms for the inventory or you can simply develop your own. Listing the garments under general categories should help you get organized. Some categories might include shirts, blouses, sweaters, jackets, pants, skirts, or dresses. If you live in an area of changing climates, you may want to take inventory as you get out your seasonal clothing in the fall and spring.

To do a thorough inventory, follow a procedure. Begin by going through your clothing and separating it into three categories—clothing you like and wear, clothing that needs repair or alteration, and clothing you don't wear. Carefully analyze the clothing that needs repair or alteration. Are the repairs and alterations simple, or are they quite extensive? Will they take up a lot of your time or require the services of a paid alterations person? Do you have the skill and time needed to make the changes? How much money do you have available for repairs and alterations? How important is that garment in your wardrobe? The way you answer these questions will influence what you decide to do with the garment.

Next, analyze the clothing you don't wear and decide why you don't wear each garment. The reason may be fit, color, or style. Can you do anything to make the garment wearable? If not, dispose of the garment in some way.

Now you have narrowed down to clothing you like and wear or clothing that could be made wearable. You are ready to inventory your accessories. *Accessories* include shoes, stockings, belts, bags, scarves, ties, and jewelry. See 27-8. Decide what accessories go with each of your garments and what accessories you need to buy. When you are analyzing separates, such as skirts and blouses or pants and shirts, consider what separates you can combine. Do some separates go with nothing else? What accessories can you wear with your separates?

27-8 **This colorful scarf would go with a variety of outfits from this suit to a fun casual outfit.**

Clothing Needs

In developing a wardrobe plan, consider your clothing needs for your lifestyle. Teenagers may need clothes for school, work, social activities, and sports activities.

Clothing needs vary greatly from person to person. The young man who is a host at a nice restaurant needs different clothing than the young man who will be washing dishes in the same restaurant. Clothing needs vary depending upon a person's age, health, occupation, activities, and lifestyle.

You may find it helpful to make a list of your specific clothing needs and compare that list with your final clothing inventory list. Analyze your lists to decide where you have the greatest need. If you need clothing in several areas, you may want to list your needs in order of their priority. Keep in mind that you can wear many clothes for a variety of activities and combine separates in many ways. Buying separates in colors that blend together will give you many possible combinations. See 27-9.

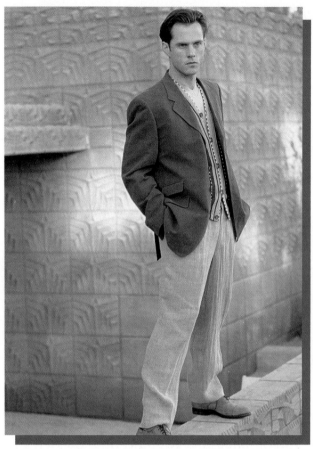

The Fashion Association

27-9 Separates like these are likely to blend well with other separates in your wardrobe.

Personal Analysis

After establishing the clothing you have and the clothing you need, a personal analysis is the next step toward a wardrobe plan. Carrying out a personal analysis will make you aware of what personal features to consider when selecting clothing.

Brainstorming

As a class, develop a questionnaire to help you analyze why people choose the clothing they do. Distribute the questionnaire among classmates. Then tally the results and discuss them with others.

First, analyze your size and body type. Some body features can't be changed, such as height and bone structure. However, you can use clothing and accessories to emphasize your positive features and to camouflage your less desirable features.

Other things about your body type can be controlled. What you eat and how much you exercise affects your looks more than any choice of clothing. Having poor posture can detract from your appearance as much as being obese or being underweight. Having an exercise routine and good eating habits can greatly improve how your clothes look on you and how you feel about yourself. When you take care of your appearance, your self-confidence increases. Your clothing choices become a pleasant challenge instead of a threat.

Your hair, face shape, and skin coloring each affect how you look to others. Learning about the elements of design, especially line and color, will help you choose clothing to bring out the positive aspects of these personal features.

The Elements of Design

Line, color, and texture are the **elements of design** that apply to clothing. These resources are arranged to create certain effects in clothing. Knowing about the elements of design gives you the power to create the look or style you feel is best for you. Later in this book, you will learn how these elements can also be used to create certain effects in the home.

Line

Line in clothing is used in a variety of ways. There are both structural lines and decorative lines. **Structural lines** are formed as the garment is sewn by seams, darts, collars, pleats, pockets, gathers, tucks, or draping. **Decorative lines** make the garment more appealing to the eye. They are present in fabric patterns or texture and in accessories such as buttons, trims, piping, and ruffles. Fabric pattern lines include stripes, plaids, herringbone, and checks. See 27-10. The outer lines of a garment form a silhouette, a prominent line in clothing.

Line is a design element that can have a strong effect on how a garment looks on you. Different types of lines and shapes create certain feelings. The effect of line depends on length, direction, straightness, and width. Some lines suggest a graceful quality, while others suggest severity, stiffness, and formality.

You can use line to accent your best features and de-emphasize the features you do not like. A person can be made to look

27-10 The horizontal stripes in this sweater are an example of decorative lines.

taller, shorter, heavier, or thinner through use of line in clothing. For instance, vertical lines tend to make a body look taller and thinner. Horizontal lines tend to make a body look shorter and heavier. Considering your figure type—your strengths and weaknesses—which lines would be helpful to you?

Color

People probably notice color of clothing more than any other design element. Some people seem to instinctively know how to use colors together successfully. Others do not. However, most people need an understanding of color in order to use it to enhance their appearance.

Understanding Color

When a beam of white light passes through a prism, the colors are separated into a band. The colors appear in a certain order—violet, blue, green, yellow, orange, and red. Colors also appear in the same order on the color wheel. For this reason, the color wheel is used to study color. See 27-11. Red, yellow, and blue are the three primary colors. They cannot be created by mixing other colors. These colors are equally spaced around the color wheel. The primary colors are used to produce the rest of the colors on the color wheel.

When you mix equal amounts of any two primary colors, a secondary color is produced. Green, orange, and violet are secondary colors. Green is produced by mixing yellow and blue. Orange is produced by mixing red and yellow. Violet is

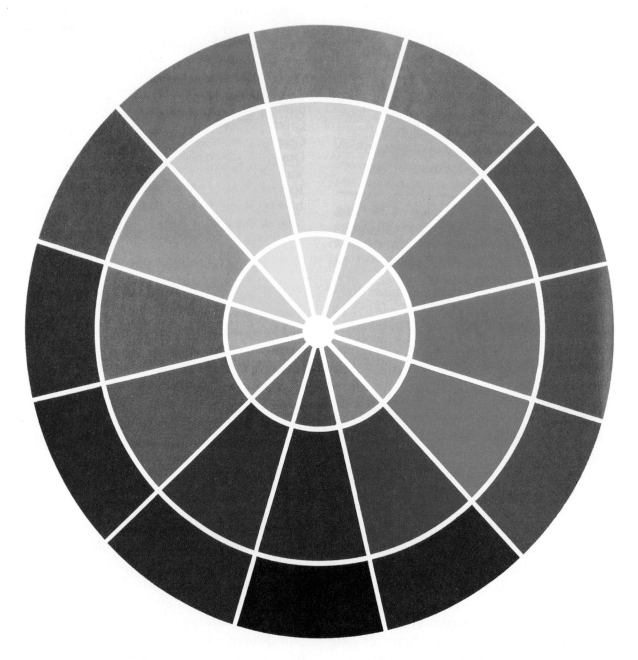

27-11 The color wheel is used to study relationships between colors. Normal values are shown in the center ring. Tints are shown in the inner ring, and shades are shown in the outer ring.

produced by mixing red and blue. Each of the secondary colors lies halfway between the primary colors that were mixed.

Mixing a primary color with the secondary color next to it produces an intermediate color. The names of intermediate colors come from the colors that produced them. They are yellow-green, blue-green, blue-violet, red-violet, red-orange, and yellow-orange.

Characteristics of Color

The three characteristics of color are hue, value, and intensity.

Hue is the characteristic that gives a color a name and makes it unique. It makes red different from blue, yellow, or any combination of colors.

Value is the lightness or darkness of a hue. Normal hues are shown in the middle ring on the color wheel. Adding white to any normal hue makes it lighter and produces a **tint**. Tints, also described as high values, are shown in the inner ring of the color wheel. Adding black to any normal value makes it darker and produces a **shade** or a low value. See 27-12. Low values are shown in the outer ring on the

color wheel. Using value contrasts can make a design more interesting, while lack of contrast can create a monotonous effect. For instance, wearing gray pants with a gray shirt and gray shoes would be monotonous.

Intensity, the brightness or dullness of a color, is the final characteristic. Strong, bright colors have a high intensity, while dull, grayed, neutral colors are of low intensity. The intensity of a hue can be lowered or grayed by mixing it with its complement—the color across from it on the color wheel.

Intensity affects the overall appearance of your clothing. Bright colors tend to advance, attract attention, and increase apparent size. See 27-13. Duller colors tend to recede and decrease in size.

Similar intensities look best together. In other words, a dull color looks best with other dull colors. However, bright and dull colors can be combined if the dull color is neutral or nearly a neutral. White, black, and gray are the neutral colors. Dull colors such as beige, dark brown, tan, gray, or dark navy could be combined with bright colors.

You can use colors to achieve a certain effect or to change your appearance. Certain colors are described as warm or cool colors. The **warm colors** are related to red, yellow, or orange. They create feelings

Pendelton

27-12 Shades of green and red are used in this skirt and sweater.

27-13 The colors in this scarf are intense and attract attention.

Getting Involved

of liveliness, cheer, and excitement. They appear to advance and make things look larger. The **cool colors** are related to blue and green. They give a more subdued, quiet feeling. These colors seem to recede and make things look smaller.

White and light colors reflect light and tend to make things look larger. Black and dark colors absorb light and make things appear smaller.

Color, You, and Your Wardrobe

When you get dressed, your skin, hair, and eyes become part of the color combination. Consider how certain colors affect these body features. One way to do this is to drape fabrics or different colors near your face. Look at how each color affects your skin, hair, and eyes. Build your wardrobe around those colors that do the most for you. See 27-14.

27-14 **This man has chosen clothing that flatters his natural coloring.**

Texture

Texture describes the feel of fabric as well as the surface appearance. Texture is found both in the thickness of the fabric and on the surface of the fabric. Variations in fibers, yarn structure, and finishes produce a great variety of textures. They range from the heavy, rough appearance of a wool winter jacket to the smooth, shiny appearance of a silk blouse. Words such as smooth, bulky, fuzzy, shiny, soft, coarse, stiff, and crisp describe varying textures.

You can use texture just as you use line and color to create the appearance you desire. Soft, clingy fabrics tend to reveal the contours of the body and are best for people who are not heavy. Stiff fabrics tend to stand away from the body and hide figure irregularities. However, they can also add bulk and weight. Bulky fabrics add volume to the body due to their weight and bulkiness. See 27-15. A tiny person may be overpowered by extreme bulk. Shiny textures, which reflect light, make a person look larger. However, dull textures seem suitable for all figure types. Which textures seem best for your figure type?

decisions are made as a part of a process that includes careful considerations. Your considerations determine the success of the final choice. Making decisions in clothing selection consists of the following five steps:

1. clarifying the choice
2. considering alternatives
3. evaluating the alternatives
4. making a choice
5. evaluating that choice

Clarifying the Choice

The first step in clothing selection is to be specific in terms of what you need to buy. For instance, an office executive might say he or she needs new clothes for work. Does he or she mean suits, casual wear, or shoes? If that person has developed a thorough wardrobe plan, he or she will know what specific items are needed. He or she will have conducted a clothing inventory, discovered needs, and set priorities.

Considering Alternatives

After clearly identifying clothing needs, the next step is to consider alternatives. Shopping at a variety of stores and trying on a variety of styles gives you more complete knowledge of what is available. Don't limit your shopping to one store unless you find the perfect garment at an unbelievable price. That seldom happens.

Evaluating the Alternatives

In this step of the decision-making process, you weigh the advantages and disadvantages of each alternative. This step is difficult for the shopper who lacks knowledge related to clothing selection. To make a good decision, you need a basic knowledge of fabrics and the care they require. In addition, you should know how to tell when a

Mark Hayward

27-15 **Bulky fabrics look good on thin people.**

Knowledge and Skill in Clothing Selection

In managing clothing, you control your use of resources to help you reach certain clothing goals. If you have been working on a wardrobe plan, you may also be starting to set specific goals in clothing selection. A variety of resources can help you reach these goals.

The Decision-Making Process in Clothing Selection

Effective clothing decisions involve more than just suddenly making a decision to buy a certain garment. These clothing garment is constructed well. Without this knowledge, you can only guess which garment is the best buy. See 27-16.

Making a Choice

The choice you make will be based on your personal values as well as your evaluation of the alternatives. Sometimes the final choice is based on economic values, perhaps the amount of money allotted for the purchase. Another time, the choice might be based on social or psychological values. For instance, you might choose one outfit over another because it is "the latest style."

Over time, your needs, interests, and values change. The values that influence your clothing choices will vary as you gain knowledge and maturity and as your resources change.

27-16 Pausing to evaluate your choices can help you make the best possible purchasing decision.

Evaluating the Choice

After you have had the opportunity to wear a garment several times, evaluate your choice. Was that garment a good choice? Would any of the other alternatives have been better? If so, why? How can you use this decision-making experience to help you make future decisions related to clothing selection?

Careful evaluation of each clothing purchase gives you helpful information for making future decisions. As part of the evaluation, you must consider what values led you to make that choice. Were those values high priorities?

Your available resources might also have influenced your choice. Time, money, energy, knowledge, and skill are some of the resources that might influence clothing selection.

Sewing Skills

Skill in clothing construction is one resource that may influence how you select clothing. The desire to customize clothing provides the incentive for some people to develop this skill. Some people feel they can save money on specialty clothing and it is worth the time spent in clothing construction. Others, whose time is quite limited, prefer to use that time in a different way.

Learning to operate and care for a sewing machine is a valuable skill. The owner's manual that comes with the sewing machine is a valuable resource in learning how to operate the machine safely and properly.

Many patterns are available to make a variety of garments. The pattern guide sheet that comes with the pattern provides step-by-step directions on how to construct the garment.

If you have sewing skills, clothing construction allows you to create the exact garment you want in terms of style, fabric, color, and fit. See 27-17.

Shopping Guidelines

Other decisions made in clothing selection deal with where and when to shop. If you have developed a wardrobe plan and know your specific needs, those decisions will be simple.

Where to Shop

Clothing is available in many types of stores. Each of these stores is different, having both advantages and disadvantages for consumers. Knowing about each type of store will help you decide where to shop. See 27-18.

Chain or independent stores that sell a large variety of goods and services are called *department stores*. They usually offer a wide selection with an extensive choice of styles, colors, sizes, qualities, and price ranges. Department stores are usually divided into special departments for

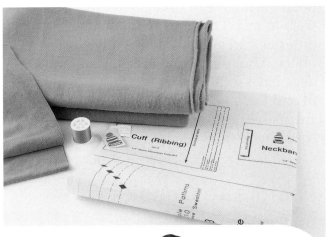

Pineapple Appeal

27-17 If you decide to sew your clothes, you can use your skill and creativity to transform a pattern and fabric into an outfit.

27-18 A mall offers a variety of stores at which to shop for clothing.

various types of garments. They offer a variety of customer services and usually have return privileges. Personal service may be limited because of the large size.

Specialty stores are chain or independent stores that specialize in a limited type of merchandise. A store might specialize in jewelry, shoes, lingerie, or leather goods. Specialty stores usually offer a wide selection within their specialty, and they have different price levels. The salespeople generally know their merchandise. They are usually well-trained and experienced.

Variety stores are chain or independent stores that sell a variety of consumer goods in a low price range. There is usually a large amount of self-service. Variety stores offer many types of merchandise in open display. Few customer services are offered. There are usually very few salespeople who have a minimum amount of training.

Manufacturer's outlet stores are stocked with extra merchandise from a manufacturer's normal production. Prices are usually lower than in variety stores. Much of the merchandise may be imperfect although the flaws may be small. Because returns may not be allowed, you should carefully inspect a product before buying it. You may be required to pay cash at an outlet store. Low prices are their chief feature.

Chain or independent stores that attempt to undersell other merchants on certain lines and types of merchandise are called *discount stores*. They generally offer convenient parking facilities, few customer services, and evening shopping hours. High-volume selling is typical.

Used clothing stores are sometimes referred to as thrift or secondhand shops. They usually have clothing in various qualities for all ages. However, sizes, colors, and styles are limited. They can be a good source of bargains.

Internet and mail-order businesses are popular with consumers. Many companies have Web sites on the Internet. *Mail-order businesses* consist of companies who offer clothing for sale in catalogs, magazines, and newspapers. The Internet and mail-order are convenient ways to shop. It is great for people who live in rural areas or do not wish to travel to do their shopping. The ordering can often be done online or by telephone. Shopping by Internet or mail-order does have some disadvantages. Judging the fit and the quality effectively can be difficult. Also, returning unwanted merchandise costs money and can be a nuisance.

Factors to Consider

Consider the following factors in selecting stores at which to shop for clothing: range of merchandise offered, types of services offered, the convenience in shopping, and business practices.

- *Range of merchandise offered.* Although some stores carry a variety in price ranges, others may have very limited price ranges. You may go into some stores and find nothing within your price range. Not only do price ranges vary, but stores also vary in the number of styles they offer. Some stores offer only limited lines of styles and sizes.

- *Types of service provided.* Stores may provide a variety of services including efficient, courteous salespeople, charge accounts, delivery service, gift wrapping, guarantees, or return privileges. However, these services will add to the cost of your purchases.

◆ *Convenience in shopping.* Convenience is important to many people. A store near your home, is easy to get to, and has convenient parking is a definite advantage. See 27-19. The way a store is arranged inside also affects its convenience.

◆ *Business practices.* The ethics of businesses show in many ways. Do they present information in advertisements honestly and accurately? Are the salespeople truthful and competent? Does the business management stand behind their goods? Answers to these questions will give you a good idea of whether or not a business is ethical.

When to Buy

When you have developed a wardrobe plan, you know specifically what you need. With this knowledge, you can take advantage of sales.

Clearance sales are held to get rid of seasonal items that have not sold. For instance, sales on winter coats are usually held in late December and early January. Clearance sales usually offer the biggest price reductions.

Occasionally, there are special purchase sales on a particular item. These sales may be due to overproduction of that particular item. Be sure to watch for slight imperfections because that could also be the reason for the sale. If the imperfections are minor—if they don't affect the looks or durability of a garment—you may have a bargain.

Because so many different types of sales are advertised, you may have difficulty knowing how good they are. The newspaper advertises anniversary sales, holiday sales, back-to-school sales, President's Day sales, and many others. Although these sales may represent some reductions in cost, they are not the drastic reductions found in clearance sales.

27-19 **Nearby parking will be especially important when you are carrying many shopping bags to your car.**

More expensive stores often have an original markup price that is from 30 to 50 percent higher than their cost. Their one-third off sale may bring the price down so it compares with the original price in other stores. You will learn how different stores use the price markup through experience. As you shop in various stores, you will begin to notice the same or similar items at different prices. In a short time, you will discover which stores tend to have a high markup.

Skill in Judging Performance

Knowing as much as you can about the product you are buying is likely to ensure a good buy. The performance of a garment refers to how it will meet your needs. This includes the way it looks on you, comfort, durability, and the amount of care required. See 27-20. These things depend upon the fiber content and fabric characteristics, finishes, care required, fit, and the quality of construction. Quality is usually related to price, but this is not always true. Therefore, you have an advantage when you have developed skill in judging performance.

27-20 **When investing in clothing that you plan to wear for some time, the performance of the garment is very important.**

The fiber used, construction methods, and finish applied all determine if a garment is suitable for its intended use. Having a basic knowledge of each of these areas can be extremely helpful to you in clothing selection.

Fibers and Yarns

Fabrics are constructed of yarns, which are made up of thread-like strands called fibers. Fibers are either natural or synthetic. The **natural fibers** are wool, cotton, flax (linen), silk, and hair fibers such as cashmere. Natural fibers come from plants or animals. Fur and leather are also natural clothing materials, but they are not textiles because they are not made of fibers. Some commonly used **synthetic fibers** are nylon, rayon, acetate, acrylic, and polyester. Most synthetic fibers are manufactured from chemicals.

Each fiber has certain characteristics that affect whether it will be suitable for certain garments. Fibers vary in their length, luster, resiliency, strength, and reaction to moisture and temperature.

Learning fiber properties may be easier if you group them according to common characteristics. For instance, cotton, linen, and rayon have many characteristics in common. They are highly absorbent, wrinkle easily, and are subject to mildew.

Fibers are twisted together into yarns. The strength of the fiber and the way the yarns are twisted together contributes to the strength of the yarn. Yarns may be monofilament, meaning one yarn, as in nylon hosiery. However, most yarns are made up of two or more yarns twisted together. A two-ply yarn refers to one in which two yarns were twisted together. A three-ply yarn is made of three yarns, and so on. If the same fiber is used, the larger ply yarn is the stronger yarn. The fabric appearance is affected by the size of the yarn and the tightness of the twist. A looser twist creates a softer yarn, while a tighter twist develops a firmer, but stronger yarn.

Blending yarns is a way to combine different fibers. A blend can combine the best characteristics of different fibers. Polyester and cotton are two commonly blended fibers. The absorbency of cotton is combined with the wrinkle resistance of polyester. Advances in the textile industry have made fiber blending highly sophisticated. Consumers must rely on garment labels for accurate information on fiber content.

Fabric Construction

Fibers and yarns can be converted into cloth by various methods. However, weaving and knitting are the most common.

Weaving is done by interlacing two or more sets of yarns at right angles. The yarns that run up and down are called the **warp yarns** and are referred to as the lengthwise grain. Those passing across the warp yarns are called the **filling yarns** and are referred to as the crosswise grain.

The strength of the woven fabric depends on the fiber used, thread count, and type of weave. The thread count, or closeness of the weave, is often measured in number of threads per inch. Because closely woven fabrics have a higher thread count, they usually keep their shape better, slip less at the seams, and last longer.

Basic Weaves

There are three basic weaves: the plain weave, twill weave, and satin weave. See 27-21. In the **plain weave**, each filler yarn is placed over one warp yarn, under the next, over the next, under the next, and so on. Gingham and percale are examples of this weave. The **twill weave** has a distinct characteristic of the diagonal line created. This line is created when a yarn in one direction floats or passes over two or more yarns in the opposite direction. Denim is a popular example of the use of this weave. Other examples include gabardine and herringbone, a twill variation. The twill weave is often used to produce strong, durable fabrics. The **satin weave** has a smooth surface created by using long float yarns on the surface. Silk and acetate are often used in satin weave construction. Sateen is the cotton fabric made using the satin weave. The satin weave does not normally produce durable fabrics since the floats tend to snag easily.

Many variations of these three weaves are produced. By combining variations in weaves, fibers, and the twist of the yarn, possibilities are almost unlimited.

Knits

Knitting is the other common method of converting yarn to cloth. Knits are made

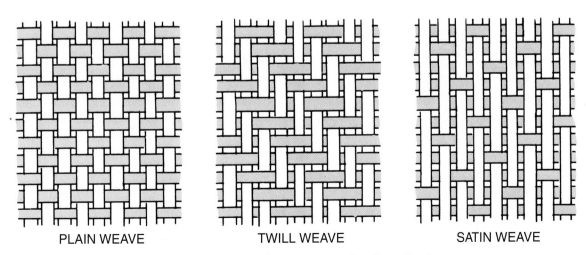

PLAIN WEAVE   TWILL WEAVE   SATIN WEAVE

▤ **27-21 The plain weave, twill weave, and satin weave are the three basic weaves.**

from a continuous yarn or set of yarns that form rows of loops. A **warp knit** can be made only by machine. One or more sets of yarn the width of the fabric are used. Loops are formed vertically, and an entire row is made at one time. Although warp knits will not run, any knit can snap easily if a loop is caught or pulled. See 27-22. A **weft knit** may be made on a knitting machine or may be made by hand. The loops are made as the yarn is added in a horizontal direction. See 27-23. Double knit is a variation of the weft knit that is firmer and will not ravel. Most knit fabrics are comfortable and wrinkle-resistant. They easily adjust to the shape of the body.

Many factors determine the wearing qualities of a fabric. Loosely woven or knitted fabrics usually snag more easily. They do not hold their shape as well as fabrics with a higher thread count or a tighter knit. Loosely woven fabrics may fray at the seams and pull out around button-holes. Knits have greater elasticity, which contributes to their comfort and fit. However, loose knits may tend to bag or stretch.

Fabric Finishes

A **fabric finish** is a treatment or process that alters the appearance, feel, or performance of a fabric. Some finishes make the

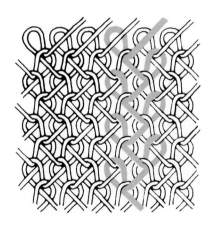

M. Bruce

27-22 Loops are formed vertically in warp knitting.

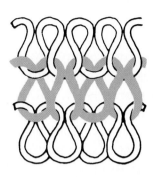

27-23 Loops are formed as yarn is added in a horizontal direction in weft knitting.

material more attractive by giving it some specific appearance. Dyeing and printing are finishes that add color to fabric. Some fabrics are constructed of fiber-dyed or yarn-dyed yarns. However, most fabrics are piece-dyed. The color is added after the fabric is constructed. At first glance, you may have difficulty telling if a fabric is printed or yarn-dyed. This might be true in looking at a striped fabric. You can usually identify a printed fabric because the wrong side is much lighter than the right side.

In general, yarn-dyed fabric tends to hold the color better than a printed fabric. However, there are great variations in quality of printing of fabrics.

Other finishes are more functional. They may make the fabric more durable, more comfortable, or so that it will require less care. Permanent press and water proofing are examples of functional finishes.

Some finishes are permanent—lasting the lifetime of the garment. Temporary finishes last only until the garment is washed or dry-cleaned. Others are referred to as durable finishes. Although they are not permanent, they will last a few washings or dry cleanings.

When you know what to expect from fabrics that have certain finishes, you can select the garment that best suits your needs. Remember to consider any extra care that may be necessary because of a finish used.

Care Required

The *Permanent Care Labeling Rule* requires that a garment include instructions on caring properly for the garment. This includes information such as whether it can be machine washed and dried, if ironing is required, or if it must be dry-cleaned.

Manufacturers may provide other valuable information that is not required. Hang tags may point out special performance characteristics such as being antistatic, water repellent, or permanently pleated.

Fit

The way clothing fits your body is an important factor in clothing selection. Even the most expensive garment does not give the appearance of quality if it does not fit properly.

When you are considering a garment purchase, check the fit in front of a triple full-length mirror. If possible, try it on with the accessories you plan to wear with it. In particular, the height of your shoe heel should be the same as the shoes you will wear with the garment. Different heel heights can change how the garment hangs.

The design of the garment determines how it should fit. Some garments are designed to be loose fitting; others fit more snugly. Evaluate the fit both for comfort and appearance. Are you able to move easily? Do the armholes bind? Is there enough ease for you to move your arms? Is there enough ease to sit down without the fabric pulling? These and other factors are important in checking fit as related to performance. Many of the factors related to fit depend upon the particular garment being considered. See 27-24.

Quality of Construction

The quality of construction is as important as the quality of the fabric. Good construction makes the garment more durable and improves its overall

appearance. Being able to effectively judge quality is an important skill in clothing selection.

One way to check garment quality is to turn the garment "inside out." Turn sleeves and pants legs inside out as well. Hold the garment up to the light to look for any holes, rips, tears, or flaws in the fabric. These could be signs of fabric weakness indicating poor quality and poor durability. Be sure to check front, back, and both sides of the garment.

When evaluating seams, look for even stitching, especially on topstitching. The seams should be wide because narrow seams may fray. Narrow seams may indicate other shortcuts in construction as well. The machine stitching should be straight.

A generous hem usually hangs better than a narrow one and also allows for alterations. The hem should be even in width, and the stitching should not show on the right side. Examine patch pockets for reinforcement at the top corners. Bound and flap pockets should have firm construction at the ends. Be sure necklines lie flat and

27-24 Fit is very important in a garment such as a tailored jacket.

collars are centered with even curves or smooth corners.

Examine buttonholes to be sure that stitches are close together and deep enough not to pull out. Make sure zippers open and close easily. Check to see that buttons are firmly sewed in place. Buttons should be washable if the garment is washable. Also examine the quality of snaps, hooks and eyes, and other fasteners carefully.

Make sure the lining will take the same kind of cleaning as the outer garment. If the outer fabric is washable and the lining is not, the garment will lose its shape. Linings should be made with a firm weave and be smooth enough to slide easily over other fabrics.

To check for wrinkle resistance or a garment's ability to travel well, do the "crush test." Take an area of the hem or sleeve. Hold it tightly and crush it in the palm of your hand for at least 30 seconds. Release the fabric to observe whether or not the creases or wrinkles remain after a short time. If the wrinkles remain, this indicates that the garment will not travel well and may need to be pressed before wearing. If wrinkles seem to disappear after a few minutes, the garment will most likely be a good choice for travel and resistant to wrinkles.

Summary

People make clothing choices based upon their values. Becoming aware of the significance of clothing in people's lives will help you understand why clothing choices differ as they do. This knowledge will also help you assess your own values in relation to clothing choices.

A wardrobe plan is a valuable resource for reaching personal clothing goals. A clothing inventory, a list of specific clothing needs, and an awareness of your personal features can help you develop the wardrobe plan.

An understanding of the elements of design can help you select clothing you feel is best for you. Design elements, such as line and color, can be used to emphasize your best features.

Various resources may be helpful in selecting clothing items. The decision-making process can be used to help you make good choices. Sewing skills and being aware of the advantages and disadvantages of types of stores that sell clothing will be another aid in clothing selection.

Developing skill in judging quality in clothing will help you make a wise choice. Knowledge of fabric characteristics, fabric construction, and care required are resources that also help in clothing selection. Being able to judge the fit and quality of a garment are other valuable skills in choosing clothing.

To Review

1. Explain the difference between the following terms:
   A. Style and fashion
   B. Fad and classic
2. Describe the steps involved in developing a wardrobe plan.
3. List the elements of design that relate to clothing and describe how they affect the way your clothing looks on you.
4. Three characteristics of color are _____, _____, and _____.
5. Match the following types of stores with the appropriate descriptions.
   _____Used clothing stores
   _____Manufacturer's outlet stores
   _____Specialty store
   _____Department stores
   _____Discount stores
   _____Variety stores
   A. attempt to undersell other merchants on some known lines and types of merchandise; high-volume selling is typical
   B. are sometimes referred to as thrift shops
   C. specialize in a limited type of merchandise
   D. usually have low-price merchandise from normal production of that particular manufacturer
   E. sell a variety of consumer goods usually in a low price range and with a large amount of self-service
   F. are usually divided into special departments for various types of garments
6. Name the three basic weaves. Then indicate which weave corresponds to each of the following descriptions.
   A. Cotton woven in this method is called sateen.
   B. This weave has the characteristic of a distinct diagonal line.
   C. Denim is an example of this weave.
   D. Gingham and percale are examples of this weave.
   E. This weave gives a smooth appearance.
   F. Gabardine and herringbone are examples of this weave.
   G. Long float yarns are used in the weave.
7. Give two examples of fabric finishes.
8. What is the purpose of the Permanent Care Labeling Rule?
9. Even the most expensive garment does not give the appearance of quality if it does not _____ properly.
10. Name eight features that indicate quality in a garment.

To Challenge Your Thinking

1. Look through recent magazines to find clothing advertisments that appeal to psychological needs. Share your examples with other members of the class.
2. Suggest ways that you could use the elements of design to help emphasize or hide certain body features.
3. Decide on a piece of clothing you need and visit at least two stores to find possible choices. Although you may not be able to make the actual purchase, use the decision-making process to make a choice. Write out step three of the process, evaluating the alternatives. List the advantages and disadvantages of each choice. Which would you choose and why? What values strongly guided your choice?
4. Choose a garment from your wardrobe and inspect it for quality. List its positive and negative features.

To Do with the Class

1. Work in a group to prepare a presentation on clothing that meets physical needs. Use examples related to fit, texture, absorbency, and other functional aspects of clothing.
2. Listen to a presentation on choosing the colors that are right for you. Discuss the relationship of hair, skin, and eye color to the color of your clothing.
3. Work in pairs to develop a personal analysis. Identify personal features to consider when selecting clothing such as body type; face shape; and skin, hair, and eye color.
4. Conduct an experiment to test the performance of various types of fibers, fabric construction, or finishes.

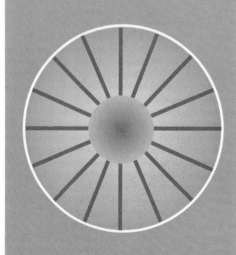

To Do with Your Community

1. Visit several types of stores that sell clothing in or near your community. Select one or more items and compare quality and cost at each of the different stores. Report findings to the class.
2. Collect any unwanted or used clothing. Donate these items to a homeless shelter as part of a class project.
3. Invite a clothing buyer or clothing store manager/owner to share information on styles, trends, and factors that determine quality in clothing.
4. Observe people in various careers or at different locations in your community. Determine the reasons they dress as they do, (status, occupation, to follow trends, etc.).

28 Caring for Clothing

To Know

care labels
soaps
detergents
water softeners
precipitating water softeners
nonprecipitating water softeners
fabric softeners
chlorine bleaches
disinfectant
oxygen bleaches

Objectives

After studying this chapter, you will be able to

- provide proper routine and periodic care and repair of your own clothing.

- suggest guidelines for clothing storage.

- demonstrate use of care labels as a resource in laundry techniques.

- explain procedures to follow in stain removal.

- describe products that contribute to better care and cleaning of clothes.

- relate specific laundry procedures to the resulting appearance of clothing.

Systematic care indicates a plan. It shows you are thorough and consistent–important qualities for a good manager. Managing your clothing care effectively can benefit you in many ways. Because proper care and maintenance will greatly extend the life of a garment, you will save money. Wearing clothing that is regularly cared for will give you a well-groomed look. See 28-1. Routine care also saves time in the long run. If clothing is cared for properly, it is fresh and ready to wear when you need it.

Techniques of Clothing Care

If done regularly and systematically, clothing care is not a time-consuming, unpleasant task. Not caring for your clothing regularly causes an accumulation of mending, pressing, laundry, and stain removal. Effective management of your clothing requires routine and periodic care of clothing as well as proper storage procedures.

Routine Care and Simple Repairs

Your daily care of clothing greatly affects its looks. For instance, the way you put a garment on and take it off will make a great

difference in how long it lasts. Carefully take your clothes off without yanking. You can avoid repair work by working zippers gently and putting pants on before you put on your shoes. Lack of care may create rips, broken fasteners, broken stitches, loose hems, or popped seams.

Proper care is important when you remove your clothing after school, after work, or at the end of the day. Hanging the clothes up or folding them and putting them away will make them ready for the next wearing. Leaving your clothes in a heap on the floor or throwing them in a chair means more work for you the next time you want to wear them. See 28-2.

As you put away your clothes, close zippers, hooks and eyes, and other fasteners that might catch and snag the garment. A variety of special hangers are

28-1 **People who take care of their clothing look fresh and well-groomed.**

28-2 **Clothes get wrinkled when thrown on a chair. They may have to be ironed before they can be worn again.**

Brainstorming

Check your wardrobe to see if you can find an article of clothing that is the victim of poor routine care. Share the problem with the class and discuss how it could have been avoided.

designed for specific garments. These include skirt hangers, pants hangers, and hangers with padded or shaped shoulder bars for jackets. Rounded plastic and wooden hangers are usually better than wire because wire hangers can leave stretch marks on fine materials. Wire hangers may also rust and leave marks on clothing. Clothing that should not be hung, such as most knit sweaters, can be folded carefully. Store these items in such a way that they will not be crushed.

Watch daily for needed repairs. Glance over each garment after you wear it. The hem might be coming out. There may be a tear, a snag, or perhaps a pulled thread in a knitted fabric. Buttons may have become loose or fallen off. Making these repairs as you notice them will help avoid a more serious problem with the garment. A small rip may become a big tear if not mended. Laundering a garment with a small rip is likely to make the rip larger.

Certain types of mending can be easily accomplished, even if you are inexperienced. Simple mending includes sewing on buttons, repairing a ripped seam, or applying a patch. Whether a mending task is easy or challenging for you, there are many resources available to help you with mending tasks. A detailed sewing book found at your local library or book store will give you step-by-step directions on performing various mending tasks. In addition, tailors and seamstresses are available if you are willing to pay to have these tasks done.

Personal cleanliness is an important part of routine care related to clothing. Using an antiperspirant will prevent perspiration from soaking through the garment. If you use hair spray after getting dressed, wrap a cloth or towel around your shoulders and neck to protect the garment.

Routine care includes laundering or cleaning your clothing when necessary. Don't throw damp clothes in a clothes hamper or down a laundry chute. Mildew can form on them in a single day.

Prompt stain removal is essential to proper clothing care. Most stains are easier to remove when they are fresh. After they have been on longer, stains are more likely to set into the fabric.

Periodic Care

A variety of clothing care procedures should be done periodically. One of these tasks is cleaning and organizing your closets and drawers. After a period of time, you may have put some items in the wrong place. Some clothing may have become wrinkled because it was put away too quickly.

Closet space for hanging garments is limited in many homes. Therefore, seasonal clothes must be stored. Often this is done in early spring and in early fall. Label the containers and keep a list of what you have stored. That way, you can find your clothing easily.

Clothing Storage

There are two important factors related to clothing storage: storing to protect garments and storing in an efficient, convenient way. You can use many convenience items to make storage more efficient.

Storage for Protection

Effectively stored clothing retains its shape; is protected from dust, moths, and mildew; and is easily accessible.

Consider the garment's shape when determining appropriate storage. Because knits stretch easily, they should be folded and stored flat. A dresser, storage box, or closet shelf storage are suitable for storing knits. See 28-3.

Wash or dry-clean clothing before putting it away for seasonal storage. Avoid using laundry aids, such as starch, that could leave deposits on the fabric. In addition to eating soil spots, silverfish are also attracted to starch.

Be sure to protect wool clothing from moths by using mothballs or crystals. Moths lay eggs. The eggs hatch, and while the moths are in the larvae stage, they eat the wool. When children or pets are present, mothballs or crystals are not recommended. Regardless, store clean woolen clothing in airtight containers with tight-fitting lids. For best results, store in cold temperatures (40°F or lower).

Protect your clothing from dampness by storing it in a clean, dry area. If you store clothing in a damp area, mildew or a musty odor may result. Because of temperature extremes and humidity, basements and attics are usually poor places to store clothing. The best places for storage are somewhere within your living area. Humidifiers, dehumidifiers, air conditioning, or heating sources can keep the temperature and humidity somewhat constant throughout the year.

Heavy and tightly constructed cedar closets and chests are considered the best storage places. The oil in cedar kills the moth larvae.

Storage for Efficiency

A good plan and system for clothing storage saves time and energy. The basic storage principles hold true for any type of storage. These are the principles you would use to store kitchen equipment, gardening equipment, and, in this case, clothing. Being aware of these principles helps you evaluate your own system of storage for efficiency.

One principle is to store each item as close as possible to the place where it will be used. Store coats, boots, hats, gloves, and umbrellas in a closet near the door.

Another storage principle is to store frequently used items where they can be easily reached. Think about the pieces of clothing you wear most often. Are they in an easy-to-reach place? Store clothing you wear daily, such as underwear and socks, where you can quickly reach it without moving other items.

Closet Maid Storage Systems by Clairson International

28-3 This closet has ample storage space for all types of garments, including knits.

Store items together if they are used together. Storing summer shorts and tops together eliminates the need to open different drawers. Underwear is another category of clothing that would logically be stored together.

Storing similar articles together is an important principle. Without doing this, you would have difficulty finding anything. If you stored sweaters in several drawers, you would waste time looking for the right sweater. Organize your closet by grouping shirts together, pants together, jackets together, and any other like items together.

You can purchase many products to help with both daily and seasonal storage. See 28-4. A creative person can also develop unique storage spaces using quality cardboard boxes

International Closet Maid Storage Systems by Clairson

28-4 Storage products are used in this closet to make the most of the available storage space.

and metal rods. Commercial storage products include shoe trees, racks, and bags; garment bags; fiberboard chests with drawers; drawer dividers; and storage boxes.

Laundry and Cleaning Techniques

To look their best, your clothes must be clean. Using certain techniques in laundry and cleaning will help maintain the original size, shape, color, and overall appearance of your clothing.

Care Labels

Care labels provide instructions for the care of the garment. Manufacturers are legally required to attach permanent care labels to all garments they make. Certain items, like sheer blouses, are exceptions because the label might detract from their appearance. However, the information is either on a removable tag or is printed on the garment's package. Care labels may be difficult to find because they are attached so they will not be seen during wearing. Even so, be sure to check the care label until you are familiar with the way a garment should be laundered.

Legislation requiring care label information was an important step toward improved clothing care. However, care labels are often misunderstood due to lack of consumer knowledge. Look for symbols in clothes such as those in 28-5.

A label marked "machine wash and dry" means you can launder and dry the garment by any method at any temperature. When this is not the case, the label must indicate the appropriate washer and dryer temperature and the wash cycle selection. It must specify air drying if needed.

Do not assume you can dry-clean a washable garment. In the past, labels had to state if dry cleaning was harmful. This information is not required on labels today. Labels are required to list only one care method, even if other methods are safe. Therefore, check with the dry cleaner before dry-cleaning a garment with a "washable" label.

If a garment needs ironing, even for a "touch up," the label must say so. Labels must also indicate the proper setting unless using a very hot iron is safe. Labels that warn "do not iron" mean ironing a garment could be harmful even at the coolest setting. See 28-6.

You can assume bleaching a garment is safe if the label doesn't warn against it. If chlorine bleach could damage the fabric, the label must say "only non-chlorine bleach." If any type of bleach might be harmful, the label must say "no bleach."

"Dry clean only" means you may use any dry-cleaning method. You should not wash the garment. Detailed instructions that specify solvent or warn against steaming must be given when necessary to protect the garment.

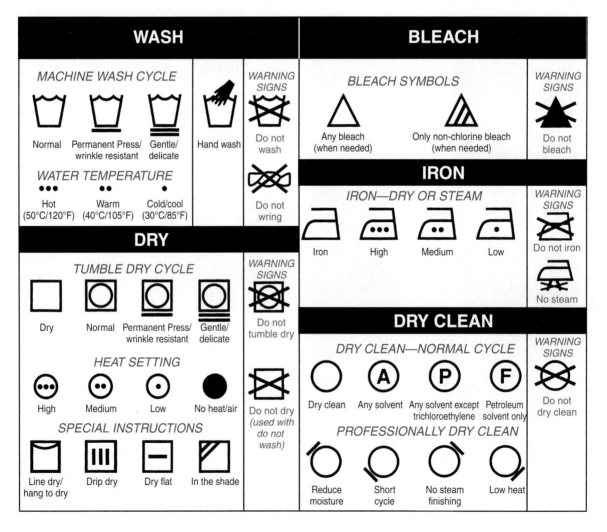

28-5 Clothing care labels indicate the proper way to wash and dry a garment.

28-6 Check the clothing care label for instructions on ironing a garment.

Fabric stores are no longer required to provide care labels with fabric you buy. Care instructions are printed only on the end of the fabric bolt. When purchasing fabric, consumers can request care labels for the fabric at the checkout counter.

Stain Removal

Stain removal is an important part of clothing care. Stains should be removed as soon as possible. Most stains do come off with either dry-cleaning fluid or detergent. However, it is important to work on them immediately while the substance is wet or still on the surface of the fabric. Washing or ironing a stained garment often makes removing the stain more difficult, if not impossible. Hot water can cause certain stains to become permanent.

Remove surface residue from the stained area as soon as possible. If the soil is dry or jellylike, it can scraped off carefully with a dull knife or spatula. If it is still wet, cotton, tissue, paper towels, or a dry white cloth can be used to absorb it. A powder can be used to absorb grease.

In the past, stain removal was quite simple. There were two basic types of stains—greasy and nongreasy. The two suggested methods for removing them were either dissolving them or washing them. The complex stains and soils of today don't fit neatly into those two categories. New fabrics and fabric finishes create additional problems in stain removal.

Before trying to remove a stain, first check the care label on the garment. Whether or not the fabric is washable will affect the way the stain is removed. Also check for the fiber content and other information that might help you.

Next, check stain removal charts for the correct procedure in removing the stain. A chart can be very helpful because it would be difficult for anyone to learn what to use for the removal of all stains. Find a good chart and keep it near your laundry area along with the basic products used in stain removal.

Once you have decided what stain removal product to use, try it out on a sample of the fabric. Use an inside seam or the edge of a hem in case it affects the color or the fiber.

As you work on the stain, place a clean, white, absorbent rag above and below the stained fabric. This gives the soil a place to go. Otherwise, the soil will just spread during spot cleaning. Change the surface of the cloth under the stain as the soil is transferred to the cloth. When you use solvents, a ring may form on the cloth. Laundering may be required to remove the ring.

If you are uncertain about how to remove a stain from a special garment, you may want to check with a dry cleaner. They have the knowledge and special equipment needed to remove most stains.

Laundry Products

The laundry aisle at the supermarket can be very confusing for some people. Laundry products are available in so many forms and quantities. See 28-7. A basic knowledge of laundry products may help clear up that confusion.

Soap and Detergents

Light-duty and heavy-duty soaps and detergents are available in both liquid and powdered forms. Light-duty soaps are used for delicate fabrics and for washing lightly soiled clothing by hand.

Mark Hayward

28-7 Many brands and types of laundry products are available. Doing the laundry becomes less challenging when you have a basic knowledge of those products.

Heavy-duty soaps and detergents are used for family wash and heavily soiled fabrics. The choice between the two depends on whether the water used for washing is hard or soft. Water hardness depends on the amount and type of minerals in the water.

Soaps are made by combining lye with fats and oils. When you use them in hard water, minerals combine with the soap and form a deposit or scum. This deposit gathers dirt from the water and sticks to the clothes and the inside of the washing machine.

Detergents are made with petroleum, natural fats, and oils. They contain chemicals that soften and tie up the water minerals to permit cleaning. Detergents are stronger and work better on synthetics and heavily soiled clothes. They are necessary in hard water.

Detergents may be high- or low-sudsing. However, the amount of suds has little to do with the product's cleaning capability. In fact, too many suds may limit the agitation of clothing as it washes and keep it from getting as clean. Follow the directions on the product to find out how much detergent to use.

Water Softeners

Water softeners inactivate or remove minerals from the water. Either mechanical softeners or water softening products can achieve this goal. Most heavy-duty detergents contain water softeners.

Packaged softeners come in two basic types: precipitating and nonprecipitating. **Precipitating water softeners** remove minerals by forming a precipitate—a solid that settles out. A film that is hard to remove will still form with the soap if you do not use enough precipitating softener.

Nonprecipitating water softeners hold the minerals in solution. You dissolve nonprecipitating types of softeners in the wash water before adding soap. Once soap hits the hard water, it forms a film that will not dissolve with the softener later. Nonprecipitating softeners are milder and less likely to change dye colors or irritate the skin.

Presoak Products

These products are made primarily for soaking stained or heavily soiled clothes before regular laundering. However, some presoak products are added to the water and used in combination with the detergent.

Presoak products are very useful when washing synthetics or synthetic blends. Oily soil penetrates those fibers so it can't be reached by detergent in a normal wash cycle. You should always presoak products on a hidden area before using them. These products may have an effect on colors.

Prewash Soil and Stain Removers

Stain removers come in aerosol, liquid, and solid stick form. They alter the soils and stains held on fibers so they can be released in the water.

Fabric Softeners

Fabric softeners reduce static electricity and wrinkling as well as making fabrics soft. Liquid softeners are added to the rinse water. Sprays, sheets, and solid bars are used in the dryer. Avoid adding a softener to the wash cycle. It may interfere with cleaning and may also lose some of its softening and antistatic qualities. See 28-8.

Bleaches

Bleaches are used to clean, whiten or brighten fabrics, and remove soils and stains. The two widely used types are liquid chlorine bleach and oxygen bleach. **Chlorine bleaches**, the strongest bleaches, disinfect and deodorize. A **disinfectant** is a product that destroys germs when used full strength. Chlorine bleaches should never be used on wool, silk, or crease-resistant or

28-8 Fabric softener should not be added to the wash cycle. However, fabric softener dispensers allow you to put softener in the dispenser before starting the washer. The softener is then released in the rinse water.

permanent-press clothes. Bleach may cause permanent discoloration on these types of fabrics. Frequent use of bleach on any fabric will cause it to weaken. **Oxygen bleaches** are much safer for general bleaching purposes and stain removal. They can be used on most washable fabrics and colors.

Read the product description on the container to find out the type of bleach. If the description doesn't mention chlorine, it is most likely an oxygen bleach. Follow directions on the product to determine how much bleach to use and when to add it to the water.

Laundry Procedures

Each laundry procedure somehow affects appearance of clothing. You will realize the importance of proper laundry procedures when you learn how they affect your clothing.

Sorting

Laundry is sorted into loads of a size suitable for the washer. Each load is sorted by color, fiber content and finish, garment construction, and degree of soil. Sorting laundry avoids the problems of color transfer, shrinkage, graying, and lint collection. See 28-9.

Separating white clothes from colored clothes prevents the whites from becoming dull, grayish, or taking on colors from other clothes. Synthetics, particularly those with a permanent press finish, should be washed in warm water with a cool rinse. They are separated from white cottons, which are best washed in hot water.

Certain delicate items should be separated because they might be stretched out of shape or roughened by agitation in the washer. Some of these items might be washed by hand. Heavily soiled clothing should be separated from clothing that is lightly soiled. This prevents the lightly soiled clothing from becoming dingy.

Prewashing Treatment

Before washing your clothes, mend any tears or rips. The agitation of the washing machine will only make them larger. Check the pockets to be sure nothing has been left in them. Close all zippers and hooks, which could damage other garments. Remove any nonwashable trimmings.

28-9 The problem of lint collection on this dark skirt would not have occurred if clothes had been sorted before they were washed.

Use a presoak product to pretreat grease and perspiration spots. Take special care with synthetics and synthetic blends. Once they have been washed with the stain, the stain may become unremovable.

Pretreat heavily soiled areas. A presoak product or thick suds of detergent can be used on a water-soluble stain. If the entire garment is soiled, a presoak product can be used. Although presoak products break down the soil, soap or detergent is still needed to remove the soil.

Wash Temperature

The water temperature is important because it directly affects cleaning, wrinkling, dye stability, and durability of fabric finishes. Cleaning, or soil removal, is most effective with hot water. The hot water can also sanitize and disinfect. It is suitable for white cottons, white linen, and heavily soiled articles that are colorfast.

Medium hot water can be used for white cottons and linens that are lightly soiled or for colorfast fabrics. Water does not sanitize at this temperature. Warm or cold water is usually recommended for permanent press fabrics. Cold water is recommended for fabrics that tend to bleed color or shrink easily, such as washable woolens.

Many washing machines offer a choice in water levels. This helps conserve energy and avoid wasting water. Be sure to use plenty of water. Using too little water will keep clothes from getting clean and will cause wrinkling.

Agitator Spin Speeds

The agitator is the part of the washing machine that creates the action during washing and rinsing. Most machines have at least two agitator and spin speeds.

When selecting washing action, consider fiber content, fabric and garment construction, and amount of soil. Faster agitation and spinning do a better job of soil removal. This also causes wrinkles in synthetic fabrics and those with a permanent press finish.

Some washers have special cycles for delicate clothes. Using these cycles automatically sets agitation and spinning speeds to move slower.

Drying Clothes

Follow the directions on the care labels for drying clothes. Do not overload the dryer because this will cause the clothes to wrinkle. When permanent press and wash-and-wear garments are dry, remove them immediately to prevent wrinkles, 28-10.

Some care labels may suggest drip-drying. This means hanging the garment to dry while dripping wet, without squeezing or wringing out water after it is rinsed. Drying flat means placing the garment on a flat surface in its original shape and allowing it to dry.

Dry Cleaning

Some fabrics require dry cleaning. Dry cleaning has many advantages. These include removal of oily stains; less shrinkage; less agitation abrasion; and safety on most colors, prints, and finishes.

The professional dry cleaner has special equipment to give a professional press to the garments.

Recently, new products have been developed to do dry cleaning at home in the dryer. These products usually include a stain kit, a bag for the items to be cleaned, and a product to be placed in the bag for freshening and dry cleaning. The main disadvantage of the do-it-yourself dry cleaning method is the lack of professional help in removing stains.

28-10 **You can avoid ironing many garments by removing them from the dryer as soon as they are dry.**

Summary

Routine care of clothing provides not only a well-groomed look but is also a timesaving resource. Laundering clothing, repairing clothing, and carefully putting clothing away are important steps in caring for your clothing so it is protected.

Using knowledge of laundry and cleaning techniques will help your clothing maintain its original size, shape, color, and overall appearance. Always follow the instructions found on care labels and remove stains properly. Understanding the features of available laundry products will help you choose the best product for your needs. The appearance of clothing is greatly affected by laundry procedures. Understanding the effects of laundry procedures will help you make wise choices related to the care of your clothing.

To Review

1. Name five things you can do daily as a part of routine clothing care.
2. Describe what may happen to clothing stored in each of the following circumstances.
   A. It is stored in a damp place.
   B. Wool clothing is stored without protection from moths.
   C. Starched clothing is stored.
3. True or false? All garments must have care labels.
4. Explain why prompt removal of stains is important.
5. Two basic types of stains are _____ and _____.
6. Describe the difference between soaps and detergents as related to hard water.
7. Name two reasons to presoak clothing.
8. Why should bleach be used with caution?
9. Describe how to sort clothes to be laundered. Explain why certain clothes are put in separate piles.
10. What are four advantages of dry cleaning?

To Do with the Class

1. Develop a bulletin board that displays pictures of items available for efficient clothing storage.
2. Plan a class demonstration that will show the difference between each of the following:
   A. The difference between soaps and detergents in hard water.
   B. The difference between precipitating and non-precipitating water softeners in hard water.
   C. The difference between removing certain stains with a solvent or a detergent.
3. Watch a demonstration on stain removal. Then discuss the techniques used.
4. Develop a display of laundry products. Label them to clearly identify the type of product and function.

To Do with Your Community

1. Visit a dry-cleaning establishment. Talk with the manager to learn about typical consumer misunderstandings related to dry cleaning. Share what you learn with the class.
2. As a class project to practice repair and mending skills, offer to inspect collected clothing to repair as needed for a homeless shelter.
3. If there are needy or elderly families in the community, share and practice your repair skills and offer to sew on buttons or repair rips for them.
4. Visit local clothing stores. Inspect clothing hangtags and care labels. Analyze clothing for ease of care.

To Challenge Your Thinking

1. Think about all the clothes you own. What would be the best way to store various items?
2. Check the care labels on various garments in your wardrobe to see if you are caring for them as suggested.
3. Bring a good stain removal chart to class to show other students.
4. Determine which stains are toughest to remove. What guidelines are recommended for treating them?

Part Ten
Managing Housing

Chapter 29
Planning and Selecting Housing
Housing satisfies physical, psychological, and functional needs. You need to know the legal and financial requirements of buying or renting a home before choosing a housing alternative.

Chapter 30
Furnishing and Caring for the Home
The furnishings you choose for your home will depend on design as well as function. Cleaning and preventive maintenance can help save your home from costly repairs.

29 Planning and Selecting Housing

To Know

humidity
special needs
universal design
traffic pattern
lease
security deposit
single-family dwelling
condominium
cooperative
mortgage
Federal Housing Administration-insured
    loans (FHA-insured loans)
Veterans Administration-guaranteed loans
    (VA-guaranteed loans)
conventional loan
foreclosure
binder
earnest money
abstract of title

Objectives

After studying this chapter, you will be able to

◇ describe ways housing can help satisfy human needs.

◇ explain factors that affect satisfaction with housing.

◇ identify the advantages and disadvantages of various housing alternatives.

◇ describe the legal aspects of renting an apartment or home.

◇ explain how a home purchase may be financed and the legal aspects of purchasing housing.

Where you live—whether in an apartment, a duplex, manufactured housing, or a house—may be referred to as your home, housing, or home environment. See 29-1. Home means different things to different

29-1 An apartment, a townhouse, and a house are examples of just three places people call home.

people. To many, the home environment represents special experiences and memories. To others, home is just a place to eat and sleep. People's needs and wants in relation to housing can be very different.Understanding how housing influences people will help you create a satisfying home environment. Knowing what factors affect satisfaction with the home helps you set positive goals related to your home. Another helpful resource for future housing decisions is knowledge and understanding of housing alternatives. Keep in mind that basic housing needs vary throughout the family life cycle. For instance, people in the expanding stage of the life cycle would most likely require a home with more space than people in the later or aging stage of the life cycle.

The Home–Meeting Human Needs

A home is much more than a place to live. Your home can provide you with comfort and safety. It can be a place for you to grow, develop, and satisfy your basic needs as well as any special needs. The home environment makes lasting impressions on children during their early years. The physical care, social experiences, and learning opportunities provided in the home all greatly affect a child's development.

All family members can be affected by housing. Opportunities for social growth in the home can help adults, as well as children, to grow. The mental or emotional health of family members can be greatly influenced by the atmosphere within the home. See 29-2. The home environment can provide intellectual stimulation for both children and adults. The home provides a place for a variety of social, personal, and

29- 2 **Both parents and children benefit from sharing special interests with each other.**

work activities. The selection and arrangement of home furnishings, equipment, and accessories can further encourage these activities.

Physical Needs

Various physical needs are affected by your housing. These include good health, physical comfort, and personal safety.

Health and Comfort

Any home encourages good health if it provides facilities for eating and for adequate sleep and rest. Housing protects your health by sheltering you from the weather.

Physical comfort is greatly affected by the temperature and humidity of the home. Tolerance for heat and cold varies.

However, most people are comfortable with inside temperatures of 68 to 70 degrees in the winter and 75 to 78 degrees in the summer. Older people might need warmer winter temperatures.

Humidity refers to the moisture that is absorbed into the air as vapor. Humidity that is either very high or very low is uncomfortable. Too little humidity causes the nose and throat to become dry, increasing your susceptibility to disease. Low humidity also causes a loss of moisture from the skin, which results in roughness and itchiness. Also, static electricity results from low humidity.

High humidity can be harmful to furnishings and the structure of the home. For instance, high humidity shows up as condensation on windows and drips onto the woodwork. Another hazard of high humidity is the condensation that may occur as moisture is caught between the inner and outer walls. This causes deterioration of the insulation, mold, and may cause paint to peel.

A variety of heating and cooling systems is used in homes today. Today's advancing technology creates constant changes and improvements in these systems. Appliances, such as single unit air conditioners, humidifiers, and dehumidifiers, are available to help create a more comfortable home environment.

Using air cleaners or air filters is another step toward a more healthful home environment. They remove particles that pollute the air, such as dirt, pollen, lint, hair, grease particles, and pollutants, such as odors from tobacco smoke. Although an air cleaner will not get rid of all polluting substances, it will help reduce them.

Technology has provided energy-saving resources in home building. However, this same technology may make the home too airtight. Indoor pollutants can be trapped inside a home creating a health hazard. As a result of polluted air in the home, people may develop allergies, feel fatigue, or become very ill. Fuels such as wood and gas emit polluting chemicals. Insulating materials also contain pollutants. Personal and household cleaning products add to the indoor pollution problem. Stagnant water left in containers like vaporizers and humidifiers can pollute the air. Ventilation reduces the pollution level. Attic vents, exhaust fans, and ceiling fans can help ventilate the home.

The lighting in your home also affects your physical comfort. See 29-3. Inadequate or poorly planned lighting may cause glares and shadows, which can result in eyestrain and fatigue.

Special Needs

Millions of people are considered to have **special needs**. These people may include older persons, families with children, and people of all ages with disabilities. Persons with special needs require homes with certain structural features or adaptations to their homes in order to make housing more functional for their living needs. In other words, their homes need to be modified to accommodate their individual situations.

Universal design is the concept of making all homes easier to use for everyone. See 29-4. As our population ages, these will become more important factors when choosing housing or remodeling existing homes. For example, older persons may have reduced vision and need larger or lit keypads on phones or thermostat

29-4 **This house was designed with wider doorways and hardwood floors. This makes it more accessible for a person who uses a wheelchair.**

29-3 **These fixtures provide adequate lighting over the kitchen table and also add to the décor of the room.**

display panels. Because of limited range of motion, door handles may need to be lowered or appliances placed at more convenient levels for easier use.

Persons with disabilities can be in any age group. They can have physical, sensory, or mental disabilities that may impair or limit their ability to carry out day-to-day activities. These disabilities can be temporary or permanent. In choosing appropriate housing, a goal is to allow persons who have limitations to become or remain as independent as possible with few or no limitations or restrictions to their daily living habits.

Ground level housing, wider doorways, ramps, non-skid steps, stair rails, and good lighting help make homes safer and more accessible for all persons and especially for those with special needs. Kitchens and bathrooms present additional considerations for the elderly and the disabled because of the important daily tasks that take place in those rooms.

Bathrooms may have showers that are wheelchair-accessible. Tubs may have vertical and horizontal guard rails. In kitchens, pull-out cabinet shelves, easy grasp handles, and wheelchair- or walker-accessible sink areas can help people maintain their independence. See 29-5.

Homes with young children will need to adapt as the children grow older. Bright, well-lit areas with durable, easy-to-clean and maintain materials are essential as children grow and develop their various hobbies, activities, and interests. The home environment can help all family members develop their potential and to live as comfortably as possible.

Home Safety

Housing can provide you with security against intruders, theft, and vandalism. A safe home has secure locks, outside lights at the entryway, and a way to see outside

Cheryl Pekul

29-5 **The lower freezer and slide-out drawer make it easy for a person with disabilities to use this appliance.**

without opening the door. The more difficult it is to enter a home, the less attractive the attempt will seem to an intruder. An alarm system is one resource to protect your home. However, there are other techniques that are not as expensive that can also be helpful. Leaving a radio turned on uses little electricity and gives the impression that someone is home. A dog is also helpful in deterring robbers, creating enough of a commotion to scare off an intruder.

A safe, secure home environment protects you against potential accidents and hazards. When you anticipate possible accidents and take precautions against them, you have a safer home. To make your home safer, you could install childproof latches in places where dangerous supplies are stored. You might adjust the water heater so the water does not get too hot and cause burns. Other precautions might include installing nonskid stickers in the bathtub or shower and securely fastening runners and treads on stairways.

A clean, orderly home is often safer than a messy one. Fewer health problems and accidents occur in a clean home. Cluttered hallways or stairs can cause accidents. Accumulated food wastes can attract insects, mice, or rats. A safe home has garbage containers that are removed and cleaned regularly. See 29-6.

The safe home environment has properly maintained electrical equipment, which is used correctly. Have your house wiring checked periodically for damage. When using any electrical appliance, take special care to avoid a shock. Using a three-prong grounded plug attached to a grounded outlet with any electrical appliance will reduce the chance of shock. Be sure to use appliances that meet industry safety and performance standards.

Smoke detectors and fire extinguishers can provide your home with security from fire. Smoke detectors sound an alarm when smoke particles are in the air around the detector. These detectors will sound an alarm even if a fire is just producing smoke without much heat. Early detection of a fire increases the chance of getting people out safely and reduces the amount of property damage. A definite routine for changing the batteries is important.

Never use water to put out an electrical fire or a fire that is feeding on flammable liquids such as gasoline or grease. Every home should have at least one fire extinguisher. Dry chemical and carbon dioxide extinguishers come in a variety of sizes and can be used on flammable liquids or electrical fires. The dry chemical type uses a powder that coats the burning surface and

29-6 A sanitary kitchen is essential in preventing health problems caused by foodborne illnesses.

smothers the fire. The carbon dioxide extinguisher smothers the fire with a heavy gas.

Carbon monoxide detectors can provide security from carbon monoxide poisoning. Carbon monoxide is a deadly, odorless gas. Keeping the furnace well maintained and good ventilation can help to prevent a build-up of carbon monoxide in the home. Make sure that outside vent pipes are unobstructed. Also, check fireplace chimney stacks and remove any animal nests that may have been built.

Psychological Needs

Home environment can greatly affect a person's mental health. A variety of factors in this environment influence psychological well-being.

The home environment provides belongingness and security. Home is a place of your own away from constant contact with others. Home is a place where you can be yourself and "do your own thing." Both children and adults need a private place where they can pursue their own interests and rest. See 29-7.

Home is a place for social development as well as privacy. Your home affects the social development and social behavior of your entire family. Interacting and relating with others is a basic human need. Your home environment can provide social contacts and growth. The home atmosphere can help you gain skill in interpersonal relationships.

Your home environment is an expression of your family's values. One family's home might express values of comfort and security. Another family might value status and prestige related to their housing. Another home might indicate the family values of neatness and cleanliness.

Your home environment also influences the values you develop. A neat, clean, well organized home environment is likely to encourage an appreciation of those values. On the other hand, growing up in a messy, disorganized home might have the same effect. A person who finds this type of environment unpleasant might be motivated to develop habits related to neatness, cleanliness, and organization. You learn to appreciate the task of routine cleaning. It can be seen as a necessary step toward the goal of a neat and clean home.

Many people have values related to the attractiveness of their home environment. Although people have different reactions to design and color, most people do appreciate housing with well-planned design features.

Functional Needs

Space and storage needs are two functional needs related to housing. You need

29-7 **Privacy is especially important during the teen years.**

space to carry on activities of daily living—sleeping, eating, working, and socializing. You need adequate storage to have orderliness in your home. Lack of sufficient storage may cause you to waste time and become frustrated when looking for misplaced items. You can achieve orderliness if each item has a storage place and family members know and use this place.

Space Needs

You may like your home for many reasons—maybe it's the location, the surroundings, a favorite room, or a cozy atmosphere. However, your satisfaction probably results from the way the space in your home is organized. In other words, does the space satisfy your needs and the needs of other family members? Space needs differ for each individual and family. The stage in the family life cycle affects space needs. A family with teenagers might like to have a family room. Teenagers could use this separate room to have friends in and watch a baseball game on TV. At the same time, parents could be in the living room relaxing in a quiet atmosphere. As the family stages change, their housing needs also change.

Social Activities

Social activities of families vary. A family may eat together, watch TV, talk with friends, or just relax. Providing space for social or group activities encourages positive relationships. See 29-8. As a result of these group activities, family members develop warmth and compatibility. Without the space to enjoy group activities, it is more difficult for families to develop companionship. Of course, many other factors also affect the way a family gets along together.

Social activities take place in various rooms of the house. The living room is a

place where family members may gather and where they may entertain guests. The furniture arrangement will affect how well the room works for socializing. Most living rooms can be arranged to provide a conversation grouping.

Personal Activities

Private or personal activities also require unique housing space. The home can provide space for sleeping, bathing, dressing, grooming, resting, hobbies, and leisure activities.

The private or personal activities of adults are similar to those of the children. They need space to sleep, rest, and to have a quiet moment to think. Adults have similar bathing and grooming needs as children. However, adults may need more

John Hartman Adams, D. Edmunds Interiors

29-8 A family room that is open to the dining area encourages social interaction.

storage space for personal grooming items, such as razors, blow dryers, curling irons, deodorants, and cosmetics.

Space for sleeping should be quiet, comfortable, and dark. See 29-9. This area should be separated from noise that might be coming from the kitchen or a recreation area. Although most people would prefer a bedroom of their own, that is not always possible. When you must share a bedroom, you can be creative and divide it using screens, dividers, or bookcases. Daybeds or convertible sofas are furnishings that can create extra sleeping places almost anywhere. Some housing designs today feature unconventional bedroom designs such as a sleeping loft.

Childhood Activities

When planning private space for children, remember that children grow up rapidly. Along with sleeping space, children need a place for their possessions. As children grow, they accumulate more and larger possessions. Because children's needs change

Brainstorming

Discuss financial pros and cons related to home rental or ownership and to the various types of housing. Share personal perspectives based on your housing situation. What type of housing would you choose for yourself in the future? Explain your reasons.

so quickly, their space should be flexible. Storage space will initially hold infant care items—diapers and clothing. However, later it will be used for toys. Eventually, that same storage space may be used to store items related to hobbies and interests. Parents can encourage maturity by giving their children the opportunity to organize and take care of their own possessions.

Children need space to play where they can spread out their blocks, games, and other toys. Some homes have a playroom or a recreation room. Other homes have play areas in rooms that are used for other purposes at certain times of the day. A corner in the dining room might be a good spot for such a play area.

The school-age child needs a place to study, rest, and think. Providing this space helps a child grow and develop. Good lighting, a place to write, and a storage area are important to children. They need a space to store their books, papers, and items related to their interests and hobbies. Space for bathing and grooming is usually not a problem except in larger families with limited bathroom space. Each person requires storage space for clothing—both closet storage and storage in a dresser or on shelves.

Dupont Co.

29-9 Children need a quiet, private place to rest.

Hobbies or Special Interests

Through the years, many adults develop hobbies or special interests that have definite space needs. See 29-10. Having a sewing room or area might be important to someone who has developed talents in sewing. Some families might have a special music room.

Work Activities

Many work activities also require space in the home. These include preparing the food, doing the laundry, keeping records, taking care of household business, and caring for the home.

Kitchens are usually more than just a work area. The kitchen is often referred to as the "heart of the home." Family members gather in the kitchen to eat, talk, sit with friends, and enjoy other family activities. In many homes, food is prepared, served, and eaten in the kitchen. In other homes, eating takes place in a dining room or a combination family room/dining room. Space in the kitchen is usually allotted for the three work centers—the preparation center, cooking center, and cleaning center. The food preparation center requires adequate counter space or work space. The kitchen should also include space for major appliances and equipment—the stove, refrigerator, sink, and often, a dishwasher.

Another work activity in the home is the laundry. The laundry area may include space for storing laundry supplies, sorting and folding laundry, and ironing. See 29-11.

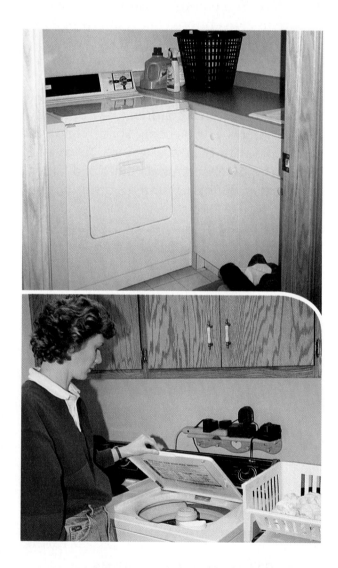

29-11 **These two laundry rooms have plenty of space for storing laundry supplies, but limited space for sorting, folding, and ironing.**

29-10 **Enthusiasm for a hobby increases when there is adequate space to work.**

The location of the laundry area may differ in various types of housing. In apartments, each unit may have its own laundry facilities or the laundry area may be shared with others. Laundry facilities may be located on each floor of the building or in the basement. Other types of homes may have laundry facilities in the kitchen, bathroom, or basement. In general, the best place for a laundry area is away from the quiet part of the house.

Your home environment should also include space to take care of the household business. A place is needed to pay bills, keep records, take care of financial accounts, and plan menus. See 29-12. You may need more than one place for these activities. The kitchen might provide a space for menu planning and storing cookbooks, recipes, and coupons for shopping. Your financial planning might be done at a desk in another room.

Other Space Considerations

Space is also necessary for the care and upkeep of the home. It is used for storing cleaning supplies, cleaning equipment, or tools. The size of this space will vary depending on the type of housing. Apartment dwellers need little space since the apartment owner or manager is usually responsible for upkeep of common areas. However, the owner of a single-family dwelling often owns equipment and tools to use in the upkeep of the home.

A very important space consideration is the traffic or circulation pattern. The **traffic pattern** refers to the circulation from one room to another and from place to place within a room. The traffic pattern indicates the way people move around their home. This pattern is planned for safety and efficiency. A good plan avoids interference with general activities. For instance, a convenient traffic pattern allows you to go from the entryway to the bedrooms and kitchen without going through the living room.

A well-planned traffic pattern moves through a room without interfering with conversation. Furniture can be placed so you do not have to walk in front of chairs or through the center of a seated group. See 29-13. Traffic lanes should be wide

Techline
29-12 A small area like this near the kitchen can be used to pay bills as well as to plan menus.

Broyhill Furniture
29-13 You could easily walk through this room and not interrupt conversation.

enough to pass through comfortably. In an existing home, you can improve traffic patterns without construction changes. The furniture can be moved to more suitable positions.

In reality, many families have limited space. They may have to be creative and try new ideas to meet their space needs. They may want to consider ways to make full use of rooms that would normally be used for only a few hours each day. For instance, a bedroom might double as an office, a study, or a sewing room. A dining room with enough space for a desk could be used as an office area or a play area with a toy storage box. See 29-14.

Storage Needs

The word "storage" indicates a place to put all the items that accumulate in your home. People store items for many different reasons. Perhaps you want to get an item out of the way, to provide care and protection for that item, or to make it easier to find.

Whether or not storage space is adequate depends upon the needs and possessions of family members. Ideally, every item has a special storage place. Each family member knows where that item is stored and puts the item back after using it. However, most homes do not have this much storage space.

The problem of lack of storage space can often be resolved by simply making better use of available space. Careful analysis and planning can greatly increase the capacity of storage spaces. See 29-15.

Begin by deciding what group activities take place in your home. Activities common to most families are eating, relaxing, and visiting together. Your family might participate in other group activities, such as playing games, listening to music, reading, and watching television.

Cheryl Pekul

29-15 These containers are an example of inexpensive storage.

Techline

29-14 This hallway area at the top of the stairs also serves as a home office.

Next, think of the items for each activity you would want to store in that area. To plan exactly where and how you store these items, you may want to consider several factors. You may want to ask yourself why you need to store them. Do you want to get them out of the way, protect them, make them simple to locate, or have them easily accessible? The answer to that question may help you decide on the best location. This may also indicate to you if the items should be stored in a "live" storage area. A live storage area would contain items you might use every day and would be easily accessible. See 29-16.

Because some items in the home are used only occasionally, they could be stored in a less convenient area. Other items are used rarely, if ever, but they are being saved for some reason. These items could be put in "dead" storage. This could be in the corner of an attic or in a less accessible spot in a hall closet.

The size, purpose, and how often you use an item influence how and where you will store it. The type of storage available also significantly affects where each item is stored. In some homes, space for storage may be very inadequate. In homes like this, you may not be able to store items in a logical, convenient area. Fortunately, a creative person can devise many inexpensive and attractive methods of storage.

In the past, storage furnishings consisted mainly of closets, chests, and bookcases. Today, an endless variety of storage furniture and accessories is available to help make efficient use of storage space. Being aware of all your storage options will help you make decisions about the items you need to store. See 29-17.

Because families differ greatly by their size, interests, lifestyle, and home environment, their storage needs differ also. One

Techline

29-16 **This closet is considered a live storage area because it contains clothes a person might use every day.**

29-17 **By taking a trip to the hardware store, you can learn a great deal about available storage aids.**

Broyhill Furniture

29-18 This storage unit allows family members to have easy access to entertainment options.

Closets by Techline

29-19 Open storage units provide a place to store clothing neatly when there is no closet.

family might have a very formal living room and require little storage except for some books and figurines. Another family might have a well-used living room that is very informal. They might need storage space for a television, a CD player, DVD player, a VCR, CDs, DVDs, tapes, books, magazines, and games. See 29-18. While the first family uses their living room mainly for formal entertaining, the second family "lives" in their living room. Therefore, the storage needs of the two families are very different.

Storage needs related to private or personal activities usually involve storage in bedrooms, linen closets, and bathrooms. Closets and dressers are basic features in a bedroom used for clothing storage. Open storage units are very convenient to use in a child's room because they can be expanded as the child grows. See 29-19. The bathroom may be used to store soap, shampoo, other personal care items, and bathroom cleaning supplies. Towels and

washcloths may also be stored in the bathroom if there is no linen closet.

The various work activities of the family create other storage requirements. The kitchen provides adequate storage for food products, utensils, and the equipment used to prepare and serve meals. The vacuum cleaner, brooms, mops, and other cleaning equipment and supplies require a storage place. The laundry area will store laundry supplies, such as boxes or bottles of detergents, softeners, and bleaches. If the laundry area is large enough, it is a convenient place to store the iron and ironing board.

Financial management is another work activity of the family. This activity requires storage space for financial records and other important items like warranties on appliances. Lawn care, another work activity of the family, requires storage space for lawn mowers, garden tools, snow shovels, and perhaps some lawn furniture. The families in single-family dwellings also need space to store tools and equipment to use in the upkeep of the home.

Factors Affecting Satisfaction with Housing

You may have already heard that the three most important points in choosing a place to live are location, location, and location. Satisfaction with your home is influenced not only by the interior of your housing but also by the exterior surroundings. The neighborhood and the community are important as well as the housing site.

Community Influences

Facilities and services the community offers will greatly affect your satisfaction with housing. The taxes paid by the residents are used to fund many of these facilities and services.

For most people, the location of housing in relation to work, schools, churches, shopping, and recreational facilities is very important. Saving time and transportation costs are both priorities for many people. Of course, individual and family interests vary greatly. These will determine which facilities should be accessible to you and your family.

For many people, schools are an important factor in selecting housing. Local newspapers are a good guide for information about schools. Some community groups, such as the League of Women Voters, may have information to share about schools. Parents may want to walk to school in the area they are considering living to inspect the route their children would take. See 29-20. It is a good idea for parents to talk with a school administrator to learn more about the school.

When considering location, also keep in mind nuisances you want to avoid. Noisy

29-20 **The nearness of a school may influence the housing decisions made by parents.**

railroads, freight yards, airports, and traffic are some examples. Most people also prefer to avoid noisy, smoky, or smelly factories or dumps and water treatment plants.

Community services and utilities also affect satisfaction with your housing choice. Efficient garbage removal is often a priority. In some areas, garbage removal is not a community service, and owners of housing must privately contract for it. See 29-21. Waste removal, such as leaf removal and snow removal, are other possible services. You can evaluate police and fire protection by inquiring about the kind of service they have provided others in the past. You want to live in an area where you feel safe.

As a potential renter or buyer, inquire about utilities and their annual costs. Find out if water comes from a public water supply or a private well and pump system. Also inquire about regulations on water usage, such as lawn watering restrictions. Find out how reliable the water supply is. Some communities have trouble meeting the demand.

Inquire about the electric power supply and its reliability, particularly during stormy weather. Also ask about local fuel supplies and the type of telephone service offered. If your family enjoys television, you may want to check on the availability of cable TV.

29-21 **When choosing housing, be sure to check on the cost and regulations for utilities and services such as garbage removal.**

Protective Restriction

Zoning laws and codes related to the building, electrical work, plumbing, and sanitation could be important to your protection. Building codes may specify materials, the strength required of materials, and particular construction techniques. Codes are important in preventing slum conditions, protecting your physical safety, and protecting your housing investment.

Many communities have developed master plans aimed at controlling growth. These communities have zoning regulations limiting the number of homes or apartment buildings that can be constructed in a specific area. These zoning regulations may be designed to hold down growth in the school population or to avoid traffic congestion. Zoning regulations might also keep the demand for extra police and fire protection from growing.

Getting **Involved**

Ask a local city official to discuss zoning and building and housing codes in your community. How many students were aware of these codes?

Although zoning laws are aimed at helping people, they can work against you in certain situations. For instance, check the zoning laws if you are planning to buy a small house and build an addition later. In some communities, zoning laws might not allow the addition.

Neighborhood Influences

Neighborhoods differ greatly, just as people differ. People's needs and wants in relation to a neighborhood vary also. See 29-22. Some people like a neighborhood where people have different incomes, professions, interests, and personalities. Others prefer a group where people have more in common.

The population of the area may influence your housing choice. In a densely populated area, more people live in less space. Large apartment buildings are dense areas. In areas of low density, there is more space for each person. People often prefer the privacy offered in areas of low density. However, housing in areas of low density is likely to be more expensive.

You can get an idea of the standards of the neighborhood simply by noticing the condition of other homes in the neighborhood. Spending some time in a neighborhood will give you an indication of the atmosphere or the mood of that area.

Looking around can also give you an indication of the local zoning practices. You

Hennepin Technical Centers

29-22 **The type of neighborhood you prefer is a personal matter. Some people would rather live in a city or a suburb than in a small town or in the country.**

can probably tell whether that area allows commercial establishments. If any large tracts of land are nearby, try to find out if there are plans for future development. Although this land might be used for housing, it might also be used for a factory or a landfill.

Housing Alternatives

Many American families want to own a single-family home. Unfortunately, most potential home buyers cannot afford to make today's typical monthly mortgage payments. See 29-23. Many people give up the goal of a single-family home by deciding the rewards are not worth the financial sacrifice.

Hennepin Technical Centers

29-23 **Many families dream of buying a large single-family home. Unfortunately, the mortgage payments of these homes are often so high that they prevent the average family from making a purchase.**

The number of people who live in rented apartments is increasing rapidly. New apartment complexes are springing up all over the country. Other dwellings, such as row houses, single houses, and even old factories and barns are being converted into apartments.

Whether you decide to buy or rent housing, your decision will be based on many factors, not just financial concerns. In fact, some people may rent even though they could afford to buy a house. The extra care and responsibility of home ownership is something you avoid when you rent. Both buying and renting have advantages and disadvantages. The first step toward making intelligent housing decisions is to learn as much as you can about the choices available. After learning about the choices and considering your special needs, you should be able to make a rational decision.

Renting Housing

The key to successful renting is in finding the right place to rent. Consider your personal needs, space needs, and storage needs. Also consider the neighborhood and community influences. Each apartment or house you may consider renting has many features to examine carefully. Refer to 29-24 for suggestions in finding rental housing.

Legal Matters

Once you have selected an apartment, you will likely sign a lease. A **lease** is an agreement between a renter and the landlord. If either of you breaks the lease, the other party can take legal action.

Leases can be written or verbal. Most verbal agreements are month-to-month leases where either party can end the

What You Should Know Before Renting

What is the floor or level of the apartment?

Basement apartments are usually least expensive, with the ground floor next, and the floors above most expensive. The basement gets the least natural light, and it tends to be damp. Each floor except the top floor may get noise from both above and below. These floors also get entry and street noise, usually not a problem on the top floor.

Who is responsible for paying for the heat, and who controls it?

As costs rise, more and more apartment landlords are having tenants pay for their own heat. Some landlords who pay for the heat also control it. If this is done, check to see at what temperature the thermostat is usually set. If you are expected to pay for the heat, check to see what fuel is required. Electric heat is very expensive.

Does the apartment have air-conditioning, and if so, who pays for it?

Just because a landlord provides the heat, this does not mean the air-conditioning will also be provided. You may want to provide your own air-conditioner if it is not provided. Ask to see if wiring is sufficient for individual room units.

Is wiring safe and adequate?

Some cities have ordinances that require property owners to update the wiring in their buildings to meet certain standards. You won't be happy in an apartment where you can't watch TV while cooking something in an electric skillet.

Check the wall outlets to be sure they are grounded. This is indicated by a third hole, the ground hole, in the outlet. Most areas require a minimum of one on each wall, but having more is convenient. More outlets will mean less need for dangerous extension cords and multiple plugs.

Is plumbing acceptable?

Plumbing is difficult to check visually because modern fixtures may be connected to old pipes that would leak any time. However, you can check for signs of plumbing problems. See if plumbing fixtures work and are clean. Also check the floors and walls around fixtures to see if they seem damp or moldy. Most apartment owners fix plumbing problems quickly because they are so damaging to their property.

What is the type of floor treatment?

Many apartments have wall-to-wall carpeting. This can mean a major savings for you if you don't own rugs. However, it is of little advantage to you if you are not satisfied with the color or quality of the carpet. Be sure to check what is underneath the carpet. A good pad adds comfort and warmth. If the carpet is laid directly on a concrete slab, it is less comfortable and less warm.

Are there signs of insects, pests, or rodents?

Older rental units may have persistent pest problems, especially in warmer climates. Look for signs of rodents, cockroaches, or other health-affecting pests.

Is cable television available?

Some landlords may include the cost of a cable hookup in your rent. Others may require that you make the arrangements with the cable company yourself. Check to see how many cable hookups you can have. You may be allowed only one.

29-24 Before you rent an apartment, be sure to get answers to some important questions.

What You Should Know Before Renting

What are the laundry facilities?

Most large apartment buildings have laundry facilities, but some do not. Laundry facilities in an apartment building are usually coin-operated and owned by an outside firm.

Check the laundry area to see if it is clean and if there is a place to fold and hang clothes. Also see how many families use each washer and dryer and what hours the laundry is open.

What types of major appliances are furnished?

Most apartments include the major appliances, but you will want to be sure of this. Check to see what type of refrigerator is furnished. Although frost-free or self-defrosting refrigerator-freezers are convenient, they cost up to twice as much to run as a conventional refrigerator. Refrigerators with a separate outside door for the freezer compartment are more efficient than those with only one door.

Is extra storage space available?

There may be available storage space in the basement or somewhere else in an apartment building. Check to see if the storage room is open to anyone or if it is locked and accessible only to tenants with keys.

Is trash pickup furnished?

You will want to know who pays for trash pickup and when it is collected. In an apartment complex, the location of the dumpster may be important. If your apartment is near the dumpster, you may find the noise and odor unpleasant.

What type of parking is available?

Many apartment complexes assign parking spaces to their tenants. Before you rent, find out how many spaces are allotted per apartment and if extra spaces are available. If you are sharing an apartment with someone who has a car, you may need two spaces. In some apartment buildings, special parking is not provided, and tenants must park in the street. This is another factor to consider.

Are any recreational facilities provided?

Many apartment complexes offer recreational facilities such as swimming pools or tennis courts. If you are considering one of these complexes, ask about obligations and rights of tenants. Is the cost of maintaining these facilities included in your rent? Do you plan on using the facilities? If you do not intend to use them, you may want to choose a complex that charges a fee to people who use those facilities.

29-24 (Continued).

agreement on a 30-day written notice. With a lease of this type, the rent can be raised or lowered at any time.

A written lease is often a better option. A written lease guards against misunderstandings and disputes by spelling out the responsibilities of the landlord or owner and the renter or tenant. See 29-25. Leases can be written for any length of time, although one-year leases are most common. A lease must include the renter's name, the landlord's name, the apartment address, the amount of rent, and when rent payments are due. Usually, the landlord cannot raise the rent until it is time to sign a new lease.

A variety of clauses may be included in the lease. Be sure that certain clauses are included. An example might be a sublet clause. This clause allows you to rent your apartment to another person if you decide to move out before your lease expires.

APARTMENT LEASE
UNFURNISHED

DATE OF LEASE	TERM OF LEASE		MONTHLY RENT	SECURITY DEPOSIT *
	BEGINNING	ENDING		

* IF NONE, WRITE "NONE". Paragraph 2 of this Lease then INAPPLICABLE.

LESSEE   **LESSOR**

NAME •   NAME •

APT. NO. •   BUSINESS •
                                                    ADDRESS
ADDRESS OF •
PREMISES

In consideration of the mutual covenants and agreements herein stated, Lessor hereby leases to Lessee and Lessee hereby leases from Lessor for a private dwelling the apartment designated above (the "Premises"), together with the appurtenances thereto, for the above Term.

ADDITIONAL COVENANTS AND AGREEMENTS *(if any)*

LEASE COVENANTS AND AGREEMENTS

RENT

1. Lessee shall pay Lessor or Lessor's agent as rent for the Premises the sum stated above, monthly in advance, until termination of this lease, at Lessor's address stated above or such other address as Lessor may designate in writing.

SECURITY DEPOSIT

2. Lessee has deposited with Lessor the Security Deposit stated above for the performance of all covenants and agreements of Lessee hereunder. Lessor may apply all or any portion thereof in payment of any amounts due Lessor from Lessee, and upon Lessor's demand Lessee shall in such case during the term of the lease promptly deposit with Lessor such additional amounts as may then be required to bring the Security Deposit up to the full amount stated above. Upon termination of the lease and full performance of all matters and payment of all amounts due by Lessee, so much of the Security Deposit as remains unapplied shall be returned to Lessee. This deposit does not bear interest unless and except as required by law. Where all or a portion of the Security Deposit is applied by Lessor as compensation for property damage, Lessor when and as required by law shall provide to Lessee an itemized statement of such damage and of the estimated or actual cost of repairing same.

CONDITION OF PREMISES; REDELIVERY TO LESSOR

3. Lessee has examined and knows the condition of Premises and has received the same in good order and repair except as herein otherwise specified, and no representations as to the condition or repair thereof have been made by Lessor or his agent prior to, or at the execution of this lease, that are not herein expressed or endorsed hereon; and upon the termination of this lease in any way, Lessee will immediately yield up Premises to Lessor in as good condition as when the same were entered upon by Lessee, ordinary wear and tear only excepted, and shall then return all keys to Lessor.

LIMITATION OF LIABILITY

4. Except as provided by Illinois statute, Lessor shall not be liable for any damage occasioned by failure to keep Premises in repair, and shall not be liable for any damage done or occasioned by or from plumbing, gas, water, steam or other pipes, or sewerage, or the bursting, leaking or running of any cistern, tank, wash-stand, water-closet or waste-pipe, in, above, upon or about said building or Premises, nor for damage occasioned by water, snow or ice being upon or coming through the roof, sky-light, trap-door or otherwise, nor for damages to Lessee or others claiming through Lessee for any loss or damage of or to property wherever located in or about said building or Premises, nor for any damage arising from acts or neglect of co-tenants or other occupants of the same building, or of any owners or occupants of adjacent or contiguous property.

29-25 A lease clearly states the responsibilities of both you and the owner of the apartment.

USE; SUBLET; ASSIGNMENT	5. Lessee will not allow Premises to be used for any purpose that will increase the rate of insurance thereon, nor for any purpose other than that hereinbefore specified, nor to be occupied in whole or in part by any other persons, and will not sublet the same, nor any part thereof, nor assign this lease, without in each case the written consent of the Lessor first had, and will not permit any transfer, by operation of law, of the interest in Premises acquired through this lease, and will not permit Premises to be used for any unlawful purpose, or purpose that will injure the reputation of the same or of the building of which they are part or disturb the tenants of such building or the neighborhood.
USE AND REPAIR	6. Lessee will take good care of the apartment demised and the fixtures therein, and will commit and suffer no waste therein; no changes or alterations of the Premises shall be made, nor partitions erected, nor walls papered, nor locks on doors installed or changed, without the consent in writing of Lessor; Lessee will make all repairs required to the walls, ceilings, paint, plastering, plumbing work, pipes and fixtures belonging to Premises, whenever damage or injury to the same shall have resulted from misuse or neglect; no furniture filled or to be filled wholly or partially with liquids shall be placed in the Premises without the consent in writing of Lessor; the Premises shall not be used as a "boarding" or "lodging" house, nor for a school, nor to give instructions in music, dancing or singing, and none of the rooms shall be offered for lease by placing notices on any door, window or wall of the building, nor by advertising the same directly or indirectly, in any newspaper or otherwise, nor shall any signs be exhibited on or at any windows or exterior portions of the Premises or of the building without the consent in writing of Lessor; there shall be no lounging, sitting upon, or unnecessary tarrying in or upon the front steps, the sidewalk, railing, stairways, halls, landing or other public places of the said building by Lessee, members of the family or other persons connected with the occupancy of Premises; no provisions, milk, ice, marketing, groceries, furniture, packages or merchandise shall be taken into the Premises through the front door of said building except where there is no rear or service entrance; cooking shall be done only in the kitchen and in no event on porches or other exterior appurtenances; Lessee, and those occupying under Lessee, shall not interfere with the heating apparatus, or with the lights, electricity, gas, water or other utilities of said building which are not within the apartment hereby demised, nor with the control of any of the public portions of said building; use of any master television antenna hookup shall be strictly in accordance with regulations of Lessor or Lessor's agent; Lessee and those occupying under Lessee shall comply with and conform to all reasonable rules and regulations that Lessor or Lessor's agent may make for the protection of the building or the general welfare and the comfort of the occupants thereof, and shall also comply with and conform to all applicable laws and governmental rules and regulations affecting the Premises and the use and occupancy thereof.
ACCESS	7. Lessee will allow Lessor free access to the Premises at all reasonable hours for the purpose of examining or exhibiting the same, or to make any needful repairs on the Premises which Lessor may deem fit to make; also Lessee will allow Lessor to have placed upon the Premises, at all times, notice of "For Sale" and "To Rent", and will not interfere with the same.
RIGHT TO RELET	8. If Lessee shall abandon or vacate the Premises, the same may be re-let by Lessor for such rent and upon such terms as Lessor may see fit; and if a sufficient sum shall not thus be realized, after paying the expenses of such reletting and collecting, to satisfy the rent hereby reserved, Lessee agrees to satisfy and pay all deficiency.
HOLDING OVER	9. If the Lessee retains possession of the Premises or any part thereof after the termination of the term by lapse of time or otherwise, then the Lessor may at Lessor's option within thirty days after the termination of the term serve written notice upon Lessee that such holding over constitutes either (a) renewal of this lease for one year, and from year to year thereafter, at double the rental specified under Section 1 for such period, or (b) creation of a month to month tenancy, upon the terms of this lease except at double the monthly rental specified under Section 1, or (c) creation of a tenancy at sufferance, at a rental of _____ dollars per day for the time Lessee remains in possession. If no such written notice is served then a tenancy at sufferance with rental as stated at (c) shall have been created, and in such case if specific per diem rental shall not have been inserted herein at (c), such per diem rental shall be one-fifteenth of the monthly rental specified under Section 1 of this lease. Lessee shall also pay to Lessor all damages sustained by Lessor resulting from retention of possession by Lessee.
RESTRICTIONS ON USE	10. Lessee will not permit anything to be thrown out of the windows, or down the courts or light shafts in said building; nothing shall be hung from the outside of the windows or placed on the outside window sills of any window in the building; no parrot, dog or other animal shall be kept within or about said apartment; the front halls and stairways and the back porches shall not be used for the storage of carriages, furniture or other articles.
WATER AND HEAT	11. The provisions of subsection (a) only hereof shall be applicable and shall form a part of this lease unless this lease is made on an unheated basis and that fact is so indicated on the first page of this lease, in which case the provisions of subsection (b) only hereof shall be applicable and form a part of this lease. (a) Lessor will supply hot and cold water to the Premises for the use of Lessee at all faucets and fixtures provided by Lessor therefor. Lessor will also supply heat, by means of the heating system and fixtures provided by Lessor, in reasonable amounts and at reasonable hours, when necessary, from October 1 to April 30, or otherwise as required by applicable municipal ordinance. Lessor shall not be liable or responsible to Lessee for failure to furnish water or heat when such failure shall result from causes beyond Lessor's control, nor during periods when the water and heating systems in the building or any portion thereof are under repair. (b) Lessor will supply cold water to the Premises for the use of Lessee at all faucets and fixtures provided by Lessor therefor. Lessor shall not be liable or responsible to Lessee for failure to furnish water when such failure shall result from causes beyond Lessor's control, nor during periods when the water system in the building or any portion thereof is under repair. All water heating and all heating of the Premises shall be at the sole expense of Lessee. Any equipment provided by Lessee therefor shall comply with applicable municipal ordinances.
STORE ROOM	12. Lessor shall not be liable for any loss or damage of or to any property placed in any store room or any storage place in the building, such store room or storage place being furnished gratuitously and not as part of the obligations of this lease.

29-25 (Continued).

Usually when your lease period is over, you either move out of the apartment or negotiate a new lease. However, your lease may include a provision that allows you to automatically renew for another set period.

This renewal clause is optional. It might be for the same rent you are now paying, or it might include the possibility of an increase.

Many other items might be included in a lease. The landlord may agree to make

FORCIBLE DETAINER	13. If default be made in the payment above reserved or any part thereof, or in any of the covenants or agreements herein contained, to be kept by Lessee, it shall be lawful for Lessor or his legal representatives, at his or their election, to declare said term ended, to re-enter the Premises or any part thereof and to expel, remove or put out the Lessee or any other person or persons occupying the same, using such force as he may deem necessary in so doing, and again to repossess and enjoy the Premises as in his first estate; and in order to enforce a forfeiture of this lease for default in any of its conditions it shall not be necessary to make demand or to serve notice on Lessee and Lessee hereby expressly waives all right to any demand or notice from Lessor of his election to declare this lease at an end on declaring it so to be; but the fact of the non-performance of any of the covenants of this lease shall in itself, at the election of Lessor, without notice or demand constitute a forfeiture of said lease, and at any and all times, after such default, the Lessee shall be deemed guilty of a forcible detainer of the Premises.
CONFESSION OF JUDGMENT	14. Lessee hereby irrevocably constitutes any attorney of any court of record of this state to enter Lessee's appearance in such court, waive process and service thereof, and confess judgment from time to time, for any rent which may be due to Lessor or his assignees by the terms of this lease, with costs and reasonable attorney's fees, and to waive all errors and right of appeal from said judgment and to file a consent in writing that a proper writ of execution may be issued immediately.
RENT AFTER NOTICE OR SUIT	15. It is further agreed, by the parties hereto, that after the service of notice, or the commencement of a suit or after final judgment for possession of the Premises, Lessor may receive and collect any rent due, and the payment of said rent shall not waive or affect said notice, said suit, or said judgment.
PAYMENT OF COSTS	16. Lessee will pay and discharge all reasonable costs, attorney's fees and expenses that shall be made and incurred by Lessor in enforcing the covenants and agreements of this lease.
RIGHTS CUMULATIVE	17. The rights and remedies of Lessor under this lease are cumulative. The exercise or use of any one or more thereof shall not bar Lessor from exercise or use of any other right or remedy provided herein or otherwise provided by law, nor shall exercise nor use of any right or remedy by Lessor waive any other right or remedy.
FIRE AND CASUALTY	18. In case the Premises shall be rendered untenantable during the term of this lease by fire or other casualty, Lessor at his option may terminate the lease or repair the Premises within 60 days thereafter. If Lessor elects to repair, this lease shall remain in effect provided such repairs are completed within said time. If Lessor shall not have repaired the Premises within said time, then at the end of such time the term hereby created shall terminate. If this lease is terminated by reason of fire or casualty as herein specified, rent shall be apportioned and paid to the day of such fire or other casualty.
PLURALS; SUCCESSORS	19. The words "Lessor" and "Lessee" wherever herein occurring and used shall be construed to mean "Lessors" and "Lessees" in case more than one person constitutes either party to this lease; and all the covenants and agreements herein contained shall be binding upon, and inure to, their respective successors, heirs, executors, administrators and assigns and be exercised by his or their attorney or agent.
SEVERABILITY	20. If any clause, phrase, provision or portion of this lease or the application thereof to any person or circumstance shall be invalid or unenforceable under applicable law, such event shall not affect, impair or render invalid or unenforceable the remainder of this lease nor any other clause, phrase, provision or portion hereof, nor shall it affect the application of any clause, phrase, provision or portion hereof to other persons or circumstances.

WITNESS the hands and seals of the parties hereto, as of the Date of Lease stated above.

LESSEE: LESSOR:

_____ (seal)   _____ (seal)

_____ (seal)   _____ (seal)

ASSIGNMENT BY LESSOR

On this _____ , _____ , for value received, Lessor hereby transfers, assigns and sets over to

_____ all right, title and interest in and to the above lease and the rent thereby reserved,

except rent due and payable prior to _____ , _____ .

_____ (seal)

GUARANTEE   _____ (seal)

On this _____ , _____ , in consideration of Ten Dollars ($10.00) and other good and valuable consideration, the receipt and sufficiency of which is hereby acknowledged, the undersigned Guarantor hereby guarantees the payment of rent and performance by Lessee, Lessee's heirs, executors, administrators, successors or assigns of all covenants and agrements of the above lease.

_____ (seal)

_____ (seal)

29-25 (Continued).

some repairs or changes in the apartment. Pets may not be permitted. Parking may be restricted.

Be aware that some leases are loaded with objectionable clauses. These clauses could put the renter at a great disadvantage should any disagreements occur. The renter can simply refuse to sign a lease that contains such clauses. Then the renter and the landlord can negotiate the lease. The renter can cross out the offending provisions and each person can initial the changes.

Notice to Terminate Tenancy*

To: Name _____

Address _____

City _____ State _____

You are hereby notified that I (we) shall be terminating my (our) tenancy of –

Apartment _____ at _____ Street _____

State of _____ on _____ day of _____ , 20 _____

Dated: _____ , 20 _____ .

Name _____

Address _____

City _____ State _____

* This form may be used by tenant as a 30 day notice to landlord to terminate month-to-month tenancy, or to give landlord 30 day notice prior to end of term created by rental agreement. It is also suggested that you retain a fully executed, and conformed copy of this notice, and on your copy, make a note of the name on whom same was served, and date and time of service.

29-25 (Continued).

When agreements are complicated, get everything in writing. This is the best way to avoid misunderstandings and to prove what has been agreed upon. Read the entire document carefully before signing. If you do not fully understand any clause, you may wish to consult a lawyer for clarification.

Security Deposits

The landlord will probably ask you to provide a **security deposit**. This refundable payment is equal to one or two months rent. A security deposit covers any damage you might do to the apartment. It also substitutes for rent if you fail to pay rent or leave before the end of the lease.

All security deposits are refundable if you comply with the lease agreement. This money is refunded when your lease period has expired and you have moved out. The landlord must submit a written list of deductions to you within a certain number of days if you aren't receiving a complete refund.

Most lawsuits and other problems involving security deposits result from disagreements about whether or not the renter has damaged the apartment. The problem becomes even more unpleasant because very often, neither party has proof.

A simple way to avoid these conflicts is to thoroughly inspect the apartment you are about to rent. Make a list of all faults or flaws and other comments on the state of the apartment. You may want to take photographs. If you omit anything from your list, you may have to pay for it when you move out through your security deposit. Include comments about the cleanliness of the apartment on your list, too. This is a good time to make a list of repairs that need to be done. Prepare the list and discuss it with the landlord. Sign and date it, have the landlord sign and date it, and make copies for you and the landlord. Keep your copy of the list in a safe place. If a dispute occurs when your deposit should be refunded, you can produce the list as proof.

Advantages and Disadvantages of Renting

The advantages and disadvantages of each type of housing differ for each individual or family depending upon their needs, wants, and resources. The major advantage of renting for most people is that it does not require major cash outlays. Renting might be the best choice if you have little savings or feel your savings would not see you through an emergency. One monthly payment provides housing and often some utilities with no further charges for upkeep and repairs. A renter pays no property taxes, and the regular monthly payments can help establish a good consumer credit rating. See 29-26.

The flexibility of renting is another advantage. Renting is a good option for people who move frequently or do not want to make a housing commitment. Attractive facilities are often another advantage of renting. Security systems, laundry facilities, swimming pools, tennis courts, and other recreational facilities offer the opportunity to relax and meet other people. Freedom from responsibilities often makes renting an attractive option. Renters don't have to worry about home repairs, gardening, or maintenance.

29-26 A young single person can establish his or her credit rating while enjoying the flexibility of renting.

Renting has certain financial disadvantages. The money you spend for rent is gone. You never recover it. There is no financial tax break related to renting. Rent helps cover the owner's payments on property taxes, but the renter receives no benefit from this contribution. Another disadvantage may become obvious in a housing shortage. If no local ordinance governs rent control, your rent may rise higher and faster than your salary. Without a lease or rent control, landlords can raise rent whenever they wish.

Another disadvantage of renting is that it is not permanent. You sign a lease for a certain period of time. At the end of that period, you can be asked to leave unless there is a special clause in the lease. In addition, landlords can let the property deteriorate and refuse to make repairs. As a renter, you may be restricted or even prohibited from making inside or outside changes to suit your preferences.

Buying Housing

Buying a home is one of life's major decisions. Whether you make a good choice or a costly mistake, deciding to buy a home can have a major effect on your life. Buying a home has become a very complicated procedure. The average person has difficulty both in judging the quality of the structures and in understanding the legalities involved. For this reason, you may wish to hire the services of professionals. You might consider hiring someone in the real estate business and a lawyer for legal protection.

Types of Home Ownership

There are several types of home ownership. You may choose to buy a single-family dwelling, a condominium, or a cooperative.

Single-Family Dwelling

The **single-family dwelling** might be a one-family home detached from any other building, or it might be a townhouse or manufactured housing. You may choose to contract to have a home built according to your specifications. See 29-27.

The manufactured housing industry has undergone profound changes in the last three decades. Manufactured homes today are similar to site-built homes in terms of quality, safety, and appearance. More people are turning to manufactured housing because it is the most affordable choice. There are two types of manufactured homes. The single section manufactured home is built to completion in a factory and

transported to the home site. The modular home is also built in the factory, but is transported to the home site in sections.

There are three types of sites available to owners of manufactured homes. In the land-lease community, homeowners lease the land on which their manufactured home sits. In a subdivision, the developer sells lots to individual manufactured home-owners who then construct their homes on the lots. Many families own their own parcels of land and choose to construct manufactured homes on them. This is known as "on your lot" manufactured housing. See 29-28.

Some manufactured homes can be moved by attaching wheels to them. Manufactured housing units vary considerably. Some contain only the basic fixtures and features: stove, refrigerator, bathroom facilities, bedroom and kitchen furniture, cabinets, and closets. More elaborate units may have two or more bedrooms, a separate dining area, built-in television, washer and dryer, and dishwasher.

Mark Hayward

29-27 People who choose to have their home built may work with an architect to design plans for the home.

Cheryl Pekul

29-28 Manufactured housing offers the independence of a single-family home, but is a less costly option.

The quality of construction is an important factor in selecting manufactured housing. The safety of these homes in relation to high winds and fire has been a great concern. Standards for construction, plumbing, heating, and electrical systems have been established.

Condominiums and Cooperatives

A **condominium** is an apartment you buy, usually in a multibuilding complex or a high-rise building. They range from very expensive sites to those that are quite reasonable. Owning a condominium is different from owning a house. In condominium ownership, each unit is owned individually with joint interest in the common property. All condominium dwellers jointly own the lot on which the building stands. They jointly own the grounds and the exterior facilities including the parking lots and recreational areas. These outside areas usually are maintained by a co-owners' association.

Financial responsibilities of condominium living are both for personal units and for the common areas. Condominium owners must provide their own fire, personal property, and liability insurance. They must meet payments on their own home and also pay real estate taxes on their dwelling. Condominium owners pay a monthly fee to maintain common property.

This money finances trash collection, repairs, lawn care, snow removal, and upkeep of recreational facilities. The owners select a board of directors to make decisions about maintenance operations and other decisions that affect all owners.

The basic concept of cooperative ownership is different from a condominium. When you buy into a **cooperative**, you are part of a group of people who have bought a building or complex. You share in the financial success of the building. The members don't actually own their own cooperative. Instead, they purchase stock in the corporation that owns the complex. See 29-29. Members of a cooperative have many

29-29 Members of a cooperative neither pay rent as in an apartment nor own their unit as in a condominium. Instead, they share the ownership of the cooperative with other cooperative members.

privileges of home owners. The apartment is theirs for a lifetime. In a cooperative, there is only one mortgage bill and one tax bill. The corporation pays these bills. Individual members of the cooperative make monthly payments that are used to meet these mortgage and tax expenses. This payment also finances the maintenance of the common areas of the cooperative. A member of a cooperative owns a share of stock or a membership certificate in the total enterprise. The stockholders elect a board of directors to operate the corporation.

Responsibility in a cooperative is similar to responsibility when renting. Cooperative members are responsible for keeping home furnishings in good condition and for any internal damages in their units.

Advantages and Disadvantages of Home Ownership

Unlike automobiles and appliances, which depreciate in value, home ownership is often a good investment. See 29-30. In ordinary economic conditions, a home is normally a safe investment, rising in value. Because real estate taxes and the interest paid on a mortgage are deductible expenses when figuring income taxes, this means a savings.

Other advantages of home ownership involve your feelings about the property. Ownership ensures continued possession, which gives you a feeling of security. It also gives you a feeling of independence and privacy. You can live as you want, decorate as you want, and enjoy as much privacy as you want. Home ownership gives you the sense of belonging—you feel a part of a neighborhood or community.

Home ownership is a major commitment in time and expense. Home ownership involves considerable financial responsibilities. First come the initial down payment and closing costs, then the monthly mortgage payment and property taxes. Home owners must also pay insurance, heat and other utilities, and mainte-

Masonite Corp.

29-30 An older home can be a great investment for people who have the building and carpentry skills needed to remodel it themselves.

nance and repair costs. A home owner might also be charged a special tax if specific property improvements are made in the area. Improved streets, a new sewer system, or new sidewalks are examples.

Upkeep of a home can take a lot of time and money. Repairs are often expensive and usually unexpected, but postponing them may increase damage or threaten safety. Therefore, most home owners are forced to spend money on home repairs before wants like recreation or new furnishings. See 29-31.

Condominiums and cooperatives have certain advantages over a single-family dwelling. Owners can enjoy the grounds and use the recreational areas without being responsible for their maintenance. The owners are also protected by a governing group—the home owners' association or the board of directors.

A member of a cooperative, like a stockholder in a business, may be subject to more rigid restrictions than an owner of a condominium. Many decisions a cooperative member makes about living quarters must be cleared through the governing group. For instance, a cooperative member cannot sublease the apartment without the permission of the other cooperative members. That tenant has a say as to who buys a share in the cooperative. In addition to owning a share of the cooperative, the owner also shares the liabilities. If certain members fail to pay their share of the taxes or mortgage, the group as a whole assumes that responsibility.

The biggest advantage of cooperative living is that owners share in the success of the total project. If the property has increased in value, the owners will make a profit on their investment and still have the security of their cooperative living situation.

Using a Real Estate Agent

Most people use the services of a real estate agent when buying a home. These licensed professionals bring home buyers and sellers together. They are paid only when the sale is completed. Therefore, it is in their best interest to make arrangements that are agreeable to both parties. The seller usually pays the real estate commission, which is from 5 to 10 percent of the purchase price.

Using a real estate agent has many advantages. Real estate agents have considerable knowledge about market values of homes. They know what homes are available in your price range and what homes are most likely to fit your needs. They can tell you about schools, churches, recreational facilities, and other services in the neighborhood. They can lead you to real estate appraisers, licensed engineers, and specialists in various building trades. You may want to consult with these people before making a final choice about a home.

29-31 Home owners may find that quite a bit of their time is taken up by the hard work of upkeep and repairs.

The real estate agent can help you in all stages of the home-buying process. See 29-32.

Financing a Home Purchase

When most people decide to buy a single-family house, a condominium, or a cooperative, they must arrange for a home mortgage loan. When you borrow money to purchase real estate, you are required to sign a mortgage. A **mortgage** is a legal document that acts as security for the lender until the debt is repaid. There are a variety of sources of home mortgage loans.

Government Loans

Government loans were designed to promote the construction or buying of housing. There are a variety of government loans, but the most common ones are the Federal Housing Administration-insured loan (FHA-insured loan) and the Veterans Administration-guaranteed loan (VA-guaranteed loan).

Federal Housing Administration-insured loans (FHA-insured loans) are provided by an approved independent lending institution and insured by the FHA. The FHA does not actually make the loan. Applications are normally available through lending agencies. The lending agency reviews the application and may or may not approve it. If the application is approved, the lending agency sends it on to the FHA for approval. If the FHA approves the loan, the applicant can borrow the money from the lending agency. As a result of this procedure, FHA loans take longer to process than conventional loans.

Two advantages of the FHA loan involve the down payment and repayment time of the loan. The down payments required are substantially lower than on most other loans. Also, the repayment period for FHA loans is longer than for conventional loans.

⊟ **29-32 A real estate agent has all the information to make buying or selling a home much easier.**

The interest rates on these loans are regulated by law. Although the rates change over time, they are usually slightly lower than for other real estate loans because the federal government insures them.

Veterans Administration-guaranteed loans (VA-guaranteed loans) are special loans granted to qualified veterans of the U.S. Armed Forces. These loans are obtained through a regular lending agency and are guaranteed by the federal government. Applications for VA loans are very strictly reviewed so that money will not be lost on the transaction. The VA loans are guaranteed by the Veterans Administration. If a veteran fails to repay the loan, the Veterans Administration can deduct this amount from any pension or other compensation the borrower might receive as a veteran.

Interest rates are generally lower on VA loans than other loans including the FHA loans. A down payment is recommended but not required. If there is no down payment, the loan is for the full amount of the purchase price.

Conventional Loans

The **conventional loan** is used most commonly in home financing. The government does not insure these loans. The home is the security of the loan. If the borrower fails to make the agreed monthly payments, the lender has the right to foreclose. **Foreclosure** means seizing the property and selling it to pay off the debt.

Usually the length of a conventional loan is no more than 30 years. Conventional loans require a sizable down payment, and interest rates vary with the economy.

Typical sources of conventional loans are savings and loan associations, commercial banks, and private lenders. See 29-33. Savings and loan associations are usually liberal in their lending. They extend loans for periods of 15 to 30 years. The down payment required for a single-family home is usually 10 to 20 percent of the cost.

Commercial banks tend to specialize in short-term loans rather than real estate loans. If they do grant real estate loans, the loans are usually for a 5- to 15-year period.

Private lenders may include your relatives or the seller of the property. A form of financing often used is called a land contract. This is when the seller of the property finances the buyer. The seller permits the buyer to make a down payment and pay off the balance owed in monthly payments. The interest and down payment are usually lower than at a commercial bank or a savings and loan. However, the title of the property remains in the name of the seller until payments are complete.

Legal Aspects of Buying Housing

Using the services of a lawyer when buying a home is a worthwhile investment.

29-33 Applying for a loan requires a down payment and a great deal of paperwork.

Although the lending institution and the seller have lawyers, they will not be looking after the buyer's best interests. The purchase of a home is a major investment and the legalities involved are quite complex. See 29-34.

Binder or Preliminary Contract

The first legal document that is signed when a home is purchased is often the **binder**. This is a tentative agreement between the buyer and the seller that indicates they are both willing to reach a final settlement. At this time, the buyer must provide **earnest money**—often a certain percentage of the selling price. This payment shows that the buyer is acting in good faith and expects to make the purchase final. Eventually, this earnest money will be credited toward the down payment.

29-34 **A lawyer can help a home buyer deal with the intricate details of the purchase.**

The binder covers a detailed description of the property, total purchase price, amount of the down payment, and date for closing the sale and delivering the deed to the new owner. This agreement remains in effect from the time it is signed until the closing of the purchase. During this time period, the buyer can investigate the title and arrange for financing.

Investigating the Title

The title in real estate is the proof of ownership of the property. The loan lending agency usually requires a title search. This search involves reviewing legal documents and public records to be sure no one else has a prior claim to the property. The lawyer may discover certain facts about zoning ordinances or problems with back taxes while reviewing the title. The report of the title search is referred to as an **abstract of title**.

The Closing

At the closing date indicated in the binder, the buyer and seller meet with their lawyers and a representative of the lending agency. This is when ownership of the property is formally transferred.

The typical closing procedure includes certain activities. The representative of the lending agency will ask to see the buyer's home owners insurance. The lender's representative will list the cost adjustments. This includes what the buyer owes the seller. Examples are the remainder of the down payment, prepaid taxes, and the costs of any appliances the buyer is purchasing. These adjustments may also include some items that the seller owes the buyer, such as unpaid taxes.

Use *Your* Reasoning Skills

Analyze your home environment. How does it meet your family's values, goals, needs, and wants? In what ways does your home need improvement in order to better meet needs? In what ways might different types of housing also meet your goals, needs, and wants?

The buyer will sign the papers for the new mortgage. This document gives the lender the right to take back the property if the buyer fails to make the mortgage payments.

The title then passes from the seller to the buyer. It is usually in the form of a deed, which contains a complete description of the property and all conditions concerning the property. The deed must be signed and dated by both buyer and seller and witnessed by a notary public. The deed and the mortgage are recorded in the city or county registry of deeds. The lending agency often keeps the original deed until the mortgage payments are completed.

The lender's representative collects the closing costs from the buyer, usually in the form of a certified check. Closing costs are quite substantial. Buyers may want to inquire about closing costs when shopping for a home mortgage loan. These costs will vary from lender to lender.

32
31
30
29
28
27
26
25
24
23
22
21
20
19
18
17
16
15
14
13
12
11
10
9
8
7
6
5
4
3
2
1

Summary

The home environment is more than the structure in which a person lives. It also involves the furnishings in the home, how they are arranged and used, and how family members use the home. To help create a positive home environment, it is helpful to understand how this home environment influences human needs.

The exterior surroundings of the home—the neighborhood and community—can greatly affect satisfaction with housing. The facilities and services offered and restrictions that may exist will also influence a family's satisfaction with their home.

Intelligent housing decisions are based on an understanding of the choices available. Knowledge of the advantages and disadvantages of renting and buying will help in decision making. Many legalities are involved in housing selection. Professionals, such as lawyers and real estate agents, can provide guidance concerning these legalities. For those buying homes, financing the purchase is very important. An understanding of loan alternatives is important for people who are buying a home.

To Review

1. List three ways a home may satisfy each of the following physical needs:
   A. Good health.
   B. Physical comfort.
   C. Personal safety.
2. True or false? The home environment can provide opportunities for social contact and growth.
3. Name the three categories of activities that have space needs. Then list three specific needs for space in each category.
4. Briefly explain how the community influences housing decisions.
5. True or false? Although zoning laws were intended to help people, they can work against you in certain situations.
6. Explain three clauses that might be included in a lease when renting an apartment.
7. The type of ownership that involves purchasing stock in the corporation that owns the complex is called _____.
   A. condominium ownership
   B. cooperative ownership
   C. town house ownership
   D. single-family dwelling ownership
8. FHA-insured loans _____.
   A. take less time to process than conventional loans
   B. usually require a larger down payment than conventional loans
   C. are provided by the Federal Housing Administration and insured by approved lending institutions
   D. are provided by approved lending institutions and insured by the Federal Housing Administration
9. When buying housing, what is covered in a binder or preliminary contract?
10. What is the main purpose of the closing?

To Do with the Class

1. Discuss situations that illustrate a person's need for privacy in a home.
2. Brainstorm activities that take place in a home and categorize each as a social activity, private activity, or work activity.
3. Search housing, building, or architectural magazines for examples of good and poor home designs or features that would help or hinder those persons with special needs. Create posters or a bulletin board showing various modifications made to help meet the needs of families and individuals throughout their lives.
4. Discuss how condominiums and cooperatives offer a combination of the advantages of owning a home and renting.

To Challenge Your Thinking

1. Copy a house plan from a magazine or book and evaluate it in terms of use of space and traffic patterns.
2. Using a hygrometer (a gauge that measures humidity), conduct an experiment to determine how different levels of humidity affect comfort.
3. Investigate Web sites to research specific trends in housing, such as current housing legislation, environmental factors, etc.
4. Find pictures of various housing types. List the advantages and disadvantages of each. Identify family characteristics as to who would be most likely to select this type of housing.

To Do with Your Community

1. Interview real estate agents to find out how they "educate" buyers.
2. Go to a library or lumberyard and find out what resources are available to help people judge home construction. Share this information with others in the class.
3. Talk with five people who are renting apartments to learn tips they would suggest in apartment hunting. Share their ideas with the class.
4. Take a walk through your community. What housing options do you see? Consider types of houses, environment, location and potential for renting or buying in your community.

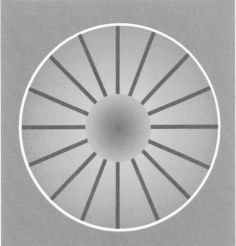

30

Furnishing and Caring for the Home

To Know

principles of design
form
color scheme
formal balance
informal balance
proportion
rhythm
emphasis
double-hung windows
casement windows
picture window
draperies
curtains
solid wood
veneer
pressed wood
incandescent lights
fluorescent lights
general lighting
directed lighting
accent lighting
preventive maintenance

Objectives

After studying this chapter, you will be able to

◇ relate the use of the elements and principles of design to an attractive home.

◇ explain characteristics that may influence selection of various home furnishings.

◇ list tips on how to maintain a clean home.

◇ describe ways maintenance helps avoid housing problems and repair.

The dictionary defines the word *attractive* as *arousing interest or pleasure*. You may have visited homes you think are attractive although you would not have chosen the same furnishings for yourself. People differ in what they like in home furnishings. Attractive homes have a pleasing appearance to many people. See 30-1.

30-1 **These two kitchens express very different ideas in decorating.**

of line, form, color, and texture. Your preferences continue to develop throughout life as you have new experiences. Learning about the elements and principles of design is a starting point for developing your skill in creating an attractive home.

Decorating involves the functional as well as the design aspects of furnishings. For instance, does a certain piece of furniture serve the purpose for which it was intended? Does the furniture meet the physical and lifestyle needs of the family? Another aspect of function involves maintenance. For a home to be functional, its furnishings and equipment must be constantly cared for and kept in working order.

Design in Home Furnishings

Studying the natural environment is a good way to learn about design. Through the years, people have observed the *elements of design*–line, form, color, and texture–in nature. They have learned to apply these elements to design in clothing, home furnishings, and home decorating.

Certain rules and guidelines have evolved to help in the use of the elements of design. These guidelines are referred to as **principles of design**. They include balance, proportion, rhythm, and emphasis. Understanding the use of the elements and principles of design in home furnishings can help in creating an attractive, personally pleasing home environment.

Elements of Design

The elements are combined to create design in the home. Although using these elements does not guarantee an attractive combination, understanding them will help you reach your decorating goals.

The ability to create an attractive home is not acquired by simply following certain rules in decorating. Your preferences will develop and change throughout the years. Values and home life influence the development of your likes and dislikes. Daily observations help you develop an awareness

Line

Line, a basic element of design, can be highly expressive. A line may be horizontal, vertical, diagonal, or curved. Line can be used to create forms or shapes in the furnishings of a room. Line creates patterns for flooring materials, wall coverings, fabrics, and accessories.

Line creates a human response. If understood, this response can help you reach certain decorating goals. *Horizontal lines* make an object look wider. They also suggest feelings of rest, steadiness, and masculinity. *Vertical lines* add height. They tend to suggest strength and formality. *Curved lines* are graceful and feminine while *diagonal lines* give a feeling of action and stimulation. One look around a room shows line used in various ways. Lines can be seen in the straight folds of draperies, a bookshelf, a staircase, and the furniture. See 30-2.

Form

Any object that is three-dimensional has form or shape. In decorating, furniture and accessories have **form**. A room looks more attractive when it contains many forms that are related while still providing variety.

In general, the form of an object is determined by its function. For instance, a chair would be designed for comfortable sitting. It is not unusual to see chairs that may look attractive, but are not functional in terms of comfort.

Color

The first thing most people notice when they enter a room is the **color scheme**–the combinations of colors used. Color creates the atmosphere and sets the mood of a room. Color is created by the walls, flooring, furniture, and accessories used in a room.

Anderson Corp.

30-2 Notice how the straight lines in this living room are dominant.

Using Color

The colors you choose to decorate a room depend on a variety of factors. You may wish to use a favorite color. See 30-3. A color choice may be based on the colors in a painting or a woven wall hanging. You may want to create a particular mood in a room.

Techline

30-3 Children often like bright primary colors in their bedrooms.

Research shows color creates a response in people. Warm colors give you a feeling of warmth and activity. They are often used in family rooms and kitchens. Because cool colors are considered more restful and relaxing, they may be more appropriate for a living room or a bedroom.

Consider the size of the room when choosing colors to use. Because warm colors advance and cool colors recede, color can be used to make a room look smaller or larger.

If the goal is to create a feeling of spaciousness, use cool colors such as blue and green. Because pale, dull colors are much less dominant, they work better to give an illusion of space than clear, bright colors. Other visual tricks can be used to change apparent room size. Warm colors on the wall make a room seem smaller than it really is. See 30-4. A long narrow room looks shorter if the ends are in warm colors.

The orientation of a room makes it warmer or cooler and greatly affects its comfort. When the sun shines in a room with southern exposure, it becomes physically warmer. Colors can also be used to make a room seem warmer or cooler. However, this is only a psychological reaction. Warm colors can make a cool room with northern or eastern exposure seem warmer. Reds, yellows, oranges, and browns have a warming effect because of their association with nature–the warm sun and the hot red flame. Cool colors, such as blue, green, and lavender, are associated with icy streams, cool grass, and majestic mountains. In warm rooms with southern or western exposure, these colors can create a cooler, more soothing atmosphere.

Color Schemes

Certain color combinations seem more successful than others. Although beautiful rooms are created using many daring combinations of color, a person who feels less secure about use of color might prefer using basic, reliable color schemes as guidelines.

The *monochromatic scheme* uses only one hue or color. Various values and intensities of the color are used to avoid monotony. Using varieties in textures and materials such as wood, metal, or glass can also make this color scheme more interesting. The monochromatic color scheme makes a room feel more spacious and presents a simple background for objects in a room. When using the monochromatic color scheme, small accents of another color are usually added for variety and excitement.

Accented neutral schemes are similar to monochromatic schemes, but they use a

30-4 **The warm red color used on the walls makes this area even smaller and cozier.**

neutral color such as brown, gray, or white as their main color. That base color may be combined with a variety of values and intensities and is supplemented with an accent color. See 30-5. This decorating scheme is easy to use. Accented neutral schemes are particularly successful when certain objects in the room are to be accented or highlighted.

The *analogous scheme* is made up of colors that are next to each other on the color wheel. Using three colors that are side by side on the color wheel seems to create a pleasing effect. Using too many colors may make a room unattractive.

With the analogous scheme, using one dominant color and smaller amounts of the others adds interest and variety. Another technique is using various values and intensities. Colors in this type of color scheme blend very well because they have one primary color in common. Analogous color schemes have a harmonious, calming effect and can be seen everywhere in nature.

The *complementary scheme* is made up of two colors that are opposite each other on the color wheel. Blue and orange or yellow-green and red-violet could be used to create a complementary color scheme. The values and intensities of the colors may vary. In fact, using two colors in full intensity to decorate a room is usually too intense. Using shades and tints creates a more pleasant combination, 30-6. Like the analogous color scheme, the complementary color scheme works best using one dominant color. Because complementary colors tend to make each other look brighter and more intense, these color schemes tend to be more dramatic than the others.

As you work more with color, you will develop a sense of harmony in different color combinations. By noticing the color schemes just described, you will become more familiar with the effects they create and will be more confident in experimenting with various color combinations. You will be able to create pleasing color schemes with a unique, personal touch.

Texture

Texture involves the surface quality of a material. The way a surface feels when you touch it and looks when light strikes it is its *texture*.

Lexington Homes

30-5 Mauve and blue are the accent colors in this accented neutral color scheme.

30-6 This complementary color scheme uses shades of green and red.

The textures of home furnishings and building materials range from smooth to rough and from hard to soft. Some woods, tweed fabrics, pottery, brick, and stucco are examples of rough textures. Smooth textures include glass, silver, chrome, polished wood, and satin fabrics. Brick, wood, slate, tile, marble, chrome, and plastics are examples of hard textures. Velvet, plush, and leather indicate soft textures.

People react to textures both physically and psychologically. When you touch a smooth surface, your physical reaction is different from your reaction when you touch a rough surface. Texture is an important quality to consider when selecting textiles for furnishings. Sitting on a hard, rough surface is uncomfortable to most people. The reflection of light from different textures also causes physical reactions. Polished metal and glass surfaces have reflective qualities. However, rough textures such as brick floors tend to absorb light. Textures cause psychological reactions as well. Smooth textures suggest refinement, sophistication, and formality. Rougher textures create a more casual, informal atmosphere.

A careful balance of textures is important in decorating. Try to choose one texture to dominate and add a few compatible textures to keep it from being overwhelming. Like color, texture can be used to play visual tricks in a room. Rough-textured materials seem to advance while smooth textures tend to recede. Rough, rich textures make a room seem smaller. A room seems larger when you use light, smooth textures that reflect light. Rough textures work in large rooms with many windows. However, small rooms would be overwhelmed.

Textures also affect color. The color of flooring looks less intense when it is made of a heavy, rough material like brick. A smooth, shiny flooring material of the same color looks much brighter.

Remember to consider the functional qualities of texture as well as the visual qualities. For instance, some materials such as plastic or leather can be very uncomfortable on hot days. Also consider the care required of certain textures. Shiny, glasslike textures are easy to clean, but they also show spots very easily. Rough textures don't show dirt as quickly, but they are harder to clean.

Principles of Design

Guidelines for combining the elements of design in decorating have been developed over time. These principles of design can help you design a room effectively.

Balance

When there is a sense of equilibrium in a room, the design is balanced. A lack of balance is sensed in a room with too much furniture on one side or an unbalanced picture grouping on a wall.

The two types of balance used in decorating are formal balance and informal balance. **Formal balance** is the arrangement of identical objects in a mirror image on either side of the center. **Informal balance** is more casual. No obvious center point divides the arrangement. Instead, this design is like a teeter-totter on which varied weights are placed at different distances from the balancing point. Informal balance is more difficult to achieve, but is considered more interesting. See 30-7.

Proportion

The relationship of one part to another or one part to the whole is **proportion**. For instance, the legs, arms, back, and seat of a chair are in a certain proportion to one another. The chair as a whole is also in a certain proportion to the other furniture in the room. Good proportion creates a pleasing relationship between parts. Unfortunately, no definite rule or formula can be used to create the "right proportion." However, unequal proportions seem to be more pleasing to the eye than equal

Hart Denoble

30-7 The room in this picture illustrates informal balance.

proportions. Ratios of 2:3, 3:5, 4:7, or 5:8 seem to create a pleasant effect.

Large furniture looks best in large rooms and smaller furniture looks best in smaller rooms. Some of the most common decorating problems occur when people mix small and large items. Keep this in mind when creating a picture grouping on a wall, choosing a lampshade, or selecting a piece of furniture to fit into a grouping. When selecting furniture, such as chairs or sofas, consider the size of the human form and its relationship to the furniture. Select furniture that is the right size for the people who will be using it. For example, chairs vary greatly both in the size of the chair and the depth of the seating area. A chair appropriate for a very tall person might not be appropriate for someone who is petite.

Rhythm

The movement of the eye across the design is called **rhythm**. The eye moves according to the arrangement of shape, color, or pattern. Rhythm can be created by repetition, gradation, transition, opposition, and radiation.

Repetition is an easy way to create rhythm that is often used in decorating. The color of a sofa may be repeated in the chairs, and a series of pictures may show repetition in shape. Remember that horizontal movement of the eye creates a feeling of width while vertical movement creates height. See 30-8.

Gradation creates eye movement by using a variety of sizes of objects or a color that changes gradually from light to dark. Gradation is found in a series of similarly shaped candles arranged from smallest to largest on a mantel over a fireplace. You might observe gradation in color when a color gradually changes from light to dark in a bedspread or a wall hanging.

Transition is rhythm found in curved lines such as an arched window, circular chair, or spiral staircase.

Seabrook Wallcoverings

30-8 This room illustrates rhythm through repetition. The pattern in the chairs is repeated in the wallpaper. The color blocks in the wallpaper also create rhythm.

Opposition occurs when lines come together to form right angles, such as in a fireplace or a picture frame.

Rhythm through *radiation* occurs when lines or patterns extend outward from a central axis. This type of rhythm in design is most often found in accessories, such as lampshades. It is also seen whenever a round table is surrounded by chairs.

Emphasis

The focal point of a room, the center of interest, is its **emphasis**. The point of interest in a living room might be the fireplace, a nice view, or a piece of art. A point of emphasis is not essential. However, if you are planning a point of emphasis, be sure the room's remaining furnishings do not compete with it for attention.

The Selection of Home Furnishings

Walls, ceilings, and floorings or floor coverings create a background for other furnishings. The design elements used on these surfaces will blend together with other choices in furnishings to create the room's overall atmosphere or character. The design of windows, window treatments, and accessories in a room can also be used to reach harmony in the design of your home.

Walls and Wall Treatments

Wall treatments are an important decorating choice. Walls occupy the largest area of a room and also determine the general atmosphere of the room. Walls may simply be background, or they may become an active part of the design plan through patterned wallpaper or built-in bookcases. Traditionally, walls were stationary and supported ceilings. Today, some walls stop short of the ceiling. This creates privacy while still allowing air to flow from room to room and perhaps allowing more light. Walls may also be made of glass or plastic, and they may slide away or fold.

For many years, plaster was the most common wall surfacing found in housing, but most new walls are of drywall construction. Because drywall is light and not very dense, it will not support a heavy weight. To suspend heavy objects from drywall, locate the wood studs in the inner structure of the wall and use them as a base. Also, special types of screws called molly bolts can be used. These screws go all the way through the drywall panel and clamp on the inner side. This provides support for the suspended object.

A wide variety of materials can be used for wall treatments or finishes. Each material has both advantages and disadvantages. Paint, wallpaper, and wood paneling are the most common finishes used, 30-9. Consider two factors when deciding on a wall finish. First, what is the condition of the walls? Second, what part will the wall play in the design of the room? If a wall is in perfect condition, almost any finish can be selected. If walls are a textured plaster, then paint is the best finish. If there are defects in the walls, wallpaper or paneling can be used to hide them. Paneling or wallpaper can be used on one wall or the entire room.

Paint is one of the most popular wall finishes. The choice of color is almost limitless. Paint is easy to apply and maintain, and its cost is relatively low.

Wallpaper is available in a wide range of textures and designs. It is more expensive than paint, and installation costs will add to the expense unless you apply it yourself.

Wood paneling is available in many forms and surface finishes. Solid wood paneling is more expensive. Paneling may also be made of plywood or manufactured materials, such as hardboard, plastic laminate, or gypsum board. Manufactured panels look like wood because they are covered with a photo-processed wood grain. A protective finish is applied to make the panels durable.

Other wall finishes include fabric, burlap, and cork. Ceramic tile, plastic tile,

30-9 **The wood paneling adds texture and color to the background of this room.**

brick, and glass are also used as finishes. See 30-10.

When decorating a room, decide whether the walls will be strictly background or a vital part of the decoration. Almost any mood can be created with the appropriate wall treatment. Depending on the treatment used, walls can make a room appear spacious or smaller, formal or informal, exciting or relaxing.

Ceilings

Most ceilings are plastered or drywalled and may be painted white or another pale color. Various types of paneling and tiles with textured surfaces may also be used. Translucent panels covering fluorescent light fixtures are used on some ceilings, particularly kitchens.

Decide whether to treat the ceiling simply or emphasize it. The height of the ceiling can greatly affect the general feeling of the room. The average height is near eight feet. In a home with ceilings much higher or lower than average, a different general feeling is created. A high ceiling emphasizes space and may suggest formality. A low ceiling, on the other hand, creates a more cozy, informal atmosphere.

A ceiling painted white or another light color makes a room look lighter and more spacious, 30-11. To soften the contrast between the walls and the ceiling, some of the wall color can be added to the white ceiling paint. Painting the ceiling with a dark color, using patterned wallpaper, or using dark beams across the room can make the ceiling look lower.

Floors and Floor Coverings

Floors are both physically and visually the foundation of any room. Because floors receive so much wear, considering the cost,

Manton Cork Corp.

30-10 A variety of materials can be used as wall treatments.

30-11 The white color, beams, and molding of this ceiling all add to the illusion of height in this room.

maintenance, and ease of replacement is important when choosing a floor. Like walls and ceilings, floors may be a background to the room or an important part of the design of the room.

A variety of materials are available for flooring. Choice of flooring may depend on many factors. For example, the type of subflooring used is important. Certain floorings would not be suitable on a concrete base. The problem is related to passage of moisture. The amount of care required will also influence your choice. The flooring you choose might depend on the kind of mood you want to create in a room. Each type of flooring has certain advantages and disadvantages.

Hard flooring materials include wood, marble, flagstone, slate, brick, terrazzo, and tile. Wood is a popular choice because of its color, grain, and possibilities for refinishing and repair. Each of the hard flooring materials has particular advantages and disadvantages, but all are quite durable.

Resilient floorings are also available. They are not as hard as wood, brick, or stone, but not nearly as soft as carpeting. Resilient floorings include vinyl, asphalt, cork, and rubber. They may be available in sheets, rolls, or tiles. Resilient floor coverings in tile form have become very popular because of their ease of installation.

Carpeting as a soft floor covering has both decorative and functional values. It can have impact on the design of the room while insulating the floor against drafts, muffling noise, and giving a feeling of comfort. Rugs, which are made in finished sizes and are seldom fastened to the floor, have many of the same characteristics as carpeting. Carpeting can be either a major part of interior design or part of the subtle background depending on the colors, textures, and patterns chosen. Carpets are available in a wide range of colors, patterns, and textures. See 30-12. Some carpets are made of low-level, tightly woven loops.

Burlington Industries

30-12 **Carpets are available in a variety of colors and patterns.**

Sculptured piles are made of different fiber lengths that create a pattern. Shags have long, twisted fibers that are much longer than the fibers in other weaves.

Carpeting has certain advantages over rugs. It gives a room a finished look, covering the floor completely. Carpeting can be used to hide flooring that is undesirable. Carpeting simplifies arranging and rearranging furniture because it does not define special areas within a room as rugs do. Carpeting also tends to make a room look more spacious.

A disadvantage of carpeting is that it is fastened down and cannot be shifted as rugs can. Carpeting tends to show wear in the heavily traveled areas after it has been used for some time. Carpeting must be cleaned in place while rugs can be sent out to be cleaned.

Rugs range from room size to area rugs that define a particular space. They can be used on hard surface floorings or on top of carpeting. The mobility of rugs is one of their greatest advantages. They can be shifted to wear and fade equally and can even be changed with the seasons.

Windows and Window Treatments

Windows control light and air and add beauty. Because of the changes in light and temperature, some kind of window treatment is usually necessary. Consider the window's primary role when choosing a window treatment. For instance, if the main function of a large picture window is to let in light or provide a beautiful view, a heavy curtain would not be a good choice. See 30-13. The window treatment selected also depends on the type of window.

Three common types of windows are double-hung windows, casement windows, and picture windows. See 30-14. **Double-hung windows** have two panels of window that slide up and down in the frame. Double-hung windows can be opened either at the bottom or the top. **Casement windows** are hinged and open like a door

Anderson Corp.

30-13 Covering this window with a drapery would prevent the plants from getting the light they need.

in the center or at the sides. French doors with windows are like casement windows that extend to the floor. Casement windows are often found in a combination of panels. The **picture window** is a large single paneled window designed to frame an exterior view.

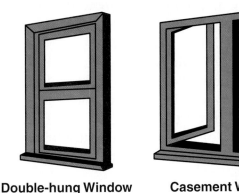
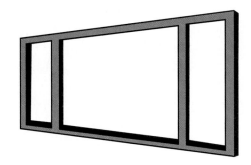

Double-hung Window   **Casement Window**   **Picture Window**

30-14 The windows illustrated here are often found in people's homes.

There are many variations of these three windows. *Ranch* or *strip windows* may be a small picture window but are often like casement windows. They are placed high on the wall so furniture can be placed under them. *Bay windows* have at least three sides that project out from the house wall, 30-15. They may be a combination of windows, such as a casement window on either side of a picture window. *Sliding windows* and sliding glass doors feature two large panes of glass. One of the panes slides across the other, which is usually in a fixed position. *Jalousie windows*, also called *louvered windows*, are composed of many horizontal slats of glass. These slats can be moved so the entire area of window can be opened. This type of window is common in warm climates.

Many variations of window treatments can be used. The function of the window is a major consideration in deciding on a window treatment. The placement, type, and size of the window will also affect the room's appearance.

Draperies and curtains are soft treatments often used on windows. **Draperies** usually refer to heavier curtains. They may cover a window completely or be pulled to the side.

Curtains have a pocket hem at the top, which slips onto a curtain rod. There are a variety of types of curtains. Glass curtains or sheers are made of a thin material and hang next to the window. *Tailored curtains* always hang straight while *ruffled curtains* may be crisscrossed or used with tiebacks. *Cafe curtains* are hung with rings from cafe rods. They may cover the whole window or only the lower half. The hardware you choose for hanging draperies or curtains can have a significant impact on the window treatment.

Other window treatments referred to as hard window treatments include shades, venetian blinds, and shutters. The use of shades has greatly increased and many varieties are available, 30-16. Fabric roller shades are available in many colors, textures, and patterns. Bamboo, plastic, or woven wood shades are available in a variety of materials and weaves. Roman shades are complicated in construction. They are usually pulled up on cords and fall into soft horizontal folds. They may also feature poufs of fabric that balloon gracefully when pulled up. Austrian shades operate like Roman shades but feature graceful scallops of fabric between the vertical cords.

Both horizontal and vertical venetian blinds are made of wood, metal, or plastic slats. Louvered shutters with stationary or movable slats are a versatile window treatment. Some shutters have spaces in the wooden frame where you can insert fabric. An energy-saving window quilt has been developed. This product is like an insulated type of roll-up blind. The side facing the inside of the room is usually fabric and is available in many different colors and designs.

Windows, like the floor and walls, may either blend in with the other background

Lexington Homes

30-15 The bay window in this inviting eating area features four double-hung windows.

elements or be one of the focal points of the room. See 30-17. With imagination, you can do many exciting things with window treatments. If windows are too big or small, too high or low, or badly proportioned, window treatments can disguise these problems. For example, a small window can easily be made to look much larger. Just use sheers that cover the window and draperies that extend from near the edge of the window over a part of the wall.

Furniture

Furniture gives a room meaning. It helps make life comfortable and convenient. Personal tastes can be expressed through the design of furniture chosen. Comfort and convenience mean different things to different people. Some people are very satisfied with a particular furniture style while others dislike it. Your personal choice should fit your taste, lifestyle, budget, and home furnishings plan.

Few people are financially able to decorate a room and buy all the furniture for it at one time. Most people add furniture gradually and are likely to have both old and new furnishings. A thorough knowledge of furniture styles is not necessary to choose good furniture or create an attractive home. Regardless of the style, furniture can be thought of in two categories. Most pieces are either heavy, strong, and bold or lightweight and more refined. The furniture is likely to blend if pieces are selected from one category or the other. Within each category, some pieces are plain and some are more ornamental. The color of the wood and the finish also influence whether the pieces go well together.

Furniture Styles

A basic knowledge of furniture styles helps develop an appreciation of relation to good design. Furniture is likely to fall into one of three categories of styles—traditional, country, or contemporary.

The *traditional styles* have European influences. Traditional styles are sometimes referred to as *period furniture* because the furniture was designed during a particular historical period.

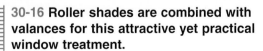
Joann Hartman Adams, D. Edmunds Interiors

30-16 Roller shades are combined with valances for this attractive yet practical window treatment.

Drexel-Heritage Furnishings, Inc.

30-17 Interesting architectural features make this window a focal point of this room.

Many *country* or *casual styles* were actually copied from the traditional styles in simplified forms by furniture makers. See 30-18. These styles have simple lines and use native woods of America, such as maple and pine.

Contemporary styles have simple, clean lines and combine well with Oriental designs. See 30-19. Many contemporary designs have a Scandinavian influence.

Another style, *eclectic*, is a combination of the other furniture styles. This style can be successful if all the pieces of furniture have some characteristic in common, such as material or shape.

People vary in their preferences for furniture styles. Some prefer to use only one style in their room design while others prefer a combination of styles.

Buying Furniture

Furniture buying is extremely challenging. When buying furniture, consider its compatibility with your other furnishings, personal preferences, and budget. Remember when choosing furniture that decorating is a continuous process. As your circumstances change, you may want to add more furniture. If careful choices are made, keeping the decorating plan in mind, the choices may be satisfying for years. Resist the temptation to buy furniture that seems appealing but is not related to other furnishings in any way. To become a discriminating customer and learn to make good choices takes time and effort. When you understand the principles of design and how a quality piece of furniture is made, you can make a more satisfactory choice. See 30-20.

Many aids are available to help with furniture selection. Any labeling on the furniture will be helpful. Consumers may not understand some terms on the label. Books and pamphlets on furniture buying are available through consumer groups and private groups such as the American Furniture Manufacturers Association. Libraries or the Internet will have many of these resources.

Broyhill Furniture

30-18 Many people like the homey look created by country furniture.

30-19 This could be described as a contemporary living room. The furniture blends perfectly with the accessories.

30-20 **Most furniture showrooms arrange furniture into settings. This may help you get a better idea of how you can decorate your own room.**

Case Goods

Preparing to buy furniture is not an easy task. There are many terms to understand. For instance, a large category of nonupholstered items made of wood, such as cabinets, chests, desks, and dressers, are called *case goods*. It is also important for consumers to understand terms that describe the way a piece of furniture is made. Furniture may be either solid wood, veneered wood, or pressed wood.

When a piece is marked **solid wood**, it is indeed made of completely solid wood. A piece of furniture may instead be labeled *veneered wood*. **Veneer** refers to a panel of wood made by gluing several layers of wood on top of one another with the grain at right angles. This results in a "wood sandwich." Inside layers are made of inexpensive wood while the outside is a more expensive, attractively grained wood. Veneering techniques often produce wood that is actually stronger than solid wood and more resistant to warping. A piece of furniture could also be made of pressed wood. **Pressed wood** is the least expensive type of wood. It is made of wood scraps, chips, and shavings. Pressed woods may be used to make inexpensive furniture and on parts of furniture that do not show. Pressed wood is sometimes covered with a more expensive type of wood or laminate to make it look more attractive. See 30-21.

Whether the furniture is made of hardwood or softwood may also affect your choice. Well-seasoned hardwoods such as walnut, oak, maple, birch, cherry, and teak are good choices in furniture. The seasoning or drying of the wood is important because it may warp and shrink badly if it is not well seasoned.

Good-quality furniture construction also depends on how well the parts are joined together. Whether the pieces are glued, screwed, nailed, or joined can be extremely significant in terms of quality furniture. The exterior finish of the wood is also important to quality.

The construction features of the drawers in case goods are another important factor to consider. More satisfactory drawer construction features grooved sides, which allow the drawers to glide in and out easily. The best but most expensive drawer construction is a ballbearing feature. This

O'Sullivan Industries, Inc.

30-21 **This bedroom furniture is made of laminated pressed wood. It is attractive and considerably less expensive than solid wood furniture.**

feature allows drawers to glide very smoothly. Quality case goods have dust panels between the drawers.

Lighting

Most interior designers feel lighting is as important to any decorating scheme as furniture, color, window treatments, and floor coverings. Lighting is functional as well as decorative. Certain levels of lighting are helpful in performing specific tasks, such as cooking, reading, or sewing. Activities that require specific lighting are performed in each room of the home. A family room might be used most often for relaxing and watching television, activities that require more general lighting. However, family members may occasionally get involved in a hobby project or a game that requires direct lighting. Lighting should be flexible enough to take into account the various activities that take place in a room.

To make the most effective use of lighting, it is helpful to understand the functional aspects of light along with its possibilities as a decorating tool. When you understand lighting, you can use it to alter, subdue, highlight, or dramatize any aspect of the room design. The quality of light—its tone, color, and intensity—affects a room's design. See 30-22. In a well-lit room, the light calls attention to its most interesting features and may conceal some of the room's less appealing aspects.

Lighting can create the atmosphere of a room. It can make colors come alive. Bright light creates a stimulating, cheerful feeling. Low levels of light tend to create a peaceful atmosphere of relaxation. Light can play visual tricks as well. A room that is very light seems larger and the ceiling seems higher. High ceilings seem lower if light is kept away from the ceiling.

Considering how natural daylight will affect the room is important in developing

American Lighting Association

30-22 **The lighting gives this room a cozy feeling despite the formality of the furniture.**

a good decorating plan. Many rooms are very attractive during the evening because artificial lighting can be planned and controlled. However, natural light can also be used effectively in a room and can even be a dramatic emphasis.

The visual comfort and mood of a room are influenced by the amount, source, and quality of the light. Glare is a major lighting problem that often exists. Glare is sometimes caused by exposed bulbs in a lamp or by the dramatic contrast between a very bright light and darkness. To diminish the contrast, every room should have both high and low levels of lights.

There are two basic sources of light—incandescent and fluorescent lighting elements. **Incandescent lights** have a tungsten filament that is heated by electricity to the temperature at which it glows. These lights are not very efficient in terms of energy consumption because more energy is converted into heat than light. However, the incandescent light gives off a pleasant warm golden glow. Incandescent lights are usually preferred to fluorescent lights.

Fluorescent lights produce light by releasing electricity through a mercury vapor sealed within the tube rather than by heat. Fluorescent tubes come in white, warm, and cool tints. Although white light is the most natural light, the warm light is the most flattering to people. Fluorescent lights seem to distort colors. On the other hand, they are less expensive to use. They work well in kitchens, bathrooms, and workrooms where the lights are used often. The life of a fluorescent light is shortened each time you turn it on. Remember this when you are leaving the room for only a short while. More energy can be saved by leaving the fluorescent light turned on while you are gone. Incandescent light is just the opposite because it produces heat. To save energy, be sure to turn off incandescent lights when you leave a room.

The best lighting effect is often achieved by having a mixture of both incandescent and fluorescent lights. This mixture seems to be easier on the eyes. Advances in technology and product design have created a variety of lighting possibilities.

Types of Lighting

Three basic types of lighting may be used in a home. **General lighting**, which maintains a low level of light throughout the room, assures safety and ease in moving about. General lighting also provides the background light for the directed lighting to avoid a glare caused by the contrast of light and dark. Ceiling fixtures, chandeliers, or recessed fixtures like down lights and luminous ceilings are examples of general lighting. Lighted valances and cornices are also common methods of producing general lighting.

Directed lighting, sometimes referred to as local or task lighting, is the second type of lighting used. Light is directed on a particular object or area and is used for activities such as reading, washing dishes, and playing the piano. Portable lamps are most often used for direct lighting although wall and ceiling fixtures are also used. See 30-23.

The third type of lighting used is **accent lighting** or decorative lighting. This type of

American Lighting Association

30-23 **These ceiling fixtures act as directed lighting for the kitchen counter.**

lighting is used to create focal points in the room. It is more decorative than functional, although it does create some general lighting for the room. Track lighting, recessed fixtures, and spotlights are often used for accent lighting.

Selecting Lighting Fixtures

Lighting can become part of the decorative design of the room through structural lighting or through portable lamps and ceiling or wall fixtures. Structural lighting is usually installed during building or remodeling. It is often a type of general lighting concealed in coves, cornices, or valances. Structural lighting also includes down lights or spotlights installed in the ceiling.

There have been many new developments in nonarchitectural lighting. These types of lighting are both economical and easy to install. A variety of ceiling and wall fixtures and portable lamps are now available. You can easily find lighting that fits into a variety of decorative schemes yet also meets functional needs.

Because personal taste in decorating differs from person to person, it is difficult to establish specific rules for selecting quality portable lamps. However, some simple guidelines might be helpful.

First, does the lamp meet the functional needs for which you chose it? For instance, a reading lamp should project enough light to read comfortably while sitting in the chair next to it. It is possible the design of the shade limits the light projection so reading becomes difficult.

Second, are the materials appropriate and well made? As long as the lamp is sturdy, the base can be made of metal, wood, marble, or ceramic. The lampshade is appropriate when it shields your eyes from the bulb when you are sitting or standing anywhere in the room. Many lamps have translucent glass bowls that help shade the bulb and diffuse the light. Because translucent shades let some light through, they contribute to general lighting as well as specific lighting. On the other hand, opaque shades do not let light through. They concentrate all of the light on the area below except for a small amount of light that escapes upward through the opening at the top.

Third, does the overall design of the lamp harmonize with other furnishings in the room and is it well proportioned? Any lamp should harmonize with the background of the room in color, shape, or texture. The lamp design can enhance the overall effect of the room.

Accessories

Accessories strongly affect a room's design. They add charm, interest, and individuality. Accessories give the room its finishing touches.

The accessories you choose will probably be related to your interests and your individuality. However, some guidelines might help you choose effective accessories.

Accessories tend to be either functional or decorative. Functional accessories are practical. They are chosen because of their usefulness in the home. Functional accessories include lamps, mirrors, clocks, pillows, and wastebaskets. Plants, paintings, sculptures, photographs, baskets, and collections are considered decorative accessories. See 30-24. Whether accessories are decorative or functional, they will enhance the decorating scheme of the room.

Maintaining a Clean Home

A clean home means different things to different people. People have varying standards for cleanliness. Nevertheless, certain cleaning tasks must be accomplished to

Marvin Windows and Doors

30-24 What accessories do you see in this room? Are they decorative or functional?

keep a home safe and to avoid deterioration. See 30-25.

Engineering advances have changed household cleaning. Synthetic fibers have been developed that resist soil and staining. Cookware coatings make cleaning much easier. Plastic laminates for furniture surfaces and countertops are resistant to soiling. Paints and coated wall coverings can be scrubbed. Some lacquer-coated metals stay brightly polished for long periods of time without further attention. Good cleaning products have been developed for specific jobs. Special-purpose brushes, synthetic sponges, and treated dustcloths are examples of products that

30-25 **Keeping a home sanitary not only makes the home look well kept, but also helps protect the health of the people who live there.**

help speed housekeeping tasks.

The many new products, however, present difficulties in selecting the appropriate tool or cleaner for a specific function and using it properly. For instance, although most plastic countertops are resistant to abrasion and soil, the incorrect use of an abrasive cleaner could scratch the surface and cause it to stain more easily. A powerful upright vacuum cleaner with a rotary brush might damage a braided rug, loosening the threads. Choose cleaners and equipment carefully to avoid damaging results.

Although there are some excellent new cleaning products available, many cleaning methods and formulas used 50 to 100 years ago are still good. The results achieved with vinegar, baking soda, or even plain table salt or lemon juice compare favorably with what the most sophisticated cleaning agents can do.

In selecting and using cleaning products, read the label carefully. Improper use of certain products can be dangerous. For instance, ammonia is an excellent cleaner when diluted with water. However, ammonia is a powerful chemical that reacts with other chemicals to form poisonous gases. Never mix ammonia with chlorine bleach, toilet bowl cleaners, rust removers, oven cleaners, or anything else that is not specifically recommended. Read all labels carefully before using any cleaning product. Some are toxic and must be kept out of the reach of children.

Cleaning done systematically following a schedule is a way to prevent being overburdened with too many cleaning tasks at one time. However, circumstances vary with each family. The time available, number of people helping, size of the home, and supplies available are just a few factors that will affect how the cleaning process is organized. A problem-solving approach to organizing cleaning can be helpful, 30-26.

Busy families sometimes employ professional cleaning services, 30-27. Some cleaning services might have one person cleaning for a half day or a full day. Other services have a group of three or four persons who work together for a shorter period of time. Many of these services supply the cleaning equipment and supplies. Before hiring a cleaning service, check out reliable references.

ServiceMASTER

30-27 A reliable cleaning service can perform cleaning tasks professionally and efficiently.

Cleaning Checklist

Some families use a checklist to accomplish various cleaning tasks. See 30-28. This way, tasks can be shared and assigned to family members. The cleaning schedule may vary from day to day or week to week. Highly used areas will require more regular cleaning. Lesser used areas can go a few days or weeks with less cleaning if necessary.

Cleaning Tools

The right tools or supplies will help make the cleaning tasks easier. The following items will help clean most all areas of your home:

- broom/dust pan
- dust mop
- vacuum cleaner with special attachments
- cloth and paper wipes
- hard bristle cleaning brushes
- scrubbing sponges/pads
- window squeegees
- buckets
- stepladder
- rubber or vinyl gloves to protect hands

A Problem-Solving Approach to Cleaning

1. **Define the problem.** List all the jobs that must be done in your home.

2. **Set your goal.** Determine how much you can realistically expect to accomplish. It is extremely important to have a goal as motivation and standards by which to measure the success of your efforts.

3. **Set priorities.** Determine which problems or jobs should get preferential treatment. It might help when listing jobs to put them under headings such as *very important*, *important, but not urgent*, and *nice, but not necessary*.

4. **Make out a timetable.** Prepare a schedule indicating whether the jobs should be done daily, weekly, occasionally, or seasonally. If necessary, break the list down even further, such as morning, afternoon, or evening for the daily jobs. The object is to establish habits.

5. **Make good use of people power.** Use some method, such as a chart, so everyone knows what is expected of him or her.

6. **Use the proper supplies.** Many resources are available to help you select the proper materials for various cleaning tasks. Ask other people what they have found to be most effective. Read labels carefully. Many books and newspaper columns available at your local library offer excellent suggestions.

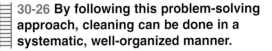

30-26 By following this problem-solving approach, cleaning can be done in a systematic, well-organized manner.

Checklist for Cleaning Tasks

Daily Tasks	Weekly Tasks	Monthly Tasks	Semiannual Tasks
• Make bed.	• Change bed linens.	• Clean closets.	• Clean closets.
• Straighten bedroom, bathroom, living area, and eating area.	• Do laundry and mending.	• Dry-clean or wash bedding.	• Dry-clean or wash bedding.
• Wash dishes or load dishwasher.	• Wash kitchen garbage pail or change liner.	• Clean drapes thoroughly.	• Clean drapes thoroughly.
• Wipe kitchen counters and cooking surface.	• Wash kitchen floor.	• Wash seldom-used glasses and dinnerware.	• Wash seldom-used glasses and dinnerware.
• Sweep kitchen floor.	• Clean bathroom sink, tub, and toilet.	• Clean silverware.	• Clean silverware.
• Empty wastebaskets and other garbage containers.	• Wash bathroom floor.	• Replace shelf liners.	• Replace shelf liners.
• Discard clutter, especially junk mail.	• Dust decorative items.	• Wash walls.	• Wash walls.
• Wipe out bathroom sinks.	• Dust and polish furniture.	• Clean woodwork.	• Clean woodwork.
• Pick up wet/damp towels and take to laundry area.	• Vacuum lamp shades.	• Wash mattress pad.	
• Use squeegee or towel to dry walls after showering to remove excess moisture.	• Vacuum carpet.	• Vacuum mattress.	
	• Shake out small rugs.	• Damp mop hard floors.	
		• Vacuum drapes and wipe blinds.	
		• Vacuum upholstered furniture.	
		• Clean kitchen shelves.	
		• Clean refrigerator and defrost if needed.	
		• Clean range, including oven.	
		• Wash bathroom walls surrounding tub.	

30-28 **This is a sample checklist of typical cleaning tasks.**

Cleaning Products

Basic cleaning products include chemicals that help in the cleaning process. Cleaning products fit into the following categories:

- *Abrasive:* rubs dirt away in dry form or with water.

- *Nonabrasive, all purpose:* penetrates and loosens soil, softens water and prevents soil from redepositing on cleaned surface.

- *Acids such as ammonia, vinegar, and lemon juice:* cuts grease and acts as a mild bleach. Can be mixed with water and sprayed on oven surfaces.

- *Specialty/spot cleaners:* designed for soil found on specific surfaces such as metal, glass, tile, or fabrics.

- *Mildew remover:* removes mold and mildew buildup, especially in bathrooms.

- *Soap and scum removers:* Removes buildup of minerals and soap scum in kitchens and bathrooms, especially by faucets and drains.

- *Furniture polish:* Lifts soil, removes old wax and forms a new coating.

The type of cleaning product to choose is based on the material of which the item is made. For example, spot cleaners can be used to treat stains on upholstery or rugs. If a surface is glass, metal, or ceramic, a general all-purpose cleaner is a good choice. Read labels on cleaning products to know the intended use(s) for best results.

Brainstorming

Brainstorm activities done in your home that contribute to preventive maintenance. How are these activities effective? What might happen in your home if these activities were not completed?

According to the Soap and Detergent Association, the three steps to choosing the right cleaning product are to:

1. Analyze the soil and the surface. Identify the dirt and then determine what type of surface needs to be cleaned.

2. Consider your own cleaning needs. What type of cleaning schedule fits your family's needs? Homes with young children need more frequent cleaning. Which types of products will meet your cleaning needs? Which forms of products do you prefer (sprays, gels, foams, powders, or liquids)?

3. Read labels on cleaning products. Labels provide information for the safe and effective use of products.

Manufacturers will also include care and maintenance information plus cleaning instructions as a guide with their products or appliances. As technology improves surfaces and products, be aware of the proper and most efficient ways to clean various household areas.

Preventive Maintenance

Many housing problems and repairs can be avoided by routine maintenance care. This is commonly called **preventive maintenance**. Preventive maintenance does not require the technical skills many repairs require. Most people are not able to fix everything themselves, but they will recognize when repairs need to be made. Skill in preventive maintenance involves both common sense and basic knowledge about systems and equipment in the home. Not only can preventive maintenance save time and money, but it can also help create a safer living environment.

Although preventive maintenance sounds ideal, many people have difficulty practicing it. Preventive maintenance often involves checking or cleaning items that are presently in working order. This type of work is not as satisfying as repairing something that is broken. Many preventive maintenance tasks are cleaning jobs that most people find boring. Therefore, these tasks are easy to forget or avoid doing. See 30-29.

Preventive maintenance is important to both the renter and owner of housing. When a renter reports a watermark on the ceiling, the owner discovers the cause before major repairs are necessary. This also helps the renter avoid a nuisance and possible damage to his or her belongings.

Schrader

30-29 **Though people may not enjoy washing windows, it is a necessary maintenance task.**

For the homeowner, preventive mainte-nance can actually mean a great savings. The time spent learning about systems, equipment, and potential problems will be quite worthwhile.

Maintenance of the Housing Structure

A basic knowledge of the housing struc-ture and the terms used to describe the various parts will help in preventive mainte-nance. This knowledge will help in following any directions on maintenance and accu-rately describe signs of possible problems.

The outside of a house is under constant attack from rain, wind, ice, or snow. The sun's rays, rodents, and insects such as termites may also cause damage. Some preventive maintenance steps to take on the outside of the house are listed in 30-30.

Many people fail to thoroughly inspect the inside of their homes because they expect to just notice any problems that develop. This attitude unfortunately does not work. Potential problems may be left unseen or ignored until it is too late.

Preventive Maintenance Outside the House

- When inspecting areaways for proper drainage, check basement windows for signs of decay or termite problems.
- Check the condition of any brickwork to be sure the mortar is firm and has not crumbled. The top of the chimney or wall should be covered with a cap of concrete to prevent water from seeping down into the mortar joints and creating damp spots. If this should freeze, damage can result.
- Check exterior doors to see if the finish or paint has worn off. If it has, moisture gets into the door and causes it to expand and stick. Moisture in a door can also cause the door to warp. If the house has wood siding, be sure the siding is well clear of the earth. Decay and termites may cause damage.
- Check for any blistering or peeling on a painted house. These are signs that water is getting into the wall. You should locate the source of water and correct the situation.
- Check the grading of the earth around the foundation walls. It should slope gently away from the walls so the water will drain that way.
- Check gutters and downspouts during a rain to see if they are draining correctly. If water is pouring over the sides, there is a problem. This may mean the gutter is full of leaves or debris, or the opening into the downspout may be clogged. The hangers holding the gutter in place may have broken loose. In that case, the gutter would no longer be able to carry the water away properly.
- Check any metal parts, such as a storm window, awning, or gutter, to see if there is any rust or corrosion.
- Check the roof regularly for loose shingles and any other damage. Look at the underside of the roof from the attic or crawl space to see if there are any water stains. These would indicate leaks.
- Check the windows for the condition of the putty or glazing compound that is applied around the edge of the glass. Moisture can get into cracks and cause decay.
- Label branch shut-off valves to indicate hot and cold water lines.
- In winter climates, turn off water lines to prevent pipes from freezing and bursting. Drain the water by opening spigot.
- Remove air conditioner units and store them inside or apply a winter cover.
- Clean up debris around central air conditioning units.
- Clean out the garage or shed to remove anything that might freeze, such as paint or adhesives.

30-30 Taking these maintenance steps will help you keep the outside of your home in good shape.

See 30-31 for a list of preventive maintenance steps that can be taken inside the house.

Housing Repairs

No matter how careful you are about preventive maintenance, there will be necessary repairs. Whether you make the repairs yourself or have someone make them for you will depend upon your time and ability. You can save a lot of money by doing some of the more common home repair jobs yourself. See 30-32. Many books offer detailed instructions on how to handle common household repair jobs. Employees at a hardware store can also give instructions on various jobs. Many products available for doing household repairs have

helpful instructions printed right on them. Short courses on simplified repairs have become popular. These courses are inexpensive in terms of both time and money when compared with the repair expenses saved.

A few basic tools will be necessary to make some of the minor repairs and practice preventive maintenance. It is helpful to have a hammer, handsaw, adjustable wrench, pliers, electric drill, flashlight, force cup, and several screwdrivers on hand. In addition to these tools, nails and screws in assorted sizes may be needed. Work will be more efficient if tools are kept in good condition and stored in a special place when not in use. See 30-33.

Certain repairs require the services of an expert. Try to plan ahead and find service people before you need them. The

---

Preventive Maintenance Inside the House

- Check the attic often for water stains, which may indicate a leaky roof.
- Check the attic in cold weather to see if there is moisture accumulating. This moisture may be caused by the warm air in the house striking the cold roof. Moisture can cause problems such as decay, but it can be eliminated by proper ventilation of the attic.
- Thoroughly check your basement at least once a month and after any heavy rain and spring thaws. Check the walls and floors for cracks, signs of termites, and decaying wood.
- Look for any possible leaks in the bathroom. Moisture can be a problem in various spots. For instance, certain leaks might allow water to get under the flooring or into the walls. There might also be a leak under the bathroom sink or around the base of the toilet bowl.
- If you have a fireplace, be sure the chimney flue is not obstructed and the damper is in working order before building the first fire of the year. Otherwise, the house may be filled with smoke.
- Notice your wooden furniture. If any wood joint has weakened, it may indicate dry air in your house. Along with heat, this dry air may have caused the wood to shrink and the joints to fail.
- Notice the effect of sun exposure on both wood and upholstered furniture. The warm sun can dry the wood, and the rays can cause the fabric to fade. If this has happened, you may want to consider a different room arrangement or close the draperies when the sun is most intense.
- Schedule an annual heating system inspection to make sure your unit is running properly.
- Periodically change or clean the furnace filter and make sure air ducts are leak free.
- Replace batteries in smoke and carbon monoxide detectors.
- Check to see that fire extinguishers work. These should be in the kitchen and family rooms.
- Change batteries and reset programmable thermostats.
- In winter climates, any indoor water pipes that could freeze should be wrapped with insulation material.

30-31 These are just a few steps you can take to prevent major problems from developing in the interior of your home.

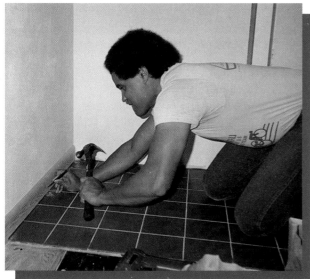

Schrader

30-32 **Many common home repair jobs are not that difficult, and doing them yourself can save a lot of money.**

Knape and Vogt Mfg.

30-33 **If tools are neatly stored, locating them will be much easier.**

best way to find a good service person is to talk with other people. Ask friends, neighbors, or employees at a hardware store or lumberyard to give you names of people who do good repair work.

A large part of the money spent on repairs goes for labor. Always check in advance to learn the hourly rate. You will also be paying for the time it takes the service person to come to your house and get back to the shop. When you call for repair work, give the model number and serial number of the equipment to be repaired. Talk to the service manager or one of the service people. They may be able to tell you how to get your equipment working.

Be sure to check what your homeowner's or personal property insurance policy covers. Policies may cover such items as damage to electrical equipment due to lightning or damage caused from frozen pipes. Insurance agents can supply a simple list of what a policy covers.

Signs of Problems

Learn to recognize signs and signals that warn of impending trouble. Doing this can

keep small problems from becoming crisis situations. Learn to depend on your eyes, ears, and nose to help you. For example, use your eyes to notice the finish on the floor is getting thin in a traffic area. You can see when a roof shingle has been pulled loose by a high wind or when paint is peeling from the windows outside the house.

Listen for changes in sound that might indicate a problem. For instance, the refrigerator may be running longer and more frequently than usual. This might indicate that dust and dirt need to be removed from the condenser. A gurgling sound as the water runs down the drain might indicate a problem in the drainage system.

Your sense of smell can help you identify possible problems, too. Take note of any unfamiliar or unpleasant odor around electric motor driven equipment, such as a refrigerator, washing machine, or vacuum cleaner. This odor tells you something is wrong. Be sure to turn off the motor until you find the reason for the odor. Immediately check any unusual odor that indicates sewer gas or natural gas. This may create a safety concern.

Getting **Involved**

Analyze the school environment. Invite someone from the maintenance department to share principles and techniques he or she uses to keep the school clean and safe. Also ask what steps students could take on a daily basis to help with upkeep. Write suggestions in a pamphlet to be distributed throughout the school. .

Maintenance for Energy Efficiency

Energy conservation is a worthwhile goal for everyone. Since energy is a limited resource, it must be used efficiently in order to avoid waste. Some solutions to the problem of energy waste must come from the governmental level. However, individual families can have a major impact on this problem. Every measure that is taken to help reduce energy waste, from turning off a light to installing a solar energy system, will help achieve both personal and national goals.

Many families pay for a lot of extra energy to make up for the waste caused by poor-quality home construction and bad personal habits. By making an effort to develop an energy-efficient household, each family can take steps in saving both money and energy. Most homes use a combination of energy sources. The following are the common household services and the forms of energy you can conserve:

- heating—gas, oil, or electricity
- cooling—electricity
- water heating—gas, oil, or electricity
- appliances—electricity or gas
- lighting—electricity

There are many possibilities available to help with energy conservation. These are listed in 30-34. Many "do-it-yourself" products are available that can help make a difference in utility costs. The money spent

Home Energy Conservation Tips

- Use the sun, wind, and trees for heating, ventilation, and protection.
- Add insulation to keep the heat inside in winter and outside in the summer.
- Reduce the amount of air leaking into the house through cracks and loose joints by repairing cracks and caulking.
- Maintain heating and cooling equipment for efficient operation.
- Reduce the use of hot water.
- Use fewer lights and more efficient lighting products.
- Operate appliances more efficiently.
- Reduce water usage from leaky faucets.
- Use solar energy systems to supplement existing heating and hot water equipment.
- Investigate ways to keep from losing heat up the fireplace chimney.
- Install a wind generator to supplement the supply of electricity.

30-34 **Home energy conservation can be accomplished by following these tips. Can you think of other ways?**

for these products will actually be saved by lowering future utility bills as a result of the energy conservation steps. In many communities, local power companies provide an energy audit service. The power company employee goes through homes inspecting them both inside and outside. Families are then given specific suggestions for making their homes more energy efficient. Many suggestions may require minor changes that are not costly. Others, such as replacing storm windows or a heating system, involve major costs and may have to be considered for the future.

Many energy conservation books and pamphlets are available at your local library or utility company. They can be extremely helpful in guiding you in energy conservation around your home.

Summary

The elements and principles of design are resources that can help create an attractive home environment. Because people have varying tastes, they will use line, form, color, and texture to create an environment that is pleasing to them. The principles of design are guidelines for combining the elements that have traditionally been helpful in decorating.

There are many decisions to make in selecting home furnishings. Being informed about these decisions will help in obtaining satisfaction related to the attractiveness and efficiency of the home.

Routine cleaning and preventive maintenance of the home is important in maintaining an attractive and efficiently functioning home. This requires a basic knowledge of the housing structure and the terms that describe various parts. Routine inspections of the interior and exterior of housing are important for preventive maintenance and protecting a housing investment.

To Review

1. List the principles of design.
2. List two adjectives that describe the kind of feeling each of the following lines suggests.
   A. horizontal line
   B. vertical line
   C. diagonal line
   D. curved line
3. The _____ color scheme makes a room feel spacious, while the colors in the _____ color scheme tend to make each other look brighter.
4. Describe the difference between formal and informal balance.
5. Describe two major advantages rugs have over carpeting.
6. Match the following furniture styles with their characteristics.
   _____traditional
   _____country
   _____contemporary
   _____eclectic
   A. Combination of styles.
   B. Simple, clean lines.
   C. Sometimes referred to as period furniture.
   D. Copied from traditional furniture, but in simplified forms.
   E. Often shows Scandinavian influence.
   F. Have European influences.
7. _____ wood is made of scraps, chips, and shavings. _____ wood is a panel made by gluing several layers of wood on top of one another with the grain at right angles.
8. Describe the differences between incandescent and fluorescent lights.
9. True or false? Preventive maintenance means you fix problems as they occur.
10. List three ways you can conserve energy at home.

To Do with the Class

1. Find pictures of accessories, rooms, and homes you like. Share these pictures in a small group within the class. Discuss how tastes, personal preferences, and concepts related to beauty differ among individuals.
2. Bring three pictures of rooms to share with others in class. Identify the color scheme and discuss the effects created by using those colors.
3. Find examples of different window styles and treatments. Analyze the effects of the designs and share your thoughts with the class.
4. Have a mini-maintenance day where tools are identified along with possible home repairs that can be done using them.

To Challenge Your Thinking

1. Develop a display that illustrates each of the standard color schemes.
2. Investigate a Web site that has information on current decorating trends. Which ideas are practical and follow good design principles?
3. Conduct an experiment to determine how different types of lighting affect the ability to complete different tasks such as reading.
4. Work with your family to develop a planned maintenance schedule for your home.

To Do with Your Community

1. Visit a retail business where floorings and floor coverings are sold to become familiar with the varieties available. Discuss your observations with the class.
2. Invite a representative from a furniture business to speak to your class on skills in furniture buying.
3. Invite a panel of service people or people from the construction industry to discuss suggestions for preventive maintenance.
4. Invite people from a professional cleaning service to share cleaning strategies and shortcuts. Have them share information about their jobs as well.

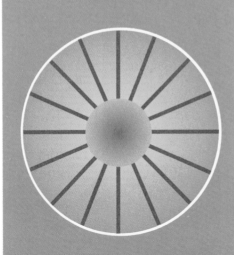

📖 **Using the decision-making process can help you choose furnishings for your home.**

Part Eleven
Preparing for Your Career

Chapter 31
Career Planning

Planning ahead is an important part of finding the best career for you. By doing research and evaluating your interests, abilities, and personal characteristics, you can determine suitable career options in the world of work.

Chapter 32
Finding a Job

Job-seeking skills are necessary in order to obtain a job you desire. Once you get a job, be sure to demonstrate the traits that lead to job success.

31

Career Planning

To Know

career
interests
abilities
aptitude
achievement
career and technical student organizations
cooperative education
career clusters
entry-level position
apprenticeship program
compressed workweek
entrepreneurship

Objectives

After studying this chapter, you will be able to

◇ explain the importance of career planning.

◇ recognize how attitudes about careers develop.

◇ explain how interests, abilities, and personality may relate to career choices.

◇ describe a variety of sources of career information.

◇ explain how management relates to careers.

Most people will live 50 to 60 years after high school graduation. Many people are involved in the world of work for as many as 25 to 40 of those years. During your working years, most of your waking hours will be involved in some kind of work activity. Therefore, spending time and effort to plan a career you will enjoy is important. See 31-1.

Good things usually don't just happen. Most worthwhile accomplishments are the result of a plan. This includes building a **career**, the succession of jobs a person has throughout life that results in professional growth and personal satisfaction. A plan indicates that goals are involved—goals based on your important values. Planning to reach a goal means making decisions.

Everyone makes many decisions throughout life. Some decisions are more critical than others. The decisions you make will create a certain lifestyle. Decisions about people, things, and ideas greatly affect your lifestyle.

Because a career will be a central activity in your life, it is important to make

Brainstorming

Discuss the meaning of the following statement: "An interest in a career isn't enough. You must also have the necessary aptitude or ability." What might happen to a person's career if he or she has limited aptitude or abilities in that career area? How can other people be affected? .

a maximum effort to make wise decisions relating to it. Understanding career development, career choices, and the relationship between lifestyle and career will help you recognize the value of decision making in career planning.

Career Planning

Most people begin giving serious thought to their future in the world of work while they are in high school. Young children often fantasize about wanting to be a movie star, sports star, or astronaut. However, during the mid-teens, ideas about careers become a more serious concern and career plans become more realistic.

Career Planning and Career Development

You will begin to think seriously about career plans during your teen years. Much of what has happened in your life before that time will affect your feelings and decisions about careers. Career development actually begins when a person is very young, 31-2. Young children first learn about careers through their parents or other people close to them. They often are read

31-1 **Life is much more pleasant when people enjoy their work.**

31-2 **Childhood interests can expand and develop into career interests.**

stories about firefighters, police officers, nurses, or teachers. Children begin to form feelings and ideas about various careers at a young age. Television and other media have a strong influence on the impressions young people form.

As children grow older, they develop their own unique hobbies and interests. A special experience such as a weekend at camp or a special presentation at school may introduce new and appealing ideas they will want to pursue. All these could be part of career development experiences. A 10-year-old boy may develop an interest in aviation while flying to visit his grandmother. The opportunity to travel in a large aircraft is an exciting experience. The boy is motivated to get a paper route and save his money so he can afford flying lessons. At 16 years of age, the boy takes flying lessons and begins to develop more specific plans toward a career in aviation. Numerous factors have influenced development of this career interest. At this point, career planning has begun.

One of the first steps in career planning is to become aware of your attitudes and behaviors about certain careers and why these have developed. This will help you understand whether your feelings are based on facts and experiences or if they developed from more emotional decisions.

Careers and Family

Your career and family roles and responsibilities are interrelated. People who enjoy their jobs tend to have good attitudes about their family lives. Pressures and problems at work can sometimes interfere with family roles. Having a balance between family and work helps make life more satisfying for all family members. See 31-3.

The husband and wife are working outside the home in more families. Most careers in today's world are available to both males and females. In the past there were

31-3 **Coming home after a satisfying day on the job can make the time you spend at home even more pleasant.**

stereotypes associated with certain career choices. For instance, the nursing career usually involved females, and doctors were usually men. This is no longer true. Many women are combining families and careers by working full-time or part-time. Many women work due to economic necessity.

Meeting family needs can be challenging when both parents work outside the home. Finding the time and energy to care for children, prepare meals, and maintain the home can be difficult. Many families need to make adjustments, such as choosing child care services for children, buying more prepared foods, and contracting a home cleaning service.

Families need to determine the importance of careers in relationship to family needs. For instance, one parent may make more money in a job that requires a great deal of travel. However, he or she may feel it is more important to be able to spend time with the children. Therefore, this parent may take a lower-paying job that does not require travel. A parent may enjoy the satisfaction of a career, but may want to spend more time caring for the children. He or she may choose to have a part-time job or work from the home. See 31-4.

31-4 **Working from home or part-time allows parents to spend even more time with their children.**

Some fathers are choosing to stay at home to become more involved with their children as they grow up. Dads want to be a more important part of their children's lives. Some fathers are more committed to spending time with their children on a daily basis, especially when the children are very young. This can save the family expense of child care costs. Children and parents can benefit from this arrangement.

Due to changing economic times, some dads may be forced to stay at home due to job loss. Others choose to stay at home because they are dissatisfied with their jobs. Some dads are able to use technology to work from the home. Sometimes it is more economical for a family to reduce child care costs by having the father stay at home, especially if the wife has a financially stable job. Regardless, families with stay at home dads must be willing to communicate clearly and manage their finances appropriately. In this way, these families are no different from dual-career families and families with stay at home moms.

Careers and Satisfaction

Your home life and work life are affected in other ways by your career. Your career helps determine your income. As a result, it has an effect on your lifestyle and hobbies. Your career may determine where you live and the friends you meet.

Your personal satisfaction is also affected by your career. If you are happy with your work, you are more likely to be happy in your personal life. However, pressures, conflicts with other employees, and even boredom with a job can lead to problems in your personal and family life.

In turn, having a satisfying personal life can help make your work life more pleasant. Having a chance to relax and do things you enjoy can help you take a positive attitude about your job. Problems in your personal life, however, can result in a lack of concentration on the job, decreasing productivity.

Most people find a balance between the rewards and disappointments of work and personal life. They look to both for support and encouragement. They also make adjustments as needed to handle problems at home or at work.

Jobs and a Career

Having a job is different from having a career. Many people drift from one job to another. They do not have a career. Instead, they just have jobs. No planning has been involved.

Career planning begins with your own concept of career. A career can be seen as a sequence of productive experiences that make your life more satisfying. A career belongs to only one person. It involves goals based on your values and is achieved through work that is meaningful and rewarding. Give each job opportunity careful consideration, looking at features, conditions, advantages, and disadvantages of the job in relation to your career goals. A job may be described as either good or bad for you depending on whether it helps move you toward your career goals. See 31-5.

To wisely consider job opportunities, first have a fairly clear picture of your career goals. Self-assessment is the first step in clarifying career goals. You will need to find out what is important to you in relation to the world of work.

A Self-Study in Relation to Career Plans

Every person has a unique definition of a successful career. Some people want to enjoy their work while others are mainly interested in the money they will earn. Because success in a career is such a

Carl Karchner Enterprises

31-5 **Some jobs provide income to help pay for education or training for a career.**

personal matter, you need to take a long hard look at yourself. Consider the person you are and the person you would like to be. The way you see yourself will greatly affect your choices related to a career and your overall lifestyle.

Through a self-study, you learn more about yourself—your interests, your abilities, and other influences on your lifestyle. The self-study should help guide you toward a career goal you can reach and one that will be satisfying to you.

Interests

Your **interests** are what you like—your preferences for activities, events, and ideas. Becoming more aware of your interests can guide you toward a career you will like.

Make a list of your interests by asking yourself some of these questions: In what kinds of activities are you involved? What activities do you enjoy most? What are your hobbies? What school courses do you like most? What topics do you talk about most? If you could spend a weekend doing what you enjoy most, what would you do?

In what activities do you perform well? See 31-6.

After you have listed your interests, try to classify them. You can do this in a variety of ways. Your interests might fall into categories such as artistic, mechanical, outdoor, social, or scientific. Another way to classify interests has to do with the type of activities they involve. Activities might involve objects, people, and the communication of ideas, or they might be activities of a scientific or technical nature. Some activities are routine, concrete, and organized. Others are abstract and creative. Certain activities result in prestige or the esteem of others, while other activities result in personal satisfaction. Some activities relate to machines and mechanical techniques.

A simple way to classify interests is to think of them in relation to data, people, or things. Interests involving numbers, symbols, and information are related to data. If you enjoy the company of others and prefer not to be alone, your interests relate to being with people. On the other hand, your interests may be more related to producing something. Perhaps you enjoy baking a cake, building a model car, or repairing broken objects. These interests are more related to things. See 31-7.

By classifying your interests, you will be able to see how those interests relate to various types of occupations. Not only will this help you select potential occupations, but it will also encourage you to learn more about those areas of work. You might get to know people working in jobs related to your major interest. Ask them questions about what they do, how they got involved in that field, their educational background, and what their career plans are. You might also like to know the entry-level salary for a person in that field.

Classifying your interests will also guide you toward developing skills related to those interests. If you are interested in a particular subject, you are usually motivated to learn more about that subject. The same is true of skills. If you enjoy a particular skill, you are likely to enjoy other skills that are closely related to it. Having a variety of skills related to a particular area may lead to a successful career. If you have trouble identifying your interests, you might be able to use an interest inventory to help. These tests are usually available through a school counselor.

31-6 **If you look forward most to classes in the computer lab, you may want to consider this interest in technology as a future career option.**

Schrader

31-7 **Making jewelry as a hobby may lead to a successful career in the same area.**

Interest inventories and surveys can be found online. To find sites, use such terms or phrases such as *career planning*, *interest inventory*, *interest survey*, *aptitude test*, and *career cluster*. College links, the *Dictionary of Occupational Titles*, and business Web sites may assist in your career investigation. State and federal government Web sites can also be helpful.

Abilities

Interests indicate activities you like and enjoy while **abilities** indicate skills and activities you can perform successfully. In order to set realistic career goals, you will need to consider your abilities in relation to those goals.

Some abilities are gained through hard work; others seem to come naturally. When someone seems to be born with a talent, it is said that he or she has an **aptitude** for that activity. One person may have a musical aptitude, while another person may have a mechanical aptitude. See 31-8.

31-8 What careers might be developed from a person's aptitude in music?

There are both mental and physical aptitudes and abilities. If you make an honest effort to do your work at school, your grades are an indication of your abilities. If you do not try very hard, you may have more aptitude than your grades indicate.

Various standardized tests measure mental abilities. Some measure your verbal ability or how well you understand the meaning of words. Others measure your reading ability—your ability to understand written materials. Your math ability is measured by how fast and how accurately you can solve mathematical problems. There are also tests to measure reasoning abilities. These tests measure your ability to see how things do or do not fit together and why. They may also involve the ability to see relationships and draw conclusions.

Tests can measure your aptitude for various mental activities. These tests can show whether you could easily develop ability in certain areas of work. Special aptitude tests can help determine if you will succeed in certain careers.

Various tests measure physical abilities as well. Some measure finger dexterity, or how well you can use your fingers to move small articles rapidly and accurately. Others measure manual dexterity, or the ability to move your hands easily and skillfully. These abilities are important in many kinds of work. Other physical abilities are not so easily measured.

One way to learn more about your abilities is to consider your achievements. Your **achievements** are goals you have accomplished—things you feel you did well. You may have achievements in your work, hobbies, school activities, or sports and social activities.

Begin by making a list of your achievements. Think about how you have influenced other people or what contributions you have made to organizations. Consider your part-time job and your extracurricular activities. See 31-9. Try to list these achievements using an action verb such as *developed, planned, organized, presented, improved, helped, created, presented,* or *managed.* With careful thought, decide what your actual achievements were. For instance, you may have had a job at a hardware store. Just saying you worked as a salesperson at a hardware store doesn't make your achievements clear. Instead, you might say "I arranged store merchandise in an attractive, logical order. I advised customers regarding consumer decisions to best meet their needs. I also assumed responsibility for counting and collecting the money from the cash registers each day."

After you have listed specific achievements, analyze each by writing down skills

31-9 **Involvement in clubs or sports indicates a willingness to work with others to reach common goals.**

Use Your Reasoning Skills

Research current occupational trends and predictions for occupations of the future. Do any of the occupations with high potential for growth seem attractive to you? How might you adjust your school course schedule to start preparing now for a career in this area? For what part-time, entry-level jobs might you apply?

used in each accomplishment. This will help you recognize the skills you have and use.

While considering the variety of skills you have used, indicate which skills you do very well. Also indicate which skills you find particularly enjoyable or exciting.

Becoming more aware of your abilities is an important step in career planning. Every career requires certain combinations of skills. An awareness of your skills will help you plan a career at which you are likely to be successful.

Personal Characteristics

Your personality is an important personal characteristic that can affect your success in a career. Your personality is the most important influence on whether or not people like you. It is a combination of personal traits that make up your own unique self, including your habits and mannerisms. It is also the way you react to people and situations. No matter what skills you have that are important to your career, your personality is more important. Unless your personality is compatible with your work and your coworkers, succeeding on your job may be difficult. See 31-10.

You show your values to others through your personality traits. Values guide your life. They influence your choice of friends

Madison Public Schools

31-10 A girl who has patience and a love for children may enjoy a career as a teacher.

and activities as well as your choices in the work world. In making choices, you are forced to set priorities and place some values ahead of others.

Choices and decisions are ideally made on the basis of values. However, if people are not clear about their values, how can they make the right decisions? Being able to identify and clarify your values is an important skill. The more clearly you understand them, the easier it will be to make choices leading toward your goals.

People's values in relation to their work vary greatly. Some value their jobs primarily because it pays the bills. Others value companionship. They enjoy working in part because they share many interests with others at work. Self-esteem is another value related to work. If you like your job and do it well, your self-esteem will be enhanced. This will happen not only through your own awareness of your accomplishments,

but also through the recognition and praise from others.

Most people have goals for the future. When you were young, you probably had some unrealistic goals about what you would be when you grew up. As you grow older, though, your goals tend to become more realistic. You begin to learn more about your abilities and about the world.

You have already developed some general lifestyle goals. You have an idea of how you would like to live and what you would like to be able to do. The way you see yourself is closely related to certain career goals. Consider how your career goal would be influenced if your lifestyle goals are to be famous and earn a lot of money. On the other hand, how might your lifestyle goals change if your career goal is to teach children in an underdeveloped country? As you continue to learn about career choices, think of various alternatives in relation to your own lifestyle goals.

Learning About Career Options

Many people do not make wise career choices because they are not aware of career possibilities in today's rapidly changing world. Therefore, developing an awareness of career possibilities is very important. You can do this by becoming involved in career and technical student organizations and seeking out career information on your own.

Career and Technical Student Organizations

In many high schools, vocational schools, and junior colleges, there are career and technical organizations for students with common career goals, 31-11. **Career and technical student organizations** provide an opportunity for students to learn more about career choices, participate in activities related to a particular career, and become involved in competition

Career and Technical Student Organization	
Organization	Purpose
Business Professionals of America (BPA)	For students enrolled in business and office programs
DECA—An Association of Marketing Students	For students interested in the field of marketing, management, and entrepreneurship
Future Business Leaders of America (FBLA)	For students interested in business careers
Family, Career and Community Leaders of America (FCCLA)	For students interested in family issues and careers in the field of family and consumer sciences
Health Occupations Students of America (HOSA)	For students interested in career opportunities in health care and enhancing the delivery of quality health care to all people
National FFA Organization	For students preparing to enter careers in agriculture, agribusiness, and horticulture
Technology Student Association (TSA)	For students interested in careers in the technology field
SkillsUSA—VICA	For students enrolled in trade, industrial, and technical courses

31-11 Career and technical student organizations allow you to explore careers of interest to you.

related to that area. Through participation in career and technical student organizations, leadership skills can be acquired and practiced. Students have the opportunity to learn how to participate in meetings, practice parliamentary procedure, and serve as leader of a group. See 31-12.

Employers look for employees who have had these kinds of leadership experiences. They know these experiences, which indicate skill in creativity, organization, and relationships, are a sign of quality in an employee.

Sources of Information

You can find a vast amount of career information in books, pamphlets, magazine articles, and on the Internet. Most public libraries have a special area for career information. There are also career information centers in many schools. Both libraries and schools have career resource directories such as the *Occupational Outlook Handbook* and the *Occupational Outlook Quarterly*. The *Occupational Outlook Handbook* is published every two years by the United States Department of Labor. It provides a wide range of information about occupations,

31-12 Thinking about your achievements in leadership positions at school may help you learn about your abilities.

salaries, training, and employment trends. The *Occupational Outlook Quarterly*, also published by the United States Department of Labor, contains articles on jobs and labor market conditions. It also includes articles on subjects such as how to look for a job and how to match personal and job characteristics. Both the *Occupational Outlook Handbook* and the U.S. Department of Labor have Web sites.

The Department of Labor has other helpful publications and leaflets that are available in libraries or by writing the United States Department of Labor. Trade associations, professional organizations, and labor unions are also good information sources. Most of them publish newsletters or journals, and many also publish career-related materials. Some of these materials are written specifically for young people.

Helpful information can be obtained from resource persons such as career or guidance counselors. Technical and four-year colleges usually offer career planning assistance. Specialty schools, which focus on specific careers, can help you plan your career in that specific area.

One of the best ways to learn details about a certain career is to talk to people who are working in those fields. Try to talk with several people who work within a specific career area. Then you can compare information from a variety of sources. Online mentoring with professionals is also available by contacting individual businesses that have a Web page.

Schools and businesses in some occupational areas offer career fairs. These are opportunities to collect career and educational information to help with your decision-making process. Often professionals are available in person to answer questions and provide first-hand information about specific jobs. The military also has extensive information and opportunities for young adults to investigate a multitude of career areas.

When talking with professionals, give some prior thought to the questions you want to ask. Most people are flattered by a genuine interest in what they do. Questions that are too simple or general might give you little information. Before you talk to someone, make a list of questions to ask. What is a typical workday like? What personal traits are required for your occupation? If you were launching your career today, what steps would you take? The answers to questions like these should provide you with very helpful information about a career.

Another excellent way to learn about the demands and opportunities of a career is to experience them. A summer job or part-time job is one way of gaining this experience. Some high schools and colleges offer opportunities to combine on-the-job work experience with traditional classwork. These programs are usually referred to as **cooperative education**. They give the student an opportunity to learn about the occupation, earn money, and take courses related to that occupation. Many schools and businesses offer internships and apprenticeships, which are work experiences in a particular occupation or organization. See 31-13. Internships often offer a well-organized look at a possible occupation. For instance, an internship at a local newspaper might involve writing stories, helping with research, and covering

M.T. Crave

31-13 An internship allows you to experience a career firsthand.

*Getting*Involved

meetings or news happenings at the side of an experienced reporter.

Many volunteer positions are also available to high school students or young adults. By being a volunteer, you gain work experience and learn special skills. Doing volunteer work exposes you to the variety of human experiences involved in that type of work. You might consider volunteering in a hospital or helping in community recreation. Teaching a craft or working with people who have physical disabilities are other options. Local libraries often maintain listings of volunteer opportunities. In addition, you might check Web sites for additional listings of volunteer opportunities and activities or projects.

Careers

Thousands of career opportunities are available in the world today. Fortunately, they are classified into groups. This makes decision making about careers and matching them to your interests and abilities somewhat easier.

Lists of careers are often divided into **career clusters**, such as business, health, communication, and public service. Each group of careers has something in common. The various career clusters may involve different work environments, different types of skills, and special vocabularies. Career possibilities may be categorized in many ways. See 31-14.

31-14 Which of the career clusters represented here interests you most?

This is an extremely challenging step of your career search. Careers vary widely as do the interests and abilities they require. From a more positive standpoint, remember this is an exploratory step in your career search. It gives you the chance to consider careers that might not have otherwise entered your mind. It takes a great effort to look at so many careers from various viewpoints. That effort will be worthwhile if it leads you toward a career path that is exciting and meaningful.

Management-Related Careers

Management goes on at all times both in daily living and the world of work. This textbook has explained resource management as related to the following areas of daily living:

- achievement of personal and family goals
- your relationships with others
- your physical and mental health
- child care and guidance
- meal planning and preparation
- clothing selection and care
- housing
- finances
- consumer issues
- career search

Management Skills and Your Career

Many of the same management skills used in daily living will directly transfer to your career. Successful managers in the world of work have problem-solving and decision-making skills, planning and organizational skills, time management skills, and communication skills. All workers solve problems, plan and organize their work, and work with others cooperatively to get the job done.

Managers are leaders in their particular group, organization, or business. You will find the same skills listed as you look at both management skills and leadership skills.

Problem-Solving and Decision-Making Skills

Although specific job responsibilities differ, all jobs deal with problems. A person who can analyze a situation and apply problem-solving and decision-making skills has a valuable skill. The stock clerk in a business uses problem-solving and decision-making skills to decide how, when, and where to store certain supplies. The warehouse manager in that same business uses those skills to guide the organization of the warehouse and direct the work of employees like the stock clerk. In that same company, an executive makes major management decisions.

The Management Process

Workers at all levels use the management process—planning, implementing, controlling, and evaluating.

Planning is the process of establishing goals and deciding what steps will be taken to reach the goal. An effective manager at any level is able to identify what must be done and then implement, or carry out, the plans. Once the plan is implemented, the manager is responsible for checking the plan's progress, evaluating and controlling it, and making adjustments when necessary. The manager evaluates the outcome of the management process and uses that information in future planning. By evaluating the process, the manager learns from both mistakes and successes.

The management process takes place at all levels. The cook in a restaurant plans what ingredients are needed and controls the steps involved in creating the items on the menu. The cook then evaluates each product and decides what might be done differently when preparing that item again. See 31-15.

At the other end of the career ladder is an executive of the corporation who owns the restaurant chain. Like the cook, the executive also uses the management process to make decisions. Major decisions about expansion of the business and its progress are made using the management process.

Organizational Skills

Organizing is the process of arranging in sequence the steps that must be taken to achieve a goal. This may involve grouping activities, coordinating different parts of a plan, or managing time and energy to reach the desired goal effectively. The primary purpose of organizing work is to divide it into smaller units that can be handled more effectively.

Organizational skills are used at all levels of employment. The person who is a cashier at a supermarket uses these skills to follow procedures in running the cash register and organizing supplies. The manager of the same supermarket uses organizational skills in assigning work to specific employees so the store will be fully stocked and run efficiently.

Communication Skills

Because very few people work in isolation, success at a job often depends on a person's ability to communicate. This communication often occurs over the telephone. Speaking in a pleasant, clear, courteous voice is appropriate.

Managers are often responsible for the work performed by other employees. The most successful managers communicate ideas effectively and listen attentively, interpreting what others say and responding to them. A manager's plans tend to be carried through effectively if that manager has strong communication skills. See 31-16.

A good manager is assertive. This is not the same as being aggressive. *Assertiveness* means expressing your feelings directly— asking for what you want and refusing what you do not want in a respectful manner.

Attitude-Related Skills

Workers at all levels use these skills. They involve the way you perceive situations

31-15 **Cooks must use management tools such as advance planning and evaluation.**

31-16 **Clear communication in the workplace results in smoother teamwork and greater accomplishments.**

and respond to others. These skills include a positive attitude, cheerfulness, optimism, and a sense of humor. They also include a healthy attitude toward yourself, an openness to change, and the ability to accept responsibility for your own decisions. Research indicates these traits increase productivity and quality of work.

Management Levels and Training Required

Seldom are people employed strictly as managers. Instead, they are taken into an organization because they have knowledge or skills in some field other than management or supervision. This means most managers are trained in another area.

Perhaps a young man has developed specialized skills through a job he had in high school. He may have had a hobby of photography and a part-time job in a camera shop. Through this job he learned even more about cameras, film, and film processing. He may decide to further his formal education by going to college and studying for a degree in science. This could eventually lead to a career in the film industry and perhaps a managerial position.

There is an advantage to becoming a manager through this kind of process. Managers are expected to be familiar with the work performed by the people they supervise. Studies have shown clearly that people tend to reject supervisors who are not familiar with the work being done. One clear advantage of "coming up through the ranks" is the manager and workers are working toward goals they all realize and understand. They are able to communicate with each other on well-recognized terms.

People who work at any level and in any subject matter area can have careers in management. See 31-17 for examples of management-related careers in the subject

Careers in Management			
	Positions Requiring a High School Diploma	**Positions Requiring Additional Training Beyond High School**	**Positions Requiring a College Degree or More**
Individual and Family Development, Relationships, Communication	Child care aide Nursery school worker Playground supervisor Teacher's aide	Assistant caseworker Broadcast technician Recreational director*	Caseworker Counselor* Child care director Extension home economist Labor negotiator* Member of the clergy Personnel manager Public relations specialist* Teacher Vocational counselor
Health	Exercise instructor* Home health aide Nurse's aide Receptionist or secretary for a doctor or hospital	Dental hygienist Emergency medical technician Health inspector Licensed practical nurse Physical therapy assistant	Dentist* Medical records supervisor Pharmacist Physician* Physical therapist* Pollution control engineer Registered nurse Safety director

31-17 This chart shows a sampling of management careers related to various subject matter areas.

Careers in Management

	Positions Requiring a High School Diploma	Positions Requiring Additional Training Beyond High School	Positions Requiring a College Degree or More
Food	Cake decorator* Caterer* Cook Food service worker Stock clerk Waiter/waitress	Appliance or food demonstrator* Chef Customer service representative Dietary consultant* Food columnist* Food inspector Restaurant manager	Dietitian Food chemist Food editor Food technologist Food stylist* Market researcher* Test kitchen home economist
Clothing	Alterations employee Fabric salesperson Pattern cutter Seamstress* Sewing machine operator Sewing machine salesperson	Fashion coordinator Fashion model Pattern designer Tailor* Textile inspector	Advertising design artist* Fashion buyer Fashion editor Fashion illustrator* Textile designer Textile lab technician
Housing	Cleaner Custodian Decorator's assistant Furniture refinisher* Maid Painter* Rug and upholstery cleaner* Wallpaper hanger*	Carpenter* Electrician* Home furnishings consultant Housing construction supervisor* Interior decorator* Plumber* Property manager Real estate agent* Upholsterer*	Architect* Engineer Interior designer* Land use planner
Financial Planning	Bank teller Credit investigator	Credit counselor Credit manager Financial consultant* Insurance agent* Investment advisor Loan officer	Banker Budget director Financial analyst* Insurance underwriter Stockbroker*
Business and Consumer Education	Bookkeeper* Cashier Computer operator Consumer advocate File clerk Inventory clerk Salesperson	Customer service representative Department store manager Magazine writer Office manager Purchasing agent Sales representative Sales supervisor	Computer programmer* Consumer information specialist* Home economist in business* Management consultant* Publicity director*

*These careers offer good opportunities for entrepreneurship.

31-17 **(Continued).**

matter areas discussed in this text. You can choose the area in which you want to work according to your interests. However, your career level is basically determined by education and experience. The amount of training and education you are willing to work toward can either limit or expand your career options. See 31-18.

Entry-Level Positions

Positions you are qualified for after graduating from high school are **entry-level positions**. Additional training is not needed. A custodian, salesperson, cashier, and food service worker have entry-level positions.

If you plan to begin your career by obtaining one of these positions after graduation, get as much managerial experience as possible while in school. If you are the officer of a club, have a part-time job, or take on responsibilities at home, you are gaining management experience. The more experience you have while in high school, the easier it will be to obtain an entry-level position related to management.

31-18 Obtaining a college degree or other training beyond high school may broaden a person's career opportunities.

Management Positions That Require Some Training Beyond High School

Continuing your education beyond high school allows you to begin a management-related career at a higher level. The training you receive may be related to a specific area of interest or to the development of specific skills. For instance, a dental hygienist and a chef both must have training beyond high school before they can become employed in those positions. A vocational school, technical school, community college, or courses on the Internet might provide the training they need.

Apprenticeship programs are another form of training. This training is often used to prepare new workers in the skilled trades, such as plumbing. Many skilled trades require workers to complete an apprenticeship program of one to four years. This includes on-the-job training and additional school in the evenings. Much of the learning is passed from the experienced person to the trainee. This method of training is accepted by most of the leading labor unions.

Other ways to learn job skills for management positions involve self-study through books and visual aids, correspondence courses, and conferences and seminars.

Management Positions That Require a College Degree or More

Many higher-level management positions require at least a four year college degree. Some require additional experience and/or education. A teacher, architect, and dietitian must all have college degrees. Generally, people who have higher-level management positions use specific vocational skills less than people who have lower-level positions. People in higher-level management positions rely more on the management skills of communicating, planning, organizing, negotiating, and delegating. See 31-19.

Occupational Trends— The Ever-Changing World of Work

Becoming aware of the current trends in employment and those predicted for the future will be valuable to you. Many of these trends are due to changing technology. Another influence on employment changes is an increase in the workforce over age 65.

More families are earning two paychecks. People in dual-career families eat out more and spend more money on leisure activities and travel. This will cause resort, hotel, and restaurant management jobs to increase. Because the number of older people in this nation is increasing, there will be more jobs in caring for the elderly, health care, and

31-19 **People who succeed in higher level management positions have well-developed management skills as well as the required education.**

hospital administration. Home maintenance services and security have better-than-average prospects for rewarding careers. Of course, computers remain a growing area. A vast number of jobs have only begun to open up for people who are trained to enter the computer field.

Having a career does not always mean having an 8:00 a.m. to 5:00 p.m. job. Career hours today are more flexible than ever. Flextime allows employees to adjust their work hours to meet their personal needs and energy peaks. Flextime can reduce frictions between family and job demands. Another variation is the **compressed workweek**. Under this system the employee can divide the hours of a standard workweek into three or four days instead of five. Factory workers, police officers, and firefighters are most likely to have a compressed workweek. Another variation is job sharing, where two workers share the hours of one job.

Another option within a career is to open and run your own business. This option is called **entrepreneurship**. Many entrepreneurs open their own stores. Others do freelance work for businesses, or manufacture and sell products from their homes. Entrepreneurs must be willing to take risks, and they must be able to handle the legal and financial aspects of running the business. Entrepreneurship is not for everyone but it can be rewarding for people who are able to take on the risks and responsibilities. See 31-20.

With the use of fax machines, copiers, and Internet access, some people can work more easily from their homes. Families may choose to move to desired areas anywhere in the country and be able to keep their jobs. Some workers may have a mobile van or

31-20 **This entrepreneur has opened and runs her own florist shop.**

vehicle from which they conduct their business. Entrepreneurship ventures may become more and more common as technology improves or changes your view of work.

Mobility affects careers in some families when they have to move due to job relocation. Other families may move closer to relatives in need of care, which affects the types of jobs they may find. The ability to work from home has helped some families avoid moving when they must change jobs due to job loss.

A wide new world of career choices is open to you. Take the time to investigate the careers that interest you most. Do library research and talk to people you know who have interesting careers in management. Knowing specific qualifications for certain positions will help you make your career decision.

32
31
30
29
28
27
26
25
24
23
22
21
20
19
18
17
16
15
14
13
12
11
10
9
8
7
6
5
4
3
2
1

Summary

Each decision you make that relates to career planning is an important one. You will realize this even more as you continue to learn about career planning and development.

Career and technical student organizations can help you explore career areas. A self-study is one resource that can help you develop career plans and set the right career goals for you. Consider your interests, skills, and personal characteristics. Then try to make the career choices best suited to you.

You will be able to apply the management skills you use in daily living to any career you choose. Management careers are available in any subject matter area and at any level. The level at which you work depends on your experience and education.

In today's rapidly changing society, career possibilities are almost limitless. Becoming familiar with the demands and opportunities of many of these careers will help you make your career decisions.

To Review

1. Explain the difference between a job and a career.
2. Explain how classifying your interests can be helpful to you in career planning.
3. Skills and activities you perform successfully are called _____.
4. List four sources of career information.
5. What steps in the management process transfer from daily living to work?
6. Why is it so important for managers to have communication skills?
7. What are the advantages of becoming a manager by "coming up through the ranks"?
8. True or false?
   A. Apprenticeship training is always necessary to enter the skilled trades.
   B. In apprenticeship training, knowledge is passed from an experienced person to the trainee.
9. List six factors affecting current occupational trends.
10. Describe what is meant by *compressed workweek*.

To Do with the Class

1. Review the basic needs of all people. Discuss the relationship of a person's career to these needs.
2. Invite a speaker to discuss personalities as related to career choices.
3. Discuss the meaning of the following: The career plans of most successful people have a common factor. They know what they want to achieve; they have goals.
4. As a class, develop a bulletin board that displays a variety of careers or division of careers.

To Challenge Your Thinking

1. Interview four people who have different careers. Ask them how their careers affect their lifestyles. Share your findings with the class.
2. Select a career area and list four positions within that career at various levels. Explain how a person in each position would use management skills.
3. Research to find statistics on women in the labor force. What percentage of working women are married, unmarried, and mothers?
4. Visit someone who does work you think might be interesting. Ask questions about job duties and responsibilities, working conditions, starting salary, and special skills necessary.

To Do with Your Community

1. Visit a business that interests you and observe working conditions and work activities. Report this and any other up-to-date information on that occupation to the class.
2. Volunteer to help in a career area or cluster in which you are interested. Some examples might be Habitat for Humanity, a soup kitchen, or a recreation program.
3. Invite a panel of people representing careers within a particular cluster or representing several clusters. Have them share their backgrounds and outlook for their careers.
4. Select a local organization. Interview several people within the organization. Identify the management levels and the similarities and differences for these levels.

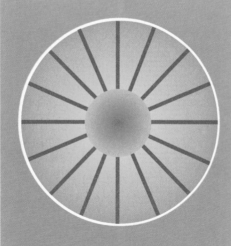

32 # Finding a Job

To Know

cover letter
resume
chronological resume
functional resume
job portfolio
digital portfolio
attitude
capability
initiative
dependability
fringe benefits

Objectives

After studying this chapter, you will be able to

◇ recognize sources of job leads and how to use them.

◇ explain job-seeking skills.

◇ write a cover letter and develop a resume.

◇ describe personal traits leading to job success.

◇ list several responsibilities of the employer to the employee.

You have now considered your interests, skills, and personal characteristics in relation to the world of work. You have looked at various careers and the skills they require. You may have even decided on one or several career goals. Now you are ready to look for a job that will help lead you to one of those goals. A variety of sources can help you find job vacancies, and specific skills will help assure you of getting a job.

Sources of Job Leads

The first available job that comes along may be just that—a job. It may be completely unrelated to your career goals. The more job opportunities from which you have to choose, the more likely you will be to find the type of work you desire. Job leads may come from many sources.

Family and Friends

Some of the best sources of job leads may be friends or family members. Although they may not be able to offer you a job, they may know of job opportunities for which you qualify. Do not be embarrassed that you are using this influence or "pull" as long as you are qualified for the position.

School Placement Office

Most high schools and colleges have placement offices. These are sometimes referred to as job placement offices or work experience offices. Placement services are especially helpful to the student for several reasons. The jobs that a placement office has available are usually ones for which their students qualify. The school knows a lot about you. They have records of your abilities, aptitudes, grades, and attendance records. The personnel may know you well enough to have information about your attitudes and your personality. The school is interested in getting a job for you because they are proud of a good employment placement record. Their service is convenient, and it is free.

Newspaper Advertisements

Daily newspapers list job openings in the classified ads. Sunday papers generally contain the most. Each paper serves a specific geographical area. Be sure to check the local papers if you are looking for a job in a certain city.

Most job openings are listed in the paper under categories, 32-1. For instance, professional technical jobs are for people with college degrees and advanced training. Sales jobs include all kinds of jobs that involve selling. The medical category covers all types of jobs in hospitals, nursing homes, and doctors' offices. Because newspapers are not consistent in the way they list ads, study all the advertisements. Sometimes jobs are even listed alphabetically by title.

Listings of job openings also appear in trade papers, journals, magazines, newsletters, and bulletins. Copies of these publications are usually found in larger public libraries. Many job openings are also listed on the Internet, either at Web sites of businesses or job placement message boards.

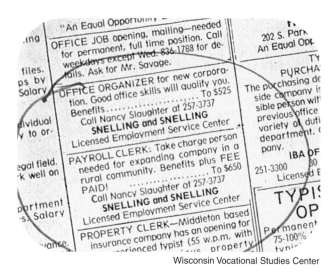

Wisconsin Vocational Studies Center

32-1 Employment opportunities are listed in daily newspapers. Sunday papers usually contain the most employment ads.

Brainstorming

Brainstorm a list of ways employees might show their work attitudes throughout the workday. How many attitudes in your list, and how many are negative? What does this show about the attitudes of employees? How might these attitudes affect job performance and coworkers?

Employment Agencies

Employment agencies usually fall into one of two groups–private or public agencies. Private agencies are privately owned businesses whose income is based on collecting a fee for placing a person on a job. Public agencies are set up under federal and state laws. They are known according to the name of the state in which their office is located. The Kansas Department of Human Resources and the Indiana Department of Workforce Development are examples of public agencies.

The operation and registration procedures are similar in both types of agencies. An employer notifies the agency of a job to be filled, and the agency searches for a person who is qualified for the position. A person might apply to the agency for assistance in finding a job. Then the agency attempts to find job opportunities appropriate for that person's qualifications.

When you first register with an employment agency, you will be asked to complete an application form. You will be interviewed by a counselor to determine your interests and qualifications. Your completed application and the comments of the counselor will be included in your file. When the agency receives a job offer for which you might qualify, you will be notified of the job location and who to contact.

An employment agency offers some advantages. Some job openings are listed only through an agency. Also, many agencies give you advice on interviewing and help you prepare your resume. Agencies can also save you time by screening out the jobs that are not right for you.

The way you deal with an employment agency can determine whether you succeed in securing a job. When you visit the agency and talk with the counselor, conduct yourself as though you were interviewing for a job. It is important for this person to be favorably impressed with your personality and job qualifications. Then the counselor will work to place you in a job. It is better not to place all your confidence in a single agency. After you apply, return to the agencies frequently to permit them to get to know you. This will indicate you are sincere in wanting to work.

Private Employment Agencies

Private or commercial agencies are listed in the Yellow Pages of the telephone directory. They are also listed in the classified ad and business opportunities sections of newspapers, especially the Sunday editions. These agencies are licensed under the laws of the state in which they operate. State laws usually control the fees charged.

When working with a private agency, be sure to ask who is responsible for paying the fee. At some private agencies, you sign an agreement to pay a certain amount or a certain percentage of your first few months' salary. At other agencies, the fee is paid by the company who hires you.

Private agencies tend to specialize in certain kinds of work, types of business, or skill areas. You are wasting your time to apply to one that does not operate in your field of interest. If you are not sure what kinds of jobs a particular agency handles, just call and ask. Also check on an agency's reputation before you register. Have family members, friends, or school counselors heard of this agency? Perhaps you know someone who has used the agency's services. Some agencies are run better than others, so it might be wise to do some checking.

Public Employment Agencies

State employment services are found in major towns and cities. In addition to being free, the state service has the advantage of providing a broad coverage in the area. See 32-2. When you register with a branch office of a state-operated employment agency, you usually qualify for consideration by all its branches.

State agencies often give you information about the kinds of jobs needing applicants. If your job goals are flexible, this information can help you make them more specific. Some state services also run training sessions in job search skills. They may be able to refer you to special training or work programs offered by the state, major unions, and employers.

Employees of state services are paid salaries, not commissions, as they are in private agencies. This is a disadvantage for the job hunter because state employees are under less pressure to fill vacancies. The private agency has another advantage over the state agency because it offers a more specialized service. Employees of private agencies deal with a small area of work and certain employers. In turn, they are more likely to get their job requests.

Mark Hayward

32-2 **State employment agencies can be a good source of job information.**

The Internet

The Internet has numerous sites to help in job and career searches. You can access employment listings based on career area, specific types of business or industry, and areas of career interest. Some sites may list regions of the country or locations where you can find jobs. Some sites feature all types of jobs. Even unusual jobs, which may require specific interests or skills of those looking for employment, can be found on the Internet. Key words related to a career, business names, industry categories, or simply the phrase *employment agencies* may be used to search for such employment opportunities.

Civil Service

Local, state, and federal government services provide jobs for thousands of people. All civil service positions require a competitive examination to qualify for appointment. To be eligible for appointment, an applicant must meet the minimum age, training, and experience requirements for a particular position. Check Internet Web sites for these positions.

Civil service examinations vary depending on the type of position. After the examination, the applicant is notified whether he or she received eligible or ineligible scores. Names of the eligible applicants are entered on a list in order of their scores. When a government agency requests the names of eligible applicants for a job vacancy, the area office sends those names at the top of the appropriate list.

All civil service positions must be prominently announced so any person interested can know it is available. Posters are placed in civil service offices, on school bulletin boards, in courthouses, and in government offices.

Mark Hayward

32-3 If you are looking for a part-time job, you may be able to apply without making an appointment.

Direct Approach

Applying directly to a business or industry is another way to find a job. Looking for a job in this way is difficult. You do not know if there are any openings, and you may not know anyone to contact in the company. However, you may find someone who is looking for workers with your skills.

The way you contact a potential employer directly will differ depending on the type of job you are seeking. If you are looking for a part-time or summer job, it is acceptable to walk in without an appointment. See 32-3. Just ask to see the owner or manager and make your request. For a full-time or more responsible position, it is better to arrange for an interview in advance. You could do this by phone or by letter.

Job-Seeking Skills

Once you have located job possibilities, you are ready to put your job-seeking skills to work. Basic skills are easily learned and can make the difference between getting a job and not getting a job.

Contacting the Potential Employer

Your first communication with a potential employer is often through a letter and resume or a telephone call requesting an interview.

Cover Letter

The letter of application or **cover letter** is your letter to the employer that states your interest in an interview. Since the cover letter is your first contact with the potential employer, it is extremely important. It gives you an opportunity to set yourself apart from all other applicants. Give careful consideration to the purpose and content of the letter before you write it. You might consider your overall goal to be an interview. Another goal is to get the prospective employer to read your resume. It is extremely important that the cover letter emphasizes how you can use your skills to meet the employer's needs. Do not use the letter to discuss your own needs, such as how much you need the job.

The letter should be brief, containing no more than three or four paragraphs. It should be clear, honest, and friendly. See 32-4. The opening paragraph might refer to the particular position in which you are interested and tell how you learned this position is available.

Write another paragraph emphasizing any of your qualifications that might appeal to the reader. Include an attention-getting statement indicating why your training, education, and experience would benefit the prospective employer. The more you know about the employer's organization, the better you can emphasize the part of your background that relates to the position. You might cite an accomplishment that relates to the position you are seeking. This will convey the message that you will be a productive employee.

In the final paragraph, call attention to your attached resume if you have not already done so. Request an interview at the employer's convenience. Indicate that you will call within a few days to learn if an interview can be arranged. It is wise to take control of the follow-up move yourself. In this case, you will be calling back

452 Maple Ave.
Blacksburg, MD 13628
May 31, 20XX

Mr. Darrell Richman, Personnel Manager
First National Bank of Blacksburg
1620 W. Harrington Blvd.
Blacksburg, MD 13628

Dear Mr. Richman:

Mr. Harvey Edmundson, director of the work-study program at Blacksburg High School, has informed me that you plan to hire a customer service trainee. I will be graduating from high school on June 7 and would like to apply for this position.

As the enclosed resume states, I have participated in the work-study program at Blacksburg High School for the past two years, and it has been a great experience. During this time, I have been able to combine my schoolwork with a part-time job as a salesperson at Zimmerman Department Store. I have taken several business classes, such as accounting. These classes have helped me with the record keeping and handling of money I do on my job. I enjoy daily contact with people and the chance to help them meet their needs. I believe I have the skills and qualities a successful customer service trainee needs.

I would like to meet with you to discuss my qualifications and interest in this position in greater detail. I will telephone you on June 5 to set up a time for an interview. If you would like further information before that time, you may contact me at (243) 555-1689. I look forward to speaking with you.

Sincerely,

Raquel A. Lewis

Raquel A. Lewis

Enclosure

32-4 A potential employer's first impression of you may be based on your cover letter. Therefore, it is important to write your cover letter carefully.

about the appointment. This is much better than sitting by the phone waiting for the employer to call.

Your cover letter is a sales letter meant to sell yourself. As with any sales, a good first impression is important. Businesses may receive dozens of application letters for each job. To get the attention you want, your letter must stand out. Interviews are often given to applicants whose letters are neat, well-written, and show they are qualified for the position.

Resume

A **resume** is a concise summary of your qualifications documented by past accomplishments, 32-5. Beneath your name, address, and telephone number, list your education, work experience, and other qualifications for employment. The purpose of the resume is to organize all relevant facts about yourself and your work capabilities in a single written presentation. Make every effort to keep your resume as concise

Raquel A. Lewis
452 Maple Ave.
Blacksburg, MD 13628
(243) 555-1689

Job Objective	An entry-level position as a customer service trainee.
Education 2002-2006	Blacksburg High School, Blacksburg, MD Will graduate June 7, 2006. Grade point average: 3.5. Took several elective courses in business.
Work Experience 2004-2006	Salesperson for Zimmerman Department Store, Blacksburg, MD. As a participant in the work-study program, I was a salesperson. I helped customers locate products to meet their needs and helped them make consumer decisions. I ran the cash register and helped do inventory.
Summers of 2002 and 2003	Babysitter for Mrs. Winona Clayton, Blacksburg, MD. I was responsible for caring for Mrs. Clayton's two young children during the summers while she and her husband were at work.
Honors and Activities	Member of Family, Career and Community Leaders of America (FCCLA) for four years and treasurer of the group during junior year. Member of the volleyball team for four years. Member of the high school band for four years.
Hobbies and Interests	Volleyball, swimming, playing the flute, reading, cooking, photography

References available upon request.

32-5 A resume shows the most important facts about you in a way that is easy to read.

as possible. Because the average employer spends only about five seconds scanning a resume, your best selling points need to stand out clearly.

Planning your resume takes time for gathering the information, organizing it, and preparing it in its final form. See 32-6.

Help with developing resumes may be found on the Internet. Numerous help sites are available. Some are set up in a format to have you simply insert the information to produce a basic resume in a short period of time. Some sites will charge a fee for additional professional services. These may be valuable alternatives when more than a basic resume is needed for a particular employment search.

To begin a resume, start by assembling material under the following headings: *career goals*, *education*, *work history*, *skills*, and *references*.

Under *career goals*, describe the type of work you hope to be doing in the future and list the jobs that would help you reach those goals.

Under *education*, list the schools you attended and degrees you received. Also list any special courses you have taken outside of formal schooling and any academic honors or awards you have received.

Work history includes any full-time, part-time, or volunteer jobs you have held. If you are still in school or are a recent graduate, you may have little to list under the work history category. Don't forget to include valuable experience you may have gained through clubs or other organizations at school, or in the community. Through these experiences, you may have gained leadership skills and other important skills in dealing with people.

Describe *skills* you consider your strongest work assets. Try to give examples of how you have successfully used these skills in the past.

You may include a list of *references* on your resume, or you may write "References available upon request." Friends, teachers, school counselors, and previous employers are possible references. Avoid using relatives as references. Be sure to ask the permission of these people ahead of time. You'll need to know the name, address, occupation, and telephone number of each reference. List only references who really know you and can provide meaningful information about you and your abilities. Choose references who represent a cross section of people. In other words, a good list of references might include a former teacher, a member of the clergy, a coworker, and a former employer. References that represent a more limited viewpoint are not as suitable. Three friends from work or three of your teachers would be less appropriate references. They could only refer to your work or school performance.

Arrange the information in your resume in a way that will "sell" you to a prospective employer. The strongest resume is developed with a particular job in mind and emphasizes skills and experiences related to that job. You may wish to emphasize different skills and experience depending on the type of job. It may be

32-6 **Writing your resume on a computer can save you time.**

helpful to develop a master resume. You can then modify it for each job opening.

In general, there are two types of resumes–chronological and functional. **Chronological resumes** list the jobs you have held beginning with the most recent job. They list the dates of employment, the employer and type of firm, and the duties performed. **Functional resumes** describe the functions or job skills you have demonstrated successfully and give specific illustrations of your experiences. Try doing your resume both ways to see which one works better for you.

The chronological resume is often easier to prepare, quicker to read, and more familiar to employers than the functional resume. However, it does tend to point out any employment gaps. The functional resume emphasizes marketable skills without the emphasis of time related to work history. Many people choose to develop a resume that is a combination of the two, bringing out the advantages of both.

No matter which format you use, the resume should be well organized and neatly typed. A poorly prepared resume is a bad reflection on you. If you need additional copies, have them reproduced in a way that will maintain a look of quality. Never use photocopies that make it obvious someone else has received the original.

Application

Many employers don't schedule job interviews until they have received application forms. These forms are used to select the people they want to see. Applications are quite standardized except for minor variations. They usually require the following information: name, address, social security number, educational background, previous employment record, hobbies and interests, the type of employment desired, and references.

Because the application blank is the first impression your potential employer has of you, it should be prepared carefully, accurately, and neatly. Some employers believe applicants will work in the same way they complete their job applications. For instance, an applicant who hurriedly completes the form without following instructions might work that way, too. An applicant's messy handwriting might be an indication of sloppy work habits.

You may be able to take the application blank home to fill it out. Of course, the longer you take to return the application form, the more likely the job will already be filled. If you do have the chance to fill out the form at the employer's office, be prepared to do so. You may be able to get an immediate interview if the application is good and the employer is available.

Some companies and service industries prefer online application processes using the Internet. This saves time for both the employer and potential employee. Web sites can be accessed at any time for greater convenience.

When applying in person, be sure to prepare a listing of the types of information you will need for the application in advance, 32-7. Carry a good pen, perhaps a black fine felt-tip pen that stands out on the

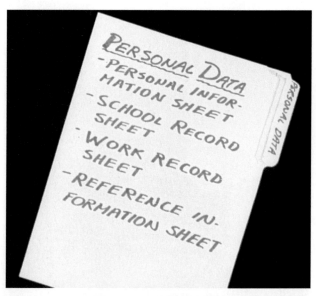

Wisconsin Vocational Studies Center

32-7 Listing this information in advance will help you fill out a job application.

written page. Unless your handwriting is very clear, print the entire application. Read the application form carefully all the way through before you fill it out. Then you'll know just what information you need without having to guess or erase.

Certain parts of the application will require some extra thought. Your application will be more impressive if you have given some thought to these items ahead of time. Write in the specific position for which you are applying. Instead of filling in an expected salary, it is better to say "open or negotiable." This keeps you from being eliminated and gives you a chance to discuss salary with the employer. List all education from grade school to the present. Your employment listing will be one of the most important parts of the application to many employers. Listing interests, hobbies, and skills is particularly important to young people who have had little or no work experience. Hobbies and skills can show responsibility or initiative depending upon their complexity. Most job applications also ask that you provide from three to five references. You can use the same references you use on your resume.

The Job Interview

The interview is probably the most important event in the entire job-seeking process. This 15 to 30 minutes is so important because it could have an important influence on your future. However, many people do nothing to prepare for a job interview.

There are many ways to prepare for an interview. One is to learn as much as you can about the firm or company that is interviewing you. Learn about its products and/or services and how long it has been in business. What are its prospects for the future, and what qualities does that employer look for in employees? If you are having several interviews, you may find it helpful to record information about each

firm on a separate sheet. This will help avoid confusion or forgetfulness.

Learning as much as possible about the job for which you are applying will also be helpful. Find out what the position involves and think about how to convince the employer that you are qualified for the job. If you cannot get information on the job, the library will have information on similar jobs that will help you.

Prepare questions to ask the interviewer. You will probably have a chance to ask these questions at the end of the interview. By having several questions planned, you will be showing your interest in the job and the company. Think of questions about the company. Don't just ask about the salary. This may make the interviewer think you are more concerned with money than the job. This would be a good time to ask about opportunities for advancement in the company.

Make plans for your grooming and dress ahead of time. Dress for the occasion so that you make the impression you really want to make. First impressions are still very important to many employers. Poor personal appearance and careless dress may influence an interviewer to reject an applicant. It is worthwhile to spend some time thinking about what your appearance may tell a potential employer about you.

Always be on time for an interview. If the interview is in an unfamiliar area, you might want to find it ahead of time. You might plan to go to the interview early in case you have a problem finding the place. When you arrive, you will probably speak with a receptionist or the employer's secretary first. Be pleasant and cooperative with all the people you meet as the employer may ask their opinions of you.

During the interview, conduct yourself in a confident, positive manner. See 32-8. If you are nervous about the interview, you may feel more comfortable by admitting it to the employer rather than trying to hide it.

Although the questions you will be asked will vary from employer to employer, most interviewers ask certain standard questions. Considering how you will answer these questions before the interview will be helpful. Be polite, accurate, honest, and frank in your answers. Make your answers brief and to the point. Try to relate all your answers to the job for which you are applying.

To prepare your answers, you may want to consider the employer's reasons for asking each question. For instance, the interviewer may ask how much money you expect to be earning in 10 years. That question is really being asked to determine your ambition, your ability to plan ahead, and the soundness of your thinking. The interviewer may ask you to tell him or her about yourself. To get prepared, put yourself in the interviewer's place. If you were an interviewer, what would you want to know about the applicant? The interviewer will be most interested in skills that relate directly to the job.

Ask questions during the interview if you do not understand something the interviewer is saying. In addition, ask the questions you prepared before the interview if they have not already been answered. See 32-9.

Before the interview is over, let the interviewer know if you are still interested in the job. You might say you have something valuable to contribute. This may give the interviewer the feeling you will work

Schrader

32-8 **You are likely to make a good impression on the interviewer if you are confident and positive.**

32-9 **Asking questions during an interview shows your interest in the job and the company. It also demonstrates your ability to communicate with coworkers in a direct, straightforward manner.**

hard and stay on the job. On the other hand, also let the interviewer know if you are not interested in the job. It is better to be truthful than to mislead a person.

Be sure the interviewer has the telephone number where you can be reached during business hours. If you are currently employed, you may wish to set a time when you can call the interviewer back. After an interview, jot down details concerning that interview as soon as possible. This will help you accurately recall what happened at that interview. You may need this information for future communications with the potential employer or for considering various job possibilities. Send a follow-up letter to the interviewer indicating your interest in the position and expressing your thanks for the interview. This may reinforce a positive impression you have made on the interviewer's mind.

Don't be discouraged if you are not hired on your first interview. It will be a useful experience anyway. After the first interview, you will have more confidence for the interviews to come. If the interviewer phones you to say someone else was hired, feel free to ask why you were not hired. The answer to that question will certainly help you plan for your next interview.

Employment Tests

Many job applicants are required to take some type of test. For any government position, a civil service test is required. Many companies also give standard achievement tests to their employees. These tests measure academic achievement in language and mathematics. Some questions also involve logic and spatial perception. In addition to written tests, performance tests are sometimes required. For instance, if you are applying for a job as a secretary, you will probably be given a keyboarding test. If you are applying for a job as a welder, you may be asked to do some welding.

Sometimes job applicants are asked to take tests that do not relate specifically to their abilities. For instance, physical examinations may be given to test an applicant's physical condition. Lie detector tests, written honesty tests, and drug tests may be given to indicate an applicant's honesty and value system. Some employment tests are completed online at the employer's Web site.

Taking tests is a stressful experience for many people. Preparing for tests in advance makes them less stressful. Sample tests are available from a variety of sources. You can purchase civil service test samples at bookstores. Libraries also have samples of civil service tests and many other types of tests. Most civil service and industrial tests cover similar subject matter. They only vary by the sentence structure and approach.

Job Portfolio

Applicants in some fields are expected to have a **job portfolio**. This is an attractive presentation of work samples in some type of a folder or other container. Applicants in an area such as commercial art would be expected to have a job portfolio. See 32-10.

Apple Computer

32-10 A job portfolio would be helpful to a person who works in an area such as advertising.

Applicants in many other areas have begun using portfolios to display their work, special awards and accomplishments, recognition publications, and other materials. The portfolio might be a loose-leaf binder, folder, file box, or any other device that holds the material to be displayed.

Organize the portfolio in a logical manner. Keep the most important or most impressive material at the beginning. Review your portfolio frequently so it is kept up-to-date. It should always be neat and clean.

In today's technology-based world, some companies may use digital portfolios to determine your hiring potential. A **digital portfolio** contains digital or scanned photos, graphics, and other pertinent information. This information can be organized into a portfolio and then be electronically submitted to employers as part of the interview process. This justifies the need for workers to have technology and computer skills. Presenting yourself through an impressive, well-organized digital portfolio can give you an edge in the workplace.

Traits Leading to Job Success

Although you have completed the job-seeking process, a big challenge is still ahead of you–being successful at the job. When you accept a job offer, you become involved in a unique relationship. You become an employee, and the person who pays your salary becomes your employer. With each of these roles, certain responsibilities are assumed. Most employers expect certain traits of their employees. These traits are not unique to a particular job or company. Understanding these traits and their importance is a step toward job success.

A high percentage of employees who lose their jobs do so during their first month of employment. Most of these people lose their jobs because of certain personal traits. This often happens because either the employer or the employee has gained a false impression during the interview. This suggests how important honesty is throughout the job-hunting process. It can prevent false impressions during the interview.

Attitude

The most important factor in job success is **attitude**. You show your attitude by the way you behave in the presence of other people. It is basically your outlook on life. See 32-11.

Your attitude is partially the result of your inheritance and upbringing. However, the fact that attitude can be changed is more important. With understanding, willpower, and desire for change, you can alter and improve your attitude. A desirable attitude will help you succeed on the job. On the other hand, employers say poor attitude is the most common reason for firing employees.

Apple Computer

32-11 Your attitude can even be recognized while talking on the phone.

Positive Attitude

If you are the kind of person who looks at the bright side of life, you have a positive attitude. People with positive attitudes look at life as exciting and worthwhile. They smile easily and enjoy other people. They rarely complain or criticize others. They respect the ideas and opinions of others and have the ability to see another person's point of view. Positive people usually enjoy a variety of activities, interests, and friends.

On the other hand, you probably know people who feel that life is unfair to them. They complain a lot, are extremely critical of others, and have very few hobbies or interests. This type of attitude can be changed, but the change takes a lot of effort and practice. The younger a person is when trying to make a personality change, the easier it will be. The change is possible if a person wants to change and become a like-able person who likes others. If you want to change, you can work toward becoming the kind of person you would like to be. People who are interested in their work and enjoy it have more interesting and enjoyable lives. As a result, they become more inter-esting people.

Attitude of Cooperation

Almost everyone works with other people, and being able to get along well with others makes a job more pleasant. See 32-12. This does not mean you must

M.T. Crave

32-12 In successful businesses, workers cooperate with each other.

be friends with everyone at work, but you should be friendly toward everyone.

Much of this cooperative attitude, or getting along with others, is based simply on respect for other people. This means recognizing that everyone is different. Each person will see a situation in a unique way because of his or her own experiences. Each person has a right to his or her own feel-ings. To get along well with coworkers, you must accept all of them as worthy people even though they may be different in many ways from you.

Some coworkers may be difficult to get along with, but remember that everyone has some good qualities. By accepting people and concentrating on their positive qualities, you will be doing your part to develop good working relationships. Many people who are uncooperative are not really very happy about themselves. You might try some subtle methods to help them change negative attitudes. Asking for their advice or showing sincere interest in their accomplishments might help them feel better about themselves. Do not use exaggerated flattery or compliments. This may seem obviously phony and create even more negative feelings.

Employees who enjoy working with one another are likely to get more work done, 32-13. When some employees do not cooperate, everyone involved is affected. The amount and quality of work will be down. The mood of the workplace may be depressing. Avoid gossip and forming cliques in the workplace. This results in lining up some employees against others. Keep your own emotions under control. If you have a temper, practice the old gimmick of counting to 10 before responding. This works quite well by providing a period of time for you to cool off and prepare a more acceptable response.

Getting along well with others is a skill that takes work and can be learned. People who get along well with others are usually happier. Other people like them, and they often experience job success.

Attitude That Accepts Criticism

Everyone must be able to accept criticism, especially from employers. Employers use criticism to let employees know how they expect a job to be done. Accepting

32-13 **A team whose members communicate effectively and work together cooperatively are more productive than those who do not.**

criticism means more than just listening politely. It means using that criticism to better yourself. When you are criticized, think carefully about how you can use that criticism to become a better employee. From that criticism, create a goal for improvement.

Attitude That Accepts Change

The term *progress* is closely associated with the world of work. Progress means change. Unfortunately, many people automatically oppose change. Many of these people are actually afraid of change. They may be afraid to take responsibility for evaluating this change or too lazy to decide how they feel about the change.

Many factors that affect your job and working conditions can change. Your employer has the right to change or alter your responsibilities. In fact, evaluating and recommending change is an important responsibility of those in charge of a business.

As a member of a productive society, your responsibility is to evaluate all types of change. Change may be for the better or for the worse. After carefully examining change, help promote changes you feel will be good and oppose changes you feel will be damaging.

People who constantly oppose change just because it is different are soon recognized by their employer and coworkers. People who oppose change are seldom asked their opinions, and they rarely advance in their job situation.

Attitude of Teamwork

In the world of work, whether you are caring for patients in a hospital or working in business on a marketing project, teamwork plays a large role. People who can work successfully as part of a team are valued. Working and being able to communicate well with all types of people, including those with difficult personalities, are assets on the job. Refusing to cooperate or having a poor attitude may result in the loss of a job. If you work as a team player, it could mean a pay raise or a job promotion. Companies and businesses look for people with an attitude of teamwork throughout the job application and interview process.

Capability

One of your major responsibilities as an employee is to do your job to the best of your ability, 32-14. The employer hired you because he or she feels you are capable of doing your job. Your **capability**, your potential for doing the job, is important to the employer. In most cases, the way you do your job affects the work of others in the

business. Ultimately, it affects the success of the business as a whole.

When you first begin a job, follow directions and do your work exactly as you are told. See 32-15. You may not understand the reason for doing each task in a certain way, but your employer does have a reason for giving you those directions. After you have shown your ability, you may be able to suggest other ways of doing certain tasks. This will indicate your capability and also your initiative.

Remember that it can take from three to four months to become comfortable with and skilled at most new jobs, even within the same career cluster. In training with new job mentors or supervisors, patience and a willingness to learn will help you to become comfortable in a new job situation.

Initiative

Employees demonstrate **initiative** when they complete a given task, find something else that needs to be done, and

32-14 **Employers depend on employees to do their work thoroughly and well.**

32-15 **When learning a new job, follow the instructions your supervisor gives you. At the same time, asking questions can help you learn about the job and improve your performance.**

do it. Employees who are successful at their jobs are promoted to jobs with greater responsibility. These are usually the employees who have taken extra steps. They have found other work that needed to be done or learned more than what they were required to learn.

Honesty and Dependability

There are various aspects of honesty on the job. Honesty could mean not stealing company property, such as office supplies or shop supplies. Honesty also means not using company supplies for personal benefit, such as using office postage for personal letters. Honesty refers to both what you say and what you write regarding the business.

Your employer has the right to expect that anything in an oral or written report about your work is correct. Another aspect of honesty is related to the "stealing of time." This can happen through expanding breaks, leaving early, or arriving late. Your employer has the right to expect you to be working every day you are to be there and to be on time. This is related to your **dependability**. See 32-16. If you cannot be at work, you have the responsibility to inform your employer that you will not be there. Many workers lose their jobs because they do not call their employers when they must be absent due to illness or other circumstances.

Employer Responsibilities

In the unique relationship between employee and employer, your employer also has certain responsibilities. Sometimes these obligations are quite complex and carefully written out in contracts. However, they are usually implied by the employer-employee relationship.

32-16 Being on time and performing the job accurately are behaviors demonstrated by a dependable employee.

Prompt Payment of Salary

Your employer is responsible for seeing that you receive your salary when it is due. The employer is obligated to meet payroll responsibilities over any other financial obligation. If you are not paid your salary when it is due, you can appeal to the Department of Labor in your state for assistance. The Department of Labor then has the responsibility to help solve this problem between employee and employer.

Safe Working Conditions

Employers are obligated to provide employees with a safe place to work. The workplace must be safe in terms of health and accident prevention. Federal and state laws, as well as some local laws, carefully spell out what conditions are necessary to meet safety regulations. These laws require the employer to develop an aggressive safety program that is constantly checked, reviewed, and revised. State inspectors make periodic safety inspections. Employers who have unsafe conditions are subject to harsh fines and possible arrest. Federal law prohibits those under 18 years of age from working in certain dangerous occupations. Coal mining and some jobs requiring the use of power machinery are examples.

Training Procedures

Before you begin your job, your employer is obligated to make you aware of accepted procedures and performance. The employer should also provide you with any on-the-job training that is needed, 32-17. The employer should inform all new employees of related information, such as services available, limitations on time, and daily procedures.

Evaluation

The fact that you are receiving a regular salary indicates a type of evaluation. Many employers use annual performance reviews that point out what the employees are doing well and how they could improve in other areas. Some employers hold periodic meetings to discuss the employee's contribution in private. This evaluation helps the employee see the need for improvement, which may not have otherwise been realized.

Information Related to Fringe Benefits

The employee should also be notified of the fringe benefits available. **Fringe benefits** are extra features granted to an employee above and beyond regular salary. Group health insurance and group life insurance are typical fringe benefits. Many employees ask about fringe benefits during the job-seeking process. They may choose one job opportunity over another because better benefits are offered. The number and types of benefits offered greatly vary among businesses.

Legal Responsibilities

An employer is legally required to withhold income tax from each employee's pay in each pay period. The number of allowances claimed by the employee is one of the factors used in determining the amount of tax to be withheld. Employees indicate the number of allowances claimed on a Form W-4 known as the Employee's Withholding Allowance Certificate. You will probably fill out this form during your first day at work.

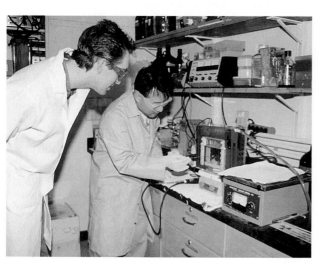

D. Riehle

32-17 **Employers provide their new employees with the training they need to do a good job.**

32
31
30
29
28
27
26
25
24
23
22
21
20
19
18
17
16
15
14
13
12
11
10
9
8
7
6
5
4
3
2
1

Summary

You can learn about job vacancies from a variety of sources. Once you have learned of job possibilities, you can learn some specific job-seeking skills that can make the difference between getting the job and not getting the job. Skills in contacting and communicating with potential employers and skills in interviewing for a job are valuable resources.

Certain personal traits tend to lead to job success. Your attitude, ability, initiative, honesty, and dependability are resources that can help you be successful on the job.

Being aware of employer responsibilities can also help you succeed. Employers have certain responsibilities to the employee that may be written out in a formal contract or implied by the employee-employer relationship.

To Review

1. Name six sources of job leads and explain how you can use each source to find a job.
2. True or false?
   A. The cover letter is very important since it is usually your first contact with a potential employer.
   B. In a cover letter, it is a good idea to stress your own needs, such as how much you need the job.
3. A resume presents your _____ to a prospective employer. The two forms of resumes are _____ and _____.
4. When filling out a job application, why is putting "open or negotiable" in the salary blank a good response?
5. Describe three steps you can take to prepare for a job interview ahead of time.
6. Describe three types of qualifying tests that may be given at job interviews.
7. What is the main purpose of a job portfolio?
8. Many people lose their jobs during the first month of employment because of _____.
9. Match the traits that are important in successful employment to the actions listed below.
   _____ Initiative.
   _____ Willingness to accept change.
   _____ Honesty and dependability.
   _____ Willingness to accept criticism.
   _____ Attitude of cooperation.
   _____ Positive attitude.
   A. Scott always starts the workday in a pleasant mood.
   B. After finishing the typing Linda was asked to do, she started straightening the office.
   C. Although his manager is rather unfriendly, Darrell accepts this and tries to be friendly to others.
   D. Lucylle always reports to work on time.
   E. After Joyce's employer showed her what she was doing wrong, she worked hard to improve that skill.
   F. Because Cleo had worked at the store for 30 years the new system of doing inventory was difficult for him, but he worked hard to learn it.
10. What are six employer responsibilities?

To Do with the Class

1. Imagine you are an employer. What qualities would you look for in a person you want to hire? Discuss this with the class.
2. Review and discuss copies of several employment tests.
3. Discuss the meaning of the following: To improve the quality of work, employees must have their work evaluated by the employer or supervisor.
4. Discuss the responsibilities of the employer and the employee.

To Challenge Your Thinking

1. Find examples of actual employee portfolios. Which ones exhibit qualities of better portfolios? How might others be improved?
2. Find examples of resumes written by people with little work experience. List both positive and negative characteristics of each resume. Share your findings with others in the class.
3. Search newspapers and magazines for stories about people who have met or have failed to meet their job responsibilities. Write a paper summarizing why these people succeeded or failed.
4. Keep a log or journal of skills you have learned that can be transferred to a job or career. Refer to them when developing your job portfolio or when interviewing for a job.

To Do with Your Community

1. Interview 10 people who are successful at their jobs. What did they learn about the position before they began work? What procedures did they go through to get their jobs? Draw conclusions from your findings and discuss them in class.
2. Talk with employers and employees at four businesses to learn how fringe benefits vary. Discuss your findings with the class.
3. Invite people from unions and professional organizations to discuss the advantages of belonging to their groups and explain the differences between groups.
4. Invite a representative from a job placement service to share information on trends in the workplace and information on job availability, employment skills, and job-seeking strategies.

Glossary

A

abilities. Skills and activities a person can perform successfully. (31)

absorption. The process in which nutrients are taken into the bloodstream throughout the walls of the intestine. (17)

abstract of title. The report of the property title search. (29)

accent lighting. Decorative lighting used to create focal points in a room. (30)

accepting. Accepting is the third aspect of openness. This means respecting the other person's right to his or her own opinions and feelings, even if you don't agree. (11)

accidents. Unplanned events that cause injury or death. (19)

achievements. Goals that have been accomplished. (31)

Acquired Immune Deficiency Syndrome (AIDS). Fatal disease caused by HIV, which breaks down the immune system and leaves the body vulnerable to diseases a healthy body could resist. (16)

actual cash value. Type of homeowner's insurance policy in which the company is responsible for the replacement cost less depreciation. (22)

additives. Chemical substances added to food for a specific purpose. (19)

adjustable life insurance. Type of insurance in which the insured can alter coverage as his or her needs change. (22)

aesthetic values. Values related to the five senses: feeling, smelling, tasting, seeing, and hearing. The senses combine with thoughts to develop an appreciation of beauty. (2)

alcoholism. A progressive disease that involves loss of control over drinking alcoholic beverages. (16)

alternatives. The various options available from which to choose. (1)

annuity. An investment product sold by life insurance companies that provides payments for a fixed number of years or over a lifetime. (22)

anorexia nervosa. Eating disorder in which victims avoid food to the point of starvation. (16)

antioxidants. Substances that protect the body's cells from damage that can be caused by pollution, exposure to chemicals, tobacco smoke, alcohol, and the by-products of normal metabolism. (16)

apprenticeship programs. Training often used to prepare new workers in the skilled trades. This includes on-the-job training and additional school in the evenings. Much of the learning is passed from the experienced person to the trainee. (31)

aptitude. An ability that seems to come naturally. (31)

attitude. A person's outlook on life. (32)

automated teller machine (ATM). A type of electronic fund transfer where you can do banking without the assistance of a teller to obtain cash or make deposits, pay bills, or transfer funds from one account to another electronically. (20)

avocational interests. Interests a person has outside his or her occupation. (8)

B

bait and switch. Deceptive practice in which an item is offered at a low price as bait to get consumers in the store. Once consumers are there, advertisers attempt to switch consumers to another, more expensive item. (23)

bank statement. A record of the checks, deposits, and charges on a bank account for a specific length of time, usually monthly. It also may include canceled checks. (20)

bartering. A way of getting what you want by exchanging goods or services instead of spending money. (15)

basic checking account. A checking account in which you are charged a fee for every check you write and/or a monthly service charge. You are not required to keep a minimum balance. (20)

behavioral level. This level of communication involves doing. (10)

beneficiary. The person receiving the death benefit from a life insurance policy. (22)

Better Business Bureau (BBB). Nonprofit organization sponsored by private businesses that attempt to settle consumer complaints against local businesses. (23)

binder. A tentative agreement between the buyer and the seller that indicates they are both willing to reach a final settlement. (29)

biodegradable waste. Waste materials that can be changed into useful substances by natural processes. (19)

biotechnology. Applying technological advances to biological science. (4)

blank endorsement. An endorsement that requires a signature. A check with this type of endorsement can be cashed by anyone who holds it. (20)

body language. Consists of body movements, facial expressions, and posture. (10)

bond. A promise to pay an investor a certain amount of money plus interest at a specific time in the future (date of maturity). (22)

budget. A spending plan. (20)

buffet service. Type of food service in which people serve themselves quickly from the serving dishes and carry their plates to the table. (26)

bulimia. Eating disorder in which victims go on food binges, then get rid of the food by vomiting or purging. (16)

C

calories. Units that indicate the amount of energy burned. (17)

capability. A person's potential for doing a job. (32)

capacity. Your ability to repay debt from your regular income. (21)

capital. Your financial resources. (21)

capitalism. The form of government that allows private ownership of land and producer goods. This system offers people the freedom to use productive resources and purchase consumer goods on their own initiative. (24)

carbohydrates. Nutrients that provide energy and heat to maintain the body's temperature. (17)

carcinogenic. Cancer-producing. (19)

cardiovascular disease. Disease of the heart and blood vessels. (16)

career. The succession of jobs a person has throughout life that results in professional growth and personal satisfaction. (31)

career and technical student organizations. Groups that provide an opportunity for students to learn more about career choices, participate in activities related to a particular career, and become involved in competition related to that area. (31)

career clusters. Lists of careers in which each group of careers has something in common. (31)

care labels. Labels that provide instructions for the care of a garment. (28)

caring family. A family in which each person sees the relationship between his or her behavior and the success of the family as a unit. (11)

casement windows. Windows that are hinged and open like a door in the center or at the sides. (30)

cash credit. Used to borrow money. It is often used to purchase goods and services from sellers who do not give credit. Types of cash credit include installment loans, single-payment loans, and credit card or check credit loans. (21)

cash value. The sum of the savings portion of a premium payment in a permanent life insurance policy. Part of it may be borrowed, used to pay the premium, or converted into a retirement income, or it can be taken in a lump sum. (22)

character. Traits and qualities that make each individual unique. These include trustworthiness, respect, responsibility, fairness, caring, and citizenship. (5)

child abuse. The physical or mental injury, sexual abuse, negligent treatment, or maltreatment of a child under the age of 18. (11)

Child and Dependent Care Tax Credit. A significant type of federal support for child care. Families who pay taxes can offset a portion of their tax bill with the expenses they have incurred from paying others to look after their children. (15)

child neglect. Failure to meet a child's physical or emotional needs. (11)

children in self-care. School-age children who are regularly left alone during some period of the day. (15)

chlamydia. The most widespread STD which attacks the urinary and reproductive systems and can lead to sterility if left untreated. (16)

chlorine bleaches. Bleaches used to clean, whiten or brighten fabrics, and remove soils and stains. They also disinfect and deodorize. (28)

cholesterol. Fatlike substance found in every cell in the body; it is consumed in foods from animal sources and is also manufactured in the body. (17)

chromosome. Threadlike structures that contain a person's genes. (5)

chronological resume. Resume organized according to jobs a person has held beginning with the most recent job. (32)

classics. Styles worn year after year by a large segment of the public. (27)

cleanup center. Kitchen work center that includes the sink area, dishwasher, garbage disposal, storage space for equipment, wastebasket, and dishcloths and towels. (26)

clothing inventory. A list of your clothing and accessories. (27)

coagulate. To thicken; often caused by heat. (26)

coinsurance feature. Policy in which the insured pays a percentage of major medical expenses in addition to the deductible amount and the company pays the rest of the costs. (22)

color scheme. The combinations of colors used. (30)

commitment. Similar to a pledge or a promise. (12)

common stock. Stock that entitles the stockholder to share in any profits of the firm. (22)

communication. Involves sharing ideas and feelings with other people both verbally and nonverbally. (10)

communism. A system of government in which the government owns the land and almost all industries and plans all production. (24)

community resources. Resources shared by all people. (3)

companionship. When people share similar interests and enjoy doing activities together. (12)

comparative advertising. Advertising in which the company compares its brand with another competing brand. (23)

comparison shopping. Looking at different brands or models of the same or similar products in several stores to compare prices, features, and store services. (25)

compensation. Counteracting a weakness by emphasizing a desirable characteristic. (16)

competition. Situation in which similar goods and services are offered by more than one seller. (23)

complementary protein foods. Incomplete protein foods that when combined supplement one another in the contribution of amino acids to the diet. (17)

complete protein. Protein food that contains an adequate amount of all the essential amino acids. (17)

complete self-concept. A view of yourself based on much knowledge of yourself and many experiences. (5)

compressed workweek. A system in which the employee can divide the hours of a standard workweek into three or four days instead of five. (31)

compromise. Occurs when each person involved in a conflict is willing to give up something in order to resolve it. (14)

concern. Having a special interest in what happens in the lives of other family members. (11)

concession. When one person gives in completely. (14)

condominium. An apartment you buy, usually in a multi-building complex or a high-rise building. (29)

conduction. The transference of heat from the heat source to the container to the substance that is being heated. (26)

conflict. Occurs in a relationship when there is disagreement. (10)

conforming. Being similar to others; providing a sense of security and belonging. (27)

consequences. The end results of each option. (1)

consolidation loans. Loans that cover a variety of debts. The borrower arranges for one loan to pay off the total amount of a variety of debts. After paying off these debts, the consumer makes one payment each month to the finance company or other lender. (21)

consumer finance companies. Institutions that specialize in small consumer loans. (21)

Consumer Product Safety Commission (CPSC). Agency that protects consumers from dangerous products and encourages safe product use in the home, schools, and recreational areas. (23)

controlling. Checking the progress regularly and adjusting a plan where necessary. (3)

convection. Cooking method in which circulating currents of hot air heat the food. (26)

convenience foods. Foods that have had a service added to them. (25)

conventional loan. The type of loan used most commonly in home financing. The government does not insure these loans. The home is the security of the loan. If the borrower fails to make the agreed monthly payments, the lender has the right to foreclose. (29)

628

conventional standards. Standards that are generally accepted in our society. These often are related to traditions, social customs, and social behavior. (2)

convertible term. Type of coverage that allows the insured to exchange a term policy for permanent life insurance within a certain amount of time without taking a medical exam. (22)

cooking and serving center. Kitchen work center located around the range that includes storage space for pots, pans, other cooking utensils, pot holders, and serving pieces. (26)

cool colors. Colors related to blue and green. They give a more subdued, quiet feeling. These colors seem to recede and make things look smaller. (27)

cooperative. A type of home ownership where people are part of a group who have bought a building or complex. They share in the financial success of the building. The members don't actually own their own cooperative. Instead, they purchase stock in the corporation that owns the complex. (29)

cooperative education. Programs that combine on-the-job work experience with traditional classwork. (31)

cooperative play. Type of play in which children interact with others. (6)

coping. Any response to a stressful situation that helps prevent, avoid, or control physical and emotional stress. (18)

cover letter. A letter to an employer stating interest in an interview. (32)

credit. A promise to pay later for goods or services used now. (3, 21)

credit bureau. Also referred to as a consumer reporting agency, it is a firm that assembles credit information and other information about consumers. They sell this information to creditors, landlords, insurers, employers, and other businesses that are interested in a consumer's ability and willingness to repay loans. (21)

credit life insurance. Insurance that covers repayment of a loan should the borrower die. (22)

creditor. A person or business who supplies money, goods, or services to debtors. (21)

credit unions. Financial institutions that are run as a cooperative-owned and operated for the benefit of their members. (21)

crises. Major problems that have a great effect on the people involved. (11)

culture. Refers to the beliefs, social customs, and traits of a particular social group. (2)

curdle. Creation of small, soft lumps in milk. (26)

curtains. Window coverings with a pocket hem at the top that slips onto a curtain rod. (30)

custody. The assumption by a parent of the responsibility for the day-to-day decisions affecting the health, education, and welfare of the children. (11)

D

dating. Gives the opportunity to become close to someone of the opposite sex outside a person's own family. (9)

death benefit. A specified amount of money paid to the beneficiary if the insured dies while the policy is in force. (22)

debit card. Used like credit cards in making purchases. They transfer money from a checking account to the account of a store or service provider. The bank's computer verifies whether there is enough money to cover the purchase and the sum is deducted from the checking account immediately. (20)

debtor. A person who uses credit. (21)

deceptive practices. Fraudulent, illegal advertising methods. (23)

decision-making process. A valuable resource to help you solve problems and reach your goals. (1)

decorative lines. Lines that make a garment more appealing to the eye. They are present in fabric patterns or texture and in accessories such as buttons, trims, piping, and ruffles. (27)

decreasing term. Coverage in which the premiums stay the same, but the amount of coverage becomes smaller. (22)

deductible clause. A clause in an insurance policy that states the insured must pay up to a certain point before the insurance company will pay. (22)

deductions. Part of earnings that are deducted (subtracted) by an employer for tax payments and other expenses. (20)

defense mechanisms. Methods people use to deal with real-life situations and adjust to frustrations. (16)

deflation. An undesirable condition that exists when prices are falling. (24)

demand feeding. Type of feeding schedule in which a child's "inner clock" determines feeding, and it may differ slightly from day to day. (7)

department stores. Stores that are usually divided into special departments. (27)

dependability. Doing what you are expected to do. (32)

dependence. Relying on others to satisfy your needs. (13)

detergents. Made with petroleum, natural fats, and oils. They contain chemicals that soften and tie up the water minerals to permit cleaning. (28)

developing resources. Increasing or expanding resources. (3)

developmental tasks. Certain behaviors and skills expected to be learned at each stage of development. (7)

dietary fiber. A carbohydrate that is not digested, also referred to as cellulose. (17)

Dietary Guidelines for Americans. Recommendations to help people choose healthful eating and fitness patterns. (16)

Dietary Reference Intakes (DRIs). Guidelines for nutrition planning. (17)

digestion. The process that modifies and reduces foods mechanically or chemically so they can pass through the intestinal wall into the bloodstream. (17)

digital portfolio. Digital or scanned photos, graphics, and other pertinent information organized into a portfolio that can be electronically submitted to employers as part of the interview process. (32)

directed lighting. Light directed on a particular object or area and used for activities such as reading, washing dishes, and playing the piano; sometimes referred to as local or task lighting. (30)

discipline. A process aimed at self-control and self-direction. (13)

discount stores. Chain or independent stores that attempt to undersell other merchants on certain lines and types of merchandise. (27)

disinfectant. A product that destroys germs when used full strength. (28)

displacement. Transferring negative feelings toward a threatening person or situation to someone else. (16)

dividend. Money paid to stockholders out of the company's earnings. (22)

divorce. Occurs as a result of stress in various areas, such as tension in marriage, financial problems, family violence, and substance abuse. (11)

domestic violence. Family violence. (11)

double-hung windows. Windows that have two panels of window that slide up and down in the frame and can be opened either at the bottom or the top. (30)

dovetailing. Fitting several tasks together to save time. (26)

draperies. Heavier curtains that may cover a window completely or be pulled to the side. (30)

drug abuse. Using illegal drugs or prescription or over-the-counter drugs in ways other than their intended medical use. (16)

drugs. Substances other than food that chemically alter the body's structure or functioning. (16)

dual-career family. Family in which both husband and wife pursue careers. (15)

E

earnest money. A certain percentage of the selling price, provided by the buyer, which is eventually credited toward the down payment. (29)

eating disorders. Abnormal eating behaviors. (16)

e-commerce. Shopping online. (24)

economic efficiency. Making the most efficient use of limited resources. (24)

economics. The study of the process people and societies use to make choices about making and spending their money. (24)

economic stability. State of the economy when there is a high level of employment without inflation or deflation. (24)

economy brands. A form of house brand distributed by many large supermarket chains. (25)

electronic funds transfer (EFT). A system of carrying out financial transactions by computer rather than using checks and cash. (4)

Electronic Funds Transfer Act (EFT Act). Legislation that functions to protect and inform the consumer. The act points out that if you use an ATM of a debit card, you can get a receipt showing the amount of the transfer, the date it was made, and other information. (20)

elements of design. Line, color, and texture. (27)

emotional abuse. Purposely harming the self-concept of a family member by insulting and undermining a person's confidence. The abused individual may suffer personality changes. Most suffer low self-esteem. (11)

emotional advertising. Ads that aim to satisfy psychological needs. (23)

emotional growth and development. Growth in feelings or emotions and their control. (5)

emotional level. This level of communication involves communicating feelings. (10)

emotional maturity. Involves your ability to understand and control your emotions. It also involves being able to express your emotions, such as anger, in appropriate ways. (12)

emotional neglect. Failure to provide children with love and affection. (11)

empathy. Trying to understand someone's feelings without judging whether the person is right or wrong. (9)

emphasis. The focal point of a room or the center of interest. (30)

emulsifying agent. An ingredient that acts to keep the oil suspended in the water-based liquid. (26)

emulsion. A mixture that forms when liquids that do not ordinarily mix, such as oil and vinegar, are combined. (26)

endowment insurance. A form of insured savings. The policyholder makes payments for a certain number of years. After that period of time, the policyholder receives the face value of the policy. If the policyholder dies during that period of time, the beneficiary gets the face value. (22)

entrepreneurship. Opening and running a business independently. (31)

entry-level positions. Positions a person is qualified for after graduating from high school. (31)

environmental influences. Everything around you that affects you, including your family, home, friends, community, and all your life experiences. (5)

Environmental Protection Agency (EPA). Agency that protects the nation's land, air, and water systems. (23)

enzymes. Proteins that are found in digestive juices and help break down foods so the body can use them. (17)

equity investment. Ownership of stock in a company. The investor will benefit from the company's growth and profits. (22)

essential amino acids. Amino acids your body cannot produce that must be supplied through certain foods. (17)

evaluating. The process of judging and the end result. (3)

evaluation. Judging a decision based on standards. (1)

exchanging resources. Trading one resource for another. (3)

exemption. Reduces the amount of income on which a person must pay taxes. (20)

extended self. Ideas or images outside the individual self. (5)

extenders. Less-costly food mixtures that are often combined with meat to make a main dish. (25)

eye-hand coordination. Coordination of what is seen with the way the hands are moved. (6)

F

fabric finish. A treatment or process that alters the appearance, feel, or performance of a fabric. (27)

fabric softeners. A laundry product used to reduce static electricity and wrinkling as well as making fabrics soft. (28)

fads. Certain styles that are accepted by a large number of people for only a short period of time. (27)

family child care. Child care provided in a private home other than the child's own home. (15)

family composition. The number of people in the family, and the spacing in age of the children. (14)

family life cycle. Basic stages families go through as they grow and develop. (14)

family management. Occurs when members of a family help make choices and assume responsibilities for the group. (14)

family management tasks. Include all activities that contribute to the well-being of the family. (14)

Family Medical Leave Act. Law that entitles workers in businesses of 50 or more employees up to 12 weeks a year of unpaid leave for the birth or adoption of a child, care of a family member with a serious health condition, or the employee's own health condition. (15)

family rituals. Events or activities observed at certain times by the family. (7)

family style service. Type of food service in which foods are placed on the table in serving dishes and passed. (26)

fashion. Refers to the style that is popular at a certain time. (27)

fats. Nutrients that are the most concentrated source of calories. They help maintain a constant body temperature by providing effective insulation under the skin. They also cushion vital organs against injury and carry fat-soluble vitamins through the bloodstream. (17)

fat-soluble vitamins. Vitamins that tend to accompany fats as they are absorbed in the digestive process and can be stored in the body. (17)

Federal Housing Administration-insured loans (FHA-insured loans). Loans provided by an approved independent lending institution and insured by the FHA. (29)

Federal Trade Commission (FTC). Agency that enforces laws encouraging fair competition among businesses. It also handles consumer problems with credit; price-fixing and fraud; and television, radio, and printed advertising. (23)

feedback. Provides a "mirror" that helps the sender decide if the message has been received. (10)

fiber. A type of complex carbohydrate that humans cannot digest. (16)

filling yarns. The yarns in fabric that pass across the warp yarns. They are referred to as the crosswise grain. (27)

finance charge. What the consumer pays for the use of credit, including interest charges and any other fees. (21)

financial records. Records that show how money is spent, such as cash flow records, bank records, evidence of debt, savings and investment records, insurance records, and tax records. (20)

financial responsibility laws. Laws that require a driver to have coverage for a minimum amount of damage for which he or she is liable. (22)

finished foods. Convenience foods that are ready to eat immediately or after heating or thawing them. (25)

first aid. Immediate and temporary care required when someone is injured or suddenly becomes ill. (19)

fiscal policies. Policies that involve the way the federal government adjusts taxes and government spending to influence economic conditions. (24)

fixed expenses. Expenses that occur regularly and stay the same or nearly the same. Rent or house payments, loan payments, insurance, or property taxes are examples of fixed expenses. (20)

fixed income investment. An investment through which a person is actually lending money to a corporation or a government agency that issues bonds. (22)

flexible expenses. Expenses that vary both in amount and frequency of occurrence. Items such as food, clothing, utilities, transportation, medical care, personal expenses, and recreational expenses are flexible expenses. (20)

flexible standards. Standards you are willing to adapt when necessary. (2)

flexplace. A type of alternative work arrangement in which people work at home via computer technology. (15)

flextime. Work arrangement in which employees determine their own working hours within certain guidelines and limits. (15)

fluorescent lights. Type of light that produces light by releasing electricity through a mercury vapor sealed within the tube rather than by heat. (30)

Food and Drug Administration (FDA). Agency that assures all food (other than meat and poultry), food additives, and cosmetics are safe and wholesome. It also assures that drugs and medical devices are properly labeled and safe for intended use. (23)

foodborne illness. A disease transmitted through a food product. (19)

food cooperative. A group of people who have enough buying power to buy directly from the wholesaler. (25)

foreclosure. Seizing property and selling it to pay off the debt. (29)

form. The shape of a three-dimensional object. (30)

formal balance. The arrangement of identical objects in a mirror image on either side of the center. (30)

fringe benefits. Extra features granted to an employee above and beyond regular salary. (32)

full warranty. A warranty with no specific limitations. Both materials and labor are totally guaranteed for the length of time specified. (23)

functional relationships. Relationships such as those with your teachers, employer, or fellow employees. Relationships that involve everyday needs and interests. (9)

functional resume. Type of resume that describes the functions or job skills a person has demonstrated successfully and gives specific illustrations of the person's experiences. (32)

G

gelatinization. The swelling and subsequent thickening of starch granules as they are heated in water and absorb liquid. (26)

gene. The basic unit of heredity in which the potential for specific traits is carried. (5)

general lighting. A low level of light maintained throughout a room, assuring safety and ease in moving about. (30)

generics. Products that have plain labels with bold black lettering that state the name of the products. Although the price of generics can be much lower, the quality is usually well below national brand level. (25)

genetic counseling. A service provided to people who need to understand birth defects and their causes. (5)

genetic disease. An inherited disability. (19)

genetic mutation. When a person's genes are damaged or altered. (19)

genetics. The study of inherited traits in living things. (4)

genital warts. Very contagious STD in which warts occur on or around the sex organs. (16)

goals. The ends toward which you work— what you desire to achieve. (1)

gonorrhea. A commonly occurring STD that can cause sterility, heart disease, crippling arthritis, or blindness if left untreated. (16)

gross pay. The total amount earned for a pay period before any deductions are subtracted from a paycheck. (20)

guidance. All the words and actions used to influence a child's behavior. (13)

H

health maintenance organization (HMO). A form of health insurance in which members pay a flat fee each year that entitles them to a specific range of health care services. (22)

healthy self-concept. An honest, accurate, and positive view of yourself. (5)

hemoglobin. A protein in the blood that carries oxygen to the tissues and carries some of the carbon dioxide from the tissues back to the lungs. (17)

heredity. The process of passing on biological characteristics from one generation to the next. (5)

hidden messages. Messages that occur when someone says one thing, but is really implying another. (10)

higher values. Values that generally fit into three categories: moral values, human need values, and aesthetic values. (2)

high fashion. A term used in the business and fashion world to describe the latest designs. These designs are often extreme and of high quality. (27)

hotlines. Telephone service people can call when they need help of any kind. (15)

house brands. Products processed to be distributed by a supermarket chain, an association of independent stores, or other stores with numerous outlets. (25)

household inventory. A list of personal property including household furniture, furnishings, and equipment. For each item, the date of purchase and the purchase price or appraised value are included. Photos or videos can be a valuable part of the household inventory to help prove ownership and value claims. (20)

hue. The characteristic that gives a color a name and makes it unique. (27)

Human Immunodeficiency Virus (HIV). AIDS-causing virus that breaks down the immune system, leaving the body vulnerable to diseases a healthy body could resist. (16)

human need values. Values related to basic fundamental needs, both physical and psychological. (2)

human resources. The resources that come from within a person. These resources include your time, energy, personal qualities, knowledge, talents, and skills. (3)

humidity. Refers to the moisture that is absorbed into the air as vapor. (29)

hypertension. High blood pressure. (16)

I

ideal self. The image you have of the person you would like to be. (5)

identification. Extension of self indicating a feeling of oneness with a person, group of people, or object. (5) A defense mechanism in which a sense of self-worth is gained by identifying with a person, group, or institution considered special. (16)

"I" messages. Messages that help the other person understand how you perceive the situation. (10)

implementing. Moving ahead with the activities planned. (3)

impulse buying. Buying items that are not really needed. (21)

incandescent lights. Lights that have a tungsten filament heated by electricity to the temperature at which it glows. (30)

incest. Sexual activity between persons who are closely related. (11)

income. All the money you receive from salaries or wages, money gifts, tips, allowances, and interest earned on a savings account. It may also include dividends or stocks, income from securities, or income from rental property. (20)

incomplete protein. Protein food that lacks one or more of the essential amino acids. (17)

independence. Not requiring of relying on the help of others. (13)

infatuation. A powerful, but short-lived, attraction to another person. This experience is sometimes referred to as "puppy love." It is highly self-centered and temporary. (9)

inflation. State of the economy that exists when the prices of goods and services rise without a corresponding increase in the production of goods and services. (24)

informal balance. A casual arrangement that is not divided by any obvious center point. (30)

informational level. This level of communication involves communicating thoughts, ideas, plans, beliefs, or stories. (10)

informative advertising. Advertising that informs and not simply persuades people about products. (23)

initiative. Completing a given task, finding something else that needs to be done, and doing it. (32)

inner communication. Involves getting in touch with yourself—with your own feelings. (10)

installment credit. A form of credit that may be used to purchase expensive items like cars or major appliances. With installment credit, the buyer makes payments in regular installments that include the finance charges. (21)

installment loan. A loan where you borrow a set amount of money and repay it plus finance charges in a series of scheduled payments. (21)

institutional advertising. Advertising that appeals to values of Americans, such as patriotism, caring for others, and importance of family. (23)

instrumental values. Values that are the means of attaining higher level values. (2)

insurance. Protects you against financial risks related to life, health, and property. (22).

intellectual growth and development. Growth in a person's ability to learn, adapt to new situations, and solve problems. (5)

intellectual maturity. Refers to your ability to communicate, to solve problems, and to reason. It also includes your ability to learn from daily experiences and to adapt to new situations. (12)

intensity. The brightness or dullness of a color. (27)

interdependence. A balance between dependence and independence. (13)

interdependent. A situation where events that affect one member of the family often affect others either consciously or unconsciously. (11)

interest. A certain annual percentage of the amount of money in an account generally paid daily, monthly, or quarterly. (22)

interest-bearing checking account. A checking account in which you earn interest and are allowed to write checks on the same account. This is a savings and checking account. There is usually a minimum balance requirement. (21)

interests. A person's preferences for activities, events, and ideas. (31)

Internet. A global network of computers also known as the "Information Superhighway." (4)

investment. The use of money for the purpose of making money. (22)

J

job portfolio. An attractive presentation of work samples in some type of a folder or other container. (32)

job sharing. Work situation in which two people share the responsibilities of one full-time job but have different schedules. (15)

joint custody. Custody in which the parents share equally in the responsibility for the children, with each parent having equal rights in decision making and spending time with the children. (11)

L

lactose. The sugar in the milk solids. (26)

lease. An agreement between a renter and the landlord. (29)

leavening agents. Substances that cause a product to increase in volume. (26)

leveling. The second aspect of open expression. Letting others know how you feel about them and their behavior. (11)

level term. Type of insurance in which the amount of protection stays the same throughout the term and the death benefit remains a fixed amount. (22)

life insurance. Insurance purchased to limit the risk of financial loss if the insured should die. (22)

lifestyle. Refers to the way you live your life. (12)

lifestyle diseases. Diseases more closely related to a person's behavior than to infectious agents. (16)

limited payment insurance. Type of insurance policy in which policyholders pay the principal for only a certain length of time. (22)

limited purpose credit cards. Credit cards that are used only at a specific business or any of its locations. Large department stores have limited purpose cards as do other large businesses such as petroleum companies. (21)

limited warranty. Warranty in which the limitations are stated. (23)

liquidity. The ease with which an investment can be converted into cash when needed. (22)

listening. Requires a conscious, active effort to understand a message. (10)

long-term goals. Goals you want to accomplish later. (2)

M

mail-order businesses. Businesses that consist of companies who offer items for sale in catalogs, magazines, newspapers, and over the Internet. (27)

management process. A resource managers use each day to make decisions and solve problems. The management process involves three steps: (1) planning, (2) implementing and controlling, and (3) evaluating. (3)

managers. People who make choices or decisions that move them toward specific goals. (1)

manufacturer's outlet stores. Stores that are stocked with extra merchandise from a manufacturer's normal production. (27)

marbling. Flecks of fat evenly distributed throughout lean meat. (26)

market economy. Type of economy in which consumers have freedom of choice. Consumer choices influence what will be produced, how much will be produced, and the price that will be paid for goods and services. (24)

market value. The price of a stock. (22)

maternity leave. A leave of absence for a mother to care for her newborn child. (15)

maturation. Process during which growth occurs and certain personal and behavioral characteristics begin to appear. (5)

mature love. Is characterized by mutual trust-feelings of confidence and security in one another. (12)

maturity. Indicates moving toward full development. (12)

menopause. Physical change that occurs when a woman's menstrual periods cease and she is no longer able to have children. (8)

metabolism. The processes that take place after food compounds have been absorbed into the bloodstream. (17)

microwaves. High-frequency radio waves that generate heat in the food itself. (26)

minerals. Substances that mainly function to help regulate body processes. (17)

minimum-balance checking account. A checking account in which you are required to keep a minimum amount of money in the account at all times to avoid paying a service charge. If your account falls below the minimum, there is a charge. (20)

mixed economy. Economic system in which individuals make most decisions, but the economy is in part regulated by the government. (24)

mobile homes. A kind of manufactured house that can be moved by attaching wheels to them. (29)

monetary policies. Policies that involve the way the Federal Reserve Board regulates money and credit to achieve a stable and growing economy. (24)

money market accounts. Accounts that pay interest at rates based on U.S. Treasury Bill rates. (22)

monopoly. Exclusive control of a good or service by only one seller. (23)

monounsaturated fats. Usually liquid at room temperature, but may start to solidify in the refrigerator. (17)

moral development. A sense of right or wrong. (6)

moral values. Values having to do with conduct. They are what you feel is proper and worthwhile. They indicate what is right, what is just, and what is good. (2)

mortgage. A legal document that acts as security for the lender until the debt is repaid. (29)

motivation. Having a strong desire to achieve a goal. (3)

motor skills. Voluntary, directed movements. (6)

multimedia. The combination of sound, graphics, animation, and information in one presentation. (4)

multipurpose credit cards. Credit cards that are accepted by a variety of businesses, stores, and restaurants. Some companies charge cardholders an annual fee. There is usually no finance charge if the total bill is paid within 30 days of the billing date. (21)

multitasking. When you do several tasks at the same time. (26)

mutual fund. Companies that invest their funds in a wide variety of stocks and bonds. When you buy shares you become part owner of investments included in the fund. (22)

mutual fund money market accounts. Type of account that offers investors the convenience of writing checks for immediate cash. These check-writing privileges are usually unlimited. (22)

mutual respect. Shows that each of you accepts the other as a worthwhile person. (9)

MyPyramid. A food guidance system designed to help you choose a healthful diet and be active every day. (16)

N

national brands. Quality products that are widely advertised across the country. (25)

National Highway Traffic Safety Administration. Agency that works to reduce highway deaths, injuries, and property losses by enforcing the Federal Motor Vehicle Safety Standards for vehicles and vehicle equipment. (23)

natural fibers. Fibers that come from plants or animals, such as wool, cotton, flax (linen), silk, and hair fibers such as cashmere. (27)

natural resources. Water, energy, air, and other resources that occur in nature. (3)

needs. Basic items that a person must have to live. (2)

negotiation. Working with one another to find a solution to a problem. (14)

net pay. The gross pay minus the deductions. (20)

network. A group of computers linked together to share data. (4)

neurons. Nerve cells in the brain.

no-fault insurance. Type of insurance in which victims are simply reimbursed for their medical expenses by their own insurance companies no matter who caused the accident. (22)

noise pollution. Sound of any intensity or quality that harms or distresses a person. (19)

nonhuman resources. Include material possessions, money or purchasing power, and community resources. (3)

nonprecipitating water softeners. Water softeners that hold the minerals in solution. (28)

nonverbal communication. Communication that includes the inflection of the voice, movements of the body, and emotions shown. Eye contact with others, facial expressions, and gestures are also examples. (10)

nutrients. Substances supplied by the diet the body needs in order to function. (16)

O

obesity. Being 20 percent or more above desirable weight. (16)

objective standards. Standards that are specific and easy to measure. (2)

omega-3 fatty acids. A type of polyunsaturated fat that can be beneficial to a person's health. (17)

open communication. Being honest and letting the other person know your true thoughts and feelings. It also involves accepting the other person's ideas and feelings. (10)

open expression. Sharing, leveling, and accepting. (11)

openness. Letting another person know your thoughts, opinions, and feelings. (9)

osteoporosis. A disease which causes the bones to deteriorate and become porous as the body takes the calcium it needs from the bones. (16)

oxidation. Exposure to oxygen. (26)

oxygen bleaches. Bleaches that are much safer than chlorine bleaches for general bleaching purposes and stain removal. (28)

P

parallel play. Playing next to another child but not with the child in a cooperative way. (6)

parental responsibilities. Responsibilities that involve meeting basic physical and psychological human needs. (13)

passbook account. Account in which deposits and withdrawals can be made in varying amounts at any time. (22)

paternity leave. Time allowed for a father to be absent from his job immediately following the birth of his child. (15)

patterns of development. Certain characteristics displayed by children in an orderly and predictable sequence as they develop. (6)

paycheck stub. Attached to a paycheck, it lists the total amount of money earned as well as deductions. (20)

peer group. Persons similar to you in age or status. (2)

peer pressure. Both positive and negative influence communicated through a person's peers. (5)

peers. Friends and classmates in a person's age group. (5)

perception. Formation of a relationship between an impression from the senses and some past experience. (6)

permanent life insurance. Cash value life insurance. The annual premium usually remains constant as long as the policy is in force. In addition to the death insurance, a savings account increases in value throughout the life of the policy. If the policyholder dies while the policy is in force, only the death benefit is paid. However, if the policyholder survives, the policy serves as a kind of savings account. (22)

personal records. Records that include personal documents, health records, education records, and employment records. (20)

personal relationships. Relationships you may have with your parents, close friends, and eventually with a marriage partner and your own children. Relationships that fulfill basic human needs such as the need to belong, to be cared for, and to be loved. (9)

personal resources. A person's personal qualities, capabilities, talents, and skills. (8)

personal self. The way a person sees himself or herself physically. (5)

persuasive advertising. Advertising that tries to persuade consumers to buy goods or services using arguments that may or may not be valid. (23)

physical abuse. Abuse that involves hitting, kicking, tripping, choking, biting, or threatening with a weapon. (11)

physical growth and development. Body changes affecting the outside appearance of the body and the internal structure. (5)

physical needs. The needs for warmth, shelter, food, clothing, and safety. (13)

physical neglect. Neglect that occurs if parents or persons legally responsible don't supply food, clothing, shelter, education, and medical care. (11)

picture window. A large single-panel window designed to frame an exterior view. (30)

plain weave. A weave where each filler yarn is placed over one warp yarn, under the next, over the next, under the next, and so on. (27)

planning. Guidance to reach the desired outcome. It involves first identifying the activities necessary to carry out the plan. It also includes arranging activities in a logical sequence. Finally, it involves grouping activities and coordinating different parts of the plan. (3)

planning center. Kitchen area that includes a desk or some counter space, a recipe file, cookbooks, and record-keeping supplies. (26)

pollution. Anything that makes the environment dirty or contaminated. (19)

polyunsaturated fats. A type of unsaturated fat that helps lower blood cholesterol levels. (17)

preauthorized transfer. A method of automatically depositing or withdrawing funds from a person's account when the account holder authorizes the bank or a third party to do so. (20)

precipitating water softeners. Water softeners that remove minerals by forming a precipitate—a solid that settles out. (28)

preferred provider organizations (PPOs). A type of health insurance in which doctors and hospitals provide reduced fees for services to insured members. (22)

preferred stock. A stock in which the annual dividend is fixed by the corporation and never changes. Dividends for this type of stock are paid before any of the other stockholders receive dividends. (22)

Pregnancy Discrimination Act. Law that prohibits discrimination against pregnant women in all areas of employment from hiring to firing. (15)

premium. The amount of money paid by the policy owner, usually the insured. (22)

preparation center. Kitchen work center that includes the refrigerator, freezer, storage cabinets, and counter space for food preparation. (26)

pressed wood. The least expensive type of wood, made of wood scraps, chips, and shavings. (30)

preventive health care. Maintaining wellness in order to prevent diseases from developing. (16)

preventive maintenance. Routine maintenance care done to avoid housing problems and repairs. (30)

principal. The amount of an investment minus the interest. (21)

principles of design. Guidelines for the use of the elements of design, including balance, proportion, rhythm, and emphasis. (30)

private property. The portion of income people keep in the form of material assets, money, or investments. (24)

problem ownership. Often used in conflict situations. Trying to determine whose problem it is. (10)

profit motivation. The motive to work in order to earn an income. (24)

projection. Shifting the blame for an undesirable act or thought to someone else. (16)

promotions. Temporary price advantages over other products. (25)

property records. Records that include real estate records, household inventory, and records of ownership. They can prove ownership, indicate monetary value of possessions, and help determine insurance needs. (20)

proportion. The relationship of one part to another or one part to the whole. (30)

protein. Nutrient important to the growth and maintenance of body tissues. (17)

psychological needs. Needs that relate to mental well-being and a sense of worth. (13)

R

radiation. Transference of heat directly from the source to the food being heated. (26)

rationalization. Offering socially acceptable reasons for a failure or negative situation. (16)

realistic self-concept. An accurate view of yourself; seeing yourself as you really are, not what you would like to be. (5)

recycling. Taking a used product and turning it back into something that can be used again. (19)

reflexes. Automatic, unlearned behaviors. (6)

regression. Reverting to immature, childish behavior when difficulties or frustrations occur. (16)

regular charge accounts. A type of sales credit that allows customers to purchase goods and services on credit and pay the bill in full in 30 days. If you do this, you are not charged interest. However, you may be charged interest if you do not pay the full amount. (21)

renewable term. Type of insurance policy in which the company will extend beyond the first term without requiring a medical examination. (22)

replacement cost. Type of homeowner's insurance policy in which the company is responsible for the full cost of repair or replacement. (22)

resources. The ways and means of reaching specific goals. (1)

respect. Seeing someone as a worthwhile individual. Showing consideration by accepting each person's rights to have opinions and feelings. (9, 11)

responsible. Being dependable and reliable. (11)

restrictive endorsement. An endorsement that states what is to be done with the check. Common restrictive endorsements include: "For deposit only" and a signature or "Pay to the order of," the name of the party to receive the check, and a signature. (20)

resume. A concise summary of a person's qualifications for a job documented by past accomplishments. (32)

reverse annuity mortgage. This is a loan based on the equity a homeowner has accumulated. The loan is disbursed as a line of credit in monthly installments over a period of years or as a lump sum. The amount usually depends on the borrower's age and the amount of equity in the home. (21)

revolving charge accounts. A form of credit in which the total amount of the bill does not have to be paid each month. However, a finance charge will be figured on the amount not paid. Additional purchases can be made even though money is owed on previous purchases. The customer's line of credit is usually limited. Credit cards are usually revolving charge accounts. (21)

rhythm. The movement of the eye across a design. (30)

role. Refers to a certain function you assume in life. (1)

role expectations. Behaviors expected in certain positions of responsibility. (14)

role model. A person who, through his or her actions, affects the attitude and actions of another person. (13)

S

safe deposit box. A rented metal box in a fireproof vault, usually at a bank. Records that are irreplaceable or difficult and costly to replace should be kept in a safe deposit box. (20)

sales credit. Credit used to purchase goods and services. (21)

satin weave. A weave that has a smooth surface created by using long float yarns on the surface. (27)

saturated fats. Fats that contain the most hydrogen atoms and are usually solid at room temperature; found mostly in meat and dairy products. (17)

scorching. The result of overheating milk which causes the lactose in the milk to turn brown, creating an undesirable flavor. (26)

searing. Process by which meat is exposed to intense, direct heat long enough to cook the outer layer and form a crust. (26)

seasonal foods. Foods that have a peak season during the year. At that time, the price is reduced because the supply is greater than the demand. (25)

secure attachments. Strong relationship between children and the adults who take care of them. They are the basis of a child's future relationships. (5)

security deposit. A refundable payment that is equal to one or two months rent. It covers any damage a renter might do to the property. It also substitutes for rent if the renter fails to pay rent or leaves before the end of the lease. (29)

security objects. Items children carry that make them feel safe and protected. (7)

self-concept. Ideas or impressions people acquire about themselves as they develop physically, socially, emotionally, and intellectually. (5)

self-concept core. Foundation of a person's self-concept that is developed in the early years and changes only over a long period of time through repeated daily experiences. (5)

self-esteem. The way a person feels about himself or herself. (5)

self-imposed stress. Stress that occurs when a person imposes unrealistic expectations on himself or herself. (18)

semiprepared foods. Convenience foods that require you to perform some additional service. (25)

sequence. Placing activities in a logical order. (3)

sexual abuse. Abuse that involves unwanted sexual contact. (11)

sexually transmitted diseases (STDs). Infections that are almost always transmitted by intimate sexual contact with an infected person. (16)

shade. Produced by adding black to any normal value making it darker and producing a low value. (27)

sharing. The first aspect of open expression. Letting others in the family know your personal thoughts, feelings, and opinions. (11)

sharing resources. More than one person using resources. (3)

short-term goals. Goals you want to accomplish soon. (2)

sibling rivalry. Competition between two or more children in a family. (6)

single-family dwelling. A one-family home detached from any other building, or it might be a townhouse or a mobile home. (29)

single-payment loan. A loan where you borrow an amount of money and repay that amount plus finance charges in one payment. (21)

situational stress. Stress caused by events that happen to or around a person. (18)

smart card. A type of debit card in which a computer chip is placed. This chip stores personal information about the cardholder. The cardholder must have money in an account to use the card. As the card is used, money is automatically transferred from the user's account. (4)

soaps. Made by combining lye with fats and oils. (20)

social growth and development. Development in the way people behave and react to others. (5)

socialism. A system of government in which there is considerable government planning to promote well-being of the citizens. The government owns and operates most industries. (24)

social maturity. Indicates you have moved from a dependent self to a more independent self. You have become less self-centered and more concerned about others. (12)

social self. The way a person views himself or herself in relation to other people. (5)

solid wood. Term used to describe furniture made of completely solid wood. (30)

special needs. Persons who require homes with certain structural features or adaptations to their homes in order to make housing more functional for their living needs. (29)

specialty stores. Stores that feature specific types of products. (25) (27)

stages in life. Periods in life such as infant, preschooler, teenager, young adult, middle-aged adult, and senior citizen. (1)

standards. Certain measures or clues that help measure performance and tell you when a goal has been reached to your satisfaction. They help you identify what is acceptable and what is not acceptable to you. (2)

stereotype. A belief that all members of a group share characteristics that may only belong to some members of the group. (9)

stock. A share of ownership in a corporation. (22)

stockbroker. The person who acts as a consumer's agent and handles details of transactions when buying or selling stocks or bonds. (22)

stranger anxiety. A feeling of anxiety or fear children often get around unfamiliar people. (6)

stress. Emotional, mental, or physical tension. (18)

structural lines. Lines formed as a garment is sewn by seams, darts, collars, pleats, pockets, gathers, tucks, or draping. (27)

style. Refers to specific characteristics or the form or shape of clothing. (27)

subjective standards. Standards that come from your own value system and are based on your own experiences. These standards cannot be specifically measured. (2)

substance abuse. Involves misusing drugs, including alcohol, to a potentially harmful level. (11)

suicide. The taking of one's own life. (11)

support group. A group of people who share a similar problem or concern. (11)

symbolic play. The ability to hold mental images from past experience. (6)

synthetic fibers. Fibers manufactured from chemicals, such as nylon, rayon, acetate, acrylic, and polyester. (27)

syphilis. A destructive STD that spreads through the bloodstream and can cause mental illness, blindness, heart attack, and ultimately death if left untreated. (16)

T

technology. A constantly changing body of scientific knowledge that is used to solve practical problems. (4)

telecommuters. People working as employees from their own homes. (4)

telephone transfer. Used by consumers to transfer funds from one account to another. They can also be used to order payment of specific bills by phone. (20)

term insurance. Type of insurance policy in which an individual's life is insured against death for a certain period of time. The policy terminates at the end of the term period. Benefits are paid only if the policyholder dies within the term. (22)

testimonial advertising. Ads that present a recommendation for a product or service from either a celebrity or a typical consumer. (23)

texture. The way a surface feels when you touch it and looks when light strikes it. (27)

time accounts. Accounts in which the money must remain in the account for a fixed period of time. A penalty will result with an early withdrawal. (22)

tint. Produced by adding white to any normal hue making it lighter. (27)

toilet training. The time when children learn bladder and bowel control. (7)

trace minerals. Minerals present in the body in relatively small amounts. (17)

traffic pattern. Refers to the circulation from one room to another and from place to place within a room. (29)

trans fatty acids. A specific type of fat formed when liquid oils are made solid at room temperature through a process called hydrogenation. (17)

trust. Believing a person is honest and reliable. (9)

twill weave. A weave that has a distinct characteristic diagonal line. This line is created when a yarn in one direction floats or passes over two or more yarns in the opposite direction. (27)

type II herpes. A highly contagious STD that causes blisters to form on the lips and mouth. (16)

U

United States Department of Agriculture (USDA). Agency that supervises food safety and inspection services. (23)

unit pricing. A pricing method that tells what a product costs per standard unit, such as per pound or per quart. (25)

universal design. The concept of making all homes easier to use for everyone. (29)

universal life insurance. Type of insurance that combines the flexibility of an adjustable policy with an investment feature. The cash value is invested to earn interest at current market rates. Premiums, face value, and level of protection can be altered as needed. (22)

unsaturated fats. Fats that contain less hydrogen and are usually liquid at room temperature. (17)

use-cost. Use of a resource that reduces the amount that is available for future use. A resource that is important, but is limited, has a high use-cost. A resource that is readily available has a low use-cost. (3)

V

vaccine. A small amount of dead or weakened bacteria or virus that may be given by mouth or by injection. This stimulates a person's body to build up resistance to a disease. (19)

value. The lightness or darkness of a hue. (27)

value indicators. Things that reveal a person's values including what they say and do, and their attitudes, beliefs, interests, actions, and activities.

values. A motivating force—what is important to a person. (1)

variable life insurance. Type of insurance in which the premiums are fixed but the face amount varies with the performance of a fund in which the premiums are invested. (22)

variety stores. Chain or independent stores that sell a variety of consumer goods in a low price range. (27)

veneer. A panel of wood made by gluing several layers of wood on top of one another with the grain at right angles. (30)

verbal communication. Communication that involves speaking and/or writing. (10)

vesting. A process by which the employee earns rights over the employer's contributions to the pension plan. (22)

Veterans Administration-guaranteed loans (VA-guaranteed loans). Special loans granted to qualified veterans of the U.S. Armed Forces. These loans are obtained through a regular lending agency and are guaranteed by the federal government. (29)

villi. Fingerlike projections found all along the lining of the small intestine that increase the surface area to help the blood pick up nutrients and transport them to the cells of the body. (17)

vitamins. Compounds required in the diet in extremely small amounts. (17)

W

wants. Something unnecessary but desired.

warehouse stores. Stores that are able to reduce prices by cutting their overhead costs. (25)

warm colors. Colors related to red, yellow, or orange. They create feelings of liveliness, cheer, and excitement. They appear to advance and make things look larger. (27)

warp knit. A knit that can be made only by machine. One or more sets of yarn the width of the fabric are used. Loops are formed vertically, and an entire row is made at one time. (27)

warp yarns. The yarns in fabric that run up and down. They are referred to as the lengthwise grain. (27)

warranty. A guarantee that a product is in good working order and will give good service for a reasonable amount of time. (23)

water softeners. Used to inactivate or remove minerals from water. (28)

water-soluble vitamins. Vitamins that dissolve in water and are not stored in the body. (17)

weaning. When babies learn to drink from a container instead of from the bottle or breast. (7)

weft knit. A knit that may be made on a knitting machine or may be made by hand. The loops are made as the yarn is added in a horizontal direction. (27)

wellness. A state of good health. (16)

whole life insurance. Type of insurance in which the amount of the premium is set at the time the policy is bought. (22)

will. A legal document used to designate heirs, identify the property they are to receive, and indicate who will act as administrator of the estate. (22)

work centers. The three areas of the kitchen related to meal preparation, serving, and cleanup. (26)

work simplification. Breaking down an activity into a detailed listing of what needs to be done. (3)

Y

"you" messages. Messages that tend to attack the person rather than the problem. (10)

Index